LOEB CLASSICAL LIBRARY
FOUNDED BY JAMES LOEB 1911

EDITED BY
JEFFREY HENDERSON

ARISTOTLE

XX

LCL 285

ARISTOTLE

THE ATHENIAN CONSTITUTION

THE EUDEMIAN ETHICS

ON VIRTUES AND VICES

WITH AN ENGLISH TRANSLATION BY

H. RACKHAM

HARVARD UNIVERSITY PRESS
CAMBRIDGE, MASSACHUSETTS
LONDON, ENGLAND

First published 1935
Revised and reprinted 1952

ISBN 978-0-674-99315-0

Printed on acid-free paper and bound by
The Maple-Vail Book Manufacturing Group

CONTENTS

PREFACE

In contributing to the Loeb series, my object is to provide a translation primarily designed as an assistance to the reader of the text on the opposite page, and not as a substitute for it. My versions therefore aim at being interpretative, not at reproducing the form of the original as literally as possible, nor yet at conveying its meaning in idiomatic English while entirely ignoring its form.

In translating Aristotle, to retain the classical English equivalents of his technical terms, which have mostly come down to us from the Latin writers on philosophy, is often misleading to the modern reader, who attaches quite un-Aristotelian meanings to such words as for instance "temperance," "speculation," and "mean" (except in the phrase "Greenwich mean time"). Even "virtue" has now a much narrower signification than ἀρετή, which is often best rendered by "goodness."

Moreover in a translation that faces the Greek it is unnecessary to keep the same English rendering for a Greek word wherever it occurs. The Greek may have different shades of meaning in different contexts; or the traditional English equivalent may sound inappropriate to some particular context. Moreover no English word may be quite adequate to convey the meaning and associations of a Greek word; and perhaps the best way to warn the student of this inadequacy may be deliberately to avoid adopting the same rendering throughout.

1935

ARISTOTLE
THE ATHENIAN CONSTITUTION

INTRODUCTION

The *Politeiai*

The place of *The Athenian Constitution* in the encyclopedia of Aristotle's writings is known to us from the concluding paragraph of *The Nicomachean Ethics.* That work forms the first volume of a treatise on the welfare of man as a social being, of which *Politics* forms the second volume; and at the end of the former (*N.E.* x. ix. 21, 23) a prefatory outline of the latter is given, in which occur the phrases 'the collections of constitutions,' 'the collected constitutions'; it is stated that on these will be based that division of *Politics* (*i.e.* Books III.-VI.) which will deal with the stability of states in general and of the various special forms of constitution, and with the causes of good and bad government.

These treatises are said in ancient lists of Aristotle's writings to have been a hundred and fifty-eight in number. Each no doubt consisted, like the volume before us, of a constitutional history of the state in question followed by a description of its constitution at the time of writing. They are frequently spoken of[a] as the work of Aristotle, but he may well have

[a] *E.g.* by the historians Philochorus (before 306 B.C.) and Timaeus (about 300 B.C.), and often later, *e.g.* Cicero, *De Finibus* vii. and others down to the 5th century A.D.

employed the aid of pupils in their compilation. They were not preserved through the Middle Ages in the Aristotelian Corpus, and until fifty years ago were only known to modern students from numerous references and quotations in later writers.

The Athenian Constitution: MSS.

But in 1880 two small and much damaged sheets of papyrus were found in the sands of Egypt which scholars eventually proved to come from a copy of the most important of all these constitutional treatises, the one on the Constitution of Athens. These sheets are now in the Berlin Museum. Palaeographers ascribe them to the fourth century A.D. Ten years later, among some papyrus rolls acquired from Egypt by the British Museum, the Librarian F. G. Kenyon recognized four sheets as containing a copy of almost the whole treatise. These sheets have writing on both sides. On the front are some accounts of receipts and expenses kept by a farm bailiff named Didymus for his master Epimachus, near the Egyptian town of Hermopolis, in the tenth and eleventh years of Vespasian, A.D. 78 and 79. On the back is the Aristotelian treatise ; its beginning is wanting, and the first page of the book is blank, showing that it was copied from a damaged copy of the work ; and the last roll is very fragmentary. Different parts are written in different hands, four in all ; the script is said to date the copy at about A.D. 100. It was doubtless made for a private person (perhaps the writer of one of the four hands), and probably buried with its owner at his death.

ARISTOTLE

Editions

In 1891 Sir Frederick Kenyon published a facsimile of the papyrus, and a printed edition of the text with an introduction and notes. In 1893 a revised text with a full and valuable commentary was put out by Sandys. Kenyon prepared an edition for the Royal Academy of Berlin, published in 1903, in which he included the fragments of the fourth roll conjecturally arranged in a consecutive text; and his latest edition was published at Oxford in 1920. Of several published abroad, the latest is the Teubner text of 1928 by Oppermann, based on the previous editions of Blass and Thalheim.

Text

The text of the present edition is based on the *editio princeps* of Kenyon, but it has been corrected by later scholars' readings of the papyrus. A few critical notes and suggested emendations are appended; but in regard to inaccuracies of grammar and arithmetic and trifling inelegancies of phrase (*e.g.* τόνδε τρόπον, for which most editors substitute τόνδε τὸν τρόπον), exactly how many are due to a copyist's carelessness and how many are to be saddled on the author, no two scholars will agree. To the papyrus text have here been prefixed and appended the principal passages from the lost beginning and end of the treatise that the learned industry of scholars has gleaned from the quotations of later Greek authors.

Sources

The sources of the historical part of the book are studied in Sandys's edition, pp. liv. ff. The author sometimes gives his evidence, quoting Solon's poetry (xii.), popular verse (xix., xx.), proverbial phrases (xvi. 7, xxi. 2). He mentions Herodotus once (xiv.) and follows his narrative, with some variations, as to Peisistratus and Cleisthenes (xiv. f., xx.). Thucydides he does not name, but he is following him, with modifications, as to Harmodius and Aristogeiton (xviii.) and the Four Hundred (xxix., xxxiii.). Later his authority is probably Ephorus, but a few statements may come from the Ἀτθίδες of Cleidemus, Phanodemus and Androtion.

He professes to make critical use of his authorities (vi., xviii. 4, xxviii.); but his own chronology and accuracy in details have been challenged, *e.g.* as to the period of Peisistratus, and as to the presence of Themistocles in Athens in 426 B.C. (xxv. 3). He cites official documents (xxvi. fin., xxix., xxx., xxxi., xxxix.); reconstructs the past by inference from the present (iii. 5, viii. 1, xvi. 5, xxii. 3); and quotes the use of this method by others (iii. 3, vii. 4).

Date of Composition

The latest event mentioned in *The Athenian Constitution* (liv. 7) is the archonship of Cephisophon, 329 B.C. The book also mentions (xlvi. 1) triremes and quadriremes, but not quinquiremes; and the earliest date at which quinquiremes in the Athenian navy are recorded is 325 B.C. The treatise can thus be dated between 328 and 325 B.C. Moreover it speaks (lxii. 16) of officials still being sent to Samos, and Samos ceased to be under the control of Athens in the autumn of 322 B.C., the year of Aristotle's death.

OUTLINE OF CONTENTS

Part I. Constitutional History of Athens to 403 B.C.

(1) *Fr.* 1. Original hereditary absolute monarchy. Military command transferred from king to war-lord in time of Ion.

Fr. 2. Local division of royal power among four sons of Pandion.

Fr. 3. Unity restored by Theseus.

Fr. 4. Growth of popular power under Theseus.

(2) *Fr.* 5. Constitution in time of Theseus: four Tribes, Thirds, Brotherhoods, Clans.

Fr. 6. Murder of Theseus. Recovery of his bones by Athens.

Fr. 7. End of hereditary monarchy.

Fr. 8. Conspiracy of Cylon put down by Megacles.

MS. c. i. Pollution and purification of Athens.

c. ii. Civil disorders from forced labour of debtors.

c. iii. Constitution before Draco. Third archon instituted, the king retaining religious functions. Three archonships finally made annual, and six Thesmothetae added. An aristocracy, the nine archons being elected by the Areopagus, whose members were ex-archons. Conspiracy of Cylon. Discontent and poverty of lower orders.

(3) c. iv. Constitution of Draco, the first code of laws. Council of Four Hundred and One. Punishment of Alcmaeonidae.

(4) cc. v.-ix. Constitution of Solon: four property-classes with graded functions, the fourth takes part in the assembly and law-courts.

c. x. Solon's cancellation of debts, and system of weights and measures.

cc. xi., xii. Ten years of party strife. Solon's poems.

(5) cc. xiii.-xix. Tyranny of Peisistratus and his sons.

(6) cc. xx.-xxii. Reforms of Cleisthenes. Creation of democracy.

(7) cc. xxiii., xxiv. Supremacy of Areopagus after Persian wars. Aristeides and Themistocles. Confederacy of Delos ; taxation of allies.

(8) cc. xxv., xxvi. Democracy restored by Ephialtes, and extended by Pericles.

c. xxviii. Popular leadership, historical review.

(9) cc. xxix., xxx. Revolution of the Four Hundred ; after failure of Sicilian expedition Athens forced to abandon democracy; citizenship to be limited to Five Thousand.

c. xxxi. The Council of Four Hundred govern as an oligarchy.

(10) cc. xxxii.-xxxiv. Counter-revolution : democracy restored. Then Sparta defeats Athens in the war and sets up the Thirty.

(11) cc. xxxv.-xxxviii. Despotic rule of the Thirty. They are put down by exiles led by Thrasybulus.

(12) cc. xxxix., xl. Extreme democracy restored : the people supreme; payment for attending Assembly.

c. xli. The eleven revolutions recapitulated.

Part II. The Existing Constitution

c. xlii. The franchise.

cc. xliii.-lx. The officials (*a*) elected by lot—the Council, archons, and others;

c. lxi. (*b*) elected by vote—military officers.

c. lxii. Payment of officials.

c lxiii. and foll. The law-courts : procedure.

ΑΡΙΣΤΟΤΕΛΟΥΣ ΑΘΗΝΑΙΩΝ ΠΟΛΙΤΕΙΑ

Primae partis Epitoma Heraclidis

[*Heracleides Lembos in the second century* B.C. *compiled a book called* Ἱστορίαι *which contained quotations from Aristotle's* Constitutions. *Excerpts made from this book, or from a later treatise by another author based upon it, have come down to us in a fragmentary form in a Vatican* MS. *of the 8th century, now at Paris, under the title* Ἐκ τῶν Ἡρακλείδου περὶ Πολιτειῶν. *These were edited by Schneidewin in* 1847 *and by others later.*

1. Ἀθηναῖοι τὸ μὲν ἐξ ἀρχῆς ἐχρῶντο βασιλείᾳ. συνοικησάντος δὲ Ἴωνος αὐτοῖς τότε πρῶτον Ἴωνες ἐκλήθησαν.

⟨Τούτου γὰρ οἰκήσαντος τὴν Ἀττικήν, ὥς Ἀριστοτέλης φησί, τοὺς Ἀθηναίους Ἴωνας κληθῆναι, καὶ Ἀπόλλωνα Πατρῷον αὐτοῖς ὀνομασθῆναι. (Harpocration *s.v.* Ἀπόλλων Πατρῷος.)

Πατρῷον τιμῶσιν Ἀπόλλωνα Ἀθηναῖοι ἐπεὶ Ἴων ὁ πολέμαρχος Ἀθηναίων ἐξ Ἀπόλλωνος καὶ Κρεούσης τῆς Ξούθου[1] ἐγένετο. (Schol. Aristoph. *Av.* 1537.)⟩

[1] Ξούθου ⟨γυναικὸς⟩ Rose.

[a] A word has perhaps been lost in the Greek, giving 'the wife of Xuthus'—unless indeed the text is a deliberate

ARISTOTLE—THE ATHENIAN CONSTITUTION

Heracleides' Epitome of the first part

For a complete study of these contributions to the reconstruction of The Athenian Constitution *readers must consult the standard commentators on the latter; only those fragments which belong to the lost early part of the treatise are given here. Quotations of the same passages of Aristotle made by other writers have been collected by scholars, and are inserted in the text in brackets* ⟨ ⟩ *where they fill gaps in Heracleides.*]

Fr. 1. The Athenians originally had a royal government. It was when Ion came to dwell with them that they were first called Ionians.

⟨For when he came to dwell in Attica, as Aristotle says, the Athenians came to be called Ionians, and Apollo was named their Ancestral god.

The Athenians honour Ancestral Apollo because their War-lord Ion was the son of Apollo and Creusa the daughter [a] of Xuthus.⟩

bowdlerization of the legend. Xuthus, King of Peloponnesus, married Creusa, daughter of Erechtheus, King of Athens, after whose death he was banished; but Creusa's son Ion was recalled to aid Athens in war with Eleusis, won them victory, and died and was buried in Attica.

2. Πανδίων δὲ βασιλεύσας μετὰ Ἐρεχθέα διένειμε τὴν ἀρχὴν τοῖς υἱοῖς ⟨Αἰγεῖ μὲν δοὺς τὴν περὶ τὸ ἄστυ χώραν, Λύκῳ δὲ τὴν διακρίαν, Πάλλαντι δὲ τὴν παραλίαν, Νίσῳ δὲ τὴν Μεγαρίδα (Id. *Vesp.* 1223.)⟩ 3. καὶ διετέλουν οὗτοι στασιάζοντες· Θήσευς δὲ ἐκήρυξε καὶ συνεβίβασε τούτους ἐπ' ἴσῃ καὶ ὁμοίᾳ.[1] ⟨ἐκάλει πάντας ἐπὶ τοῖς ἴσοις καὶ τὸ "δεῦρ' ἴτε, πάντες λεῴ" κήρυγμα Θήσεως γενέσθαι φασὶ πανδημίαν τινὰ καθιστάντος. (Plutarch, *Theseus* 25.)⟩

4. ⟨ὅτι δὲ πρῶτος ἀπέκλινε πρὸς τὸν ὄχλον, ὡς Ἀριστοτέλης φησίν, καὶ ἀφῆκε τὸ μοναρχεῖν, ἔοικε μαρτυρεῖν καὶ Ὅμηρος ἐν νεῶν καταλόγῳ μόνους Ἀθηναίους δῆμον προσαγορεύσας. (Plutarch, *ib.*)⟩

5. ⟨Ὡς ἱστορεῖ ἐν τῇ Ἀθηναίων Πολιτείᾳ Ἀριστοτέλης λέγων οὕτως· φυλὰς δὲ αὐτῶν συννενεμῆσθαι δ', ἀπομιμησαμένων τὰς ἐν τοῖς ἐνιαυτοῖς ὥρας, ἑκάστην δὲ διῃρῆσθαι εἰς τρία μέρη τῶν φυλῶν, ὅπως γίνηται τὰ πάντα δώδεκα μέρη, καθάπερ οἱ μῆνες εἰς τὸν ἐνιαυτόν, καλεῖσθαι δὲ αὐτὰ τριττῦς καὶ φρατρίας· εἰς δὲ τὴν φρατρίαν τριάκοντα γένη διακεκοσμῆσθαι, καθάπερ αἱ ἡμέραι εἰς τὸν μῆνα, τὸ δὲ γένος εἶναι τριάκοντα ἀνδρῶν. (*Lexicon Patm.* p. 152 Sakkel.)⟩

6. Οὗτος ἐλθὼν εἰς Σκῦρον ⟨Ἀριστοτέλης ἱστορεῖ ὅτι ἐλθὼν Θήσευς εἰς Σκῦρον ἐπὶ κατασκοπὴν εἰκότως διὰ τὴν Αἰγέως συγγένειαν . . . (Schol. Vatic. ad Eurip. *Hipp.* 11)⟩ ἐτελεύτησεν

[1] Schneidewin: ὁμοίᾳ μοίρᾳ (aut τιμῇ) codd.

[a] Perhaps the formula of the crier sent round to announce the meetings of the Ecclesia: *cf.* ἀκούετε, λεῴ ('Oyez').

Fr. 2. Erechtheus was succeeded as king by Pandion, who divided up his realm among his sons ⟨giving the citadel and its neighbourhood to Aegeus, the hill country to Lycus, the coast to Pallas and the district of Megara to Nisus⟩. *Fr.* 3. And these sections were continually quarrelling; but Theseus made a proclamation and brought them together on an equal and like footing. ⟨He summoned all on equal terms, and it is said that the phrase 'Come hither, all ye folks'[a] was the proclamation of Theseus made when he was instituting an assembly of the whole people.⟩

Fr. 4. ⟨And that Theseus first leant towards the mob, as Aristotle says, and relinquished monarchical government, even Homer seems to testify, when he applies the term 'people'[b] in the Catalogue of Ships to the Athenians only.⟩

Fr. 5. ⟨. . . As Aristotle narrates in his *Athenian Constitution*, where he says: 'And they were grouped in four tribal divisions in imitation of the seasons in the year, and each of the tribes was divided into three parts, in order that there might be twelve parts in all, like the months of the year, and they were called Thirds and Brotherhoods; and the arrangement of clans was in groups of thirty to the brotherhood, as the days to the month, and the clan consisted of thirty men.'⟩[c]

Fr. 6. He having come to Scyros ⟨probably in order to inspect it because of his kinship with Aegeus[d]⟩

[b] *Iliad*, ii. 547.

[c] After Cleisthenes' reforms, 510 B.C., there were ten tribes, each divided into Thirds and also into ten or more Demes; each Deme was divided into Brotherhoods (number unknown), and these perhaps into Clans.

[d] Aegeus, King of Athens, father of Theseus, is not connected in any extant myth with the Aegean island of Scyros.

ὠσθεὶς κατὰ πετρῶν ὑπὸ Λυκομήδους, φοβηθέντος μὴ σφετερίζηται τὴν νῆσον. Ἀθηναῖοι δὲ ὕστερον μετὰ τὰ Μηδικὰ μετεκόμισαν αὐτοῦ τὰ ὀστᾶ. ⟨Ἀθηναῖοι μετὰ τὰ Μηδικὰ κατὰ μαντείαν ἀνελόντες αὐτοῦ τὰ ὀστᾶ ἔθαψαν. (Schol. *l.c.*)⟩

7. Ἀπὸ δὲ Κοδριδῶν οὐκέτι βασιλεῖς ᾑροῦντο, διὰ τὸ δοκεῖν τρυφᾶν καὶ μαλακοὺς γεγονέναι. Ἱππομένης δὲ εἷς τῶν Κοδριδῶν βουλόμενος ἀπώσασθαι τὴν διαβολήν, λαβὼν ἐπὶ τῇ θυγατρὶ Λειμώνῃ μοιχόν, ἐκεῖνον μὲν ἀνεῖλεν ὑποζεύξας μετὰ τῆς θυγατρὸς[1] τῷ ἅρματι, τὴν δὲ ἵππῳ συνέκλεισεν ἕως ἀπώλετο.

8. Τοὺς μετὰ Κύλωνος διὰ τὴν τυραννίδα ἐπὶ τὸν βωμὸν τῆς θεοῦ πεφευγότας οἱ περὶ Μεγακλέα ἀπέκτειναν. καὶ τοὺς δράσαντας ὡς ἐναγεῖς ἤλαυνον.

Incipit codex

1 I. . . . ⟨κατηγοροῦντος⟩[2] Μύρωνος, καθ' ἱερῶν ὀμόσαντες, ἀριστίνδην. καταγνωσθέντος δὲ τοῦ ἄγους, αὐτοὶ μὲν ἐκ τῶν τάφων ἐξεβλήθησαν, τὸ δὲ γένος αὐτῶν ἔφυγεν ἀειφυγίαν. Ἐπιμενίδης δ' ὁ Κρὴς ἐπὶ τούτοις ἐκάθηρε τὴν πόλιν.

1 II. Μετὰ δὲ ταῦτα συνέβη στασιάσαι τούς τε

[1] μετὰ τῶν ζυγίων (sic Aristoph. *Nub.* 122) coni. Blass: secl. Koehler.
[2] Wilamowitz e Plut. *Sol.* 12.

[a] King of Athens, died 1068 B.C. (by the mythical chronology).

[b] 722 B.C.; the Attic nobles deposed him in punishment.

[c] This nobleman seized the Acropolis to make himself tyrant. When blockaded he escaped. His comrades were induced to surrender by the archon, Megacles of the

met his end by being thrust down a cliff by Lycomedes, who was afraid that he might appropriate the island. But subsequently the Athenians after the Persian Wars brought back his bones. ⟨The Athenians, after the Persian Wars, in conformity with an oracle took up his bones and buried them.⟩

Fr. 7. Kings were no longer chosen from the house of Codrus,[a] because they were thought to be luxurious and to have become soft. But one of the house of Codrus, Hippomenes, who wished to repel the slander, taking a man in adultery with his daughter Leimonē, killed him by yoking him to his chariot with his daughter [? emend 'with his team'], and locked her up with a horse till she died.[b]

Fr. 8. The associates of Cylon[c] because of his 620 B.C.?
tyranny were killed by the party of Megacles when they had taken refuge at the altar of Athena. And those who had done this were then banished as being under a curse.

The MS. *begins here*

I. ⟨The Alcmaeonids were tried, on the prosecu- 1
tion⟩ of Myron, ⟨by jurymen⟩ solemnly sworn in,[d]
selected according to noble birth. The charge of 599 B.C.
sacrilege having been confirmed by the verdict, the bodies of the guilty men themselves were cast out of their tombs, and their family was sentenced to everlasting banishment. Thereupon Epimenides of
Crete purified the city. 596 B.C.

II. Afterwards it came about that a party quarrel 1

Alcmaeonid family, who promised to spare their lives, but then put them to death. From what follows in the text it appears that the movement to punish this sacrilege only came to a head after Megacles was dead and buried.

[d] Lit. 'having taken an oath over the sacred victims.'

2 γνωρίμους καὶ τὸ πλῆθος πολὺν χρόνον.[1] ἦν γὰρ αὐτῶν ἡ πολιτεία τοῖς τ' ἄλλοις ὀλιγαρχικὴ πᾶσι καὶ δὴ καὶ ἐδούλευον οἱ πένητες τοῖς πλουσίοις καὶ αὐτοὶ καὶ τὰ τέκνα καὶ αἱ γυναῖκες· καὶ ἐκαλοῦντο πελάται, καὶ ἑκτημόροι· κατὰ ταύτην γὰρ τὴν μίσθωσιν ἠργάζοντο τῶν πλουσίων τοὺς ἀγρούς (ἡ δὲ πᾶσα γῆ δι' ὀλίγων ἦν), καὶ εἰ μὴ τὰς μισθώσεις ἀποδιδοῖεν, ἀγώγιμοι καὶ αὐτοὶ καὶ οἱ παῖδες ἐγίγνοντο· καὶ οἱ δανεισμοὶ πᾶσιν ἐπὶ τοῖς σώμασιν ἦσαν μέχρι Σόλωνος· οὗτος δὲ πρῶτος ἐγένετο τοῦ δήμου προστάτης.
3 χαλεπώτατον μὲν οὖν καὶ πικρότατον ἦν τοῖς πολλοῖς τῶν κατὰ τὴν πολιτείαν τὸ δουλεύειν· οὐ μὴν ἀλλὰ καὶ ἐπὶ τοῖς ἄλλοις ἐδυσχέραινον, οὐδενὸς γὰρ ὡς εἰπεῖν ἐτύγχανον μετέχοντες.

1 III. Ἦν δ' ἡ τάξις τῆς ἀρχαίας πολιτείας τῆς πρὸ Δράκοντος τοιάδε. τὰς μὲν ἀρχὰς καθίστασαν ἀριστίνδην καὶ πλουτίνδην· ἦρχον δὲ τὸ μὲν πρῶτον
2 διὰ βίου, μετὰ δὲ ταῦτα δεκαέτειαν. μέγισται δὲ καὶ πρῶται τῶν ἀρχῶν ἦσαν βασιλεὺς καὶ πολέμαρχος καὶ ἄρχων. τούτων δὲ πρώτη μὲν ἡ τοῦ βασιλέως, αὕτη γὰρ ἦν πάτριος. δευτέρα δ' ἐπικατέστη πολεμαρχία διὰ τοῦ γενέσθαι τινὰς τῶν βασιλέων τὰ πολέμια μαλακούς· ὅθεν καὶ τὸν
3 Ἴωνα μετεπέμψαντο χρείας καταλαβούσης. τελευταία δ' ἡ τοῦ ἄρχοντος· οἱ μὲν γὰρ πλείους ἐπὶ

[1] χρονοντονδημον cod.: secl. Kenyon.

---

[a] πελάτης, 'one who *approaches* as a dependent,' was later used as the Greek for *cliens*.

[b] Apparently this became almost an official title, see c. xxviii.

took place between the notables and the multitude
that lasted a long time. For the Athenian constitu- 2
tion was in all respects oligarchical, and in fact the poor themselves and also their wives and children were actually in slavery to the rich; and they were called Clients,[a] and Sixth-part-tenants (for that was the rent they paid for the rich men's land which they farmed, and the whole of the country was in few hands), and if they ever failed to pay their rents, they themselves and their children were liable to arrest; and all borrowing was on the security of the debtors' persons down to the time of Solon: it was
he who first became head[b] of the People. Thus the 3
most grievous and bitter thing in the state of public affairs for the masses was their slavery; not but what they were discontented also about everything else, for they found themselves virtually without a share in anything.

III. The form of the ancient constitution that 1
existed before Draco was as follows. Appointment to the supreme offices of state went by birth and wealth; and they were held at first for life, and
afterwards for a term of ten years. The greatest and 2
oldest of the offices were the King, the War-lord and the Archon. Of these the office of King was the oldest, for it was ancestral. The second established was the office of War-lord, which was added because some of the Kings proved cowardly in warfare (which was the reason why the Athenians had summoned Ion to their aid in an emergency).[c]
The last of these three offices established was 3
that of the Archon, the institution of which is dated by a majority of authorities in the time of

[c] See Fr. 1 above.

Μέδοντος, ἔνιοι δ' ἐπὶ Ἀκάστου φασὶ γενέσθαι ταύτην· τεκμήριον δ' ἐπιφέρουσιν ὅτι οἱ ἐννέα ἄρχοντες ὀμνύουσιν ἦ τὰ[1] ἐπὶ Ἀκάστου ὅρκια[2] ποιήσειν, ὡς ἐπὶ τούτου τῆς βασιλείας παραχωρησάντων τῶν Κοδριδῶν ἀντὶ τῶν δοθεισῶν[3] τῷ ἄρχοντι δωρεῶν. τοῦτο μὲν οὖν ὁποτέρως ποτ' ἔχει μικρὸν ἂν παραλλάττοι τοῖς χρόνοις· ὅτι δὲ τελευταία τούτων ἐγένετο τῶν ἀρχῶν, σημεῖον καὶ τὸ μηδὲν τῶν πατρίων τὸν ἄρχοντα διοικεῖν, ὥσπερ ὁ βασιλεὺς καὶ ὁ πολέμαρχος, ἀλλ' ἁπλῶς τὰ ἐπίθετα· διὸ καὶ νεωστὶ γέγονεν ἡ ἀρχὴ μεγάλη,
4 τοῖς ἐπιθέτοις αὐξηθεῖσα. θεσμοθέται δὲ πολλοῖς ὕστερον ἔτεσιν ᾑρέθησαν, ἤδη κατ' ἐνιαυτὸν αἱρουμένων τὰς ἀρχάς, ὅπως ἀναγράψαντες τὰ θέσμια φυλάττωσι πρὸς τὴν τῶν ἀμφισβητούντων κρίσιν· διὸ καὶ μόνη τῶν ἀρχῶν οὐκ ἐγένετο πλείων
5 ἐνιαυσίας. τοῖς μὲν οὖν χρόνοις τοσοῦτον προέχουσιν ἀλλήλων. ἦσαν δ' οὐχ ἅμα πάντες οἱ ἐννέα ἄρχοντες, ἀλλ' ὁ μὲν βασιλεὺς εἶχε τὸ νῦν καλούμενον Βουκόλιον, πλησίον τοῦ πρυτανείου (σημεῖον δέ· ἔτι καὶ νῦν γὰρ τῆς τοῦ βασιλέως γυναικὸς ἡ σύμμειξις ἐνταῦθα γίνεται τῷ Διονύσῳ καὶ ὁ γάμος), ὁ δὲ ἄρχων τὸ πρυτανεῖον, ὁ δὲ πολέμαρχος τὸ Ἐπιλυκεῖον (ὃ πρότερον μὲν ἐκαλεῖτο πολεμ-

[1] ἦ ⟨μὴν⟩ τὰ Wilamowitz.
[2] δίκαια (cf. lv. 5 δικαίως ἄρξειν) Richards.
[3] αντιτωνδοθεισων literis valde obscuris scriptum: ἀνταποδοθεισῶν ? Sandys.

[a] Son of Codrus (see Fr. 7 above) and life-archon.
[b] Medon's successor.
[c] Or, with Sandys's reading, 'corresponding privileges being (at the same time) assigned to the Archon.'
[d] The official title of the six junior Archons.

Medon,[a] though some put it in that of Acastus,[b] ad-
ducing in evidence the fact that the Nine Archons
swear that they will perform their oaths even as in
the time of Acastus, showing that in his time the
house of Codrus retired from the Kingship in return
for the privileges bestowed on the Archon.[c] Whichever of the two accounts is true, it would make very
little difference in the dates; but that this was the
last of these offices to be instituted is also indicated
by the fact that the Archon does not administer any
of the ancestral rites, as do the King and the War-
lord, but merely the duties added later; on account of which also the Archonship only became
great in recent times, when augmented by the
added duties. Legislators[d] were elected many years 4
later, when the elections to the offices were now 683 B.C.
yearly, to perform the function of publicly recording
the ordinances and to preserve them for the trial of
litigants; hence this alone of the supreme offices was
never tenable for more than a year. These are the 5
intervals between the dates of the institution of the
various supreme offices. And the Nine Archons[e]
were not all together, but the King had what is now
called the Bucolium,[f] near the town hall[g] (as is indicated by the fact that even at the present day the
union and marriage[h] of the King's Wife with Dionysus
takes place there), while the Archon had the President's Hall, and the War-lord the Epilyceum (which
formerly used to be called the War-lord's House, but

[e] *i.e.* their official residences and courts.

[f] Otherwise unknown.

[g] Position uncertain.

[h] An annual ceremony by which the god Dionysus was incorporated as an Athenian: the lady personifying his consort passed a night in his temple.

αρχεῖον, ἐπεὶ δὲ Ἐπίλυκος ἀνῳκοδόμησε καὶ κατεσκεύασεν αὐτὸ πολεμαρχήσας, Ἐπιλυκεῖον ἐκλήθη), θεσμοθέται δ' εἶχον τὸ θεσμοθετεῖον. ἐπὶ δὲ Σόλωνος ἅπαντες εἰς τὸ θεσμοθετεῖον συνῆλθον. κύριοι δ' ἦσαν καὶ τὰς δίκας αὐτοτελεῖς κρίνειν, καὶ οὐχ ὥσπερ νῦν προανακρίνειν. τὰ μὲν οὖν
6 περὶ τὰς ἀρχὰς τοῦτον εἶχε τὸν τρόπον. ἡ δὲ τῶν Ἀρεοπαγιτῶν βουλὴ τὴν μὲν τάξιν εἶχε τοῦ διατηρεῖν τοὺς νόμους, διῴκει δὲ τὰ πλεῖστα καὶ τὰ μέγιστα τῶν ἐν τῇ πόλει, καὶ κολάζουσα καὶ ζημιοῦσα πάντας τοὺς ἀκοσμοῦντας κυρίως· ἡ γὰρ αἵρεσις τῶν ἀρχόντων ἀριστίνδην καὶ πλουτίνδην ἦν, ἐξ ὧν οἱ Ἀρεοπαγῖται καθίσταντο, διὸ καὶ μόνη τῶν ἀρχῶν αὕτη μεμένηκε διὰ βίου καὶ νῦν. ἡ μὲν οὖν πρώτη πολιτεία ταύτην εἶχε τὴν ὑπογραφήν.

1 IV. Μετὰ δὲ ταῦτα, χρόνου τινὸς οὐ πολλοῦ διελθόντος, ἐπ' Ἀρισταίχμου ἄρχοντος Δράκων τοὺς θεσμοὺς ἔθηκεν· ἡ δὲ τάξις αὕτη τόνδε τὸν
2 τρόπον εἶχε. ἀπεδέδοτο μὲν ἡ πολιτεία τοῖς ὅπλα παρεχομένοις· ᾑροῦντο δὲ τοὺς μὲν ἐννέα ἄρχοντας καὶ τοὺς ταμίας οὐσίαν κεκτημένους οὐκ ἐλάττω δέκα μνῶν ἐλευθέραν, τὰς δ' ἄλλας ἀρχὰς τὰς[1] ἐλάττους ἐκ τῶν ὅπλα παρεχομένων, στρατηγοὺς δὲ καὶ ἱππάρχους οὐσίαν ἀποφαίνοντας οὐκ ἔλαττον' ἢ ἑκατὸν μνῶν ἐλευθέραν[2] καὶ παῖδας ἐκ γαμετῆς γυναικὸς γνησίους ὑπὲρ δέκα ἔτη γεγονό-

[1] τὰς suppletum a Richards et aliis.
[2] edd.: ελευθερων cod.

[a] Draco was presumably one of the Thesmothetae, Aristaechmus being Archon Eponymus. For Draco's work see

because Epilycus on becoming War-lord rebuilt and furnished it, it received the name of Epilyceum); and the Legislators had the Legislators' Court. But in Solon's time they all came together in the Legislators' Court. They also had power to give final judgement in lawsuits, and not as now merely to hold a preliminary trial. Such then were the regulations relating to the supreme offices. The Council of 6
Areopagus had the official function of guarding the laws, but actually it administered the greatest number and the most important of the affairs of state, inflicting penalties and fines upon offenders against public order without appeal; for the elections of the Archons went by birth and wealth, and the members of the Areopagus were appointed from them, owing to which this alone of the offices has remained even to the present day tenable for life. This, then, was the outline of the first form of the constitution.

IV. And after this when a certain moderate length 1
of time had passed, in the archonship of Aristaechmus, 621 B.C.
Draco enacted his ordinances[a]; and this system was on the following lines. Citizenship had already been 2
bestowed on those who provided themselves with arms; and these elected as the Nine Archons and the Treasurers,[b] who were owners of an unencumbered estate worth not less than 10 minae,[c] and the other minor offices from those who provided themselves with arms, and as Generals and Masters of the Horse persons proving their possession of unencumbered estate worth not less than 100 minae and sons legitimately born in wedlock over ten years of age. The

Politics 1274 b 15 ff.; it is there said that he 'adapted his laws to a constitution that already existed.'

[b] For the Treasurers of Athena see xlvii. 1.

[c] Say £40.

τας· τούτους δ' ἔδει διεγγυᾶν τοὺς πρυτάνεις καὶ τοὺς στρατηγοὺς καὶ τοὺς ἱππάρχους τοὺς ἕνους μέχρι εὐθυνῶν, ἐγγυητὰς δ' ἐκ τοῦ αὐτοῦ τέλους δεχομένους οὗπερ οἱ στρατηγοὶ καὶ οἱ ἵππαρχοι.
3 βουλεύειν δὲ τετρακοσίους καὶ ἕνα τοὺς λαχόντας ἐκ τῆς πολιτείας· κληροῦσθαι δὲ καὶ ταύτην καὶ τὰς ἄλλας ἀρχὰς τοὺς ὑπὲρ τριάκοντα ἔτη γεγονότας· καὶ δὶς τὸν αὐτὸν μὴ ἄρχειν πρὸ τοῦ πάντας ἐξελθεῖν, τότε δὲ πάλιν ἐξ ὑπαρχῆς κληροῦν. εἰ δέ τις τῶν βουλευτῶν, ὅταν ἕδρα βουλῆς ἢ ἐκκλησίας ᾖ,[1] ἐκλείποι[2] τὴν σύνοδον, ἀπέτινον ὁ μὲν πεντακοσιομέδιμνος τρεῖς δραχμάς, ὁ δὲ ἱππεὺς δύο,
4 ζευγίτης[3] δὲ μίαν. ἡ δὲ βουλὴ ἡ ἐξ Ἀρείου πάγου φύλαξ ἦν τῶν νόμων, καὶ διετήρει τὰς ἀρχὰς ὅπως κατὰ τοὺς νόμους ἄρχωσιν. ἐξῆν δὲ τῷ ἀδικουμένῳ πρὸς τὴν τῶν Ἀρεοπαγιτῶν βουλὴν εἰσαγγέλλειν, ἀποφαίνοντι παρ' ὃν ἀδικεῖται νόμον. ἐπὶ δὲ τοῖς σώμασιν ἦσαν οἱ δανεισμοί, καθάπερ εἴρηται, καὶ ἡ χώρα δι' ὀλίγων ἦν.

1 V. Τοιαύτης δὲ τῆς τάξεως οὔσης ἐν τῇ πολιτείᾳ καὶ τῶν πολλῶν δουλευόντων τοῖς ὀλίγοις, ἀντέστη
2 τοῖς γνωρίμοις ὁ δῆμος. ἰσχυρᾶς δὲ τῆς στάσεως οὔσης καὶ πολὺν χρόνον ἀντικαθημένων ἀλλήλοις, εἵλοντο κοινῇ διαλλακτὴν καὶ ἄρχοντα Σόλωνα καὶ τὴν πολιτείαν ἐπέτρεψαν αὐτῷ, ποιήσαντι τὴν ἐλεγείαν ἧς ἐστὶν ἀρχή·

[1] ὅταν . . . ᾖ] ὅτε . . . εἴη ? Richards.
[2] ἐκλίποι Heerwerden-Leeuwen.
[3] ⟨ὁ⟩ ζευγίτης Kontos.

[a] Probably before Solon's time this denotes the Archons.
[b] See vii. 3. A drachma (say 9½d. or 1 franc) was a hundredth part of a mina (say £4).
[c] On these quotations from Solon see Edmonds, *Elegy and*

new officials had to bail the outgoing Presidents[a] and
Generals and Masters of the Horse till the audit,
accepting four sureties from the same rating as
that to which the Generals and Masters of the Horse
belonged. And the Council was to be formed of four 3
hundred and one members chosen by lot from the
citizen body, and lots were to be cast both for this
and for the other offices by the citizens over thirty
years of age; and the same person was not to hold
office twice until the whole number had been gone
through, and then lots were to be cast among them
again from the beginning. And if any Councillor,
whenever there was a sitting of the Council or
Assembly, failed to attend the meeting, he paid a
fine of 3 drachmae if of Five-hundred-measure rank,
2 drachmae if a Knight, and 1 if a Teamster.[b] The 4
Council of Areopagus was guardian of the laws, and
kept a watch on the magistrates to make them
govern in accordance with the laws. A person unjustly treated might lay a complaint before the
Council of the Areopagites, stating the law in contravention of which he was treated unjustly. Loans
were secured on the person, as has been said, and the ii. 2.
land was divided among few owners.

V. Such being the system in the constitution, and 1
the many being enslaved to the few, the people rose
against the notables. The party struggle being 2
violent and the parties remaining arrayed in opposition to one another for a long time, they jointly
chose Solon as arbitrator and Archon, and entrusted 594 B.C.?
the government to him, after he had composed the
elegy[c] that begins:

Iambus (L.C.L.), vol. i. pp. 104 ff., especially pp. 120-121, 142-143, and 148-153.

γινώσκω, καί μοι φρενὸς ἔνδοθεν ἄλγεα κεῖται
 πρεσβυτάτην ἐσορῶν γαῖαν Ἰαονίας
καινομένην[1]·

ἐν ᾗ πρὸς ἑκατέρους ὑπὲρ ἑκατέρων μάχεται καὶ διαμφισβητεῖ, καὶ μετὰ ταῦτα κοινῇ παραινεῖ
3 καταπαύειν τὴν ἐνεστῶσαν φιλονικίαν. ἦν δ' ὁ Σόλων τῇ μὲν φύσει καὶ τῇ δόξῃ τῶν πρώτων, τῇ δ' οὐσίᾳ καὶ τοῖς πράγμασι τῶν μέσων, ὡς ἔκ τε τῶν ἄλλων ὁμολογεῖται καὶ αὐτὸς ἐν τοῖσδε τοῖς ποιήμασιν μαρτυρεῖ, παραινῶν τοῖς πλουσίοις μὴ πλεονεκτεῖν·

ὑμεῖς δ' ἡσυχάσαντες ἐνὶ φρεσὶ καρτερὸν ἦτορ,
 οἳ πολλῶν ἀγαθῶν ἐς κόρον ἠλάσατε,
ἐν μετρίοισι[2] τίθεσθε μέγαν νόον· οὔτε γὰρ ἡμεῖς
 πεισόμεθ', οὔθ' ὑμῖν ἄρτια ταῦτ'[3] ἔσεται.

καὶ ὅλως αἰεὶ τὴν αἰτίαν τῆς στάσεως ἀνάπτει τοῖς πλουσίοις· διὸ καὶ ἐν ἀρχῇ τῆς ἐλεγείας δεδοικέναι φησὶ

τήν τε φιλαργυρίαν[4] τήν θ' ὑπερηφανίαν,

ὡς διὰ ταῦτα τῆς ἔχθρας ἐνεστώσης.

1 VI. Κύριος δὲ γενόμενος τῶν πραγμάτων Σόλων τόν τε δῆμον ἠλευθέρωσε καὶ ἐν τῷ παρόντι καὶ εἰς τὸ μέλλον, κωλύσας δανείζειν ἐπὶ τοῖς σώμασιν, καὶ νόμους ἔθηκε, καὶ χρεῶν ἀποκοπὰς ἐποίησε καὶ τῶν ἰδίων καὶ τῶν δημοσίων, ἃς σεισάχθειαν

[1] κλινομένην, καρφομένην nonnulli legunt: καιομένην? Edmonds.

[2] μέτροισι Wilamowitz-Kaibel metri gratia (et τέμεσθε, 'cut to measure,' Edmonds).

[3] πάντ' nonnulli legunt: τᾶστ' Edmonds.

I mark, and sorrow fills my breast to see,
Ionia's oldest land being done to death,—

in which he does battle on behalf of each party against the other and acts as mediator, and after this exhorts them jointly to stop the quarrel that prevailed between them. Solon was by birth and re- 3
putation of the first rank, but by wealth and position belonged to the middle class, as is admitted on the part of the other authorities, and as he himself testifies in these poems, exhorting the wealthy not to be covetous :

Refrain ye in your hearts those stubborn moods,
Plunged in a surfeit of abundant goods,
And moderate your pride ! We'll not submit,
Nor even you yourselves will this befit.[a]

And he always attaches the blame for the civil strife wholly to the rich ; owing to which at the beginning of the elegy he says that he fears

Both love of money and o'erweening pride—,

implying that these were the causes of the enmity that prevailed.

VI. Solon having become master of affairs made 1
the people free both at the time and for the future by prohibiting loans secured on the person, and he laid down laws, and enacted cancellations of debts both private and public, the measures[b] that are known

[a] 'Nor shall ye possess what ye have now without decrease' (Edmonds).

[b] Their actual provisions are quite uncertain.

---

[1] φιλοχρηίαν legit Edmonds (cf. φιλοχρηματιᾶν Plutarch, *Solon* 14).

2 καλοῦσιν, ὡς ἀποσεισαμένων[1] τὸ βάρος. ἐν οἷς πειρῶνταί τινες διαβάλλειν αὐτόν· συνέβη γὰρ τῷ Σόλωνι μέλλοντι ποιεῖν τὴν σεισάχθειαν προειπεῖν τισὶ τῶν γνωρίμων, ἔπειθ', ὡς μὲν οἱ δημοτικοὶ λέγουσι, παραστρατηγηθῆναι διὰ τῶν φίλων, ὡς δ' οἱ βουλόμενοι βλασφημεῖν, καὶ αὐτὸν κοινωνεῖν. δανεισάμενοι γὰρ οὗτοι συνεπρίαντο πολλὴν χώραν, καὶ μετ' οὐ πολὺ τῆς τῶν χρεῶν ἀποκοπῆς γενομένης[2] ἐπλούτουν· ὅθεν φασὶ γενέσθαι τοὺς
3 ὕστερον δοκοῦντας εἶναι παλαιοπλούτους. οὐ μὴν ἀλλὰ πιθανώτερος ὁ τῶν δημοτικῶν λόγος· οὐ γὰρ εἰκὸς ἐν μὲν τοῖς ἄλλοις οὕτω μέτριον γενέσθαι καὶ κοινὸν ὥστ', ἐξὸν αὐτῷ τοὺς ἑτέρους ὑποποιησάμενον τυραννεῖν τῆς πόλεως, ἀμφοτέροις ἀπεχθέσθαι καὶ περὶ πλείονος ποιήσασθαι τὸ καλὸν καὶ τὴν τῆς πόλεως σωτηρίαν ἢ τὴν αὑτοῦ πλεονεξίαν, ἐν οὕτω δὲ μικροῖς καὶ ἀναξίοις[3] καταρρυπαί-
4 νειν ἑαυτόν. ὅτι δὲ ταύτην ἔσχε τὴν ἐξουσίαν, τά τε πράγματα νοσοῦντα μαρτυρεῖ, καὶ ἐν τοῖς ποιήμασιν αὐτὸς πολλαχοῦ μέμνηται, καὶ οἱ ἄλλοι συνομολογοῦσι πάντες. ταύτην μὲν οὖν χρὴ νομίζειν ψευδῆ τὴν αἰτίαν εἶναι.

1 VII. Πολιτείαν δὲ κατέστησε καὶ νόμους ἔθηκεν ἄλλους, τοῖς δὲ Δράκοντος θεσμοῖς ἐπαύσαντο χρώμενοι πλὴν τῶν φονικῶν. ἀναγράψαντες δὲ τοὺς

[1] Mayor: αποσισαμενοι cod.
[2] Rutherford: γινομενης cod.
[3] φανεροῖς incerte legit Rutherford.

as 'the Shaking-off of Burdens,' meaning that the people shook off their load. In these matters some people try to misrepresent him; for it happened 2
that when Solon was intending to enact the Shaking-off of Burdens, he informed some of the notables beforehand, and afterwards, as those of popular sympathies say, he was out-manœuvred by his friends, but according to those who want to malign him he himself also took a share. For these persons borrowed money and bought up a quantity of land, and when not long afterwards the cancellation of debts took place they were rich men; and this is said to be the origin of the families subsequently reputed to be ancestrally wealthy.[a] Nevertheless, 3
the account of those of popular sympathies is more credible; for considering that he was so moderate and public-spirited in the rest of his conduct that, when he had the opportunity to reduce one of the two parties to subjection and so to be tyrant of the city, he incurred the enmity of both, and valued honour and the safety of the state more than his own aggrandizement, it is not probable that he besmirched himself in such worthless trifles. And that he got 4
this opportunity is testified by the disordered state of affairs, and also he himself alludes to it in many places in his poems, and everybody else agrees with him. We are bound therefore to consider this charge to be false.

VII. And he established a constitution and made 1
other laws, and they ceased to observe the ordinances of Draco, except those relating to homicide. They

[a] Apparently certain well-known families, but not alluded to elsewhere.

νόμους εἰς τοὺς κύρβεις ἔστησαν ἐν τῇ στοᾷ τῇ
βασιλείῳ καὶ ὤμοσαν χρήσεσθαι πάντες· οἱ δ'
ἐννέα ἄρχοντες ὀμνύντες πρὸς τῷ λίθῳ κατεφάτιζον
ἀναθήσειν ἀνδριάντα χρυσοῦν ἐάν τινα παραβῶσι
τῶν νόμων· ὅθεν ἔτι καὶ νῦν οὕτως ὀμνύουσι.
2 κατέκλεισεν δὲ τοὺς νόμους εἰς ἑκατὸν ἔτη. καὶ
3 διέταξε τὴν πολιτείαν τόνδε τρόπον· τιμήματι
διεῖλεν[1] εἰς τέτταρα τέλη, καθάπερ διῄρητο καὶ
πρότερον, εἰς πεντακοσιομέδιμνον καὶ ἱππέα καὶ
ζευγίτην καὶ θῆτα· καὶ τὰς μὲν ἄλλας[2] ἀρχὰς
ἀπένειμεν ἄρχειν ἐκ πεντακοσιομεδίμνων καὶ ἱππέων καὶ ζευγιτῶν, τοὺς ἐννέα ἄρχοντας καὶ
τοὺς ταμίας καὶ τοὺς πωλητὰς καὶ τοὺς ἕνδεκα
καὶ τοὺς κωλακρέτας, ἑκάστοις ἀνὰ λόγον τῷ μεγέθει τοῦ τιμήματος ἀποδιδοὺς ἑκάστην[3] ἀρχήν·
τοῖς δὲ τὸ θητικὸν τελοῦσιν ἐκκλησίας καὶ δικα-
4 στηρίων μετέδωκε μόνον. ἔδει δὲ τελεῖν πεντακοσιομέδιμνον μὲν ὃς ἂν ἐκ τῆς[4] οἰκείας ποιῇ
πεντακόσια μέτρα τὰ συνάμφω ξηρὰ καὶ ὑγρά,
ἱππάδα δὲ τοὺς τριακόσια ποιοῦντας—ὡς δ' ἔνιοί
φασι, τοὺς ἱπποτροφεῖν δυναμένους· σημεῖον δὲ
φέρουσι τό τε ὄνομα τοῦ τέλους, ὡς ἀπὸ[5] τοῦ
πράγματος κείμενον, καὶ τὰ ἀναθήματα τῶν
ἀρχαίων· ἀνάκειται γὰρ ἐν ἀκροπόλει εἰκὼν
Διφίλου[6] ἐφ' ᾗ ἐπιγέγραπται τάδε·

[1] διεῖλεν ⟨αὐτὴν⟩ ? Rutherford.
[2] μὲν ἄλλας Diels: μ . . . ας cod.: μεγίστας Blass olim.
[3] Rackham: την cod.
[4] γῆς Bywater.
[5] ἀπὸ Rackham: αναπω cod.
[6] [Διφίλου] Thompson.

[a] Three-sided (or perhaps four-sided) structures of wood (or perhaps stone) revolving on pivots; set up in the Stoa Basilike, the court of the King-Archon, on the west side of the Agora.

wrote up the laws on the Boards[a] and set them in the Royal Colonnade, and all swore to observe them; and the Nine Archons used to make affirmation on oath at the Stone[b] that if they transgressed any one of the laws they would dedicate a gold statue of a man; owing to which they are even now still sworn in with this oath. And he fixed the laws to stay unaltered for 2
a hundred years. And he arranged the constitution in the following way: he divided the people by assess- 3
ment into four classes, as they had been divided before, Five-hundred-measure man, Horseman, Teamster and Labourer, and he distributed the other offices to be held from among the Five-hundred-measure men, Horsemen and Teamsters—the Nine Archons, the Treasurers,[c] the Vendors of Contracts,[d] the Eleven[e] and the Paymasters, assigning each office to the several classes in proportion to the amount of their assessment; while those who were rated in the Labourer class he admitted to the membership of the assembly and law-courts alone. Any man had 4
to be rated as a Five-hundred-measure man the produce from whose estate was five hundred dry and liquid measures jointly,[f] and at the cavalry-rate those who made three hundred,—or as some say, those who were able to keep a horse, and they adduce as a proof the name of the rating as being derived from the fact, and also the votive offerings of the ancients; for there stands dedicated in the Acropolis a statue of Diphilus[g] on which are inscribed these lines:

[b] Perhaps the altar of Zeus Agoraios.

[c] See xlvii. 1. [d] See xlvii. 2. [e] See lii. 1.

[f] *i.e.* measures of corn and of wine and oil amounting in all to five hundred.

[g] 'Of Diphilus' is probably a mistaken insertion; presumably the statue was of Anthemion himself.

Διφίλου Ἀνθεμίων τήνδ' ἀνέθηκε θεοῖς . . .
θητικοῦ ἀντὶ τέλους ἱππάδ' ἀμειψάμενος—

καὶ παρέστηκεν ἵππος ἐκμαρτυρῶν[1] ὡς τὴν ἱππάδα τοῦτο σημαίνουσαν. οὐ μὴν ἀλλ' εὐλογώτερον τοῖς μέτροις διῃρῆσθαι καθάπερ τοὺς πεντακοσιομεδίμνους. ζευγίσιον δὲ τελεῖν τοὺς διακόσια τὰ συνάμφω ποιοῦντας· τοὺς δ' ἄλλους θητικόν, οὐδεμιᾶς μετέχοντας ἀρχῆς, διὸ καὶ νῦν ἐπειδὰν ἔρηται τὸν μέλλοντα κληροῦσθαί τιν' ἀρχὴν ποῖον τέλος τελεῖ, οὐδ' ἂν εἷς εἴποι θητικόν.

1 VIII. Τὰς δ' ἀρχὰς ἐποίησε κληρωτὰς ἐκ προκρίτων οὓς ἑκάστη προκρίνειε[2] τῶν φυλῶν. προὔκρινεν δ' εἰς τοὺς ἐννέα ἄρχοντας ἑκάστη δέκα, καὶ[3] τούτων ἐκλήρουν[4]· ὅθεν ἔτι διαμένει ταῖς φυλαῖς τὸ δέκα κληροῦν ἑκάστην, εἶτ' ἐκ τούτων κυαμεύειν. σημεῖον δ' ὅτι κληρωτὰς ἐποίησεν[5] ἐκ τῶν τιμημάτων ὁ περὶ τῶν ταμιῶν νόμος ᾧ χρώμενοι διατελοῦσιν ἔτι καὶ νῦν· κελεύει γὰρ κληροῦν τοὺς ταμίας ἐκ πεντακοσιομεδίμνων.
2 Σόλων μὲν οὖν οὕτως ἐνομοθέτησεν περὶ τῶν ἐννέα ἀρχόντων· τὸ γὰρ ἀρχαῖον ἡ ἐν Ἀρείῳ πάγῳ βουλὴ ἀνακαλεσαμένη καὶ κρίνασα καθ' αὑτὴν τὸν ἐπιτήδειον ἐφ' ἑκάστῃ τῶν ἀρχῶν ἐπ'
3 ἐνιαυτὸν ἄρξοντα[6] ἀπέστελλεν. φυλαὶ δ' ἦσαν δ'

[1] εἰς μαρτύριον coni. Blass. [2] Gertz: προκρινει cod.
[3] κἀκ Gomperz (sed cf. xxx. 1, xxxi. 1).
[4] Kaibel-Wilamowitz: του . . . λη̣ρουν cod.
[5] Bury: ιποιησαν cod.
[6] Kaibel: διατάξασα Kenyon: . . . τα vel . . . σα cod.

[a] Apparently the property qualification was ignored, without being formally repealed.

[b] *i.e.* nine were taken by lot out of forty elected by vote

Anthemion Diphilus's son dedicated this statue to the gods
. . . having exchanged the Labourer rating for the Cavalry—

and a horse stands beside him, in evidence that 'cavalry' meant the class able to keep a horse. Nevertheless it is more probable that the cavalry were distinguished by their amounts of produce as the Five-hundred-measure men were. And men had to be rated in the Teamster class who made two hundred measures, wet and dry together; while the rest were rated in the Labourer class, being admitted to no office: hence even now when the presiding official asks a man who is about to draw lots for some office what rate he pays, no one whatever would say that he was rated as a Labourer.[a]

VIII. For the offices of state he instituted election 1
by lot from candidates selected by the tribes severally by a preliminary vote. For the Nine Archons each tribe made a preliminary selection of ten, and the election was made from among these by lot[b]; hence there still survives with the tribes the system that each elects ten by lot and then they choose from among these by ballot.[c] And a proof that he made the offices elective by lot according to assessments is the law in regard to the Treasurers that remains in force even at the present day; for it orders the Treasurers to be elected by lot from the Five-hundred-measure
men. Solon, therefore, legislated thus about the Nine 2
Archons; for in ancient times the Council on the Areopagus used to issue a summons and select independently the person suitable for each of the offices,
and commission him to hold office for a year. And 3

by the four tribes; whereas in the writer's day the preliminary election was also by lot and produced one hundred from the ten tribes.

[c] *i.e.* by lot again.

καθάπερ πρότερον καὶ φυλοβασιλεῖς τέσσαρες. ἐκ δὲ τῆς φυλῆς ἑκάστης ἦσαν νενεμημέναι τριττύες μὲν τρεῖς, ναυκραρίαι δὲ δώδεκα καθ' ἑκάστην, ἐπὶ δὲ τῶν[1] ναυκραριῶν ἀρχὴ καθεστηκυῖα ναύκραροι, τεταγμένη πρός τε τὰς εἰσφορὰς καὶ τὰς δαπάνας τὰς γινομένας· διὸ καὶ ἐν τοῖς νόμοις τοῖς Σόλωνος, οἷς οὐκέτι χρῶνται, πολλαχοῦ γέγραπται τοὺς ναυκράρους εἰσπράττειν, καὶ ἀνα-
4 λίσκειν ἐκ τοῦ ναυκραρικοῦ ἀργυρίου. βουλὴν δ' ἐποίησε τετρακοσίους, ἑκατὸν ἐξ ἑκάστης φυλῆς, τὴν δὲ τῶν Ἀρεοπαγιτῶν ἔταξεν ἐπὶ τὸ νομοφυλακεῖν, ὥσπερ ὑπῆρχεν καὶ πρότερον ἐπίσκοπος οὖσα τῆς πολιτείας, ἣ τά τε ἄλλα καὶ τὰ πλεῖστα καὶ τὰ μέγιστα τῶν πολιτικῶν[2] διετήρει καὶ τοὺς ἁμαρτάνοντας ηὔθυνεν κυρία οὖσα καὶ ζημιοῦν καὶ κολάζειν, καὶ τὰς ἐκτίσεις ἀνέφερεν εἰς πόλιν οὐκ ἐπιγράφουσα τὴν πρόφασιν τοῦ ἐκτίνεσθαι,[3] καὶ τοὺς ἐπὶ καταλύσει τοῦ δήμου συνισταμένους ἔκρινεν, Σόλωνος θέντος νόμον εἰσαγγελίας
5 περὶ αὐτῶν. ὁρῶν δὲ τὴν μὲν πόλιν πολλάκις στασιάζουσαν τῶν δὲ πολιτῶν ἐνίους διὰ τὴν ῥᾳθυμίαν ἀγαπῶντας τὸ αὐτόματον, νόμον ἔθηκε πρὸς αὐτοὺς ἴδιον, ὃς ἂν στασιαζούσης τῆς πόλεως μὴ θῆται τὰ ὅπλα μηδὲ μεθ' ἑτέρων ἄτιμον εἶναι καὶ τῆς πόλεως μὴ μετέχειν.

1 IX. Τὰ μὲν οὖν περὶ τὰς ἀρχὰς τοῦτον εἶχε τὸν τρόπον. δοκεῖ δὲ τῆς Σόλωνος πολιτείας τρία

[1] ἦν δ' ἐπὶ τῶν nonnulli legunt.
[2] πολιτικῶν coni. Richards: πολιτων cod.
[3] εὐθύνεσθαι nonnulli legunt, δι' ὃ τὸ ἐκτίνεσθαι alii.

[a] The *Naucrariae* were forty-eight administrative districts into which the country was divided for taxation, each having

there were four Tribes, as before, and four Tribal Kings. And from each Tribe there had been assigned three Thirds and twelve Ship-boards [a] to each, and over the Ship-boards there was established the office of Ship-commissioners, appointed for the levies and the expenditures that were made ; because of which in the laws of Solon, which are no longer in force, the clauses frequently occur, 'the Ship-commissioner to levy' and 'to spend out of the Ship-commission
Fund.' And he made a Council of four hundred 4
members, a hundred from each tribe, but appointed the Council of the Areopagus to the duty of guarding the laws, just as it had existed even before as overseer of the constitution, and it was this Council that kept watch over the greatest number and the most important of the affairs of state, in particular correcting offenders with sovereign powers both to fine and punish, and making returns of its expenditure to the Acropolis without adding a statement of the reason for the outlay, and trying persons that conspired to put down the democracy, Solon having laid down a
law of impeachment in regard to them. And as he 5
saw that the state was often in a condition of party strife, while some of the citizens through slackness were content to let things slide, he laid down a special law to deal with them, enacting that whoever when civil strife prevailed did not join forces with either party was to be disfranchised and not to be a member of the state.

IX. This then was the nature of his reforms in 1
regard to the offices of state. And the three most

to defray the equipment of one battle-ship. Their presidents were *Naucrari*. Every four *Naucrariae* formed a *Trittys*, of which there were three in each Tribe.

ταῦτ' εἶναι τὰ δημοτικώτατα, πρῶτον μὲν καὶ μέγιστον τὸ μὴ δανείζειν ἐπὶ τοῖς σώμασιν, ἔπειτα τὸ ἐξεῖναι τῷ βουλομένῳ τιμωρεῖν ὑπὲρ τῶν ἀδικουμένων, τρίτον δέ, ᾧ[1] μάλιστά φασιν ἰσχυκέναι τὸ πλῆθος, ἡ εἰς τὸ δικαστήριον ἔφεσις· κύριος γὰρ ὢν ὁ δῆμος τῆς ψήφου κύριος γίνεται τῆς πολι-
2 τείας. ἔτι δὲ καὶ διὰ τὸ μὴ γεγράφθαι τοὺς νόμους ἁπλῶς μηδὲ σαφῶς, ἀλλ' ὥσπερ ὁ περὶ τῶν κλήρων καὶ ἐπικλήρων, ἀνάγκη πολλὰς ἀμφισβητήσεις γίνεσθαι καὶ πάντα βραβεύειν καὶ τὰ κοινὰ καὶ τὰ ἴδια τὸ δικαστήριον. οἴονται μὲν οὖν τινὲς ἐπίτηδες ἀσαφεῖς αὐτὸν ποιῆσαι τοὺς νόμους ὅπως ᾖ τῆς κρίσεως ὁ δῆμος κύριος· οὐ μὴν εἰκός, ἀλλὰ διὰ τὸ μὴ δύνασθαι καθόλου περιλαβεῖν τὸ βέλτιστον· οὐ γὰρ δίκαιον ἐκ τῶν νῦν γινομένων ἀλλ' ἐκ τῆς ἄλλης πολιτείας θεωρεῖν τὴν ἐκείνου βούλησιν.
1 X. Ἐν μὲν οὖν τοῖς νόμοις ταῦτα δοκεῖ θεῖναι δημοτικά, πρὸ δὲ τῆς νομοθεσίας ποιήσας[2] τὴν τῶν χρεῶν ἀποκοπὴν καὶ μετὰ ταῦτα τήν τε τῶν μέτρων καὶ σταθμῶν καὶ τὴν τοῦ νομίσματος
2 αὔξησιν. ἐπ' ἐκείνου γὰρ ἐγένετο καὶ τὰ μέτρα μείζω[3] τῶν Φειδωνείων,[4] καὶ ἡ μνᾶ πρότερον ἔχουσα σταθμὸν ἑβδομήκοντα δραχμὰς ἀνεπληρώθη ταῖς ἑκατόν. ἦν δ' ὁ ἀρχαῖος χαρακτὴρ δίδραχμον. ἐποίησε δὲ καὶ σταθμὰ πρὸς τὸ νόμισμα, τρεῖς καὶ

[1] δέ, ᾧ Lipsius : δε cod. [2] ποιῆσαι legit Kenyon.
[3] μείω (Heerwerden-Leeuwen) ? Johnston.
[4] Αἰγιναίων (φειδωνείων *gloss. prav.*) ? id.

[a] King of Argos, probably early 7th century B.C., see *Politics* 1310 b 26. His standards of coinage and weights and measures came to prevail through most of Greece.

[b] *i.e.* seventy of the new drachmae: the drachma coin

democratic features in Solon's constitution seem to be these: first and most important the prohibition of loans secured upon the person, secondly the liberty allowed to anybody who wished to exact redress on behalf of injured persons, and third, what is said to have been the chief basis of the powers of the multitude, the right of appeal to the jury-court—for the people, having the power of the vote, becomes
sovereign in the government. And also, since the 2
laws are not drafted simply nor clearly, but like the law about inheritances and heiresses, it inevitably results that many disputes take place and that the jury-court is the umpire in all business both public and private. Therefore some people think that Solon purposely made his laws obscure, in order that the people might be sovereign over the verdict. But this is unlikely—probably it was due to his not being able to define the ideal in general terms; for it is not fair to study his intention in the light of what happens at the present day, but to judge it from the rest of his constitution.

X. Solon therefore seems to have laid down these 1
enactments of a popular nature in his laws; while before his legislation his democratic reform was his cancellation of debts, and afterwards his raising the standard of the measures and weights and of the
coinage. For it was in his time that the measures 2
were made larger than those of Pheidon,[a] and that the mina, which previously had a weight of seventy drachmae,[b] was increased to the full hundred. The ancient coin-type was the two-drachma piece. Solon also instituted weights corresponding to the cur-

was also enlarged, so that seventy of the new equalled one hundred of the old; and see note on iv. 3.

ἑξήκοντα μνᾶς τὸ τάλαντον ἀγούσας, καὶ ἐπιδιενεμήθησαν αἱ τρεῖς μναῖ τῷ στατῆρι καὶ τοῖς ἄλλοις σταθμοῖς.

1 XI. Διατάξας δὲ τὴν πολιτείαν ὅνπερ εἴρηται τρόπον, ἐπειδὴ προσιόντες αὐτῷ περὶ τῶν νόμων ἐνώχλουν τὰ μὲν ἐπιτιμῶντες τὰ δὲ ἀνακρίνοντες, βουλόμενος μήτε ταῦτα κινεῖν μήτ' ἀπεχθάνεσθαι παρών, ἀποδημίαν ἐποιήσατο κατ' ἐμπορίαν ἅμα καὶ θεωρίαν εἰς Αἴγυπτον, εἰπὼν ὡς οὐχ ἥξει δέκα ἐτῶν, οὐ γὰρ οἴεσθαι δίκαιον εἶναι τοὺς νόμους ἐξηγεῖσθαι παρὼν ἀλλ' ἕκαστον τὰ γεγραμμένα
2 ποιῆσαι. ἅμα δὲ καὶ συνέβαινεν αὐτῷ τῶν τε γνωρίμων διαφόρους γεγενῆσθαι πολλοὺς διὰ τὰς τῶν χρεῶν ἀποκοπάς, καὶ τὰς στάσεις ἀμφοτέρας μεταθέσθαι διὰ τὸ παρὰ δόξαν αὐτοῖς γενέσθαι τὴν κατάστασιν. ὁ μὲν γὰρ δῆμος ᾤετο πάντ' ἀνάδαστα ποιήσειν αὐτόν, οἱ δὲ γνώριμοι πάλιν ἢ τὴν αὐτὴν τάξιν ἀποδώσειν ἢ μικρὸν παραλλάξαντα· ὁ δὲ Σόλων ἀμφοτέροις ἠναντιώθη, καὶ ἐξὸν αὐτῷ μεθ' ὁποτέρων ἠβούλετο συστάντα τυραννεῖν εἵλετο πρὸς ἀμφοτέρους ἀπεχθέσθαι[1] σώσας τὴν πατρίδα καὶ τὰ βέλτιστα νομοθετήσας.

1 XII. Ταῦτα δ' ὅτι τοῦτον τρόπον ἔσχεν[2] οἵ τ' ἄλλοι συμφωνοῦσι πάντες καὶ αὐτὸς ἐν τῇ ποιήσει μέμνηται περὶ αὐτῶν ἐν τοῖσδε·

δήμῳ μὲν γὰρ ἔδωκα τόσον γέρας ὅσσον ἀπαρκεῖ,
τιμῆς οὔτ' ἀφελὼν οὔτ' ἐπορεξάμενος,

[1] Wyse: απεχθεσθηναι cod. [2] εἶχεν Wilamowitz-Kaibel.

[a] The weight of a fiftieth part of a mina.
[b] See v. 2 n.

rency, the talent weighing sixty-three minae, and a fraction proportionate to the additional three minae was added to the stater [a] and the other weights.

XI. When Solon had organized the constitution 1
in the manner stated, people kept coming to him and worrying him about his laws, criticizing some points and asking questions about others ; so as he did not wish either to alter these provisions or to stay and incur enmity, he went abroad on a journey to Egypt, for the purpose both of trading and of seeing the country, saying that he would not come back for ten years, as he did not think it fair for him to stay and explain his laws, but for everybody to carry out their provisions for himself. At the same time 2
it befell him that many of the notables had become at variance with him because of the cancellations of debts, and also that both the factions changed their attitude to him because the settlement had disappointed them. For the people had thought that he would institute universal communism of property, whereas the notables had thought that he would either restore the system in the same form as it was before or with slight alteration ; but Solon went against them both, and when he might have been tyrant if he had taken sides with whichever of the two factions he wished, he chose to incur the enmity of both by saving the country and introducing the legislation that was best.

XII. That this is how it happened is the unanimous 1
account of everybody, and in particular Solon himself in his poetry [b] recalls the matter in these words :

For to the people gave I grace enough,
Nor from their honour took, nor proffered more ;

οἳ δ' εἶχον δύναμιν καὶ χρήμασιν ἦσαν ἀγητοί,
καὶ τοῖς ἐφρασάμην μηδὲν ἀεικὲς ἔχειν·
ἔστην δ' ἀμφιβαλὼν κρατερὸν σάκος ἀμφοτέροισι
νικᾶν δ' οὐκ εἴασ' οὐδετέρους ἀδίκως.

2 πάλιν δ' ἀποφαινόμενος περὶ τοῦ πλήθους ὡς αὐτῷ δεῖ χρῆσθαι·

δῆμος δ' ὧδ' ἂν ἄριστα σὺν ἡγεμόνεσσιν ἕποιτο,
μήτε λίαν ἀνεθεὶς μήτε βιαζόμενος·
τίκτει γὰρ κόρος ὕβριν ὅταν πολὺς ὄλβος ἕπηται
ἀνθρώποισιν ὅσοις μὴ νόος ἄρτιος ᾖ.

3 καὶ πάλιν δ' ἑτέρωθί που λέγει περὶ τῶν διανείμασθαι τὴν γῆν βουλομένων·

οἳ δ' ἐφ' ἁρπαγαῖσιν ἦλθον ἐλπίδ' εἶχον[1] ἀφνεάν,
κἀδόκουν ἕκαστος αὐτῶν ὄλβον εὑρήσειν πολύν,
καί με κωτίλλοντα λείως τραχὺν ἐκφανεῖν νόον.
χαῦνα μὲν τότ' ἐφράσαντο, νῦν δέ μοι χολούμενοι
λοξὸν ὀφθαλμοῖσ' ὁρῶσι πάντες ὥστε δήιον,
οὐ χρεών· ἃ μὲν γὰρ εἶπα σὺν θεοῖσιν ἤνυσα,
ἄλλα δ' οὐ μάτην ἔερδον, οὐδέ μοι τυραννίδος
ἡνδάνεν[2] βίᾳ τι ῥέζειν, οὐδὲ πιείρας χθονὸς
πατρίδος κακοῖσιν ἐσθλοὺς ἰσομοιρίαν ἔχειν.

4 πάλιν[3] δὲ καὶ περὶ τῆς ἀποκοπῆς τῶν χρεῶν καὶ τῶν δουλευόντων μὲν πρότερον ἐλευθερωθέντων δὲ διὰ τὴν σεισάχθειαν·

[1] ἐφ' ἁρπαγῇ συνῆλθον κἀλπίδ' εἶχον (commate infra post νόον posito) Ziegler: ἐφ' ἁρπαγαῖς ἔχοντες ἐλπίδ' ἦλθον Richards.
[2] Richards: ανδανει cod.
[3] πάλιν Kenyon: λέγει Kontos: lacunam cod.

While those possessing power and graced with wealth,
These too I made to suffer nought unseemly;
I stood protecting both with a strong shield,
And suffered neither to prevail unjustly.

And again, when declaring about how the multi- 2
tude ought to be treated:

Thus would the people with the chiefs best follow,
With neither too much freedom nor compulsion;
Satiety breeds insolence when riches
Attend the men whose mind is not prepared.

And again in a different place he says about those 3
who wish to divide up the land:

They that came on plunder bent were filled with over-lavish hope,
Each and all imagining that they would find abundant wealth,
And that I, though smoothly glozing, would display a purpose rough.
Vain and boastful then their fancies; now their bile 'gainst me is stirred,
And with eyes askance they view me, and all deem me as a foe—
Wrongly: for the things I promised, those by heaven's aid I did,
And much else, no idle exploits; nothing did it please my mind
By tyrannic force to compass, nor that in our fatherland
Base and noble should have equal portion in her fertile soil.

And again about the cancellation of debts, and 4
those who were in slavery before but were liberated
by the Shaking-off of Burdens:

ἐγὼ δὲ τῶν μὲν οὕνεκα ξυνήγαγον
δῆμον, τί τούτων πρὶν τυχεῖν ἐπαυσάμην;
συμμαρτυροίη ταῦτ᾽ ἂν ἐν δίκῃ Χρόνου
μήτηρ μεγίστη δαιμόνων Ὀλυμπίων ·
ἄριστα, Γῆ μέλαινα, τῆς ἐγώ ποτε
ὅρους ἀνεῖλον πολλαχῇ πεπηγότας,
πρόσθεν δὲ δουλεύουσα, νῦν ἐλευθέρα.[1]
πολλοὺς δ᾽ Ἀθήνας πατρίδ᾽ εἰς θεόκτιτον
ἀνήγαγον πραθέντας, ἄλλον ἐκδίκως,
ἄλλον δικαίως, τοὺς δ᾽ ἀναγκαίης ὕπο
χρειοῦς φυγόντας, γλῶσσαν οὐκέτ᾽ Ἀττικὴν
ἱέντας, ὡς ἂν[2] πολλαχῇ πλανωμένους,
τοὺς δ᾽ ἐνθάδ᾽ αὐτοῦ δουλίην ἀεικέα
ἔχοντας, ἤθη δεσποτῶν τρομευμένους,
ἐλευθέρους ἔθηκα. ταῦτα μὲν κρατεῖν,
ὁμοῦ[3] βίαν τε καὶ δίκην συναρμόσας,
ἔρεξα καὶ διῆλθον ὡς ὑπεσχόμην·
θεσμούς θ᾽ ὁμοίως τῷ κακῷ τε κἀγαθῷ,
εὐθεῖαν εἰς ἕκαστον ἁρμόσας δίκην,
ἔγραψα. κέντρον δ᾽ ἄλλος ὡς ἐγὼ λαβών,
κακοφραδής τε καὶ φιλοκτήμων ἀνήρ,
οὐκ ἂν κατέσχε δῆμον· εἰ γὰρ ἤθελον
ἃ τοῖς ἐναντίοισιν ἥνδανεν τότε,
αὖθις δ᾽ ἃ τοῖσιν οὕτεροι φρασαίατο,
πολλῶν ἂν ἀνδρῶν ἥδ᾽ ἐχηρώθη πόλις.
τῶν οὕνεκ᾽ ἀλκὴν πάντοθεν ποιούμενος
ὡς ἐν κυσὶν πολλῇσιν ἐστράφην λύκος.

5 καὶ πάλιν ὀνειδίζων πρὸς τὰς ὕστερον αὐτῶν μεμψιμοιρίας ἀμφοτέρων·

δήμῳ μὲν εἰ χρὴ διαφραδὴν[4] ὀνειδίσαι,
ἃ νῦν ἔχουσιν οὔποτ᾽ ὀφθαλμοῖσιν ἂν

But what did I leave unachieved, of all
The ends for which I did unite the people?
Whereof before the judgement-seat of Time
The mighty mother of the Olympian gods,
Black Earth, would best bear witness, for 'twas I
Removed her many boundary-posts[a] implanted:
Ere then she was a slave, but now is free.
And many sold away I did bring home
To god-built Athens, this one sold unjustly,
That other justly; others that had fled
From dire constraint of need, uttering no more
Their Attic tongue, so widely had they wandered,
And others suffering base slavery
Even here, trembling before their masters' humours,
I did set free. These deeds I made prevail,
Adjusting might and right to fit together,
And did accomplish even as I had promised.
And rules of law alike for base and noble,
Fitting straight justice unto each man's case,
I drafted. Had another than myself
Taken the goad, unwise and covetous,
He'd not have held the people! Had I willed
Now that pleased one of the opposing parties,
And then whate'er the other party bade them,
The city had been bereft of many men.
Wherefore I stood at guard on every side,
A wolf at bay among a pack of hounds!

And again in his taunting reply to the later 5
querulous complaints of both the parties:

If openly I must reprove the people,
Ne'er in the dreams of sleep could they have seen

[a] *i.e.* posts marking mortgaged estates.

---

[1] *πρόσθεν δεδουλευκυῖα νῦν δ' ἐλευθέρα* Ziegler.
[2] *ωσαν* cod. et fr. Berol.: *ὥς γε* ? Rackham.
[3] *κρατεειιομου* cod., *κρ·τηομου* fr. Berol.: *κράτει | νόμου* edd. nonnulli; *cf.* vi. 1.
[4] *διαφάδην* coni. edd.

εὕδοντες εἶδον. . . .
ὅσοι δὲ μείζους καὶ βίαν ἀμείνονες
αἰνοῖεν ἄν με καὶ φίλον ποιοίατο·

εἰ γάρ τις ἄλλος, φησί, ταύτης τῆς τιμῆς ἔτυχεν,

οὐκ ἂν κατέσχε δῆμον, οὐδ' ἐπαύσατο
πρὶν ἀνταράξας πῖαρ[1] ἐξεῖλεν γάλα·
ἐγὼ δὲ τούτων ὥσπερ ἐν μεταιχμίῳ
ὅρος κατέστην.

1 XIII. Τὴν μὲν οὖν ἀποδημίαν ἐποιήσατο διὰ ταύτας τὰς αἰτίας. Σόλωνος δ' ἀποδημήσαντος, ἔτι τῆς πόλεως τεταραγμένης, ἐπὶ μὲν ἔτη τέτταρα διῆγον ἐν ἡσυχίᾳ· τῷ δὲ πέμπτῳ μετὰ τὴν Σόλωνος ἀρχὴν οὐκ κατέστησαν ἄρχοντα διὰ τὴν στάσιν, καὶ πάλιν ἔτει πέμπτῳ διὰ[2] τὴν αὐτὴν αἰτίαν
2 ἀναρχίαν ἐποίησαν. μετὰ δὲ ταῦτα διὰ τῶν αὐτῶν χρόνων Δαμασίας αἱρεθεὶς ἄρχων ἔτη δύο καὶ δύο μῆνας ἦρξεν, ἕως ἐξηλάθη βίᾳ τῆς ἀρχῆς. εἶτ' ἔδοξεν αὐτοῖς διὰ τὸ στασιάζειν ἄρχοντας ἑλέσθαι δέκα, πέντε μὲν εὐπατριδῶν τρεῖς δὲ ἀγροίκων δύο δὲ δημιουργῶν, καὶ οὗτοι τὸν μετὰ Δαμασίαν ἦρξαν ἐνιαυτόν. ᾧ καὶ δῆλον ὅτι μεγίστην εἶχεν δύναμιν ὁ ἄρχων· φαίνονται γὰρ αἰεὶ στασιάζοντες
3 περὶ ταύτης τῆς ἀρχῆς. ὅλως δὲ διετέλουν νοσοῦντες τὰ πρὸς ἑαυτούς, οἱ μὲν ἀρχὴν καὶ πρόφασιν ἔχοντες τὴν τῶν χρεῶν ἀποκοπήν (συνεβεβήκει γὰρ αὐτοῖς γεγονέναι πένησιν), οἱ δὲ τῇ πολιτείᾳ δυσχεραίνοντες διὰ τὸ μεγάλην[3] γεγονέναι μεταβολήν, ἔνιοι δὲ διὰ τὴν πρὸς ἀλλήλους φιλονικίαν.

The things that they have now . . .
While all the greater and the mightier men
Might praise me and might deem me as a friend;

for had another, he says, won this office,

He had not checked the people nor refrained,
Ere he had churned and robbed the milk of cream;
But I as 'twere betwixt their armèd hosts
A frontier-post did stand.

XIII. Accordingly Solon made his journey abroad 1
for these reasons. And when he had gone abroad,
though the city was still disturbed, for four years
they kept at peace; but in the fifth year after Solon's 589 B.C.?
archonship because of party strife they did not
appoint an archon, and again in the fifth year after 585 B.C.?
that they enacted a suspension of the archonship for
the same cause. After this at the same interval of 2
time Damasias was elected Archon, and held the 581 B.C.?
post for two years and two months, until he was
driven out of the office by force. Then because of
the civil strife they decided to elect ten Archons,
five from the nobles, three from the farmers and two
from the artisans, and these held office for the year 579 B.C.?
after Damasias. This shows that the Archon had
very great power; for we find that they were always
engaging in party strife about this office. And they 3
continued in a state of general internal disorder,
some having as their incentive and excuse the cancellation of debts (for it had resulted in their having
become poor), others discontented with the constitution because a great change had taken place, and
some because of their mutual rivalry. The factions 4

[1] πῖαρ edd. ex Plutarcho: πυαρ cod.
[2] διὰ fr. Berol.: om. cod.
[3] ⟨οὐ⟩ μεγάλην Vollgraf.

4 ἦσαν δ' αἱ στάσεις τρεῖς· μία μὲν τῶν παραλίων, ὧν προειστήκει Μεγακλῆς ὁ Ἀλκμέωνος, οἵπερ ἐδόκουν μάλιστα διώκειν τὴν μέσην πολιτείαν· ἄλλη δὲ τῶν πεδιακῶν, οἳ τὴν ὀλιγαρχίαν ἐζήτουν, ἡγεῖτο δ' αὐτῶν Λυκοῦργος· τρίτη δ' ἡ τῶν διακρίων, ἐφ' ᾗ τεταγμένος ἦν Πεισίστρατος,
5 δημοτικώτατος εἶναι δοκῶν. προσεκεκόσμηντο δὲ τούτοις οἵ τε ἀφῃρημένοι τὰ χρέα διὰ τὴν ἀπορίαν, καὶ οἱ τῷ γένει μὴ καθαροὶ διὰ τὸν φόβον· σημεῖον δ' ὅτι μετὰ τὴν τῶν τυράννων κατάλυσιν ἐποίησαν διαψηφισμὸν[1] ὡς πολλῶν κοινωνούντων τῆς πολιτείας οὐ προσῆκον. εἶχον δ' ἕκαστοι τὰς ἐπωνυμίας ἀπὸ τῶν τόπων ἐν οἷς ἐγεώργουν.

1 XIV. Δημοτικώτατος δ' εἶναι δοκῶν ὁ Πεισίστρατος καὶ σφόδρ' εὐδοκιμηκὼς ἐν τῷ πρὸς Μεγαρέας πολέμῳ, κατατραυματίσας ἑαυτὸν συνέπεισε τὸν δῆμον, ὡς ὑπὸ τῶν ἀντιστασιωτῶν ταῦτα πεπονθώς, φυλακὴν ἑαυτῷ δοῦναι τοῦ σώματος, Ἀριστίωνος γράψαντος τὴν γνώμην. λαβὼν δὲ τοὺς κορυνηφόρους καλουμένους, ἐπαναστὰς μετὰ τούτων τῷ δήμῳ κατέσχε τὴν ἀκρόπολιν ἔτει δευτέρῳ[2] καὶ τριακοστῷ μετὰ τὴν τῶν
2 νόμων θέσιν, ἐπὶ Κωμέου ἄρχοντος. λέγεται δὲ Σόλωνα Πεισιστράτου τὴν φυλακὴν αἰτοῦντος ἀντιλέξαι, καὶ εἰπεῖν ὅτι τῶν μὲν εἴη σοφώτερος τῶν δ' ἀνδρειότερος· ὅσοι μὲν γὰρ ἀγνοοῦσι Πεισί-

[1] διαψηφισμὸν edd.: διαφημισμον cod.
[2] δ' (i.e. τετάρτῳ) coni. Bauer.

[a] *i.e.* by Solon's legislation.
[b] Perhaps the hostilities that ended in the Athenians' capture of Nisaea about 570 B.C.

were three: one was the party of the Men of the
Coast, whose head was Megacles the son of Alcmaeon,
and they were thought chiefly to aim at the middle
form of constitution; another was the party of the
Men of the Plain, who desired the oligarchy, and their
leader was Lycurgus; third was the party of the
Hillmen, which had appointed Peisistratus over it,
as he was thought to be an extreme advocate of the
people. And on the side of this party were also 5
arrayed, from the motive of poverty, those who had
been deprived [a] of the debts due to them, and, from
the motive of fear, those who were not of pure
descent; and this is proved by the fact that after the
deposition of the tyrants the Athenians enacted a
revision of the roll, because many people shared the
citizenship who had no right to it. The different
parties derived their names from the places where
their farms were situated.

XIV. Peisistratus, being thought to be an extreme 1
advocate of the people, and having won great fame
in the war against Megara,[b] inflicted a wound on
himself with his own hand and then gave out that
it had been done by the members of the opposite
factions, and so persuaded the people to give him a
bodyguard, the resolution being proposed by Aristo-
phon. He was given the retainers called Club-bearers,
and with their aid he rose against the people and
seized the Acropolis, in the thirty-second year after
the enactment of his laws, in the archonship of 560 B.C.
Comeas. It is said that when Peisistratus asked for 2
the guard Solon opposed the request, and said that
he was wiser than some men and braver than others
—he was wiser than those who did not know that

στρατον ἐπιτιθέμενον τυραννίδι, σοφώτερος εἶναι τούτων, ὅσοι δ' εἰδότες κατασιωπῶσιν, ἀνδρειότερος. ἐπεὶ δὲ λέγων οὐκ ἔπειθεν, ἐξαράμενος τὰ ὅπλα πρὸ τῶν θυρῶν αὐτὸς μὲν ἔφη βεβοηθηκέναι τῇ πατρίδι καθ' ὅσον ἦν δυνατὸς (ἤδη γὰρ σφόδρα πρεσβύτης ἦν), ἀξιοῦν δὲ καὶ τοὺς ἄλλους ταὐτὸ
3 τοῦτο ποιεῖν. Σόλων μὲν οὖν οὐδὲν ἤνυσεν τότε παρακαλῶν· Πεισίστρατος δὲ λαβὼν τὴν ἀρχὴν διῴκει τὰ κοινὰ πολιτικῶς μᾶλλον ἢ τυραννικῶς. οὔπω δὲ τῆς ἀρχῆς ἐρριζωμένης ὁμοφρονήσαντες οἱ περὶ τὸν Μεγακλέα καὶ τὸν Λυκοῦργον ἐξέβαλον αὐτὸν ἕκτῳ ἔτει μετὰ τὴν πρώτην κατάστασιν,
4 ἐφ' Ἡγησίου ἄρχοντος. ἔτει δὲ δωδεκάτῳ[1] μετὰ ταῦτα περιελαυνόμενος ὁ Μεγακλῆς τῇ στάσει πάλιν ἐπικηρυκευσάμενος πρὸς τὸν Πεισίστρατον, ἐφ' ᾧ τε τὴν θυγατέρα αὐτοῦ λήψεται κατήγαγεν αὐτὸν ἀρχαίως καὶ λίαν ἁπλῶς. προδιασπείρας γὰρ λόγον ὡς τῆς Ἀθηνᾶς καταγούσης Πεισίστρατον, καὶ γυναῖκα μεγάλην καὶ καλὴν ἐξευρών, ὡς μὲν Ἡρόδοτός φησιν ἐκ τοῦ δήμου τῶν Παιανέων, ὡς δ' ἔνιοι λέγουσιν ἐκ τοῦ Κολυττοῦ στεφανόπωλιν Θρᾷτταν ᾗ ὄνομα Φύη, τὴν θεὸν ἀπομιμησάμενος τῷ κόσμῳ συνεισήγαγεν μετ' αὐτοῦ, καὶ ὁ μὲν Πεισίστρατος ἐφ' ἅρματος εἰσήλαυνε παραιβατούσης τῆς γυναικός, οἱ δ' ἐν τῷ ἄστει προσκυνοῦντες ἐδέχοντο θαυμάζοντες.

1 XV. Ἡ μὲν οὖν πρώτη κάθοδος ἐγένετο τοιαύτη. μετὰ δὲ ταῦτα ὡς[2] ἐξέπεσε τὸ δεύτερον ἔτει μάλιστα ἑβδόμῳ μετὰ τὴν κάθοδον,—οὐ γὰρ πολὺν χρόνον

[1] τετάρτῳ Thompson.
[2] ὡς del. Wilamowitz-Kaibel.

Peisistratus was aiming at tyranny, and braver than those who knew it but held their tongues. But as he failed to carry them with him by saying this, he brought his armour out [a] in front of his door and said that for his part he had come to his country's aid as far as he could (for he was now a very old man), and that he called on the others also to do the same.
Solon's exhortations on this occasion had no effect; 3
and Peisistratus having seized the government proceeded to carry on the public business in a manner more constitutional than tyrannical. But before his government had taken root the partisans of Megacles and Lycurgus made common cause and expelled him,
in the sixth year after his first establishment, in the 556 B.C.?
archonship of Hegesias. In the twelfth year after 4
this Megacles, being harried by party faction, made overtures again to Peisistratus, and on terms of receiving his daughter in marriage brought him back, in an old-fashioned and extremely simple manner. Having first spread a rumour that Athena was bringing Peisistratus back, he found a tall and beautiful woman, according to Herodotus [b] a member of the Paeanian deme, but according to some accounts a Thracian flower-girl from Collytus named Phyē, dressed her up to look like the goddess, and brought her to the city with him, and Peisistratus drove in a chariot with the woman standing at his side, while the people in the city marvelled and received them with acts of reverence.

XV. In this way his first return took place. After- 1
wards, as he was expelled a second time in about the
seventh year after his return—for he did not main- 539 B.C.?
tain his hold for long, but came to be afraid of both

[a] Apparently, for some younger man to use. [b] i. 60.

κατέσχεν, ἀλλὰ διὰ τὸ μὴ βούλεσθαι τῇ τοῦ Μεγακλέους θυγατρὶ συγγίνεσθαι φοβηθεὶς ἀμφοτέρας
2 τὰς στάσεις ὑπεξῆλθεν—· καὶ[1] πρῶτον μὲν συνῴκισε περὶ τὸν Θέρμαιον κόλπον χωρίον ὃ καλεῖται Ῥαίκηλος, ἐκεῖθεν δὲ παρῆλθεν εἰς τοὺς περὶ Πάγγαιον τόπους, ὅθεν χρηματισάμενος καὶ στρατιώτας μισθωσάμενος, ἐλθὼν εἰς Ἐρετρίαν ἑνδεκάτῳ πάλιν ἔτει τὸ[2] πρῶτον ἀνασώσασθαι βίᾳ τὴν ἀρχὴν ἐπεχείρει, συμπροθυμουμένων αὐτῷ πολλῶν μὲν καὶ ἄλλων μάλιστα δὲ Θηβαίων καὶ Λυγδάμιος τοῦ Ναξίου, ἔτι δὲ τῶν ἱππέων τῶν
3 ἐχόντων ἐν Ἐρετρίᾳ τὴν πολιτείαν. νικήσας δὲ τὴν ἐπὶ Παλληνίδι μάχην καὶ λαβὼν τὴν πόλιν καὶ παρελόμενος τοῦ δήμου τὰ ὅπλα, κατεῖχεν ἤδη τὴν τυραννίδα βεβαίως, καὶ Νάξον ἑλὼν ἄρχοντα
4 κατέστησε Λύγδαμιν. παρεῖλε[3] δὲ τοῦ δήμου τὰ ὅπλα τόνδε τὸν τρόπον· ἐξοπλασίαν ἐν τῷ Θησείῳ[4] ποιησάμενος ἐκκλησιάζειν ἐπεχείρει, τῆς δὲ φωνῆς ἐχάλασεν[5] μικρόν, οὐ φασκόντων δὲ κατακούειν ἐκέλευσεν αὐτοὺς προσαναβῆναι πρὸς τὸ πρόπυλον τῆς ἀκροπόλεως ἵνα γεγώνῃ μᾶλλον· ἐν ᾧ δ' ἐκεῖνος διέτριβε δημηγορῶν, ἀνελόντες οἱ ἐπὶ τούτῳ τεταγμένοι τὰ ὅπλα καὶ κατακλῄσαντες εἰς τὰ πλησίον οἰκήματα τοῦ Θησείου διεσήμηναν
5 ἐλθόντες πρὸς τὸν Πεισίστρατον. ὁ δὲ ἐπεὶ τὸν ἄλλον λόγον ἐπετέλεσεν, εἶπε καὶ περὶ τῶν ὅπλων τὸ γεγονὸς ὡς οὐ χρὴ θαυμάζειν οὐδ' ἀθυμεῖν,

[1] καὶ fortasse delendum Kenyon.
[2] τότε Blass.
[3] παρείλετο Rutherford.
[4] Ἀνακείῳ legunt nonnulli.
[5] Kontos: τ . . . . ασεν (?) cod.: φθέγγεσθαι δ' ἐσπούδασεν Wilamowitz-Kaibel: καὶ χρόνον προσηγόρευεν Kenyon.

the factions owing to his unwillingness to live with Megacles' daughter as his wife, and secretly withdrew—; and first he collected a settlement at a place 2
near the Gulf of Thermae called Rhaecelus, but from there he went on to the neighbourhood of Pangaeus, from where he got money and hired soldiers, and in the eleventh year went again to Eretria, and now for 528 B.C.?
the first time set about an attempt to recover his power by force, being supported in this by a number of people, especially the Thebans and Lygdamis of Naxos, and also the knights who controlled the government of Eretria. Winning the battle of 3
Pallenis,[a] he seized the government and disarmed the people; and now he held the tyranny firmly, and he took Naxos and appointed Lygdamis ruler. The 4
way in which he disarmed the people was this: he held an armed muster at the Temple of Theseus, and began to hold an Assembly, but he lowered his voice a little, and when they said they could not hear him, he told them to come up to the forecourt of the Acropolis, in order that his voice might carry better; and while he used up time in making a speech, the men told off for this purpose gathered up the arms,[b] locked them up in the neighbouring buildings of the Temple of Theseus, and came and informed Peisistratus. He, 5
when he had finished the rest of his speech, told his audience not to be surprised at what had happened about their arms, and not to be dismayed, but to go

[a] The deme Pallene, dedicated to Athena Pallenis, lay just N.E. of Athens.

[b] The citizens had piled their arms when Peisistratus began to make a speech, and left them behind when they went up the hill.

ἀλλ' ἀπελθόντας ἐπὶ τῶν ἰδίων εἶναι, τῶν δὲ κοινῶν αὐτὸς ἐπιμελήσεσθαι πάντων.

1 XVI. Ἡ μὲν οὖν Πεισιστράτου τυραννὶς ἐξ ἀρχῆς τε κατέστη τοῦτον τὸν τρόπον καὶ μετα-
2 βολὰς ἔσχε τοσαύτας. διῴκει δ' ὁ Πεισίστρατος, ὥσπερ εἴρηται, τὰ περὶ τὴν πόλιν μετρίως καὶ μᾶλλον πολιτικῶς ἢ τυραννικῶς· ἔν τε γὰρ τοῖς ἄλλοις φιλάνθρωπος ἦν καὶ πρᾶος καὶ τοῖς ἁμαρτάνουσι συγγνωμονικός, καὶ δὴ καὶ τοῖς ἀπόροις προεδάνειζε χρήματα πρὸς τὰς ἐργασίας, ὥστε
3 διατρέφεσθαι γεωργοῦντας. τοῦτο δ' ἐποίει δυοῖν χάριν, ἵνα μήτε ἐν τῷ ἄστει διατρίβωσιν ἀλλὰ διεσπαρμένοι κατὰ τὴν χώραν, καὶ ὅπως εὐποροῦντες τῶν μετρίων καὶ πρὸς τοῖς ἰδίοις ὄντες μήτ' ἐπιθυμῶσι μήτε σχολάζωσιν ἐπιμελεῖσθαι
4 τῶν κοινῶν. ἅμα δὲ συνέβαινεν αὐτῷ καὶ τὰς προσόδους γίνεσθαι μείζους ἐξεργαζομένης τῆς χώρας· ἐπράττετο γὰρ ἀπὸ τῶν γιγνομένων δεκά-
5 την. διὸ καὶ τοὺς κατὰ δήμους κατεσκεύασε[1] δικαστάς, καὶ αὐτὸς ἐξῄει πολλάκις εἰς τὴν χώραν ἐπισκοπῶν καὶ διαλύων τοὺς διαφερομένους, ὅπως μὴ καταβαίνοντες εἰς τὸ ἄστυ παραμελῶσι τῶν
6 ἔργων. τοιαύτης γάρ τινος ἐξόδου τῷ Πεισιστράτῳ γιγνομένης συμβῆναί φασι τὰ περὶ τὸν ἐν τῷ Ὑμηττῷ γεωργοῦντα τὸ κληθὲν ὕστερον χωρίον ἀτελές. ἰδὼν γάρ τινα παντελῶς πέτρας σκάπτοντα καὶ ἐργαζόμενον, διὰ τὸ θαυμάσαι τὸν παῖδα ἐκέλευσεν ἐρέσθαι τί γίγνεται ἐκ τοῦ χωρίου· ὁ δὲ "ὅσα κακὰ καὶ ὀδύναι" ἔφη, "καὶ τούτων τῶν κακῶν καὶ τῶν ὀδυνῶν[2] Πεισίστρατον δεῖ

[1] Wilamowitz-Kaibel: κατεσκευαζε cod.
[2] [τῶν κακῶν καὶ ὀδυνῶν] Hude.

away and occupy themselves with their private affairs, while he would attend to all public business.

XVI. This was the way, therefore, in which the 1
tyranny of Peisistratus was originally set up, and this is a list of the changes that it underwent.
Peisistratus's administration of the state was, as has 2
been said,[a] moderate, and more constitutional than tyrannic; he was kindly and mild in everything, and in particular he was merciful to offenders, and moreover he advanced loans of money to the poor for their industries, so that they might support themselves by
farming. In doing this he had two objects, to pre- 3
vent their stopping in the city and make them stay scattered about the country, and to cause them to have a moderate competence and be engaged in their private affairs, so as not to desire nor to have time
to attend to public business.[b] And also the land's 4
being thoroughly cultivated resulted in increasing his revenues; for he levied a tithe from the produce.
And for this reason he organized the Local Justices,[c] 5
and often went to the country on circuit in person, inspecting and settling disputes, in order that men might not neglect their agriculture by coming into
the city. For it was when Peisistratus was making 6
an expedition of this kind that the affair of the man on Hymettus cultivating the farm afterwards called Tax-free Farm is said to have occurred. He saw a man at farm-work, digging mere rocks, and because of his surprise ordered his servant to ask what crop the farm grew; and the man said, "All the aches and pains that there are, and of these aches and pains

[a] ch. xiv. § 3.

[b] This policy will be found expressed in general formulae in *Politics* 1311 a 13, 1318 b 6, 1319 a 30, 1320 b 7.

[c] See xxvi. 5, liii. 1.

λαβεῖν τὴν δεκάτην." ὁ μὲν οὖν ἄνθρωπος ἀπεκρίνατο ἀγνοῶν, ὁ δὲ Πεισίστρατος ἡσθεὶς διὰ τὴν παρρησίαν καὶ τὴν φιλεργίαν ἀτελῆ ἁπάντων
7 ἐποίησεν αὐτόν. οὐδὲν δὲ τὸ πλῆθος οὐδ' ἐν τοῖς ἄλλοις παρηνώχλει[1] κατὰ τὴν ἀρχήν, ἀλλ' αἰεὶ παρεσκεύαζεν εἰρήνην καὶ ἐτήρει τὴν ἡσυχίαν· διὸ καὶ πολλάκις ἀκούειν ἦν[2] ὡς ἡ Πεισιστράτου τυραννὶς ὁ ἐπὶ Κρόνου βίος εἴη· συνέβη γὰρ ὕστερον διαδεξαμένων τῶν υἱέων πολλῷ γενέσθαι τρα-
8 χυτέραν τὴν ἀρχήν. μέγιστον δὲ πάντων ἦν τῶν εἰρημένων τὸ δημοτικὸν εἶναι τῷ ἤθει καὶ φιλάνθρωπον. ἔν τε γὰρ τοῖς ἄλλοις ἐβούλετο πάντα διοικεῖν κατὰ τοὺς νόμους οὐδεμίαν ἑαυτῷ πλεονεξίαν διδούς, καί ποτε προσκληθεὶς φόνου δίκην εἰς Ἄρειον πάγον αὐτὸς μὲν ἀπήντησεν ὡς ἀπολογησόμενος ὁ δὲ προσκαλεσάμενος φοβηθεὶς
9 ἔλιπεν. διὸ καὶ πολὺν χρόνον ἔμεινεν ἐν[3] τῇ ἀρχῇ, καὶ ὅτ' ἐκπέσοι πάλιν ἀνελάμβανε ῥᾳδίως. ἐβούλοντο γὰρ καὶ τῶν γνωρίμων καὶ τῶν δημοτικῶν οἱ πολλοί· τοὺς μὲν γὰρ ταῖς ὁμιλίαις τοὺς δὲ ταῖς εἰς τὰ ἴδια βοηθείαις προσήγετο, καὶ πρὸς ἀμ-
10 φοτέρους ἐπεφύκει καλῶς. ἦσαν δὲ καὶ τοῖς Ἀθηναίοις οἱ περὶ τῶν τυράννων νόμοι πρᾷοι κατ' ἐκείνους τοὺς καιροὺς οἵ τ' ἄλλοι καὶ δὴ καὶ ὁ μάλιστα καθήκων πρὸς τὴν τῆς τυραννίδος κατάστασιν.[4] νόμος γὰρ αὐτοῖς ἦν ὅδε· θέσμια τάδε Ἀθηναίων καὶ πάτρια, ἐάν τινες τυραννεῖν

[1] Wyse: παρωχλει cod.
[2] ἀκούειν ἦν Blass e [Plat.] *Hipparch.* 229 B: abrasus cod.
[3] ἐν supplevit Blass.
[4] κατάστασιν insertum a Wilamowitz-Kaibel.

Peisistratus has to get the tithe." The man did not know who it was when he answered, but Peisistratus was pleased by his free speech and by his industry, and made him free from all taxes. And in all other 7
matters too he gave the multitude no trouble during his rule, but always worked for peace and safeguarded tranquillity; so that men were often to be heard saying that the tyranny of Peisistratus was the Golden Age of Cronos; for it came about later when his sons had succeeded him that the government became much harsher. And the greatest of all the things 8
said of him was that he was popular and kindly in temper. For he was willing to administer everything according to the laws in all matters, never giving himself any advantage; and once in particular when he was summoned to the Areopagus to be tried on a charge of murder, he appeared in person to make his defence, and the issuer of the summons was frightened and left. Owing to this he remained in his office for 9
a long period, and every time that he was thrown out of it he easily got it back again. For both the notables and the men of the people were most of them willing for him to govern, since he won over the former by his hospitality and the latter by his assistance in their private affairs, and was good-natured to both. And also the laws of Athens concerning 10
tyrants were mild at those periods, among the rest particularly the one that referred to the establishment of tyranny. For they had the following law: 'These are the ordinances and ancestral principles of Athens: if any persons rise in insurrection in

ἐπανιστῶνται [ἐπὶ τυραννίδι][1] ἢ συγκαθιστῇ τὴν τυραννίδα ἄτιμον εἶναι αὐτὸν καὶ γένος.[2]

1 XVII. Πεισίστρατος μὲν οὖν ἐγκατεγήρασε τῇ ἀρχῇ καὶ ἀπέθανε νοσήσας ἐπὶ Φιλόνεω ἄρχοντος, ἀφ' οὗ μὲν κατέστη τὸ πρῶτον τύραννος ἔτη τριάκοντα καὶ τρία βιώσας, ἃ δ' ἐν τῇ ἀρχῇ διέμεινεν ἑνὸς δέοντα εἴκοσι, ἔφευγε γὰρ τὰ λοιπά.
2 διὸ καὶ φανερῶς ληροῦσι[3] φάσκοντες ἐρώμενον εἶναι Πεισίστρατον Σόλωνος καὶ στρατηγεῖν ἐν τῷ πρὸς Μεγαρέας πολέμῳ περὶ Σαλαμῖνος· οὐ γὰρ ἐνδέχεται ταῖς ἡλικίαις, ἐάν τις ἀναλογίζηται τὸν ἑκατέρου βίον καὶ ἐφ' οὗ ἀπέθανεν ἄρχοντος. τελευτήσαντος δὲ Πεισιστράτου κατεῖχον οἱ υἱεῖς τὴν ἀρχήν, προαγαγόντες[4] τὰ πράγματα τὸν αὐτὸν τρόπον. ἦσαν δὲ δύο μὲν ἐκ τῆς γαμετῆς Ἱππίας καὶ Ἵππαρχος, δύο δ' ἐκ τῆς Ἀργείας Ἰοφῶν καὶ Ἡγησίστρατος ᾧ παρωνύμιον ἦν Θέτταλος.
3 ἔγημεν[5] γὰρ Πεισίστρατος ἐξ Ἄργους ἀνδρὸς Ἀργείου θυγατέρα ᾧ ὄνομα ἦν Γόργιλος, Τιμώνασσαν, ἣν πρότερον ἔσχεν γυναῖκα Ἀρχῖνος ὁ Ἀμπρακιώτης τῶν Κυψελιδῶν· ὅθεν καὶ ἡ πρὸς τοὺς Ἀργείους ἐνέστη φιλία, καὶ συνεμαχέσαντο χίλιοι τὴν ἐπὶ Παλληνίδι μάχην, Ἡγησιτράτου κομίσαντος. γῆμαι δέ φασι τὴν Ἀργείαν οἱ μὲν ἐκπεσόντα τὸ πρῶτον, οἱ δὲ κατέχοντα τὴν ἀρχήν.

1 XVIII. Ἦσαν δὲ κύριοι μὲν τῶν πραγμάτων διὰ τὰ ἀξιώματα καὶ διὰ τὰς ἡλικίας Ἵππαρχος καὶ Ἱππίας, πρεσβύτερος δ' ὢν ὁ Ἱππίας καὶ τῇ

[1] Keil.
[2] ἦσαν δὲ . . . γένος] totus locus conflatus et interpolatus ? ed.
[3] ληροῦσιν <οἱ> edd.
[4] προάγοντες edd.
[5] <ἐπ>έγημεν edd., coll. Plut. *Cato mai.* 24.

order to govern tyrannically, or if any person assists in establishing the tyranny, he himself and his family shall be disfranchised.'[a]

XVII. Peisistratus, therefore, grew old in office, and 1
died of disease in the archonship of Philoneos, having 528 B.C.
lived thirty-three years since he first established himself as tyrant, but the time that he remained in office was nineteen[b] years, as he was in exile for the
remainder. Therefore the story that Peisistratus was 2
a lover of Solon and that he commanded in the war against Megara for the recovery of Salamis is clearly nonsense, for it is made impossible by their ages, if one reckons up the life of each and the archonship in which he died. When Peisistratus was dead, his sons held the government, carrying on affairs in the same way. He had two sons by his wedded wife, Hippias and Hipparchus, and two by his Argive consort, Iophon and Hegesistratus surnamed
Thettalus. For Peisistratus married a consort from 3
Argos, Timonassa, the daughter of a man of Argos named Gorgilus, who had previously been the wife of Archinus, a man of Ambracia of the Cypselid family. This was the cause of Peisistratus's friendship with Argos, and a thousand Argives brought by Hegesistratus fought for him in the battle of Pallenis.[c] Some people date his marriage with the Argive lady during his first banishment, others in a period of office.

XVIII. Affairs were now under the authority of 1
Hipparchus and Hippias, owing to their station and their ages, but the government was controlled by

[a] The genuineness of § 10 may be questioned.

[b] *Politics* 1315 b 31 says 'seventeen.'

[c] See xv. 3.

φύσει πολιτικὸς καὶ ἔμφρων ἐπεστάτει τῆς ἀρχῆς· ὁ δὲ Ἵππαρχος παιδιώδης καὶ ἐρωτικὸς καὶ φιλόμουσος ἦν (καὶ τοὺς περὶ Ἀνακρέοντα καὶ Σιμωνίδην καὶ τοὺς ἄλλους ποιητὰς οὗτος ἦν ὁ
2 μεταπεμπόμενος), Θέτταλος δὲ νεώτερος πολὺ καὶ τῷ βίῳ θρασὺς καὶ ὑβριστής, ἀφ' οὗ καὶ συνέβη τὴν ἀρχὴν αὐτοῖς γενέσθαι πάντων τῶν κακῶν. ἐρασθεὶς γὰρ τοῦ Ἁρμοδίου καὶ διαμαρτάνων τῆς πρὸς αὐτὸν φιλίας οὐ κατεῖχε τὴν ὀργήν, ἀλλ' ἔν τε τοῖς ἄλλοις ἐνεσημαίνετο πικρῶς καὶ τὸ τελευταῖον μέλλουσαν αὐτοῦ τὴν ἀδελφὴν κανηφορεῖν Παναθηναίοις ἐκώλυσεν, λοιδορήσας τι τὸν Ἁρμόδιον ὡς μαλακὸν ὄντα· ὅθεν συνέβη παροξυνθέντα τὸν Ἁρμόδιον καὶ τὸν Ἀριστογείτονα
3 πράττειν τὴν πρᾶξιν μετεχόντων[1] πολλῶν.[2] ἤδη δὲ παρατηροῦντες ἐν ἀκροπόλει τοῖς Παναθηναίοις Ἱππίαν (ἐτύγχανεν γὰρ οὗτος μὲν δεχόμενος ὁ δ' Ἵππαρχος ἀποστέλλων τὴν πομπήν), ἰδόντες τινὰ τῶν κοινωνούντων τῆς πράξεως φιλανθρώπως ἐντυγχάνοντα τῷ Ἱππίᾳ καὶ νομίσαντες μηνύειν, βουλόμενοί τι δρᾶσαι πρὸ τῆς συλλήψεως, καταβάντες καὶ προεξαναστάντες τῶν ἄλλων, τὸν μὲν Ἵππαρχον διακοσμοῦντα τὴν
4 πομπὴν παρὰ τὸ Λεωκόρειον ἀπέκτειναν, τὴν δ' ὅλην ἐλυμήναντο πρᾶξιν, αὐτῶν δ' ὁ μὲν Ἁρμόδιος εὐθέως ἐτελεύτησεν ὑπὸ τῶν δορυφόρων,

[1] μετὰ πολιτῶν nonnulli legunt.
[2] ⟨οὐ⟩ πολλῶν Kaibel e Thuc.

Hippias, who was the elder and was statesmanlike and wise by nature; whereas Hipparchus was fond of amusement and love-making, and had literary tastes: it was he who brought to Athens poets such as
Anacreon and Simonides, and the others. Thettalus 2
was much younger, and bold and insolent in his mode of life, which proved to be the source of all their misfortunes. For he fell in love with Harmodius, and when his advances were continually unsuccessful he could not restrain his anger, but displayed it bitterly in various ways, and finally when Harmodius's sister was going to be a Basket-carrier[a] in the procession at the Panathenaic Festival he prevented her by uttering some insult against Harmodius as being effeminate; and the consequent wrath of Harmodius led him and Aristogeiton to enter on their plot with a
number[b] of accomplices. At the Panathenaic Festival 3
on the Acropolis they were already keeping a watch 514 B.C.?
on Hippias (who happened to be receiving the procession, while Hipparchus was directing its start), when they saw one of their partners in the plot conversing in a friendly way with Hippias. They thought that he was giving information, and wishing to do something before their arrest they went down and took the initiative without waiting for their confederates, killing Hipparchus as he was arranging the
procession by the Leocoreum.[c] This played havoc with 4
the whole plot. Of the two of them Harmodius was at once dispatched by the spearmen, and Aristogeiton

[a] Baskets holding the requisites for the religious service were carried by maidens of high birth.

[b] Thucydides (vi. 56. 3) says 'not many.'

[c] A monument to three daughters of Leon who in obedience to an oracle gave their lives for their country by running against the enemy's ranks in battle.

ὁ δ' Ἀριστογείτων ὕστερον, συλληφθεὶς καὶ πολὺν χρόνον αἰκισθείς. κατηγόρησεν δ' ἐν ταῖς ἀνάγκαις πολλῶν οἳ καὶ τῇ φύσει τῶν ἐπιφανῶν καὶ φίλοι τοῖς τυράννοις ἦσαν. οὐ γὰρ ἐδύναντο παραχρῆμα λαβεῖν οὐδὲν ἴχνος τῆς πράξεως, ἀλλ' ὁ λεγόμενος λόγος ὡς ὁ Ἱππίας ἀποστήσας ἀπὸ τῶν ὅπλων τοὺς πομπεύοντας ἐφώρασε τοὺς τὰ ἐγχειρίδια ἔχοντας οὐκ ἀληθής ἐστιν· οὐ γὰρ ἔπεμπον τότε[1] μεθ' ὅπλων, ἀλλ' ὕστερον τοῦτο
5 κατεσκεύασεν ὁ δῆμος. κατηγόρει δὲ τῶν τοῦ
τυράννου φίλων, ὡς μὲν οἱ δημοτικοί φασιν, ἐπίτηδες ἵνα ἀσεβήσαιεν ἅμα καὶ γένοιντο ἀσθενεῖς ἀνελόντες τοὺς ἀναιτίους καὶ φίλους ἑαυτῶν, ὡς δ' ἔνιοι λέγουσιν, οὐχὶ πλαττόμενος ἀλλὰ τοὺς
6 συνειδότας ἐμήνυεν. καὶ τέλος ὡς οὐκ ἐδύνατο
πάντα ποιῶν ἀποθανεῖν, ἐπαγγειλάμενος ὡς ἄλλους μηνύσων πολλοὺς καὶ πείσας αὐτῷ τὸν Ἱππίαν δοῦναι τὴν δεξιὰν πίστεως χάριν, ὡς ἔλαβεν ὀνειδίσας ὅτι τῷ φονεῖ τοῦ ἀδελφοῦ τὴν δεξιὰν δέδωκε, οὕτω παρώξυνε τὸν Ἱππίαν ὥσθ' ὑπὸ τῆς ὀργῆς οὐ κατεῖχεν ἑαυτὸν ἀλλὰ σπασάμενος τὴν μάχαιραν διέφθειρεν αὐτόν.

1 XIX. Μετὰ δὲ ταῦτα συνέβαινεν πολλῷ τραχυ-
τέραν εἶναι τὴν τυραννίδα· καὶ γὰρ διὰ τὸ τιμωρῶν[2] τῷ ἀδελφῷ [καὶ διὰ τὸ][3] πολλοὺς ἀνῃρηκέναι καὶ
2 ἐκβεβληκέναι πᾶσιν ἦν ἄπιστος καὶ πικρός. ἔτει
δὲ τετάρτῳ μάλιστα μετὰ τὸν Ἱππάρχου θάνατον, ἐπεὶ κακῶς εἶχεν τὰ ἐν τῷ ἄστει, τὴν Μουνυχίαν

[1] ἔπεμπον τότε Rutherford: επεμποντο cod.
[2] Kokalos: τιμωρειν cod. [3] Kokalos.

[a] A hill above the sea S. of the city, commanding Peiraeus and the two other harbours.

died later, having been taken into custody and
tortured for a long time. Under the strain of the
tortures he gave the names of a number of men that
belonged by birth to families of distinction, and were
friends of the tyrants, as confederates. For they
were not able immediately to find any trace of the
plot, but the current story that Hippias made the
people in the procession fall out away from their arms
and searched for those that retained their daggers is
not true, for in those days they did not walk in the
procession armed, but this custom was instituted
later by the democracy. According to the account 5
of people of popular sympathies, Aristogeiton accused
the tyrants' friends for the purpose of making his
captors commit an impiety and weaken themselves
at the same time by making away with men who were
innocent and their own friends, but others say that
his accusations were not fictitious but that he dis-
closed his actual accomplices. Finally, as do what 6
he would he was unable to die, he offered to give
information against many more, and induced Hippias
to give him his right hand as a pledge of good faith,
and when he grasped it he taunted him with giving
his hand to his brother's murderer, and so enraged
Hippias that in his anger he could not control himself
but drew his dagger and made away with him.

XIX. After this it began to come about that the 1
tyranny was much harsher; for Hippias's numerous
executions and sentences of exile in revenge for his
brother led to his being suspicious of everybody and
embittered. About four years after Hipparchus's 2
death the state of affairs in the city was so bad that
he set about fortifying Munychia,[a] with the intention

ἐπεχείρησε τειχίζειν, ὡς ἐκεῖ[1] μεθιδρυσόμενος. ἐν τούτοις δ' ὢν ἐξέπεσεν ὑπὸ Κλεομένους τοῦ Λακεδήμονος βασιλέως, χρησμῶν γινομένων ἀεὶ τοῖς Λάκωσι καταλύειν τὴν τυραννίδα διὰ τοιάνδ' αἰτίαν.
3 οἱ φυγάδες ὧν οἱ Ἀλκμεωνίδαι προειστήκεσαν αὐτοὶ μὲν δι' αὑτῶν οὐκ ἐδύναντο ποιήσασθαι τὴν κάθοδον, ἀλλ' αἰεὶ προσέπταιον· ἔν τε γὰρ τοῖς ἄλλοις οἷς ἔπραττον διεσφάλλοντο, καὶ τειχίσαντες ἐν τῇ χώρᾳ Λειψύδριον τὸ ὑπὲρ Πάρνηθος, εἰς ὃ συνεξῆλθόν τινες τῶν ἐκ τοῦ ἄστεως, ἐξεπολιορκήθησαν ὑπὸ τῶν τυράννων, ὅθεν ὕστερον εἰς[2] ταύτην τὴν συμφορὰν ᾖδον ἐν τοῖς σκολίοις[3]·

αἰαῖ Λειψύδριον προδωσέταιρον,
οἵους ἄνδρας ἀπώλεσας, μάχεσθαι
ἀγαθούς τε καὶ εὐπατρίδας,
οἳ τότ' ἔδειξαν οἵων πατέρων ἔσαν.

4 ἀποτυγχάνοντες οὖν ἐν ἅπασι τοῖς ἄλλοις ἐμισθώσαντο τὸν ἐν Δελφοῖς νεὼν οἰκοδομεῖν, ὅθεν ηὐπόρησαν χρημάτων πρὸς τὴν τῶν Λακώνων βοήθειαν. ἡ δὲ Πυθία προέφερεν αἰεὶ τοῖς Λακεδαιμονίοις χρηστηριαζομένοις ἐλευθεροῦν τὰς Ἀθήνας, εἰς τοῦθ' ἕως[4] προὔτρεψε τοὺς Σπαρτιάτας, καίπερ ὄντων ξένων αὐτοῖς τῶν Πεισιστρατιδῶν· συνεβάλλετο δὲ οὐκ ἐλάττω μοῖραν τῆς ὁρμῆς τοῖς Λάκωσιν ἡ πρὸς τοὺς Ἀργείους τοῖς Πεισιστρατί-
5 δαις ὑπάρχουσα φιλία. τὸ μὲν οὖν πρῶτον Ἀγχίμολον ἀπέστειλαν κατὰ θάλατταν ἔχοντα στρατιάν·

1 ἐκεῖ<σε> Mayor.
2 εἰς Wilamowitz-Kaibel ex *Etym. Mag.*: μετα cod.
3 σκολίοις edd.: σκολιοισαιει cod.
4 τοῦθ' ἕως Blass: τουτευθεως cod.

of moving his establishment there. While engaged 511 B.C.
in this he was driven out by the king of Sparta, Cleomenes, as oracles were constantly being given to the Spartans to put down the tyranny, for the
following reason. The exiles headed by the Alcmeon- 3
idae were not able to effect their return by their own unaided efforts, but were always meeting reverses; for besides the other plans that were complete failures, they built the fort of Leipsydrion[a] in the country, on the slopes of Parnes, where some of their friends in the city came out and joined them, but they were besieged and dislodged by the tyrants, owing to which afterwards they used to refer to this disaster in singing their catches:

> Faithless Dry Fountain! Lackaday,
> What good men's lives you threw away!
> True patriots and fighters game,
> They showed the stock from which they came!

So as they were failing in everything else, they con- 4
tracted to build the temple at Delphi,[b] and so acquired a supply of money for the assistance of the Spartans. And the Pythian priestess constantly uttered a command to the Spartans, when they consulted the oracle, to liberate Athens, until she brought the Spartiates to the point, although the Peisistratidae were strangers to them; and an equally great amount of incitement was contributed to the Spartans by the friendship that subsisted between the Argives and
the Peisistratidae. As a first step, therefore, they 5
dispatched Anchimolus with a force by sea; but he

[a] The name suggests 'water-failure.' Parnes is a mountain in N.E. Attica.

[b] It had been burnt down in 548 B.C. Apparently they made a profit on the contract, but rebuilt it to the satisfaction of the priestess.

ἡττηθέντος δ' αὐτοῦ καὶ τελευτήσαντος διὰ τὸ Κινέαν βοηθῆσαι τὸν Θεσσαλὸν ἔχοντα χιλίους ἱππεῖς, προσοργισθέντες τῷ γενομένῳ Κλεομένην ἐξέπεμψαν τὸν βασιλέα στόλον ἔχοντα μείζω κατὰ γῆν, ὃς ἐπεὶ τοὺς τῶν Θεσσαλῶν ἱππεῖς ἐνίκησεν κωλύοντας αὐτὸν εἰς τὴν Ἀττικὴν παριέναι, κατακλείσας τὸν Ἱππίαν εἰς τὸ καλούμενον Πελαργικὸν
6 τεῖχος ἐπολιόρκει μετὰ τῶν Ἀθηναίων. προσκαθημένου δ' αὐτοῦ συνέπεσεν ὑπεξιόντας ἁλῶναι τοὺς τῶν Πεισιστρατιδῶν υἱεῖς· ὧν ληφθέντων ὁμολογίαν ἐπὶ τῇ τῶν παίδων σωτηρίᾳ ποιησάμενοι καὶ τὰ ἑαυτῶν ἐν πένθ' ἡμέραις ἐκκομισάμενοι παρέδωκαν τὴν ἀκρόπολιν τοῖς Ἀθηναίοις ἐπὶ Ἁρπακτίδου ἄρχοντος, κατασχόντες τὴν τυραννίδα μετὰ τὴν τοῦ πατρὸς τελευτὴν ἔτη μάλιστα ἑπτακαίδεκα, τὰ δὲ σύμπαντα σὺν οἷς ὁ πατὴρ ἦρξεν ἑνὸς δεῖν[1] πεντήκοντα.

1 XX. Καταλυθείσης δὲ τῆς τυραννίδος ἐστασίαζον πρὸς ἀλλήλους Ἰσαγόρας ὁ Τεισάνδρου, φίλος ὢν τῶν τυράννων, καὶ Κλεισθένης τοῦ γένους ὢν τῶν Ἀλκμεονιδῶν. ἡττημένος[2] δὲ[3] ταῖς ἑταιρείαις ὁ Κλεισθένης προσηγάγετο[4] τὸν δῆμον, ἀποδιδοὺς
2 τῷ πλήθει τὴν πολιτείαν. ὁ δὲ Ἰσαγόρας ἐπιλειπόμενος τῇ δυνάμει, πάλιν ἐπικαλεσάμενος τὸν Κλεομένην ὄντα ἑαυτῷ ξένον συνέπεισεν ἐλαύνειν τὸ ἄγος, διὰ τὸ τοὺς Ἀλκμεωνίδας δοκεῖν εἶναι τῶν
3 ἐναγῶν. ὑπεξελθόντος δὲ τοῦ Κλεισθένους, μετ'

[1] Mayor: δεῖ cod.
[2] ἡττώμενος edd. ex Herod. v. 66.
[3] δ' ἐν? Rackham.
[4] προσήγετο Thalheim.

[a] The fortification surrounding the west end of the Acropolis.

was defeated and lost his life, because the Thessalian Cineas came to the defence with a thousand cavalry. Enraged at this occurrence, they dispatched their king Cleomenes by land with a larger army; he won a victory over the Thessalian cavalry who tried to prevent his reaching Attica, and so shut up Hippias in the fortress called the Pelargicum[a] and began to lay siege to it with the aid of the Athenians. While he 6
was sitting down against it, it occurred that the sons of the Peisistratidae were caught when trying secretly to get away; and these being taken they came to terms on the condition of the boys' safety, and conveyed away their belongings in five days, surrendering the Acropolis to the Athenians; this was in the archonship of Harpactides, and Peisistratus's sons 511 B.C.
had retained the tyranny for about seventeen years after their father's death, making when added to the period of their father's power a total of forty-nine years.

XX. When the tyranny had been put down, there 1
was a period of faction-strife between Isagoras son of Teisander, who was a friend of the tyrants, and Cleisthenes, who belonged to the family of the Alcmaeonidae. Cleisthenes having been worsted by the Comradeships[b] enlisted the people on his side, offering to hand over the government to the multitude. Isagoras began to lose power, so he again 2
called in the aid of Cleomenes, who was a great friend of his, and jointly persuaded him to drive out the curse,[c] because the Alcmaeonidae were reputed to be a family that was under a curse. Cleisthenes 3
secretly withdrew, and Cleomenes with a few troops

[b] Political clubs with anti-democratic leanings.
[c] *Cf.* ch. i.

ὀλίγων[1] ἡγηλάτει τῶν Ἀθηναίων ἑπτακοσίας οἰκίας· ταῦτα δὲ διαπραξάμενος τὴν μὲν βουλὴν ἐπειρᾶτο καταλύειν Ἰσαγόραν δὲ καὶ τριακοσίους τῶν φίλων μετ' αὐτοῦ κυρίους καθιστάναι τῆς πόλεως. τῆς δὲ βουλῆς ἀντιστάσης καὶ συναθροισθέντος τοῦ πλήθους οἱ μὲν περὶ τὸν Κλεομένην καὶ Ἰσαγόραν κατέφυγον εἰς τὴν ἀκρόπολιν, ὁ δὲ δῆμος δύο μὲν ἡμέρας προσκαθεζόμενος ἐπολιόρκει, τῇ δὲ τρίτῃ Κλεομένην μὲν καὶ τοὺς μετ' αὐτοῦ πάντας ἀφεῖσαν ὑποσπόνδους, Κλεισθένην δὲ καὶ
4 τοὺς ἄλλους φυγάδας μετεπέμψαντο. κατασχόντος δὲ τοῦ δήμου τὰ πράγματα Κλεισθένης ἡγεμὼν ἦν καὶ τοῦ δήμου προστάτης. αἰτιώτατοι γὰρ σχεδὸν ἐγένοντο τῆς ἐκβολῆς τῶν τυράννων οἱ Ἀλκμεωνίδαι, καὶ[2] στασιάζοντες τὰ πολλὰ διετέλεσαν.
5 ἔτι δὲ πρότερον τῶν Ἀλκμεονιδῶν Κήδων ἐπέθετο τοῖς τυράννοις· διὸ καὶ ᾖδον καὶ εἰς τοῦτον ἐν τοῖς σκολίοις·

ἔγχει καὶ Κήδωνι, διάκονε, μηδ' ἐπιλήθου,
εἰ χρὴ τοῖς ἀγαθοῖς ἀνδράσιν οἰνοχοεῖν.

1 XXI. Διὰ μὲν οὖν ταύτας τὰς αἰτίας ἐπίστευεν ὁ δῆμος τῷ Κλεισθένει. τότε δὲ τοῦ πλήθους προεστηκὼς ἔτει τετάρτῳ μετὰ τὴν τῶν τυράννων
2 κατάλυσιν ἐπὶ Ἰσαγόρου ἄρχοντος, πρῶτον μὲν συνένειμε[3] πάντας εἰς δέκα φυλὰς ἀντὶ τῶν τεττάρων, ἀναμεῖξαι βουλόμενος, ὅπως μετάσχωσι πλείους τῆς πολιτείας· ὅθεν ἐλέχθη καὶ τὸ μὴ

[1] <ἀφικόμενος ὁ Κλεομένης> μετ' ὀλίγων Wilamowitz-Kaibel ex Herod. v. 72.

[2] <οἱ> καὶ Richards.

[3] συνένειμε Newman: ουνενειμε cod.

proceeded to expel as accursed seven hundred Athenian households; and having accomplished this he tried to put down the Council and set up Isagoras and three hundred of his friends with him in sovereign power over the state. But the Council resisted, and the multitude banded together, so the forces of Cleomenes and Isagoras took refuge in the Acropolis, and the people invested it and laid siege to it for two days. On the third day they let Cleomenes and his comrades go away under a truce, and sent for
Cleisthenes and the other exiles to come back. The 4
people having taken control of affairs, Cleisthenes was their leader and was head of the People. For almost the chief initiative in the expulsion of the tyrants was taken by the Alcmaeonids, and they accomplished
most of it by party faction. And even before the 5
Alcmaeonids Cedon had attacked the tyrants, owing to which people also sang in his honour in their catches:

> Now fill to Cedon, boy! let's drink him too,
> If duty bids us toast good men and true.

XXI. These were the causes, therefore, that led the 1
people to trust in Cleisthenes. And when this time
he had become Chief of the multitude, in the fourth 508 B.C.
year after the deposition of the tyrants, in the archonship of Isagoras, he first divided the whole body into 2
ten tribes instead of the existing four, wishing to mix them up, in order that more might take part in the government[a]; from which arose the saying, 'Don't draw distinctions between tribes,' addressed

[a] Less incompletely stated in *Politics* iii. 275 b 37 ff. Members of the same class might now belong to different tribes; and a number of new citizens were enrolled (see § 4), free-born aliens and emancipated slaves, who were not members of clans.

φυλοκρινεῖν, πρὸς τοὺς ἐξετάζειν τὰ γένη βουλο-
3 μένους. ἔπειτα τὴν βουλὴν πεντακοσίους ἀντὶ τετρακοσίων κατέστησεν, πεντήκοντα ἐξ ἑκάστης φυλῆς· τότε δ' ἦσαν ἑκατόν. διὰ τοῦτο δὲ οὐκ εἰς δώδεκα φυλὰς συνέταξεν, ὅπως αὐτῷ μὴ συμβαίνῃ μερίζειν κατὰ τὰς προϋπαρχούσας τριττῦς (ἦσαν γὰρ ἐκ δ' φυλῶν δώδεκα τριττύες), ὥστ' οὐ συνέπιπτεν ἂν[1] ἀναμίσγεσθαι τὸ πλῆθος.
4 διένειμε δὲ καὶ τὴν χώραν κατὰ δήμους τριάκοντα μέρη, δέκα μὲν τῶν περὶ τὸ ἄστυ, δέκα δὲ τῆς παραλίας, δέκα δὲ τῆς μεσογείου· καὶ ταύτας ἐπονομάσας τριττῦς ἐκλήρωσεν τρεῖς εἰς τὴν φυλὴν ἑκάστην, ὅπως ἑκάστη μετέχῃ πάντων τῶν τόπων. καὶ δημότας ἐποίησεν ἀλλήλων τοὺς οἰκοῦντας ἐν ἑκάστῳ τῶν δήμων, ἵνα μὴ πατρόθεν προσαγορεύοντες ἐξελέγχωσιν τοὺς νεοπολίτας, ἀλλὰ τῶν δήμων ἀναγορεύωσιν· ὅθεν καὶ καλοῦσιν
5 Ἀθηναῖοι σφᾶς αὐτοὺς τῶν δήμων. κατέστησε δὲ καὶ δημάρχους τὴν αὐτὴν ἔχοντας ἐπιμέλειαν τοῖς πρότερον ναυκράροις· καὶ γὰρ τοὺς δήμους ἀντὶ τῶν ναυκραριῶν ἐποίησεν. προσηγόρευσε δὲ τῶν δήμων τοὺς μὲν ἀπὸ τῶν τόπων, τοὺς δὲ ἀπὸ τῶν κτισάντων, οὐ γὰρ ἅπαντες ὑπῆρχον ἐν[2] τοῖς
6 τόποις. τὰ δὲ γένη καὶ τὰς φρατρίας καὶ τὰς ἱερωσύνας εἴασεν ἔχειν ἑκάστους κατὰ τὰ πάτρια.

[1] ἂν supplevit Hude.
[2] ἐν fr. Berol.: in cod. alii εν, alii ετι legunt.

[a] See viii. 3 n.

[b] *i.e.* he made the deme a social group, united by almost a family feeling.

[c] *Cf.*, *e.g.*, xxviii. 3 'Callicrates of the Paeanian deme,' and subsequent designations of persons by their demes; up to that point the father's name is used.

to those who want to inquire into people's clans.
Next he made the Council to consist of five hundred 3
members instead of four hundred, fifty from each Tribe, whereas under the old system there had been a hundred. This was the reason why he did not arrange them in twelve tribes, in order that he might not have to use the existing division of the Thirds[a] (for the four Tribes contained twelve Thirds), with the result that the multitude would not have been
mixed up. He also portioned out the land among the 4
demes into thirty parts, ten belonging to the suburbs, ten to the coast, and ten to the inland district; and he gave these parts the name of Thirds, and assigned them among the Tribes by lot, three to each, in order that each Tribe might have a share in all the districts. And he made all the inhabitants in each of the demes fellow-demesmen of one another,[b] in order that they might not call attention to the newly enfranchised citizens by addressing people by their fathers' names, but designate people officially by their demes; owing to which Athenians in private life also use the names of their demes as surnames.[c]
And he also appointed Demarchs, having the same 5
duties as the former Ship-commissioners,[d] for he put the demes in the place of the Ship-commissions. He named some of the demes from their localities, but others from their founders, for the demes were no
longer all corresponding to the places. The clans 6
and brotherhoods[e] and priesthoods belonging to the various demes he allowed to remain on the ancestral

[d] See viii. 3 n.

[e] In *Politics* 1319 b 23 it is said that 'Cleisthenes increased the number of the brotherhoods,' but that no doubt refers to the new citizens.

ταῖς δὲ φυλαῖς ἐποίησεν ἐπωνύμους ἐκ τῶν προκριθέντων ἑκατὸν ἀρχηγετῶν οὓς ἀνεῖλεν ἡ Πυθία δέκα.

1 XXII. Τούτων δὲ γενομένων δημοτικωτέρα πολὺ τῆς Σόλωνος ἐγένετο ἡ πολιτεία· καὶ γὰρ συνέβη τοὺς μὲν Σόλωνος νόμους ἀφανίσαι τὴν τυραννίδα διὰ τὸ μὴ χρῆσθαι, καινοὺς δ' ἄλλους θεῖναι τὸν Κλεισθένη στοχαζόμενον τοῦ πλήθους, ἐν οἷς ἐτέθη
2 καὶ ὁ περὶ τοῦ ὀστρακισμοῦ νόμος. πρῶτον μὲν οὖν ἔτει πέμπτῳ[1] μετὰ ταύτην τὴν κατάστασιν ἐφ' Ἑρμοκρέοντος ἄρχοντος τῇ βουλῇ τοῖς πεντακοσίοις τὸν ὅρκον ἐποίησαν ὃν ἔτι καὶ νῦν ὀμνύουσιν. ἔπειτα τοὺς στρατηγοὺς ᾑροῦντο κατὰ φυλάς, ἐξ ἑκάστης φυλῆς ἕνα, τῆς δὲ ἁπάσης
3 στρατιᾶς ἡγεμὼν ἦν ὁ πολέμαρχος. ἔτει δὲ μετὰ ταῦτα δωδεκάτῳ νικήσαντες τὴν ἐν Μαραθῶνι μάχην, ἐπὶ Φαινίππου ἄρχοντος, διαλιπόντες ἔτη δύο μετὰ τὴν νίκην, θαρροῦντος ἤδη τοῦ δήμου, τότε πρῶτον ἐχρήσαντο τῷ νόμῳ τῷ περὶ τὸν ὀστρακισμόν, ὃς ἐτέθη διὰ τὴν ὑποψίαν τῶν ἐν ταῖς δυνάμεσιν ὅτι[2] Πεισίστρατος δημαγωγὸς καὶ
4 στρατηγὸς ὢν τύραννος κατέστη. καὶ πρῶτος ὠστρακίσθη τῶν ἐκείνου συγγενῶν Ἵππαρχος Χάρμου Κολλυτεύς, δι' ὃν καὶ μάλιστα τὸν νόμον ἔθηκεν ὁ Κλεισθένης, ἐξελάσαι βουλόμενος αὐτόν. οἱ γὰρ Ἀθηναῖοι τοὺς τῶν τυράννων φίλους, ὅσοι μὴ συνεξαμαρτάνοιεν[3] ἐν ταῖς ταραχαῖς, εἴων οἰκεῖν τὴν πόλιν, χρώμενοι τῇ εἰωθυίᾳ τοῦ δήμου

[1] πέμπτῳ (=ε') cod.: ὀγδόῳ (=η')? Kenyon.
[2] Kenyon: οτε cod.
[3] Poste: συνεξαμαρτανον cod.

plan. As eponymous deities of the Tribes he instituted ten tutelary heroes selected by an oracle of the Pythian priestess from a previously chosen list of a hundred.

XXII. These reforms made the constitution much 1
more democratic than that of Solon; for it had come about that the tyranny had obliterated the laws of Solon by disuse, and Cleisthenes aiming at the multitude had instituted other new ones, including the enactment of the law about ostracism. First of 2
all, in the fifth year[a] after these enactments, in the archonship of Hermocreon, they instituted the oath of induction for the Council of Five Hundred that is still in use. Next they began to elect the Generals by tribes, one from each tribe, while the whole army was under the command of the War-lord. Eleven years afterwards came their victory in the 3
battle of Marathon; and in the archonship of Phaen- 490 B.C.
ippus, two years after the victory, the people being 488 B.C.
now in high courage, they put in force for the first time the law about ostracism, which had been enacted owing to the suspicion felt against the men in the positions of power because Peisistratus when leader of the people and general set himself up as tyrant. The first person banished by ostracism was one of his 4
relatives, Hipparchus son of Charmus of the deme of Collytus, the desire to banish whom had been Cleisthenes' principal motive in making the law. For the Athenians permitted all friends of the tyrants that had not taken part with them in their offences during the disorders to dwell in the city,—in this the customary mildness of the people was displayed; and

[a] *i.e.* in 504 B.C.; but if Marathon (490 B.C.) was eleven years later (§ 3), perhaps the Greek should be altered here to give 'in the eighth year after.'

πραότητι· ὧν ἡγεμὼν καὶ προστάτης ἦν Ἵππαρχος.
5 εὐθὺς δὲ τῷ ὑστέρῳ ἔτει ἐπὶ Τελεσίνου ἄρχοντος
ἐκυάμευσαν τοὺς ἐννέα ἄρχοντας κατὰ φυλὰς ἐκ
τῶν προκριθέντων ὑπὸ τῶν δημοτῶν[1] πεντακοσίων
τότε[2] μετὰ τὴν τυραννίδα πρῶτον· οἱ δὲ πρότεροι
πάντες ἦσαν αἱρετοί. καὶ ὠστρακίσθη Μεγακλῆς
6 Ἱπποκράτους Ἀλωπεκῆθεν. ἐπὶ μὲν οὖν ἔτη γʹ
τοὺς τῶν τυράννων φίλους ὠστράκιζον, ὧν χάριν
ὁ νόμος ἐτέθη, μετὰ δὲ ταῦτα τῷ τετάρτῳ ἔτει
καὶ τῶν ἄλλων εἴ τις δοκοίη μείζων εἶναι μεθίστατο·
καὶ πρῶτος ὠστρακίσθη τῶν ἄπωθεν τῆς τυραν-
7 νίδος Ξάνθιππος ὁ Ἀρίφρονος. ἔτει δὲ τρίτῳ
μετὰ ταῦτα Νικομήδου[3] ἄρχοντος, ὡς ἐφάνη[4] τὰ
μέταλλα τὰ ἐν Μαρωνείᾳ καὶ περιεγένετο τῇ
πόλει τάλαντα ἑκατὸν ἐκ τῶν ἔργων, συμβουλευ-
όντων τινῶν τῷ δήμῳ διανείμασθαι τὸ ἀργύριον
Θεμιστοκλῆς ἐκώλυσεν, οὐ λέγων ὅ τι χρήσεται
τοῖς χρήμασιν, ἀλλὰ δανεῖσαι κελεύων τοῖς πλου-
σιωτάτοις Ἀθηναίων ἑκατὸν ἑκάστῳ τάλαντον,
εἶτ' ἐὰν μὲν ἀρέσκῃ τὸ ἀνάλωμα, τῆς πόλεως
εἶναι,[5] εἰ δὲ μή, κομίσασθαι τὰ χρήματα παρὰ
τῶν δανεισαμένων. λαβὼν δ' ἐπὶ τούτοις ἐναυ-
πηγήσατο τριήρεις ἑκατόν, ἑκάστου ναυπηγου-
μένου τῶν ἑκατὸν μίαν, αἷς ἐναυμάχησαν ἐν
Σαλαμῖνι πρὸς τοὺς βαρβάρους. ὠστρακίσθη δ'
ἐν τούτοις τοῖς καιροῖς Ἀριστείδης ὁ Λυσιμάχου.

[1] δήμων fr. Berol. [2] τότε Whibley: τοις cod.
[3] Νικοδημου fr. Berol.
[4] ⟨λυσιτελέστερα⟩ ἐφάνη Richards coll. Xen. *Red.* 4. 31.
[5] post εἶναι, in cod. alia manus τηνδαπανην supra lineam scripsit.

Hipparchus was the leader and chief of these persons.
But directly afterwards, in the next year, in the 5
archonship of Telesinus, they elected the Nine 487 B.C.
Archons by lot, tribe by tribe, from a preliminary
list of five hundred chosen by the demesmen: this
was the date of the first election on these lines, after
the tyranny, the previous Archons having all been
elected by vote. And Megacles son of Hippocrates
of the deme Alopekē was ostracized. For three years 6
they went on ostracizing the friends of the tyrants,
at whom the legislation had been aimed, but afterwards in the fourth year it was also used to remove
any other person who seemed to be too great; the
first person unconnected with the tyranny to be
ostracized was Xanthippus son of Ariphron. Two 7
years later, in the archonship of Nicomedes, in con- 483 B.C.
sequence of the discovery of the mines at Maronea,[a]
the working of which had given the state a profit of a hundred talents, the advice was given by some persons that the money should be distributed among the people; but Themistocles prevented this, not saying what use he would make of the money, but recommending that it should be lent to the hundred richest Athenians, each receiving a talent, so that if they should spend it in a satisfactory manner, the state would have the advantage, but if they did not, the state should call in the money from the borrowers. On these terms the money was put at his disposal, and he used it to get a fleet of a hundred triremes built, each of the hundred borrowers having one ship built, and with these they fought the naval battle at Salamis against the barbarians. And it was during this period that Aristeides son of Lysimachus was

[a] Possibly five miles north of Cape Sunium.

8 τετάρτῳ[1] δ' ἔτει κατεδέξαντο πάντας τοὺς ὠστρακισμένους ἄρχοντος Ὑψηχίδου, διὰ τὴν Ξέρξου στρατείαν· καὶ τὸ λοιπὸν ὥρισαν τοῖς ὀστρακιζομένοις ἐντὸς Γεραιστοῦ καὶ Σκυλλαίου μὴ[2] κατοικεῖν ἢ ἀτίμους εἶναι καθάπαξ.

1 XXIII. Τότε μὲν οὖν μέχρι τούτου προῆλθεν ἡ πόλις, ἅμα τῇ δημοκρατίᾳ κατὰ μικρὸν αὐξανομένη· μετὰ δὲ τὰ Μηδικὰ πάλιν ἴσχυσεν ἡ ἐν Ἀρείῳ πάγῳ βουλὴ καὶ διῴκει τὴν πόλιν, οὐδενὶ δόγματι λαβοῦσα τὴν ἡγεμονίαν ἀλλὰ διὰ τὸ γενέσθαι τῆς περὶ Σαλαμῖνα ναυμαχίας αἰτία. τῶν γὰρ στρατηγῶν ἐξαπορησάντων τοῖς πράγμασι καὶ κηρυξάντων σῴζειν ἕκαστον ἑαυτόν, πορίσασα δραχμὰς ἑκάστῳ ὀκτὼ διέδωκε καὶ
2 ἐνεβίβασεν εἰς τὰς ναῦς. διὰ ταύτην δὴ τὴν αἰτίαν παρεχώρουν αὐτῆς[3] τῷ ἀξιώματι καὶ ἐπολιτεύθησαν Ἀθηναῖοι καλῶς κατὰ[4] τούτους τοὺς καιρούς· συνέβη γὰρ αὐτοῖς κατὰ τὸν χρόνον τοῦτον τά τε εἰς τὸν πόλεμον ἀσκῆσαι καὶ παρὰ τοῖς Ἕλλησιν εὐδοκιμῆσαι καὶ τὴν τῆς θαλαττης ἡγεμονίαν λαβεῖν ἀκόντων τῶν Λακεδαιμονίων.
3 ἦσαν δὲ προστάται τοῦ δήμου κατὰ τούτους τοὺς καιροὺς Ἀριστείδης ὁ Λυσιμάχου καὶ Θεμιστοκλῆς ὁ Νεοκλέους, ὁ μὲν τὰ πολέμια ἀσκῶν[5] ὁ δὲ τὰ πολιτικὰ δεινὸς εἶναι καὶ δικαιοσύνῃ τῶν

[1] τρίτῳ Wilamowitz-Kaibel collato Plut. *Aristid.* 8.
[2] μὴ supplevit Kaibel (ἐκτὸς pro ἐντὸς Wyse).
[3] Blass: αυτην cod.
[4] κατὰ (vel καὶ <μετρίως> κατὰ ?) Kenyon: καικατα cod.
[5] δοκῶν Richards: δοκῶν ἀσκεῖν Kenyon.

ostracized. Three years later in the archonship of 8
Hypsechides they allowed all the persons ostracized
to return, because of the expedition of Xerxes ; and 480 B.C.
they fixed a boundary thenceforward for persons ostracized, prohibiting them from living[a] within a line drawn from Geraestus[b] to Scyllaeum[c] under penalty of absolute loss of citizenship.

XXIII. At this date, therefore, the state had 1
advanced to this point, growing by slow stages with the growth of the democracy ; but after the Persian Wars the Council on the Areopagus became powerful again, and carried on the administration, having gained the leadership by no definite resolution but owing to its having been the cause of the naval battle of Salamis. For the Generals had been reduced to utter despair by the situation and had made a proclamation that every man should see to his own safety ; but the Council provided a fund and distributed eight drachmas a head and got them to man the
ships. For this reason, therefore, the Generals gave 2
place to the Council in esteem. And Athens was well governed in these periods ; for during this time it occurred that the people practised military duties and won high esteem among the Greeks and gained the supremacy of the sea against the will of the Lacedaemonians. The heads of the People[d] in these periods 3
were Aristeides son of Lysimachus and Themistocles son of Neocles, the latter practising to be skilful in military pursuits, and the former in politics,[e] and to excel

[a] The MS. gives 'enacting that they must live.'

[b] The S. point of Euboea.

[c] The S.E. point of Argolis.

[d] See ii. 3 n.

[e] The Greek should perhaps be altered to give 'the latter practising military pursuits, and the former esteemed to be skilful in politics.'

καθ' ἑαυτὸν διαφέρειν· διὸ καὶ ἐχρῶντο τῷ μὲν
4 στρατηγῷ τῷ δὲ συμβούλῳ. τὴν μὲν οὖν τῶν
τειχῶν ἀνοικοδόμησιν κοινῇ διῴκησαν, καίπερ δια-
φερόμενοι πρὸς ἀλλήλους· ἐπὶ δὲ τὴν ἀπόστασιν
τὴν τῶν Ἰώνων ἀπὸ τῆς τῶν Λακεδαιμονίων συμ-
μαχίας[1] Ἀριστείδης ἦν ὁ προτρέψας, τηρήσας τοὺς
5 Λάκωνας διαβεβλημένους διὰ Παυσανίαν. διὸ καὶ
τοὺς φόρους οὗτος ἦν ὁ τάξας ταῖς πόλεσιν τοὺς
πρώτους ἔτει τρίτῳ μετὰ τὴν ἐν Σαλαμῖνι ναυμαχίαν ἐπὶ Τιμοσθένους ἄρχοντος, καὶ τοὺς ὅρκους
ὤμοσε τοῖς Ἴωσι ὥστε τὸν αὐτὸν ἐχθρὸν εἶναι καὶ
φίλον, ἐφ' οἷς καὶ τοὺς μύδρους ἐν τῷ πελάγει
καθεῖσαν.

1 XXIV. Μετὰ δὲ ταῦτα θαρρούσης ἤδη τῆς
πόλεως καὶ χρημάτων ἠθροισμένων πολλῶν, συν-
εβούλευεν ἀντιλαμβάνεσθαι τῆς ἡγεμονίας καὶ κατα-
βάντας ἐκ τῶν ἀγρῶν οἰκεῖν ἐν τῷ ἄστει· τροφὴν
γὰρ ἔσεσθαι πᾶσι, τοῖς μὲν στρατευομένοις τοῖς δὲ
φρουροῦσι τοῖς δὲ τὰ κοινὰ πράττουσι, εἶθ' οὕτω
2 κατασχήσειν τὴν ἡγεμονίαν. πεισθέντες δὲ ταῦτα
καὶ λαβόντες τὴν ἀρχὴν τοῖς[2] συμμάχοις δε-
σποτικωτέρως ἐχρῶντο πλὴν Χίων καὶ Λεσβίων
καὶ Σαμίων· τούτους δὲ φύλακας εἶχον τῆς ἀρχῆς,
ἐῶντες τάς τε πολιτείας παρ' αὐτοῖς καὶ ἄρχειν
3 ὧν ἔτυχον ἄρχοντες. κατέστησαν δὲ καὶ τοῖς
πολλοῖς εὐπορίαν τροφῆς, ὥσπερ Ἀριστείδης

[1] καιτηντωνλακεδαιμονιωνσυμμαχιαν cod., corr. Blass.
[2] τοῖς Blass: τοιστε cod.

---

[a] The city fortifications were rebuilt, the harbour of Peiraeus completed and the Long Walls built to link Peiraeus and Phalerum with the city.

[b] The parties swore to keep the covenant until the iron

his contemporaries in justice; hence the Athenians
employed the one as general and the other as
counsellor. So the rebuilding of the walls[a] was directed 4
by both these statesmen jointly, although they were
at variance with one another; but the secession of
the Ionian states from the Lacedaemonian alliance
was promoted by Aristeides, who seized the opportunity when the Lacedaemonians were discredited
because of Pausanias. Hence it was Aristeides who 5
assessed the tributes of the allied states on the first
occasion, two years after the naval battle of Salamis, 478 B.C.
in the archonship of Timosthenes, and who administered the oaths to the Ionians when they swore to
have the same enemies and friends, ratifying their
oaths by letting the lumps of iron sink to the bottom
out at sea.[b]

XXIV. Afterwards, now that the state was em- 1
boldened and much money had been collected, he began to advise them to aim at the leadership, and to come down from their farms and live in the city, telling them that there would be food for all, some serving in the army and others as frontier-guards and others conducting the business of the community, and then by this method they would keep the leadership. Having taken this advice and won the empire, 2
they treated the allies too masterfully, except Chios, Lesbos and Samos, which they kept as outposts of empire, and allowed to have their own governments and to rule the subjects that they had at the time.
They also established a plentiful food-supply for the 3
multitude, as Aristeides had proposed; for the com-

appeared again on the surface, *πρὶν ἢ τὸν μύδρον τοῦτον ἀναφῆναι* Hdt. i. 165, and Hor. *Epodes* 16. 25—

> sed iuremus in haec: 'simul imis saxa renarint
> vadis leuata, ne redire sit nefas.'

εἰσηγήσατο· συνέβαινεν γὰρ ἀπὸ τῶν φόρων καὶ τῶν τελῶν καὶ τῶν συμμάχων πλείους ἢ δισμυρίους ἄνδρας τρέφεσθαι. δικασταὶ μὲν γὰρ ἦσαν ἑξακισχίλιοι, τοξόται δ' ἑξακόσιοι καὶ χίλιοι καὶ πρὸς τούτοις ἱππεῖς χίλιοι καὶ διακόσιοι, βουλὴ δὲ πεντακόσιοι, καὶ φρουροὶ νεωρίων πεντακόσιοι καὶ πρὸς τούτοις ἐν τῇ πόλει φρουροὶ ν', ἀρχαὶ δ' ἔνδημοι μὲν εἰς ἑπτακοσίους ἄνδρας ὑπερόριοι δ' εἰς ἑπτακοσίους[1]· πρὸς δὲ τούτοις, ἐπεὶ συνεστήσαντο[2] τὸν πόλεμον ὕστερον, ὁπλῖται μὲν δισχίλιοι καὶ πεντακόσιοι, νῆες δὲ φρουρίδες εἴκοσι, ἄλλαι δὲ νῆες αἱ τοὺς φρούρους[3] ἄγουσαι τοὺς ἀπὸ τοῦ κυάμου δισχιλίους ἄνδρας· ἔτι δὲ πρυτανεῖον καὶ ὀρφανοὶ καὶ δεσμωτῶν φύλακες· ἅπασι γὰρ τούτοις ἀπὸ τῶν κοινῶν ἡ διοίκησις ἦν.

1 XXV. Ἡ μὲν οὖν τροφὴ τῷ δήμῳ διὰ τούτων ἐγίνετο. ἔτη δὲ ἑπτακαιδέκα μάλιστα μετὰ τὰ Μηδικὰ διέμεινεν ἡ πολιτεία προεστώτων τῶν Ἀρεοπαγιτῶν, καίπερ ὑποφερομένη κατὰ μικρόν. αὐξανομένου δὲ τοῦ πλήθους γενόμενος τοῦ δήμου προστάτης Ἐφιάλτης ὁ Σωφωνίδου καὶ δοκῶν[4] ἀδωροδόκητος εἶναι καὶ δίκαιος πρὸς τὴν πολι-
2 τείαν, ἐπέθετο τῇ βουλῇ. καὶ πρῶτον μὲν ἀνεῖλεν πολλοὺς τῶν Ἀρεοπαγιτῶν ἀγῶνας ἐπιφέρων περὶ τῶν διῳκημένων· ἔπειτα τῆς βουλῆς ἐπὶ Κόνωνος ἄρχοντος ἅπαντα περιεῖλε[5] τὰ ἐπίθετα δι' ὧν ἦν ἡ τῆς πολιτείας φυλακή, καὶ τὰ μὲν τοῖς πεντα-

[1] numerum e priore versu male repetitum notant Wilamowitz-Kaibel.
[2] συνέστησαν τὰ ⟨εἰς⟩? Rackham: συνεστήσαντο τὰ εἰς Wilamowitz-Kaibel.
[3] Blass, cf. lxii. 1: φορους cod.
[4] δοκῶν καὶ Kaibel.
[5] περιείλετο Richards.

bined proceeds of the tributes and the taxes and the allies served to feed more than twenty thousand men. For there were six thousand jurymen, one thousand six hundred archers and also one thousand two hundred cavalry, five hundred members of the Council, five hundred guardians of the docks, and also fifty watchmen in the city, as many as seven hundred officials at home and as many as seven hundred [a] abroad; and in addition to these, when later they settled into the war, two thousand five hundred hoplites, twenty guard-ships and other ships conveying the guards to the number of two hundred elected by lot; and furthermore the prytaneum,[b] orphans, and warders of prisoners—for all of these had their maintenance from public funds.

XXV. By these means the people were provided 1
with their food-supply. The constitution remained under the leadership of the Areopagites for about seventeen years after the Persian War, although it was being gradually modified. But as the population increased, Ephialtes son of Sophonides, having become head of the People [c] and having the reputation of being incorruptible and just in regard to the constitution, attacked the Council. First he made away with 2
many of the Areopagites by bringing legal proceedings against them about their acts of administration;
then in the archonship of Conon he stripped the 462 B.C.
Council of all its added powers which made it the safeguard of the constitution, and assigned some of

[a] The number is probably repeated from the previous line by mistake; otherwise 'also' would be added.

[b] The town-hall, probably in the old Agora, south of the Acropolis; in it a fire was kept continually burning, and the Prytaneis dined.

[c] See ii. 3 n.

κοσίοις τὰ δὲ τῷ δήμῳ καὶ τοῖς δικαστηρίοις
3 ἀπέδωκεν. ἔπραξε δὲ ταῦτα συναιτίου γενομένου Θεμιστοκλέους, ὃς ἦν μὲν τῶν Ἀρεοπαγιτῶν ἔμελλε δὲ κρίνεσθαι μηδισμοῦ. βουλόμενος δὲ καταλυθῆναι τὴν βουλὴν ὁ Θεμιστοκλῆς πρὸς μὲν τὸν Ἐφιάλτην ἔλεγεν ὅτι συναρπάζειν αὐτὸν ἡ βουλὴ μέλλει, πρὸς δὲ τοὺς Ἀρεοπαγίτας ὅτι δείξει τινὰς συνισταμένους ἐπὶ καταλύσει τῆς πολιτείας. ἀγαγὼν δὲ τοὺς αἱρεθέντας[1] τῆς βουλῆς οὗ διέτριβεν ὁ Ἐφιάλτης ἵνα δείξῃ τοὺς ἀθροι-
4 ζομένους, διελέγετο μετὰ σπουδῆς αὐτοῖς. ὁ δ' Ἐφιάλτης ὡς εἶδεν καταπλαγεὶς καθίζει μονοχίτων ἐπὶ τὸν βωμόν. θαυμασάντων δὲ πάντων τὸ γεγονὸς καὶ μετὰ ταῦτα συναθροισθείσης τῆς βουλῆς τῶν πεντακοσίων κατηγόρουν τῶν Ἀρεοπαγιτῶν ὅ τ' Ἐφιάλτης καὶ ὁ[2] Θεμιστοκλῆς, καὶ πάλιν ἐν τῷ δήμῳ τὸν αὐτὸν τρόπον, ἕως περιείλοντο αὐτῶν τὴν δύναμιν. καὶ[3] ἀνῃρέθη δὲ καὶ ὁ Ἐφιάλτης δολοφονηθεὶς μετ' οὐ πολὺν χρόνον δι' Ἀριστοδίκου τοῦ Ταναγραίου.

1 XXVI. Ἡ μὲν οὖν τῶν Ἀρεοπαγιτῶν βουλὴ τοῦτον τὸν τρόπον ἀπεστερήθη τῆς ἐπιμελείας. μετὰ δὲ ταῦτα συνέβαινεν ἀνίεσθαι μᾶλλον τὴν πολιτείαν διὰ τοὺς προθύμως δημαγωγοῦντας. κατὰ γὰρ τοὺς καιροὺς τούτους συνέπεσε μηδ' ἡγεμόνα ἔχειν τοὺς ἐπιεικεστέρους, ἀλλ' αὐτῶν προεστάναι Κίμωνα τὸν Μιλτιάδου νεώτερον[4] ὄντα καὶ πρὸς

[1] Kenyon: αφαιρεθεντας cod.
[2] ὁ suppletum a Wilamowitz-Kaibel.
[3] [καὶ] Mayor: καὶ <ὁ μὲν Θεμιστοκλῆς . . .> Wilamowitz-Kaibel.
[4] νωθρὸν Blass: νωθρώτερον Wilamowitz-Kaibel.

them to the Five Hundred and others to the People and to the jury-courts. For these acts of Ephialtes, 3
Themistocles[a] was partly responsible; he was a member of the Areopagus, but was destined to be put on trial for treasonable dealings with Persia. Themistocles desiring the Council to be destroyed used to tell Ephialtes that the Council was going to arrest him, while he told the Areopagites that he would give information about certain persons who were conspiring to destroy the constitution. And he used to take selected members of the Council to the place where Ephialtes resided to show them the people collecting there, and conversed with them seriously. Ephialtes was dismayed when he saw 4
this, and took his seat at the altar in only his shirt. Everybody was amazed at what had happened, and afterwards when the Council of Five Hundred assembled Ephialtes and Themistocles kept on denouncing the Areopagites, and again similarly at the meetings of the people, until they deprived them of their power. And also Ephialtes was actually made away with not long after, being craftily murdered by Aristodicus of Tanagra.

XXVI. In this way the Council of the Areopagites 1
was deprived of the superintendence of affairs. After this there came about an increased relaxation of the constitution, due to the eagerness of those who were the leaders of the People. For it so happened that during these periods the better classes[b] had no leader at all, but the chief person among them, Cimon son of Miltiades, was a rather young man who had only

[a] In *Politics* ii. xii. the place assigned here to Themistocles is taken by Pericles.

[b] Or 'more respectable': it is a vague term of social approval, *cf.* § 1 fin, xxvii. 4, xxviii. 1, xxxvi. 9.

τὴν πόλιν ὀψὲ προσελθόντα, πρὸς δὲ τούτοις ἐφθάρθαι τοὺς πολλοὺς κατὰ πόλεμον· τῆς γὰρ στρατείας γινομένης ἐν τοῖς τότε χρόνοις ἐκ καταλόγου καὶ στρατηγῶν ἐφισταμένων ἀπείρων μὲν τοῦ πολεμεῖν τιμωμένων δὲ διὰ τὰς πατρικὰς δόξας, αἰεὶ συνέβαινεν τῶν ἐξιόντων ἀνὰ δισχιλίους ἢ τρισχιλίους ἀπόλλυσθαι, ὥστε ἀναλίσκεσθαι τοὺς ἐπιεικεῖς καὶ τοῦ δήμου καὶ τῶν εὐπόρων.
2 τὰ μὲν οὖν ἄλλα πάντα διῴκουν οὐχ ὁμοίως καὶ πρότερον τοῖς νόμοις προσέχοντες, τὴν δὲ τῶν ἐννέα ἀρχόντων αἵρεσιν οὐκ ἐκίνουν ἀλλ' ἢ[1] ἕκτῳ ἔτει μετὰ τὸν Ἐφιάλτου θάνατον ἔγνωσαν καὶ ἐκ ζευγιτῶν προκρίνεσθαι τοὺς κληρωσομένους τῶν ἐννέα ἀρχόντων· καὶ πρῶτος ἦρξεν ἐξ αὐτῶν Μνησιθείδης. οἱ δὲ πρὸ τούτου πάντες ἐξ ἱππέων καὶ πεντακοσιομεδίμνων ἦσαν, οἱ δὲ[2] ζευγῖται τὰς ἐγκυκλίους ἦρχον, εἰ μή τι παρ-
3 εωρᾶτο τῶν ἐν τοῖς νόμοις. ἔτει δὲ πέμπτῳ μετὰ ταῦτα ἐπὶ Λυσικράτους ἄρχοντος οἱ τριάκοντα δικασταὶ κατέστησαν πάλιν οἱ καλούμενοι κατὰ δήμους· καὶ τρίτῳ μετὰ τοῦτον ἐπὶ Ἀντιδότου διὰ τὸ πλῆθος τῶν πολιτῶν Περικλέους εἰπόντος ἔγνωσαν μὴ μετέχειν τῆς πόλεως ὃς ἂν μὴ ἐξ ἀμφοῖν ἀστοῖν ᾖ γεγονώς.

1 XXVII. Μετὰ δὲ ταῦτα πρὸς τὸ δημαγωγεῖν ἐλθόντος Περικλέους καὶ πρῶτον[3] εὐδοκιμήσαντος ὅτε κατηγόρησε τὰς εὐθύνας Κίμωνος στρατηγοῦντος νέος ὤν, δημοτικωτέραν ἔτι συνέβη

[1] ἢ supplevit Blass. [2] δὲ supplevit Kenyon.
[3] πρῶτον Blass: πωτου cod.: πρὸ τοῦ Jackson.

[a] *Cf.* xvi. 5.

lately entered public life ; and in addition, that the multitude had suffered seriously in war, for in those days the expeditionary force was raised from a muster-roll, and was commanded by generals with no experience of war but promoted on account of their family reputations, so that it was always happening that the troops on an expedition suffered as many as two or three thousand casualties, making a drain on the numbers of the respectable members both of the
people and of the wealthy. Thus in general all 2
the administration was conducted without the same attention to the laws as had been given before, although no innovation was made in the election of the Nine Archons, except that five years after the death of Ephialtes they decided to extend to the Teamster class eligibility to the preliminary roll from which the Nine Archons were to be selected by lot ; and the first of the Teamster class to hold
the archonship was Mnesitheides. All the Archons 457 B.C.
hitherto had been from the Knights and Five-hundred-measure-men, while the Teamsters held the ordinary offices, unless some provision of the laws was ignored.
Four years afterwards, in the archonship of Lysicrates, 3
the thirty judges called the Local Justices were in- 453 B.C.
stituted again[a] ; and two years after Lysicrates, in 451 B.C.
the year of Antidotus, owing to the large number of the citizens an enactment was passed on the proposal of Pericles confining citizenship to persons of citizen birth on both sides.

XXVII. After this when Pericles advanced to the 1
leadership of the people, having first distinguished 463 B.C.
himself when while still a young man he challenged the audits of Cimon who was a general, it came about that the constitution became still more democratic.

γενέσθαι τὴν πολιτείαν. καὶ γὰρ τῶν Ἀρεοπαγιτῶν ἔνια παρείλετο, καὶ μάλιστα προὔτρεψεν τὴν πόλιν ἐπὶ τὴν ναυτικὴν δύναμιν, ἐξ ἧς συνέβη θαρρήσαντας τοὺς πολλοὺς ἅπασαν τὴν πολιτείαν
2 μᾶλλον ἄγειν εἰς αὑτούς. μετὰ δὲ τὴν ἐν Σαλαμῖνι ναυμαχίαν ἑνὸς δεῖ πεντηκοστῷ ἔτει ἐπὶ Πυθοδώρου ἄρχοντος ὁ πρὸς Πελοποννησίους ἐνέστη πόλεμος, ἐν ᾧ κατακλεισθεὶς ὁ δῆμος ἐν τῷ ἄστει καὶ συνεθισθεὶς ἐν ταῖς στρατείαις μισθοφορεῖν, τὰ μὲν ἑκὼν τὰ δὲ ἄκων προῃρεῖτο[1] τὴν πολιτείαν διοικεῖν αὐτός. ἐποίησε δὲ καὶ μισθοφόρα τὰ δικαστήρια Περικλῆς πρῶτος, ἀντιδημαγωγῶν
3 πρὸς τὴν Κίμωνος εὐπορίαν. ὁ γὰρ Κίμων ἅτε τυραννικὴν ἔχων οὐσίαν πρῶτον μὲν τὰς κοινὰς λῃτουργίας ἐλῃτούργει λαμπρῶς, ἔπειτα τῶν δημοτῶν ἔτρεφε πολλούς· ἐξῆν γὰρ τῷ βουλομένῳ Λακιαδῶν καθ' ἑκάστην τὴν ἡμέραν ἐλθόντι παρ' αὐτὸν ἔχειν τὰ μέτρια, ἔτι δὲ τὰ χωρία πάντα ἄφρακτα ἦν, ὅπως ἐξῇ[2] τῷ βουλομένῳ τῆς ὀπώρας
4 ἀπολαύειν. πρὸς δὴ ταύτην τὴν χορηγίαν ἐπιλειπόμενος ὁ Περικλῆς τῇ οὐσίᾳ, συμβουλεύσαντος αὐτῷ Δαμωνίδου τοῦ Οἴηθεν (ὃς ἐδόκει τῶν πολλῶν εἰσηγητὴς εἶναι τῷ Περικλεῖ, διὸ καὶ ὠστράκισαν αὐτὸν ὕστερον) ἐπεὶ τοῖς ἰδίοις ἡττᾶτο διδόναι τοῖς πολλοῖς τὰ αὑτῶν, κατεσκεύασε μισθοφορὰν τοῖς δικαστηρίοις[3]· ἀφ' ὧν αἰτιῶνταί τινες χείρω[4] γενέσθαι, κληρουμένων ἐπιμελῶς ἀεὶ μᾶλλον τῶν
5 τυχόντων ἢ τῶν ἐπιεικῶν ἀνθρώπων. ἤρξατο δὲ

[1] προήγετο Richards.
[2] ἐξῇ Kenyon: εξην cod.
[3] Blass: δικασταις cod.
[4] χείρους Wilamowitz-Kaibel (servato δικασταῖς).

For he took away some of the functions of the Areopagus, and he urged the state very strongly in the direction of naval power, which resulted in emboldening the multitude,[a] who brought all the government more into their own hands. Forty-eight years after 2
the naval battle of Salamis, in the archonship of 432 B.C.
Pythodorus, the war against the Peloponnesians broke out, during which the people being locked up in the city, and becoming accustomed to earning pay on their military campaigns, came partly of their own will and partly against their will to the decision to administer the government themselves. Also Pericles first made service in the jury-courts a paid office, as a popular counter-measure against Cimon's wealth. For as Cimon had an estate large enough for a 3
tyrant, in the first place he discharged the general public services in a brilliant manner, and moreover he supplied maintenance to a number of the members of his deme; for anyone of the Laciadae who liked could come to his house every day and have a moderate supply, and also all his farms were unfenced, to enable anyone who liked to avail himself of the harvest. So as Pericles' means were insufficient for 4
this lavishness, he took the advice of Damonides of Oea (who was believed to suggest to Pericles most of his measures, owing to which they afterwards ostracized him), since he was getting the worst of it with his private resources, to give the multitude what was their own, and he instituted payment for the jury-courts; the result of which according to some critics was their deterioration, because ordinary persons always took more care than the respectable to cast lots for the duty. Also it was after this that the organized 5

[a] *Cf.* xxii. 7, xxiv. 1.

μετὰ ταῦτα καὶ τὸ δεκάζειν, πρώτου καταδείξαντος Ἀνύτου μετὰ τὴν ἐν Πύλῳ στρατηγίαν· κρινόμενος γὰρ ὑπό τινων διὰ τὸ ἀποβαλεῖν Πύλον, δεκάσας τὸ δικαστήριον ἀπέφυγεν.

1 XXVIII. Ἕως μὲν οὖν Περικλῆς προειστήκει τοῦ δήμου βελτίω τὰ κατὰ τὴν πολιτείαν ἦν, τελευτήσαντος δὲ Περικλέους πολὺ χείρω. πρῶτον γὰρ τότε προστάτην ἔλαβεν ὁ δῆμος οὐκ εὐδοκιμοῦντα παρὰ τοῖς ἐπιεικέσιν, ἐν δὲ τοῖς πρότερον χρόνοις ἀεὶ διετέλουν οἱ[1] ἐπιεικεῖς δημαγωγοῦντες.
2 ἐξ ἀρχῆς μὲν γὰρ καὶ πρῶτος ἐγένετο προστάτης τοῦ δήμου Σόλων, δεύτερος δὲ Πεισίστρατος, τῶν εὐγενῶν καὶ γνωρίμων· καταλυθείσης δὲ τῆς τυραννίδος Κλεισθένης τοῦ γένους ὢν τῶν Ἀλκμεονιδῶν, καὶ τούτῳ μὲν οὐδεὶς ἦν ἀντιστασιώτης ὡς ἐξέπεσον οἱ περὶ τὸν Ἰσαγόραν· μετὰ δὲ ταῦτα τοῦ μὲν δήμου προειστήκει Ξάνθιππος, τῶν δὲ γνωρίμων Μιλτιάδης· ἔπειτα Θεμιστοκλῆς καὶ Ἀριστείδης· μετὰ δὲ τούτους Ἐφιάλτης μὲν τοῦ δήμου, Κίμων δ' ὁ Μιλτιάδου τῶν εὐπόρων· εἶτα Περικλῆς μὲν τοῦ δήμου, Θουκυδίδης δὲ τῶν ἑτέρων, κηδεστὴς ὢν Κίμωνος.
3 Περικλέους δὲ τελευτήσαντος τῶν μὲν ἐπιφανῶν προειστήκει Νικίας ὁ ἐν Σικελίᾳ τελευτήσας, τοῦ δὲ δήμου Κλέων ὁ Κλεαινέτου, ὃς δοκεῖ μάλιστα διαφθεῖραι τὸν δῆμον ταῖς ὁρμαῖς,[2] καὶ πρῶτος ἐπὶ τοῦ βήματος ἀνέκραγε καὶ ἐλοιδορήσατο καὶ περιζωσάμενος ἐδημηγόρησε, τῶν ἄλλων ἐν κόσμῳ

[1] [οἱ] Richards.
[2] *διανομαῖς* Sandys: *νομαῖς* Thalheim.

---

[a] Pylos (Navarino) on the W. coast of Peloponnesus, had been taken by Athens 425 B.C., but was retaken by Sparta

bribery of juries began, Anytus having first shown the way to it after his command at Pylos[a]; for when he was brought to trial by certain persons for having lost Pylos he bribed the court and got off.

XXVIII. So long, then, as Pericles held the head- 1
ship[b] of the People, the affairs of the state went better, but when Pericles was dead they became much worse. For the People now for the first time adopted a head who was not in good repute with the respectable classes, whereas in former periods those
always continued to lead the people. For Solon 2
was the first and original head of the People, and the second was Peisistratus, who was one of the men of nobility and note. After the tyranny had been put down, Cleisthenes, a member of the family of the Alcmaeonidae, was head of the People, and he had no opponent, since the party of Isagoras was banished; but after this Xanthippus held the headship of the People, and Miltiades of the notables; and then Themistocles and Aristeides; and after them Ephialtes held the headship of the People, and Cimon son of Miltiades of the wealthy; and then Pericles of the People and Thucydides of the others, he being a
relation of Cimon. When Pericles died, Nicias, who 3
died in Sicily, held the headship of the men of distinction, and the head of the People was Cleon son of Cleaenetus, who is thought to have done the most to corrupt the people by his impetuous outbursts, and was the first person to use bawling and abuse on the platform, and to gird up his cloak before making a public speech, all other persons speaking in orderly

409 B.C. Anytus (see also xxxiv. 3, one of the prosecutors of Socrates) was sent with 30 triremes to its relief, but owing to weather never got round Cape Malea.

[b] See note on ii. 3.

λεγόντων. εἶτα μετὰ τούτους τῶν μὲν ἑτέρων Θηραμένης ὁ Ἅγνωνος, τοῦ δὲ δήμου Κλεοφῶν ὁ λυροποιός, ὃς καὶ τὴν διωβολίαν[1] ἐπόρισε πρῶτος· καὶ χρόνον μέν τινα διεδίδου,[2] μετὰ δὲ ταῦτα κατέλυσε Καλλικράτης Παιανιεὺς πρῶτος ὑποσχόμενος ἐπιθήσειν πρὸς τοῖν δυοῖν ὀβολοῖν ἄλλον ὀβολόν. τούτων μὲν οὖν ἀμφοτέρων θάνατον κατέγνωσαν ὕστερον· εἴωθεν γὰρ κἂν ἐξαπατηθῇ τὸ πλῆθος ὕστερον μισεῖν τούς τι προαγαγόντας ποιεῖν

4 αὐτοὺς τῶν μὴ καλῶς ἐχόντων. ἀπὸ δὲ Κλεοφῶντος ἤδη διεδέχοντο συνεχῶς τὴν δημαγωγίαν οἱ μάλιστα βουλόμενοι θρασύνεσθαι καὶ χαρίζεσθαι τοῖς πολλοῖς πρὸς τὸ παραυτίκα βλέποντες.

5 δοκοῦσι δὲ[3] βέλτιστοι γεγονέναι τῶν Ἀθήνησι πολιτευσαμένων μετὰ τοὺς ἀρχαίους Νικίας καὶ Θουκυδίδης καὶ Θηραμένης. καὶ περὶ μὲν Νικίου καὶ Θουκυδίδου πάντες σχεδὸν ὁμολογοῦσιν ἄνδρας γεγονέναι οὐ μόνον καλοὺς κἀγαθοὺς ἀλλὰ καὶ πολιτικοὺς καὶ τῇ πόλει πάσῃ πατρικῶς χρωμένους, περὶ δὲ Θηραμένους διὰ τὸ συμβῆναι κατ' αὐτὸν ταραχώδεις τὰς πολιτείας εἶναι[4] ἀμφισβήτησις τῆς κρίσεώς ἐστι. δοκεῖ μέντοι[5] τοῖς μὴ παρέργως ἀποφαινομένοις οὐχ ὥσπερ αὐτὸν διαβάλλουσι πάσας τὰς πολιτείας καταλύειν, ἀλλὰ πάσας προάγειν ἕως μηδὲν παρανομοῖεν, ὡς δυνάμενος πολιτεύεσθαι κατὰ πάσας, ὅπερ ἐστὶν ἀγαθοῦ πολίτου ἔργον, παρανομούσαις δὲ οὐ συγχωρῶν ἀλλ' ἀπεχθανόμενος.

[1] διωβελίαν edd. [2] διεδίδοτο Wyse.
[3] δὲ: δοι (= δ' οἱ) cod., ε superscripto.
[4] εἶναι supplevit Richards. [5] μέντοι Kenyon: μεν cod.

[a] By instituting the 'theatre-fund' (τὸ θεωρικόν), which was

fashion. Then after these Theramenes son of Hagnon was chief of the others and Cleophon the lyre-maker of the People, who first introduced the two-obol dole[a]; he went on distributing this for a time, but afterwards Callicrates of the Paeanian deme abolished it, being the first person to promise to add to the two obols another obol. Both of these two leaders were afterwards condemned to death; for even though the multitude may be utterly deceived, subsequently it usually hates those who have led it
to do anything improper. From Cleon onward the 4
leadership of the People was handed on in an unbroken line by the men most willing to play a bold part and to gratify the many with an eye to immediate
popularity. And it is thought that the best of the 5
politicians at Athens after those of early times were Nicias, Thucydides and Theramenes. As to Nicias and Thucydides, almost everybody agrees that they were not only honourable gentlemen but also statesmanlike and patriotic servants of the whole state, but about Theramenes, owing to the confused nature of the constitutional changes that took place in his time, the verdict is a matter of dispute. However, the view of writers not making mere incidental references is that he was not a destroyer of all governments, as critics charge him with being, but guided them all forward into a fully law-abiding course, since he was capable of serving the state under all of them, which is the duty of a good citizen, but did not give in to them when they acted illegally, but faced their enmity.

a state fund for defraying the cost of an ordinary seat at the theatre, 2 obols. Plutarch attributes its institution to Pericles. An obol was about 1½d., 6 to a drachma.

1 XXIX. Ἕως μὲν οὖν ἰσόρροπα τὰ πράγματα κατὰ τὸν πόλεμον ἦν διεφύλαττον τὴν δημοκρατίαν. ἐπεὶ δὲ μετὰ τὴν ἐν Σικελίᾳ γενομένην συμφορὰν[1] ἰσχυρότατα[2] τὰ τῶν Λακεδαιμονίων ἐγένετο διὰ τὴν πρὸς βασιλέα συμμαχίαν, ἠναγκάσθησαν κινήσαντες τὴν δημοκρατίαν καταστῆσαι τὴν ἐπὶ τῶν τετρακοσίων πολιτείαν, εἰπόντος τὸν μὲν πρὸ[3] τοῦ ψηφίσματος λόγον Μηλοβίου, τὴν δὲ γνώμην γράψαντος Πυθοδώρου τοῦ Ἀναφλυστίου,[4] μάλιστα δὲ συμπεισθέντων τῶν πολλῶν διὰ τὸ νομίζειν βασιλέα μᾶλλον ἑαυτοῖς συμπολεμήσειν ἐὰν δι' ὀλίγων
2 ποιήσωνται τὴν πολιτείαν. ἦν δὲ τὸ ψήφισμα τοῦ Πυθοδώρου τοιόνδε· τὸν δῆμον ἑλέσθαι μετὰ τῶν προϋπαρχόντων δέκα προβούλων ἄλλους εἴκοσι ἐκ τῶν ὑπὲρ τετταράκοντα ἔτη γεγονότων, οἵτινες ὀμόσαντες ἦ μὴν συγγράψειν ἃ ἂν ἡγῶνται βέλτιστα εἶναι τῇ πόλει συγγράψουσι περὶ τῆς
3 σωτηρίας· ἐξεῖναι δὲ καὶ τῶν ἄλλων τῷ βουλομένῳ γράφειν, ἵν' ἐξ ἁπάντων αἱρῶνται τὸ ἄριστον. Κλειτοφῶν δὲ τὰ μὲν ἄλλα καθάπερ Πυθόδωρος εἶπεν, προσαναζητῆσαι δὲ τοὺς αἱρεθέντας ἔγραψεν καὶ τοὺς πατρίους νόμους οὓς Κλεισθένης ἔθηκεν ὅτε καθίστη τὴν δημοκρατίαν, ὅπως[5] ἀκούσαντες καὶ τούτων βουλεύσωνται τὸ ἄριστον, ὡς οὐ δημοτικὴν ἀλλὰ παραπλησίαν οὖσαν τὴν Κλει-
4 σθένους πολιτείαν τῇ Σόλωνος. οἱ δ' αἱρεθέντες πρῶτον μὲν ἔγραψαν ἐπάναγκες εἶναι τοὺς πρυ-

[1] Richards: διαφοραν cod.
[2] ἰσχυρότερα Mayor.
[3] πρὸ] περὶ Wyse.
[4] Blass: . . . υ.τιου cod.
[5] ὅπως <ἂν> Wilamowitz-Kaibel.

[a] Or ' before the resolution.'

XXIX. In the period of the war therefore, so long 1
as fortunes were evenly balanced, they continued to preserve the democracy. But when after the occurrence of the disaster in Sicily the Lacedaemonian side 413 B.C.
became very strong owing to the alliance with the king of Persia, they were compelled to overthrow the democracy and set up the government of the Four Hundred, Melobius making the speech on behalf of the resolution [a] but Pythodorus of the deme Anaphlystus having drafted the motion, and the acquiescence of the mass of the citizens being chiefly due to the belief that the king would help them more in the war if they limited their constitution. The resolution of Pytho- 2
dorus was as follows: 'That in addition to the ten Preliminary Councillors [b] already existing the people choose twenty others from those over forty years of age, and that these, after taking a solemn oath to draft whatever measures they think best for the state, shall draft measures for the public safety; and that 3
it be open to any other person also that wishes, to frame proposals, in order that they may choose the one that is best out of them all.' Cleitophon moved an amendment to the resolution of Pythodorus, that the commissioners elected should also investigate the ancestral laws laid down by Cleisthenes when he was establishing the democracy, in order that they might decide on the best course to advise after hearing these laws also, on the ground that the constitution of Cleisthenes was not democratic but similar to that of Solon. The commissioners when elected first pro- 4

[b] The ten commissioners appointed at Athens after the Sicilian disaster to deal with the emergency (Thuc. viii. 1), and later instructed to reform the constitution (*ib.* lxvii.).

τάνεις ἅπαντα τὰ λεγόμενα περὶ τῆς σωτηρίας ἐπιψηφίζειν, ἔπειτα τὰς τῶν παρανόμων γραφὰς καὶ τὰς εἰσαγγελίας καὶ τὰς προσκλήσεις[1] ἀνεῖλον, ὅπως ἂν οἱ ἐθέλοντες Ἀθηναῖοι συμβουλεύωσι περὶ τῶν προκειμένων· ἐὰν δέ τίς τινα[2] τούτων χάριν ἢ ζημιοῖ ἢ προσκαλῆται ἢ εἰσάγῃ εἰς δικαστήριον, ἔνδειξιν αὐτοῦ εἶναι καὶ ἀπαγωγὴν πρὸς τοὺς στρατηγούς, τοὺς δὲ στρατηγοὺς παρα-
5 δοῦναι τοῖς ἕνδεκα θανάτῳ ζημιῶσαι. μετὰ δὲ ταῦτα τὴν πολιτείαν διέταξαν τόνδε τρόπον· τὰ μὲν προσιόντα[3] μὴ ἐξεῖναι ἄλλοσε δαπανῆσαι ἢ εἰς τὸν πόλεμον, τὰς δ' ἀρχὰς ἀμίσθους ἄρχειν ἁπάσας ἕως ἂν ὁ πόλεμος ᾖ, πλὴν τῶν ἐννέα ἀρχόντων καὶ τῶν πρυτανέων οἳ ἂν ὦσιν, τούτους δὲ φέρειν τρεῖς ὀβολοὺς ἕκαστον τῆς ἡμέρας· τὴν δ' ἄλλην πολιτείαν ἐπιτρέψαι πᾶσαν[4] Ἀθηναίων τοῖς δυνατωτάτοις καὶ τοῖς σώμασιν καὶ τοῖς χρήμασιν λῃτουργεῖν μὴ ἔλαττον ἢ πεντακισχιλίοις[5] ἕως ἂν ὁ πόλεμος ᾖ· κυρίους δ' εἶναι τούτους καὶ συνθήκας συντίθεσθαι πρὸς οὓς ἂν ἐθέλωσιν· ἑλέσθαι δ' ἐκ[6] τῆς φυλῆς ἑκάστης δέκα ἄνδρας ὑπὲρ τετταράκοντα ἔτη γεγονότας οἵτινες καταλέξουσι τοὺς πεντακισχιλίους ὀμόσαντες καθ' ἱερῶν τελείων.

1 XXX. Οἱ μὲν οὖν αἱρεθέντες ταῦτα συνέγραψαν· κυρωθέντων δὲ τούτων εἵλοντο σφῶν αὐτῶν οἱ

[1] Blass: προκλησεις cod.

[2] τίς τινα Richards: τις cod.

[3] προσίοντα Richards (cf. xxxix. 2): χρηματαπροσιοντα cod.: χρ. ⟨τὰ⟩ πρ. Kenyon.

[4] πᾶσαν Mayor: πασιν cod.

[5] -ων (i.e. ἔλαττον πεντακισχιλίων) v.l. adscr. cod.

[6] δ' ἐκ edd.: δεκαι cod.

posed that it should be compulsory for the Presidents[a] to put to the vote all proposals made for the public safety, and then repealed the procedures of impeachment for illegal proposals, information and summons, in order that those Athenian citizens who wished might give advice about the matters before them; and enacted that, if anybody attempted to punish or summon or bring them into court for so doing, he be liable to information and summary arrest before the Generals, and that the Generals should hand him
over to the Eleven to be punished with death. After 5
this they framed the constitution in the following way: that it should not be permissible to spend the revenues on any other object than the war; that all the officers of state should be unpaid for the duration of the war, excepting those who held the posts of the Nine Archons and the Presidents, and these should draw three obols[b] per man per day; and that all the rest of the functions of government should be entrusted to those Athenians who in person and property were most capable of serving the state, not less than five thousand, for the duration of the war; and that the powers of this body should include competence to contract treaties with whatever people they wished; and that they should elect ten men over forty years of age from each tribe, who should enroll the Five Thousand after taking oath over unblemished victims.

XXX. So the Commissioners drafted these pro- 1
posals; and these being ratified, the Five Thousand

[a] The Presidents of the Council, see xliii. 2.
[b] Half a drachma, see iv. 3 n.

πεντακισχίλιοι τοὺς ἀναγράψοντας τὴν πολιτείαν
ἑκατὸν ἄνδρας. οἱ δ’ αἱρεθέντες ἀνέγραψαν καὶ
2 ἐξήνεγκαν τάδε· βουλεύειν μὲν κατ’ ἐνιαυτὸν τοὺς[1]
ὑπὲρ τριάκοντα ἔτη γεγονότας ἄνευ μισθοφορᾶς·
τούτων δ’ εἶναι τοὺς στρατηγοὺς καὶ τοὺς ἐννέα
ἄρχοντας καὶ τὸν ἱερομνήμονα καὶ τοὺς ταξιάρχους
καὶ ἱππάρχους καὶ φυλάρχους καὶ ἄρχοντας εἰς τὰ
φρούρια καὶ ταμίας τῶν ἱερῶν χρημάτων τῇ θεῷ
καὶ τοῖς ἄλλοις θεοῖς δέκα καὶ ἑλληνοταμίας[2] καὶ
τῶν ἄλλων ὁσίων[3] χρημάτων ἁπάντων εἴκοσιν οἳ
διαχειριοῦσιν,[4] καὶ ἱεροποιοὺς καὶ ἐπιμελητὰς δέκα
ἑκατέρους· αἱρεῖσθαι δὲ πάντας τούτους ἐκ προκρίτων, ἐκ τῶν ἀεὶ βουλευόντων πλείους προκρίνοντας,
τὰς δ’ ἄλλας ἀρχὰς ἁπάσας κληρωτὰς εἶναι καὶ
μὴ ἐκ τῆς βουλῆς· τοὺς δὲ ἑλληνοταμίας οἳ ἂν
3 διαχειρίζωσι τὰ χρήματα μὴ συμβουλεύειν. βουλὰς
δὲ ποιῆσαι τέτταρας ἐκ τῆς ἡλικίας τῆς εἰρημένης
εἰς τὸν λοιπὸν χρόνον, καὶ τούτων τὸ λαχὸν μέρος
βουλεύειν, νεῖμαι δὲ καὶ τοὺς ἄλλους πρὸς τὴν
λῆξιν ἑκάστην. τοὺς δ’ ἑκατὸν ἄνδρας διανεῖμαι
σφᾶς τε αὐτοὺς καὶ τοὺς ἄλλους τέτταρα μέρη
ὡς ἰσαίτατα καὶ διακληρῶσαι, καὶ εἰς ἐνιαυτὸν
4 βουλεύειν τοὺς λαχόντας[5]· βουλεύεσθαι[6] δὲ ᾗ ἂν

[1] τοὺς] τετρακοσίους Niemeyer.
[2] [καὶ ἑλληνοταμίας] Sandys.
[3] [ὁσίων] ? Rackham.
[4] [-ν οἳ διαχειριοῦσιν] Thompson.
[5] τοὺς λαχόντας suppletum a Wilamowitz-Kaibel.
[6] βουλεύεσθαι suppletum a Sandys.

[a] The secretary or registrar who with the actual representative, the Pylagoras, was sent by Athens, as by the other members, to the Amphictyonic Council.

elected a hundred of their members as a committee to draw up the constitution. This committee drew up and published the following resolutions: 'The 2
Council to consist of members over thirty years of age holding office for a year and drawing no pay; these members to include the Generals, the Nine Archons, the Sacred Remembrancer,[a] the Company-commanders,[b] Officers of the Horse,[c] Officers of Tribes[d] and officers in command of the Guards,[e] the Treasurers of the Sacred Funds of the Goddess[f] and the ten Treasurers of the other gods, the Greek Treasurers,[g] and twenty Treasurers of all the secular funds as well, who shall manage them,[h] and Sacrificial Officers and Superintendents, ten of each; and the Council to elect all of these from a larger preliminary list of candidates proposed by it from its members at the time, but all other offices to be elected by lot and not from the Council; and the Greek Treasurers[i] that are to manage the funds not to be members of the Council.
And four Councils to be formed for the future from 3
persons of the stated age, and a division of these selected by lot to officiate, but the others also to be included in each such selection. And the Hundred Men to divide themselves and the others[j] into four divisions as nearly equal as possible, and to cast lots among them, and those on whom the lot falls to form the Council for a year. And the Council to frame 4

[b] See lxi. 3. [c] See *ib.* 4. [d] See *ib.* 5.

[e] See xxiv. 3. [f] Athena.

[g] This contradicts the end of the section, and the text seems to be corrupt.

[h] This clause seems to be interpolated from below.

[i] The managers of the funds paid as tribute by the Confederacy of Delos.

[j] *i.e.* the rest of the Five Thousand.

δοκῇ αὐτοῖς ἄριστα ἕξειν περί τε τῶν χρημάτων
ὅπως ἂν σῶα ᾖ καὶ εἰς τὸ δέον ἀναλίσκηται, καὶ
περὶ τῶν ἄλλων ὡς ἂν δύνωνται ἄριστα· ἐὰν δὲ[1]
τι θέλωσιν βουλεύσασθαι μετὰ πλειόνων, ἐπεισ-
καλεῖν ἕκαστον ἐπείσκλητον ὃν ἂν ἐθέλῃ τῶν ἐκ
τῆς αὐτῆς ἡλικίας. τὰς δ' ἕδρας ποιεῖν τῆς
βουλῆς κατὰ πενθήμερον, ἐὰν μὴ δέωνται πλειόνων.
5 κληροῦν δὲ τὴν βουλὴν τοὺς ἐννέα ἄρχοντας, τὰς
δὲ χειροτονίας κρίνειν πέντε τοὺς λαχόντας ἐκ
τῆς βουλῆς, καὶ ἐκ τούτων ἕνα κληροῦσθαι καθ'
ἑκάστην ἡμέραν τὸν ἐπιψηφιοῦντα. κληροῦν δὲ
τοὺς λαχόντας πέντε τοὺς ἐθέλοντας προσελθεῖν
ἐναντίον τῆς βουλῆς, πρῶτον μὲν ἱερῶν, δεύτερον
δὲ κήρυξιν, τρίτον πρεσβείαις, τέταρτον τῶν ἄλλων·
τὰ δὲ τοῦ πολέμου ὅταν δέῃ ἀκληρωτὶ προσαγα-
6 γόντας τοὺς στρατηγοὺς χρηματίζεσθαι.[2] τὸν δὲ
μὴ ἰόντα εἰς τὸ βουλευτήριον τῶν βουλευόντων
τὴν ὥραν τὴν προρρηθεῖσαν ὀφείλειν δραχμὴν τῆς
ἡμέρας ἑκάστης, ἐὰν μὴ εὑρισκόμενος[3] ἄφεσιν τῆς
βουλῆς ἀπῇ.
1 XXXI. Ταύτην μὲν οὖν εἰς τὸν μέλλοντα χρόνον
ἀνέγραψαν τὴν πολιτείαν, ἐν δὲ τῷ παρόντι καιρῷ
τήνδε· βουλεύειν μὲν τετρακοσίους κατὰ τὰ
πάτρια, τετταράκοντα ἐξ ἑκάστης φυλῆς ἐκ προκρίτων οὓς ἂν ἕλωνται οἱ φυλέται τῶν ὑπὲρ
τριάκοντα ἔτη γεγονότων. τούτους δὲ τάς τε
ἀρχὰς καταστῆσαι, καὶ περὶ τοῦ ὅρκου ὅντινα
χρὴ ὀμόσαι γράψαι, καὶ[4] περὶ τῶν νόμων καὶ
τῶν εὐθυνῶν καὶ τῶν ἄλλων πράττειν ᾗ ἂν
2 ἡγῶνται συμφέρειν. τοῖς δὲ νόμοις οἳ ἂν τεθῶσιν

[1] δὲ suppletum a Mayor. [2] χρηματίζειν Blass.
[3] εὑρόμενος Tyrrell. [4] καὶ supplevit Kenyon.

such resolutions as may seem to them likely to be
best to secure the safe preservation of the funds and
their expenditure upon necessary objects, and about
the other affairs to the best of their ability ; and in
case of their desiring to consider some matter with
added numbers, each member to summon as a co-
opted member anybody of the same age as himself
that he may wish. To hold the sittings of the
Council every five days, unless more sittings are required. The Nine Archons to apply sortition to the 5
Council, and five persons elected by lot from the
Council to be tellers, and one of these to be chosen by
lot to serve daily as putter of the question. And the
five tellers elected to cast lots among those who
desire an audience of the Council, first about matters
of religion, second for Heralds, third for embassies,
fourth about other business ; but whenever questions
relating to war need consideration they are to introduce the Generals without casting lots and take their
business. A member of the Council not coming to the 6
Council-chamber at the time previously announced
to be liable to a fine of a drachma for each day, unless
he obtain leave of absence from the Council.'

XXXI. This constitution, therefore, they drew up 1
for the future, but the following to be in force in
the present crisis : 'The Council to consist of four
hundred members according to the ancestral regulations, forty from each tribe taken from a preliminary
list of any persons over thirty years of age that the
members of the tribe may elect. These to appoint
the officials, and to draft a proposal about the form of
oath to be taken, and to take action about the laws
and the audits and other matters as they may think
good. And to follow any laws that may be enacted 2

περὶ τῶν πολιτικῶν χρῆσθαι, καὶ μὴ ἐξεῖναι μετακινεῖν μηδ' ἑτέρους θέσθαι. τῶν δὲ στρατηγῶν τὸ νῦν εἶναι τὴν αἵρεσιν ἐξ ἁπάντων ποιεῖσθαι τῶν πεντακισχιλίων, τὴν δὲ βουλὴν ἐπειδὰν καταστῇ[1] ποιήσασαν ἐξέτασιν ἐν[2] ὅπλοις ἑλέσθαι δέκα ἄνδρας καὶ γραμματέα τούτοις, τοὺς δὲ αἱρεθέντας ἄρχειν τὸν εἰσιόντα ἐνιαυτὸν αὐτοκράτορας, καὶ ἄν τι δέωνται συμβουλεύεσθαι μετὰ τῆς βουλῆς.
3 ἑλέσθαι δὲ καὶ ἵππαρχον ἕνα[3] καὶ φυλάρχους δέκα· τὸ δὲ λοιπὸν τὴν αἵρεσιν ποιεῖσθαι τούτων τὴν βουλὴν κατὰ τὰ γεγραμμένα. τῶν δ' ἄλλων ἀρχῶν πλὴν τῆς βουλῆς καὶ τῶν στρατηγῶν μὴ ἐξεῖναι μήτε τούτοις μήτε ἄλλῳ μηδενὶ πλεῖον ἢ ἅπαξ ἄρξαι τὴν αὐτὴν ἀρχήν. εἰς δὲ τὸν ἄλλον χρόνον, ἵνα νεμηθῶσιν οἱ τετρακόσιοι εἰς τὰς τέτταρας λήξεις, ὅταν ἑκάστοις[4] γίγνηται μετὰ τῶν ἄλλων βουλεύειν, διανειμάντων αὐτοὺς οἱ ἑκατὸν ἄνδρες.

1 XXXII. Οἱ μὲν οὖν ἑκατὸν οἱ ὑπὸ τῶν πεντακισχιλίων αἱρεθέντες ταύτην ἀνέγραψαν τὴν πολιτείαν. ἐπικυρωθέντων δὲ τούτων ὑπὸ τοῦ πλήθους ἐπιψηφίσαντος Ἀριστομάχου, ἡ μὲν βουλὴ ἡ[5] ἐπὶ Καλλίου πρὶν διαβουλεῦσαι κατελύθη μηνὸς Θαργηλιῶνος τετράδι ἐπὶ δέκα, οἱ δὲ τετρακόσιοι εἰσῇσαν ἐνάτῃ φθίνοντος Θαργηλιῶνος· ἔδει δὲ τὴν εἰληχυῖαν τῷ κυάμῳ βουλὴν εἰσιέναι δ' ἐπὶ
2 δέκα Σκιροφοριῶνος. ἡ μὲν οὖν ὀλιγαρχία τοῦτον κατέστη τὸν τρόπον ἐπὶ Καλλίου μὲν ἄρχοντος ἔτεσιν δ' ὕστερον τῆς τῶν τυράννων ἐκβολῆς

[1] Wyse: καταστησηι cod. [2] ἐν supplevit Wyse.
[3] ἕνα <καὶ ταξιάρχους δέκα> Wilamowitz.
[4] ἑκάστοις (vel τοῖς αὐτοῖς, αὐτοῖς) edd.: τοισαστοις cod.
[5] ἡ supplevit Rutherford.

about the affairs of state, and not to have powers to alter them nor to enact others. The election of the Generals for the time being to be made from among all the Five Thousand, and the Council as soon as it is appointed to hold a review under arms and elect ten men to the post, and a secretary for them, and those elected to hold office for the ensuing year with autocratic powers, and to consult with the Council about any matter if they require. And also to elect 3
one Master of the Horse and ten Tribe-commanders; and for the future the Council to conduct the election of these according to the procedure enacted. And none of the other officials except the Council and the Generals, nor anybody else, to be allowed to hold the same office more than once. And for the future, in order that the Four Hundred may be divided into the four lists,[a] when each division takes its turn to form the Council with the rest, let the Hundred Men divide them into sections.'

XXXII. This then was the constitution drawn up by 1
the Hundred elected by the Five Thousand. These proposals were carried by the multitude, being put to the vote by Aristomachus, and the Council in Callias's year was dissolved on the 14th day of the 412 B.C.
month of Thargelion before it had completed its term of office; while the Four Hundred came into office on Thargelion the 21st; and the Council elected by lot was due to enter office on Scirophorion the 14th.[b] In this way therefore the oligarchy was set 2
up, in the archonship of Callias, about a hundred years after the expulsion of the tyrants, the chief

[a] *Cf.* xxx. 3.

[b] The three dates are about May 31, June 7, and June 30.

μάλιστα ἑκατόν, αἰτίων μάλιστα γενομένων Πεισάνδρου καὶ Ἀντιφῶντος καὶ Θηραμένους, ἀνδρῶν καὶ γεγενημένων εὖ καὶ συνέσει καὶ γνώμῃ δοκούν-
3 των διαφέρειν. γενομένης δὲ ταύτης τῆς πολιτείας οἱ μὲν πεντακισχίλιοι λόγῳ μόνον ᾑρέθησαν, οἱ δὲ τετρακόσιοι μετὰ τῶν δέκα τῶν αὐτοκρατόρων εἰσελθόντες εἰς τὸ βουλευτήριον ἦρχόν τε[1] τῆς πόλεως καὶ πρὸς Λακεδαιμονίους πρεσβευσάμενοι κατελύοντο τὸν πόλεμον ἐφ᾽ οἷς ἑκάτεροι τυγχάνουσιν ἔχοντες, οὐχ ὑπακουόντων δ᾽ ἐκείνων εἰ μὴ καὶ τὴν ἀρχὴν τῆς θαλάττης ἀφήσουσιν, οὕτως ἀπέστησαν.

1 XXXIII. Μῆνας μὲν οὖν ἴσως τέτταρας διέμεινεν ἡ τῶν τετρακοσίων πολιτεία, καὶ ἦρξεν ἐξ αὐτῶν Μνασίλοχος δίμηνον ἐπὶ Θεοπόμπου ἄρχοντος, ὃς[2] ἦρξε τοὺς ἐπιλοίπους δέκα μῆνας. ἡττηθέντες δὲ τῇ περὶ Ἐρετρίαν ναυμαχίᾳ καὶ τῆς Εὐβοίας ἀποστάσης ὅλης πλὴν Ὠρεοῦ, χαλεπῶς ἐνεγκόντες ἐπὶ τῇ συμφορᾷ μάλιστα τῶν προγεγενημένων (πλείω γὰρ ἐκ τῆς Εὐβοίας ἢ τῆς Ἀττικῆς ἐτύγχανον ὠφελούμενοι) κατέλυσαν τοὺς τετρακοσίους καὶ τὰ πράγματα παρέδωκαν τοῖς πεντακισχιλίοις τοῖς ἐκ τῶν ὅπλων, ψηφισά-
2 μενοι μηδεμίαν ἀρχὴν εἶναι μισθοφόρον. αἰτιώτατοι δ᾽ ἐγένοντο τῆς καταλύσεως Ἀριστοκράτης καὶ Θηραμένης, οὐ συναρεσκόμενοι τοῖς ὑπὸ τῶν τετρακοσίων γιγνομένοις· ἅπαντα γὰρ δι᾽ αὑτῶν ἔπραττον, οὐδὲν ἐπαναφέροντες τοῖς πεντακισχιλίοις. δοκοῦσι δὲ καλῶς πολιτευθῆναι κατὰ τούτους τοὺς καιρούς, πολέμου τε καθεστῶτος καὶ ἐκ τῶν ὅπλων τῆς πολιτείας οὔσης.

[1] τε supplevit Hude.

[2] ὃς supplevit Kenyon.

movers having been Peisander, Antiphon and Theramenes, men of good birth and of distinguished reputation for wisdom and judgement. But when this con- 3
stitution had been set up, the Five Thousand were only nominally chosen, but the Four Hundred with the aid of the Ten with autocratic powers[a] entered the Council-chamber and governed the state. They also sent envoys to the Lacedaemonians and proposed to conclude peace on terms of *uti possidetis*; but the Lacedaemonians would not consent unless Athens would also relinquish the empire of the sea, so that they finally abandoned the project.

XXXIII. The constitution of the Four Hundred 1
lasted perhaps four months, for two of which Mnesilochus was archon, in the year of the archonship of 411 B.C.
Theopompus, who received the office for the remaining ten months. But when they had been worsted in the naval battle off Eretria and the whole of Euboea except Oreum had revolted, they were more distressed at the misfortune than by any previous disaster (for they were actually getting more support from Euboea than from Attica), and they dissolved the Four Hundred and handed over affairs to the Five Thousand that were on the armed roll,[b] having passed by vote a resolution that no office should receive pay.
The persons chiefly responsible for the dissolution 2
were Aristocrates and Theramenes, who disapproved of the proceedings of the Four Hundred; for they did everything on their own responsibility and referred nothing to the Five Thousand. But Athens seems to have been well governed during this critical period, although a war was going on and the government was confined to the armed roll.

[a] The Ten Generals, see xxxi. 2. [b] *Cf.* iv. 2, xxix. 5.

1 XXXIV. Τούτους μὲν οὖν ἀφείλετο τὴν πολιτείαν ὁ δῆμος διὰ τάχους· ἔτει δ' ἑβδόμῳ[1] μετὰ τὴν τῶν τετρακοσίων κατάλυσιν, ἐπὶ Καλλίου τοῦ Ἀγγελῆθεν ἄρχοντος, γενομένης τῆς ἐν Ἀργινούσαις ναυμαχίας, πρῶτον μὲν τοὺς δέκα στρατηγοὺς τοὺς τῇ ναυμαχίᾳ νικῶντας συνέβη κριθῆναι μιᾷ χειροτονίᾳ πάντας, τοὺς μὲν οὐδὲ συνναυμαχήσαντας, τοὺς δ' ἐπ' ἀλλοτρίας νεὼς σωθέντας, ἐξαπατηθέντος τοῦ δήμου διὰ τοὺς παροργίσαντας· ἔπειτα βουλομένων Λακεδαιμονίων ἐκ Δεκελείας ἀπιέναι[2] ἐφ' οἷς ἔχουσιν ἑκάτεροι καὶ εἰρήνην ἄγειν,[3] ἔνιοι μὲν ἐσπούδαζον, τὸ δὲ πλῆθος οὐχ ὑπήκουσεν, ἐξαπατηθέντες ὑπὸ Κλεοφῶντος, ὃς ἐκώλυσε γενέσθαι τὴν εἰρήνην ἐλθὼν εἰς τὴν ἐκκλησίαν μεθύων καὶ θώρακα ἐνδεδυκώς, οὐ φάσκων ἐπιτρέψειν ἐὰν μὴ πάσας ἀφιῶσι Λακεδαι-
2 μόνιοι τὰς πόλεις. οὐ χρησάμενοι δὲ καλῶς τότε τοῖς πράγμασι μετ' οὐ πολὺν χρόνον ἔγνωσαν τὴν ἁμαρτίαν. τῷ γὰρ ὕστερον ἔτει ἐπ' Ἀλεξίου ἄρχοντος ἠτύχησαν τὴν ἐν Αἰγὸς ποταμοῖς ναυμαχίαν, ἐξ ἧς συνέβη κύριον γενόμενον τῆς πόλεως Λύσανδρον καταστῆσαι τοὺς τριάκοντα τρόπῳ
3 τοιῷδε· τῆς εἰρήνης γενομένης αὐτοῖς ἐφ' ᾧ τε πολιτεύσονται τὴν πάτριον πολιτείαν, οἱ μὲν δημοτικοὶ διασῴζειν ἐπειρῶντο τὸν δῆμον, τῶν δὲ

[1] ἕκτῳ edd. [2] Mayor: ανιεναι cod.
[3] ἐφ' οἷς . . . ἄγειν cum schol. Wilamowitz-Kaibel: καιεφοισεχουσινιρηνηνεκατεροιαγειν cod.

[a] 'Sixth' (in Greek arithmetic 'seventh') is a mistake for 'fifth' (Greek 'sixth'): the Four Hundred fell in 411, Callias was archon 406 B.C.

[b] *i.e.* with his courage artificially stimulated and with armour to protect him against assassination (unless we adopt

XXXIV. So the people speedily took the government out of these men's hands; and in the sixth[a] year after the dissolution of the Four Hundred, in the archonship of Callias of the deme of Angelē, after the occurrence of the naval battle at Arginusae, it came about first that the ten Generals to whom victory in the naval battle was due were all condemned by a single vote, some of them not even having been in the engagement at all and the others having escaped on board a ship not their own, the people being completely deceived through the persons who provoked their anger; and then, when the Lacedaemonians were willing to evacuate Decelea on terms of both parties retaining what they held, and to make peace, though some persons were eager to accept, yet the mass of the people refused to consent, being completely deceived by Cleophon, who prevented the conclusion of peace by coming into the assembly, drunk and wearing a corslet,[b] and protesting that he would
1
not allow it unless the Lacedaemonians surrendered
all the cities.[c] But though on this occasion they had 2
managed their affairs ill, they realized their mistake
not long afterwards. For in the next year, when 405 B.C.
Alexius was Archon, they met with the disaster in the naval battle of Aegospotami which resulted in the city's falling into the hands of Lysander, who
set up the Thirty in the following way. The peace 3
having been concluded on terms of their carrying on the government according to the ancestral constitution, the popular party endeavoured to preserve the

the conjecture that μεθύων καὶ θώρακα ἐνδεδυκώς is a mistaken paraphrase of some original record giving θώρακα ἔχων in the slang sense of 'well primed with liquor,' *cf.* Aristoph. *Ran.* 1504).

[c] *i.e.* those that they had taken in the war.

γνωρίμων οἱ μὲν ἐν ταῖς ἑταιρείαις ὄντες, καὶ τῶν φυγάδων οἱ μετὰ τὴν εἰρήνην κατελθόντες, ὀλιγαρχίας ἐπεθύμουν, οἱ δ' ἐν ἑταιρείᾳ μὲν οὐδεμιᾷ συγκαθεστῶτες ἄλλως δὲ δοκοῦντες οὐδενὸς ἐπιλείπεσθαι τῶν πολιτῶν τὴν πάτριον πολιτείαν ἐζήτουν· ὧν ἦν μὲν καὶ Ἀρχῖνος καὶ Ἄνυτος καὶ Κλειτοφῶν καὶ Φορμίσιος καὶ ἕτεροι πολλοί, προειστήκει δὲ μάλιστα Θηραμένης. Λυσάνδρου δὲ προσθεμένου τοῖς ὀλιγαρχικοῖς καταπλαγεὶς ὁ δῆμος ἠναγκάσθη χειροτονεῖν τὴν ὀλιγαρχίαν. ἔγραψε δὲ τὸ ψήφισμα Δρακοντίδης Ἀφιδναῖος.

1 XXXV. Οἱ μὲν οὖν τριάκοντα τοῦτον τὸν τρόπον κατέστησαν ἐπὶ Πυθοδώρου ἄρχοντος. γενόμενοι δὲ κύριοι τῆς πόλεως τὰ μὲν ἄλλα τὰ δόξαντα περὶ τῆς πολιτείας παρεώρων, πεντακοσίους δὲ βουλευτὰς καὶ τὰς ἄλλας ἀρχὰς καταστήσαντες ἐκ προκρίτων ἐκ τῶν χιλίων,[1] καὶ προσελόμενοι σφίσιν αὐτοῖς τοῦ Πειραιέως ἄρχοντας δέκα καὶ τοῦ δεσμωτηρίου φύλακας ἕνδεκα καὶ μαστιγοφόρους τριακοσίους ὑπηρέτας κατεῖχον
2 τὴν πόλιν δι' ἑαυτῶν. τὸ μὲν οὖν πρῶτον μέτριοι τοῖς πολίταις ἦσαν καὶ προσεποιοῦντο διοικεῖν[2] τὴν πάτριον πολιτείαν, καὶ τούς τ' Ἐφιάλτου καὶ Ἀρχεστράτου νόμους τοὺς περὶ τῶν Ἀρεοπαγιτῶν καθεῖλον ἐξ Ἀρείου πάγου καὶ τῶν Σόλωνος θεσμῶν ὅσοι διαμφισβητήσεις εἶχον, καὶ τὸ κῦρος ὃ ἦν ἐν τοῖς δικασταῖς κατέλυσαν, ὡς ἐπανορ-

[1] [ἐκ τῶν] χιλίων Herwerden: [ἐκ τῶν χιλίων] Rutherford: φυλῶν pro χιλίων Hude.
[2] διώκειν edd.

democracy, but the notables who belonged to the Comradeships and those exiles who had returned after the peace were eager for oligarchy, while those notables who were not members of any Comradeship but who otherwise were inferior in reputation to none of the citizens were aiming at the ancestral constitution; members of this party were Archinus, Anytus, Cleitophon and Phormisius, while its chief leader was Theramenes. And when Lysander sided with the oligarchical party, the people were cowed and were forced to vote for the oligarchy. The motion was proposed by Dracontides of Aphidna.

XXXV. So in this manner the Thirty were estab- 1
lished, in the archonship of Pythodorus. Having be- 404 B.C.
come masters of the state they neglected most of the measures that had been resolved on in regard to the constitution, but appointed five hundred Councillors and the other offices from among persons previously selected from the Thousand,[a] and also chose for themselves ten governors of Peiraeus, eleven guardians of the prison, and three hundred retainers carrying
whips, and so kept the state in their own hands. At 2
first, then, they were moderate towards the citizens and pretended to be administering the ancestral form of constitution, and they removed from the Areopagus the laws of Ephialtes and Archestratus[b] about the Areopagites, and also such of the ordinances of Solon as were of doubtful purport, and abolished the sovereignty vested in the jurymen, claiming to be rectifying the constitution and removing its un-

[a] *i.e.* from the knights; but the text can hardly be correct, and may be emended to give 'from among a thousand persons previously selected.'

[b] Probably a supporter of Ephialtes, for whose legislation see ch. xxv.

θοῦντες καὶ ποιοῦντες ἀναμφισβήτητον τὴν πολιτείαν, οἷον περὶ τοῦ δοῦναι τὰ ἑαυτοῦ ᾧ ἂν ἐθέλῃ κύριον ποιήσαντες καθάπαξ, τὰς δὲ προσούσας δυσκολίας "ἐὰν μὴ μανιῶν ἢ γήρως ⟨ἕνεκα⟩[1] ἢ γυναικὶ πιθόμενος" ἀφεῖλον ὅπως μὴ ᾖ τοῖς συκοφάνταις ἔφοδος· ὁμοίως δὲ τοῦτ᾽ ἔδρων καὶ
3 ἐπὶ τῶν ἄλλων. κατ᾽ ἀρχὰς μὲν οὖν ταῦτ᾽ ἐποίουν καὶ τοὺς συκοφάντας καὶ τοὺς τῷ δήμῳ πρὸς χάριν ὁμιλοῦντας παρὰ τὸ βέλτιστον καὶ κακοπράγμονας ὄντας καὶ πονηροὺς ἀνῄρουν, ἐφ᾽ οἷς ἔχαιρεν[2] ἡ πόλις γιγνομένοις, ἡγούμενοι τοῦ βελτίστου
4 χάριν ποιεῖν αὐτούς. ἐπεὶ δὲ τὴν πόλιν ἐγκρατέστερον ἔσχον, οὐδενὸς ἀπείχοντο τῶν πολιτῶν, ἀλλ᾽ ἀπέκτειναν τοὺς καὶ ταῖς οὐσίαις καὶ τῷ γένει καὶ τοῖς ἀξιώμασιν προέχοντας, ὑπεξαιρούμενοί τε τὸν φόβον καὶ βουλόμενοι τὰς οὐσίας διαρπάζειν· καὶ χρόνου διαπεσόντος βραχέος οὐκ ἐλάττους ἀνῃρήκεσαν ἢ χιλίους πεντακοσίους.

1 XXXVI. Οὕτως δὲ τῆς πόλεως ὑποφερομένης Θηραμένης ἀγανακτῶν ἐπὶ τοῖς γινομένοις τῆς μὲν ἀσελγείας αὐτοῖς παρῄνει παύσασθαι μεταδοῦναι δὲ τῶν πραγμάτων τοῖς βελτίστοις. οἱ δὲ πρῶτον[3] ἐναντιωθέντες, ἐπεὶ διεσπάρησαν οἱ λόγοι πρὸς τὸ πλῆθος καὶ πρὸς τὸν Θηραμένην οἰκείως εἶχον οἱ πολλοί, φοβηθέντες μὴ προστάτης γενόμενος τοῦ δήμου καταλύσῃ τὴν δυναστείαν καταλέγουσιν τῶν πολιτῶν τρισχιλίους[4] ὡς μετα-
2 δώσοντες τῆς πολιτείας. Θηραμένης δὲ πάλιν

[1] ἕνεκα γήρως Wyse: γηρων cod.
[2] Sidgwick (cf. xxxiv. 1 τὸ δὲ πλῆθος οὐχ ὑπήκουσεν, ἐξαπατηθέντες): εχαιρον cod.
[3] edd.: πρωτοι cod.
[4] edd.: δισχιλιους cod.

certainties: for example, in regard to the bestowal of one's property on whomsoever one wishes, making the single act of donation valid absolutely, while they removed the tiresome qualifications 'save when in consequence of insanity or of old age, or under the influence of a woman,' in order that there might be no opening for blackmailers; and similarly they did
this in the other matters as well. At the outset, there- 3
fore, they were engaged in these matters, and in removing the blackmailers and the persons who consorted undesirably with the people to curry favour and were evil-doers and scoundrels; and the state was delighted at these measures, thinking that they
were acting with the best intentions. But when 4
they got a firmer hold on the state, they kept their hands off none of the citizens, but put to death those of outstanding wealth or birth or reputation, intending to put that source of danger out of the way, and also desiring to plunder their estates; and by the end of a brief interval of time they had made away with not less than fifteen hundred.

XXXVI. While the state was thus being under- 1
mined, Theramenes, resenting what was taking place, kept exhorting them to cease from their wantonness and to admit the best classes to a share in affairs. At first they opposed him, but since these proposals became disseminated among the multitude, and the general public were well disposed towards Theramenes, they grew afraid that he might become head of the People and put down the oligarchy, and so they enrolled three thousand of the citizens with the intention of giving them a share in the government.
But Theramenes again criticized this procedure also, 2

ἐπιτιμᾷ καὶ τούτοις, πρῶτον μὲν ὅτι βουλόμενοι μεταδοῦναι τοῖς ἐπιεικέσι τρισχιλίοις μόνοις μεταδιδόασι, ὡς ἐν τούτῳ τῷ πλήθει τῆς ἀρετῆς ὡρισμένης, ἔπειθ' ὅτι δύο τὰ ἐναντιώτατα ποιοῦσιν, βίαιόν τε τὴν ἀρχὴν καὶ τῶν ἀρχομένων ἥττω κατασκευάζοντες. οἱ δὲ τούτων μὲν ὠλιγώρησαν, τὸν δὲ κατάλογον τῶν τρισχιλίων πολὺν μὲν χρόνον ὑπερεβάλλοντο[1] καὶ παρ' αὑτοῖς ἐφύλαττον τοὺς ἐγνωσμένους, ὅτε δὲ καὶ δόξειεν αὐτοῖς ἐκφέρειν τοὺς μὲν ἐξήλειφον τῶν ἐγγεγραμμένων[2] τοὺς δ' ἀντενέγραφον τῶν ἔξωθεν.

1 XXXVII. Ἤδη δὲ τοῦ χειμῶνος ἐνεστῶτος, καταλαβόντος Θρασυβούλου μετὰ τῶν φυγάδων Φυλὴν καὶ κατὰ τὴν στρατιὰν ἣν ἐξήγαγον οἱ τριάκοντα κακῶς ἀποχωρήσαντες, ἔγνωσαν τῶν μὲν ἄλλων τὰ ὅπλα παρελέσθαι Θηραμένην δὲ διαφθεῖραι τόνδε τρόπον. νόμους εἰσήνεγκαν εἰς τὴν βουλὴν δύο κελεύοντες ἐπιχειροτονεῖν, ὧν ὁ μὲν εἷς αὐτοκράτορας ἐποίει τοὺς τριάκοντα τῶν πολιτῶν ἀποκτεῖναι τοὺς μὴ τοῦ καταλόγου μετέχοντας τῶν τρισχιλίων, ὁ δ' ἕτερος ἐκώλυε κοινωνεῖν τῆς παρούσης πολιτείας ὅσοι τυγχάνουσιν τὸ ἐν Ἠετιωνείᾳ τεῖχος κατασκάψαντες ἢ τοῖς τετρακοσίοις ἐναντίον τι πράξαντες τοῖς[3] κατασκευάσασι τὴν προτέραν ὀλιγαρχίαν· ὧν ἐτύγχανεν ἀμφοτέρων κεκοινωνηκὼς ὁ Θηραμένης, ὥστε συνέβαινεν ἐπικυρωθέντων τῶν νόμων ἔξω

[1] ὑπερεβάλλοντο ⟨ἐκφέρειν⟩ Gertz.
[2] ἐγγεγραμμένων Herwerden: γεγραμμενων cod.
[3] τοῖς Herwerden: ητοις cod.

first on the ground that although willing to share the government with the respectable they were only giving a share to three thousand, as though moral worth were limited to that number, and next because they were doing two absolutely incompatible things, making their rule one of force and at the same time weaker than those they ruled. But they despised these remonstrances, and for a long time went on postponing the roll of the Three Thousand and keeping to themselves those on whom they had decided, and even on occasions when they thought fit to publish it they made a practice of erasing some of the names enrolled and writing in others instead from among those outside the roll.[a]

XXXVII. Winter had already set in, when Thrasy- 1
bulus with the exiles occupied Phylē, and things went badly with the Thirty on the expedition that they led out against them; so they decided to disarm the others and to destroy Theramenes in the following way. They introduced two laws into the Council, with orders to pass them; one was to give the Thirty absolute powers to execute any citizens not members of the roll of Three Thousand, and the other prohibited admission to citizenship under the present constitution for all who had actually taken part in the demolition of the fort[b] on Eëtionea, or in any act of opposition to the Four Hundred who had instituted the former oligarchy; in both of these proceedings Theramenes had in fact participated, so that the result was that when the laws had been ratified he

[a] So that no one would be sure of being on it.

[b] A projecting mole on the northern side of Peiraeus harbour, commanding the entrance. It had been begun, but was then demolished at the instigation of Theramenes (Thuc. viii. 90-92).

τε γίγνεσθαι τῆς πολιτείας αὐτὸν καὶ τοὺς τριά-
2 κοντα κυρίους εἶναι θανατοῦντας. ἀναιρεθέντος δὲ Θηραμένους τά τε ὅπλα παρείλοντο πάντων πλὴν τῶν τρισχιλίων καὶ ἐν τοῖς ἄλλοις πολὺ πρὸς ὠμότητα καὶ πονηρίαν ἐπέδοσαν. πρέσβεις δὲ[1] πέμψαντες εἰς Λακεδαίμονα τοῦ τε Θηραμένους κατηγόρουν καὶ βοηθεῖν αὐτοῖς ἠξίουν· ὧν ἀκούσαντες οἱ Λακεδαιμόνιοι Καλλίβιον ἀπέστειλαν ἁρμοστὴν καὶ στρατιώτας ὡς ἑπτακοσίους, οἳ τὴν ἀκρόπολιν ἐλθόντες ἐφρούρουν.

1 XXXVIII. Μετὰ δὲ ταῦτα καταλαβόντων τῶν ἀπὸ Φυλῆς τὴν Μουνιχίαν καὶ νικησάντων μάχῃ τοὺς μετὰ τῶν τριάκοντα βοηθήσαντας, ἐπαναχωρήσαντες μετὰ τὸν κίνδυνον οἱ ἐκ τοῦ ἄστεως καὶ συναθροισθέντες εἰς τὴν ἀγορὰν τῇ ὑστεραίᾳ, τοὺς μὲν τριάκοντα κατέλυσαν αἱροῦνται δὲ δέκα τῶν πολιτῶν αὐτοκράτορας ἐπὶ τὴν τοῦ πολέμου κατάλυσιν. οἱ δὲ παραλαβόντες τὴν ἀρχὴν ἐφ'[2] οἷς μὲν ᾑρέθησαν οὐκ ἔπραττον, ἔπεμπον δ' εἰς Λακεδαίμονα βοήθειαν μεταπεμπόμενοι καὶ χρή-
2 ματα δανειζόμενοι. χαλεπῶς δὲ φερόντων ἐπὶ τούτοις τῶν ἐν τῇ πολιτείᾳ, φοβούμενοι μὴ καταλυθῶσιν τῆς ἀρχῆς καὶ βουλόμενοι καταπλῆξαι τοὺς ἄλλους (ὅπερ ἐγένετο), συλλαβόντες Δημάρετον οὐδενὸς ὄντα δεύτερον τῶν πολιτῶν ἀπέκτειναν, καὶ τὰ πράγματα βεβαίως[3] εἶχον, συναγωνιζομένου Καλλιβίου τε καὶ τῶν Πελοποννησίων τῶν παρόντων καὶ πρὸς τούτοις ἐνίων τῶν ἐν τοῖς ἱππεῦσι· τούτων γάρ τινες μάλιστα τῶν πολιτῶν ἐσπούδαζον μὴ κατελθεῖν τοὺς ἀπὸ

[1] δὲ supplevit Mayor.
[2] ἐφ' edd.: εν cod.
[3] βιαίως Mayor.

became outside the constitution and the Thirty had authority to put him to death. Theramenes having 2
been put out of the way, they disarmed everybody except the Three Thousand, and in the rest of their proceedings went much further in the direction of cruelty and rascality. And they sent ambassadors to Sparta to denounce Theramenes and call upon the Spartans to assist them; and when the Spartans heard this message they dispatched Callibius as governor and about seven hundred troops, who came and garrisoned the Acropolis.

XXXVIII. After this the refugees in Phylē took 1
Munichia, and defeated in action the force that came with the Thirty to the defence; and the force from the city, on their return after this dangerous expedition, held a meeting in the market-place the day after, deposed the Thirty, and elected ten of the citizens as plenipotentiaries to bring the war to a conclusion. These, however, having obtained this office did not proceed to do the things for the purpose of which they had been elected, but sent to Sparta
to procure help and to borrow funds. But this was 2
resented by those within the constitution, and the Ten, in their fear of being deposed from office and their desire to terrify the others (which they succeeded in doing), arrested one of the most leading citizens, Demaretus, and put him to death, and kept a firm hold upon affairs, while Callibius and the Peloponnesians at Athens actively supported them, and so did some members of the corps of Knights as well; for some of the Knights were the most eager of all the citizens that the men at Phylē should not

3 Φυλῆς. ὡς δ' οἱ τὸν Πειραιέα καὶ τὴν Μουνυχίαν
ἔχοντες ἀποστάντος ἅπαντος τοῦ δήμου πρὸς
αὐτοὺς[1] ἐπεκράτουν τῷ πολέμῳ, τότε καταλύσαν-
τες τοὺς δέκα τοὺς πρώτους αἱρεθέντας, ἄλλους
εἵλοντο δέκα τοὺς βελτίστους εἶναι δοκοῦντας, ἐφ'
ὧν συνέβη καὶ τὰς διαλύσεις γενέσθαι καὶ κατελθεῖν τὸν δῆμον, συναγωνιζομένων καὶ προθυμου-
μένων τούτων. προειστήκεσαν δ' αὐτῶν μάλιστα
Ῥίνων τε ὁ Παιανιεὺς καὶ Φάυλλος ὁ Ἀχερδούσιος·
οὗτοι γὰρ πρίν τε Πανσανίαν[2] ἀφικέσθαι δι-
επέμποντο πρὸς τοὺς ἐν Πειραιεῖ καὶ ἀφικομένου
4 συνεσπούδασαν τὴν κάθοδον. ἐπὶ πέρας γὰρ ἤγαγε
τὴν εἰρήνην καὶ τὰς διαλύσεις Παυσανίας ὁ τῶν
Λακεδαιμονίων βασιλεὺς μετὰ τῶν δέκα διαλ-
λακτῶν τῶν ὕστερον ἀφικομένων ἐκ Λακεδαί-
μονος οὓς αὐτὸς ἐσπούδασεν ἐλθεῖν. οἱ δὲ περὶ
τὸν Ῥίνωνα διά τε τὴν εὔνοιαν τὴν εἰς τὸν δῆμον
ἐπῃνέθησαν, καὶ λαβόντες τὴν ἐπιμέλειαν ἐν ὀλιγ-
αρχίᾳ τὰς εὐθύνας ἔδοσαν ἐν δημοκρατίᾳ, καὶ
οὐδεὶς οὐδὲν ἐνεκάλεσεν αὐτοῖς οὔτε τῶν ἐν ἄστει
μεινάντων οὔτε τῶν ἐκ Πειραιέως κατελθόντων,
ἀλλὰ διὰ ταῦτα καὶ στρατηγὸς εὐθὺς ᾑρέθη Ῥίνων.
1 XXXIX. Ἐγένοντο δ' αἱ διαλύσεις ἐπ' Εὐ-
κλείδου ἄρχοντος κατὰ τὰς συνθήκας τάσδε. τοὺς
βουλομένους Ἀθηναίων τῶν ἐν ἄστει μεινάντων
ἐξοικεῖν ἔχειν Ἐλευσῖνα ἐπιτίμους ὄντας καὶ
κυρίους καὶ αὐτοκράτορας ἑαυτῶν καὶ τὰ αὐτῶν
2 καρπουμένους. τὸ δ' ἱερὸν εἶναι κοινὸν ἀμφο-

[1] Blass: αυτην cod.
[2] τε Πανσανίαν Richards: ηπαυσανιαντε cod.

return. But the party holding Peiraeus and Munichia, 3
now that the whole of the people had come over to their side, began to get the upper hand in the war, and so finally they deposed the ten who had been elected first, and chose ten others whom they thought to be the best men, and while these were in power there took place the reconciliation and the return of the people, with the active and eager support of the ten. The most prominent among them were Rhinon of the Paeanian deme and Phayllus of the Acherdusian; for these men had repeatedly gone on missions to the men at Peiraeus before Pausanias's arrival, and after his arrival they zealously supported the return.
For it was Pausanias the king of the Lacedaemonians 4
who brought the peace and reconciliation to fulfilment, with the aid of the ten mediators who later arrived from Sparta, and whose coming was due to the efforts of the king himself. Rhinon and his companions were commended for their goodwill towards the people, and having been appointed to superintend these negotiations under an oligarchy they gave in their accounts under a democracy, and no one made any charge against them whatever, whether of those who had remained in the city or of those who had returned from Peiraeus; indeed, on the contrary Rhinon was immediately elected general because of his conduct in this office.

XXXIX. The reconciliation took place in the 1
archonship of Eucleides on the following terms: 403 B.C.
'That those of the Athenians who have remained in the city that desire to emigrate do have Eleusis, retaining their full rights, and having sovereignty and self-government, and enjoying their own revenues.
And that the temple be the common property of both 2

τέρων, ἐπιμελεῖσθαι δὲ Κήρυκας καὶ Εὐμολπίδας κατὰ τὰ πάτρια. μὴ ἐξεῖναι δὲ μήτε τοῖς Ἐλευσίνοθεν εἰς τὸ ἄστυ μήτε τοῖς ἐκ τοῦ ἄστεως Ἐλευσίναδ' εἰσιέναι πλὴν μυστηρίοις ἑκατέρους. συντελεῖν δὲ ἀπὸ τῶν προσιόντων εἰς τὸ συμ-
3 μαχικὸν καθάπερ τοὺς ἄλλους Ἀθηναίους. ἐὰν δέ τινες τῶν ἀπιόντων οἰκίαν λαμβάνωσιν Ἐλευσῖνι, συμπείθειν τὸν κεκτημένον· ἐὰν δὲ μὴ συμβαίνωσιν ἀλλήλοις τιμητὰς ἑλέσθαι τρεῖς ἑκάτερον,[1] καὶ ἥντιν' ἂν οὗτοι τάξωσι τιμὴν λαμβάνειν. Ἐλευσινίων δὲ συνοικεῖν οὓς ἂν οὗτοι[2] βούλωνται.
4 τὴν δ' ἀπογραφὴν εἶναι τοῖς βουλομένοις ἐξοικεῖν, τοῖς μὲν ἐπιδημοῦσιν ἀφ' ἧς ἂν ὀμόσωσιν τοὺς ὅρκους δέκα ἡμερῶν, τὴν δ' ἐξοίκησιν εἴκοσι, τοῖς δ' ἀποδημοῦσιν ἐπειδὰν ἐπιδημήσωσιν κατὰ ταὐτά.
5 μὴ ἐξεῖναι δὲ ἄρχειν μηδεμίαν ἀρχὴν τῶν ἐν τῷ ἄστει τὸν Ἐλευσῖνι κατοικοῦντα πρὶν ἀπογράψηται πάλιν ἐν τῷ ἄστει κατοικεῖν. τὰς δὲ δίκας τοῦ φόνου εἶναι κατὰ τὰ πάτρια, εἴ τίς τινα αὐτόχειρ
6 ἀπέκτεινεν ἢ ἔτρωσεν.[3] τῶν δὲ παρεληλυθότων μηδενὶ πρὸς μηδένα μνησικακεῖν ἐξεῖναι πλὴν πρὸς τοὺς τριάκοντα καὶ τοὺς δέκα καὶ τοὺς ἕνδεκα καὶ τοὺς τοῦ Πειραιέως ἄρξαντας, μηδὲ πρὸς τούτους ἐὰν διδῶσιν εὐθύνας. εὐθύνας δὲ δοῦναι τοὺς μὲν ἐν Πειραιεῖ ἄρξαντας ἐν τοῖς ἐν Πειραιεῖ, τοὺς δ' ἐν τῷ ἄστει ἐν τοῖς[4] τὰ τιμήματα παρ-

[1] ἑκάτερον Bury: εκατερων cod.
[2] αὐτοὶ Richards.
[3] εἴ τίς . . . ἔτρωσεν Blass, partim ex aliis: valde confusa cod.
[4] ἐν τοῖς <ἐν τῷ ἄστει> ? Kenyon.

[a] See lvii. 1.
[b] Perhaps ' in the city ' should be inserted after ' property.'

sections, and be under the superintendence of the Heralds and the Eumolpidae[a] according to the ancestral practice. But that it be not lawful for those at Eleusis to go into the city, nor for those in the city to go to Eleusis, except in either case at a celebration of the Mysteries. And that they contribute from their revenues like the other Athenians to the fund
for the common defence. And that any of those who 3
go away that take a house at Eleusis be helped to obtain the consent of the owner; and if they cannot come to terms with one another, each party to choose three valuers, and to accept whatever price these valuers assess. And that of the people of Eleusis those whom the settlers may be willing to
allow do dwell in the place with them. And that the 4
registration of those that wish to migrate be, for those who are in the country, within ten days of the date of their swearing the oaths of peace, and their migration within twenty days, and for those abroad
similarly from the date when they return. And that 5
it be not permitted for anyone residing at Eleusis to hold any of the offices in the city until he removes himself from the roll in order to reside again in the city. And that trials for homicide be in accordance with the ancestral ordinances, if a man has killed or
wounded another with his own hand. And that there 6
be a universal amnesty for past events, covering everybody except the Thirty, the Ten, the Eleven, and those that have been governors of Peiraeus, and that these also be covered by the amnesty if they render account. And that those who had been governors in Peiraeus render account before the courts held in Peiraeus, but those in the city before a court of persons that can produce ratable property[b];

εχομένοις· εἶθ' οὕτως ἐξοικεῖν τοὺς μὴ[1] ἐθέλοντας. τὰ δὲ χρήματα ἃ ἐδανείσαντο εἰς τὸν πόλεμον ἑκατέρους ἀποδοῦναι χωρίς.

1 XL. Γενομένων δὲ τοιούτων τῶν διαλύσεων, καὶ φοβουμένων ὅσοι μετὰ τῶν τριάκοντα συνεπολέμησαν, καὶ πολλῶν μὲν ἐπινοούντων ἐξοικεῖν ἀναβαλλομένων δὲ τὴν ἀπογραφὴν[2] εἰς τὰς ἐσχάτας ἡμέρας, ὅπερ εἰώθασιν ποιεῖν ἅπαντες, Ἀρχῖνος συνιδὼν τὸ πλῆθος καὶ βουλόμενος κατασχεῖν αὐτοὺς ὑφεῖλε τὰς ὑπολοίπους ἡμέρας τῆς ἀπογραφῆς, ὥστε συναναγκασθῆναι μένειν πολλοὺς ἄκοντας
2 ἕως ἐθάρρησαν. καὶ δοκεῖ τοῦτό τε πολιτεύσασθαι καλῶς Ἀρχῖνος, καὶ μετὰ ταῦτα γραψάμενος τὸ ψήφισμα τὸ Θρασυβούλου παρανόμων, ἐν ᾧ μετεδίδου τῆς πολιτείας πᾶσι τοῖς ἐκ Πειραιέως συγκατελθοῦσι, ὧν ἔνιοι φανερῶς ἦσαν δοῦλοι, καὶ τρίτον, ἐπεί τις ἤρξατο τῶν κατεληλυθότων μνησικακεῖν, ἀπαγαγὼν τοῦτον ἐπὶ τὴν βουλὴν καὶ πείσας ἄκριτον ἀποκτεῖναι, λέγων ὅτι νῦν δείξουσιν εἰ βούλονται τὴν δημοκρατίαν σῴζειν καὶ τοῖς ὅρκοις ἐμμένειν· ἀφέντας μὲν γὰρ τοῦτον προτρέψειν καὶ τοὺς ἄλλους, ἐὰν δ' ἀνέλωσιν παράδειγμα ποιήσειν ἅπασιν. ὅπερ καὶ συνέπεσεν· ἀποθανόντος γὰρ οὐδεὶς πώποτε ὕστερον ἐμνησικάκησεν, ἀλλὰ δοκοῦσιν κάλλιστα δὴ καὶ πολιτικώτατα ἁπάντων καὶ ἰδίᾳ καὶ κοινῇ χρήσασθαι ταῖς προ-
3 γεγενημέναις συμφοραῖς· οὐ γὰρ μόνον τὰς περὶ

[1] τοὺς μὴ Blass: τους δ cod. (δ supra lineam).
[2] Jackson: αναγραφην cod.

or that those who will not render account on these terms do migrate.[a] And that each party separately repay their loans contracted for the war.'

XL. The reconciliation having been made on these 1
terms, all those who had fought on the side of the
Thirty were alarmed, and many intended to migrate,
but put off their registration to the latest days,
as everybody usually does; so Archinus perceiving
their numbers and wishing to retain them, cancelled
the remainder of the days allowed for registration,
so that many should be jointly compelled to stay
against their will until they recovered courage. This 2
seems to have been a statesmanlike act of Archinus ;
as was also later his indicting as unconstitutional
the decree of Thrasybulus admitting to citizenship
all those who had come back together from Peiraeus,
some of whom were clearly slaves ; and his third act
of statesmanship was that when somebody began
to stir up grudges against the returned citizens, he
arraigned him before the Council and persuaded it
to execute him without trial, saying that this was
the moment for them to show if they wished to save
the democracy and keep their oaths ; for by letting
this man off they would incite the others too, but if
they put him out of the way they would make him
an example to everybody. And this is what actually
occurred ; for never since he was put to death has
anybody broken the amnesty, but the Athenians
appear both in private and public to have behaved
towards the past disasters in the most completely
honourable and statesmanlike manner of any people
in history ; for they not only blotted out recrimina- 3

[a] A variant reading (*εἶθ' οὕτως ἐξοικεῖν τοὺς ἐθέλοντας*) gives 'then those who wish are to emigrate on these terms.'

τῶν προτέρων αἰτίας ἐξήλειψαν ἀλλὰ καὶ τὰ χρήματα Λακεδαιμονίοις ἃ οἱ τριάκοντα πρὸς τὸν πόλεμον ἔλαβον ἀπέδοσαν κοινῇ, κελευουσῶν τῶν συνθηκῶν ἑκατέρους ἀποδιδόναι χωρίς, τούς τ' ἐκ τοῦ ἄστεως καὶ τοὺς ἐκ τοῦ Πειραιέως, ἡγούμενοι τοῦτο πρῶτον ἄρχειν δεῖν τῆς ὁμονοίας· ἐν δὲ ταῖς ἄλλαις πόλεσιν οὐχ οἷον ἔτι προστιθέασιν τῶν οἰκείων οἱ δημοκρατήσαντες[1] ἀλλὰ καὶ τὴν
4 χώραν ἀνάδαστον ποιοῦσιν. διελύθησαν δὲ καὶ πρὸς τοὺς ἐν Ἐλευσῖνι κατοικήσαντας ἔτει τρίτῳ μετὰ τὴν ἐξοίκησιν ἐπὶ Ξεναινέτου ἄρχοντος.

1 XLI. Ταῦτα μὲν οὖν ἐν τοῖς ὕστερον συνέβη γενέσθαι καιροῖς, τότε δὲ κύριος ὁ δῆμος γενόμενος τῶν πραγμάτων ἐνεστήσατο τὴν νῦν οὖσαν πολιτείαν ἐπὶ Πυθοδώρου μὲν ἄρχοντος δοκοῦντος δὲ δικαίως[2] τοῦ δήμου λαβεῖν τὴν πολιτείαν διὰ τὸ ποιήσασθαι τὴν κάθοδον δι' αὑτοῦ τὸν δῆμον.
2 ἦν δὲ τῶν μεταβολῶν ἑνδεκάτη τὸν ἀριθμὸν αὕτη. πρώτη μὲν γὰρ ἐγένετο ἡ κατάστασις[3] τῶν ἐξ ἀρχῆς Ἴωνος καὶ τῶν μετ' αὐτοῦ συνοικισάντων· τότε γὰρ πρῶτον εἰς τὰς τέτταρας συνενεμήθησαν φυλὰς καὶ τοὺς φυλοβασιλέας κατέστησαν. δευτέρα δέ, καὶ πρώτη μετὰ ταύτην ἔχουσά τι πολιτείας τάξις[4] ἡ ἐπὶ Θησέως γενομένη, μικρὸν παρεγκλίνουσα τῆς βασιλικῆς. μετὰ δὲ ταύτην ἡ ἐπὶ Δράκοντος, ἐν ᾗ καὶ νόμους ἀνέγραψαν πρῶτον. τρίτη δ' ἡ μετὰ τὴν στάσιν ἡ ἐπὶ Σόλωνος, ἀφ'

[1] οἱ δῆμοι κρατήσαντες edd.

[2] δικαίου Richards.

[3] μετάστασις alii legunt.

[4] Wilamowitz: εχουσαιπολιτειαντaξιν cod.

[a] The Greek text is very doubtful, but apparently the constitution in the time of Ion is taken as the starting-point,

tions with regard to the past, but also publicly restored to the Spartans the funds that the Thirty had taken for the war, although the treaty ordered that the parties in the city and in Peiraeus were each to make restitution separately. The Athenians thought that they must take this as a first step to concord, whereas in the other states those who have set up democracy not only do not pay any more out of their own property but even make a redistribution
of the land. They also made a reconciliation with 4
those that had settled at Eleusis two years after the
migration, in the archonship of Xenaenetus. 401 B.C.

XLI. These events then came about in the follow- 1
ing periods; but at the date mentioned the people having become sovereign over affairs established the now existing constitution, in the archonship of Pythodorus, when the People's having accomplished
its return by its own efforts made it appear just for 402 B.C.
it to assume the government. In the list of reforms 2
this was the eleventh in number. There first occurred the organization of the original constitution after the settlement at Athens of Ion and his companions, for it was then that the people were first divided into the four Tribes and appointed the Tribal Kings. The second constitution, and the first subsequent one that involved a constitutional point,[a] was the reform that took place in the time of Theseus, which was a slight divergence from the royal constitution. After that one came the reform in the time of Draco, in which a code of laws was first published. Third was the one that followed the civil disturbance in the time of Solon, from which democracy took its beginning.

and the eleven revolutions follow. Draco's reform is not numbered as one of them.

ἧς ἀρχὴ δημοκρατίας ἐγένετο. τετάρτη δ᾿ ἡ ἐπὶ Πεισιστράτου τυραννίς. πέμπτη δ᾿ ἡ μετὰ τὴν τῶν[1] τυράννων κατάλυσιν ἡ Κλεισθένους, δημοτικωτέρα τῆς Σόλωνος. ἕκτη δ᾿ ἡ μετὰ τὰ Μηδικά, τῆς ἐξ Ἀρείου πάγου βουλῆς ἐπιστατούσης. ἑβδόμη δὲ καὶ[2] μετὰ ταύτην ἣν Ἀριστείδης μὲν ὑπέδειξεν Ἐφιάλτης δ᾿ ἐπετέλεσεν καταλύσας τὴν Ἀρεοπαγῖτιν βουλήν, ἐν ᾗ πλεῖστα συνέβη τὴν πόλιν διὰ τοὺς δημαγωγοὺς ἁμαρτάνειν διὰ[3] τὴν τῆς θαλάττης ἀρχήν. ὀγδόη δ᾿ ἡ τῶν τετρακοσίων κατάστασις, καὶ μετὰ ταύτην ἐνάτη δὲ ἡ δημοκρατία πάλιν. δεκάτη δ᾿ ἡ τῶν τριάκοντα καὶ ἡ τῶν δέκα τυραννίς. ἑνδεκάτη δ᾿ ἡ μετὰ τὴν ἀπὸ Φυλῆς καὶ ἐκ Πειραιέως κάθοδον· ἀφ᾿ ἧς διαγεγένηται μέχρι τῆς νῦν, ἀεὶ προσεπιλαμβάνουσα τῷ πλήθει τὴν ἐξουσίαν. ἁπάντων γὰρ αὐτὸς αὑτὸν πεποίηκεν ὁ δῆμος κύριον καὶ πάντα διοικεῖται ψηφίσμασιν καὶ δικαστηρίοις ἐν οἷς ὁ δῆμός ἐστιν ὁ κρατῶν, καὶ γὰρ αἱ τῆς βουλῆς κρίσεις εἰς τὸν δῆμον ἐληλύθασιν. καὶ τοῦτο δοκοῦσι ποιεῖν ὀρθῶς· εὐδιαφθορώτεροι γὰρ ὀλίγοι τῶν
3 πολλῶν εἰσὶν καὶ κέρδει καὶ χάρισιν. μισθοφόρον δ᾿ ἐκκλησίαν τὸ μὲν πρῶτον ἀπέγνωσαν ποιεῖν· οὐ συλλεγομένων δ᾿ εἰς τὴν ἐκκλησίαν, ἀλλὰ πολλὰ σοφιζομένων τῶν πρυτάνεων ὅπως προσιστῆται τὸ πλῆθος πρὸς τὴν ἐπικύρωσιν τῆς χειροτονίας, πρῶτον μὲν Ἀγύρριος ὀβολὸν ἐπόρισεν, μετὰ δὲ

[1] τὴν τῶν Kenyon: των cod.
[2] καὶ secl. Blass: ἡ coni. Mayor.
[3] ⟨καὶ⟩ διὰ, κατὰ, διὰ . . . ἀρχὴν ⟨θαρρήσασαν⟩ coni. edd.

Fourth was the tyranny in the time of Peisistratus. Fifth the constitution of Cleisthenes, following the deposition of the tyrants, which was more democratic than the constitution of Solon. Sixth the reform after the Persian War, under the superintendence of the Council of Areopagus. Seventh followed the reform outlined by Aristeides but completed by Ephialtes when he put down the Areopagite Council, during which it came about because of the demagogues that the state made many mistakes, because of the empire of the sea.[a] Eighth was the establishment of the Four Hundred, and after that, ninth, democracy again. Tenth was the tyranny of the Thirty and that of the Ten. Eleventh was the constitution established after the return from Phylē and from Peiraeus, from which date the constitution has continued down to its present form, constantly taking on additions to the power of the multitude. For the people has made itself master of everything, and administers everything by decrees and by jury-courts in which the people is the ruling power, for even the cases tried by the Council have come to the people. And they seem to act rightly in doing this, for a few are more easily corrupted by gain and by influence than the many. The proposal to introduce 3
payment for attendance at the Assembly was on the first occasion rejected ; but as people were not attending the Assembly but the presidents kept contriving a number of devices to get the multitude to attend for the passing of the resolution by show of hands, first Agyrrhius introduced a fee of an obol, and after

[a] Here again the exact text is doubtful.

τοῦτον Ἡρακλείδης ὁ Κλαζομένιος ὁ Βασιλεὺς ἐπικαλούμενος διώβολον, πάλιν δ' Ἀγύρριος τριώβολον.

1 XLII. Ἔχει δ' ἡ νῦν κατάστασις τῆς πολιτείας τόνδε τὸν τρόπον. μετέχουσιν μὲν τῆς πολιτείας οἱ ἐξ ἀμφοτέρων γεγονότες ἀστῶν, ἐγγράφονται δ' εἰς τοὺς δημότας ὀκτωκαίδεκα ἔτη γεγονότες. ὅταν δ' ἐγγράφωνται διαψηφίζονται περὶ αὐτῶν ὀμόσαντες οἱ δημόται, πρῶτον μὲν εἰ δοκοῦσι γεγονέναι τὴν ἡλικίαν τὴν ἐκ τοῦ νόμου, κἂν μὴ δόξωσι ἀπέρχονται πάλιν εἰς παῖδας, δεύτερον δ' εἰ ἐλεύθερός ἐστι καὶ γέγονε κατὰ τοὺς νόμους· ἔπειτ' ἂν[1] ἀποψηφίσωνται[2] μὴ εἶναι ἐλεύθερον, ὁ μὲν ἐφίησιν εἰς τὸ δικαστήριον, οἱ δὲ δημόται κατηγόρους αἱροῦνται πέντε ἄνδρας ἐξ αὐτῶν, κἂν μὲν μὴ δόξῃ δικαίως ἐγγράφεσθαι, πωλεῖ τοῦτον ἡ πόλις· ἐὰν δὲ νικήσῃ, τοῖς δημόταις
2 ἐπάναγκες ἐγγράφειν. μετὰ δὲ ταῦτα δοκιμάζει τοὺς ἐγγραφέντας ἡ βουλή, κἄν τις δόξῃ νεώτερος ὀκτωκαίδεκα ἐτῶν εἶναι, ζημιοῖ τοὺς δημότας τοὺς ἐγγράψαντας. ἐπὰν δὲ δοκιμασθῶσιν οἱ ἔφηβοι, συλλεγέντες οἱ πατέρες αὐτῶν κατὰ φυλὰς ὀμόσαντες αἱροῦνται τρεῖς ἐκ τῶν φυλετῶν τῶν ὑπὲρ τετταράκοντα ἔτη γεγονότων οὓς ἂν ἡγῶνται βελτίστους εἶναι καὶ ἐπιτηδειοτάτους ἐπιμελεῖσθαι τῶν ἐφήβων, ἐκ δὲ τούτων ὁ δῆμος ἕνα τῆς φυλῆς ἑκάστης χειροτονεῖ σωφρονιστήν, καὶ κοσμητὴν ἐκ
3 τῶν ἄλλων Ἀθηναίων ἐπὶ πάντας. συλλαβόντες δ' οὗτοι τοὺς ἐφήβους, πρῶτον μὲν τὰ ἱερὰ περιῆλθον, εἶτ' εἰς Πειραιέα πορεύονται καὶ φρουροῦ-

[1] ἂν Papageorgios: αν μεν cod. [2] Wyse: επιψ. cod.

him Heracleides of Clazomenae, surnamed[a] King, two obols, and Agyrrhius again three obols.

XLII. The present form of the constitution is as 1
follows. Citizenship belongs to persons of citizen parentage on both sides, and they are registered on the rolls of their demes at the age of eighteen. At the time of their registration the members of the deme make decision about them by vote on oath, first whether they are shown to have reached the lawful age, and if they are held not to be of age they go back again to the boys, and secondly whether the candidate is a freeman and of legitimate birth; after this, if the vote as to free status goes against him, he appeals to the jury-court, and the demesmen elect five men from among themselves to plead against him, and if it is decided that he has no claim to be registered, the state sells him, but if he wins, it is
compulsory for the demesmen to register him. After 2
this the Council revises the list of persons that have been registered, and if anyone is found to be under eighteen years of age, it fines the demesmen that registered him. And when the cadets have been passed by this revision, their fathers hold meetings by tribes and after taking oath elect three members of the tribe of more than forty years of age, whom they think to be the best and most suitable to supervise the cadets, and from them the people elects by show of hands one of each tribe as disciplinary officer, and elects from the other citizens a marshal over
them all. These take the cadets in a body, and 3
after first making a circuit of the temples then go to

[a] Or 'nicknamed' (as was Peisistratus in Eupolis's comedy *Demos*); but perhaps his family claimed royal descent in Asia Minor.

σιν οἱ μὲν τὴν Μουνιχίαν οἱ δὲ τὴν Ἀκτήν. χειροτονεῖ δὲ καὶ παιδοτρίβας αὐτοῖς δύο καὶ διδασκάλους οἵτινες ὁπλομαχεῖν καὶ τοξεύειν καὶ ἀκοντίζειν καὶ καταπάλτην ἀφιέναι διδάσκουσιν.[1] δίδωσι δὲ καὶ εἰς τροφὴν τοῖς μὲν σωφρονισταῖς δραχμὴν α′ ἑκάστῳ, τοῖς δ' ἐφήβοις τέτταρας ὀβολοὺς ἑκάστῳ· τὰ δὲ τῶν φυλετῶν τῶν αὑτοῦ λαμβάνων ὁ σωφρονιστὴς ἕκαστος ἀγοράζει τὰ ἐπιτήδεια πᾶσιν εἰς τὸ κοινόν (συσσιτοῦσι γὰρ κατὰ φυλάς), καὶ τῶν ἄλλων ἐπιμελεῖται πάντων.
4 καὶ τὸν μὲν πρῶτον ἐνιαυτὸν οὕτως διάγουσι· τὸν δ' ὕστερον, ἐκκλησίας ἐν τῷ θεάτρῳ γενομένης ἀποδειξάμενοι τῷ δήμῳ τὰ περὶ τὰς τάξεις καὶ λαβόντες ἀσπίδα καὶ δόρυ παρὰ τῆς πόλεως, περιπολοῦσι τὴν χώραν καὶ διατρίβουσιν ἐν τοῖς
5 φυλακτηρίοις. φρουροῦσι δὲ τὰ δύο ἔτη· χλαμύδας ἔχοντες· καὶ ἀτελεῖς εἰσὶ πάντων· καὶ δίκην οὔτε διδόασιν οὔτε λαμβάνουσιν, ἵνα μὴ πρόφασις ᾖ τοῦ ἀπιέναι,[2] πλὴν περὶ κλήρου καὶ ἐπικλήρου κἄν τινι κατὰ[3] γένος ἱερωσύνη γένηται. διεξελθόντων δὲ τῶν δυεῖν ἐτῶν ἤδη μετὰ τῶν ἄλλων εἰσίν.

1 XLIII. Τὰ μὲν οὖν περὶ τὴν τῶν πολιτῶν ἐγγραφὴν καὶ τοὺς ἐφήβους τοῦτον ἔχει τὸν τρόπον. τὰς δ' ἀρχὰς τὰς περὶ τὴν ἐγκύκλιον διοίκησιν ἁπάσας ποιοῦσι κληρωτάς, πλὴν ταμίου στρατιωτικῶν καὶ τῶν ἐπὶ τῶν θεωρικῶν καὶ τοῦ τῶν κρηνῶν ἐπιμελητοῦ· ταύτας δὲ χειροτονοῦσιν, καὶ οἱ χειροτονηθέντες ἄρχουσιν ἐκ Παναθηναίων

[1] διδάξουσιν Rutherford.
[2] πρόφασις . . . ἀπιέναι legit Blass, sed incertus cod.
[3] κατὰ Wilamowitz-Kaibel: κατατο cod.

Peiraeus, and some of them garrison Munichia,[a] others the Point.[b] And the people also elects two athletic trainers and instructors for them, to teach them their drill as heavy-armed soldiers, and the use of the bow, the javelin and the sling. It also grants the disciplinary officers one drachma a head for rations, and the cadets four obols a head; and each disciplinary officer takes the pay of those of his own tribe and buys provisions for all in common (for they mess together
by tribes), and looks after everything else. They go 4
on with this mode of life for the first year; in the following year an assembly is held in the theatre, and the cadets give a display of drill before the people, and receive a shield and spear from the state; and they then serve on patrols in the country and are
quartered at the guard-posts. Their service on 5
patrol goes on for two years; the uniform is a mantle; they are exempt from all taxes; and they are not allowed to be sued nor to sue at law, in order that they may have no pretext for absenting themselves, except in cases concerning estate, marriage of an heiress, and any priesthood that one of them may have inherited. When the two years are up, they now are members of the general body of citizens.

XLIII. Such, then, are the regulations about the 1
registration of the citizens and about the cadets. All the officials concerned with the regular administration are appointed by lot, except a Treasurer of Military Funds, the Controllers of the Spectacle Fund, and the Superintendent of Wells; these officers are elected by show of hands, and their term of office runs from

[a] See xix. 2 n.
[b] The southern promontory of Peiraeus.

εἰς Παναθήναια. χειροτονοῦσι δὲ καὶ τὰς πρὸς τὸν πόλεμον ἁπάσας.

2 Βουλὴ δὲ κληροῦται φ′, ν′ ἀπὸ φυλῆς ἑκάστης. πρυτανεύει δ' ἐν μέρει τῶν φυλῶν ἑκάστη καθ' ὅ τι ἂν λάχωσιν, αἱ μὲν πρῶται τέτταρες ϛ′ καὶ λ′ ἡμέρας ἑκάστη, αἱ δὲ ϛ′ αἱ ὕστεραι πέντε καὶ λ′ ἡμέρας ἑκάστη· κατὰ σελήνην γὰρ ἄγουσιν τὸν
3 ἐνιαυτόν. οἱ δὲ πρυτανεύοντες αὐτῶν πρῶτον μὲν συσσιτοῦσιν ἐν τῇ θόλῳ, λαμβάνοντες ἀργύριον παρὰ τῆς πόλεως, ἔπειτα συνάγουσιν καὶ τὴν βουλὴν καὶ τὸν δῆμον, τὴν μὲν οὖν[1] βουλὴν ὅσαι ἡμέραι,[2] πλὴν ἐάν τις ἀφέσιμος ᾖ, τὸν δὲ δῆμον τετράκις τῆς πρυτανείας ἑκάστης. καὶ ὅσα δεῖ χρηματίζειν τὴν βουλήν, καὶ ὅ τι ἐν ἑκάστῃ τῇ ἡμέρᾳ, καὶ ὅπου καθίζειν,[3] οὗτοι προγράφουσι.
4 προγράφουσι δὲ καὶ τὰς ἐκκλησίας οὗτοι· μίαν μὲν κυρίαν, ἐν ᾗ δεῖ τὰς ἀρχὰς ἐπιχειροτονεῖν εἰ δοκοῦσι καλῶς ἄρχειν, καὶ περὶ σίτου καὶ περὶ φυλακῆς τῆς χώρας χρηματίζειν, καὶ τὰς εἰσαγγελίας ἐν ταύτῃ τῇ ἡμέρᾳ τοὺς βουλομένους ποιεῖσθαι, καὶ τὰς ἀπογραφὰς τῶν δημευομένων ἀναγινώσκειν, καὶ τὰς λήξεις τῶν κλήρων καὶ τῶν ἐπικλήρων ἀναγινώσκειν,[4] ὅπως μηδένα λάθῃ μηδὲν
5 ἐρῆμον γενόμενον· ἐπὶ δὲ τῆς ἕκτης πρυτανείας πρὸς τοῖς εἰρημένοις καὶ περὶ τῆς ὀστρακοφορίας ἐπιχειροτονίαν διδόασιν εἰ δοκεῖ ποιεῖν ἢ μή, καὶ συκοφαντῶν προβολὰς τῶν Ἀθηναίων καὶ τῶν με-

[1] [οὖν] edd. [2] ὁσημέραι Kenyon.
[3] Wilamowitz-Kaibel: οτιουκαθιζει cod.
[4] [ἀναγινώσκειν] Gennadios.

[a] *i.e.* in every four years; the Great Panathenaic Festival, as also the Pythian, was held in the third Olympic year.

one Panathenaic Festival to the next.[a] All military officers also are elected by show of hands.

The Council is elected by lot, and has five hundred 2
members, fifty from each tribe. The Presidency is filled by each tribe in turn, in an order settled by lot, each of the first four selected holding the office for thirty-six days and each of the latter six for thirty-five days; for their year is divided into lunar months.[b]
Those of them serving as Presidents first dine to- 3
gether in the Round-house,[c] receiving a sum of money from the state, and then convene meetings of the Council and the People, the Council indeed meeting on every day excepting holidays, but the People four times in each presidency. And the Presidents put up written notice of the business to be dealt with by the Council, and of each day's agenda, and of the place of
meeting. They also put up written notice of the 4
meetings of the Assembly: one[d] sovereign meeting, at which the business is to vote the confirmation of the magistrates in office if they are thought to govern well, and to deal with matters of food supply and the defence of the country; and on this day informations have to be laid by those who wish, and the inventories of estates being confiscated read, and the lists of suits about inheritance and heiresses, so that all may have cognizance of any vacancy in
an estate that occurs. In the sixth presidency in 5
addition to the business specified they take a vote on the desirability of holding an ostracism, and on preliminary informations against persons charged as malicious informers, citizens and resident aliens, up

[b] Alternate months of 29 and 30 days make a year of 354 days, as does $36 \times 4 + 35 \times 6$.

[c] At the N.E. of the Areopagus, near the Council-chamber.

[d] One in each presidential term of office.

τοίκων μέχρι τριῶν ἑκατέρων, κἄν τις ὑποσχόμενός
6 τι μὴ ποιήσῃ τῷ δήμῳ. ἑτέραν δὲ ταῖς ἱκετηρίαις,
ἐν ᾗ θεὶς ὁ βουλόμενος ἱκετηρίαν ὑπὲρ ὧν ἂν
βούληται καὶ ἰδίων καὶ δημοσίων διαλέξεται πρὸς
τὸν δῆμον. αἱ δὲ δύο περὶ τῶν ἄλλων εἰσίν, ἐν
αἷς κελεύουσιν οἱ νόμοι τρία μὲν ἱερῶν χρηματίζειν,
τρία δὲ κήρυξιν καὶ πρεσβείαις, τρία δ' ὁσίων.
χρηματίζουσιν δ' ἐνίοτε καὶ ἄνευ προχειροτονίας.
προσέρχονται δὲ καὶ οἱ κήρυκες καὶ οἱ πρέσβεις
τοῖς πρυτάνεσιν πρῶτον, καὶ οἱ τὰς ἐπιστολὰς
φέροντες τούτοις ἀποδιδόασι.

1 XLIV. Ἔστι δ' ἐπιστάτης τῶν πρυτάνεων εἷς ὁ
λαχών· οὗτος δ' ἐπιστατεῖ νύκτα καὶ ἡμέραν, καὶ
οὐκ ἔστιν οὔτε πλείω χρόνον οὔτε δὶς τὸν αὐτὸν
γενέσθαι. τηρεῖ δ' οὗτος τάς τε κλεῖς τὰς τῶν
ἱερῶν ἐν οἷς τὰ χρήματ' ἐστὶν καὶ τὰ[1] γράμματα
τῇ πόλει, καὶ τὴν δημοσίαν σφραγῖδα, καὶ μένειν
ἀναγκαῖον ἐν τῇ θόλῳ τοῦτόν ἐστιν καὶ τριττὺν
2 τῶν πρυτάνεων ἣν ἂν οὗτος κελεύῃ. καὶ ἐπειδὰν
συναγάγωσιν οἱ πρυτάνεις τὴν βουλὴν ἢ τὸν δῆμον
οὗτος κληροῖ προέδρους ἐννέα, ἕνα ἐκ τῆς φυλῆς
ἑκάστης πλὴν τῆς πρυτανευούσης, καὶ πάλιν ἐκ
τούτων ἐπιστάτην ἕνα, καὶ παραδίδωσι τὸ πρό-
3 γραμμα αὐτοῖς· οἱ δὲ παραλαβόντες τῆς τ' εὐ-
κοσμίας ἐπιμελοῦνται καὶ ὑπὲρ ὧν δεῖ χρηματίζειν
προτιθέασιν καὶ τὰς χειροτονίας κρίνουσιν καὶ τὰ
ἄλλα πάντα διοικοῦσιν καὶ τοῦ[2] ἀφεῖναι κύριοί εἰσιν.

[1] τὰ suppletum ab edd.
[2] τοῦ Richards: τουτ cod.: τοῦ δ' Hude.

to the number of not more than three cases of either class, and charges of failure to perform a service promised to the People. Another meeting 6
is given to petitions, at which anyone who wishes, after placing a suppliant-branch,[a] may speak to the People about any matter he may wish whether public or private. The two other meetings deal with all other business, at which the laws enact that three cases of sacred matters are to be dealt with, three audiences for heralds and embassies, and three cases of secular matters. And sometimes they do business without a preliminary vote being taken. Also the Presidents give a first audience to heralds and to ambassadors, and to the Presidents dispatches are delivered by their bearers.

XLIV. The Presidents have a single Head elected 1
by lot; he holds office for a day and a night, and may not hold office longer, nor serve a second time. He is keeper of the keys of the temples in which the money and documents of the state are lodged, and of the state seal, and he is required to stay in the Round-house, and so is whichever Third[b] of the Presidential Boards he orders. And whenever the 2
Presidents call a meeting of the Council or of the People, this official selects by lot nine Chairmen, one from each tribe except the tribe presiding, and again from these a single Head, and he hands over the list of agenda to them; and after receiving it they super- 3
intend procedure, bring forward the business to be dealt with, act as tellers, direct all the other business and have power to dismiss the meeting. A man

[a] An olive-branch wreathed with wool was carried by the 'suppliant' and placed on the altar in the assembly.

[b] See viii. 30 n.

καὶ ἐπιστατῆσαι μὲν οὐκ ἔξεστιν πλεῖον ἢ ἅπαξ ἐν τῷ ἐνιαυτῷ, προεδρεύειν δ' ἔξεστιν ἅπαξ ἐπὶ τῆς πρυτανείας ἑκάστης.

4 Ποιοῦσι δὲ καὶ ἀρχαιρεσίας[1] στρατηγῶν καὶ ἱππάρχων καὶ τῶν ἄλλων τῶν πρὸς τὸν πόλεμον ἀρχῶν ἐν τῇ ἐκκλησίᾳ, καθ' ὅ τι ἂν τῷ δήμῳ δοκῇ· ποιοῦσι δ' οἱ μετὰ τὴν ϛʹ πρυτανεύοντες ἐφ' ὧν ἂν εὐσημία γένηται. δεῖ δὲ προβούλευμα γενέσθαι καὶ περὶ τούτων.

1 XLV. Ἡ δὲ βουλὴ πρότερον μὲν ἦν κυρία καὶ χρήμασιν ζημιῶσαι καὶ δῆσαι καὶ ἀποκτεῖναι. καὶ Λυσίμαχον δ'[2] αὐτῆς ἀγαγούσης ὡς τὸν δήμιον, καθήμενον ἤδη μέλλοντα ἀποθνήσκειν Εὐμηλίδης ὁ Ἀλωπεκῆθεν ἀφείλετο, οὐ φάσκων δεῖν ἄνευ δικαστηρίου γνώσεως οὐδένα τῶν πολιτῶν ἀποθνήσκειν· καὶ κρίσεως ἐν δικαστηρίῳ γενομένης ὁ μὲν Λυσίμαχος ἀπέφυγεν, καὶ ἐπωνυμίαν ἔσχεν ὁ ἀπὸ τοῦ τυπάνου· ὁ δὲ δῆμος ἀφείλετο τῆς βουλῆς τὸ θανατοῦν καὶ δεῖν καὶ χρήμασι ζημιοῦν, καὶ νόμον ἔθετο, ἄν τινος ἀδικεῖν ἡ βουλὴ καταγνῷ ἢ ζημιώσῃ, τὰς καταγνώσεις καὶ τὰς ἐπιζημιώσεις εἰσάγειν τοὺς θεσμοθέτας εἰς τὸ δικαστήριον, καὶ ὅ τι ἂν οἱ δικασταὶ ψηφίσωνται τοῦτο κύριον εἶναι.

2 Κρίνει δὲ τὰς ἀρχὰς ἡ βουλὴ τὰς πλείστας, καὶ μάλισθ' ὅσαι χρήματα διαχειρίζουσιν· οὐ κυρία δ' ἡ κρίσις ἀλλ' ἐφέσιμος εἰς τὸ δικαστήριον. ἔξεστι δὲ καὶ τοῖς ἰδιώταις εἰσαγγέλλειν ἣν ἂν βούλωνται

[1] edd.: δεκαιδεκαρχαιρεσιας (dittographia) cod.
[2] Λυσίμαχον δ' Papageorgios: καιλυσιμαχον codex.

cannot become Head more than once a year, but he can be Chairman once in each presidency.

They also conduct elections of Generals, and 4
Cavalry Commanders and the other military officers in the Assembly, in whatever manner seems good to the People ; and these elections are held by the first board of Presidents, after the sixth Presidency,[a] in whose term of office favourable weather-omens may occur. These matters also require a preliminary resolution of the Council.

XLV. The Council formerly had sovereign power 1
to pass sentences of fine, imprisonment and death. But once it had brought Lysimachus to the public executioner, when, as he already sat awaiting death, Eumelides of the deme Alopecē rescued him, saying that no citizen ought to die without sentence by a jury ; and when a trial was held in a jury-court Lysimachus got off, and he got the nickname of 'the man from the drum-stick'[b] ; and the People deprived the Council of the power to sentence to death and imprisonment and to impose fines, and made a law that all verdicts of guilty and penalties passed by the Council must be brought before the jury-court by the Legislators, and that any vote of the jurymen should be sovereign.

Trials of officials are held in most cases by the 2
Council, particularly those of the officials who handle funds ; but the verdict of the Council is not sovereign, but subject to appeal to the jury-court. Private persons also have the right to lay an information

[a] *i.e.* the Presidents holding the seventh or a later term of office, see xliii. 2. Rain, thunder, etc., were bad omens, but the regulation had a practical value for the open-air meetings in the Pnyx.

[b] *i.e.* the man who escaped the bastinado.

τῶν ἀρχῶν μὴ χρῆσθαι τοῖς νόμοις· ἔφεσις δὲ καὶ τούτοις ἐστὶν εἰς τὸ δικαστήριον ἐὰν αὐτῶν ἡ βουλὴ καταγνῷ.

3 Δοκιμάζει δὲ καὶ τοὺς βουλευτὰς τοὺς τὸν ὕστερον ἐνιαυτὸν βουλεύσοντας καὶ τοὺς ἐννέα ἄρχοντας. καὶ πρότερον μὲν ἦν ἀποδοκιμάσαι κυρία, νῦν δὲ τούτοις[1] ἔφεσίς ἐστιν εἰς τὸ δικαστήριον.

4 Τούτων μὲν οὖν ἄκυρός ἐστιν ἡ βουλή, προβουλεύει δ' εἰς τὸν δῆμον, καὶ οὐκ ἔξεστιν οὐδὲν ἀπροβούλευτον οὐδ' ὅ τι ἂν μὴ προγράψωσιν οἱ πρυτάνεις ψηφίσασθαι τῷ δήμῳ· κατ' αὐτὰ γὰρ ταῦτα ἔνοχός ἐστιν ὁ νίκησας γραφῇ παρανόμων.

1 XLVI. Ἐπιμελεῖται δὲ καὶ τῶν πεποιημένων τριήρων καὶ τῶν σκευῶν καὶ τῶν νεωσοίκων, καὶ ποιεῖται καινὰς[2] τριήρεις ἢ τετρήρεις, ὁποτέρας ἂν ὁ δῆμος χειροτονήσῃ, καὶ σκεύη ταύταις καὶ νεωσοίκους· χειροτονεῖ δ' ἀρχιτέκτονας ὁ δῆμος ἐπὶ τὰς ναῦς. ἂν δὲ μὴ παραδῶσιν ἐξειργασμένα ταῦτα τῇ νέᾳ βουλῇ, τὴν δωρεὰν οὐκ ἔστιν αὐτοῖς λαβεῖν· ἐπὶ γὰρ τῆς ὕστερον βουλῆς λαμβάνουσιν. ποιεῖται δὲ τὰς τριήρεις, δέκα ἄνδρας ἐξ αὐτῆς
2 ἑλομένη τριηροποιούς. ἐξετάζει δὲ καὶ τὰ οἰκοδομήματα τὰ δημόσια πάντα, κἄν τις ἀδικεῖν αὐτῇ δόξῃ τῷ τε δήμῳ τοῦτον ἀποφαίνει καὶ καταγνοῦσα[3] παραδίδωσι δικαστηρίῳ.

1 XLVII. Συνδιοικεῖ δὲ καὶ ταῖς ἄλλαις ἀρχαῖς τὰ πλεῖστα. πρῶτον μὲν γὰρ οἱ ταμίαι τῆς Ἀθηνᾶς εἰσὶ μὲν δέκα, κληροῦται δ' εἷς ἐκ τῆς φυλῆς, ἐκ πεντακοσιομεδίμνων κατὰ τὸν Σόλωνος

[1] ⟨καὶ⟩ τούτοις Wilamowitz-Kaibel.
[2] καινὰς Kenyon: καινασδε cod.
[3] καταγνόντος Wilamowitz-Kaibel.

of illegal procedure against any official they may wish; but in these cases also there is an appeal to the People if the Council passes a verdict of guilty.

The Council also checks the qualifications of the 3
Councillors who are to hold office for the following year, and of the Nine Archons. And formerly it had sovereign power to reject them as disqualified, but now they have an appeal to the jury-court.

In these matters therefore the Council is not 4
sovereign, but it prepares resolutions for the People, and the People cannot pass any measures that have not been prepared by the Council and published in writing in advance by the Presidents; for the proposer who carries such a measure is *ipso facto* liable to penalty by indictment for illegal procedure.

XLVI. The Council also inspects triremes after 1
construction, and their rigging, and the naval sheds, and has new triremes or quadriremes, whichever the People votes for, built and rigged, and naval sheds built; but naval architects are elected by the People. If the outgoing Council does not hand over these works completed to the new Council, the members cannot draw their honorarium, which is payable when the next Council is in office. For the building of triremes it elects ten of its own members as Naval Constructors. It also inspects all public buildings, 2
and if it finds any commissioner in default it reports him to the People, and if it gets a verdict of guilty hands him over to a jury-court.

XLVII. The Council also shares in the administra- 1
tion of the other offices in most affairs. First there are the ten Treasurers of Athena, elected one from a tribe by lot, from the Five-hundred-bushel class, according to the law of Solon (which is still in force),

νόμον (ἔτι γὰρ ὁ νόμος κύριός ἐστιν), ἄρχει δ' ὁ λαχὼν κἂν πάνυ πένης ᾖ. παραλαμβάνουσι δὲ τό τε ἄγαλμα τῆς Ἀθηνᾶς καὶ τὰς Νίκας καὶ τὸν ἄλλον κόσμον καὶ τὰ χρήματα ἐναντίον τῆς βουλῆς.

2 Ἔπειθ' οἱ πωληταὶ ι' μέν εἰσι, κληροῦται δ' εἷς ἐκ τῆς φυλῆς. μισθοῦσι δὲ τὰ μισθώματα πάντα καὶ τὰ μέταλλα πωλοῦσι καὶ τὰ τέλη μετὰ τοῦ ταμίου τῶν στρατιωτικῶν καὶ τῶν ἐπὶ τὸ θεωρικὸν ᾑρημένων ἐναντίον τῆς βουλῆς, καὶ κυροῦσιν ὅτῳ ἂν ἡ βουλὴ χειροτονήσῃ, καὶ τὰ πραθέντα μέταλλα τά τ' ἐργάσιμα[1] τὰ εἰς τρία ἔτη πεπραμένα καὶ τὰ συγκεχωρημένα τὰ εἰς . . .[2] ἔτη πεπραμένα. καὶ τὰς οὐσίας τῶν ἐξ Ἀρείου πάγου φευγόντων καὶ τῶν ἄλλων ἐναντίον τῆς βουλῆς πωλοῦσιν, κατακυροῦσι δ' οἱ θ' ἄρχοντες. καὶ τὰ τέλη τὰ εἰς ἐνιαυτὸν πεπραμένα ἀναγράψαντες εἰς λελευκωμένα γραμματεῖα τόν τε πριάμενον καὶ ὅσου[3] ἂν πρίηται τῇ
3 βουλῇ παραδιδόασιν. ἀναγράφουσιν δὲ χωρὶς μὲν οὓς δεῖ κατὰ πρυτανείαν ἑκάστην καταβάλλειν εἰς δέκα γραμματεῖα, χωρὶς δ' οὓς τρὶς τοῦ ἐνιαυτοῦ, γραμματεῖον κατὰ τὴν καταβολὴν ἑκάστην ποιήσαντες, χωρὶς δ' οὓς ἐπὶ τῆς ἐνάτης πρυτανείας. ἀναγράφουσι δὲ καὶ τὰ χωρία καὶ τὰς οἰκίας τἀπογραφέντα καὶ πραθέντα ἐν τῷ δικαστηρίῳ· καὶ γὰρ ταῦθ' οὗτοι πωλοῦσιν. ἔστι δὲ τῶν μὲν οἰκιῶν ἐν ε' ἔτεσιν ἀνάγκη τὴν τιμὴν ἀποδοῦναι,

[1] τά τ' ⟨ἄργα καὶ τὰ⟩ ἐργάσιμα Sandys.
[2] numerum rasum alii ι', alii γ' legunt.
[3] erasum supplevit Wilamowitz.

[a] Golden figures, kept in the Parthenon; probably there

and the one on whom the lot falls holds office even though he is quite a poor man. They take over the custody of the statue of Athena and the Victories[a] and the other monuments and the funds in the presence of the Council.

Then there are the ten Vendors, elected by lot 2
one from a tribe. They farm out all public contracts and sell the mines and the taxes, with the co-operation of the Treasurer of Military Funds and those elected to superintend the Spectacle Fund, in the presence of the Council, and ratify the purchase for the person for whom the Council votes, and the mines sold and the workings that have been sold for three years and the concessions sold for . . .[b] years. And the estates of persons banished by the Areopagus and of the others they sell at a meeting of the Council, but the sale is ratified by the Nine Archons. And they draw up and furnish to the Council a list written on whitened tablets[c] of the taxes sold for a year, showing the purchaser and the price that he is paying. And 3
they draw up ten separate lists of those who have to pay in each presidency, and separate lists of those who have to pay three times in the year, making a list for each date of payment, and a separate list of those who have to pay in the ninth presidency. They also draw up a list of the farms and houses written off[d] and sold in the jury-court; for these sales are also conducted by these officials. Payment must be made for purchases of houses within five years, and for

had been ten, but eight were melted down for coinage towards the end of the Peloponnesian War.

[b] The number half erased may be 10 or 3.

[c] Wooden boards coated with chalk, on which notices were scratched; they could be easily rubbed off, *cf.* xlviii. 1.

[d] *i.e.* registered as confiscated.

τῶν δὲ χωρίων ἐν δέκα· καταβάλλουσιν δὲ ταῦτα
4 ἐπὶ τῆς ἐνάτης πρυτανείας. εἰσφέρει δὲ καὶ ὁ
βασιλεὺς τὰς μισθώσεις τῶν τεμενῶν ἀναγράψας
ἐν γραμματείοις λελευκωμένοις. ἔστι δὲ καὶ τούτων ἡ μὲν μίσθωσις εἰς ἔτη δέκα, καταβάλλεται
δ' ἐπὶ τῆς θ' πρυτανείας· διὸ καὶ πλεῖστα χρή-
5 ματα ἐπὶ ταύτης συλλέγεται τῆς πρυτανείας. εἰσ-
φέρεται μὲν οὖν εἰς τὴν βουλὴν τὰ γραμματεῖα
κατὰ τὰς καταβολὰς ἀναγεγραμμένα, τηρεῖ δ' ὁ
δημόσιος· ὅταν δ' ᾖ χρημάτων καταβολή, παραδίδωσι τοῖς ἀποδέκταις αὐτὰ ταῦτα καθελὼν ἀπὸ
τῶν ἐπιστυλίων ὧν ἐν ταύτῃ τῇ ἡμέρᾳ δεῖ τὰ
χρήματα καταβληθῆναι καὶ ἀπαλειφθῆναι, τὰ δ'
ἄλλα ἀπόκειται χωρὶς ἵνα μὴ προεξαλειφθῇ.

1 XLVIII. Εἰσὶ δ' ἀποδέκται δέκα κεκληρωμένοι
κατὰ φυλάς· οὗτοι δὲ παραλαβόντες τὰ γραμματεῖα
ἀπαλείφουσι τὰ καταβαλλόμενα χρήματα ἐναντίον
τῆς βουλῆς ἐν τῷ βουλευτηρίῳ καὶ πάλιν ἀποδιδόασιν τὰ γραμματεῖα τῷ δημοσίῳ· κἄν τις ἐλλίπῃ
καταβολήν, ἐνταῦθ' ἐγγέγραπται, καὶ διπλασίαν
ἀνάγκη τὸ ἐλλειφθὲν καταβάλλειν ἢ δεδέσθαι·
καὶ ταῦτα εἰσπράττειν ἡ βουλὴ καὶ δῆσαι κυρία
2 κατὰ τοὺς νόμους ἐστίν. τῇ μὲν οὖν προτεραίᾳ
δέχονται τὰς καταβολὰς[1] καὶ μερίζουσι ταῖς ἀρχαῖς,
τῇ δ' ὑστεραίᾳ τόν τε μερισμὸν εἰσφέρουσι γράψαντες
ἐν σανίδι καὶ καταλέγουσιν ἐν τῷ βουλευτηρίῳ,
καὶ προτιθέασιν ἐν τῇ βουλῇ εἴ τίς τινα οἶδεν
ἀδικοῦντα περὶ τὸν μερισμὸν ἢ ἄρχοντα ἢ ἰδιώτην,
καὶ γνώμας ἐπιψηφίζουσιν ἐάν τίς τι δοκῇ ἀδικεῖν.

[1] τὰς καταβολὰς (vel τὰς πάσας) Kaibel: τα . . . . . . s cod.

farms within ten; and they make these payments in the ninth presidency.
Also the King-archon intro- 4
duces the letting of domains, having made a list of them on whitened tablets. These also are let for ten years, and the rent is paid in the ninth presidency; hence in that presidency a very large revenue comes in.
The tablets written up with the list of pay- 5
ments are brought before the Council, but are in the keeping of the official clerk; and whenever a payment of money is made, he takes down from the pillars and hands over to the receivers just these tablets showing the persons whose money is to be paid on that day and wiped off the record, but the other tablets are stored away separately in order that they may not be wiped off before payment is made.

XLVIII. There are ten Receivers elected by lot, 1
one from each tribe; these take over the tablets and wipe off[a] the sums paid in the presence of the Council in the Council-chamber, and give the tablets back again to the official clerk; and anybody that has defaulted in a payment is entered on them, and has to pay double the amount of his arrears or go to prison; and the legal authority to impose this fine and imprisonment is the Council.
On the first day, 2
therefore, they receive the payments and apportion them among the magistrates, and on the second day they introduce the apportionment, written on a wooden tablet, and recount it in the Council-chamber, and bring forward in the Council any case in which somebody knows of anyone, either an official or a private person, having committed a wrong in relation to the apportionment, and put resolutions to the vote in case anyone is found to have committed any wrong.

[a] See xlvii. 2 n.

3 Κληροῦσι δὲ καὶ λογιστὰς ἐξ αὑτῶν οἱ βουλευταὶ δέκα τοὺς λογιουμένους ταῖς ἀρχαῖς κατὰ τὴν
4 πρυτανείαν ἑκάστην. κληροῦσι δὲ καὶ εὐθύνους, ἕνα τῆς φυλῆς ἑκάστης, καὶ παρέδρους β′ ἑκάστῳ τῶν εὐθύνων, οἷς ἀναγκαῖόν ἐστι ταῖς ἀγοραῖς[1] κατὰ τὸν ἐπώνυμον τὸν τῆς φυλῆς ἑκάστης καθῆσθαι, κἄν τις βούληταί τινι τῶν τὰς εὐθύνας ἐν τῷ δικαστηρίῳ δεδωκότων ἐντὸς γ′ ἡμερῶν ἀφ᾽ ἧς ἔδωκε τὰς εὐθύνας εὔθυναν ἄν τ᾽ ἰδίαν ἄν τε δημοσίαν ἐμβαλέσθαι, γράψας εἰς πινάκιον λελευκωμένον τοὔνομα τό θ᾽ αὑτοῦ καὶ τὸ τοῦ φεύγοντος καὶ τὸ ἀδίκημ᾽ ὅ τι ἂν ἐγκαλῇ, καὶ τίμημα ἐπιγραψάμενος ὅ τι ἂν αὐτῷ δοκῇ, δίδωσιν τῷ εὐθύνῳ·
5 ὁ δὲ λαβὼν τοῦτο καὶ ἀναγνούς, ἐὰν[2] καταγνῷ παραδίδωσιν τὰ μὲν ἴδια τοῖς δικασταῖς τοῖς κατὰ δήμους τοῖς τὴν φυλὴν ταύτην εἰσάγουσιν,[3] τὰ δὲ δημόσια τοῖς θεσμοθέταις ἐπιγράφει. οἱ δὲ θεσμοθέται ἐὰν παραλάβωσιν πάλιν εἰσάγουσιν ταύτην τὴν[4] εὔθυναν εἰς τὸ δικαστήριον, καὶ ὅ τι ἂν γνῶσιν οἱ δικασταὶ τοῦτο κύριόν ἐστιν.

1 XLIX. Δοκιμάζει δὲ καὶ τοὺς ἵππους ἡ βουλή, κἂν μέν τις καλὸν ἵππον ἔχων κακῶς δοκῇ τρέφειν, ζημιοῖ τῷ σίτῳ, τοῖς δὲ μὴ δυναμένοις ἀκολουθεῖν ἢ μὴ θέλουσι μένειν ἀλλ᾽ ἀνάγουσι[5] τροχὸν ἐπὶ τὴν γνάθον ἐπιβάλλει, καὶ ὁ τοῦτο[6] παθὼν ἀδόκιμός ἐστι. δοκιμάζει δὲ καὶ τοὺς

[1] Kenyon, sed γ incertum, ορ desunt.
[2] ἐὰν Herwerden: εανμεν cod.
[3] δικάζουσιν Richards.
[4] ταύτην ante τὴν supplet Blass.
[5] ἀλλ᾽ ἀνάγουσι Blass, sed incertum: ἀλλ᾽ ἀναγ⟨ώγοις⟩ οὖσι ('unbroken') Wyse.
[6] γνάθον . . . τοῦτο Blass (et partim alii): γναθ . . . ουτο cod.

The Council also elect by lot ten of their own body 3
as Accountants, to keep the accounts of the officials
for each presidency. Also they elect by lot Auditors, 4
one for each tribe, and two Assessors for each Auditor,
who are required to sit at the tribal meetings according to the hero after whom each tribe is named,[a] and if anyone wishes to prefer a charge, of either a private or a public nature, against any magistrate who has rendered his accounts before the jury-court, within three days from the day on which he rendered his accounts, he writes on a tablet his own name and that of the defendant, and the offence of which he accuses him, adding whatever fine he thinks suitable, and gives it to the Auditor;
and the Auditor takes it and reads it, and if he con- 5
siders the charge proved, he hands it over, if a private case, to those jurymen in the villages who introduced this tribe, and if a public suit, he marks it to the Legislators. And the Legislators, if they receive it, introduce this audit again before the jury-court, and the verdict of the jurymen holds good.

XLIX. The Council also inspects the Knights' 1
chargers, and if anybody having a good horse keeps it in bad condition, it fines him the cost of the feed, and horses that cannot keep up with the squadron or will not stay in line but jib it brands on the jaw with the sign of a wheel, and a horse so treated has failed to pass the inspection. It also inspects

[a] *i.e.* one Auditor and two Assessors are assigned to each tribe, the assignment being indicated by the name of the hero after whom the tribe was named. See liii. 5 n.

προδρόμους ὅσοι ἂν αὐτῇ δοκῶσιν ἐπιτήδειοι προδρομεύειν εἶναι, κἄν τιν' ἀποχειροτονήσῃ, καταβέβηκεν οὗτος. δοκιμάζει δὲ καὶ τοὺς ἁμίππους, κἄν τινα ἀποχειροτονήσῃ, πέπαυται μισθοφορῶν

2 οὗτος. τοὺς δ' ἱππέας καταλέγουσιν οἱ καταλογεῖς, οὓς ἂν ὁ δῆμος χειροτονήσῃ δέκα ἄνδρας· οὓς δ' ἂν καταλέξωσι παραδιδόασι τοῖς ἱππάρχοις καὶ φυλάρχοις, οὗτοι δὲ παραλαβόντες εἰσφέρουσι τὸν κατάλογον εἰς τὴν βουλὴν καὶ τὸν πίνακα ἀνοίξαντες ἐν ᾧ κατασεσημασμένα τὰ ὀνόματα τῶν ἱππέων ἐστί, τοὺς μὲν ἐξομνυμένους τῶν πρότερον ἐγγεγραμμένων μὴ δυνατοὺς εἶναι τοῖς σώμασιν ἱππεύειν ἐξαλείφουσι, τοὺς δὲ κατειλεγμένους καλοῦσι, κἂν μέν τις ἐξομόσηται μὴ δύνασθαι τῷ σώματι ἱππεύειν ἢ τῇ οὐσίᾳ τοῦτον ἀφιᾶσιν, τὸν δὲ μὴ ἐξομνύμενον διαχειροτονοῦσιν οἱ βουλευταὶ πότερον ἐπιτήδειός ἐστιν ἱππεύειν ἢ οὔ· κἂν μὲν χειροτονήσωσιν, ἐγγράφουσιν εἰς τὸν πίνακα, εἰ δὲ μή, καὶ τοῦτον ἀφιᾶσιν.

3 Ἔκρινεν δέ ποτε καὶ τὰ παραδείγματα καὶ[1] τὸν πέπλον ἡ βουλή, νῦν δὲ τὸ δικαστήριον τὸ λαχόν· ἐδόκουν γὰρ οὗτοι καταχαρίζεσθαι τὴν κρίσιν. καὶ τῆς ποιήσεως τῶν Νικῶν καὶ τῶν ἄθλων τῶν εἰς τὰ Παναθήναια συνεπιμελεῖται μετὰ τοῦ ταμίου τῶν στρατιωτικῶν.

4 Δοκιμάζει δὲ καὶ τοὺς ἀδυνάτους ἡ βουλή· νόμος γάρ ἐστιν ὃς κελεύει τοὺς ἐντὸς τριῶν μνῶν κεκτημένους καὶ τὸ σῶμα πεπηρωμένους ὥστε

[1] καὶ] τὰ εἰς coniecit Blass.

[a] Woven for Athena at every Panathenaic Festival and carried in the procession.

the mounted skirmishers, to see which it considers fit for skirmishing duty, and any that it votes to reject are thereby deposed from that rank. It also inspects the foot-soldiers that fight in the ranks of the cavalry, and anyone it votes against is thereby stopped from drawing his pay. The Knights' 2
roll is made by the ten Roll-keepers elected by the People; and they pass on the names of all whom they enroll to the Cavalry Commanders and Tribe Commanders, and these take over the roll and bring it into the Council, and opening the tablet on which the names of the Knights have been inscribed, they delete those among the persons previously entered who claim on oath exemption from cavalry service on the ground of bodily incapacity, and summon those enrolled, and grant discharge to anyone who claims exemption on oath on the ground of bodily incapacity for cavalry service or lack of means, and as to those who do not claim exemption the Councillors decide by vote whether they are fit for cavalry service or not; and if they vote for them as fit they enter them on the tablet, but if not, these also they dismiss.

At one time the Council used also to judge the 3
patterns for the Robe,[a] but now this is done by the jury-court selected by lot, because the Council was thought to show favouritism in its decision. And the Council has joint supervision with the Steward of the Army Funds over the construction of the Victories and over the prizes for the Panathenaic Games.

The Council also inspects the Incapables; for 4
there is a law enacting that persons possessing less than 3 minae [b] and incapacitated by bodily infirmity

[b] See iv. 4 n.

μὴ δύνασθαι μηδὲν ἔργον ἐργάζεσθαι δοκιμάζειν μὲν τὴν βουλήν, διδόναι δὲ δημοσίᾳ τροφὴν δύο ὀβολοὺς ἑκάστῳ τῆς ἡμέρας. καὶ ταμίας ἐστὶν αὐτοῖς κληρωτός.

Συνδιοικεῖ δὲ καὶ ταῖς ἄλλαις ἀρχαῖς τὰ πλεῖσθ' ὡς ἔπος εἰπεῖν.

1 L. Τὰ μὲν οὖν ὑπὸ τῆς βουλῆς διοικούμενα ταῦτ' ἐστίν. κληροῦνται δὲ καὶ ἱερῶν ἐπισκευασταὶ δέκα ἄνδρες, οἳ λαμβάνοντες τριάκοντα μνᾶς παρὰ τῶν ἀποδεκτῶν ἐπισκευάζουσιν τὰ μάλιστα
2 δεόμενα τῶν ἱερῶν, καὶ ἀστυνόμοι δέκα· τούτων δὲ ε′ μὲν ἄρχουσιν ἐν Πειραιεῖ πέντε δ' ἐν ἄστει, καὶ τάς τε αὐλητρίδας καὶ τὰς ψαλτρίας καὶ τὰς κιθαριστρίας οὗτοι σκοποῦσιν ὅπως μὴ πλείονος ἢ δυεῖν δραχμαῖς μισθωθήσονται, κἂν πλείους τὴν αὐτὴν σπουδάσωσι λαβεῖν οὗτοι διακληροῦσι καὶ τῷ λαχόντι μισθοῦσιν. καὶ ὅπως τῶν κοπρολόγων μηδεὶς ἐντὸς ι′ σταδίων τοῦ τείχους καταβαλεῖ κόπρον ἐπιμελοῦνται, καὶ τὰς ὁδοὺς κωλύουσι κατοικοδομεῖν καὶ δρυφάκτους ὑπὲρ τῶν ὁδῶν ὑπερτείνειν καὶ ὀχετοὺς μετεώρους εἰς τὴν ὁδὸν ἔκρουν ἔχοντας ποιεῖν καὶ τὰς θυρίδας εἰς τὴν ὁδὸν ἀνοίγειν· καὶ τοὺς ἐν ταῖς ὁδοῖς ἀπογιγνομένους ἀναιροῦσιν, ἔχοντες δημοσίους ὑπηρέτας.

1 LI. Κληροῦνται δὲ καὶ ἀγορανόμοι ι′,[1] πέντε μὲν εἰς Πειραιέα, ε′ δ' εἰς ἄστυ. τούτοις δὲ ὑπὸ τῶν νόμων προστέτακται τῶν ὠνίων ἐπιμελεῖσθαι πάντων, ὅπως καθαρὰ καὶ ἀκίβδηλα πωλῆται.

2 Κληροῦνται δὲ καὶ μετρονόμοι ι′,[1] πέντε μὲν εἰς ἄστυ, ε′ δὲ εἰς Πειραιέα· καὶ οὗτοι τῶν μέτρων

[1] numerum ι′ bis supplevit Papageorgios.

from doing any work are to be inspected by the Council, which is to give them a grant for food at the public expense at the rate of 2 obols[a] a day each. And there is a Treasurer for these persons, elected by lot.

The Council also shares in the administration of virtually the greatest number of the duties of the other offices.

L. These then are the matters administered by the 1
Council. Also ten men are elected by lot as Restorers of Temples, who draw 30 minae[b] from the Receivers and repair the temples that most require it; and ten
City Controllers, five of whom hold office in Peiraeus 2
and five in the city; it is they who supervise the flute-girls and harp-girls and lyre-girls to prevent their receiving fees of more than two drachmas,[b] and if several persons want to take the same girl these officials cast lots between them and hire her out to the winner. And they keep watch to prevent any scavenger from depositing ordure within a mile and a quarter of the wall; and they prevent the construction of buildings encroaching on and balconies overhanging the roads, of overhead conduits with an overflow into the road, and of windows opening outward on to the road; and they remove for burial the bodies of persons who die on the roads, having public slaves for this service.

LI. Also Market-controllers are elected by lot, five 1
for Peiraeus and five for the city. To these the laws assign the superintendence of all merchandise, to prevent the sale of adulterated and spurious articles.

Also ten Controllers of Measures are appointed by 2
lot, five for the city and five for Peiraeus, who super-

[a] Say threepence.
[b] See iv. 4 n.

καὶ τῶν σταθμῶν ἐπιμελοῦνται πάντων, ὅπως οἱ πωλοῦντες χρήσωνται[1] δικαίοις.

3 Ἦσαν δὲ καὶ σιτοφύλακες κληρωτοὶ ι′,[2] πέντε μὲν εἰς Πειραιέα, πέντε δ' εἰς ἄστυ, νῦν δ' εἴκοσι μὲν εἰς ἄστυ, πεντεκαίδεκα δ' εἰς Πειραιέα. οὗτοι δ' ἐπιμελοῦνται πρῶτον μὲν ὅπως ὁ ἐν ἀγορᾷ σῖτος ἀργὸς ὤνιος ἔσται δικαίως, ἔπειθ' ὅπως οἵ τε μυλωθροὶ πρὸς τὰς τιμὰς τῶν κριθῶν τὰ ἄλφιτα πωλήσουσιν καὶ οἱ ἀρτοπῶλαι πρὸς τὰς τιμὰς τῶν πυρῶν τοὺς ἄρτους, καὶ τὸν σταθμὸν ἄγοντας ὅσον ἂν οὗτοι τάξωσιν· ὁ γὰρ νόμος τούτους κελεύει τάττειν.

4 Ἐμπορίου δ' ἐπιμελητὰς δέκα κληροῦσιν· τούτοις δὲ προστέτακται τῶν τ' ἐμπορίων ἐπιμελεῖσθαι, καὶ τοῦ σίτου τοῦ καταπλέοντος εἰς τὸ σιτικὸν[3] ἐμπόριον τὰ δύο μέρη τοὺς ἐμπόρους ἀναγκάζειν εἰς τὸ ἄστυ κομίζειν.

1 LII. Καθιστᾶσι δὲ καὶ τοὺς ἕνδεκα κληρωτούς, ἐπιμελησομένους τῶν ἐν τῷ δεσμωτηρίῳ, καὶ τοὺς ἀπαγομένους κλέπτας καὶ τοὺς ἀνδραποδιστὰς καὶ τοὺς λωποδύτας ἂν μὲν ὁμολογῶσι θανάτῳ ζημιώσοντας, ἂν δ' ἀμφισβητῶσιν εἰσάξοντας εἰς τὸ δικαστήριον, κἂν μὲν ἀποφύγωσιν ἀφήσοντας, εἰ δὲ μὴ τότε θανατώσοντας, καὶ τὰ ἀπογραφόμενα χωρία καὶ οἰκίας εἰσάξοντας εἰς τὸ δικαστήριον καὶ τὰ δόξαντα δημόσια εἶναι παραδώσοντας τοῖς πωληταῖς, καὶ τὰς ἐνδείξεις εἰσάξοντας—καὶ γὰρ ταύτας εἰσάγουσιν οἱ ἕνδεκα· εἰσάγουσι δὲ τῶν ἐνδείξεών τινας καὶ οἱ θεσμοθέται.

[1] χρήσονται Rutherford.

[2] ι′ suppletum ex Harpocratione a Wilamowitz-Kaibel.

[3] ἀστικὸν vel Ἀττικὸν edd. (v.ll. ex Harpocratione).

intend all measures and weights, in order that sellers may use just ones.

Also there used to be ten Corn-wardens elected by 3
lot, five for Peiraeus and five for the city, but now there are twenty for the city and fifteen for Peiraeus. Their duties are first to see that unground corn in the market is on sale at a fair price, and next that millers sell barley-meal at a price corresponding with that of barley, and bakers loaves at a price corresponding with that of wheat, and weighing the amount fixed by the officials—for the law orders that these shall fix the weights.

They elect by lot ten Port-superintendents, whose 4
duty is to superintend the harbour-markets and to compel the traders to bring to the city two-thirds of the sea-borne corn that reaches the corn-market.

LII. They also appoint the Eleven, officers chosen 1
by lot to superintend the persons in the prison, and to punish with death people arrested as thieves and kidnappers and footpads that confess their guilt, but if they deny the charge to bring them before the Jury-court, and if they are acquitted discharge them, but if not then to execute them ; and to bring before the Jury-court lists of farms and houses declared to be public property and to hand over to the Vendors [a] those that it is decided to confiscate ; and to bring in informations—for these too are brought in by the Eleven, though the Legislators also bring in some informations.

[a] See xlvii. 2.

2 Κληροῦσι δὲ καὶ εἰσαγωγέας ε´ ἄνδρας, οἳ τὰς ἐμμήνους εἰσάγουσι δίκας, δυοῖν φυλαῖν ἕκαστος. εἰσὶ δ᾽ ἔμμηνοι προικός, ἐάν τις ὀφείλων μὴ ἀποδῷ, κἄν τις ἐπὶ δραχμῇ δανεισάμενος ἀποστερῇ, κἄν τις ἐν ἀγορᾷ βουλόμενος ἐργάζεσθαι δανείσηται παρά τινος ἀφορμήν· ἔτι δ᾽ αἰκείας καὶ ἐρανικὰς καὶ κοινωνικὰς καὶ ἀνδραπόδων καὶ ὑποζυγίων
3 καὶ τριηραρχίας καὶ τραπεζιτικάς.[1] οὗτοι μὲν οὖν ταύτας δικάζουσιν ἐμμήνους εἰσάγοντες, οἱ δ᾽ ἀποδέκται τοῖς τελώναις καὶ κατὰ τῶν τελωνῶν, τὰ μὲν μέχρι δέκα δραχμῶν ὄντες κύριοι, τὰ δ᾽ ἄλλ᾽ εἰς τὸ δικαστήριον εἰσάγοντες ἔμμηνα.

1 LIII. Κληροῦσι δὲ καὶ[2] τετταράκοντα, τέτταρας ἐκ τῆς φυλῆς ἑκάστης, πρὸς οὓς τὰς ἄλλας δίκας λαγχάνουσιν· οἳ πρότερον μὲν ἦσαν τριάκοντα καὶ κατὰ δήμους περιόντες[3] ἐδίκαζον, μετὰ δὲ τὴν ἐπὶ τῶν τριάκοντα ὀλιγαρχίαν τετταράκοντα γεγό-
2 νασιν. καὶ τὰ μὲν μέχρι δέκα δραχμῶν αὐτοτελεῖς εἰσὶ δικάζειν, τὰ δ᾽ ὑπὲρ τοῦτο τὸ τίμημα τοῖς διαιτηταῖς παραδιδόασιν. οἱ δὲ παραλαβόντες ἐὰν μὴ δύνωνται διαλῦσαι γιγνώσκουσι, κἂν μὲν ἀμφοτέροις ἀρέσκῃ τὰ γνωσθέντα καὶ ἐμμένωσιν, ἔχει τέλος ἡ δίκη. ἂν δ᾽ ὁ ἕτερος ἐφῇ τῶν ἀντιδίκων εἰς τὸ δικαστήριον, ἐμβαλόντες τὰς μαρτυρίας καὶ τὰς προκλήσεις καὶ τοὺς νόμους εἰς ἐχίνους, χωρὶς μὲν τὰς τοῦ διώκοντος χωρὶς δὲ τὰς τοῦ φεύγοντος, καὶ τούτους κατασημηνάμενοι

[1] ἐρανικαὶ . . . κοινωνικαὶ . . . τραπεζιτικαὶ Bury.
[2] καὶ <τοὺς> Wilamowitz-Kaibel.
[3] περιιόντες Kenyon.

[a] A drachma a mina a month = 12 per cent per annum.
[b] *i.e.* particularly an action to recover expenses, brought

They also elect by lot five men as Introducers, who 2
introduce the cases to be tried within a month, each official those of two tribes. These cases include prosecutions for non-payment of dowry due, actions for the recovery of loans borrowed at a drachma interest,[a] and of capital borrowed from one party by another wishing to do business in the market; and also actions for assault, friendly-society business, partnerships, slaves, draft animals, naval command,[b] and bank cases.
These officials, therefore, bring into court and decide 3
these suits within a month; but the Receivers [c] decide suits brought by tax-farmers or against them, having power to deal summarily with suits up to ten francs but bringing the others into the Jury-court within a month.

LIII. They also elect by lot forty persons,[d] four 1
from each tribe, who are the court before which the other suits are brought; formerly they were thirty and went on circuit trying cases in each parish, but since the oligarchy of the Thirty their number has
been raised to forty. They have summary jurisdiction 2
in claims not exceeding ten francs, but suits above that value they pass on to the Arbitrators. These take over the cases, and if they are unable to effect a compromise, they give judgement, and if both parties are satisfied with their judgement and abide by it, that ends the suit. But if one of the two parties appeals to the Jury-court, they put the witnesses' evidence and the challenges and the laws concerned into deed-boxes, those of the prosecutor and those of the defendant separately, and seal them up, and

by the captain of a trireme against his successor who had failed to relieve him when his year of office was over.

[c] See xlviii. 1.

[d] Perhaps the Greek should be altered to give 'the Forty.'

καὶ τὴν γνῶσιν τοῦ διαιτητοῦ γεγραμμένην ἐν γραμματείῳ προσαρτήσαντες, παραδιδόασι τοῖς δʹ
3 τοῖς τὴν φυλὴν τοῦ φεύγοντος δικάζουσιν. οἱ δὲ παραλαβόντες εἰσάγουσιν εἰς τὸ δικαστήριον, τὰ μὲν ἐντὸς χιλίων εἰς ἕνα καὶ διακοσίους, τὰ δ' ὑπὲρ χιλίας εἰς ἕνα καὶ τετρακοσίους. οὐκ ἔξεστι δ' οὔτε νόμοις οὔτε προκλήσεσι οὔτε μαρτυρίαις ἀλλ' ἢ ταῖς παρὰ τοῦ διαιτητοῦ χρῆσθαι ταῖς εἰς
4 τοὺς ἐχίνους ἐμβεβλημέναις. διαιτηταὶ δ' εἰσὶν οἷς ἂν ἑξηκοστὸν ἔτος ᾖ· τοῦτο δὲ δῆλον ἐκ τῶν ἀρχόντων καὶ τῶν ἐπωνύμων· εἰσὶ γὰρ ἐπώνυμοι δέκα μὲν οἱ τῶν φυλῶν, δύο δὲ καὶ τετταράκοντα οἱ τῶν ἡλικιῶν· οἱ δ' ἔφηβοι ἐγγραφόμενοι πρότερον μὲν εἰς λελευκωμένα γραμματεῖα ἐνεγράφοντο, καὶ ἐπεγράφοντο αὐτοῖς ὅ τ' ἄρχων ἐφ' οὗ ἐνεγράφησαν καὶ ὁ ἐπώνυμος ὁ τῷ προτέρῳ[1] ἔτει δεδιαιτηκώς, νῦν δ' εἰς στήλην χαλκῆν ἀναγράφονται, καὶ ἵσταται ἡ στήλη πρὸ τοῦ βουλευτηρίου
5 παρὰ τοὺς ἐπωνύμους. τὸν δὲ τελευταῖον τῶν ἐπωνύμων λαβόντες οἱ τετταράκοντα διανέμουσιν αὐτοῖς τὰς διαίτας καὶ ἐπικληροῦσιν ἃς ἕκαστος διαιτήσει· καὶ ἀναγκαῖον ἃς ἂν ἕκαστος λάχῃ διαίτας ἐκδιαιτᾶν, ὁ γὰρ νόμος ἄν τις μὴ γένηται διαιτητὴς τῆς ἡλικίας αὐτῷ καθηκούσης ἄτιμον εἶναι κελεύει, πλὴν ἐὰν τύχῃ ἀρχὴν ἄρχων τινὰ ἐν ἐκείνῳ τῷ ἐνιαυτῷ ἢ ἀποδημῶν· οὗτοι δ' ἀτελεῖς

[1] πρότερον edd. hiatus causa.

[a] Of the 100 Attic heroes 10 gave their names to the Tribes (see xxi. 6), and of the remaining 90, 42 names were affixed to the successive years of active citizenship, military service being from the age of 18 to 59, and those in their 60th year serving as *diaetetae*. As each year expired, the

attach to them a copy of the Arbitrator's verdict written on a tablet, and hand them over to the four judges taking the cases of the defendant's tribe.
When these have received them they bring them before 3
the Jury-court, claims within 1000 drachmas before a court of two hundred and one jurymen, and claims above that before one of four hundred and one. The litigants are not permitted to put in laws or challenges or evidence other than those passed on by the Arbitrator, that have been put into the deed-boxes.
Persons fifty-nine years of age may serve as Arbi- 4
trators, as appears from the regulations for the Archons and Name-heroes; for the Heroes giving their names to the Tribes are ten in number and those of the years of military age forty-two,[a] and the cadets used formerly when being enrolled to be inscribed on whitened tablets, and above them the Archon [b] in whose term of office they were enrolled and the Name-hero of those that had been Arbitrators the year before, but now they are inscribed on a copper pillar and this is set up in front of the Council-chamber
at the side of the list of Name-heroes. The Forty 5
take the last one of the Name-heroes and distribute the arbitration-cases among those of his year and assign by lot the cases that each is to arbitrate upon; and it is compulsory for each of them to complete the arbitration of the cases allotted to him, for the law enacts the disfranchisement of anybody who does not become Arbitrator when of the proper age, unless he happens to hold some office in that year or to be abroad, these being the only grounds of exemption.

Name-hero of the men now passing the age of 60 was transferred to those now just 18.

[b] *i.e.* the senior of the Nine Archons, called Ἐπώνυμος because his name dated the year.

6 εἰσὶ μόνοι. ἔστιν δὲ καὶ εἰσαγγέλλειν εἰς τοὺς
διαιτητὰς[1] ἐάν τις ἀδικηθῇ ὑπὸ τοῦ διαιτητοῦ, κἄν
τινος καταγνῶσιν ἀτιμοῦσθαι κελεύουσιν οἱ νόμοι·
7 ἔφεσις δ' ἐστὶ καὶ τούτοις. χρῶνται δὲ τοῖς
ἐπωνύμοις καὶ πρὸς τὰς στρατείας, καὶ ὅταν
ἡλικίαν ἐκπέμπωσι προγράφουσιν ἀπὸ τίνος ἄρχοντος καὶ ἐπωνύμου μέχρι τίνων δεῖ στρατεύεσθαι.
1 LIV. Κληροῦσι δὲ καὶ τάσδε τὰς ἀρχάς· ὁδο-
ποιοὺς πέντε, οἷς προστέτακται δημοσίους ἐργάτας
2 ἔχουσι τὰς ὁδοὺς ἐπισκευάζειν· καὶ λογιστὰς δέκα
καὶ συνηγόρους τούτοις δέκα, πρὸς οὓς ἅπαντας
ἀνάγκη τοὺς τὰς ἀρχὰς ἄρξαντας λόγον ἀπενεγκεῖν.
οὗτοι γάρ εἰσιν οἱ[2] μόνοι τοῖς ὑπευθύνοις λογιζόμενοι καὶ τὰς εὐθύνας εἰς τὸ δικαστήριον εἰσάγοντες. κἂν μέν τινα κλέπτοντ' ἐξελέγξωσι,
κλοπὴν οἱ δικασταὶ καταγινώσκουσι, καὶ τὸ
γνωσθὲν ἀποτίνεται δεκαπλοῦν· ἐὰν δέ τινα δῶρα
λαβόντα ἐπιδείξωσιν καὶ καταγνῶσιν οἱ δικασταί,
δώρων τιμῶσιν, ἀποτίνεται δὲ καὶ τοῦτο δεκα-
πλοῦν· ἂν δ' ἀδικεῖν καταγνῶσιν, ἀδικίου τιμῶσιν,
ἀποτίνεται δὲ τοῦθ' ἁπλοῦν ἐὰν πρὸ τῆς θ' πρυτανείας ἐκτείσῃ τις, εἰ δὲ μή, διπλοῦται· τὸ δὲ[3]
δεκαπλοῦν οὐ διπλοῦται.
3 Κληροῦσι δὲ καὶ γραμματέα τὸν κατὰ πρυτανείαν καλούμενον, ὃς τῶν γραμμάτων[4] ἐστὶ κύριος
καὶ τὰ ψηφίσματα τὰ γιγνόμενα φυλάττει καὶ
τἄλλα πάντα ἀντιγράφεται καὶ παρακάθηται τῇ
βουλῇ. πρότερον μὲν οὖν οὗτος ἦν χειροτονητός,

[1] δικαστὰς Kenyon.
[2] εἰσιν οἱ Jos. Mayor: εισι cod. [3] δὲ supplevit Kenyon.
[4] ex Harpocratione edd.: γραμματεων cod.

[a] Perhaps διαιτητάς is a mistake for δικαστάς, 'jurymen.'

Anybody unjustly dealt with by the Arbitrator may 6
indict him before the Arbitrators,[a] and the laws prescribe the penalty of disfranchisement for an Arbitrator found guilty; but the Arbitrators also have an appeal. The Name-heroes also are employed 7
to regulate military service; when soldiers of a certain age are being sent on an expedition, a notice is posted stating the years that they are to serve, indicated by the Archon and Name-hero of the earliest and latest.

LIV. They also elect by lot the following officials: 1
five Highway-constructors, whose duty is to repair the roads, with workmen who are public slaves; and 2
ten Auditors and ten Assessors with them, to whom all retiring officials have to render account. For these are the only magistrates who audit the returns of officials liable to account and bring the audits before the Jury-court. And if an official is proved by them to have committed peculation, the Jury convict him of peculation, and the fine is ten times the amount of which he is found guilty; and if they show that a man has taken bribes and the Jury convict, they assess the value of the bribes and in this case also the fine is ten times the amount; but if they find him guilty of maladministration, they assess the damage, and the fine paid is that amount only, provided that it is paid before the ninth presidency; otherwise it is doubled. But a fine of ten times the amount is not doubled.

They also appoint by lot the officer called Clerk for 3
the Presidency, who is responsible for documents, is keeper of the decrees that are passed and supervises the transcription of all other documents, and who attends the sittings of the Council. Formerly this officer was elected by show of hands, and the most

καὶ τοὺς ἐνδοξοτάτους καὶ πιστοτάτους ἐχειρο-
τόνουν, καὶ γὰρ ἐν ταῖς στήλαις πρὸς ταῖς συμ-
μαχίαις καὶ προξενίαις καὶ πολιτείαις οὗτος ἀναγρά-
4 φεται· νῦν δὲ γέγονε κληρωτός. κληροῦσι δὲ καὶ
ἐπὶ τοὺς νόμους[1] ἕτερον ὃς παρακάθηται τῇ βουλῇ,
5 καὶ ἀντιγράφεται καὶ οὗτος πάντας. χειροτονεῖ
δὲ καὶ ὁ δῆμος γραμματέα τὸν ἀναγνωσόμενον
αὐτῷ καὶ τῇ βουλῇ, καὶ οὗτος οὐδενός ἐστι κύριος
ἀλλὰ τοῦ ἀναγνῶναι.

6 Κληροῖ δὲ καὶ ἱεροποιοὺς δέκα τοὺς ἐπὶ τὰ
ἐκθύματα καλουμένους, οἳ τά τε μαντευτὰ ἱερὰ
θύουσιν, κἄν τι καλλιερῆσαι δέῃ καλλιεροῦσι μετὰ
7 τῶν μάντεων. κληροῖ δὲ καὶ ἑτέρους δέκα τοὺς
κατ᾽ ἐνιαυτὸν καλουμένους, οἳ θυσίας τέ τινας
θύουσι καὶ τὰς πεντετηρίδας ἁπάσας διοικοῦσιν
πλὴν Παναθηναίων. εἰσὶ δὲ πεντετηρίδες μία μὲν
ἡ εἰς Δῆλον (ἔστι δὲ καὶ ἑπτετηρὶς ἐνταῦθα),
δευτέρα δὲ Βραυρώνια, τρίτη δὲ Ἡράκλεια,
τετάρτη δὲ Ἐλευσίνια· ε´ δὲ Παναθήναια, καὶ
τούτων οὐδεμιᾷ[2] ἐν τῷ αὐτῷ ἐγγίνεται. νῦν δὲ
πρόσκειται καὶ Ἡφαίστια ἐπὶ[3] Κηφισοφῶντος
ἄρχοντος.

8 Κληροῦσι δὲ καὶ εἰς Σαλαμῖνα ἄρχοντα καὶ εἰς
Πειραιέα δήμαρχον, οἳ τά τε Διονύσια ποιοῦσι
ἑκατέρωθι καὶ χορηγοὺς καθιστᾶσιν· ἐν Σαλαμῖνι
δὲ καὶ τοὔνομα τοῦ ἄρχοντος ἀναγράφεται.

[1] e Polluce Kenyon: επιτουτοισνομον cod.
[2] Wilamowitz-Kaibel: ουδεμια cod. [3] ἀπὸ Blass.

[a] An honourable office assigned to a citizen of another state who represented Athenian interests there.

[b], [c] *i.e.* taking place once in every four or six years: in Greek this is called "five-yearly," "seven-yearly." At [c] both the text and the facts are most uncertain.

distinguished and trustworthy men used to be elected, for this officer's name is inscribed on the monumental slabs above records of alliances and appointments to consulships [a] and grants of citizenship; but now it has
been made an office elected by lot. They also elect 4
by lot another officer to superintend the laws, who attends the sittings of the Council, and he also has
copies made of all the laws. The People also elect 5
by show of hands a clerk to read documents to the Assembly and to the Council; he has no duties except as reader.

The People also elects by lot the ten sacrificial 6
officers entitled Superintendents of Expiations, who offer the sacrifices prescribed by oracle, and for business requiring omens to be taken watch for good
omens in co-operation with the soothsayers. It also 7
elects by lot ten others called the Yearly Sacrificial Officers, who perform certain sacrifices and administer all the four-yearly [b] festivals except the Panathenaic Festival. One of the four-yearly festivals is the Mission to Delos (and there is also a six-yearly [c] festival there), a second is the Brauronia, a third the Heraclea, and a fourth the Eleusinia; a fifth is the Panathenaic, which is not held in the same year as any of the others mentioned. There has now been added the Festival of Hephaestus, instituted in the
archonship of Cephisophon. 329 B.C.

They also elect by lot an archon for Salamis and 8
a demarch for Peiraeus, who hold the Festivals of Dionysus [d] in each of those places and appoint Choir-leaders; at Salamis the name of the archon is recorded in an inscription.

[d] τὰ Διονύσια τὰ κατ' ἀγρούς.

1 LV. Αὗται μὲν οὖν αἱ ἀρχαὶ κληρωταί τε
καὶ κύριαι τῶν εἰρημένων πάντων[1] εἰσίν. οἱ δὲ
καλούμενοι ἐννέα ἄρχοντες τὸ μὲν ἐξ ἀρχῆς ὃν
τρόπον καθίσταντο εἴρηται· νῦν δὲ κληροῦσιν θεσμοθέτας μὲν ἓξ καὶ γραμματέα τούτοις, ἔτι δ'
ἄρχοντα καὶ βασιλέα καὶ πολέμαρχον, κατὰ μέρος
2 ἐξ ἑκάστης φυλῆς. δοκιμάζονται δ' οὗτοι πρῶτον
μὲν ἐν τῇ βουλῇ τοῖς φ', πλὴν τοῦ γραμματέως,
οὗτος δ' ἐν δικαστηρίῳ μόνον, ὥσπερ οἱ ἄλλοι
ἄρχοντες (πάντες γὰρ καὶ οἱ κληρωτοὶ καὶ οἱ
χειροτονητοὶ δοκιμασθέντες ἄρχουσιν), οἱ δ' ἐννέα
ἄρχοντες ἔν τε τῇ βουλῇ καὶ πάλιν ἐν δικαστηρίῳ.
καὶ πρότερον μὲν οὐκ ἦρχεν ὅντιν' ἀποδοκιμάσειεν
ἡ βουλή, νῦν δ' ἔφεσίς ἐστιν εἰς τὸ δικαστήριον,
3 καὶ τοῦτο κύριόν ἐστι τῆς δοκιμασίας. ἐπερωτῶσιν
δ' ὅταν δοκιμάζωσιν πρῶτον μὲν "τίς σοι πατὴρ
καὶ πόθεν τῶν δήμων, καὶ τίς πατρὸς πατήρ, καὶ
τίς μήτηρ, καὶ τίς μητρὸς πατὴρ καὶ πόθεν τῶν
δήμων;" μετὰ δὲ ταῦτα εἰ ἔστιν αὐτῷ Ἀπόλλων
Πατρῷος καὶ Ζεὺς Ἑρκεῖος, καὶ ποῦ ταῦτα τὰ
ἱερά ἐστιν· εἶτα ἠρία εἰ ἔστιν καὶ ποῦ ταῦτα·
ἔπειτα γονέας εἰ εὖ ποιεῖ, κεἰ[2] τὰ τέλη τελεῖ, καὶ
τὰς στρατείας εἰ ἐστράτευται. ταῦτα δ' ἀν-
ερωτήσας "κάλει" φησὶν "τούτων τοὺς μάρ-
4 τυρας." ἐπειδὰν δὲ παράσχηται τοὺς μάρτυρας,
ἐπερωτᾷ "τούτου βούλεταί τις κατηγορεῖν;"
κἂν μὲν ᾖ τις κατήγορος, δοὺς κατηγορίαν καὶ

[1] πάντων Kenyon: πράξεων alii: . . . ων cod.
[2] Thalheim: και cod. (καὶ τὰ τέλη <εἰ> Wilamowitz-Kaibel).

[a] Chaps. iii., viii., xxii., xxvi.

LV. These offices, then, are elected by lot and have 1
authority over all the matters stated. As to the officials designated the Nine Archons, the mode of their appointment that was originally in force has been stated before[a]; but now the six Lawgivers and their clerk are elected by lot, and also the Archon,[b] King and War-lord, from each tribe in turn. The 2
qualifications of these are first checked in the Council of Five Hundred, except the Clerk, but he is checked only in a Jury-court, as are the other officials (for all of them, both those elected by lot and those elected by show of hands, have their qualifications checked before they hold office), while the Nine Archons are checked in the Council and also again in a Jury-court. Formerly any official not passed by the Council did not hold office, but now there is an appeal to the Jury-court, and with this rests the final decision as to qualification. The questions put in 3
examining qualifications are, first, 'Who is your father and to what deme does he belong, and who is your father's father, and who your mother, and who her father and what his deme?' then whether he has a Family Apollo and Homestead Zeus,[c] and where these shrines are; then whether he has family tombs and where they are; then whether he treats his parents well, and whether he pays his taxes, and whether he has done his military service. And after putting these questions the officer says, 'Call your witnesses to these statements.' And when he has 4
produced his witnesses, the officer further asks, 'Does anybody wish to bring a charge against this man?' And if any accuser is forthcoming, he is given a hearing and

[b] *i.e.* the Archon Eponymus, see liv. 4 n.

[c] The gods of the Athenian's home.

ἀπολογίαν, οὕτω δίδωσιν ἐν μὲν τῇ βουλῇ τὴν
ἐπιχειροτονίαν ἐν δὲ τῷ δικαστηρίῳ τὴν ψῆφον·
ἐὰν δὲ μηδεὶς βούληται κατηγορεῖν, εὐθὺς δίδωσι
τὴν ψῆφον· καὶ πρότερον μὲν εἷς ἐνέβαλλε τὴν
ψῆφον, νῦν δ' ἀνάγκη πάντας ἔστι διαψηφίζεσθαι
περὶ αὐτῶν, ἵνα ἄν τις πονηρὸς ὢν ἀπαλλάξῃ τοὺς
κατηγόρους ἐπὶ τοῖς δικασταῖς γένηται τοῦτον
5 ἀποδοκιμάσαι. δοκιμασθὲν[1] δὲ τοῦτον τὸν τρόπον,
βαδίζουσι πρὸς τὸν λίθον ἐφ' οὗ τὰ τόμι' ἐστιν
(ἐφ' οὗ καὶ οἱ διαιτηταὶ ὀμόσαντες ἀποφαίνονται
τὰς διαίτας καὶ οἱ μάρτυρες ἐξόμνυνται τὰς μαρτυρίας), ἀναβάντες δ' ἐπὶ τοῦτον ὀμνύουσιν δικαίως
ἄρξειν καὶ κατὰ τοὺς νόμους, καὶ δῶρα μὴ
λήψεσθαι τῆς ἀρχῆς ἕνεκα, κἄν τι λάβωσιν ἀνδριάντα ἀναθήσειν χρυσοῦν. ἐντεῦθεν δ' ὀμόσαντες
εἰς ἀκρόπολιν βαδίζουσιν καὶ πάλιν ἐκεῖ ταὐτὰ
ὀμνύουσι, καὶ μετὰ ταῦτα εἰς τὴν ἀρχὴν εἰσ-
έρχονται.

1 LVI. Λαμβάνουσι δὲ καὶ παρέδρους ὅ τε ἄρχων
καὶ ὁ βασιλεὺς καὶ ὁ πολέμαρχος δύο ἕκαστος
οὓς ἂν βούληται, καὶ οὗτοι δοκιμάζονται ἐν τῷ
δικαστηρίῳ πρὶν παρεδρεύειν, καὶ εὐθύνας διδόασιν
ἐπὰν παρεδρεύσωσιν.

2 Καὶ ὁ μὲν ἄρχων εὐθὺς εἰσελθὼν πρῶτον μὲν
κηρύττει ὅσα τις εἶχεν πρὶν αὐτὸν εἰσελθεῖν εἰς
τὴν ἀρχὴν ταῦτ' ἔχειν καὶ κρατεῖν μέχρι ἀρχῆς
3 τέλους. ἔπειτα χορηγοὺς τραγῳδοῖς καθίστησι
τρεῖς, ἐξ ἁπάντων Ἀθηναίων τοὺς πλουσιωτάτους·
πρότερον δὲ καὶ κωμῳδοῖς καθίστη πέντε, νῦν δὲ

[1] δοκιμασθέν⟨τες⟩ Rutherford.

the man on trial an opportunity of defence, and then
the official puts the question to a show of hands in the
Council or to a vote by ballot in the Jury-court; but
if nobody wishes to bring a charge against him, he
puts the vote at once; formerly one person used to
throw in his ballot-pebble, but now all are compelled to
vote one way or the other about them, in order that
if anyone being a rascal has got rid of his accusers,[a]
it may rest with the jurymen to disqualify him. And 5
when the matter has been checked in this way, they
go to the stone on which are the victims cut up for
sacrifice (the one on which Arbitrators also take oath
before they issue their decisions, and persons summoned as witnesses swear that they have no evidence
to give), and mounting on this stone they swear
that they will govern justly and according to the laws,
and will not take presents on account of their office,
and that if they should take anything they will set
up a golden statue. After taking oath they go from
the stone to the Acropolis and take the same oath
again there, and after that they enter on their office.

LVI. The Archon, the King and the War-lord also 1
take two assessors each, chosen by themselves, and
the qualifications of these are checked in the Jury-court before they hold office, and they are called to
account when they retire from office.

Immediately on coming into office the Archon first 2
makes proclamation that all men shall hold until
the end of his office those possessions and powers
that they held before his entry into office. Then he 3
appoints three Chorus-leaders for the tragedies, the
wealthiest men among all the Athenians; and formerly he used also to appoint five for the comedies,

[a] *i.e.* has bribed them to let him off.

τούτους[1] αἱ φυλαὶ φέρουσιν. ἔπειτα παραλαβὼν τοὺς χορηγοὺς τοὺς ἐνηνεγμένους ὑπὸ τῶν φυλῶν εἰς Διονύσια ἀνδράσιν καὶ παισὶν καὶ κωμῳδοῖς καὶ εἰς Θαργήλια ἀνδράσιν καὶ παισὶν (εἰσὶ δ' οἱ μὲν εἰς Διονύσια κατὰ φυλάς, εἰς Θαργήλια δὲ[2] δυεῖν φυλαῖν εἷς, παρέχει δ' ἐν μέρει ἑκατέρα τῶν φυλῶν) τούτοις τὰς ἀντιδόσεις ποιεῖ καὶ τὰς σκήψεις εἰσάγει ἐάν τις ἢ λελητουργηκέναι φῇ πρότερον ταύτην τὴν λητουργίαν ἢ ἀτελὴς εἶναι λελητουργηκὼς ἑτέραν λητουργίαν καὶ τῶν χρόνων αὐτῷ τῆς ἀτελείας μὴ ἐξεληλυθότων ἢ τὰ ἔτη μὴ γεγονέναι (δεῖ γὰρ τὸν τοῖς παισὶν χορηγοῦντα ὑπὲρ τετταράκοντα ἔτη γεγονέναι). καθίστησι δὲ καὶ εἰς Δῆλον χορηγοὺς καὶ ἀρχιθέωρον τῷ τριακοντορίῳ τῷ τοὺς ἠιθέους ἄγοντι.
4 πομπῶν δ' ἐπιμελεῖται τῆς τε τῷ Ἀσκληπιῷ
γινομένης ὅταν οἰκουρῶσι μύσται, καὶ τῆς Διονυσίων τῶν μεγάλων μετὰ τῶν ἐπιμελητῶν, οὓς
πρότερον μὲν ὁ δῆμος ἐχειροτόνει δέκα ὄντας,
καὶ τὰ εἰς τὴν πομπὴν ἀναλώματα παρ' αὑτῶν
ἀνήλισκον, νῦν δ' ἕνα τῆς φυλῆς ἑκάστης κληροῖ
5 καὶ δίδωσιν εἰς τὴν κατασκευὴν ἑκατὸν μνᾶς· ἐπιμελεῖται δὲ καὶ τῆς εἰς Θαργήλια καὶ τῆς τῷ Διῒ
τῷ Σωτῆρι. διοικεῖ δὲ καὶ τὸν ἀγῶνα τῶν Διονυσίων οὗτος καὶ τῶν Θαργηλίων. ἑορτῶν μὲν οὖν
6 ἐπιμελεῖται τούτων. γραφαὶ δὲ καὶ δίκαι λαγχά-

[1] Wyse: τουτοις cod. [2] δὲ supplent edd.

[a] A festival in May, at which there were competitions of cyclic choruses and a procession (§ 5).

[b] A citizen appointed to one of these expensive public offices could challenge another as better able to afford it,

but these are now returned by the Tribes. Afterwards he receives the Chorus-leaders nominated by the Tribes for the men's and boys' competitions and the comedies at the Dionysia and for men and boys at the Thargelia [a] (for the Dionysia one for each tribe, for the Thargelia one for two tribes, which take turns to supply them), and deals with their claims for substitution by exchange of property,[b] and brings forward their claims to exemption on the ground of having performed that public service before, or of being exempt because of having performed another service and the period of exemption not having expired, or of not being of the right age (for a man serving as Chorus-leader for the boys must be over forty). He also appoints Chorus-leaders for Delos and a Procession-leader for the thirty-oared vessel that
carries the youths.[c] He supervises processions, the 4
one celebrated in honour of Asclepius when initiates keep a watch-night, and the one at the Great Dionysia, in which he acts jointly with the Supervisors; these were formerly ten men elected by show of hands by the People, and they found the expenses of the procession out of their own pockets, but now they are elected by lot, one from each tribe,
and given 100 minae for equipment; and he also 5
supervises the procession of Thargelia, and the one in honour of Zeus the Saviour. This official also administers the competition of the Dionysia and of the Thargelia. These, then, are the festivals that he
supervises. Criminal and civil law-suits are instituted 6

and the man challenged could only escape undertaking the office by exchanging estates with the challenger.

[c] For the festival at Delos see liv. 7; boys' choruses went from Athens.

νονται πρὸς αὐτόν, ἃς ἀνακρίνας εἰς τὸ δικαστήριον εἰσάγει, γονέων κακώσεως (αὗται δέ εἰσιν ἀζήμιοι τῷ βουλομένῳ διώκειν), ὀρφανῶν κακώσεως (αὗται δ' εἰσὶ κατὰ τῶν ἐπιτρόπων), ἐπικλήρου κακώσεως (αὗται δέ εἰσι κατὰ τῶν ἐπιτρόπων καὶ τῶν συνοικούντων), οἴκου ὀρφανικοῦ κακώσεως (εἰσὶ δὲ καὶ αὗται κατὰ τῶν ἐπιτρόπων), παρανοίας, ἐάν τις αἰτιᾶταί τινα παρανοοῦντα τὰ ὑπάρχοντα[1] ἀπολλύναι, εἰς δατητῶν αἵρεσιν, ἐάν τις μὴ θέλῃ κοινὰ τὰ ὄντα νέμεσθαι, εἰς ἐπιτροπῆς κατάστασιν, εἰς ἐπιτροπῆς διαδικασίαν, εἰς ἐμφανῶν κατάστασιν, ἐπίτροπον αὐτὸν ἐγγράψαι, κλήρων καὶ
7 ἐπικλήρων ἐπιδικασίαι. ἐπιμελεῖται δὲ καὶ τῶν ὀρφανῶν καὶ τῶν ἐπικλήρων καὶ τῶν γυναικῶν ὅσαι ἂν τελευτήσαντος τοῦ ἀνδρὸς σκήπτωνται κύειν, καὶ κύριός ἐστι τοῖς ἀδικοῦσιν ἐπιβάλλειν ἢ εἰσάγειν εἰς τὸ δικαστήριον. μισθοῖ δὲ καὶ τοὺς οἴκους τῶν ὀρφανῶν καὶ τῶν ἐπικλήρων ἕως ἄν τις τετταρακαιδεκέτις[2] γένηται καὶ τὰ ἀποτιμήματα λαμβάνει, καὶ τοὺς ἐπιτρόπους[3] ἔαν μὴ διδῶσι τοῖς παισὶν τὸν σῖτον οὗτος εἰσπράττει.

1 LVII. Καὶ ὁ μὲν ἄρχων ἐπιμελεῖται[4] τούτων. ὁ δὲ βασιλεὺς πρῶτον μὲν μυστηρίων ἐπιμελεῖται μετὰ τῶν ἐπιμελητῶν οὓς ὁ δῆμος ἐχειροτονεῖ, δύο μὲν ἐξ Ἀθηναίων ἁπάντων, ἕνα δ' ἐξ Εὐμολπιδῶν, ἕνα δὲ ἐκ Κηρύκων. ἔπειτα Διονυσίων τῶν Ἐπι-

[1] Blass (alii alia): τα . . . . απολλυν . . cod.
[2] Blass: επικλ . . . . . ακαιδε . . τις cod.
[3] Brooks: και . . . . ους cod.
[4] Blass: καιο . . . αι cod.

before him, and after a preliminary trial he brings them in before the Jury-court: actions for ill-usage of parents (in which anybody who wishes may act as prosecutor without liability to penalty); for ill-usage of orphans (which lie against their guardians); for ill-usage of an heiress (which lie against the guardians or the relations that they live with); for injury to an orphan's estate (these also lie against the guardians); prosecutions for insanity, when one man accuses another of wasting his property when insane; actions for the appointment of liquidators, when a man is unwilling for property to be administered in partnership; actions for the institution of guardianship; actions for deciding rival claims to guardianship; actions for the production of goods or documents; actions for enrolment as trustee; claims to estates and to heiresses. He also supervises orphans and 7
heiresses and women professing to be with child after the husband's death, and he has absolute power to fine offenders against them or to bring them before the Jury-court. He grants leases of houses belonging to orphans and heiresses until they are fourteen years of age, and receives the rents, and he exacts maintenance for children from guardians who fail to supply it.

LVII. These are the matters superintended by the 1
Archon. But the King superintends, first, the mysteries, in co-operation with Superintendents elected by show of hands by the People, two from the whole body of the citizens, one from the Eumolpidae and one from the Heralds.[a] Next the Dionysia in

[a] The Eumolpidae and Kerykes were two ancient priestly families at Athens.

ληναίων[1]· ταῦτα δ' ἐστὶ πομπή τε καὶ ἀγών.[2] τὴν μὲν οὖν πομπὴν κοινῇ πέμπουσιν ὅ τε βασιλεὺς καὶ οἱ ἐπιμεληταί, τὸν δὲ ἀγῶνα διατίθησιν ὁ βασιλεύς. τίθησι δὲ καὶ τοὺς τῶν λαμπάδων ἀγῶνας ἅπαντας, ὡς δ' ἔπος εἰπεῖν καὶ τὰς
2 πατρίους θυσίας διοικεῖ οὗτος πάσας. γραφαὶ δὲ λαγχάνονται πρὸς αὐτὸν ἀσεβείας, κἄν τις ἱερωσύνης ἀμφισβητῇ πρός τινα. διαδικάζει δὲ καὶ τοῖς γένεσι καὶ τοῖς ἱερεῦσι τὰς ἀμφισβητήσεις τὰς ὑπὲρ τῶν γερῶν ἁπάσας οὗτος. λαγχάνονται δὲ καὶ αἱ τοῦ φόνου δίκαι πᾶσαι πρὸς τοῦτον, καὶ ὁ προαγορεύων εἴργεσθαι τῶν νομίμων οὗτός ἐστιν.
3 εἰσὶ δὲ φόνου δίκαι καὶ τραύματος, ἂν μὲν ἐκ προνοίας ἀποκτείνῃ[3] ἢ τρώσῃ, ἐν Ἀρείῳ πάγῳ, καὶ φαρμάκων, ἐὰν ἀποκτείνῃ δούς, καὶ πυρκαᾶς· ταῦτα γὰρ ἡ βουλὴ μόνα δικάζει, τῶν δ' ἀκουσίων καὶ βουλεύσεως κἂν οἰκέτην ἀποκτείνῃ τις ἢ μέτοικον ἢ ξένον, οἱ ἐπὶ Παλλαδίῳ· ἐὰν δ' ἀποκτεῖναι μέν τις ὁμολογῇ, φῇ δὲ κατὰ τοὺς νόμους, οἷον μοιχὸν λαβὼν ἢ ἐν πολέμῳ ἀγνοήσας ἢ ἐν ἄθλῳ ἀγωνιζόμενος, τούτῳ ἐπὶ Δελφινίῳ δικάζουσιν· ἐὰν δὲ φεύγων φυγὴν ὧν ἄρεσίς ἐστιν αἰτίαν ἔχῃ ἀποκτεῖναι ἢ τρῶσαί τινα, τούτῳ δ' ἐν Φρεάτου δικάζουσιν, ὁ δ' ἀπολογεῖται προσ-
4 ορμισάμενος ἐν πλοίῳ. δικάζουσι δ' οἱ λαχόντες ταῦτ' ἐφέται πλὴν[4] τῶν ἐν Ἀρείῳ πάγῳ γιγνο-

[1] ἐπὶ Ληναίῳ Bywater.
[2] Van Leeuwen: εστι . . . η . . . cod.
[3] ἀποκτείνῃ ⟨τις⟩ Papageorgios.
[4] Kenyon: τα . . . πλην cod.

[a] Held at the Limnae, S.E. of the Acropolis, at the end of January. The 7th Attic month, Gamelion (January-February), was in old Ionic called Lenaeon.

Lenaeon[a]; this festival consists of a procession and a competition, the former conducted by the King and the Superintendents jointly, the latter organized by the King. He also holds all the Torch-race Competitions; also he is the director of practically all the ancestral sacrifices. He holds the court that 2
tries charges of impiety and disputed claims to hereditary priesthoods. He adjudicates between clans and between priests in all disputed claims to privileges. Before him are also brought all murder cases, and proclamations of exclusion from customary rites are made by him. Trials for deliberate murder 3
and wounding are held in the Areopagus, and for causing death by poison, and for arson; for these only are tried by the Council, whereas involuntary homicide and plotting to murder, and murder of a slave or resident alien or foreigner, come before the court at the Palladium[b]; and one who admits homicide but declares it to have been legal (for instance when he has killed a man taken in adultery), or who in war has killed a fellow-citizen in ignorance, or in an athletic contest, is tried at the Delphinium; but if, when a man has taken refuge in exile after an offence that admits of satisfaction, he is charged with homicide or wounding, he is tried at the Precinct of Phreatus,[c] and delivers his defence from a ship anchored near the shore. Commissioners appointed by lot 4
try these cases, except those that are held on the Areopagus; the cases are introduced by the King,

[b] This shrine and the Delphinium were probably S.E. of the Acropolis.

[c] Near the harbour of Zea; doubtless the eponymous hero was fictitious, the place being really named from a well, φρέαρ. If the defendant had landed he would have been arrested for his former offence.

μένων· εἰσάγει δ' ὁ βασιλεύς, καὶ δικάζουσιν ἐν ἱερῷ καὶ ὑπαίθριοι, καὶ ὁ βασιλεὺς ὅταν δικάζῃ περιαιρεῖται τὸν στέφανον. ὁ δὲ τὴν αἰτίαν ἔχων τὸν μὲν ἄλλον χρόνον εἴργεται τῶν ἱερῶν καὶ οὐδ' εἰς τὴν ἀγορὰν νόμος ἐμβαλεῖν αὐτῷ, τότε δ' εἰς τὸ ἱερὸν εἰσελθὼν ἀπολογεῖται. ὅταν δὲ μὴ εἰδῇ τὸν ποιήσαντα, τῷ δράσαντι λαγχάνει, δικάζει δ' ὁ βασιλεὺς καὶ οἱ φυλοβασιλεῖς, καὶ τὰς τῶν ἀψύχων καὶ τῶν ἄλλων ζῴων.

1 LVIII. Ὁ δὲ πολέμαρχος θύει μὲν θυσίας τήν τε τῇ Ἀρτέμιδι τῇ Ἀγροτέρᾳ καὶ τῷ Ἐνυαλίῳ, διατίθησι δ' ἀγῶνα τὸν ἐπιτάφιον [καὶ][1] τοῖς τετελευτηκόσιν ἐν τῷ πολέμῳ, καὶ Ἁρμοδίῳ καὶ

2 Ἀριστογείτονι ἐναγίσματα ποιεῖ. δίκαι δὲ λαγχάνονται πρὸς αὐτὸν ἴδιαι μόνον,[2] αἵ τε τοῖς μετοίκοις καὶ τοῖς ἰσοτελέσι καὶ ⟨αἱ⟩[3] τοῖς προξένοις γιγνόμεναι· καὶ δεῖ τοῦτον λαβόντα καὶ διανείμαντα δέκα μέρη τὸ λαχὸν ἑκάστῃ τῇ φυλῇ μέρος προσθεῖναι, τοὺς δὲ τὴν φυλὴν δικάζοντας

3 τοῖς διαιτηταῖς ἀποδοῦναι. αὐτὸς δ' εἰσάγει δίκας τάς τε τοῦ ἀποστασίου καὶ ἀπροστασίου καὶ κλήρων καὶ ἐπικλήρων τοῖς μετοίκοις, καὶ τἄλλ' ὅσα τοῖς πολίταις ὁ ἄρχων ταῦτα τοῖς μετοίκοις ὁ πολέμαρχος.

1 LIX. Οἱ δὲ θεσμοθέται πρῶτον μὲν τοῦ προγράψαι τὰ δικαστήριά εἰσι κύριοι τίσιν ἡμέραις δεῖ δικάζειν,[4] ἔπειτα τοῦ δοῦναι ταῖς ἀρχαῖς· καθότι γὰρ ἂν οὗτοι δῶσιν, κατὰ τοῦτο χρῶνται.

[1] Kenyon secundum Pollucem.
[2] μόνον Wilamowitz-Kaibel: μεν cod.
[3] Kaibel.
[4] καθίζειν Richards.

[a] A form of Ares.

and the court sits within the sacred precinct in the open air, and when the King is acting in a case he takes off his crown. The accused man all the rest of the time is debarred from sacred places and is even forbidden by law from setting foot in the market-place, but at the trial he enters the precinct and makes his defence. When the King does not know who committed the act, he institutes proceedings against 'the guilty man,' and the King and Tribal Kings try the case, as also prosecutions of inanimate objects and animals for homicide.

LVIII. The War-lord offers sacrifices to Artemis the 1
Huntress and to Enyalius,[a] and arranges the funeral games in honour of those who have fallen in war, and makes memorial offerings to Harmodius and Aristogeiton. Only private law-suits are brought before 2
him in which resident aliens, ordinary and privileged, and foreign consuls are concerned; he has to take the list of cases and divide it into ten portions and assign one portion by lot to each tribe, and to assign the jurymen for each tribe to the Arbitrators.
He himself brings forward cases in which resident aliens 3
are concerned, on charges of acting without their protectors[b] or of lacking a protector, and as to estates and heiresses; and all other actions that in the case of citizens are brought in by the Archon, in the case of resident aliens are introduced by the War-lord.

LIX. The Lawgivers are responsible, first, for 1
preparing lists of the days on which the jury-courts are to sit, and then for giving them to the officers, for these follow the arrangements that the Lawgivers

[b] A *metoikos* (other than the *isoteleis*, who for taxation and military service ranked with citizens) had to be enrolled under a citizen, whose sanction was necessary for his actions if important.

2 ἔτι δὲ τὰς εἰσαγγελίας εἰσαγγέλλουσιν[1] εἰς τὸν δῆμον, καὶ τὰς καταχειροτονίας καὶ τὰς προβολὰς ἁπάσας εἰσάγουσιν οὗτοι, καὶ γραφὰς παρανόμων, καὶ νόμον μὴ ἐπιτήδειον θεῖναι, καὶ προεδρικὴν
3 καὶ ἐπιστατικὴν καὶ στρατηγοῖς εὐθύνας. εἰσὶ δὲ καὶ γραφαὶ πρὸς αὐτοὺς ὧν παράστασις τίθεται, ξενίας καὶ δωροξενίας (ἄν τις δῶρα δοὺς ἀποφύγῃ τὴν ξενίαν) καὶ συκοφαντίας καὶ δώρων καὶ ψευδεγγραφῆς καὶ ψευδοκλητείας καὶ βουλεύσεως
4 καὶ ἀγραφίου καὶ μοιχείας. εἰσάγουσιν δὲ καὶ τὰς δοκιμασίας ταῖς ἀρχαῖς ἁπάσαις, καὶ τοὺς ἀπεψηφισμένους ὑπὸ τῶν δημοτῶν, καὶ τὰς κατα-
5 γνώσεις τὰς ἐκ τῆς βουλῆς. εἰσάγουσι δὲ καὶ δίκας ἰδίας, ἐμπορικὰς καὶ μεταλλικάς, καὶ δούλων, ἄν τις τὸν ἐλεύθερον κακῶς λέγῃ. καὶ ἐπικληροῦσι ταῖς ἀρχαῖς οὗτοι τὰ δικαστήρια τά τ'[2] ἴδια
6 καὶ τὰ δημόσια. καὶ τὰ σύμβολα τὰ πρὸς τὰς πόλεις οὗτοι κυροῦσι, καὶ τὰς δίκας τὰς ἀπὸ τῶν συμβόλων εἰσάγουσι, καὶ τὰ ψευδομαρτύρια τὰ[3] ἐξ Ἀρείου πάγου.

7 Τοὺς δὲ δικαστὰς κληροῦσι πάντες[4] οἱ ἐννέα ἄρχοντες δέκατος δ' ὁ γραμματεὺς ὁ τῶν θεσμοθετῶν, τοὺς τῆς αὑτοῦ φυλῆς ἕκαστος.

1 LX. Τὰ μὲν οὖν περὶ τοὺς θ' ἄρχοντας τοῦτον ἔχει τὸν τρόπον. κληροῦσι δὲ καὶ ἀθλοθέτας δέκα ἄνδρας, ἕνα τῆς φυλῆς ἑκάστης. οὗτοι δὲ δοκιμασθέντες ἄρχουσι τέτταρα ἔτη, καὶ διοικοῦσι τήν τε πομπὴν τῶν Παναθηναίων καὶ τὸν ἀγῶνα

[1] ⟨ἃς ἄν τινες⟩ εἰσαγγέλλωσι Blass: εἰσ. . . . δῆμον secl. Wilamowitz-Kaibel.
[2] τ' suppletum a Kaibel.
[3] τὰ suppletum a Bernadakis.
[4] πάντες coni. Kenyon: παντας cod.

assign. Moreover it is they who bring before the 2
People indictments, and bring in all votes of re-
moval from office, preliminary informations sent on
by the Assembly, impeachments for illegal procedure,
proceedings against inexpedient legislation, a suit
against a President or a Superintendent, and audits
imposed on Generals. Also they hear indictments for 3
which a fee is paid, on charges of alien birth, alien
corruption (that is, if a person charged with alien
birth secures his acquittal by bribery), malicious
information, bribery, false entry of public debts,
personation of a witness, conspiracy, non-registration,
adultery. They also introduce[a] the tests of qualifica- 4
tion for all offices, and claims to citizenship rejected
by vote of the deme, and verdicts of guilty passed
on from the Council.[b] They also introduce private 5
actions in commercial and mining cases, and actions
against slaves for slandering a freeman. And they
assign the public and the private jury-courts by lot
among the magistrates. They ratify contracts with 6
other states, and bring into court suits arising under
those contracts, and prosecutions for false witness
instituted by the Areopagus.

All the Nine Archons with the Lawgivers' Clerk, 7
making ten, elect by lot the jurymen, each electing
those of his own tribe.

LX. These are the functions of the Nine Archons. 1
They also elect by lot ten men as Stewards of the
Games, one from each tribe, who when passed as
qualified hold office for four years, and administer the
procession of the Panathenaic Festival, and the con-

[a] *i.e.* before the bodies that checked these qualifications, see lv. 2-4.

[b] See xliv. 2 fin.

τῆς μουσικῆς καὶ τὸν γυμνικὸν ἀγῶνα καὶ τὴν ἱπποδρομίαν, καὶ τὸν πέπλον ποιοῦνται, καὶ τοὺς ἀμφορεῖς ποιοῦνται μετὰ τῆς βουλῆς, καὶ τὸ ἔλαιον
2 τοῖς ἀθληταῖς ἀποδιδόασι. συλλέγεται δὲ τὸ[1] ἔλαιον ἀπὸ τῶν μοριῶν· εἰσπράττει δὲ τοὺς τὰ χωρία κεκτημένους ἐν οἷς αἱ μορίαι εἰσὶν ὁ ἄρχων, τρί' ἡμικοτύλια ἀπὸ τοῦ στελέχους ἑκάστου. πρότερον δ' ἐπώλει τὸν καρπὸν ἡ πόλις, καὶ εἴ τις ἐξορύξειεν ἐλαίαν μορίαν ἢ κατάξειεν, ἔκρινεν ἡ ἐξ Ἀρείου πάγου βουλή, καὶ εἴ του καταγνοίη, θανάτῳ τοῦτον ἐζημίουν. ἐξ οὗ δὲ τὸ ἔλαιον ὁ τὸ χωρίον κεκτημένος ἀποτίνει, ὁ μὲν νόμος ἔστιν, ἡ δὲ κρίσις καταλέλυται· τὸ δ'[2] ἔλαιον ἐκ τοῦ κτήματος, οὐκ ἀπὸ τῶν στελεχῶν, ἐστὶ τῇ πόλει.
3 συλλέξας οὖν ὁ ἄρχων τὸ ἐφ' ἑαυτοῦ γιγνόμενον τοῖς ταμίαις παραδίδωσιν εἰς ἀκρόπολιν, καὶ οὐκ ἔστιν ἀναβῆναι πρότερον εἰς Ἄρειον πάγον πρὶν ἂν ἅπαν παραδῷ τοῖς ταμίαις. οἱ δὲ ταμίαι τὸν μὲν ἄλλον χρόνον τηροῦσιν ἐν ἀκροπόλει, τοῖς δὲ Παναθηναίοις ἀπομετροῦσι τοῖς ἀθλοθέταις, οἱ δ' ἀθλοθέται τοῖς νικῶσι τῶν ἀγωνιστῶν. ἔστι γὰρ ἆθλα τοῖς μὲν τὴν μουσικὴν νικῶσιν ἀργύριον[3] καὶ χρυσᾶ, τοῖς δὲ τὴν εὐανδρίαν ἀσπίδες, τοῖς δὲ τὸν γυμνικὸν ἀγῶνα καὶ τὴν ἱπποδρομίαν ἔλαιον.[a]

1 LXI. Χειροτονοῦσι δὲ καὶ τὰς πρὸς τὸν πόλεμον ἀρχὰς ἁπάσας, στρατηγοὺς δέκα, πρότερον μὲν ἀφ' ἑκάστης[4] φυλῆς ἕνα, νῦν δ' ἐξ ἁπάντων, καὶ τούτους διατάττουσι τῇ χειροτονίᾳ, ἕνα μὲν ἐπὶ

[1] δὲ τὸ Richards: τοδ cod. [2] δ': γὰρ coni. Blass.
[3] Wilamowitz-Kaibel: αργυρια cod.
[4] ἑκάστης supplevit Kenyon: αφφυλης cod.

[a] See xlix. 3 n.

test in music, the gymnastic contest and the horse-race, and have the Robe [a] made, and in conjunction with the Council have the vases [b] made, and assign the olive-oil to the competitors. The oil is procured from 2
the sacred trees; and the Archon levies it from the owners of the farms in which the trees are, three quarters of a pint from each trunk. Formerly the state used to sell the fruit, and anybody who dug up or cut down a sacred olive-tree was tried by the Council of Areopagus, and if found guilty punished with death; but ever since the olive-oil has been provided as rent by the owner of the farm, though the law still stands, the trial has gone out; and the state's claim to the oil is calculated on the estate and not on the number of trees.[c] So the Archon collects the tribute of oil 3
accruing in his year, and passes it on to the Treasurers at the Acropolis, and he is not allowed to go up to the Areopagus before he has handed the full quantity over to the Treasurers. These have it in their keeping in the Acropolis always, except that at the Panathenaic Festival they dole it out to the Directors of the Games and these to the victorious competitors. For the prizes are for the victors in music silver money and gold vessels, for those in manly beauty shields, and for those in the gymnastic contest and the horse-race olive-oil.

LXI. They also elect by show of hands all the 1
military officers—ten Generals, formerly one from each tribe, but now from all the citizens together, and the vote decides the assignment of duties to these

[b] In athletic contests the prize was a vase of oil and a garland of foliage from the sacred olive-trees.

[c] *i.e.* the amount per tree stated above is only approximately calculated.

τοὺς ὁπλίτας, ὃς ἡγεῖται τῶν ὁπλιτῶν ἂν ἐξίωσι, ἕνα δ' ἐπὶ τὴν χώραν, ὃς φυλάττει, κἂν πόλεμος ἐν τῇ χώρᾳ γίγνηται πολεμεῖ οὗτος· δύο δ' ἐπὶ τὸν Πειραιέα, τὸν μὲν εἰς τὴν Μουνυχίαν τὸν δ' εἰς τὴν Ἀκτήν, οἳ τῆς φυλακῆς[1] ἐπιμελοῦνται τῶν[2] ἐν Πειραιεῖ· ἕνα δ' ἐπὶ τὰς συμμορίας, ὃς τούς τε τριηράρχους καταλέγει καὶ τὰς ἀντιδόσεις αὐτοῖς ποιεῖ καὶ τὰς διαδικασίας αὐτοῖς εἰσάγει· τοὺς δ' ἄλλους πρὸς τὰ παρόντα πράγματα ἐκπέμπουσιν.

2 ἐπιχειροτονία δ' αὐτῶν ἐστὶ κατὰ τὴν πρυτανείαν ἑκάστην, εἰ δοκοῦσιν καλῶς ἄρχειν· κἄν τινα ἀποχειροτονήσωσιν, κρίνουσιν ἐν τῷ δικαστηρίῳ, κἂν μὲν ἁλῷ τιμῶσιν ὅ τι χρὴ παθεῖν ἢ ἀποτεῖσαι, ἂν δ' ἀποφύγῃ πάλιν ἄρχει. κύριοι δέ εἰσιν ὅταν ἡγῶνται καὶ δῆσαί τὸν[3] ἀτακτοῦντα καὶ ἐκκηρῦξαι[4] καὶ ἐπιβολὴν ἐπιβάλλειν· οὐκ εἰώθασι δὲ ἐπιβάλλειν.

3 Χειροτονοῦσι δὲ καὶ ταξιάρχους δέκα, ἕνα τῆς φυλῆς ἑκάστης· οὗτος δ' ἡγεῖται τῶν φυλετῶν καὶ λοχαγοὺς καθίστησιν.

4 Χειροτονοῦσι δὲ καὶ ἱππάρχους δύο ἐξ ἁπάντων· οὗτοι δ' ἡγοῦνται τῶν ἱππέων, διελόμενοι τὰς φυλὰς ε' ἑκάτερος· κύριοι δὲ τῶν αὐτῶν εἰσιν ὧνπερ[5] οἱ στρατηγοὶ κατὰ τῶν ὁπλιτῶν. ἐπιχειροτονία δὲ γίνεται καὶ[6] τούτων.

5 Χειροτονοῦσι δὲ καὶ φυλάρχους ι',[7] ἕνα τῆς

[1] φυλακῆς coni. Kenyon, φυλῆς secundum codicem dedit.
[2] τῶν Wilamowitz-Kaibel: καιτων cod.
[3] τιν cod.: corr. Wilamowitz-Kaibel.
[4] κηρυξαι cod.: corr. Blass.
[5] εἰσὶν ὧνπερ Wilamowitz-Kaibel: ωνπερεισιν cod.
[6] καὶ suppleuit Gertz.
[7] numerum ι' suppleuit Richards.

—one being appointed to the heavy infantry, who commands them on foreign expeditions; one to the country, who guards it and commands in any war that takes place in it; two to Peiraeus, one of them to Munychia and the other to the Point, who superintend the protection of the population of Peiraeus; one to the Symmories,[a] who enrols the Captains of triremes and carries out their exchanges and introduces their claims for exemption; and the others they
dispatch on expeditions as occasion arises. A con- 2
firmatory vote is taken in each presidency upon the satisfactoriness of their administration; and if this vote goes against any officer he is tried in the jury-court, and if convicted, the penalty or fine to be imposed on him is assessed, but if he is acquitted he resumes office. When in command of a force they have power to punish breach of discipline with imprisonment, exile, or the infliction of a fine; but a fine is not usual.

They also elect by show of hands ten Regimental 3
Commanders, one of each tribe; these lead their fellow-tribesmen and appoint company-commanders.

They also elect by show of hands two Cavalry 4
Commanders from the whole body of citizens; these lead the Knights, each commanding a division consisting of five tribes, and their powers are the same as those of the Generals over the heavy infantry. The Cavalry Commanders' election also is submitted to a confirmatory vote.

They also elect by show of hands ten Tribal Com- 5

[a] The 20 companies in which the 1200 richest citizens were enrolled for payment of the εἰσφορά or property-tax levied to meet emergency expenses of war.

φυλῆς, τὸν ἡγησόμενον τῶν ἱππέων[1] ὥσπερ οἱ ταξίαρχοι τῶν ὁπλιτῶν.

6 Χειροτονοῦσι δὲ καὶ εἰς Λῆμνον ἵππαρχον, ὃς ἐπιμελεῖται τῶν ἱππέων τῶν ἐν Λήμνῳ.

7 Χειροτονοῦσι δὲ καὶ ταμίαν τῆς Παράλου καὶ νῦν[2] τῆς τοῦ Ἄμμωνος.

1 LXII. Αἱ δὲ κληρωταὶ ἀρχαὶ πρότερον μὲν ἦσαν αἱ μὲν μετ' ἐννέα ἀρχόντων ἐκ τῆς φυλῆς ὅλης κληρούμεναι, αἱ δ' ἐν Θησείῳ κληρούμεναι διῃροῦντο εἰς τοὺς δήμους· ἐπειδὴ δ' ἐπώλουν οἱ δῆμοι, καὶ ταύτας ἐκ τῆς φυλῆς ὅλης κληροῦσι, πλὴν βουλευτῶν καὶ φρουρῶν· τούτους δ' εἰς τοὺς δήμους ἀποδιδόασι.

2 Μισθοφοροῦσι δὲ πρῶτον ὁ δῆμος ταῖς μὲν ἄλλαις ἐκκλησίαις δραχμήν, τῇ δὲ κυρίᾳ ἐννέα ὀβόλους[3]· ἔπειτα τὰ δικαστήρια τρεῖς ὀβολούς· εἶθ' ἡ βουλὴ πέντε ὀβολούς. τοῖς δὲ πρυτανεύουσιν εἰς σίτησιν ὀβολὸς προστίθεται [δέκα προστίθενται].[4] ἔπειτ' εἰς σίτησιν λαμβάνουσιν ἐννέα ἄρχοντες τέτταρας ὀβολοὺς ἕκαστος, καὶ παρατρέφουσι κήρυκα καὶ αὐλητήν· ἔπειτ' ἄρχων εἰς Σαλαμῖνα δραχμὴν τῆς ἡμέρας. ἀθλοθέται δ' ἐν πρυτανείῳ δειπνοῦσι τὸν Ἑκατομβαιῶνα μῆνα ὅταν ᾖ τὰ Παναθήναια, ἀρξάμενοι ἀπὸ τῆς τετράδος ἱσταμένου. ἀμφικτύονες εἰς Δῆλον δραχμὴν τῆς ἡμέρας ἑκάστης ἐκ Δήλου λαμβάνουσι.[5] λαμβάνουσι δὲ

1 τῶν ἱππέων suppleuit Kenyon.
2 νῦν Blass: erasum, δίχα legit Kenyon.
3 ὀβόλους suppletum a Wilamowitz-Kaibel.
4 Blass.
5 λαμβάνουσι suppleuit Kenyon (cf. lvii. 2).

manders, one for each tribe, to lead the cavalry as the Regimental Commanders lead the heavy infantry.

They also elect by show of hands a Cavalry Com- 6
mander for Lemnos, to take control of the cavalry in that island.

They also elect by show of hands a Treasurer of 7
the Paralus,[a] and at the present day a Treasurer of the ship of Ammon.

LXII. The officials elected by lot were formerly 1
those elected from the whole tribe together with the Nine Archons and those now elected in the temple of Theseus who used to be divided among the demes; but since the demes began to sell their offices, the latter also are elected by lot from the whole tribe, excepting members of the Council and Guards[b]; these they entrust to the demes.

Payment for public duties is as follows: first, the 2
People draw a drachma for ordinary meetings of the Assembly, and a drachma and a half for a sovereign meeting[c]; second, the Jury-courts half a drachma; third, the Council five obols; and those acting as president have an additional obol for food. Also the Nine Archons get four obols each for food, and have to keep a herald and a flute-player as well; and the archon for Salamis gets a drachma a day. Games-directors dine in the Prytaneum in the month of Hecatombaeon, during the Panathenaic Festival, from the fourth of the month onward. Amphictyons for Delos get a drachma a day from Delos. All the

[a] One of the state triremes used for embassies, etc. The other, the Salaminia, was superseded by the one named after Zeus Ammon, specially used to convey missions to Cyrene on the way to the shrine of Zeus Ammon.

[b] Possibly the guards of the docks, mentioned at xxiv. 3.

[c] See xliii. 4.

καὶ ὅσαι ἀποστέλλονται ἀρχαὶ εἰς Σάμον ἢ Σκῦρον ἢ Λῆμνον ἢ Ἴμβρον εἰς σίτησιν ἀργύριον.

3 Ἄρχειν δὲ τὰς μὲν κατὰ πόλεμον ἀρχὰς ἔξεστι πλεονάκις, τῶν δ' ἄλλων οὐδεμίαν, πλὴν βουλεῦσαι δίς.

1 LXIII. Τὰ δὲ δικαστήρια κληροῦσιν οἱ θ' ἄρχοντες κατὰ φυλάς, ὁ δὲ γραμματεὺς τῶν θεσμο-
2 θετῶν τῆς δεκάτης φυλῆς.[1] εἴσοδοι δέ εἰσιν εἰς τὰ δικαστήρια δέκα, μία τῇ φυλῇ ἑκάστῃ, καὶ κληρωτήρια εἴκοσι, δύο τῇ φυλῇ ἑκάστῃ, καὶ κιβώτια ἑκατόν, δέκα τῇ φυλῇ ἑκάστῃ, καὶ ἕτερα κιβώτια εἰς ἃ[2] ἐμβάλλεται τῶν λαχόντων δικαστῶν τὰ πινάκια, καὶ ὑδρίαι δύο καὶ βακτηρίαι παρατίθενται κατὰ τὴν εἴσοδον[3] ἑκάστην ὅσοιπερ οἱ δικασταί, καὶ βάλανοι εἰς τὴν ὑδρίαν ἐμβάλλονται ἴσαι ταῖς βακτηρίαις, γέγραπται δὲ ἐν ταῖς βαλάνοις τὰ στοιχεῖα ἀπὸ τοῦ ἑνδεκάτου, τοῦ λ,[4] ὅσαπερ ἂν
3 μέλλῃ τὰ δικαστήρια πληρωθήσεσθαι. δικάζειν δ' ἔξεστιν τοῖς ὑπὲρ λ' ἔτη γεγονόσιν, ὅσοι αὐτῶν μὴ ὀφείλουσιν τῷ δημοσίῳ ἢ ἄτιμοί εἰσιν· ἐὰν δέ τις δικάζῃ οἷς[5] μὴ ἔξεστιν, ἐνδείκνυται καὶ εἰς τὸ δικαστήριον εἰσάγεται, ἐὰν δ' ἁλῷ προστιμῶσιν αὐτῷ οἱ δικασταὶ ὅ τι ἂν δοκῇ ἄξιος εἶναι παθεῖν ἢ ἀποτῖσαι· ἐὰν δὲ ἀργυρίου τιμηθῇ δεῖ αὐτὸν δε-

[1] τῇ δεκάτῃ φυλῇ ? Richards.
[2] κιβώτια δέκα εἰς ἃ (uel οἷς) alii: κιβω . . . . . cod.
[3] Kenyon: ἔξοδον Hommel: ε . . . cod.
[4] Kenyon: post λ inserit τριακοστου (interpretans) cod.
[5] ᾧ Richards.

[a] 'The dicasts in each tribe are distributed over all the 10 divisions into which all the dicasts are divided. In each tribe all the tickets (πινάκια) bearing the names of the dicasts in the division A are placed in the first κιβώτιον, those of

officials sent to Samos, Scyros, Lemnos or Imbros also get money for food.

The military offices may be held repeatedly, but 3
none of the others, except that a man may become a member of the Council twice.

LXIII. The Jury-courts are elected by lot by the 1
Nine Archons by tribes, and the Clerk of the Law-givers from the tenth tribe. The courts have ten 2
entrances, one for each tribe, twenty rooms, two for each tribe, in which courts are allotted to jurors, a hundred small boxes, ten for each tribe,[a] and other boxes into which the tickets of the jurymen drawn by lot are thrown, and two urns. Staves are placed at each entrance, as many as there are jurymen, and acorns to the same number as the staves are thrown into the urn, and on the acorns are written the letters of the alphabet, starting with the eleventh, *lambda*, as many as the courts that are going to be filled. Right 3
to sit on juries belongs to all those over thirty years old who are not in debt to the Treasury or disfranchised. If any unqualified person sits on a jury, information is laid against him and he is brought before the jury-court, and if convicted the jurymen assess against him whatever punishment or fine he is thought to deserve; and if given a money fine, he has

division B in the second, and so on for all the 10 divisions. According to the number of dicasts required, an equal number of tickets is drawn by lot from each of the 100 κιβώτια. Each ticket so drawn has a court assigned to it by lot; and the tickets are now all placed in the second set of 10 κιβώτια, all tickets assigned to dicasts of any special court being placed in the κιβώτιον which bears the letter corresponding to that court. The names of all the dicasts selected to serve are thus distributed over the several courts that are to sit on the day in question' (Sandys). See further ch. lxiv.

δέσθαι ἕως ἂν ἐκτίσῃ τό τε πρότερον ὄφλημα ἐφ' ᾧ ἐνεδείχθη καὶ ὅ τι ἂν αὐτῷ προστιμήσῃ τὸ
4 δικαστήριον. ἔχει δ' ἕκαστος δικαστὴς ἓν πινάκιον πύξινον, ἐπιγεγραμμένον τὸ ὄνομα τὸ ἑαυτοῦ πατρόθεν καὶ τοῦ δήμου καὶ γράμμα ἓν τῶν στοιχείων μέχρι τοῦ κ· νενέμηνται γὰρ κατὰ φυλὰς δέκα μέρη οἱ δικασταί, παραπλησίως ἴσοι ἐν ἑκάστῳ τῷ γράμματι.

5 Ἐπειδὰν δὲ ὁ θεσμοθέτης ἐπικληρώσῃ τὰ γράμματα ἃ δεῖ προσπαρατίθεσθαι τοῖς δικαστηρίοις, ἐπέθηκε φέρων ὁ ὑπηρέτης ἐφ' ἕκαστον τὸ δικαστήριον τὸ γράμμα τὸ λαχόν.

. . . . . .

Only fragments of the remaining pages of the MS. *survive, much defaced. The most legible passages are here appended, gaps having been filled in without note where the restoration is generally accepted or is very probable.*

1 LXIV. Τὰ δὲ κιβώτια τὰ δέκα κεῖται ἐν τῷ ἔμπροσθεν τῆς εἰσόδου καθ' ἑκάστην τὴν φυλήν. ἐπιγέγραπται δ' ἐπ' αὐτῶν τὰ στοιχεῖα μεχρὶ τοῦ κ. ἐπειδὰν δ' ἐμβάλωσιν οἱ δικασταὶ τὰ πινάκια εἰς τὸ κιβώτιον ἐφ' οὗ ἂν ᾖ ἐπιγεγραμμένον τὸ γράμμα τὸ αὐτὸ ὅπερ ἐπὶ τῷ πινακίῳ ἐστὶν αὐτῷ τῶν στοιχείων, διασείσαντος τοῦ ὑπηρέτου ἕλκει ὁ θεσμοθέτης ἐξ ἑκάστου τοῦ κιβωτίου πινάκιον ἕν·
2 οὗτος δὲ καλεῖται ἐμπήκτης, καὶ ἐμπήγνυσι τὰ πινάκια τὰ ἐκ τοῦ κιβωτίου εἰς τὴν κανονίδα ἐφ' ἧς τὸ αὐτὸ γράμμα ἔπεστιν ὅπερ ἐπὶ τοῦ κιβωτίου. κληροῦται δὲ οὗτος ἵνα μὴ ἀεὶ ὁ αὐτὸς ἐμπηγνύων κακουργῇ. εἰσὶ δὲ κανονίδες πέντε[1]

to go to prison until he has paid both the former debt,
for which the information was laid, and whatever
additional sum has been imposed on him as a fine by
the court. Each juryman has one box-wood ticket, 4
with his own name and that of his father and deme
written on it, and one letter of the alphabet as far as
kappa; for the jurymen of each tribe are divided
into ten sections, approximately an equal number
under each letter.

As soon as the Lawgiver has drawn by lot the 5
letters to be assigned to the courts, the attendant
immediately takes them and affixes to each court its
allotted letter.

. . . . . .

LXIV. The ten boxes lie in front of the entrance for 1
each tribe. They have inscribed on them the letters
as far as *kappa*. When the jurymen have thrown
their tickets into the box on which is inscribed the
same letter of the alphabet as is on the ticket itself,
the attendant shakes them thoroughly and the Lawgiver draws one ticket from each box. This attendant 2
is called the Affixer, and he affixes the tickets taken
from the box to the ledged frame on which is the
same letter that is on the box. This attendant is
chosen by lot, in order that the same person may not
always affix the tickets and cheat. There are five

---

[1] πέντε Blass, δέκα alii: lacunam cod.

3 ἐν ἑκάστῳ τῶν κληρωτηρίων. ὅταν δὲ ἐμβάλῃ τοὺς κύβους, ὁ ἄρχων τὴν φυλὴν κληροῖ κατὰ κληρωτήριον. εἰσὶ δὲ κύβοι χαλκοῖ μέλανες καὶ λευκοί· ὅσους δ᾽ ἂν δέῃ λαχεῖν δικαστάς, τοσοῦτοι ἐμβάλλονται λευκοί, κατὰ πέντε πινάκια εἷς, οἱ δὲ μέλανες τὸν αὐτὸν τρόπον. ἐπειδὰν δ᾽ ἐξαιρῇ[1] τοὺς κύβους, καλεῖ τοὺς εἰληχότας ὁ κῆρυξ·
4 ὑπάρχει δὲ καὶ ὁ ἐμπήκτης εἰς τὸν ἀριθμόν. ὁ δὲ κληθεὶς καὶ ὑπακούσας ἕλκει βάλανον ἐκ τῆς ὑδρίας, καὶ ὀρέξας αὐτὴν ἀνέχων τὸ γράμμα, δείκνυσιν πρῶτον μὲν τῷ ἄρχοντι τῷ ἐφεστηκότι· ὁ δὲ ἄρχων ἐπειδὰν ἴδῃ, ἐμβάλλει τὸ πινάκιον αὐτοῦ εἰς τὸ κιβώτιον ὅπου ἂν ᾖ ἐπιγεγραμμένον τὸ αὐτὸ στοιχεῖον ὅπερ ἐν τῇ βαλάνῳ, ἵν᾽ εἰς οἷον ἂν λάχῃ εἰσίῃ καὶ μὴ εἰς οἷον ἂν βούληται, μηδὲ ᾖ συναγαγεῖν εἰς δικαστήριον οὓς ἂν βούληταί τις.
5 παράκειται δὲ τῷ ἄρχοντι κιβώτια ὅσαπερ ἂν μέλλῃ τὰ δικαστήρια πληρωθήσεσθαι, ἔχοντα στοιχεῖον ἕκαστον ὅπερ ἂν ᾖ ἐπὶ τοῦ δικαστηρίου ἑκάστου εἰληχός.

1 LXV. Αὐτὸς δὲ δείξας πάλιν τῷ ὑπηρέτῃ εἶτ᾽ ἐντὸς εἰσέρχεται τῆς κιγκλίδος.[2] ὁ δὲ ὑπηρέτης δίδωσιν αὐτῷ βακτηρίαν ὁμόχρων τῷ δικαστηρίῳ ἐφ᾽ οὗ τὸ αὐτὸ γράμμα ἐστὶν ὅπερ ἐν τῇ βαλάνῳ, ἵνα ἀναγκαῖον ᾖ αὐτῷ εἰσελθεῖν εἰς ὃ εἴληχε δικαστήριον· ἐὰν γὰρ εἰς ἕτερον εἰσίῃ ἐξελέγχεται ὑπὸ
2 τοῦ χρώματος τῆς βακτηρίας· τοῖς γὰρ δικαστηρίοις χρώματα[3] ἐπιγέγραπται ἑκάστῳ ἐπὶ τῷ σφηκίσκῳ τῆς εἰσόδου. ὁ δὲ λαβὼν τὴν βακτηρίαν

[1] ἐξελῇ alii: ε . . . cod.
[2] primae sententiae supersunt tantum paucae literae incertae.
[3] χρῶμα edd. e schol. Aristoph. *Plut.* 277.

ledged frames in each of the balloting-rooms. When 3
he has thrown in the dice, the Archon casts lots for
the tribe for each balloting-room; they are dice of
copper, black and white. As many white ones are
thrown in as jurymen are required to be selected, one
white die for each five tickets, and the black dice
correspondingly. As he draws out the dice the herald
calls those on whom the lot has fallen. Also the
Affixer is there corresponding to the number. The 4
man called obeys and draws an acorn from the urn
and, holding it out with the inscription upward, shows
it first to the superintending Archon; when the
Archon has seen it, he throws the man's ticket into
the box that has the same letter written on it as the
one on the acorn, in order that he may go into whatever
court he is allotted to and not into whatever
court he chooses and in order that it may not be
possible to collect into a court whatever jurymen a
person wishes. The Archon has by him as many 5
boxes as courts are going to be filled, each lettered
with whichever is the letter assigned by lot to each
court.

LXV. And the man himself having again shown it 1
to the attendant then goes inside the barrier, and the
attendant gives him a staff of the same colour as the
court bearing the same letter as the one on the acorn,
in order that it may be necessary for him to go into
the court to which he has been assigned by lot; for if
he goes into another, he is detected by the colour of
his staff, for each of the courts has a colour painted 2
on the lintel of its entrance. He takes the staff and

βαδίζει εἰς τὸ δικαστήριον τὸ ὁμόχρων μὲν τῇ βακτηρίᾳ ἔχον δὲ τὸ αὐτὸ γράμμα ὅπερ ἐν τῷ βαλάνῳ. ἐπειδὰν δ' εἰσέλθῃ, παραλαμβάνει σύμβολον δημοσίᾳ παρὰ τοῦ εἰληχότος ταύτην τὴν
3 ἀρχήν. εἶτα τήν τε βάλανον καὶ τὴν βακτηρίαν[1] ἐν τῷ δικαστηρίῳ τοῦτον τρόπον εἰσεληλυθότες. τοῖς δ' ἀπολαγχάνουσιν ἀποδιδόασιν οἱ ἐμπῆκται
4 τὰ πινάκια. οἱ δὲ ὑπηρέται οἱ δημόσιοι ἀπὸ τῆς φυλῆς ἑκάστης παραδιδόασι τὰ κιβώτια, ἓν ἐπὶ τὸ δικαστήριον ἕκαστον, ἐν ᾧ ἔνεστι τὰ ὀνόματα τῆς φυλῆς τὰ ὄντα ἐν ἑκάστῳ τῶν δικαστηρίων. παραδιδόασι δὲ τοῖς εἰληχόσι ταῦτα ἀποδιδόναι τοῖς δικασταῖς ἐν ἑκάστῳ [τῷ][2] δικαστηρίῳ ἀριθμῷ τὰ πινάκια ὅπως ἐκ τούτων σκοποῦντες ἀποδιδῶσι τὸν μισθόν.

1 LXVI. Ἐπειδὰν δὲ πάντα πλήρη ᾖ τὰ δικαστήρια, τίθεται ἐν τῷ πρώτῳ τῶν δικαστηρίων β' κληρωτήρια καὶ κύβοι χαλκοῖ ἐν οἷς ἐπιγέγραπται τὰ χρώματα τῶν δικαστηρίων, καὶ ἕτεροι κύβοι ἐν οἷς ἐστιν τῶν ἀρχῶν τὰ ὀνόματα ἐπιγεγραμμένα. λαχόντες δὲ τῶν θεσμοθετῶν δύο χωρὶς ἑκατέρων τοὺς κύβους ἐμβάλλουσιν, ὁ μὲν τὰ χρώματα εἰς τὸ ἓν κληρωτήριον, ὁ δὲ τῶν ἀρχῶν τὰ ὀνόματα εἰς τὸ ἕτερον. ᾗ δ' ἂν πρώτῃ λάχῃ τῶν ἀρχῶν, αὕτη ἀναγορεύεται ὑπὸ τοῦ κήρυκος ὅτι χρήσεται τῷ πρώτῳ λαχόντι δικαστηρίῳ. . . .

*Of cc. lxvi. 2–lxviii. 2 (*MS. *pp. 33, 34) only fragments remain, variously put together and supplemented by editors.*

goes to the court of the same colour as his staff and
having the same letter as is on the acorn. And when
he has come into it he receives a token publicly from
the person appointed by lot to this office. Then 3
with the acorn and the staff they take their seats
in the court, when they have thus entered. And to
those to whom the lot does not fall the Affixers give
back their tickets. And the public attendants from 4
each tribe hand over the boxes, one to each court,
in which are those names of the tribe that are in
each of the courts. And they hand them over to the
persons appointed by lot to restore the tickets to
the jurymen in each court by number, in order that
according to these when they examine them they
may assign the pay.

LXVI. When all the courts are full, two ballot- 1
boxes are placed in the first of the courts, and copper
dice with the colours of the courts painted on them,
and other dice with the names of the offices written
on them. And two of the Lawgivers are chosen by
lot, and throw the two sets of dice in separately, one
throwing in the coloured dice into one ballot-box and
the other the names of the offices into the other. And
to whichever of the offices the lot falls first, it is
proclaimed by the herald that this will use the first
court allotted. . . .

---

[1] βακτηρίαν <ἔχοντες καθίζουσιν> Kenyon: <ἀποτιθέασιν> Thalheim.

[2] si recte legitur, dittographiam secl. Rackham.

2 LXVIII. . . . μετὰ τὸν γʹ (ἀποδιδοὺς γὰρ γʹ λαμβάνει) ἵνα ψηφίζωνται πάντες· οὐ γὰρ ἔστι
3 λαβεῖν σύμβολον οὐδενὶ ἐὰν μὴ ψηφίζηται. εἰσὶ δὲ ἀμφορεῖς δύο κείμενοι ἐν τῷ δικαστηρίῳ, ὁ μὲν χαλκοῦς ὁ δὲ ξύλινος, διαιρετοὶ ὅπως μὴ λάθῃ ὑποβάλλων τις ψήφους, εἰς οὓς ψηφίζονται οἱ δικασταί, ὁ μὲν χαλκοῦς κύριος ὁ δὲ ξυλινὸς ἄκυρος. ἔχων ὁ χαλκοῦς ἐπίθημα διερρινημένον ὥστ' αὐτὴν μόνην χωρεῖν τὴν ψῆφον, ἵνα μὴ δύο ὁ αὐτὸς
4 ἐμβάλλῃ. ἐπειδὰν δὲ διαψηφίζεσθαι μέλλωσιν οἱ δικασταί, ὁ κῆρυξ ἀγορεύει πρῶτον ἂν ἐπισκήπτωνται οἱ ἀντίδικοι ταῖς μαρτυρίαις· οὐ γὰρ ἔστιν ἐπισκήψασθαι ὅταν ἄρξωνται διαψηφίζεσθαι. ἔπειτα πάλιν ἀνακηρύττει "ἡ τετρυπημένη τοῦ πρότερον λέγοντος ἡ δὲ πλήρης τοῦ ὕστερον λέγοντος." ὁ δὲ δικαστὴς λαβὼν ἅμα[1] ἐκ τοῦ λυχνείου τὰς ψήφους, πιέζων τὸν αὐλίσκον τῆς ψήφου καὶ οὐ δεικνύων τοῖς ἀγωνιζομένοις οὔτε τὸ τετρυπημένον οὔτε τὸ πλῆρες, ἐμβάλλει τὴν μὲν κυρίαν εἰς τὸν χαλκοῦν ἀμφορέα τὴν δὲ ἄκυρον εἰς τὸν ξύλινον.

1 LXIX. Πάντες δ' ἐπειδὰν ὦσι διεψηφισμένοι, λαβόντες οἱ ὑπηρέται τὸν ἀμφορέα τὸν κύριον ἐξερῶσι ἐπὶ ἄβακα τρυπήματα ἔχοντα ὅσαιπερ εἰσὶν αἱ ψῆφοι, ἵν' αὗται φανεραὶ προκειμέναι εὐαρίθμητοι ὦσιν, καὶ τὰ τρυπητὰ καὶ τὰ πλήρη δῆλα τοῖς ἀντιδίκοις. οἱ δὲ ἐπὶ τὰς ψήφους εἰληχότες διαριθμοῦσιν αὐτὰς ἐπὶ τοῦ ἄβακος, χωρὶς μὲν τὰς πλήρεις χωρὶς δὲ τὰς τετρυπημένας. καὶ ἀναγορεύει ὁ κῆρυξ τὸν ἀριθμὸν τῶν ψήφων,

[1] λαβόμενος alii: λα | . . . cod.

LXVIII. . . . ⟨a copper token marked with a⟩ 2
3 (for on giving this up he gets three obols), so that
they all may vote; for nobody can get a token if
he does not vote. And there are two jars placed in 3
the court, one of copper and one of wood, separate
so that a man may not secretly throw in pebbles
undetected, into which the jurymen put their votes,
the copper jar to count and the wooden jar for
pebbles not used, the copper jar having a lid with
a hole in it only large enough to take just the
pebble alone, so that the same man may not throw in
two. And when the jury are about to give their 4
verdict, the herald first asks whether the litigants
wish to challenge the evidence of the witnesses; for
they are not allowed to challenge it after the voting
has begun. Then he proclaims again, 'The pebble
with the hole through it is a vote for the first speaker,
and the whole pebble one for the second speaker.'
And the juryman when taking the pebbles out of the
ballot-box presses the hole in the pebble between his
finger and thumb and does not let the parties to the
action see either the perforation or the whole one, and
throws the one that he wishes to count into the copper
vessel and the one that he discards into the wooden one.

LXIX. And when all have voted, the attendants 1
take the vessel that is to count and empty it out on to
a reckoning-board with as many holes in it as there
are pebbles, in order that they may be set out visibly
and be easy to count, and that the perforated and
the whole ones may be clearly seen by the litigants.
And those assigned by lot to count the voting-pebbles
count them out on to the reckoning-board, in two
sets, one the whole ones and the other those perforated. And the herald proclaims the number of

τοῦ μὲν διώκοντος τὰς τετρυπημένας τοῦ δὲ φεύγοντος τὰς πλήρεις· ὁποτέρῳ δ' ἂν πλείων γένηται, οὗτος νικᾷ, ἂν δὲ ἴσαι, ὁ φεύγων.
2 ἔπειτα πάλιν τιμῶσι, ἂν δέῃ τιμῆσαι, τὸν αὐτὸν τρόπον ψηφιζόμενοι, τὸ μὲν σύμβολον ἀποδίδοντες βακτηρίαν δὲ πάλιν παραλαμβάνοντες· ἡ δὲ τίμησίς ἐστιν πρὸς ἡμίχουν ὕδατος ἑκατέρῳ. ἐπειδὰν δὲ αὐτοῖς ᾖ δεδικασμένα τὰ ἐκ τῶν νόμων, ἀπολαμβάνουσιν τὸν μισθὸν ἐν τῷ μέρει οὗ ἔλαχον ἕκαστοι. . . .

votes, the perforated pebbles being for the prosecutor, and the whole ones for the defendant ; and whichever gets the larger number wins the suit, but if the votes are equal, the defendant wins. Then again they 2
assess the damages, if this has to be done, voting in the same way, giving up their ticket and receiving back a staff; as to assessment of damages each party is allowed to speak during three pints of water. And when they have completed their legal duties as jurymen, they take their pay in the division to which each was assigned by lot. . . .

INDEX I.—PROPER NAMES

(References are to chapters except that 'fr.' denotes one of the fragments printed before c. 1.)

INDEX II.—SUBJECTS

(References are to chapters and sections. Notes will sometimes be found under the first reference.)

INDEX II. TO ATHENIAN CONSTITUTION

THE EUDEMIAN ETHICS

INTRODUCTION

I. Place of the *Eudemian Ethics* in the Aristotelian Corpus

All the extant books attributed to Aristotle (including probably the recently recovered treatise on the Athenian Constitution) belong to the group of his works designated by ancient authorities ἀκροατικοὶ λόγοι, 'lecture-courses.' These are scientific treatises, in places hardly more than mere outlines, though for the larger part fully written out arguments; presumably they are records of Aristotle's doctrine made for his pupils, and preserved in the library of the Peripatetic School. The other class of his writings, now lost, were more popular expositions intended for the general reader; some of them were in dialogue form. They were published, and they are alluded to as ἐκδεδομένοι λόγοι.

The former group includes three works on the philosophy of conduct, entitled *The Eudemian Ethics, The Nicomachean Ethics* and *Magna Moralia.* The two former are full scientific treatises, in eight and ten Books respectively. *Magna Moralia* is a smaller work, more discursive in style, of which only two Books survive, the latter part being lost; its contents correspond partly with *The Eudemian* and partly with *The Nicomachean Ethics*; it was probably compiled by a Peripatetic of the generation after Aristotle. Eudemus was the pupil of Aristotle who followed his doctrine most closely; Nicomachus was Aristotle's son, who fell in battle when a mere lad. Both may have been the compilers of the treatises that bear their names : Cicero (*De Finibus* v. 12) says that *The Nicomachean Ethics*, though attributed to Aristotle himself, can well have been by his son, and Diogenes of Laerte quotes from it as by Nicomachus. But the early commentator Porphyry speaks of both works as 'dedicated to' the persons whose names they bear. Whatever the truth may be, *The Nicomachean Ethics* has always been accepted as the authoritative exposition of Aristotle's moral science ; and it seems probable that *The Eudemian*, so far as it differs, represents an earlier stage of its development.[a] This view is not necessarily precluded by the fact that in some places *The Eudemian Ethics* is fuller in expression or more discursive than *The Nicomachean.*

II. The Eudemian–Nicomachean Books

For about one third of the whole the two works overlap, the Eudemian Books IV., V., VI. being identical with the Nicomachean V., VI., VII. ; these are given in the MSS. and editions of the latter work only. Scholars have debated to which they really belong, some holding that they fit the argument of

[a] This is the view of Jaeger, followed by Burnet in his *Essays and Addresses* and by Mansion ; but *The Eudemian Ethics* is regarded as later than *The Nicomachean* by Spengel, Susemihl 1900, and Stock (in the Oxford Aristotle vol. ix., Introduction to *M.M.* etc. p. v), as it was by Burnet in his earlier work, his edition of *N.E.* Taylor (*Aristotle*, p. 18) thinks that *The Nicomachean* is a redaction of the master's doctrine by his son, and *The Eudemian* a freer and more readable recast by his pupil. *Magna Moralia* is put last by almost all scholars, but first of the three treatises by Schleiermacher and Arnim.

the *Eudemian* and that the corresponding parts of the *Nicomachean* have been lost, others the opposite. But all Aristotle's treatises are so loosely put together that the arguments for neither view are convincing. It is more probable that the three common Books represent his final doctrine, except in so far as they are modified by other parts of his works—thus the excursus on the ethical value of pleasure in *E.E.* VI. = *N.E.* VII. was doubtless superseded by the more accurate treatment of the topic at the beginning of *N.E.* X.

III. The *Eudemian Ethics*: Outline of Contents and Comparison with the *Nicomachean*

Book I. introduces the subject—the nature of Happiness or Well-being, the supreme End or Aim of human conduct. This is a practical study: knowledge of the good is an aid to its attainment. The different views that prevail are crystallized in three typical Lives, the philosopher's life of thought, the statesman's life of action, the voluptuary's life of pleasure. The Platonic theory of an Absolute Good is of questionable philosophic validity, and in any case has no bearing on practical life.

Book II. c. i. defines Happiness as consisting in the right exercise of the functions of man's nature moral and intellectual. The contents of *E.E.* so far correspond with those of *N.E.* Book I.; the remainder of Book II. with *N.E.* II. and III. i.-v. It examines the nature of Moral Goodness, Goodness of Character, Virtue, which is defined as a fixed disposition that in action or emotion steers a middle course between too much and too little. The various virtues are tabulated, with the vices of excess and defect that correspond to each. The problem of the Freedom of the Will is studied in the light of the psychology of Volition and Purpose.

Book III. discusses the Virtues and some minor Graces of Character seriatim, each with its corresponding pair of Vices. The list tallies with that in *N.E.* III., vi. ff. and IV., except that it inserts the virtue of Mildness between Temperance and Liberality, and adds to the minor Graces of Character Nemesis (righteous indignation at another's undeserved good or bad fortune), Friendliness and Dignity, while it omits Gentleness and Agreeableness (*N.E.* IV., v., vi.).

(Books IV., V., VI. are omitted in MSS. and editions of the *Eudemian Ethics*, as they are the same as Books V., VI., VII. of the *Nicomachean*; the first of these three Books deals with Justice, thus completing the examination of the Moral Virtues; the second treats the Intellectual Virtues of Prudence or Practical Wisdom and Theoria or Speculative Wisdom; the third forms an appendix to the section on Moral Virtue—it examines Weakness of Will and studies the psychology of Pleasure—a subject again treated differently and more accurately in *N.E.* X. *init.*)

The subject of Book VII. is Friendship. The term includes all forms of friendly mutual regard, whether between equals or superior and inferior, relatives or other associates, and whether based on the motive of utility or the pleasure of society or respect for worth. The psychology of friendship is analysed in relation to that of self-love.

In *N.E.* VIII. and IX. Friendship is discussed at greater length with fuller detail; the arrangement of the topics is different but there is perhaps no striking discrepancy of view.

E.E. VIII. notices the epistemological aspect of Virtue (treated in *N.E.* I., ix., but differently); and discusses the ethical bearing of Good Luck (more fully dealt with in a different connexion in c. iii. of *N.E.* VII. = *E.E.* VI.). There follows an essay on Kalokâgathia, Moral Nobility (a virtue merely alluded to without analysis in *N.E.*, as a necessary quality of the Great-spirited man, 1124 a 4 and 1179 b 10); it is treated as the consummation of the particular virtues. In conclusion there is a glance at Theoria, the activity of Speculative Wisdom, as the highest life of man; at Book II. *init.* this was coupled with Moral Conduct as constituting happiness. There is nothing corresponding to the full treatment of Theoria as the consummation of human well-being that is given in *N.E.* X. vii., viii., or to the transition from ethics to politics (glancing at the importance of public education) which concludes that work.

IV. Text, MSS. and Editions

The *Eudemian Ethics* is not contained in the two best MSS. of Aristotle, the 10th c. Laurentianus (denoted by the sign K^b) and the 12th c. Parisiensis (L^b); we derive it chiefly from Vaticanus (P^b), a 13th c. copy of K^b, and the early 15th c. Marcianus (M^b), not so good a text as P^b but an indispensable adjunct to it—according to Jackson, who refers to the text of these two MSS. as 'the Greek tradition.' Other later copies certainly contain more errors, and are of little value as actual traditions of a sound text —some of their variants may be mere conjectural corrections ; their readings are only occasionally given in this edition.

The 13th c. Latin translation attributed to William of Moerbeke follows the Greek very closely, and is almost equivalent to another MS. ranking in value next to Vaticanus and Marcianus ; it is occasionally adduced in this edition either in Latin or in its original Greek when this can be inferred with certainty.

There is an old Latin version of Book VIII. c. ii. with *Magna Moralia* Book II. c. viii., entitled *De Bona Fortuna*, printed in a Latin Aristotle of 1482, which indicates an independent Greek text of that passage.

The earliest printed edition of Aristotle is the Aldine, Venice 1498. The foundation of all modern work on the text is the monumental Berlin edition, with a Latin translation, scholia and indices, published by the Academia Regia Borussica in 1831 and the following years. The text, edited by Bekker, forms Volumes I. and II. which are paged consecutively, the *Eudemian Ethics* occupying pp. 1214-1249 ; the Berlin pages, the columns (indicated by *a* and *b*) and the numbering of the lines are shown in the margin of the present text.

Fritsche's edition of the *Eudemian Ethics* (Ratisbon 1851) has an introduction on the authorship and contents, a text with explanatory notes, illustrative quotations and critical notes, a Latin translation and a Greek index.

The Teubner text of Susemihl (Leipzig 1884) has useful critical notes, collecting the corrections of other scholars published in the learned journals.

Henry Jackson contributed a valuable study of the text and contents of Book VII. cc. i., ii. to *The Journal of Philology* xxxii. pp. 170 ff.; and also supplied a number of printed notes to the Oxford translator, J. Solomon.

Solomon's translation, in Volume IX. of the Oxford Aristotle 1925, is the most recent work on the book. Mr. Solomon in his footnotes gives full references to the corresponding passages of the *Nicomachean Ethics* and *Magna Moralia*; and his notes on the readings of the Greek that he has adopted make his work a valuable critical edition: they include conjectures of the translator himself, of Professor Ross the general editor of the series, and of other scholars, among them the notes of Henry Jackson referred to above.

In view of the comparatively scanty amount of work on the text hitherto published, the present editor has thought himself justified in making a considerable number of conjectural emendations of his own. Some freedom has been used in incorporating these and those of other scholars in the text; it seems in keeping with the purpose of this series to present the reader directly with what Aristotle probably wrote, leaving him to glance at the critical notes to discover what he is represented as having written by his copyists. At the same time in the interests of scholarship emended passages in the text are marked by a number referring to the corresponding note.

Similarly, the style of the translation is intended to make it serve as an aid to a student reading the original. It is as interpretative as was possible without becoming a mere paraphrase; it is not intended as a substitute for the Greek, which might take the form either of a rigidly literal version or of a rendering into idiomatic English conveying the sense but ignoring the form of the original.

The following signs are used in the critical notes:

MSS.

P^b = Vaticanus.
M^b = Marcianus.
cet. = all the other MSS. collated by editors where their readings agree.
v.l. = the reading of one or some of these other MSS.
Guil. = the Latin version of William of Moerbeke.
Γ = the conjectured Greek original of this.
B^f = *De Bona Fortuna.*

The following abbreviations are used for the names of some editors and commentators quoted for the text:

Ald. = editio princeps Aldina.
Bek. = Bekker.
Bus. = Busolt.
Bz. = Bonitz.
Cas. = Casaubon.
Fr. = Fritsche.
Iac. = Henry Jackson.
Rac. = the present editor.
Ras. = Rassow.
Ric. = Richards.
Sol. = Solomon.
Sp. = Spengler.
Sus. = Susemihl.
Syl. = Sylburg.
Vict. = Victorius.

H. R.

November 1934.

ΗΘΙΚΩΝ ΕΥΔΗΜΙΩΝ Α

1214 a

I. Ὁ μὲν ἐν Δήλῳ παρὰ τῷ θεῷ τὴν αὑτοῦ 1
γνώμην ἀποφηνάμενος συνέγραψεν ἐπὶ τὸ προπύλαιον τοῦ Λητῴου διελὼν ὡς[1] οὐχ ὑπάρχοντα πάντα τῷ αὐτῷ τό τε ἀγαθὸν καὶ τὸ καλὸν καὶ τὸ ἡδύ, ποιήσας

κάλλιστον τὸ δικαιότατον, λῷστον δ' ὑγιαίνειν,
πάντων ἥδιστον δ'[2] οὗ τις ἐρᾷ τὸ τυχεῖν.

ἡμεῖς δ' αὐτῷ μὴ συγχωρῶμεν· ἡ γὰρ εὐδαιμονία κάλλιστον καὶ ἄριστον ἁπάντων οὖσα ἥδιστόν ἐστιν.

Πολλῶν δ' ὄντων θεωρημάτων ἃ περὶ ἕκαστον 2
πρᾶγμα καὶ περὶ ἑκάστην φύσιν ἀπορίαν ἔχει καὶ δεῖται σκέψεως, τὰ μὲν αὐτῶν συντείνει πρὸς τὸ γνῶναι μόνον, τὰ δὲ καὶ περὶ τὰς κτήσεις[3] καὶ περὶ τὰς πράξεις τοῦ πράγματος. ὅσα μὲν οὖν 3
ἔχει φιλοσοφίαν μόνον θεωρητικήν, λεκτέον κατὰ τὸν ἐπιβάλλοντα καιρὸν ὅ τι περ ἂν οἰκεῖον ᾖ[4] τῇ

[1] ὡς add. Sp.
[2] δ' hic Fr.: ante ἥδιστον aut om. codd.
[3] χρήσεις Sp.
[4] Ric.: ὅ τι περ οἰκεῖον ἦν.

[a] Theognis (255 f. with slight variation, quoted also in *N.E.* i., 1099 a 27).

THE EUDEMIAN ETHICS

BOOK I

Books I. IX. init. HAPPINESS. Introduction (cc. i.-vi.): the supreme good—

1 I. The man [a] who at Delos set forth in the precinct of the god his own opinion composed an inscription for the forecourt of the temple of Leto in which he distinguished goodness, beauty and pleasantness as not all being properties of the same thing. His verses are :

> Justice [b] is fairest, and Health is best,
> But to win one's desire is the pleasantest.

But for our part let us not allow that he is right ; for Happiness [c] is at once the pleasantest and the fairest and best of all things whatever.

its mode of acquisition,

2 About every thing and every natural species there
are many views that involve difficulty and require
examination ; of these some relate only to our knowledge of the thing, others deal also with modes of
3 acquiring it and of acting in relation to it. As to
all those views therefore that involve only speculative philosophy, we must say whatever may be proper
to the inquiry when the suitable occasion occurs.

[b] Or ' Righteousness ' ; the term includes more than justice.

[c] Or ' Well-being ' ; the Greek word is entirely non-committal, and does not necessarily denote a state of feeling, consciousness of welfare.

1214 a
μεθόδῳ. πρῶτον δὲ σκεπτέον ἐν τίνι τὸ εὖ ζῆν 4
καὶ πῶς κτητόν, πότερον φύσει γίνονται πάντες
εὐδαίμονες οἱ τυγχάνοντες ταύτης τῆς προσηγορίας,
ὥσπερ μεγάλοι καὶ μικροὶ καὶ τὴν χροιὰν δια-
φέροντες, ἢ διὰ μαθήσεως, ὡς οὔσης ἐπιστήμης
τινὸς τῆς εὐδαιμονίας, ἢ διά τινος ἀσκήσεως
(πολλὰ γὰρ οὔτε κατὰ φύσιν οὔτε μαθοῦσιν ἀλλ'
ἐθισθεῖσιν ὑπάρχει τοῖς ἀνθρώποις, φαῦλα μὲν
τοῖς φαύλως ἐθισθεῖσι, χρηστὰ δὲ τοῖς χρηστῶς);
ἢ τούτων μὲν κατ' οὐδένα τῶν τρόπων, δυοῖν δὲ 5
θάτερον, ἤτοι καθάπερ οἱ νυμφόληπτοι καὶ θεό-
ληπτοι τῶν ἀνθρώπων, ἐπιπνοίᾳ δαιμονίου τινὸς
ὥσπερ ἐνθουσιάζοντες, ἢ διὰ τὴν τύχην (πολλοὶ
γὰρ ταὐτόν φασιν εἶναι τὴν εὐδαιμονίαν καὶ τὴν
εὐτυχίαν).
Ὅτι μὲν οὖν ἡ παρουσία[1] διὰ τούτων ἁπάντων ἢ 6
τινῶν ἢ τινὸς ὑπάρχει τοῖς ἀνθρώποις, οὐκ ἄδηλον·
ἅπασαι γὰρ αἱ γενέσεις σχεδὸν πίπτουσιν εἰς
ταύτας τὰς ἀρχάς (καὶ γὰρ τὰς[2] ἀπὸ τῆς διανοίας
ἁπάσας πρὸς τὰς ἀπ' ἐπιστήμης ἄν τις συναγάγοι
πράξεις). τὸ δ' εὐδαιμονεῖν καὶ τὸ ζῆν μακαρίως 7
καὶ καλῶς εἴη ἂν ἐν τρισὶ μάλιστα τοῖς εἶναι
δοκοῦσιν αἱρετωτάτοις· οἱ μὲν γὰρ τὴν φρόνησιν
μέγιστον εἶναί φασιν ἀγαθόν, οἱ δὲ τὴν ἀρετήν, οἱ
δὲ τὴν ἡδονήν. καὶ πρὸς τὴν εὐδαιμονίαν ἔνιοι 8
1214 b περὶ τοῦ μεγέθους αὐτῶν διαμφισβητοῦσι, συμ-
βάλλεσθαι φάσκοντες θάτερον θατέρου μᾶλλον εἰς

[1] v.l. παρουσία τῆς εὐδαιμονίας. [2] τὰς add. Cas.

[a] The Greek term here still retains the general sense that it has in Plato. In the *Nicomachean Ethics* it is limited to

4 But we must consider first what the good life consists in and how it is to be obtained—whether all of those who receive the designation 'happy' acquire happiness by nature, as is the case with tallness and shortness of stature and differences of complexion, or by study, which would imply that there is a science of happiness, or by some form of training, for there are many human attributes that are not bestowed by nature nor acquired by study but gained by habituation—bad attributes by those trained in bad habits and good attributes by those trained in good ones.
5 Or does happiness come in none of these ways, but either by a sort of elevation of mind inspired by some divine power, as in the case of persons possessed by a nymph or a god, or, alternatively, by fortune? for many people identify happiness with good fortune.

6 Now it is pretty clear that the presence of happiness is bestowed upon men by all of these things, or by some or one of them; for almost all the modes in which it is produced fall under these principles, inasmuch as all the acts that spring from thought may be included with those that spring from knowledge.
7 But to be happy and to live blissfully and finely may consist chiefly in three things deemed to be most desirable: some people say that Wisdom [a] is the greatest good, others Goodness [b] and others
8 Pleasure. And certain persons debate about their importance in relation to happiness, declaring that one contributes more to it than another—some holding

its three main constituents,

[a] Practical Wisdom, *prudentia*, 'prudence,' as distinct from *θεωρία*, *sapientia*, 'speculative wisdom.'

[b] It must always be remembered that the Greek term is less limited in meaning than 'virtue,' and may denote excellence in any department, not only moral goodness.

1214 b αὐτήν, οἱ μὲν ὡς οὖσαν μεῖζον ἀγαθὸν τὴν
φρόνησιν τῆς ἀρετῆς, οἱ δὲ ταύτης τὴν ἀρετήν,
οἱ δ' ἀμφοτέρων τούτων τὴν ἡδονήν· καὶ τοῖς μὲν
ἐκ πάντων δοκεῖ τούτων, τοῖς δ' ἐκ δυοῖν, τοῖς δ'
ἐν ἑνί τινι τούτων εἶναι τὸ ζῆν εὐδαιμόνως.

II. Περὶ δὴ τούτων ἐπιστήσαντας ἅπαντα τὸν 1
δυνάμενον ζῆν κατὰ τὴν αὑτοῦ προαίρεσιν θέσθαι
τινὰ σκοπὸν τοῦ καλῶς ζῆν, ἤτοι τιμὴν ἢ δόξαν
ἢ πλοῦτον ἢ παιδείαν, πρὸς ὃν ἀποβλέπων ποιήσεται
πάσας τὰς πράξεις (ὡς τό γε μὴ συντετάχθαι τὸν
βίον πρός τι τέλος ἀφροσύνης πολλῆς σημεῖόν
ἐστιν), μάλιστα δὴ δεῖ πρῶτον ἐν αὑτῷ διορίσασθαι 2
μήτε προπετῶς μήτε ῥαθύμως ἐν τίνι τῶν ἡμετέρων
τὸ ζῆν εὖ καὶ τίνων ἄνευ τοῖς ἀνθρώποις οὐκ
ἐνδέχεται τοῦθ' ὑπάρχειν. οὐ γὰρ ταὐτὸν ὧν τ'
ἄνευ οὐχ οἷόν τε ὑγιαίνειν καὶ τὸ ὑγιαίνειν, ὁμοίως 3
δ' ἔχει τοῦτο καὶ ἐφ' ἑτέρων πολλῶν· ὥστ' οὐδὲ
τὸ ζῆν καλῶς καὶ ὧν ἄνευ οὐ δυνατὸν ζῆν καλῶς.
ἔστι δὲ τῶν τοιούτων τὰ μὲν οὐκ ἴδια τῆς ὑγιείας 4
οὐδὲ τῆς ζωῆς ἀλλὰ κοινὰ πάντων ὡς εἰπεῖν, καὶ
τῶν ἕξεων καὶ τῶν πράξεων, οἷον ἄνευ τοῦ ἀναπνεῖν
ἢ ἐγρηγορέναι ἢ κινήσεως μετέχειν οὐθὲν ἂν
ὑπάρξειεν ἡμῖν οὔτ' ἀγαθὸν οὔτε κακόν, τὰ δ'
ἴδια μᾶλλον περὶ ἑκάστην φύσιν, οὐ γὰρ ὁμοίως
οἰκεῖον πρὸς εὐεξίαν τοῖς εἰρημένοις κρεωφαγία
καὶ τῶν περιπάτων οἱ μετὰ δεῖπνον. ἃ δεῖ μὴ

---

[a] *Cf. N.E.* i., 1094 a 22, 1095 a 22-26.

that Wisdom is a greater good than Goodness, others the reverse, and others that Pleasure is a greater good than either of them ; and some think that the happy life comes from them all, others from two of them, others that it consists in some one of them.

1 II. Having then in regard to this subject established that everybody able to live according to his own purposive choice should set before him some object for noble living to aim at[a]—either honour or else glory or wealth or culture—on which he will keep his eyes fixed in all his conduct (since clearly it is a mark of much folly not to have one's life regulated with
2 regard to some End), it is therefore most necessary first to decide within oneself, neither hastily nor carelessly, in which of the things that belong to us the good life consists, and what are the indispensable conditions for men's possessing it. For there is a distinction between health and the things that are
3 indispensable conditions of health, and this is similarly the case with many other things ; consequently also to live finely is not the same as the things with-
4 out which living finely is impossible. And in the latter class of things some that are indispensable conditions of health and life are not peculiar to special people but common to practically all men—both some states and some actions—for instance, without breathing or being awake or participating in movement we could not possess any good or any evil at all ; whereas others are more peculiar to special types of natural constitution—for instance, eating meat and taking walking exercise after dinner are not closely related to health in the same way as the conditions mentioned. And these facts

its essential conditions.

λανθάνειν·[1] ἔστι γὰρ ταῦτ' αἴτια τῆς ἀμφισβητήσεως 5
περὶ τοῦ εὐδαιμονεῖν τί ἐστι καὶ γίνεται διὰ τίνων·
ὧν ἄνευ γὰρ οὐχ οἷόν τε εὐδαιμονεῖν ἔνιοι μέρη
τῆς εὐδαιμονίας εἶναι νομίζουσιν.

III. Πάσας μὲν οὖν τὰς δόξας ἐπισκοπεῖν ὅσας 1
ἔχουσί τινες περὶ αὐτῆς περίεργον. πολλὰ γὰρ
φαίνεται καὶ τοῖς παιδαρίοις καὶ τοῖς κάμνουσι
καὶ παραφρονοῦσι περὶ ὧν ἂν οὐθεὶς νοῦν ἔχων
διαπορήσειεν, δέονται γὰρ οὐ λόγων, ἀλλ' οἱ μὲν
ἡλικίας ἐν ᾗ μεταβαλοῦσιν[2] οἱ δὲ κολάσεως
ἰατρικῆς ἢ πολιτικῆς (κόλασις γὰρ ἡ φαρμακεία
τῶν πληγῶν οὐκ ἐλάττων ἐστίν)· ὁμοίως δὲ 2
ταύταις οὐδὲ τὰς τῶν πολλῶν, εἰκῇ γὰρ λέγουσι
σχεδὸν περὶ ἁπάντων καὶ μάλιστα περὶ ταύτης.
τὰς δὲ τῶν σοφῶν[3] ἐπισκεπτέον μόνας· ἄτοπον
γὰρ προσφέρειν λόγον τοῖς λόγου μηδὲν δεομένοις
ἀλλὰ πάθους.[4] ἐπεὶ δ' εἰσὶν ἀπορίαι περὶ ἑκάστην 3
πραγματείαν οἰκεῖαι, δῆλον ὅτι καὶ περὶ βίου τοῦ
κρατίστου καὶ ζωῆς τῆς ἀρίστης εἰσίν· ταύτας οὖν
καλῶς ἔχει τὰς δόξας ἐξετάζειν, οἱ γὰρ τῶν
ἀμφισβητούντων ἔλεγχοι τῶν ἐναντιουμένων αὐταῖς[5]
λόγων ἀποδείξεις εἰσίν.

Ἔτι δὲ πρὸ ἔργου τὸ τὰ τοιαῦτα μὴ λανθάνειν 4
μάλιστα πρὸς ἃ δεῖ συντείνειν πᾶσαν σκέψιν, ἐκ
τίνων ἐνδέχεται μετασχεῖν τοῦ εὖ καὶ καλῶς ζῆν

[1] ἃ . . . λανθάνειν hic Rac.: supra post φύσιν.
[2] Sp.: μεταβάλλουσιν.
[3] ταύτης . . . σοφῶν add. Pᵇ marg. (δὲ add. Rac.).
[4] πείθους Iac.
[5] Rac.: αὐτοῖς.

[a] In the MSS. this clause comes before the preceding one, 'for instance, eating meat . . . mentioned.'

[b] *Cf. N.E.* i., 1095 a 28-30, b 19 ff.

5 must not be overlooked,[a] for these are the causes of the disputes about the real nature of happiness and about the means of procuring it; for some people regard the things that are indispensable conditions of being happy as actual parts of happiness.

1 III. Now to examine all the opinions that any people hold about happiness is a superfluous task.[b] For children and the sick and insane have many opinions which no sensible man would discuss, for these persons need not argument but the former time in which to grow up and alter and the latter medical or official chastisement (treatment with drugs being chastisement just as much as flogging
2 is). And similarly it is also superfluous to examine the opinions of the multitude[c] either; for they talk at random about almost everything, and especially about happiness. We ought to examine only the opinions of the wise[d]; for it is out of place to apply reasoning to those who do not need reasoning at all,
3 but experience. But since every subject has special difficulties related to it, it is clear that there are such in regard to the highest life and the best mode of existence; it is then well to examine the opinions putting these difficulties, since the refutations advanced by those who challenge them are demonstrations of the theories that are opposed to them.

Considered opinions as to the nature of happiness

4 Moreover to notice such matters is especially advantageous with a view to the subjects to which all inquiry ought to be directed—the question what are the means that make it possible to participate in living well and finely (if 'blissfully' is too invidious

are of practical value for its attainment.

[c] *Cf. N.E.* i., 1095 b 19.

[d] The words translated 'happiness' and 'the opinions of the wise' are conjectural insertions in the Greek.

1215 a (εἰ τὸ[1] μακαρίως ἐπιφθονώτερον εἰπεῖν), καὶ πρὸς
τὴν ἐλπίδα τὴν περὶ ἕκαστα γενομένην ἂν τῶν
ἐπιεικῶν. εἰ μὲν γὰρ ἐν τοῖς διὰ τύχην γινομένοις 5
ἢ τοῖς διὰ φύσιν τὸ καλῶς ζῆν ἐστίν, ἀνέλπιστον
ἂν εἴη πολλοῖς, οὐ γάρ ἐστι δι' ἐπιμελείας ἡ
κτῆσις οὐδὲ[2] ἐπ' αὐτοῖς οὐδὲ[3] τῆς αὐτῶν πραγ-
ματείας· εἰ δ' ἐν τῷ αὐτὸν ποιόν τινα εἶναι καὶ 6
τὰς κατ' αὐτὸν πράξεις, κοινότερον ἂν εἴη τὸ
ἀγαθὸν καὶ θειότερον, κοινότερον μὲν τῷ πλείοσιν
ἐνδέχεσθαι μετασχεῖν, θειότερον δὲ τῷ κεῖσθαι
τὴν εὐδαιμονίαν τοῖς[4] αὐτοὺς παρασκευάζουσι
ποιούς τινας καὶ τὰς πράξεις.

IV. Ἔσται δὲ φανερὰ τὰ πλεῖστα τῶν ἀμφισ- 1
βητουμένων καὶ διαπορουμένων ἂν καλῶς ὁρισθῇ
τί χρὴ νομίζειν εἶναι τὴν εὐδαιμονίαν, πότερον ἐν
τῷ ποιόν τινα μόνον εἶναι τὴν ψυχήν, καθάπερ
τινὲς ᾠήθησαν τῶν σοφῶν καὶ πρεσβυτέρων, ἢ
δεῖ μὲν καὶ ποιόν τινα ὑπάρχειν αὐτόν, μᾶλλον δὲ
δεῖ τὰς πράξεις εἶναι ποιάς τινας.

Διῃρημένων δὲ τῶν βίων καὶ τῶν μὲν οὐδ'[5] 2
ἀμφισβητούντων τῆς τοιαύτης εὐημερίας ἀλλ'
ἄλλως[6] τῶν ἀναγκαίων χάριν σπουδαζομένων, οἷον
τῶν περὶ τὰς τέχνας τὰς φορτικὰς καὶ τὰς
βαναύσους[7] καὶ τῶν περὶ χρηματισμὸν (λέγω δὲ
φορτικὰς μὲν τὰς πρὸς δόξαν πραγματευομένας
μόνον, βαναύσους δὲ τὰς ἑδραίας καὶ μισθαρνικάς,

[1] τὸ Vict., τῷ τὸ Fr.: τῷ.

[2] οὐδὲ om. Sp. [3] οὐδὲ διὰ Pᵇ.

[4] v.l. ἐν τοῖς: ἐν τῷ . . . παρασκευάζειν ? Rac.

[5] οὐδ' add. Bz. [6] Sp. ὡς.

[7] Sp.: καὶ τὰς βαναύσους post χρηματισμόν.

[a] The word ψυχή, usually rendered 'soul,' has no term exactly corresponding to it in English, as it denotes the whole

an expression)—and with a view to the hope that we may have of the things that are good in the various
5 departments. For if living finely depends on things that come by fortune or by nature, it would be beyond the hopes of many men, for then its attainment is not to be secured by effort, and does not rest with men themselves and is not a matter of their own
6 conduct; but if it consists in oneself and one's own actions having a particular quality, the good would be more common and more divine—more common because it would be possible for more people to share it, and more divine because happiness would then be in store for those who made themselves and their actions of a particular quality.

Character or conduct?

1 IV. Most of the points debated and the difficulties raised will be clear if it be satisfactorily determined what the proper conception of happiness is—does it consist merely in a person's possessing some particular quality of spirit,[a] as some of the sages and the older thinkers held, or although a particular personal character is indeed an indispensable condition, is a particular quality of conduct even more necessary?

Three typical lives

2 There are various different modes of life, and some do not lay any claim to well-being of the kind under consideration, but are pursued merely for the sake of things necessary—for instance the lives devoted to the vulgar and mechanic arts and those dealing with business (by vulgar arts I mean those pursued only for reputation, by mechanic the sedentary and wage-earning pursuits, and by arts of business those

vitality of a living creature, with the unconscious factors of nutrition and growth as well as conscious feelings or emotions and thoughts.

1215 a
χρηματιστικὰς δὲ τὰς πρὸς ὠνὰς ἀγοραίας[1] καὶ
πράσεις καπηλικάς), τῶν δ' εἰς ἀγωγὴν εὐδαιμο-
νικὴν ταττομένων τριῶν ὄντων τῶν καὶ πρότερον
ῥηθέντων ἀγαθῶν ὡς μεγίστων τοῖς ἀνθρώποις,
ἀρετῆς καὶ φρονήσεως καὶ ἡδονῆς, τρεῖς ὁρῶμεν
καὶ βίους ὄντας οὓς οἱ ἐξουσίας[2] τυγχάνοντες
1215 b προαιροῦνται ζῆν ἅπαντες, πολιτικὸν φιλόσοφον
ἀπολαυστικόν. τούτων γὰρ ὁ μὲν φιλόσοφος 3
βούλεται περὶ φρόνησιν εἶναι καὶ τὴν θεωρίαν τὴν
περὶ τὴν ἀλήθειαν, ὁ δὲ πολιτικὸς περὶ τὰς πράξεις
τὰς καλάς (αὗται δ' εἰσὶν αἱ ἀπὸ τῆς ἀρετῆς), ὁ
δ' ἀπολαυστικὸς περὶ τὰς ἡδονὰς τὰς σωματικάς.
διόπερ ἕτερος[3] ἕτερον[4] εὐδαίμονα προσαγορεύει, 4
καθάπερ ἐλέχθη καὶ πρότερον, καὶ[5] Ἀναξαγόρας
μὲν ὁ Κλαζομένιος ἐρωτηθεὶς τίς ὁ εὐδαιμονέστατος,
"οὐθείς" εἶπεν "ὧν σὺ νομίζεις, ἀλλ' ἄτοπος ἄν
τίς σοι φανείη." τοῦτον δ' ἀπεκρίνατο τὸν τρόπον
ἐκεῖνος ὁρῶν τὸν ἐρόμενον ἀδύνατον ὑπολαμβάνοντα
μὴ μέγαν ὄντα καὶ καλὸν ἢ πλούσιον ταύτης
τυγχάνειν τῆς προσηγορίας, αὐτὸς δ' ἴσως ᾤετο
τὸν ζῶντα ἀλύπως καὶ καθαρῶς πρὸς τὸ δίκαιον
ἤ τινος θεωρίας κοινωνοῦντα θείας, τοῦτον ὡς
ἄνθρωπον εἰπεῖν[6] μακάριον εἶναι.
V. Περὶ πολλῶν μὲν οὖν καὶ ἑτέρων οὐ ῥᾴδιον 1

[1] Sol.: πρὸς ἀγορὰς μέν.
[2] Sp.: ἐπ' ἐξουσίας: ἐπ' ἐξουσίας <ὄντες> τυγχάνοντες ? Rac.
[3] ἕτερος add. Ras.
[4] ἕτερον Rac.: ἕτερον τόν.
[5] καὶ add. ? Sus.
[6] εἰπεῖν <δεῖν> ? Ric.

[a] See 1214 a 30-b 5.
[b] Perhaps the Greek should be emended to give 'those who happen to be in power.'
[c] *i.e.* active citizenship: 'statesmanship' is too lofty a term.

concerned with market purchase and retail selling); but on the other hand, the things related to the happy conduct of life being three, the things already mentioned[a] as the greatest possible goods for men—goodness, wisdom and pleasure, we see that there are also three ways of life in which those to whom fortune gives opportunity[b] invariably choose to live, the life of politics,[c] the life of philosophy, and the life
3 of enjoyment. Of these the philosophic life denotes being concerned with the contemplation of truth, the political life means being occupied with honourable activities (and these are the activities that spring from goodness), and the life of enjoyment is con-
4 cerned with the pleasures of the body. Owing to this, different people give the name of happy to different persons, as was said before too; and Anaxagoras[d] of Clazomenae when asked 'Who is the happiest man?' said 'None of those whom you think, but he would seem to you an odd sort of person.' But Anaxagoras answered in that way because he saw that the man who put the question supposed it to be impossible to receive the appellation 'happy' without being great and beautiful or rich, whereas he himself perhaps thought that the person who humanly speaking enjoys bliss is he that lives by the standard of justice without pain and in purity, or participates in some form of divine contemplation.[e]

1 V. While there are many different things as to Various opinions as to life's goods

[d] The physical philosopher, 500–428 B.C., born at Clazomenae in Ionia, taught at Athens.

[e] *i.e.* the man who displays the virtues of Temperance, Justice and Wisdom (the fourth cardinal virtue, Courage, is omitted), enhanced by pleasure or freedom from pain. This passage illustrates how Aristotle prepared the way for the hedonism of Epicurus.

1215 b τὸ κρῖναι καλῶς, μάλιστα δὲ περὶ οὗ πᾶσι ῥᾷστον
εἶναι δοκεῖ καὶ παντὸς ἀνθρώπου τὸ γνῶναι, τί
τῶν ἐν τῷ ζῆν αἱρετόν, καὶ λαβὼν ἂν τις ἔχοι
πλήρη τὴν ἐπιθυμίαν. πολλὰ γάρ ἐστι τοιαῦτα
τῶν ἀποβαινόντων δι' ἃ προΐενται τὸ ζῆν, οἷον
νόσους περιωδυνίας χειμῶνας· ὥστε δῆλον ὅτι
κἂν ἐξ ἀρχῆς αἱρετὸν ἦν, εἴ τις αἵρεσιν ἐδίδου,
διά γε ταῦτα τὸ μὴ γενέσθαι. πρὸς δὲ τούτοις ὁ[1] 2
βίος ὃν ζῶσιν ἔτι παῖδες ὄντες· καὶ γὰρ ἐπὶ τοῦτον
ἀνακάμψαι πάλιν οὐδεὶς ἂν ὑπομείνειεν εὖ φρονῶν.
ἔτι δὲ πολλὰ τῶν τε μηδεμίαν ἐχόντων ἡδονὴν ἢ 3
λύπην, καὶ τῶν ἐχόντων μὲν ἡδονὴν μὴ καλὴν
δέ, τοιαῦτ' ἐστὶν ὥστε τὸ μὴ εἶναι κρεῖττον εἶναι
τοῦ ζῆν. ὅλως δ' εἴ τις ἅπαντα συναγάγοι ὅσα 4
πράττουσι μὲν καὶ πάσχουσιν ἅπαντες, ἑκόντες
μέντοι μηθὲν αὐτῶν διὰ τὸ μηδ' αὐτοῦ χάριν, καὶ
προσθείη χρόνου πλῆθος ἀπέραντόν τι, οὐ μᾶλλον
ἕνεκ' ἂν τις τούτων ἕλοιτο ζῆν ἢ μὴ ζῆν. ἀλλὰ 5
μὴν οὐδὲ διὰ τὴν τῆς τροφῆς μόνον ἡδονὴν ἢ τὴν
τῶν ἀφροδισίων, ἀφαιρεθεισῶν τῶν ἄλλων ἡδονῶν
ἃς τὸ γινώσκειν ἢ βλέπειν ἢ τῶν ἄλλων τις
αἰσθήσεων πορίζει τοῖς ἀνθρώποις, οὐδ' ἂν εἷς
προτιμήσειε τὸ ζῆν μὴ παντελῶς ὢν ἀνδράποδον,
δῆλον γὰρ ὅτι τῷ ταύτην ποιουμένῳ τὴν αἵρεσιν
οὐθὲν ἂν διενέγκειε γενέσθαι θηρίον ἢ ἄνθρωπον·
1216 a ὁ γοῦν ἐν Αἰγύπτῳ βοῦς, ὃν ὡς Ἆπιν τιμῶσιν, ἐν 6
πλείοσι τῶν τοιούτων ἐξουσιάζει πολλῶν μονάρχων.[2]

[1] ⟨τίς⟩ ὁ . . . ; Cas. [2] Γ: μοναρχιῶν.

---

[a] *Cf.* Soph. *O.C.* 1225 μὴ φῦναι τὸν ἅπαντα νικᾷ λόγον.

which it is not easy to make a right judgement, this is especially the case with one about which everybody thinks that it is very easy to judge and that anybody can decide—the question which of the things contained in being alive is preferable, and which when attained would fully satisfy a man's desire. For many of life's events are such that they cause men to throw life away, for instance, diseases, excessive pains, storms; so that it is clear that on account of these things any way it would actually be preferable, if someone offered us the choice, not to be born at
2 all.[a] And in addition, the kind of life that people live while still children is not desirable—in fact no sensible person could endure to go back to it again.
3 And further, many of the experiences that contain no pleasure nor pain, and also of those that do contain pleasure but pleasure of an ignoble kind, are such that non-existence would be better than being alive.
4 And generally, if one collected together the whole of the things that the whole of mankind do and experience yet do and experience unwillingly, because not for the sake of the things themselves, and if one added an infinite extent of time, these things would not cause a man to choose to be alive rather than
5 not alive. But moreover, also the pleasure of food or of sex alone, with the other pleasures abstracted that knowledge or sight or any other of the senses provides for human beings, would not induce anybody to value life higher if he were not utterly slavish, for it is clear that to one making this choice there would be no difference between being born a
6 beast or a man; at all events, the ox in Egypt, which they reverence as Apis, has a greater abundance of
7 such indulgences than many monarchs. Nor like-

1216 a ὁμοίως δὲ οὐδὲ διὰ τὴν τοῦ καθεύδειν ἡδονήν· τί 7
γὰρ διαφέρει καθεύδειν ἀνέγερτον ὕπνον ἀπὸ τῆς
πρώτης ἡμέρας μέχρι τῆς τελευταίας ἐτῶν ἀριθμὸν
χιλίων ἢ ὁποσωνοῦν,[1] ἢ ζῆν ὄντα φυτόν; τὰ γοῦν
φυτὰ τοιαύτης τινὸς ἔοικε μετέχειν ζωῆς, ὥσπερ
καὶ τὰ παιδία· καὶ γὰρ ταῦτα κατὰ τὴν πρώτην
ἐν τῇ μητρὶ[2] γένεσιν πεφυκότα μὲν διατελεῖ
καθεύδοντα δὲ τὸν πάντα χρόνον. ὥστε φανερὸν 8
ἐκ τῶν τοιούτων ὅτι διαφεύγει σκοπουμένους τί
τὸ εὖ καὶ τί τὸ ἀγαθὸν τὸ ἐν τῷ ζῆν.

Τὸν μὲν οὖν Ἀναξαγόραν φασὶν ἀποκρίνασθαι 9
πρός τινα διαποροῦντα τοιαῦτ᾽ ἄττα καὶ διερωτῶντα
τίνος ἕνεκ᾽ ἄν τις ἕλοιτο γενέσθαι μᾶλλον ἢ μὴ
γενέσθαι "τοῦ" φάναι "θεωρῆσαι τὸν οὐρανὸν
καὶ τὴν περὶ τὸν ὅλον κόσμον τάξιν." οὗτος μὲν
οὖν ἐπιστήμης τινὸς ἕνεκεν τὴν αἵρεσιν ᾤετο
τιμίαν εἶναι τοῦ ζῆν· οἱ δὲ Σαρδανάπαλλον 10
μακαρίζοντες ἢ Σμινδυρίδην τὸν Συβαρίτην ἢ
τῶν ἄλλων τινὰς τῶν ζώντων τὸν ἀπολαυστικὸν
βίον, οὗτοι δὲ πάντες ἐν τῷ χαίρειν φαίνονται
τάττειν τὴν εὐδαιμονίαν· ἕτεροι δέ τινες οὔτ᾽ ἂν 11
φρόνησιν οὐδεμίαν οὔτε τὰς σωματικὰς ἡδονὰς
ἕλοιντο μᾶλλον ἢ τὰς πράξεις τὰς ἀπ᾽ ἀρετῆς·
αἱροῦνται γοῦν οὐ μόνον ἔνιοι δόξης χάριν αὐτὰς
ἀλλὰ καὶ μὴ μέλλοντες εὐδοκιμήσειν. ἀλλ᾽ οἱ 12
πολλοὶ τῶν πολιτικῶν οὐκ ἀληθῶς τυγχάνουσι

[1] v.l. ἐτῶν ἀριθμῶν χίλιον ἄριθμον ἢ ὁποσονοῦν : ἐτῶν χιλίων ἢ ὁποσωνοῦν? (exciso ἄριθμον gloss. ad ὁποσονοῦν erratum) Rac.

[2] μήτρᾳ Γ.

[a] See 1215 b 6 n.

[b] A mythical king of Assyria, proverbial for luxury, *cf.* *N.E.* i., 1295 b 22.

wise would anyone desire life for the pleasure of sleep either; for what is the difference between slumbering without being awakened from the first day till the last of a thousand or any number of years, and living a vegetable existence? any way plants seem to participate in life of that kind; and so do children too, inasmuch as at their first procreation in the mother, although alive, they stay asleep all the time.
8 So that it is clear from considerations of this sort that the precise nature of well-being and of the good in life escapes our investigation.

9 Now it is said that when somebody persisted in putting various difficulties of this sort to Anaxagoras [a] and went on asking for what object one should choose to come into existence rather than not, he replied by saying, 'For the sake of contemplating the heavens and the whole order of the universe.' Anaxagoras therefore thought that the alternative of being alive was valuable for the sake of some kind
10 of knowledge; but those who ascribe bliss to Sardanapallus [b] or Smindyrides of Sybaris [c] or some of the others living the life of enjoyment, all appear for
11 their part to place happiness in delight; while a different set would not choose either wisdom of any kind or the bodily pleasures in preference to the actions that spring from goodness: at all events, some people choose those actions not only for the sake of reputation but even when they are not going to get
12 any credit. But the majority of those engaged in politics are not correctly designated 'politicians,' for

[c] Greek colony in S. Italy. For Smindyrides, who travelled with 1000 slaves in attendance, see Herod vi. 127, Athenaeus, v. p. 273.

1216 a
τῆς προσηγορίας· οὐ γάρ εἰσι πολιτικοὶ κατὰ τὸν
ἀλήθειαν, ὁ μὲν γὰρ πολιτικὸς τῶν καλῶν ἐστὶ
πράξεων προαιρετικὸς αὐτῶν χάριν, οἱ δὲ πολλοὶ
χρημάτων καὶ πλεονεξίας ἕνεκεν ἅπτονται τοῦ
ζῆν οὕτως.

Ἐκ μὲν οὖν τῶν εἰρημένων φανερὸν ὅτι πάντες 13
ἐπὶ τρεῖς βίους φέρουσι τὴν εὐδαιμονίαν, πολιτικὸν
φιλόσοφον ἀπολαυστικόν. τούτων δ᾽ ἡ μὲν περὶ
τὰ σώματα καὶ τὰς ἀπολαύσεις ἡδονὴ καὶ τίς καὶ
ποία τις γίνεται καὶ διὰ τίνων οὐκ ἄδηλον, ὥστ᾽
οὐ τίνες εἰσὶ δεῖ ζητεῖν ἡμᾶς[1] ἀλλ᾽ εἰ συντείνουσί
τι πρὸς εὐδαιμονίαν ἢ μή, καὶ πῶς συντείνουσι,
καὶ πότερον, εἰ δεῖ προσάπτειν τῷ ζῆν καλῶς[2]
ἡδονάς τινας, ταύτας δεῖ προσάπτειν ἢ τούτων
μὲν ἄλλον τινὰ τρόπον ἀνάγκη κοινωνεῖν, ἕτεραι
δ᾽ εἰσὶν αἱ[3] ἡδοναὶ δι᾽ ἃς εὐλόγως οἴονται τὸν
εὐδαίμονα ζῆν ἡδέως καὶ μὴ μόνον ἀλύπως.

Ἀλλὰ περὶ μὲν τούτων ὕστερον ἐπισκεπτέον, 14
περὶ δ᾽ ἀρετῆς καὶ φρονήσεως πρῶτον θεωρήσωμεν
τήν τε φύσιν αὐτῶν ἑκατέρου τίς ἐστι καὶ πότερον
μόρια ταῦτα τῆς ἀγαθῆς ζωῆς ἐστὶν[4] αὐτὰ ἢ αἱ
1216 b πράξεις αἱ ἀπ᾽ αὐτῶν, ἐπειδὴ προσάπτουσιν αὐτὰ
κἂν εἰ μὴ πάντες εἰς τὴν εὐδαιμονίαν ἀλλ᾽ οὖν οἱ
λόγου ἄξιοι τῶν ἀνθρώπων πάντες.

Σωκράτης μὲν οὖν ὁ πρεσβύτης ᾤετ᾽ εἶναι τέλος 15
τὸ γινώσκειν τὴν ἀρετήν, καὶ ἐπεζήτει τί ἐστιν ἡ
δικαιοσύνη καὶ τί ἡ ἀνδρεία καὶ ἕκαστον τῶν

[1] Fr.: αὐτάς.
[2] Bz.: καλάς.
[3] αἱ add. Rac.
[4] Rac.: ἐστιν ἤ.

[a] The Greek word is specially associated with sensual pleasures.

[b] The promised discussion does not occur, but see *N.E.* vii., 1153 b 7-25.

they are not truly political, since the political man is one who purposely chooses noble actions for their own sake, whereas the majority embrace that mode of life for the sake of money and gain.

13 What has been said, therefore, demonstrates that all men ascribe happiness to three modes of life—the political, the philosophic, and the life of enjoyment.[a] Among these, the nature and quality of the pleasure connected with the body and with enjoyment, and the means that procure it, are not hard to see; so that it is not necessary for us to inquire what these pleasures are, but whether they conduce at all to happiness or not, and how they so conduce, and, if it be the case that the noble life ought to have some pleasures attached to it, whether these are the pleasures that ought to be attached, or whether these must be enjoyed in some other way, whereas the pleasures which people reasonably believe to make the happy man's life pleasant and not merely painless are different ones.

all come back to the three typical lives.

14 But these matters must be examined later.[b] Let us first consider Goodness and Wisdom[c]—what the nature of each is, and also whether they themselves or the actions that spring from them are parts of the good life, since that they are connected with happiness is asserted, if not by everybody, at all events by all of mankind who are worthy of consideration.

Ethics a practical subject.

15 Accordingly Socrates the senior[d] thought that the End is to get to know virtue, and he pursued an inquiry into the nature of justice and courage and

[c] See 1214 a 33 note; but practical wisdom is specially implied here.

[d] *Cf.* 1235 a 37. A younger Socrates was a pupil of Plato.

1216 b μορίων αὐτῆς. ἐποίει δὲ[1] ταῦτ' εὐλόγως· ἐπιστήμας
γὰρ ᾤετ' εἶναι πάσας τὰς ἀρετάς, ὥσθ' ἅμα
συμβαίνειν εἰδέναι τε τὴν δικαιοσύνην καὶ εἶναι
δίκαιον· ἅμα γὰρ μεμαθήκαμεν τὴν γεωμετρίαν
καὶ οἰκοδομίαν καὶ ἐσμὲν οἰκοδόμοι καὶ γεωμέτραι·
διόπερ ἐζήτει τί ἐστιν ἀρετὴ ἀλλ' οὐ πῶς γίνεται
καὶ ἐκ τίνων. τοῦτο δὲ ἐπὶ μὲν τῶν ἐπιστημῶν 16
συμβαίνει τῶν θεωρητικῶν, οὐθὲν γὰρ ἕτερον
τέλος[2] ἐστὶ τῆς ἀστρολογίας οὐδὲ τῆς περὶ φύσεως ἐπιστήμης οὐδὲ γεωμετρίας πλὴν τὸ γνωρίσαι
καὶ θεωρῆσαι τὴν φύσιν τῶν πραγμάτων τῶν
ὑποκειμένων ταῖς ἐπιστήμαις (οὐ μὴν ἀλλὰ κατὰ
συμβεβηκὸς οὐθὲν κωλύει πρὸς πολλὰ τῶν ἀναγκαίων εἶναι χρησίμους αὐτὰς ἡμῖν), τῶν δὲ 17
ποιητικῶν ἐπιστημῶν ἕτερον τὸ τέλος τῆς ἐπιστήμης καὶ γνώσεως, οἷον ὑγίεια μὲν ἰατρικῆς,
εὐνομία δὲ ἤ τι τοιοῦθ' ἕτερον τῆς πολιτικῆς.
καλὸν μὲν οὖν καὶ τὸ γνωρίζειν ἕκαστον τῶν 18
καλῶν, οὐ μὴν ἀλλὰ περί γ'[3] ἀρετῆς οὐ τὸ εἰδέναι
τιμιώτατον τί ἐστιν ἀλλὰ τὸ γινώσκειν ἐκ τίνων
ἐστίν. οὐ γὰρ εἰδέναι βουλόμεθα τί ἐστιν ἀνδρεία
ἀλλ' εἶναι ἀνδρεῖοι, οὐδὲ τί ἐστι δικαιοσύνη ἀλλ'
εἶναι δίκαιοι, καθάπερ καὶ ὑγιαίνειν μᾶλλον ἢ
γινώσκειν τί ἐστι τὸ ὑγιαίνειν καὶ εὖ ἔχειν τὴν
ἕξιν μᾶλλον ἢ γινώσκειν τί ἐστι τὸ εὖ ἔχειν.

[1] Fr.: γάρ. [2] τέλος add. Cas.
[3] Ric.: γε περί.

[a] The Greek term primarily denotes biology, rather than physics in the modern sense (with which contrast the modern

each of the divisions of virtue. And this was a reasonable procedure, since he thought that all the virtues are forms of knowledge, so that knowing justice and being just must go together, for as soon as we have learnt geometry and architecture, we are architects and geometricians; owing to which he used to inquire what virtue is, but not how and
16 from what sources it is produced. But although this does happen in the case of the theoretical sciences, inasmuch as astronomy and natural science [a] and geometry have no other End except to get to know and to contemplate the nature of the things that are the subjects of the sciences (although it is true that they may quite possibly be useful to us accidentally
17 for many of our necessary requirements), yet the End of the productive sciences is something different from science and knowledge, for example the End of medicine is health and that of political science ordered government, or something of that sort, different from mere knowledge of the science.
18 Although, therefore, it is fine even to attain a knowledge of the various fine things, all the same nevertheless in the case of goodness it is not the knowledge of its essential nature that is most valuable but the ascertainment of the sources that produce it. For our aim is not to know what courage is but to be courageous, not to know what justice is but to be just, in the same way as we want to be healthy rather than to ascertain what health is, and to be in good condition of body rather than to ascertain what good bodily condition is.

limitation of the term 'physiology,' and of 'physic' in the sense of medicine); accordingly it does not here include astronomy.

1216 VI. Πειρατέον δὲ περὶ τούτων πάντων[1] ζητεῖν 1
τὴν πίστιν διὰ τῶν λόγων, μαρτυρίοις καὶ παρα-
δείγμασι χρώμενον τοῖς φαινομένοις. κράτιστον
μὲν γὰρ πάντας ἀνθρώπους φαίνεσθαι συνομο-
λογοῦντας τοῖς ῥηθησομένοις, εἰ δὲ μή, τρόπον
γέ τινα πάντας,[2] ὅπερ μεταβιβαζόμενοι ποιήσουσιν·
ἔχει γὰρ ἕκαστος οἰκεῖόν τι πρὸς τὴν ἀλήθειαν,
ἐξ ὧν ἀναγκαῖον δεικνύναι πως περὶ αὐτῶν· ἐκ
γὰρ τῶν ἀληθῶς μὲν λεγομένων οὐ σαφῶς δὲ
προϊοῦσιν ἔσται καὶ τὸ σαφῶς, μεταλαμβάνουσιν
ἀεὶ τὰ γνωριμώτερα τῶν[3] εἰωθότων λέγεσθαι
συγκεχυμένως. διαφέρουσι δ' οἱ λόγοι περὶ 2
ἑκάστην μέθοδον οἵ τε φιλοσόφως λεγόμενοι καὶ οἱ
μὴ φιλοσόφως· διόπερ καὶ τῷ πολιτικῷ[4] οὐ χρὴ
νομίζειν περίεργον εἶναι τὴν τοιαύτην θεωρίαν δι'
ἧς οὐ μόνον τὸ τί φανερὸν ἀλλὰ καὶ τὸ διὰ τί·
φιλόσοφον γὰρ τὸ τοιοῦτο περὶ ἑκάστην μέθοδον.
δεῖται μέντοι τοῦτο πολλῆς εὐλαβείας. εἰσὶ γάρ 3
1217 a τινες οἳ διὰ τὸ δοκεῖν φιλοσόφου εἶναι τὸ μηθὲν
εἰκῇ λέγειν ἀλλὰ μετὰ λόγου πολλάκις λανθάνουσι
λέγοντες ἀλλοτρίους λόγους τῆς πραγματείας καὶ
κενούς (τοῦτο δὲ ποιοῦσιν ὁτὲ μὲν δι' ἄγνοιαν ὁτὲ 4
δὲ δι' ἀλαζονείαν), ὑφ' ὧν ἁλίσκεσθαι συμβαίνει
καὶ τοὺς ἐμπείρους καὶ δυναμένους πράττειν ὑπὸ
τούτων τῶν μήτ' ἐχόντων μήτε δυναμένων διάνοιαν
ἀρχιτεκτονικὴν ἢ πρακτικήν. πάσχουσι δὲ τοῦτο 5

[1] πάντα (vel 27 χρωμένους) Sp. [2] Vic.: πάντως.
[3] ⟨ἀντὶ⟩ τῶν? Ric. [4] Ric.: τῶν πολιτικῶν.

---

[a] Or perhaps 'led on step by step.'
[b] *i.e.* practical men often think that any string of arguments constitutes philosophy, though the arguers may be mere charlatans.

1 VI. And about all these matters the endeavour must be made to seek to convince by means of rational arguments, using observed facts as evidences and examples. For the best thing would be if all mankind were seen to be in agreement with the views that will be stated, but failing that, at any rate that all should agree in some way. And this they will do if led to change their ground,[a] for everyone has something relative to contribute to the truth, and we must start from this to give a sort of proof about our views ; for from statements that are true but not clearly expressed, as we advance, clearness will also be attained, if at every stage we adopt more scientific positions in exchange for the
2 customary confused statements. And in every investigation arguments stated in philosophical form are different from those that are non-philosophical ; hence we must not think that theoretical study of such a sort as to make manifest not only the nature of a thing but also its cause is superfluous even for the political student, since that is the philosophic procedure in every field of inquiry. Nevertheless this
3 requires much caution. For because to say nothing at random but use reasoned argument seems to mark a philosopher, some people often without being detected advance arguments that are not germane to the subject under treatment and that have nothing
4 in them (and they do this sometimes through ignorance and sometimes from charlatanry), which bring it about that even men of experience and practical capacity are taken in by these people, who neither possess nor are capable of constructive or practical
5 thought.[b] And this befalls them owing to lack of

The method of Ethics is to observe facts and discover their reasons.

1217 a δι' ἀπαιδευσίαν· ἀπαιδευσία γάρ ἐστι περὶ ἕκαστον
πρᾶγμα τὸ μὴ δύνασθαι κρίνειν τούς τ' οἰκείους
λόγους τοῦ πράγματος καὶ τοὺς ἀλλοτρίους.
καλῶς δ' ἔχει καὶ τὸ χωρὶς κρίνειν τὸν τῆς αἰτίας 6
λόγον καὶ τὸ δεικνύμενον, διά τε τὸ ῥηθὲν ἀρτίως,
ὅτι προσέχειν οὐ δεῖ πάντα τοῖς διὰ τῶν λόγων
ἀλλὰ πολλάκις μᾶλλον τοῖς φαινομένοις (νῦν δ'
ὁπότ' ἂν λύειν μὴ ἔχωσιν ἀναγκάζονται πιστεύειν
τοῖς εἰρημένοις), καὶ διότι πολλάκις τὸ[1] ὑπὸ τοῦ
λόγου δεδεῖχθαι δοκοῦν ἀληθὲς μέν ἐστιν οὐ μέντοι
διὰ ταύτην τὴν αἰτίαν δι' ἥν φησιν ὁ λόγος. ἔστι
γὰρ διὰ ψεύδους ἀληθὲς δεῖξαι· δῆλον δ' ἐκ τῶν
ἀναλυτικῶν.

VII. Πεπροοιμιασμένων δὲ καὶ τούτων, λέγωμεν 1
ἀρξάμενοι πρῶτον ἀπὸ τῶν πρώτων,[2] ὥσπερ
εἴρηται, οὐ σαφῶς λεγομένων, ζητοῦντες ἔπειτα[3]
σαφῶς εὑρεῖν τί ἐστιν ἡ εὐδαιμονία. ὁμολογεῖται 2
δὴ μέγιστον εἶναι καὶ ἄριστον τοῦτο τῶν ἀγαθῶν
τῶν ἀνθρωπίνων (ἀνθρώπινον δὲ λέγομεν ὅτι τάχ'
ἂν εἴη καὶ βελτίονός τινος ἄλλου τῶν ὄντων
εὐδαιμονία, οἷον θεοῦ)· τῶν[4] γὰρ ἄλλων ζῴων, ὅσα 3
χείρω τὴν φύσιν τῶν ἀνθρώπων ἐστίν, οὐθὲν
κοινωνεῖ ταύτης τῆς προσηγορίας· οὐ γάρ ἐστιν
εὐδαίμων ἵππος οὐδ' ὄρνις οὐδ' ἰχθὺς οὐδ' ἄλλο
τῶν ὄντων οὐθὲν ὃ μὴ κατὰ τὴν ἐπωνυμίαν ἐν
τῇ φύσει μετέχει θείου τινός, ἀλλὰ κατ' ἄλλην

[1] Rac.: τὸ μὲν.
[2] πρώτων <τῶν> ? Ric.
[3] ἔπειτα Ras.: ἐπὶ τὸ (<προιέναι> ἐπὶ τὸ ? Ric.).
[4] Rac.: τῶν μὲν.

---

[a] § 1 above.
[b] *i.e.* a proposition that logically follows from premisses

education—for in respect of each subject inability to distinguish arguments germane to the subject
6 from those foreign to it is lack of education. And it is also well to judge separately the statement of the cause and the demonstrated fact, both for the reason stated just now,[a] that it is not proper in regard to all things to attend to theoretical arguments, but often rather to the facts of observation (whereas now when men are unable to refute an argument they are forced to believe what has been said), and also because often, although the result that seems to have been proved by the arguments is true, it is not true because of the cause asserted in the argument. For it is possible to prove truth by falsehood, as is clear from *Analytics*.[b]

Happiness the supreme good attainable by action.

1 VII. These prefatory remarks having also been made, let us proceed by starting first from the first statements, which, as has been said,[c] are not clearly expressed, afterwards seeking to discover clearly
2 the essential nature of happiness. Now it is agreed that happiness is the greatest and best of human goods (and we say 'human' because there might very likely also be a happiness belonging to some
3 higher being, for instance a god); since none of the other animals, which are inferior in nature to men, share in the designation 'happy,' for a horse is not happy, nor is a bird nor a fish nor any other existing thing whose designation does not indicate that it possesses in its nature a share of something divine, but it is by some other mode of participating in things

that are false may be a true one: see *Anal. Pr.* ii., 53 b 26 ff., *Anal. Post.* i., 88 a 20 ff. Aristotle's simplest example is the syllogism 'A man is a stone, but a stone is an animal, therefore a man is an animal.'

[c] 1216 b 32 ff.

1217 a
τινὰ τῶν ἀγαθῶν μετοχὴν τὸ μὲν βέλτιον ζῇ τὸ
δὲ χεῖρον αὐτῶν.
Ἀλλʼ ὅτι τοῦτον ἔχει τὸν τρόπον ὕστερον 4
ἐπισκεπτέον. νῦν δὲ λέγωμεν[1] ὅτι τῶν ἀγαθῶν
τὰ μέν ἐστιν ἀνθρώπῳ πρακτὰ τὰ δʼ οὐ πρακτά.
τοῦτο δὲ λέγομεν οὕτω διότι ἔνια τῶν ὄντων οὐθὲν
μετέχει κινήσεως, ὥστʼ οὐδὲ τῶν[2] ἀγαθῶν, καὶ[3]
ταῦτʼ ἴσως ἄριστα τὴν φύσιν ἐστίν, ἔνια δὲ πρακτὰ
μέν, ἀλλὰ πρακτὰ κρείττοσιν ἡμῶν. ἐπειδὴ δὲ 5
διχῶς λέγεται τὸ πρακτόν (καὶ γὰρ ὧν ἕνεκα
πράττομεν καὶ ἃ τούτων ἕνεκα μετέχει πράξεως,
οἷον καὶ τὴν ὑγίειαν καὶ τὸν πλοῦτον τίθεμεν τῶν
πρακτῶν καὶ τὰ τούτων πραττόμενα χάριν, τά
θʼ ὑγιεινὰ καὶ τὰ χρηματιστικά), δῆλον ὅτι καὶ
τὴν εὐδαιμονίαν τῶν ἀνθρώπῳ πρακτῶν ἄριστον
θετέον.

1217 b
VIII. Σκεπτέον τοίνυν τί τὸ ἄριστον καὶ ποσαχῶς 1
λέγεται.[4] ἐν τρισὶ δὴ μάλιστα φαίνεται δόξαις
εἶναι τοῦτο. φασὶ γὰρ ἄριστον μὲν εἶναι πάντων
αὐτὸ τὸ ἀγαθόν, αὐτὸ δʼ εἶναι τὸ ἀγαθὸν ᾧ ὑπάρχει
τό τε πρώτῳ εἶναι τῶν ἀγαθῶν καὶ τὸ αἰτίῳ τῇ
παρουσίᾳ τοῖς ἄλλοις τοῦ ἀγαθοῖς[5] εἶναι· ταῦτα δʼ 2
ὑπάρχειν[6] ἀμφότερα τῇ ἰδέᾳ τοῦ ἀγαθοῦ (λέγω δὲ
ἀμφότερα τό τε πρῶτον τῶν ἀγαθῶν καὶ τὸ τοῖς
ἄλλοις αἴτιον ἀγαθοῖς τῇ παρουσίᾳ τοῦ ἀγαθοῖς

[1] vulg. λέγομεν.
[2] τῶν <πρακτῶν> ? Ric.
[3] καί<τοι> ? Ric.
[4] Rac.: λέγεται ποσαχῶς.
[5] Vic.: ἀγαθά.
[6] Fr.: ὑπάρχει.

[a] This promise is not kept.

[b] Ἰδέα is here used in its Platonic sense, as a synonym for εἶδος, class-form, to denote the permanent immaterial reality that underlies any group of things classed together in virtue of possessing a common quality. An ἰδέα is perceptible

good that one of them has a better life and another a worse.

4 But the fact that this is so must be considered later.[a] At the present let us say that among things good some are within the range of action for a human being and others are not. And we make this distinction for the reason that some existing things do not participate in change at all, and therefore some good things do not, and these are perhaps in their nature the best things; and some things, though practicable, are only practicable for beings superior
5 to us. And inasmuch as 'practicable' has two meanings (for both the Ends for which we act and the actions that we do as means to those Ends have to do with action—for example we class among things practicable both health and wealth and the pursuits that are followed for the sake of health and wealth, healthy exercise and lucrative business), it is clear that happiness must be set down as the best of the things practicable for a human being.

1 VIII. We must consider, therefore, what the best is, and in how many senses the term is used. The answer seems to be principally contained in three views. For it is said that the best of all things is the Absolute Good, and that the Absolute Good is that which has the attributes of being the first of goods and of being by its presence the cause to the other goods of
2 their being good; and both of these attributes, it is said, belong to the Form[b] of good (I mean both being the first of goods and being by its presence the cause to the other goods of their being good), since it is of that

Plato's 'Idea' of Good refuted.

only by the mind, but the word does not denote the content of a mental perception, as does the derivative 'idea' in ordinary English.

1217 b
εἶναι)· μάλιστά τε γὰρ τἀγαθὸν λέγεσθαι κατ'
ἐκείνης ἀληθῶς (κατὰ μετοχὴν γὰρ καὶ ὁμοιότητα
τἆλλα ἀγαθὰ ἐκείνης εἶναι), καὶ πρῶτον τῶν
ἀγαθῶν, ἀναιρουμένου γὰρ τοῦ μετεχομένου ἀναιρεῖσθαι καὶ τὰ μετέχοντα τῆς ἰδέας (ἃ λέγεται
τῷ μετέχειν ἐκείνης), τὸ δὲ πρῶτον[1] τοῦτον ἔχειν 3
τὸν τρόπον πρὸς τὸ ὕστερον· ὥστ' εἶναι αὐτὸ τὸ
ἀγαθὸν τὴν ἰδέαν τοῦ ἀγαθοῦ· καὶ γὰρ χωριστὴν
εἶναι τῶν μετεχόντων, ὥσπερ καὶ τὰς ἄλλας ἰδέας.
Ἔστι μὲν οὖν τὸ διασκοπεῖν περὶ ταύτης τῆς 4
δόξης ἑτέρας τε διατριβῆς καὶ τὰ πολλὰ λογικω-
τέρας ἐξ ἀνάγκης· οἱ γὰρ ἅμα ἀναιρετικοί τε καὶ
κοινοὶ λόγοι κατ' οὐδεμίαν εἰσὶν ἄλλην ἐπιστήμην.
εἰ δὲ δεῖ συντόμως εἰπεῖν περὶ αὐτῶν, λέγομεν[2] 5
ὅτι πρῶτον μὲν τὸ εἶναι ἰδέαν μὴ μόνον ἀγαθοῦ
ἀλλὰ καὶ ἄλλου ὁτουοῦν λέγεται λογικῶς καὶ
κενῶς (ἐπέσκεπται δὲ πολλοῖς περὶ αὐτοῦ τρόποις
καὶ ἐν τοῖς ἐξωτερικοῖς λόγοις καὶ ἐν τοῖς κατὰ
φιλοσοφίαν)· ἔπειτ' εἰ καὶ ὅτι μάλιστ' εἰσὶν αἱ 6
ἰδέαι καὶ ἀγαθοῦ ἰδέα, μή ποτ' οὐδὲ χρήσιμος
πρὸς ζωὴν ἀγαθὴν οὐδὲ πρὸς τὰς πράξεις.
Πολλαχῶς γὰρ λέγεται καὶ ἰσαχῶς τῷ ὄντι τὸ 7
ἀγαθόν. τό τε γὰρ ὄν, ὥσπερ ἐν ἄλλοις διῄρηται,
σημαίνει τὸ μὲν τί ἐστι τὸ δὲ ποιὸν τὸ δὲ ποσὸν
τὸ δὲ πότε καὶ πρὸς τούτοις τὸ μὲν ἐν τῷ
κινεῖσθαι τὸ δὲ ἐν τῷ κινεῖν· καὶ τὸ ἀγαθὸν ἐν
ἑκάστῃ τῶν πτώσεών ἐστι τούτων, ἐν οὐσίᾳ μὲν

[1] πρότερον Sp. [2] λέγωμεν ? Rac.

[a] The use of this phrase by Aristotle elsewhere seems to show that it denotes doctrines, recorded in books or familiar in debate, that were not peculiar to the Peripatetic school.

Form that goodness is most truly predicated (inasmuch as the other goods are good by participation in and resemblance to the Form of good) and also it is the first of goods, for the destruction of that which is participated in involves the destruction of the things participating in the Form (which get
3 their designation by participating in it), and that is the relation existing between what is primary and what is subsequent; so that the Form of good is the Absolute Good, inasmuch as the Form of good is separable from the things that participate in it, as are the other Forms also.

4 Now a thorough examination of this opinion belongs to another course of study, and one that for the most part necessarily lies more in the field of Logic, for that is the only science dealing with arguments that
5 are at the same time destructive and general. But if we are to speak about it concisely, we say that in the first place to assert the existence of a Form not only of good but of anything else is a mere idle abstraction (but this has been considered in various ways both in extraneous discourses [a] and in those
6 on philosophical lines); next, even granting that Forms and the Form of good exist in the fullest sense, surely this is of no practical value for the good life or for conduct.

A. The Idea of Good does not exist, because

7 For 'good' has many senses, in fact as many as 'being.' For the term 'is,' as it has been analysed in other works, signifies now substance, now quality, now quantity, now time, and in addition to these meanings it consists now in undergoing change and now in causing it; and the good is found in each of these cases [b]—

i. 'good' falls under several categories;

[b] *i.e.* categories. The last two specified are elsewhere designated κινεῖν and κινεῖσθαι, Action and Passion.

1217 b ὁ νοῦς καὶ ὁ θεός, ἐν δὲ τῷ ποιῷ τὸ δίκαιον, ἐν
δὲ τῷ ποσῷ τὸ μέτριον, ἐν δὲ τῷ πότε ὁ καιρός,
τὸ δὲ διδάσκον καὶ τὸ διδασκόμενον περὶ κίνησιν.
ὥσπερ οὖν οὐδὲ τὸ ὂν ἕν τι ἐστὶ περὶ[1] τὰ εἰρημένα, 8
οὕτως οὐδὲ τὸ ἀγαθόν, οὐδὲ ἐπιστήμη ἐστὶ μία
οὔτε τοῦ ὄντος οὔτε τοῦ ἀγαθοῦ. ἀλλ' οὐδὲ τὰ
ὁμοιοσχημόνως λεγόμενα ἀγαθὰ μιᾶς ἐστὶ θεωρῆσαι,
οἷον τὸν καιρὸν ἢ τὸ μέτριον, ἀλλ' ἑτέρα ἕτερον
καιρὸν θεωρεῖ καὶ ἑτέρα ἕτερον μέτριον, οἷον περὶ
τροφὴν μὲν τὸν καιρὸν καὶ τὸ μέτριον ἰατρικὴ καὶ
γυμναστική, περὶ δὲ τὰς πολεμικὰς πράξεις
στρατηγία, καὶ οὕτως ἑτέρα περὶ ἑτέραν πρᾶξιν,
1218 a ὥστε σχολῇ αὐτό γε τὸ ἀγαθὸν θεωρῆσαι μιᾶς.

Ἔτι ἐν ὅσοις ὑπάρχει τὸ πρότερον καὶ ὕστερον, 9
οὐκ ἔστι κοινόν τι παρὰ ταῦτα καὶ τοῦτο[2] χωριστόν·
εἴη γὰρ ἄν τι τοῦ πρώτου πρότερον, πρότερον γὰρ 10
τὸ κοινὸν καὶ χωριστὸν διὰ τὸ ἀναιρουμένου τοῦ
κοινοῦ ἀναιρεῖσθαι τὸ πρῶτον. οἷον εἰ τὸ διπλάσιον
πρῶτον τῶν πολλαπλασίων, οὐκ ἐνδέχεται τὸ
πολλαπλάσιον τὸ κοινῇ κατηγορούμενον εἶναι
χωριστόν· ἔσται γὰρ τοῦ διπλασίου πρότερον,[3] εἰ
συμβαίνει τὸ κοινὸν εἶναι τὴν ἰδέαν, οἷον εἰ
χωριστὸν ποιήσειέ τις τὸ κοινόν· εἰ γάρ ἐστι
δικαιοσύνη ἀγαθὸν καὶ ἀνδρεία, ἔστι τοίνυν, φασίν,
αὐτό τι ἀγαθόν· τὸ οὖν αὐτὸ πρόσκειται πρὸς τὸν 11
λόγον τὸν κοινόν. τοῦτο δὲ τί ἂν εἴη πλὴν ὅτι
ἀίδιον καὶ χωριστόν; ἀλλ' οὐδὲν μᾶλλον λευκὸν

[1] παρὰ Vic. [2] τούτων Sp.
[3] lacunam hic Sus.

in essence, as mind and God, in quality justice, in quantity moderation, in time opportunity, and as instances of change, the teacher and the taught.
8 Therefore, just as being is not some one thing in respect of the categories mentioned, so neither is the good, and there is no one science either of the real or of the good. But also even the goods predicated in the same category, for example opportunity or moderation, do not fall within the province of a single science to study, but different sorts of opportunity and of moderation are studied by different sciences, for instance opportunity and moderation in respect of food are studied by medicine and gymnastics, in respect of military operations by strategics, and similarly in respect of another pursuit by another science; so that it can hardly be the case that the Absolute Good is the subject of only one science.

ii. even in one category it is the subject of several sciences,

9 Again, wherever there is a sequence of factors, a prior and a subsequent, there is not some common element
10 beside these factors and that element separable; for then there would be something prior to the first in the series, for the common and separable term would be prior because when the common element was destroyed the first factor would be destroyed. For example, if double is the first of the multiples, the multiplicity predicated of them in common cannot exist as a separable thing, for then it will be prior to double, if it is the case that the common element is the Form, as it would be if one were to make the common element separable: for if justice is a good, and courage, there is then, they say, a Good-in-itself,
11 so the term 'in itself' is added to the common definition. But what could this denote except that the good is eternal and separable? Yet a thing that is

iii. a series has no unity separately existing;

1218 a
τὸ πολλὰς ἡμέρας λευκὸν τοῦ μίαν ἡμέραν· ὥστ᾽
οὐδὲ ⟨τὸ ἀγαθὸν μᾶλλον ἀγαθὸν τῷ ἀίδιον εἶναι·
οὐδὲ⟩[1] δὴ τὸ κοινὸν ἀγαθὸν ταὐτὸ τῇ ἰδέᾳ· πᾶσι
γὰρ ὑπάρχει κοινόν.

Ἀνάπαλιν δὲ καὶ δεικτέον ἢ ὡς νῦν δεικνύουσι 12
τὸ ἀγαθὸν αὐτό. νῦν μὲν γὰρ ἐκ τῶν μὴ[2] ὁμολογουμένων ἔχειν τὸ ἀγαθόν, ἐξ ἐκείνων τὰ
ὁμολογούμενα εἶναι ἀγαθὰ δεικνύουσιν· οἷον[3] ἐξ
ἀριθμῶν ὅτι ἡ δικαιοσύνη καὶ ἡ ὑγίεια ἀγαθόν,
τάξεις γὰρ καὶ ἀριθμοί, ὡς τοῖς ἀριθμοῖς καὶ
ταῖς μονάσιν ἀγαθὸν ὑπάρχον διὰ τὸ εἶναι τὸ ἓν
αὐτὸ τἀγαθόν.[4] δεῖ δ᾽ ἐκ τῶν ὁμολογουμένων οἷον 13
ὑγιείας ἰσχύος σωφροσύνης ὅτι καὶ ἐν τοῖς ἀκινήτοις μᾶλλον τὸ καλόν· πάντα γὰρ τάδε τάξις καὶ
ἠρεμία· εἰ ἄρα, ἐκεῖνα μᾶλλον, ἐκείνοις γὰρ ὑπάρχει ταῦτα μᾶλλον.—παράβολος δὲ καὶ ἡ ἀπό- 14
δειξις ὅτι τὸ ἓν αὐτὸ τὸ ἀγαθὸν ὅτι οἱ ἀριθμοὶ
ἐφίενται αὐτοῦ[5]· οὔτε γὰρ ὡς ἐφίενται λέγουσι[6]
φανερῶς ἀλλὰ λίαν ἁπλῶς τοῦτό φασι, καὶ ὄρεξιν
εἶναι πῶς ἄν τις ὑπολάβοι ἐν οἷς ζωὴ μὴ ὑπάρχει;
δεῖ δὲ περὶ τούτου πραγματευθῆναι, καὶ μὴ ἀξιοῦν 15
μηθὲν ἀλόγως ὃ[7] καὶ μετὰ λόγου πιστεῦσαι οὐ
ῥᾴδιον.—τό τε φάναι πάντα τὰ ὄντα ἐφίεσθαι ἑνός
τινος ἀγαθοῦ οὐκ ἀληθές· ἕκαστον γὰρ ἰδίου ἀγαθοῦ
ὀρέγεται, ὀφθαλμὸς ὄψεως, σῶμα ὑγιείας, οὕτως
ἄλλο ἄλλου.

[1] ⟨τὸ ἀγαθὸν . . . οὐδὲ⟩ Ras.
[2] μὴ add. Zeller. [3] οἷον add. Rac.
[4] Fr.: ἀγαθόν.
[5] αὐτοῦ add. ? Ric. (supra post ὅτι Fr.).
[6] Sp.: λέγονται. [7] Sp.: ἃ.

[a] The words rendered 'the good is . . . eternal' are a conjectural insertion.

iv. eternity does not affect quality;

white for many days is no more white than a thing
that is white for one day, so that the good is no more
good by being eternal[a]; nor yet therefore is the
common good the same as the Form, for it is the
common property of all the goods.

v. general should be proved from particular, not *vice versa*;

12 Also the proper method of proving the Absolute
Good is the contrary of the method now adopted. At
present it is from things not admitted to possess
goodness that they prove the things admitted to be
good, for instance, they prove from numbers that
justice and health are good, because they are arrangements and numbers—on the assumption that goodness is a property of numbers and monads because
13 the Absolute Good is unity. But the proper method
is to start from things admitted to be good, for instance health, strength, sobriety of mind, and prove
that beauty is present even more in the unchanging;
for all these admitted goods consist in order and rest,
and therefore, if that is so, the things unchanging are
good in an even greater degree, for they possess order

vi. unity of good unproved,

14 and rest in a greater degree.—And it is a hazardous
way of proving that the Absolute Good is unity to say
that numbers aim at unity; for it is not clearly stated
how they aim at it, but the expression is used in too
unqualified a manner; and how can one suppose that
15 things not possessing life can have appetition? One
ought to study this matter carefully, and not make
an unreasoned assumption about something as to
which it is not easy to attain certainty even with the
aid of reason.—And the statement that all existing
things desire some one good is not true; each thing
seeks its own particular good, the eye sight, the
body health, and similarly another thing another
good.

vii. and not true in fact.

1218 a Ὅτι μὲν οὖν οὐκ ἔστιν αὐτό τι[1] ἀγαθόν, ἔχει 16
ἀπορίας τοιαύτας, καὶ ὅτι οὐ χρήσιμον τῇ πολιτικῇ,
ἀλλ' ἴδιόν τι ἀγαθόν, ὥσπερ καὶ ταῖς ἄλλαις, οἷον
γυμναστικῇ εὐεξία.

[2]Ἔτι καὶ τὸ ἐν τῷ λόγῳ γεγραμμένον· ἢ γὰρ 17
οὐδεμιᾷ χρήσιμον αὐτὸ τὸ τοῦ ἀγαθοῦ εἶδος ἢ
πάσαις ὁμοίως.

Ἔτι οὐ πρακτόν.

Ὁμοίως δ' οὐδὲ τὸ κοινὸν ἀγαθὸν οὔτε αὐτὸ[3] 18
1218 b ἀγαθόν ἐστιν (καὶ γὰρ ἂν μικρῷ ὑπάρξαι ἀγαθῷ)
οὔτε πρακτόν· οὐ γὰρ ὅπως ὑπάρξει τὸ ὁτῳοῦν ὑπάρχον ἡ ἰατρικὴ πραγματεύεται ἀλλ' ὅπως ὑγίεια,
ὁμοίως δὲ καὶ τῶν ἄλλων τεχνῶν ἑκάστη. ἀλλὰ 19
πολλαχῶς τὸ ἀγαθόν, καὶ ἔστι τι αὐτοῦ καλόν,[4]
καὶ τὸ μὲν πρακτὸν τὸ δ' οὐ πρακτόν. πρακτὸν δὲ τὸ
τοιοῦτον ἀγαθόν, τὸ οὗ ἕνεκα, οὐκ ἔστι δὲ τὸ ἐν
τοῖς ἀκινήτοις.

Φανερὸν οὖν[5] ὅτι οὔτε ἡ ἰδέα τἀγαθοῦ τὸ
ζητούμενον αὐτὸ τὸ ἀγαθόν ἐστιν οὔτε τὸ κοινόν
(τὸ μὲν γὰρ ἀκίνητον καὶ οὐ πρακτόν, τὸ δὲ κινητὸν
μὲν ἀλλ' οὐ πρακτόν). τὸ δ' οὗ ἕνεκα ὡς τέλος
ἄριστον καὶ αἴτιον τῶν ὑφ' αὐτὸ καὶ πρῶτον
πάντων· ὥστε τοῦτ' ἂν εἴη αὐτὸ τὸ ἀγαθόν, τὸ 20
τέλος τῶν ἀνθρώπῳ πρακτῶν. τοῦτο δ' ἐστὶ τὸ
ὑπὸ τὴν κυρίαν πασῶν, αὕτη δ' ἐστὶ πολιτικὴ καὶ
οἰκονομικὴ καὶ φρόνησις· διαφέρουσι γὰρ αὗται
αἱ ἕξεις πρὸς τὰς ἄλλας τῷ τοιαῦται εἶναι (πρὸς δ'

[1] τὸ ? Rac.
[2] ἔτι . . . πρακτόν secl. Wilson.
[3] αὐτὸ τὸ ? Rac.
[4] καὶ . . . καλόν secl. Sus.
[5] οὖν add. Brandis.

[a] This sentence reads like a mere note. The reference seems to be to 1217 b 16-1218 a 32, especially 1217 a 19-25.

B. The Idea of Good of no practical use if it did exist;

16 Such then are the difficulties indicating that the Absolute Good does not exist,—and that it is of no use for political science, but that this has a special good of its own, as have the other sciences also—for instance the good of gymnastics is good bodily condition.

17 [a] Further there is also what has been written in the discourse: either the Class-form of the good is in itself useful to no science, or it is useful to all alike. Further it is not practicable.

nor is the good as universal.

18 And similarly the good as universal also is not an Absolute Good (for universal good may be realized in even a small good), and also it is not practicable; for medical science does not study how to procure an attribute that belongs to *anything*, but how to procure health, and similarly also each of the other
19 practical sciences. But 'good' has many meanings, and there is a part of it that is beautiful, and one form of it is practicable but another is not. The sort of good that is practicable is that which is an object aimed at, but the good in things unchangeable is not practicable.

For practical purposes Man's aim and End constitutes his Absolute Good.

It is manifest, therefore, that the Absolute Good we are looking for is not the Form of good, nor yet the good as universal, for the Form is unchangeable and impracticable, and the universal good though changeable is not practicable. But the object aimed at as End is the chief good, and is the cause of the subordi-
20 nate goods and first of all; so that the Absolute Good would be this—the End of the goods practicable for man. And this is the good that comes under the supreme of all the practical sciences, which is Politics and Economics and Wisdom; for these states of character differ from the others in the fact that they

1218 b ἀλλήλας εἴ τι διαφέρουσιν ὕστερον λεκτέον). ὅτι 21
δ' αἴτιον τὸ τέλος τῶν ὑφ' αὑτὸ δηλοῖ ἡ διδασκαλία·
ὁρισάμενοι γὰρ τὸ τέλος τἆλλα δεικνύουσιν ὅτι
ἕκαστον αὐτῶν ἀγαθόν, αἴτιον γὰρ τὸ οὗ ἕνεκα·
οἷον ἐπειδὴ τὸ ὑγιαίνειν τοδί, ἀνάγκη τοδὶ[1] εἶναι
τὸ συμφέρον πρὸς αὐτήν, τὸ δ' ὑγιεινὸν τῆς ὑγιείας
αἴτιον ὡς κινῆσαν, καίτοι[2] τοῦ εἶναι ἀλλ' οὐ τοῦ
ἀγαθὸν εἶναι τὴν ὑγίειαν. ἔτι οὐδὲ δείκνυσιν οὐθεὶς 22
ὅτι ἀγαθὸν ἡ ὑγίεια (ἂν μὴ σοφιστὴς ᾖ καὶ μὴ
ἰατρός, οὗτοι γὰρ τοῖς ἀλλοτρίοις λόγοις σοφίζονται),
ὥσπερ οὐδ' ἄλλην ἀρχὴν οὐδεμίαν.

Τὸ δ' ὡς τέλος[3] ἀγαθὸν ἀνθρώπῳ καὶ τὸ ἄριστον τῶν πρακτῶν σκεπτέον ποσαχῶς τὸ ἄριστον πάντων,[4] ἐπειδὴ τοῦτο ἄριστον, μετὰ ταῦτα ἄλλην λαβοῦσιν ἀρχήν.[5]

[1] τοδὶ ? Sp.: τόδε.

[2] καίτοι Ross: καὶ τότε (καὶ τόδε ? Ric.).

[3] τὸ δὲ τέλος ὡς vel ὡς δὲ τὸ τέλος Ric.

[4] πάντων <λέγεται> ? Rac.

[5] ἐπειδὴ . . . ἀρχήν secl. ? Rac. (μετὰ . . . ἀρχήν secl. Sus.).

[a] See 1141 b 21-1142 a 11 (*E.E.* v. = *N.E.* vi. viii. init.).

are supreme (whether they differ at all from one
21 another must be discussed later on [a]). And that the End stands in a causal relation to the means subordinate to it is shown by the method of teachers; they prove that the various means are each good by first defining the End, because the End aimed at is a cause: for example, since to be in health is so-and-so, what contributes to health must necessarily be so-and-so; the wholesome is the efficient cause of health, though only the cause of its existing—it is
22 not the cause of health's being a good. Furthermore nobody *proves* that health is a good (unless he is a sophist and not a physician—it is sophists that juggle with irrelevant arguments), any more than he proves any other first principle.

After this we must take a fresh starting-point [b] and consider, in regard to the good as End for man and in regard to the best of practicable goods, how many senses there are of the term 'best of all,' since this is best.

[b] This clause and the last clause of the sentence render words that look like an interpolation patched into the text from the opening sentence of Book II.

1218 b

B

I. Μετὰ δὲ ταῦτ' ἄλλην λαβοῦσιν ἀρχὴν περὶ τῶν 1
ἑπομένων λεκτέον.
Πάντα δὴ τἀγαθὰ ἢ ἐκτὸς ἢ ἐν[1] ψυχῇ, καὶ
τούτων αἱρετώτερα τὰ ἐν τῇ ψυχῇ, καθάπερ δι-
αιρούμεθα καὶ ἐν τοῖς ἐξωτερικοῖς λόγοις. φρόνησις γὰρ καὶ ἀρετὴ καὶ ἡδονὴ ἐν ψυχῇ, ὧν ἢ ἔνια ἢ
πάντα τέλος εἶναι δοκεῖ πᾶσιν. τῶν δὲ ἐν ψυχῇ
τὰ μὲν ἕξεις ἢ δυνάμεις εἰσί, τὰ δ' ἐνέργειαι καὶ
κινήσεις.
Ταῦτα δὴ οὕτως ὑποκείσθω, καὶ περὶ ἀρετῆς 2
ὅτι ἐστὶν ἡ βελτίστη διάθεσις ἢ ἕξις ἢ δύναμις
1219 a ἑκάστων ὅσων ἐστί τις χρῆσις ἢ ἔργον. δῆλον δ'
ἐκ τῆς ἐπαγωγῆς· ἐπὶ πάντων γὰρ οὕτω τίθεμεν·
οἷον ἱματίου ἀρετή ἐστιν, καὶ γὰρ ἔργον τι καὶ
χρῆσίς ἐστιν, καὶ ἡ βελτίστη ἕξις τοῦ ἱματίου
ἀρετή ἐστιν· ὁμοίως δὲ καὶ πλοίου καὶ οἰκίας καὶ
τῶν ἄλλων. ὥστε καὶ ψυχῆς, ἔστι γάρ τι ἔργον
αὐτῆς. καὶ τῆς βελτίονος δὴ ἕξεως ἔστω βέλτιον 3
τὸ ἔργον, καὶ ὡς ἔχουσιν αἱ ἕξεις πρὸς ἀλλήλας,
οὕτω καὶ τὰ ἔργα τὰ ἀπὸ τούτων πρὸς ἄλληλα
ἐχέτω. καὶ τέλος ἑκάστου τὸ ἔργον· φανερὸν 4

[1] ἐν add. Camot: ἢ ⟨ἐν σώματι ἢ ἐν⟩ Sus. (et infra αἱρετώτατα Rac.).

BOOK II

1 I. After this we must take a fresh starting-point and discuss the subjects that follow.

ETHICAL PSYCHOLOGY (c. i). Nature of Happiness deduced from function of man.

Now all goods are either external or within the spirit, and of these two kinds the latter are preferable, as we class them even in the extraneous discourses.[a] For Wisdom and Goodness and Pleasure are in the spirit, and either some or all of these are thought by everybody to be an End. And the contents of the spirit are in two groups, one states or faculties, the other activities and processes.

2 Let these assumptions, then, be made, and let it be assumed as to Goodness that it is the best disposition or state or faculty of each class of things that have some use or work. This is clear from induction, for we posit this in all cases: for instance, there is a goodness that belongs to a coat, for a coat has a particular function and use, and the best state of a coat is its goodness; and similarly with a ship and a house and the rest. So that the same is true also

Goodness means fitness for function

3 of the spirit, for it has a work of its own. And therefore let us assume that the better the state is the better is the work of that state, and that as states stand in relation to one another so do the works

4 that result from them. And the work of each thing

[a] See note on 1217 b 23.

1219 a

τοίνυν ἐκ τούτων ὅτι βέλτιον τὸ ἔργον τῆς ἕξεως· τὸ γὰρ τέλος ἄριστον ὡς τέλος, ὑπόκειται γὰρ τέλος τὸ βέλτιστον καὶ τὸ ἔσχατον οὗ ἕνεκα τἆλλα πάντα· ὅτι μὲν τοίνυν τὸ ἔργον βέλτιον τῆς ἕξεως καὶ τῆς διαθέσεως, δῆλον.

5 Ἀλλὰ τὸ ἔργον λέγεται διχῶς· τῶν μὲν γάρ ἐστιν ἕτερόν τι τὸ ἔργον παρὰ τὴν χρῆσιν, οἷον οἰκοδομικῆς οἰκία ἀλλ' οὐκ οἰκοδόμησις καὶ ἰατρικῆς ὑγίεια ἀλλ' οὐχ ὑγίανσις οὐδ' ἰάτρευσις, τῶν δ' ἡ χρῆσις ἔργον, οἷον ὄψεως ὅρασις καὶ μαθηματικῆς ἐπιστήμης θεωρία. ὥστ' ἀνάγκη ὧν ἔργον ἡ χρῆσις τὴν χρῆσιν βέλτιον εἶναι τῆς ἕξεως.

6 Τούτων δὲ τοῦτον τὸν τρόπον διωρισμένων, λέγομεν ὅτι τὸ αὐτὸ[1] ἔργον τοῦ πράγματος καὶ τῆς ἀρετῆς (ἀλλ' οὐχ ὡσαύτως), οἷον σκυτοτομικῆς καὶ σκυτεύσεως ὑπόδημα· εἰ δή τις ἐστὶν ἀρετὴ σκυτικὴ[2] καὶ σπουδαῖος σκυτεύς,[3] τὸ ἔργον ἐστὶ σπουδαῖον ὑπόδημα· τὸν αὐτὸν δὲ τρόπον καὶ ἐπὶ τῶν ἄλλων.

7 Ἔτι ἔστω ψυχῆς ἔργον τὸ ζῆν ποιεῖν, τοῦτο[4] δὲ χρῆσις καὶ ἐγρήγορσις (ὁ γὰρ ὕπνος ἀργία τις καὶ ἡσυχία)· ὥστ' ἐπεὶ τὸ ἔργον ἀνάγκη ἓν καὶ ταὐτὸ εἶναι τῆς ψυχῆς καὶ τῆς ἀρετῆς, ἔργον ἂν εἴη τῆς ἀρετῆς ζωὴ σπουδαία. τοῦτ' ἄρ' ἐστὶ τὸ

[1] αὐτὸ add. Rac. (ταὐτὸ ante τὸ ἔργον Cas.).
[2] Rac.: σκυτικῆς.
[3] Sp.: σπουδαίου σκύτεως.
[4] Wilson: τοῦ.

is its End; from this, therefore, it is plain that the work is a greater good than the state, for the End is the best as being an End, since the greatest good is assumed as an End and as the ultimate object for the sake of which all the other things exist. It is clear, therefore, that the work is a greater good than the state and disposition.

5 But the term 'work' has two meanings; for some things have a work that is something different from the employment of them, for instance the work of architecture is a house, not the act of building, that of medicine health, not the process of healing or curing, whereas with other things their work is the process of using them, for instance the work of sight is the act of seeing, that of mathematical science the contemplation of mathematical truths. So it follows that with the things whose work is the employment of them, the act of employing them must be of more value than the state of possessing them.

(which is not necessarily a *productive* process),

6 And these points having been decided in this way, we say that the same work belongs to a thing and to its goodness (although not in the same way): for example, a shoe is the work of the art of shoemaking and of the act of shoemaking; so if there is such a thing as shoemaking goodness and a good shoemaker, their work is a good shoe; and in the same way in the case of the other arts also.

7 Again, let us grant that the work of the spirit is to cause life, and that being alive is employment and being awake (for sleep is a kind of inactivity and rest); with the consequence that since the work of the spirit and that of its goodness are necessarily one and the same, the work of goodness would be good life. Therefore this is the perfect good, which

and its exercise in action constitutes Happiness.

1219 a τέλεον ἀγαθόν, ὅπερ ἦν ἡ εὐδαιμονία. δῆλον δὲ 8
ἐκ τῶν ὑποκειμένων (ἦν μὲν γὰρ ἡ εὐδαιμονία τὸ
ἄριστον, τὰ δὲ τέλη ἐν ψυχῇ καὶ τὰ ἄριστα τῶν ἀγαθῶν, τὰ ἐν αὐτῇ[1] δὲ ἢ ἕξις ἢ ἐνέργεια), ἐπεὶ βέλτιον ἡ ἐνέργεια τῆς διαθέσεως καὶ τῆς βελτίστης ἕξεως ἡ βελτίστη ἐνέργεια ἡ δ' ἀρετὴ βελτίστη ἕξις, τὴν[2] τῆς ἀρετῆς ἐνέργειαν[3] τῆς ψυχῆς ἄριστον
εἶναι. ἦν δὲ καὶ ἡ εὐδαιμονία τὸ ἄριστον· ἔστιν 9
ἄρα ἡ εὐδαιμονία ψυχῆς ἀγαθῆς[4] ἐνέργεια. ἐπεὶ δὲ ἦν ἡ εὐδαιμονία τέλεόν τι, καὶ ἔστι ζωὴ καὶ τελέα καὶ ἀτελής, καὶ ἀρετὴ ὡσαύτως (ἡ μὲν γὰρ ὅλη, ἡ δὲ μόριον), ἡ δὲ τῶν ἀτελῶν ἐνέργεια ἀτελής, εἴη ἂν ἡ εὐδαιμονία ζωῆς τελείας ἐνέργεια κατ' ἀρετὴν τελείαν.

Ὅτι δὲ τὸ γένος καὶ τὸν ὅρον αὐτῆς λέγομεν 10
καλῶς, μαρτύρια τὰ δοκοῦντα πᾶσιν ἡμῖν. τό τε
1219 b γὰρ εὖ πράττειν καὶ τὸ εὖ ζῆν τὸ αὐτὸ τῷ εὐδαιμονεῖν, ὧν ἑκάτερον[5] χρῆσίς ἐστι καὶ ἐνέργεια, καὶ ἡ ζωὴ καὶ ἡ πρᾶξις· καὶ γὰρ ἡ πρακτικὴ χρηστική ἐστιν, ὁ μὲν γὰρ χαλκεὺς ποιεῖ χαλινὸν χρῆται δ' ὁ ἱππικός. καὶ τὸ μήτε μίαν ἡμέραν εἶναι[6] εὐδαίμονα μήτε παῖδα μήθ' ἡλικίαν πᾶσαν (διὸ καὶ τὸ Σόλωνος ἔχει καλῶς, τὸ μὴ ζῶντ' εὐδαιμονίζειν ἀλλ' ὅταν λάβῃ τέλος)· οὐθὲν γὰρ
ἀτελὲς εὔδαιμον, οὐ γὰρ ὅλον. ἔτι δ' οἱ ἔπαινοι 11

[1] τὰ ἐν αὐτῇ Sus.: αὐτὴ aut αὕτη.
[2] τὴν add. ? Ric. [3] Bz.: ἐνεργεία ἡ aut ἡ.
[4] ἀγαθὴ Sp.
[5] ἑκάτερον ? Ric.: ἕκαστον
[6] ἡμέραν <εὐδαίμονα ποιεῖν μήτ'> εἶναι Fr.

[a] *Cf.* 1218 b 7-12.

8 as we saw is happiness. And it is clear from the assumptions laid down (for we said that happiness is the greatest good and that the Ends or the greatest of goods are in the spirit, but things in the spirit are either a state or an activity) that, since an activity is a better thing than a disposition and the best activity than the best state, and since goodness is the best state, the activity of goodness is the
9 spirit's greatest good. But also we saw that the greatest good is happiness. Therefore happiness is the activity of a good spirit. And since we saw [a] that happiness is something perfect, and life is either perfect or imperfect, and the same with goodness (for some goodness is a whole and some a part), but the activity of imperfect things is imperfect, it would follow that happiness is an activity of perfect life in accordance with perfect goodness.

Definition of Happiness.

10 And that our classification and definition of it are correct is evidenced by opinions that we all hold. For we think that to do well and live well are the same as to be happy; but each of these, both life and action, is employment and activity, inasmuch as active life involves employing things—the coppersmith makes a bridle, but the horseman uses it. There is also the evidence of the opinion that a person is not happy for one day only,[b] and that a child is not happy, nor any period of life [c] (hence also Solon's advice holds good, not to call a man happy while he is alive, but only when he has reached the end), for nothing incom-
11 plete is happy, since it is not a whole. And again,

Definition supported by Common Sense.

[b] A single happy day does not make one a happy (*i.e.* fortunate) man.

[c] It is a mistake to say that youth (or maturity, or old age) is the happy time of life.

1219 b
τῆς ἀρετῆς διὰ τὰ ἔργα, καὶ τὰ ἐγκώμια τῶν
ἔργων (καὶ στεφανοῦνται οἱ νικῶντες, ἀλλ' οὐχ οἱ
δυνάμενοι νικᾶν μὴ νικῶντες δέ), καὶ τὸ κρίνειν
ἐκ τῶν ἔργων ὁποῖός τις ἐστίν. ἔτι διὰ τί ἡ 12
εὐδαιμονία οὐκ ἐπαινεῖται; ὅτι διὰ ταύτην τἆλλα,
ἢ τῷ εἰς ταύτην ἀναφέρεσθαι ἢ τῷ μόρια εἶναι
αὐτῆς. διὸ ἕτερον εὐδαιμονισμὸς καὶ ἔπαινος καὶ
ἐγκώμιον· τὸ μὲν γὰρ ἐγκώμιον λόγος τοῦ καθ'
ἕκαστον ἔργου, ὁ δ' ἔπαινος τοῦ[1] τοιοῦτον εἶναι
καθόλου, ὁ δ' εὐδαιμονισμὸς τέλους.[2] καὶ τὸ 13
ἀπ ορούμενον δ' ἐνίοτε δῆλον ἐκ τούτων διὰ τί
ποτ' οὐθὲν βελτίους οἱ σπουδαῖοι τῶν φαύλων τὸν
ἥμισυν τοῦ βίου, ὅμοιοι γὰρ καθεύδοντες πάντες.
αἴτιον δ' ὅτι ἀργία ψυχῆς ὁ ὕπνος ἀλλ' οὐκ ἐνέργεια.
διὸ καὶ ἄλλο εἴ τι μόριόν ἐστι ψυχῆς, οἷον τὸ 14
θρεπτικόν, ἡ τούτου ἀρετὴ οὐκ ἔστι μόριον τῆς
ὅλης ἀρετῆς, ὥσπερ οὐδ' ἡ τοῦ σώματος· ἐν τῷ
ὕπνῳ γὰρ μᾶλλον ἐνεργεῖ τὸ θρεπτικόν, τὸ δ'
αἰσθητικὸν καὶ τὸ[3] ὀρεκτικὸν ἀτελῆ ἐν τῷ ὕπνῳ.
ὅσον δὲ τοῦ πῃ[4] κινεῖσθαι μετέχουσι, καὶ αἱ φαν-
τασίαι βελτίους αἱ τῶν σπουδαίων, ἐὰν μὴ διὰ
νόσον ἢ πήρωσιν.

Μετὰ ταῦτα περὶ ψυχῆς θεωρητέον· ἡ γὰρ ἀρετὴ 15
ψυχῆς, οὐ κατὰ συμβεβηκός. ἐπεὶ δ' ἀνθρωπίνην
ἀρετὴν ζητοῦμεν, ὑποκείσθω δύο μέρη ψυχῆς τὰ
λόγου μετέχοντα, οὐ τὸν αὐτὸν δὲ τρόπον μετέχειν
λόγου ἄμφω, ἀλλὰ τῷ μὲν τὸ ἐπιτάττειν τῷ δὲ

[1] τοῦ add. Bz. [2] Bz.: τέλος. [3] τὸ add. Rac.
[4] πῃ ? (cf. *N.E.* 1029 b 9) Cas.: μή.

there are the praises given to goodness on account of its deeds, and panegyrics describing deeds (and it is the victorious who are given wreaths, not those who are capable of winning but do not win) ; and there is the fact that we judge a man's character
12 from his actions. Also why is happiness not praised ? It is because it is on account of it that the other things are praised, either by being placed in relation to it or as being parts of it. Hence felicitation, praise and panegyric are different things : panegyric is a recital of a particular exploit, praise a statement of a man's general distinction, felicitation is bestowed on
13 an end achieved. From these considerations light is also thrown on the question sometimes raised—what is the precise reason why the virtuous are for half their lives no better than the base, since all men are alike when asleep ? The reason is that sleep is
14 inaction of the spirit, not an activity. Hence the goodness of any other part of the spirit, for instance the nutritive, is not a portion of goodness as a whole, just as also goodness of the body is not ; for the nutritive part functions more actively in sleep, whereas the sensory and appetitive parts are ineffective in sleep. But even the imaginations of the virtuous, so far as the imaginative faculty participates in any mode of motion, are better than those of the base, provided they are not perverted by disease or mutilation.

15 Next we must study the spirit ; for goodness is a property of the spirit, it is not accidental. And since it is human goodness that we are investigating, let us begin by positing that the spirit has two parts that partake of reason, but that they do not both partake of reason in the same manner, but one of them by having by nature the capacity to give orders, and the

Psychology of rational being.

1219 b
τὸ[1] πείθεσθαι καὶ ἀκούειν πεφυκέναι (εἰ δέ τι
ἐστὶν ἑτέρως ἄλογον, ἀφείσθω τοῦτο τὸ μόριον).
διαφέρει δ' οὐθὲν οὔτ' εἰ μεριστὴ ἡ ψυχὴ οὔτ' εἰ 16
ἀμερής, ἔχει μέντοι δυνάμεις διαφόρους καὶ τὰς
εἰρημένας, ὥσπερ ἐν τῷ καμπύλῳ τὸ κοῖλον καὶ
τὸ κυρτὸν ἀδιαχώριστον, καὶ τὸ εὐθὺ καὶ τὸ λευ-
κόν, καίτοι τὸ εὐθὺ οὐ λευκὸν ἀλλ' ἢ[2] κατὰ συμβεβηκὸς καὶ οὐκ οὐσίᾳ τῇ αὑτοῦ.[3] ἀφῄρηται[4] 17
δὲ καὶ εἴ τι ἄλλο ἐστὶ μέρος ψυχῆς, οἷον τὸ
φυτικόν.[5] ἀνθρωπίνης γὰρ[6] ψυχῆς τὰ εἰρημένα
μόρια ἴδια, διὸ οὐδ' αἱ ἀρεταὶ αἱ τοῦ θρεπτικοῦ
καὶ αὐξητικοῦ[7] ἀνθρώπου· δεῖ γάρ, εἰ ᾗ ἄνθρωπος,
λογισμὸν ἐνεῖναι πρὸς[8] ἀρχὴν καὶ πρᾶξιν, ἄρχει
1220 a δ' ὁ λογισμὸς οὐ λογισμοῦ ἀλλ' ὀρέξεως καὶ
παθημάτων· ἀνάγκη ἄρα ταῦτ' ἔχειν τὰ μέρη. 18
καὶ ὥσπερ ἡ εὐεξία σύγκειται ἐκ τῶν κατὰ μόριον
ἀρετῶν, οὕτω καὶ ἡ τῆς ψυχῆς ἀρετὴ ᾗ τέλος.

Ἀρετῆς δ' εἴδη δύο, ἡ μὲν ἠθικὴ ἡ δὲ διανοητική· 19
ἐπαινοῦμεν γὰρ οὐ μόνον τοὺς δικαίους ἀλλὰ καὶ
τοὺς συνετοὺς καὶ τοὺς σοφούς. ἐπαινετὸν γὰρ
ὑπέκειτο ἢ[9] ἀρετὴ ἢ τὸ ἔργον, ταῦτα δ' οὐκ
ἐνεργεῖ ἀλλ' εἰσὶν αὐτῶν ἐνέργειαι. ἐπεὶ δ' αἱ 20
διανοητικαὶ μετὰ λόγου, αἱ μὲν τοιαῦται τοῦ λόγον
ἔχοντος ὃ ἐπιτακτικόν ἐστι τῆς ψυχῆς ᾗ λόγον

[1] τῷ μὲν . . . τὸ . . . τῷ δὲ . . . τὸ Ric.: τὸ μὲν . . . τῷ . . . τὸ δὲ . . . τῷ.
[2] ἀλλ' ἢ Ric.: ἀλλὰ.
[3] Ric.: οὐσία τοῦ αὐτοῦ (οὐσία τὸ αὐτό Bz.).
[4] ἀφῃρήσθω Fr.: ἀφείσθω Bz.
[5] Vict.: φυσικόν.
[6] Γ: δὲ.
[7] Bz.: ὀρεκτικοῦ.
[8] Ric.: καὶ (ὡς Sus.).
[9] ἢ Sol.: ἡ.

[a] *i.e.* the part 'connected with nutrition and growth,' man's animal life, which is irrational absolutely, and not

other to obey and listen (let us leave out any part
16 that is irrational in another way[a]). And it makes no difference whether the spirit is divisible or is undivided yet possessed of different capacities, namely those mentioned, just as the concave and convex sides in a curve are inseparable, and the straightness and whiteness in a straight white line, although a straight thing is not white except accidentally and
17 not by its own essence. And we have also abstracted any other part of the spirit that there may be, for instance the factor of growth; for the parts that we have mentioned are the special properties of the human spirit, and hence the excellences of the part dealing with nutrition and growth are not the special property of a man, for necessarily, if considered as a man, he must possess a reasoning faculty for a principle and with a view to conduct, and the reasoning faculty is a principle controlling not reasoning but
18 appetite and passions; therefore he must necessarily possess those parts. And just as a good constitution consists of the separate excellences of the parts of the body, so also the goodness of the spirit, as being an End, is composed of the separate virtues.

Goodness of Character and Goodness of Intellect.

19 And goodness has two forms, moral virtue and intellectual excellence; for we praise not only the just but also the intelligent and the wise. For we assumed[b] that what is praiseworthy is either goodness or its work, and these are not activities but possess
20 activities. And since the intellectual excellences involve reason, these forms of goodness belong to the rational part, which as having reason is in command

merely in the sense of not possessing reason but being capable of obedience to it.

[b] *Cf.* 1218 a 37 ff., 1219 b 8 ff., 15 ff.

1220 a
ἔχει, αἱ δ᾽ ἠθικαὶ τοῦ ἀλόγου μὲν ἀκολουθητικοῦ
δὲ κατὰ φύσιν τῷ λόγον ἔχοντι· οὐ γὰρ λέγομεν
ποῖός τις τὸ ἦθος, ὅτι σοφὸς ἢ δεινός, ἀλλ᾽ ὅτι
πρᾶος ἢ θρασύς.

Μετὰ ταῦτα σκεπτέον πρῶτον περὶ ἀρετῆς ἠθι- 21
κῆς τί ἐστι καὶ ποῖα μόρια αὐτῆς (εἰς τοῦτο γὰρ
ἀνῆκται) καὶ γίνεται διὰ τίνων. δεῖ δὴ ζητεῖν ὥσπερ ἐν τοῖς ἄλλοις ἔχοντές τι ζητοῦσι πάντες,
ὥστε δεῖ διὰ τῶν ἀληθῶς μὲν λεγομένων οὐ σαφῶς
δὲ πειρᾶσθαι λαβεῖν τὸ καὶ[1] ἀληθῶς καὶ σαφῶς.
νῦν γὰρ ὁμοίως ἔχομεν ὥσπερ ἂν εἰ εἰδείημεν[2] καὶ 22
ὑγίειαν ὅτι ἡ ἀρίστη διάθεσις τοῦ σώματος καὶ
Κορίσκον[3] ὅτι[4] ὁ τῶν ἐν τῇ ἀγορᾷ μελάντατος· τί
μὲν γὰρ ἑκάτερον τούτων οὐκ ἴσμεν, πρὸς μέντοι
τὸ εἰδέναι τί ἑκάτερον αὐτοῖν[5] πρὸ ἔργου τὸ οὕτως
ἔχειν.—ὑποκείσθω δὴ πρῶτον ἡ βελτίστη διάθεσις 23
ὑπὸ τῶν βελτίστων γίγνεσθαι καὶ πράττεσθαι τὰ[6]
ἄριστα περὶ ἕκαστον ἀπὸ τῆς ἑκάστου ἀρετῆς,
οἷον πόνοι τε ἄριστοι καὶ τροφὴ ἀφ᾽ ὧν γίνεται
εὐεξία, καὶ ἀπὸ τῆς εὐεξίας πονοῦσιν ἄριστα· ἔτι 24
πᾶσαν διάθεσιν ὑπὸ τῶν αὐτῶν γίγνεσθαί τε[7] καὶ
φθείρεσθαι πὼς προσφερομένων, ὥσπερ ὑγίεια ὑπὸ
τροφῆς καὶ πόνων καὶ ὥρας· ταῦτα δὲ δῆλα ἐκ
τῆς ἐπαγωγῆς. καὶ ἡ ἀρετὴ ἄρα ἡ τοιαύτη διά-
θεσίς ἐστιν ἣ γίνεταί τε ὑπὸ τῶν ἀρίστων περὶ
ψυχὴν κινήσεων καὶ ἀφ᾽ ἧς πράττεται τὰ ἄριστα
τῆς ψυχῆς ἔργα καὶ πάθη· καὶ ὑπὸ τῶν αὐτῶν 25

[1] τὸ καὶ Ric.: καὶ τό.
[2] εἰδείημεν add. Sp.
[3] Rac.: Κορίσκος.
[4] ὅτι add. Sp.
[5] rec. M^b: αὐτῆς.
[6] τὰ add. Rac.
[7] τε add. Rac.

[a] *Cf.* 1240 b 25 n.

of the spirit; whereas the moral virtues belong to the part that is irrational but by nature capable of following the rational—for in stating a man's moral qualities we do not say that he is wise or clever but that he is gentle or rash.

GOODNESS OF CHARACTER OR VIRTUE (Bk. II. fin.) Its nature and genesis.

21 After this we must first consider Moral Goodness—its essence and the nature of its divisions (for that is the subject now arrived at), and the means by which it is produced. Our method of inquiry then must be that employed by all people in other matters when they have something in hand to start with—we must endeavour by means of statements that are true but not clearly expressed to arrive at a result that is both
22 true and clear. For our present state is as if we knew that health is the best disposition of the body and that Coriscus[a] is the darkest man in the market-place; for that is not to know what health is and who Coriscus is, but nevertheless to be in that state is a help to-
23 wards knowing each of these things.—Then let it first be taken as granted that the best disposition is produced by the best means, and that the best actions in each department of conduct result from the excellences belonging to each department—for example, it is the best exercises and food that produce a good condition of body, and a good condition of body en-
24 ables men to do the best work; further, that every disposition is both produced and destroyed by the same things applied in a certain manner, for example health by food and exercises and climate; these points are clear from induction. Therefore goodness too is the sort of disposition that is created by the best movements in the spirit and is also the source of the production of the spirit's best actions and emotions;
25 and it is in one way produced and in another way

A fuller definition of Virtue.

1220 a πῶς μὲν γίνεται πῶς δὲ φθείρεται, καὶ πρὸς ταῦτα ἡ χρῆσις αὐτῆς ὑφ' ὧν καὶ αὔξεται καὶ φθείρεται πρὸς ἃ βέλτιστα διατίθησιν. σημεῖον δ' ὅτι περὶ ἡδέα καὶ λυπηρὰ καὶ ἡ ἀρετὴ καὶ ἡ κακία· αἱ γὰρ κολάσεις ἰατρεῖαι οὖσαι καὶ γινόμεναι διὰ τῶν ἐναντίων, καθάπερ ἐπὶ τῶν ἄλλων, διὰ τούτων εἰσίν.

II. Ὅτι μὲν τοίνυν ἡ ἠθικὴ ἀρετὴ περὶ ἡδέα 1
καὶ λυπηρά ἐστι, δῆλον. ἐπεὶ δ' ἐστὶ τὸ ἦθος—
1220 b ὥσπερ καὶ τὸ ὄνομα σημαίνει ὅτι ἀπὸ ἔθους ἔχει
τὴν ἐπίδοσιν, ἐθίζεται δὲ ὑπ' ἀγωγῆς τὸ μὴ
ἔμφυτον[1] τῷ πολλάκις κινεῖσθαί πως οὕτως ἤδη[2]
ἐνεργητικόν (ὃ ἐν τοῖς ἀψύχοις οὐχ ὁρῶμεν, οὐδὲ
γὰρ ἂν μυριάκις ῥίψῃς ἄνω τὸν λίθον οὐδέποτε
ποιήσει τοῦτο μὴ βίᾳ)—διὸ ἔστω τὸ[3] ἦθος τοῦτο,
ψυχῆς κατὰ ἐπιτακτικὸν λόγον δυναμένῃ[4] ἀκολουθεῖν
τῷ λόγῳ ποιότης. λεκτέον δὴ κατὰ τί τῆς ψυχῆς 2
ποι' ἄττα[5] ἤθη. ἔσται δὲ κατά τε τὰς δύναμεις 3
τῶν παθημάτων καθ' ἃς πῶς[6] παθητικοὶ λέγονται
καὶ κατὰ τὰς ἕξεις καθ' ἃς πρὸς τὰ πάθη τοιοῦτοι[7]
λέγονται τῷ πάσχειν πως ἢ ἀπαθεῖς εἶναι.
Μετὰ ταῦτα ἡ διαίρεσις ἐν τοῖς διειλεγμένοις[8] 4
τῶν παθημάτων καὶ τῶν δυνάμεων καὶ τῶν ἕξεων.

[1] Fr.: ἐθίζεται δὲ τὸ ὑπ' ἀγωγῆς μὴ ἐμφύτου.
[2] ἤδη Rac.: ἤδη τὸ.
[3] τὸ add. Rac.
[4] Sp. (cf. Stob. *Ecl. eth.* p. 36): δυναμένου δ'.
[5] ποι' ἄττα Sol. (ποι' ἄττα τὰ ? Rac., ποιότης τὰ Sp.): ποῖ' ἄττα.
[6] Rac.: ὡς.
[7] τοιοῦτοι Ric.: ταῦτα.
[8] Ras.: ἀπηλλαγμένοις.

[a] *e.g.* fever, which is caused by heat, is cured by cold (the contrary doctrine to homoeopathy, *similia similibus curantur*).

[b] ἦθος derived from ἔθος by lengthening of ε to η: *cf. N.E.*

destroyed by the same things, and its employment of the things that cause both its increase and its destruction is directed towards the things towards which it creates the best disposition. And this is indicated by the fact that both goodness and badness have to do with things pleasant and painful; for punishments, which are medicines, and which as is the case with other cures[a] operate by means of opposites, operate by means of pleasures and pains.

The hedonistic factor.

1 II. It is clear, therefore, that Moral Goodness has to do with pleasures and pains. And since moral character is, as even its name implies that it has its growth from habit,[b] and by our often moving in a certain way a habit not innate in us is finally trained to be operative in that way (which we do not observe in inanimate objects, for not even if you throw a stone upwards ten thousand times will it ever rise upward unless under the operation of force)—let moral character then be defined as a quality of the spirit in accordance with governing reason that is capable of following
2 the reason. We have then to say what is the part of the spirit in respect of which our moral characters
3 are of a certain quality. And it will be in respect of our faculties for emotions according to which people are termed liable to some emotion, and also of the states of character according to which people receive certain designations in respect of the emotions, because of their experiencing or being exempt from some form of emotion.

The moral character.

4 After this comes the classification, made in previous discussions,[c] of the modes of emotion, the faculties

ii. iii. 4. This clause and the one following interrupt the construction of the sentence.

[c] Perhaps a reference to *N.E.* 1105 b 20, inserted in the belief that the *Eudemian Ethics* is the later work.

1220 b
λέγω δὲ πάθη μὲν τὰ τοιαῦτα, θυμὸν φόβον αἰδῶ
ἐπιθυμίαν, ὅλως οἷς ἕπεται ὡς ἐπὶ τὸ πολὺ ἡ
αἰσθητικὴ ἡδονὴ ἢ λύπη καθ' αὑτά· καὶ κατὰ μὲν 5
ταῦτα οὐκ ἔστι ποιότης [ἀλλὰ πάσχει][1], κατὰ δὲ
τὰς δυνάμεις ποιότης· λέγω δὲ[2] δυνάμεις καθ' ἃς
λέγονται κατὰ τὰ πάθη οἱ ἐνεργοῦντες, οἷον ὀργίλος
ἀνάλγητος ἐρωτικὸς αἰσχυντηλὸς ἀναίσχυντος.
ἕξεις δέ εἰσιν ὅσαι αἴτιαί εἰσι τοῦ ταῦτα ἢ κατὰ
λόγον ὑπάρχειν ἢ ἐναντίως, οἷον ἀνδρεία σωφροσύνη
δειλία ἀκολασία.

III. Διωρισμένων δὲ τούτων ληπτέον ὅτι ἐν 1
ἅπαντι συνεχεῖ καὶ διαιρετῷ ἐστὶν ὑπεροχὴ καὶ
ἔλλειψις καὶ μέσον, καὶ ταῦτα ἢ πρὸς ἄλληλα ἢ
πρὸς ἡμᾶς, οἷον ἐν γυμναστικῇ, ἐν ἰατρικῇ, ἐν
οἰκοδομικῇ, ἐν κυβερνητικῇ, καὶ ἐν ὁποιᾳοῦν πράξει
καὶ ἐπιστημονικῇ καὶ ἀνεπιστημονικῇ καὶ τεχνικῇ
καὶ ἀτέχνῳ· ἡ μὲν γὰρ κίνησις συνεχές, ἡ δὲ 2
πρᾶξις κίνησις. ἐν πᾶσι δὲ τὸ μέσον τὸ πρὸς
ἡμᾶς βέλτιστον· τοῦτο γάρ ἐστιν ὡς ἡ ἐπιστήμη
κελεύει καὶ ὁ λόγος. πανταχοῦ δὲ τοῦτο καὶ
ποιεῖ τὴν βελτίστην ἕξιν. καὶ τοῦτο δῆλον διὰ
τῆς ἐπαγωγῆς καὶ τοῦ λόγου· τὰ γὰρ ἐναντία
φθείρει ἄλληλα· τὰ δ' ἄκρα καὶ ἀλλήλοις καὶ τῷ
μέσῳ ἐναντία, τὸ γὰρ μέσον ἑκάτερον πρὸς
ἑκάτερόν ἐστιν, οἷον τὸ ἴσον τοῦ μὲν ἐλάττονος
μεῖζον τοῦ μείζονος δὲ ἔλαττον. ὥστ' ἀνάγκη 3
τὴν ἠθικὴν ἀρετὴν περὶ μέσ' ἄττα εἶναι καὶ
μεσότητά τινα. ληπτέον ἄρα ἡ ποία μεσότης

[1] pravum glossema Rac.

[2] δὲ Sus.: δὲ τάς.

[a] This interpolation was made by an editor who derived ποιότης from ποιεῖν.

and the states of character. By emotions I mean such things as anger, fear, shame, desire, and generally those experiences that are in themselves usually
5 accompanied by sensory pleasure or pain. And to these there is no quality corresponding [but they are passive].[a] But quality corresponds to the faculties: by faculties I mean the properties acting by which persons are designated by the names of the various emotions, for instance choleric, insensitive, erotic, bashful, shameless. States of character are the states that cause the emotions to be present either rationally or the opposite: for example courage, sobriety of mind, cowardice, profligacy.

Virtue and the relative mean in conduct.

1 III. These distinctions having been established, it must be grasped that in every continuum that is divisible there is excess and deficiency and a mean, and these either in relation to one another or in relation to us, for instance in gymnastics or medicine or architecture or navigation, and in any practical pursuit of whatever sort, both scientific and unscientific, both
2 technical and untechnical; for motion is a continuum, and conduct is a motion. And in all things the mean in relation to us is the best, for that is as knowledge and reason bid. And everywhere this also produces the best state. This is proved by induction and reason: contraries are mutually destructive, and extremes are contrary both to each other and to the mean, as the mean *is* either extreme in relation to the other—for example the equal is greater than the less
3 and less than the greater. Hence moral goodness must be concerned with certain means and must be a middle state. We must, therefore, ascertain what sort of middle state is goodness and with what sort of

1220 b ἀρετὴ καὶ περὶ ποῖα μέσα. εἰλήφθω δὴ παρα- 4
δείγματος χάριν, καὶ θεωρείσθω ἕκαστον ἐκ τῆς
ὑπογραφῆς·

	ὀργιλότης	ἀοργησία[1]	πραότης.
	θρασύτης	δειλία	ἀνδρεία.
1221 a	ἀναισχυντία	κατάπληξις	αἰδώς.
	ἀκολασία	ἀναισθησία	σωφροσύνη.
	φθόνος	ἀνώνυμον	νέμεσις.
	κέρδος	ζημία	δίκαιον.
	ἀσωτία	ἀνελευθερία	ἐλευθεριότης.
	ἀλαζονεία	εἰρωνεία	ἀλήθεια.
	κολακεία	ἀπέχθεια	φιλία.
	ἀρέσκεια	αὐθάδεια	σεμνότης.
	τρυφερότης	κακοπάθεια	καρτερία.
	χαυνότης	μικροψυχία	μεγαλοψυχία.
	δαπανηρία	μικροπρέπεια	μεγαλοπρέπεια.
	πανουργία	εὐήθεια	φρόνησις.

τὰ μὲν πάθη ταῦτα καὶ τοιαῦτα συμβαίνει ταῖς 5
ψυχαῖς, πάντα δὲ λέγεται τὰ μὲν τῷ ὑπερβάλλειν
τὰ δὲ τῷ ἐλλείπειν. ὀργίλος μὲν γάρ ἐστιν ὁ
μᾶλλον ἢ δεῖ ὀργιζόμενος καὶ θᾶττον καὶ πλείοσιν
ἢ οἷς δεῖ, ἀόργητος[2] δὲ ὁ ἐλλείπων καὶ οἷς καὶ
ὅτε καὶ ὥς· καὶ θρασὺς μὲν ὁ μήτε ἃ χρὴ φοβούμενος
μήθ' ὅτε μήθ' ὥς, δειλὸς δὲ ὁ καὶ ἃ μὴ δεῖ καὶ
ὅτ' οὐ δεῖ καὶ ὡς οὐ δεῖ. ὁμοίως δὲ καὶ ἀκόλαστος 6
καὶ[3] ὁ ἐπιθυμητικὸς καὶ ὁ[4] ὑπερβάλλων πᾶσιν ὅσοις

[1] Rac. (cf. *N.E.* 1108 a 7 et 1100 b 33): ἀναλγησία.
[2] Rac.: ἀνάλγητος. [3] [καὶ] Bz. [4] [καὶ ὁ] Vict.

---

[a] The MSS. give 'Insensitiveness,' 'insensitive,' but doubtless the Greek should be altered to agree with *N.E.* 1108 a 7.

4 means it is concerned. Let each then be taken by way of illustration and studied with the help of the schedule:

Irascibility	Spiritlessness [a]	Gentleness
Rashness	Cowardice	Courage
Shamelessness	Diffidence	Modesty
Profligacy	Insensitiveness	Temperance
Envy	(nameless [b])	Righteous Indignation
Profit	Loss	The Just
Prodigality	Meanness	Liberality
Boastfulness	Self-depreciation	Sincerity [c]
Flattery	Surliness	Friendliness
Subservience	Stubbornness	Dignity
Luxuriousness	Endurance [d]	Hardiness
Vanity	Smallness of Spirit	Greatness of Spirit
Extravagance	Shabbiness	Magnificence
Rascality	Simpleness	Wisdom.

5 These and such as these are the emotions that the spirit experiences, and they are all designated from being either excessive or defective. The man that gets angry more and more quickly and with more people than he ought is irascible, he that in respect of persons and occasions and manner is deficient in anger is spiritless [a]; the man that is not afraid of things of which he ought to be afraid, nor when nor as he ought, is rash, he that is afraid of things of which he ought not to be afraid, and when and as he ought not
6 to be, is cowardly.[e] Similarly also one that is a prey to his desires and that exceeds in everything possible

The Vices of excess and defect.

[b] In *N.E.* 1108 b 2 ἐπιχαιρεκακία, Malice, rejoicing in another's misfortune.

[c] *N.E.* iv. vii. shows that sincerity in asserting one's own merits is meant.

[d] 'Submission to evils' (Solomon): not in *N.E.*

[e] The shameless and diffident are omitted here: see the table above.

1221 a ἐνδέχεται, ἀναίσθητος δὲ ὁ ἐλλείπων καὶ μηδ' ὅσον βέλτιον καὶ κατὰ τὴν φύσιν ἐπιθυμῶν, ἀλλ' ἀπαθὴς ὥσπερ λίθος. κερδαλέος δὲ ὁ πανταχόθεν πλεον- 7
εκτικός, ζημιώδης δὲ ὁ εἰ μὴ[1] μηδαμόθεν ἀλλ' ὀλιγαχόθεν. ἀλαζὼν δὲ ὁ πλείω τῶν ὑπαρχόντων προσποιούμενος, εἴρων δὲ ὁ ἐλάττω. καὶ κόλαξ 8
μὲν ὁ πλείω συνεπαινῶν ἢ καλῶς ἔχει, ἀπεχθητικὸς δὲ ὁ ἐλάττω. καὶ τὸ μὲν λίαν πρὸς ἡδονὴν ἀρέσκεια, τὸ δ' ὀλίγα καὶ μόγις αὐθάδεια. ἔτι δ' 9
ὁ μὲν μηδεμίαν ὑπομένων λύπην, μηδ' εἰ βέλτιον, τρυφερός, ὁ δὲ πᾶσαν ὁμοίως ὡς μὲν ἁπλῶς εἰπεῖν ἀνώνυμος, μεταφορᾷ δὲ λέγεται σκληρὸς καὶ ταλαίπωρος καὶ κακοπαθητικός. χαῦνος δ' ὁ 10
μειζόνων ἀξιῶν αὐτόν, μικρόψυχος δ' ὁ ἐλαττόνων. ἔτι δ' ἄσωτος μὲν ὁ πρὸς ἅπασαν δαπάνην ὑπερβάλλων, ἀνελεύθερος δὲ ὁ πρὸς ἅπασαν ἐλλείπων. ὁμοίως δὲ καὶ ὁ μικροπρεπὴς καὶ ὁ 11
σαλάκων, ὁ μὲν γὰρ ὑπερβάλλει τὸ πρέπον, ὁ δ' ἐλλείπει τοῦ πρέποντος. καὶ ὁ μὲν πανοῦργος πάντως καὶ πάντοθεν πλεονεκτικός, ὁ δ' εὐήθης οὐδ' ὅθεν δεῖ. φθονερὸς δὲ τῷ λυπεῖσθαι ἐπὶ 12
πλείοσιν εὐπραγίαις ἢ δεῖ, καὶ γὰρ οἱ ἄξιοι εὖ πράττειν λυποῦσι τοὺς φθονεροὺς εὖ πράττοντες· ὁ δ' ἐναντίος ἀνωνυμώτερος, ἔστι δ' ὁ ὑπερβάλλων
1221 b τῷ[2] μὴ λυπεῖσθαι μηδ' ἐπὶ τοῖς ἀναξίοις εὖ πράττουσιν, ἀλλ' εὐχερὴς ὥσπερ οἱ γαστρίμαργοι πρὸς τροφήν, ὁ δὲ δυσχερὴς κατὰ τὸν φθόνον ἐστίν.—τὸ δὲ πρὸς ἕκαστον μὴ κατὰ συμβεβηκὸς 13

[1] εἰ μὴ add. Fr. (ἀλλ' <εἴ γε> Bussemaker).
[2] τῷ Sp.: ἐπὶ τῷ.

[a] Envy in § 12 comes here in the schedule.

is profligate, and one that is deficient and does not desire even to a proper degree and in a natural way, but is as devoid of feeling as a stone, is insensitive.[a]
7 The man that seeks gain from every source is a profiteer, and he that seeks gain if not from no source, yet from few, is a waster.[b] He that pretends to have more possessions than he really has is a boaster, and he that pretends to have fewer is a self-depreciator.
8 One that joins in approval more than is fitting is a flatterer, one that does so less than is fitting is surly. To be too complaisant is subservience; to be complaisant seldom and reluctantly is stubbornness.
9 Again, the man that endures no pain, not even if it is good for him, is luxurious; one that can endure all pain alike is strictly speaking nameless, but by metaphor
10 he is called hard, patient or enduring. He that rates himself too high is vain, he that rates himself too low, small-spirited. Again, he that exceeds in all expenditure is prodigal, he that falls short in all, mean.
11 Similarly the shabby man and the swaggerer—the latter exceeds what is fitting and the former falls below it. The rascal grasps profit by every means and from every source, the simpleton does not make
12 profit even from the proper sources. Envy consists in being annoyed at prosperity more often than one ought to be, for the envious are annoyed by the prosperity even of those who deserve to prosper; the opposite character is less definitely named, but it is the man that goes too far in not being annoyed even at the prosperity of the undeserving, and is easy-going, as gluttons are in regard to food, whereas his opposite is difficult-tempered in respect of jealousy.—
13 It is superfluous to state in the definition that the

[b] The prodigal and mean in § 10 comes here in the schedule.

1221 b
οὕτως ἔχειν περίεργον διορίζειν[1]· οὐδεμία γὰρ
ἐπιστήμη οὔτε θεωρητικὴ οὔτε ποιητικὴ οὔτε
λέγει οὔτε πράττει τοῦτο προσδιορίζουσα, ἀλλὰ
τοῦτ' ἐστὶ πρὸς τὰς συκοφαντίας τῶν τεχνῶν τὰς
λογικάς. ἁπλῶς μὲν οὖν διωρίσθω τὸν τρόπον 14
τοῦτον, ἀκριβέστερον δ' ὅταν περὶ τῶν ἕξεων
λέγωμεν τῶν ἀντικειμένων.

Αὐτῶν δὲ τούτων τῶν παθημάτων εἴδη κατ-
ονομάζεται τῷ διαφέρειν κατὰ τὴν ὑπερβολὴν ἢ
χρόνου ἢ τοῦ μᾶλλον ἢ πρός τι τῶν ποιούντων
τὰ πάθη. λέγω δ' οἷον ὀξύθυμος μὲν τῷ θᾶττον 15
πάσχειν ἢ δεῖ, χαλεπὸς δὲ καὶ θυμώδης τῷ
μᾶλλον, πικρὸς δὲ τῷ φυλακτικὸς εἶναι τῆς ὀργῆς,
πλήκτης δὲ καὶ λοιδορητικὸς ταῖς κολάσεσι ταῖς
ἀπὸ τῆς ὀργῆς. ὀψοφάγοι δὲ καὶ γαστρίμαργοι 16
καὶ οἰνόφλυγες τῷ πρὸς ὁποτέρας τροφῆς ἀπόλαυσιν
ἔχειν τὴν δύναμιν παθητικὴν παρὰ τὸν λόγον.

Οὐ δεῖ δ' ἀγνοεῖν ὅτι ἔνια τῶν λεγομένων οὐκ 17
ἔστιν ἐν τῷ πῶς λαμβάνειν, ἂν πῶς λαμβάνηται
τὸ[2] μᾶλλον πάσχειν. οἷον μοιχὸς οὐ τῷ μᾶλλον
ἢ δεῖ πρὸς τὰς γαμετὰς πλησιάζειν (οὐ γάρ ἐστιν),
ἀλλὰ μοχθηρία τις αὐτὴ ἤδη[3] ἐστίν, συνειλημμένον
γὰρ τό τε πάθος λέγεται καὶ τὸ τοιόνδε εἶναι·
ὁμοίως δὲ καὶ ἡ ὕβρις. διὸ καὶ ἀμφισβητοῦσι, 18
συγγενέσθαι μὲν φάσκοντες ἀλλ' οὐ μοιχεῦσαι,
ἀγνοοῦντες γὰρ ἢ ἀναγκαζόμενοι, καὶ πατάξαι
μὲν ἀλλ' οὐχ ὑβρίσαι· ὁμοίως δὲ καὶ ἐπὶ τὰ ἄλλα
τὰ τοιαῦτα.

[1] προσδιορίζειν ? (ut *De Interpr.* 17 a 36, *Met.* iii., 1005 b 21) Rac.
[2] Ric. τῷ.
[3] Rac.: δή.

[a] In Book III.
[b] τοιόνδε = μοχθηρόν.

specified relation to each thing must not be accidental; no science whether theoretical or productive makes this addition to the definition either in discourse or in practice, but this addition is aimed against the logical
14 quibbling of the sciences. Let us then accept these simple definitions, and let us make them more precise when we are speaking about the opposite dispositions.[a]

But these modes of emotion themselves are divided into species designated according to their difference in respect of time or intensity or in regard to one Sub-species of Vices.
15 of the objects that cause the emotions. I mean for instance that a man is called quick-tempered from feeling the emotion of anger sooner than he ought, harsh and passionate from feeling it more than he ought, bitter from having a tendency to cherish his anger, violent and abusive owing to the acts of retalia-
16 tion to which his anger gives rise. Men are called gourmands or gluttons and drunkards from having an irrational liability to indulgence in one or the other sort of nutriment.

17 But it must not be ignored that some of the vices mentioned cannot be classed under the heading of manner, if manner is taken to be feeling the emotion to excess. For example, a man is not an adulterer because he exceeds in intercourse with married women, for 'excess' does not apply here, but adultery merely in itself is a vice, since the term denoting the passion implicitly denotes that the man Some Vices absolute.
18 is vicious[b]; and similarly with outrage. Hence men dispute the charge, and admit intercourse but deny adultery on the ground of having acted in ignorance or under compulsion, or admit striking a blow but deny committing an outrage; and similarly in meeting the other charges of the same kind.

1221 b
IV. Εἰλημμένων δὲ τούτων, μετὰ ταῦτα λεκτέον 1
ὅτι ἐπειδὴ δύο μέρη τῆς ψυχῆς καὶ αἱ ἀρεταὶ κατὰ
ταῦτα διῄρηνται, καὶ αἱ μὲν τοῦ λόγον ἔχοντος
διανοητικαί,[1] ὧν ἔργον ἀλήθεια, ἢ περὶ τοῦ πῶς
ἔχει ἢ περὶ γενέσεως, αἱ δὲ τοῦ ἀλόγου ἔχοντος
δ' ὄρεξιν (οὐ γὰρ ὁτιοῦν μέρος ἔχει τῆς ψυχῆς 2
ὄρεξιν εἰ μεριστή ἐστιν), ἀνάγκη δὴ φαῦλον τὸ
ἦθος καὶ σπουδαῖον εἶναι τῷ διώκειν καὶ φεύγειν
ἡδονάς τινας καὶ λύπας. δῆλον δὲ τοῦτο ἐκ τῶν
διαιρέσεων τῶν περὶ τὰ πάθη καὶ τὰς δυνάμεις
καὶ τὰς ἕξεις. αἱ μὲν γὰρ δυνάμεις καὶ αἱ ἕξεις
τῶν[2] παθημάτων, τὰ δὲ πάθη λύπῃ καὶ ἡδονῇ
διώρισται· ὥστε διά τε ταῦτα καὶ διὰ τὰς 3
ἔμπροσθεν θέσεις συμβαίνει πᾶσαν ἠθικὴν ἀρετὴν
περὶ ἡδονὰς εἶναι καὶ λύπας. πᾶσα γὰρ ψυχὴ[3]
ὑφ' οἵων πέφυκε γίνεσθαι χείρων καὶ βελτίων,
1222 a πρὸς ταῦτα καὶ περὶ ταῦτά ἐστιν ἡ ἕξις.[4] δι' 4
ἡδονὰς δὲ καὶ λύπας φαύλους φαμὲν εἶναι, τῷ
διώκειν καὶ φεύγειν ἢ ὡς μὴ δεῖ ἢ ἃς μὴ δεῖ.
διὸ καὶ διορίζονται πάντες[5] προχείρως ἀπάθειαν
καὶ ἠρεμίαν περὶ ἡδονὰς καὶ λύπας εἶναι τὰς
ἀρετάς, τὰς δὲ κακίας ἐκ τῶν ἐναντίων.

V. Ἐπεὶ δ' ὑπόκειται ἀρετὴ εἶναι ἡ τοιαύτη 1
ἕξις ἀφ' ἧς πρακτικοὶ τῶν βελτίστων καὶ καθ' ἣν
ἄριστα διάκεινται περὶ τὸ βέλτιστον, βέλτιστον δὲ
καὶ ἄριστον τὸ κατὰ τὸν ὀρθὸν λόγον, τοῦτο δ'

[1] [διανοητικαί] ? Rac. [2] <αἰτίαι> τῶν Bus.
[3] πάσης γὰρ ψυχῆς Bz.
[4] Bz.: ἡδονή. [5] [πάντες] Spengel: τινες ? Sus.

---

[a] *Cf.* 1220 b 7-20. [b] See 1218 b 37 ff.

1 IV. These points having been taken, we must next say that since the spirit has two parts, and the virtues are divided between them, one set being those of the rational part, intellectual virtues, whose work is truth, whether about the nature of a thing or about its mode of production, while the other set belongs to the part that is irrational but possesses
2 appetition (for if the spirit is divided into parts, not any and every part possesses appetition), it therefore follows that the moral character is vicious or virtuous by reason of pursuing or avoiding certain pleasures and pains. This is clear from the classification [a] of the emotions, faculties and states of character. For the faculties and the states are concerned with the modes of emotion, and the emotions
3 are distinguished by pain and pleasure ; so that it follows from these considerations as well as from the positions already laid down that all moral goodness
4 is concerned with pleasures and pains. For our state of character is related to and concerned with such things as have the property of making every person's spirit worse and better. But we say that men are wicked owing to pleasures and pains, through pursuing and avoiding the wrong ones or in the wrong way. Hence all men readily define the virtues as insensitiveness or tranquillity in regard to pleasures and pains, and the vices by the opposite qualities.

The hedonistic factor analysed.

1 V. But since it has been assumed [b] that goodness is a state of character of a sort that causes men to be capable of doing the best actions and gives them the best disposition in regard to the greatest good, and the best and greatest good is that which is in accordance with right principle, and this is the mean be-

1222 a
ἐστὶ τὸ μέσον ὑπερβολῆς καὶ ἐλλείψεως τῆς πρὸς
ἡμᾶς, ἀναγκαῖον ἂν εἴη τὴν ἠθικὴν ἀρετὴν κατ' αὐτὴν
ἑκάστην[1] μεσότητα εἶναι καὶ[2] περὶ μέσ' ἄττα ἐν
ἡδοναῖς καὶ λύπαις καὶ ἡδέσι καὶ λυπηροῖς. ἔσται 2
δ' ἡ μεσότης ὁτὲ μὲν ἐν ἡδοναῖς (καὶ γὰρ ὑπερβολὴ
καὶ ἔλλειψις), ὁτὲ δ' ἐν λύπαις, ὁτὲ δ' ἐν ἀμφοτέραις.
ὁ γὰρ ὑπερβάλλων τῷ χαίρειν τῷ ἡδεῖ ὑπερβάλλει
καὶ ὁ τῷ λυπεῖσθαι τῷ ἐναντίῳ, καὶ ταῦτα ἢ
ἁπλῶς ἢ πρός τινα ὅρον, οἷον ὅταν μᾶλλον ἢ[3] ὡς
οἱ πολλοί· ὁ δ' ἀγαθὸς ὡς δεῖ.—ἐπεὶ δ' ἐστί τις 3
ἕξις ἀφ' ἧς τοιοῦτος ἔσται ὁ ἔχων αὐτὴν ὥστε
τοῦ αὐτοῦ πράγματος ὁ[4] μὲν ἀποδέχεσθαι τὴν
ὑπερβολὴν ὁ[4] δὲ τὴν ἔλλειψιν, ἀνάγκη ὡς ταῦτ'
ἀλλήλοις ἐναντία καὶ τῷ μέσῳ, οὕτω καὶ τὰς
ἕξεις ἀλλήλαις ἐναντίας εἶναι καὶ τῇ ἀρετῇ.

Συμβαίνει μέντοι τὰς ἀντιθέσεις ἔνθα μὲν 4
φανερωτέρας εἶναι πάσας, ἔνθα δὲ τὰς ἐπὶ τὴν
ὑπερβολήν, ἐνιαχοῦ δὲ τὰς ἐπὶ τὴν ἔλλειψιν.
αἴτιον δὲ τῆς ἐναντιώσεως ὅτι οὐκ ἀεὶ ἐπὶ ταὐτὰ[5] 5
τῆς ἀνισότητος ἡ ὁμοιότης[6] πρὸς τὸ μέσον, ἀλλ'
ὁτὲ μὲν θᾶττον ἂν μεταβαίη ἀπὸ τῆς ὑπερβολῆς
ἐπὶ τὴν μέσην ἕξιν, ὁτὲ δ' ἀπὸ τῆς ἐλλείψεως, ἧς
ὃς[7] πλέον ἀπέχει[8] οὗτος δοκεῖ ἐναντιώτερος
εἶναι, οἷον καὶ περὶ τὸ σῶμα ἐν μὲν τοῖς πόνοις
ὑγιεινότερον ἡ ὑπερβολὴ τῆς ἐλλείψεως καὶ
ἐγγύτερον τοῦ μέσου, ἐν δὲ τῇ τροφῇ ἡ ἔλλειψις

[1] Ric.: καθ' αὐτὸν ἕκαστον.
[2] καὶ Sus.: ἤ.
[3] μᾶλλον ἢ lac.: μή.
[4] ὁ (bis) Bz.: οὐ.
[5] ταὐτὰ <ἔρχεται> vel <ἥκει> Ric.
[6] Bz.: ἡ ὁμοιότητος.
[7] ὃς add. Sus.
[8] ἀπέχων Mb.

tween excess and deficiency relative to ourselves, it would necessarily follow that moral goodness corresponds with each particular middle state and is concerned with certain mean points in pleasures
2 and pains and pleasant and painful things. And this middle state will sometimes be in pleasures (for even in these there is excess and deficiency), sometimes in pains, sometimes in both. For he that exceeds in feeling delight exceeds in the pleasant, and he that exceeds in feeling pain exceeds in the opposite—and this whether his feelings are excessive absolutely or excessive in relation to some standard, for instance are felt more than ordinary men feel them; whereas the good man feels in the proper way.—
3 And since there is a certain state of character which results in its possessor's being in one instance such as to accept an excess and in another such as to accept a deficiency of the same thing, it follows that as these actions are contrary to each other and to the mean, so also the states of character that cause them are contrary to each other and to virtue.

One of the two extremes may be more opposed to the virtue than the other.

4 It comes about, however, that sometimes all the oppositions are more evident, sometimes those on the side of excess, in some cases those on the side of
5 deficiency. The cause of this contrariety is that the resemblance does not always reach the same point of inequality in regard to the middle, but sometimes it may pass over more quickly from the excess, sometimes from the deficiency, to the middle state, the person farther removed from which seems to be more contrary: for instance, with regard to the body excess is more healthy and nearer the middle than deficiency in the case of exercises but deficiency
6 than excess in the case of food. Consequently the

1222 a
ὑπερβολῆς. ὥστε καὶ αἱ προαιρετικαὶ ἕξεις αἱ 6
φιλογυμναστικαὶ φιλοϋγιεῖς μᾶλλον ἔσονται καθ'
ἑκατέραν τὴν αἵρεσιν, ἔνθα μὲν οἱ πολυπονώτεροι[1]
ἔνθα δ' οἱ ὑποστατικώτεροι,[2] καὶ ἐναντίος τῷ
μετρίῳ καὶ τῷ ὡς ὁ λόγος ἔνθα μὲν ὁ ἄπονος
καὶ οὐκ ἄμφω, ἔνθα δὲ[3] ὁ ἀπολαυστικὸς καὶ
οὐχ ὁ πεινητικός. συμβαίνει δὲ τοῦτο διότι ἡ 7
φύσις εὐθὺς οὐ πρὸς ἅπαντα ὁμοίως ἀφέστηκε τοῦ
μέσου, ἀλλ' ἧττον μὲν φιλόπονοί ἐσμεν μᾶλλον δ'
ἀπολαυστικοί· ὁμοίως δὲ ταῦτ' ἔχει καὶ περὶ
ψυχῆς. ἐναντίαν δὲ τίθεμεν τὴν ἕξιν ἐφ' ἥν τε 8
ἁμαρτάνομεν μᾶλλον καὶ ἐφ' ἣν οἱ πολλοί, ἡ δ'
ἑτέρα ὥσπερ οὐκ οὖσα λανθάνει, διὰ γὰρ τὸ ὀλίγον
ἀναίσθητός ἐστιν. οἷον ὀργὴν πραότητι καὶ τὸν 9
1222 b ὀργίλον τῷ πράῳ· καίτοι ἐστὶν ὑπερβολὴ καὶ ἐπὶ
τὸ ἵλεων εἶναι καὶ τὸ[4] καταλλακτικὸν εἶναι καὶ
μὴ ὀργίζεσθαι ῥαπιζόμενον, ἀλλ' ὀλίγοι οἱ τοιοῦτοι, ἐπ' ἐκεῖνο δὲ πάντες ῥέπουσι μᾶλλον· διὸ
καὶ οὐ κολακικὸν[5] ὁ θυμός.
Ἐπεὶ δ' εἴληπται ἡ διαλογὴ τῶν ἕξεων καθ' 10
ἕκαστα τὰ πάθη ἧ καὶ[6] ὑπερβολαὶ καὶ ἐλλείψεις,
καὶ τῶν ἐναντίων ἕξεων καθ' ἃς ἔχουσι κατὰ τὸν
ὀρθὸν λόγον (τίς δ' ὁ ὀρθὸς λόγος καὶ πρὸς τίνα
δεῖ ὅρον ἀποβλέποντας λέγειν τὸ μέσον ὕστερον
ἐπισκεπτέον), φανερὸν ὅτι πᾶσαι αἱ ἠθικαὶ ἀρεταὶ

[1] αἱ πολυπονώτεραι Bz. [2] αἱ ὑποστατικώτεραι Bz.
[3] Bz.: δὲ καὶ. [4] τὸ . . . τὸ Bz.: τῷ . . . τῷ.
[5] καταλλακτικὸν Fr., εὐκόλαστον ? Ric.
[6] ἧ καὶ Ras.: καὶ αἱ.

---

[a] In respect of amount of exercise.
[b] In respect of amount of food.
[c] A probable alteration of the Greek gives 'is not ready to make up a quarrel.'
[d] See 1249 a 21 ff.

states of will favourable to athletic training will be variously favourable to health according to the two different fields of choice—in the one case [a] the over-energetic men ⟨will be nearer the mean than the slack ones⟩, in the other [b] the too hardy ⟨will be nearer the mean than the self-indulgent ones⟩; and also the character contrary to the moderate and rational will be in the one case the slack and not both the slack and the over-energetic, and in the other case the self-indulgent and not the man who
7 goes hungry. And this comes about because from the start our nature does not diverge from the mean in the same way as regards everything, but in energy we are deficient and in self-indulgence excessive ; and this is
8 also the same with regard to the spirit. And we class as contrary to the mean the disposition to which we, and most men, are more liable to err ; whereas the other passes unnoticed as if non-existent, because its
9 rarity makes it not observed. For instance we count anger the contrary of gentleness and the passionate man the contrary of the gentle ; yet there is also excess in the direction of being gentle and placable and not being angry when struck, but men of that sort are few, and everyone is more prone to the other extreme ; on which account moreover a passionate temper is not a characteristic of a toady.[c]

10 And since we have dealt with the scheme of states of character in respect of the various emotions in which there are excesses and deficiencies, and of the opposite states in accordance with which men are disposed in accordance with right principle (though the question what is the right principle and what rule is to guide us in defining the mean must be considered later [d]), it is evident that all the

Recapitulation.

1222 b
καὶ κακίαι περὶ ἡδονῶν καὶ λυπῶν ὑπερβολὰς καὶ
ἐλλείψεις εἰσί, καὶ ἡδοναὶ καὶ λῦπαι ἀπὸ τῶν
εἰρημένων ἕξεων καὶ παθημάτων γίνονται. ἀλλὰ 11
μὴν ἥ γε βελτίστη ἕξις ἡ περὶ ἕκαστα μέση ἐστίν.
δῆλον τοίνυν ὅτι αἱ ἀρεταὶ ἢ πᾶσαι ἢ τούτων τινὲς
ἔσονται τῶν μεσοτήτων.

VI. Λάβωμεν οὖν ἄλλην ἀρχὴν τῆς ἐπιούσης 1
σκέψεως. εἰσὶ δὴ πᾶσαι μὲν αἱ οὐσίαι κατὰ
φύσιν τινὲς ἀρχαί, διὸ καὶ ἑκάστη πολλὰ δύναται τοιαῦτα γεννᾶν, οἷον ἄνθρωπος ἀνθρώπους καὶ
ζῷον[1] ὅλως ζῷα καὶ φυτὸν φυτά. πρὸς δὲ τούτοις 2
ὅ γ' ἄνθρωπος καὶ πράξεών τινών ἐστιν ἀρχὴ
μόνον τῶν ζῴων· τῶν γὰρ ἄλλων οὐθὲν εἴποιμεν
ἂν πράττειν. τῶν δ' ἀρχῶν ὅσαι τοιαῦται, ὅθεν 3
πρῶτον αἱ κινήσεις, κύριαι λέγονται, μάλιστα δὲ
δικαίως ἀφ' ὧν μὴ ἐνδέχεται ἄλλως, ἣν ἴσως ὁ
θεὸς ἄρχει. ἐν δὲ ταῖς ἀκινήτοις ἀρχαῖς, οἷον ἐν 4
ταῖς μαθηματικαῖς, οὐκ ἔστι τὸ κύριον· καίτοι
λέγεταί γε καθ' ὁμοιότητα· καὶ γὰρ ἐνταῦθα
κινουμένης τῆς ἀρχῆς πάντα μάλιστ' ἂν τὰ δει-
κνύμενα μεταβάλλοι, αὐτὰ δὲ δι'[2] αὑτὰ οὐ μεταβάλλει ἀναιρούμενον θάτερον[3] ὑπὸ θατέρου ἂν μὴ τῷ
τὴν ὑπόθεσιν ἀνελεῖν καὶ δι' ἐκείνης δεῖξαι. ὁ δ' 5
ἄνθρωπος ἀρχὴ κινήσεώς τινος· ἡ γὰρ πρᾶξις
κίνησις. ἐπεὶ δ' ὥσπερ ἐν τοῖς ἄλλοις ἡ ἀρχὴ

[1] Sus.: ζῷον ὄν.
[2] δὲ δι' ? Ric.
[3] Rieckher: ἀναιρουμένου θατέρου.

[a] The writer proceeds to distinguish the strict sense of ἀρχή, 'origin or cause of change' (which applies to man as capable of volition and action) from its secondary sense, 'cause or explanation of an unchanging state of things' (which applies to the 'first principles' of mathematics).

[b] *e.g.* if ἀρχή A led to B and C, of which C was absurd,

forms of moral goodness and badness have to do with excesses and deficiencies of pleasures and pains, and that pleasures and pains result from the states
11 of character and modes of emotion mentioned. But then the best state in relation to each class of thing is the middle state. It is clear, therefore, that the virtues will be either all or some of these middle states.

Freedom of the Will: human conduct is contingent, not necessary.

1 VI. Let us, therefore, take another starting-point for the ensuing inquiry.[a] Now all essences are by nature first principles of a certain kind, owing to which each is able to generate many things of the same sort as itself, for example a man engenders men, and in
2 general an animal animals, and a plant plants. And in addition to this, obviously man alone among animals initiates certain conduct—for we should not
3 ascribe conduct to any of the others. And the first principles of that sort, which are the first source of motions, are called first principles in the strict sense, and most rightly those that have necessary results; doubtless God is a ruling principle that acts in this
4 way. But the strict sense of 'first principle' is not found in first principles incapable of movement, for example those of mathematics, although the term is indeed used of them by analogy, for in mathematics if the first principle were changed virtually all the things proved from it would change, though they do not change owing to themselves, one being destroyed by the other, except by destroying the
5 assumption and thereby establishing a proof.[b] But man is a first principle of a certain motion, for action is motion. And since as in other matters

then C by refuting A would refute the other consequence B (Solomon).

1222 b αἰτία ἐστὶ τῶν δι᾽ αὐτὴν ὄντων ἢ γινομένων,
δεῖ νοῆσαι καθάπερ ἐπὶ τῶν ἀποδείξεων. εἰ γὰρ 6
ἔχοντος τοῦ τριγώνου δύο ὀρθὰς ἀνάγκη τὸ τετρά-
γωνον ἔχειν τέτταρας ὀρθάς, φανερὸν ὡς αἴτιον
τούτου τὸ δύο ὀρθὰς ἔχειν τὸ τρίγωνον· εἰ δέ γε
μεταβάλλοι[1] τὸ τρίγωνον, ἀνάγκη καὶ τὸ τετρά-
γωνον μεταβάλλειν, οἷον εἰ τρεῖς, ἕξ, εἰ δὲ τέτταρας,[2] ὀκτώ· κἂν εἰ μὴ μεταβάλλει[3] τοιοῦτον δ᾽
ἐστί, κἀκεῖνο τοιοῦτον ἀναγκαῖον εἶναι.

Δῆλον δ᾽ ὃ ἐπιχειροῦμεν ὅτι ἀναγκαῖον ἐκ τῶν 7
ἀναλυτικῶν· νῦν δ᾽ οὔτε μὴ λέγειν οὔτε λέγειν
ἀκριβῶς οἷόν τε πλὴν τοσοῦτον. εἰ γὰρ μηθὲν
ἄλλο αἴτιον τοῦ τὸ τρίγωνον οὕτως ἔχειν, ἀρχή
τις ἂν εἴη τοῦτο καὶ αἴτιον τῶν ὕστερον. ὥστ᾽ 8
εἴπερ ἐστὶν ἔνια τῶν ὄντων ἐνδεχόμενα ἐναντίως
ἔχειν, ἀνάγκη καὶ τὰς ἀρχὰς αὐτῶν εἶναι τοιαύτας·
1223 a ἐκ γὰρ τῶν ἐξ ἀνάγκης ἀναγκαῖον τὸ συμβαῖνόν
ἐστι, τὰ δέ γε ἐντεῦθεν ἐνδέχεται γενέσθαι ἐπὶ[4]
τἀναντία. καὶ ἃ[5] ἐφ᾽ αὐτοῖς ἐστὶ τοῖς ἀνθρώποις,
πολλὰ τῶν τοιούτων, καὶ ἀρχαὶ τῶν τοιούτων
εἰσὶν αὐτοί. ὥστε ὅσων πράξεων ὁ ἄνθρωπός 9
ἐστιν ἀρχὴ καὶ κύριος, φανερὸν ὅτι ἐνδέχεται καὶ
γίνεσθαι καὶ μή, καὶ ὅτι ἐφ᾽ αὐτῷ ταῦτ᾽ ἐστὶ
γίνεσθαι καὶ μή, ὧν γε κύριός ἐστι τοῦ εἶναι καὶ

[1] μεταβάλλει Ric.
[2] Sp.: τέτταρες.
[3] Ric.: μεταβάλλοι.
[4] ἐπὶ add. Bz.
[5] Fr.: ὅ.

[a] *Cf. Anal. Post.* I. i.

the first principle is a cause of the things that exist or come into existence because of it, we must think
6 as we do in the case of demonstrations. For example, if as the angles of a triangle are together equal to two right angles the angles of a quadrilateral are necessarily equal to four right angles, that the angles of a triangle are equal to two right angles is clearly the cause of that fact; and supposing a triangle were to change, a quadrilateral would necessarily change too—for example if the angles of a triangle became equal to three right angles, the angles of a quadrilateral would become equal to six right angles, or if four, eight; also if a triangle does not change but is as described, a quadrilateral too must of necessity be as described.

7 The necessity of what we are arguing is clear from *Analytics* [a]; at present we cannot either deny or affirm anything definitely except just this. Supposing there were no further cause of the triangle's having the property stated, then the triangle would be a sort of first principle or cause of the later stages.
8 Hence if in fact there are among existing things some that admit of the opposite state, their first principles also must necessarily have the same quality; for of things that are of necessity the result is necessary, albeit the subsequent stages may possibly happen in the opposite way. And the things that depend on men themselves in many cases belong to this class of variables, and men are themselves the first prin-
9 ciple of things of this sort. Hence it is clear that all the actions of which a man is the first principle and controller may either happen or not happen, and that it depends on himself for them to happen or not, as he controls their existence or non-existence.

Therefore virtue and vice are voluntary.

1223 a
τοῦ μὴ εἶναι. ὅσα δ' ἐφ' αὑτῷ ἐστὶ ποιεῖν ἢ μὴ
ποιεῖν, αἴτιος τούτων αὐτὸς[1] ἐστιν, καὶ ὅσων αἴτιος,
ἐφ' αὑτῷ. ἐπεὶ δ' ἥ τε ἀρετὴ καὶ ἡ κακία καὶ τὰ 10
ἀπ' αὐτῶν ἔργα τὰ μὲν ἐπαινετὰ τὰ δὲ ψεκτά
(ψέγεται γὰρ καὶ ἐπαινεῖται οὐ τὰ[2] ἐξ ἀνάγκης ἢ
τύχης ἢ φύσεως ὑπάρχοντα ἀλλ' ὅσων αὐτοὶ αἴ-
τιοί ἐσμεν, ὅσων γὰρ ἄλλος αἴτιος ἐκεῖνος καὶ τὸν
ψόγον καὶ τὸν ἔπαινον ἔχει), δῆλον ὅτι καὶ ἡ ἀρετὴ
καὶ ἡ κακία περὶ ταῦτ' ἐστὶν ὧν αὐτὸς αἴτιος καὶ
ἀρχὴ πράξεων. ληπτέον ἄρα ποίων αὐτὸς αἴτιος 11
καὶ ἀρχὴ πράξεων. πάντες μὲν δὴ ὁμολογοῦμεν,
ὅσα μὲν ἑκούσια καὶ κατὰ προαίρεσιν τὴν ἑκάστου,
ἐκείνων[3] αἴτιον εἶναι, ὅσα δ' ἀκούσια, οὐκ αὐτὸν
αἴτιον. πάντα δ' ὅσα προελόμενος, καὶ ἑκὼν δῆλον
ὅτι. δῆλον τοίνυν ὅτι καὶ ἡ ἀρετὴ καὶ ἡ κακία τῶν
ἑκουσίων ἂν εἴησαν.

VII. Ληπτέον ἄρα τί τὸ ἑκούσιον καὶ τί τὸ 1
ἀκούσιον, καὶ τί ἐστιν ἡ προαίρεσις, ἐπειδὴ ἡ
ἀρετὴ καὶ ἡ κακία ὁρίζεται τούτοις· καὶ[4] πρῶτον
σκεπτέον τὸ ἑκούσιον καὶ τὸ ἀκούσιον. τριῶν δὴ 2
τούτων ἕν τι δόξειεν ἂν[5] εἶναι, ἤτοι κατ' ὄρεξιν ἢ
κατὰ προαίρεσιν ἢ κατὰ διάνοιαν, τὸ μὲν ἑκούσιον
κατὰ τούτων τι, τὸ δ' ἀκούσιον παρὰ τούτων τι.
ἀλλὰ μὴν ἡ ὄρεξις εἰς τρία διαιρεῖται, εἰς βούλησιν 3

[1] Bz.: οὗτος. [2] Fr.: διὰ τά.
[3] Fr.: ἐκεῖνον. [4] καὶ add. Fr. [5] ἂν add. Sp.

But of things which it depends on him to do or not
to do he is himself the cause, and what he is the
10 cause of depends on himself. And since goodness
and badness and the actions that spring from them
are in some cases praiseworthy and in other cases
blameworthy (for praise and blame are not given
to things that we possess from necessity or fortune
or nature but to things of which we ourselves are
the cause, since for things of which another person
is the cause, that person has the blame and the
praise), it is clear that both goodness and badness
have to do with things where a man is himself the
11 cause and origin of his actions. We must, then, ascertain what is the kind of actions of which a man is
himself the cause and origin. Now we all agree
that each man is the cause of all those acts that are
voluntary and purposive for him individually, and
that he is not himself the cause of those that are
involuntary. And clearly he commits voluntarily
all the acts that he commits purposely. It is clear,
then, that both goodness and badness will be in the
class of things voluntary.

THE VOLUNTARY (cc. vii-ix). It is not acting by impulse, whether in the form of appetite

1 VII. We must, therefore, ascertain what voluntary
and involuntary mean, and what is purposive choice,
since they enter into the definition of goodness and
badness. And first we must consider the meaning of
2 voluntary and involuntary. Now they would seem to
refer to one of three things—conformity with appetition, or with purposive choice, or with thought:
voluntary is what conforms with one of these and in-
3 voluntary is what contravenes one of them. But
moreover there are three subdivisions of appetition—

1223 a
καὶ θυμὸν καὶ ἐπιθυμίαν, ὥστε ταῦτα διαιρετέον·
καὶ πρῶτον τὸ[1] κατ' ἐπιθυμίαν.
Δόξειε δ' ἂν πᾶν τὸ κατ' ἐπιθυμίαν ἑκούσιον 4
εἶναι. τὸ γὰρ ἀκούσιον πᾶν δοκεῖ εἶναι βίαιον,
τὸ δὲ βίαιον λυπηρόν, καὶ πᾶν ὃ ἀναγκαζόμενοι
ποιοῦσιν ἢ πάσχουσιν, ὥσπερ καὶ Εὔηνός φησι·

πᾶν γὰρ ἀναγκαῖον πρᾶγμ' ἀνιαρὸν ἔφυ·

ὥστ' εἴ τι λυπηρὸν βίαιον καὶ εἴ τι[2] βίαιον λυπη- 5
ρόν· τὸ δὲ παρὰ τὴν ἐπιθυμίαν πᾶν λυπηρόν (ἡ
γὰρ ἐπιθυμία τοῦ ἡδέος), ὥστε βίαιον καὶ ἀκούσιον.
τὸ ἄρα κατ' ἐπιθυμίαν ἑκούσιον· ἐναντία γὰρ ταῦτ'
ἀλλήλοις. ἔτι ἡ μοχθηρία ἀδικώτερον πᾶσα ποιεῖ, 6
ἡ δ' ἀκρασία μοχθηρία δοκεῖ εἶναι· ὁ δ' ἀκρατὴς
οἷος κατὰ[3] τὴν ἐπιθυμίαν παρὰ τὸν λογισμὸν
πράττειν, ἀκρατεύεται δ' ὅταν ἐνεργῇ κατ' αὐτήν·
1223 b ὥσθ' ὁ ἀκρατὴς ἀδικήσει τῷ πράττειν κατ'
ἐπιθυμίαν. τὸ δ' ἀδικεῖν ἑκούσιον[4]· ἑκὼν ἄρα
πράξει, καὶ ἑκούσιον τὸ κατ' ἐπιθυμίαν. καὶ γὰρ
ἄτοπον εἰ δικαιότεροι ἔσονται οἱ ἀκρατεῖς γινόμενοι.[5]—ἐκ μὲν τοίνυν τούτων δόξειεν ἂν τὸ κατ' 7
ἐπιθυμίαν ἑκούσιον εἶναι· ἐκ δὲ τῶνδε τοὐναντίον,
ἅπαν γὰρ ὃ ἑκών τις πράττει βουλόμενος πράττει,

[1] τὸ add. Cas. [2] εἴ τι rec. Pb: εἰ.
[3] οἷος κατὰ Sp.: ὁ κατὰ et οἷος infra ante πράττειν.
[4] τὸ δ' . . . ἑκούσιον hic Rac.: supra ante ὥσθ' ὁ ἀκρατής.
[5] καὶ γὰρ . . . γινόμενοι supra post τῷ πράττειν κατ' ἐπιθυμίαν tr. ? Rac.

[a] Quoted also *Met.* 1015 a 28 and (without author's name) *Rhet.* 1370 a 10, and = Theognidea 472 (but that has χρῆμ' ἀνιαρόν); probably by the elder Evenus of Paros, *fl.* 460 B.C. (Bowra, *Cl. Rev.* xlviii. 2).

[b] In the MSS. this sentence precedes the one before.

wish, passion and desire; so that we have to distinguish these. And first we must consider conformity with desire.

4 It would seem that everything that conforms with desire is voluntary. For everything involuntary seems to be forced, and what is forced and everything that people do or suffer under necessity is painful, as indeed Evenus says: (to yield to which can be shown as both voluntary and involuntary),

For all necessity doth cause distress—[a]

5 so that if a thing is painful it is forced and if a thing is forced it is painful; but everything contrary to desire is painful (for desire is for what is pleasant), so that it is forced and involuntary. Therefore what conforms with desire is voluntary, for things contrary to and things in conformity with desire are
6 opposite to one another. Again, all wickedness makes a man more unrighteous, and lack of self-control seems to be wickedness; and the uncontrolled man is the sort of man to act in conformity with desire contrary to calculation, and he shows his lack of control when his conduct is guided by desire; so that the uncontrolled man will act unrighteously by acting in conformity with desire. But unrighteous action is voluntary.[b] Therefore he will be acting voluntarily, and action guided by desire is voluntary. Indeed it would be strange if those who become
7 uncontrolled will be more righteous.[c]—From these considerations, then, it would appear that what is in conformity with desire is voluntary; but the opposite[d] follows from the fact that for all that a man does volun- or of anger (for the same reason),

[c] This sentence would come in better above, after 'acting in conformity with desire.'

[d] Viz. that what is against desire is involuntary.

1223 b καὶ ὃ βούλεται ἑκών, βούλεται δ' οὐθεὶς ὃ οἴεται εἶναι κακόν. ἀλλὰ μὴν ὁ ἀκρατευόμενος οὐχ ἃ βούλεται ποιεῖ, τὸ γὰρ παρ' ὃ οἴεται βέλτιστον εἶναι πράττειν δι' ἐπιθυμίαν ἀκρατεύεσθαί ἐστιν· ὥστε ἅμα συμβήσεται τὸν αὐτὸν ἑκόντα καὶ ἄκοντα
πράττειν. τοῦτο δ' ἀδύνατον. ἔτι δ' ὁ ἐγκρατὴς 8
δικαιοπραγήσει, καὶ μᾶλλον τῆς ἀκρασίας· ἡ γὰρ ἐγκράτεια ἀρετή, ἡ δ' ἀρετὴ δικαιοτέρους ποιεῖ. ἐγκρατεύεται δ' ὅταν πράττῃ παρὰ τὴν ἐπιθυμίαν κατὰ τὸν λογισμόν. ὥστ' εἰ τὸ μὲν δικαιοπραγεῖν ἑκούσιον, ὥσπερ καὶ τὸ ἀδικεῖν (ἄμφω γὰρ δοκεῖ ταῦτα ἑκούσια εἶναι, καὶ ἀνάγκη εἰ θάτερον ἑκούσιον καὶ θάτερον), τὸ δὲ παρὰ τὴν ἐπιθυμίαν ἀκούσιον, ἅμα ἄρα ὁ αὐτὸς τὸ αὐτὸ πράξει ἑκὼν καὶ ἄκων.

Ὁ δ' αὐτὸς λόγος καὶ περὶ θυμοῦ· ἀκρασία γὰρ 9
καὶ ἐγκράτεια καὶ θυμοῦ δοκεῖ εἶναι ὥσπερ καὶ ἐπιθυμίας, καὶ τὸ παρὰ τὸν θυμὸν λυπηρὸν καὶ βίαιον ἡ κάθεξις, ὥστ' εἰ τὸ βίαιον ἀκούσιον, τὸ κατὰ τὸν θυμὸν ἑκούσιον ἂν εἴη πᾶν. ἔοικε δὲ καὶ Ἡράκλειτος λέγειν εἰς τὴν ἰσχὺν τοῦ θυμοῦ βλέψας ὅτι λυπηρὰ ἡ κώλυσις αὐτοῦ· "χαλεπὸν γάρ" φησι "θυμῷ μάχεσθαι, ψυχῆς γὰρ ὠνεῖται."
εἰ δ' ἀδύνατον τὸ αὐτὸ[1] ἑκόντα καὶ ἄκοντα πράττειν 10
ἅμα καὶ[2] κατὰ τὸ αὐτὸ τοῦ πράγματος, μᾶλλον ἑκούσιον τὸ κατὰ βούλησιν τοῦ κατ' ἐπιθυμίαν

[1] Pb: τὸ αὐτὸν Mb: τὸν αὐτὸν edd. [2] καὶ Bz.: τό.

[a] The natural philosopher of Ephesus, *fl.* c. 513 B.C. His sentence ended ὅ τι γὰρ ἂν χρήζῃ γίνεσθαι, ψυχῆς ὠνεῖται, Iamblichus, *Protrepticus*, p. 140.

tarily he wishes to do, and what he wishes to do he does voluntarily, but nobody wishes what he thinks to be bad. But yet the uncontrolled man does not do what he wishes, for being uncontrolled means acting against what one thinks to be best owing to desire ; hence it will come about that the same person is acting voluntarily and involuntarily at the same
8 time. But this is impossible. And further, the self-controlled man will act righteously, or more righteously than lack of control will ; for self-control is goodness, and goodness makes men more righteous. And a man exercises self-control when he acts against his desire in conformity with rational calculation. So that if righteous action is voluntary, as also unrighteous action (for both of these seem to be voluntary, and if one of them is voluntary it follows of necessity that the other is also), whereas what is contrary to desire is involuntary, it therefore follows that the same person will do the same action voluntarily and involuntarily at the same time.

9 The same argument applies also in the case of passion ; for there appear to be control and lack of control of passion as well as of desire and what is contrary to passion is painful and restraint is a matter of force, so that if what is forced is involuntary, what is in accordance with passion will always be voluntary. Even Heracleitus [a] seems to have in view the strength of passion when he remarks that the checking of passion is painful ; for 'It is difficult (he says) to do battle with passion, for it buys its wish
10 at the price of life.' And if it is impossible to do the same act voluntarily and involuntarily at the same time and in respect of the same part of the act, action guided by one's wish is more voluntary than

or of wish (which also involves contradiction).

1223 b
καὶ θυμόν. τεκμήριον δέ· πολλὰ γὰρ πράττομεν
ἑκόντες ἄνευ ὀργῆς καὶ ἐπιθυμίας.

Λείπεται ἄρα εἰ τὸ βουλόμενον καὶ ἑκούσιον 11
ταὐτὸ σκέψασθαι. φαίνεται δὲ καὶ τοῦτο ἀδύνατον.
ὑπόκειται γὰρ ἡμῖν καὶ δοκεῖ ἡ μοχθηρία ἀδικω-
τέρους ποιεῖν, ἡ δ' ἀκρασία μοχθηρία τις φαίνεται.
συμβήσεται δὲ τοὐναντίον· βούλεται μὲν γὰρ οὐθεὶς
ἃ οἴεται εἶναι κακά, πράττει δ' ὅταν γένηται[1]
ἀκρατής· εἰ οὖν τὸ μὲν ἀδικεῖν ἑκούσιον, τὸ δ'
ἑκούσιον τὸ κατὰ βούλησιν, ὅταν ἀκρατὴς γένηται,
οὐκέτι ἀδικήσει, ἀλλ' ἔσται δικαιότερος ἢ πρὶν
γενέσθαι ἀκρατής. τοῦτο δ' ἀδύνατον. ὅτι μὲν
τοίνυν οὐκ ἔστι τὸ ἑκούσιον τὸ κατὰ ὄρεξιν πράττειν οὐδ' ἀκούσιον τὸ παρὰ τὴν ὄρεξιν φανερόν.

VIII. Ὅτι δ' οὐδὲ κατὰ προαίρεσιν, πάλιν ἐκ 1
τῶνδε δῆλον. τὸ μὲν γὰρ κατὰ βούλησιν ὡς οὐκ
ἀκούσιον[2] ἀπεδείχθη, ἀλλὰ μᾶλλον[3] πᾶν ὃ βού-
1224 a λεται καὶ ἑκούσιον· ἀλλ' ὅτι καὶ μὴ βουλόμενον
ἐνδέχεται πράττειν ἑκόντα, τοῦτο δέδεικται μόνον.[4]
πολλὰ δὲ βουλόμενοι πράττομεν ἐξαίφνης, προαιρεῖται δ' οὐδεὶς οὐδὲν ἐξαίφνης.

Εἰ δὲ ἀνάγκη μὲν ἦν τριῶν τούτων ἕν τι εἶναι 2
τὸ ἑκούσιον, ἢ κατ' ὄρεξιν ἢ κατὰ προαίρεσιν ἢ

[1] Sol.: γίνηται.
[2] οὐχ ὡς ἑκούσιον ? Rac. (οὐχ ὡς ἀκ. Ras.: ὡς ἀκ. οὐκ. Bz.).
[3] μᾶλλον <ὅτι> ? Rac.
[4] [μόνον] Sol.

[a] Or, altering the text, 'It was proved not that acting in accordance with one's wishes is the same as acting voluntarily, but rather that all one wishes is also voluntary although it is possible to act voluntarily without wishing—this is all that has been proved; but many things that we wish——'

[b] *Cf.* 1223 a 23 ff.

action guided by desire or passion. And a proof of this is that we do many things voluntarily without anger or desire.

11 It remains, therefore, to consider whether acting as we wish and acting voluntarily are the same. This also seems impossible. For it is a fundamental assumption with us, and a general opinion, that wickedness makes men more unrighteous; and lack of self-control seems to be a sort of wickedness. But from the hypothesis that acting as we wish and acting voluntarily are the same the opposite will result; for nobody wishes things that he thinks to be bad, yet he does them when he has become uncontrolled, so if to do injustice is voluntary and the voluntary is what is in accordance with one's wish, then when a man has become uncontrolled he will no longer be acting unjustly but will be more just than he was before he lost control of himself. But this is impossible. Therefore it is clear that acting voluntarily does not mean acting in accordance with appetition nor acting involuntarily acting in opposition to appetition.

1 VIII. Also it is clear from the following considerations that voluntary action does not mean acting in accordance with purposive choice. It was proved [a] that acting in accordance with one's wish is not acting involuntarily, but rather everything that one wishes is also voluntary—it has only been proved that it is possible to do a thing voluntarily without wishing; but many things that we wish we do suddenly, whereas nobody makes a purposive choice suddenly. nor is it always purposive.

2 But if as we said [b] the voluntary must necessarily be one of three things—what is in conformity with appetition, or with purposive choice, or with thought—, Therefore (by exclusion,

1224 a κατὰ διάνοιαν, τούτων δὲ τὰ δύο μή ἐστι, λείπεται
ἐν τῷ διανοούμενόν πως πράττειν εἶναι τὸ ἑκούσιον.
ἔτι δὲ μικρὸν προαγαγόντες τὸν λόγον ἐπιθῶμεν 3
τέλος τῷ περὶ τοῦ ἑκουσίου καὶ ἀκουσίου διορισμῷ.
δοκεῖ γὰρ τὸ βίᾳ καὶ μὴ βίᾳ τι ποιεῖν οἰκεῖα τοῖς
εἰρημένοις εἶναι· τό τε γὰρ βίαιον ἀκούσιον καὶ
τὸ ἀκούσιον πᾶν βίαιον εἶναι φαμέν. ὥστε περὶ
τοῦ βίᾳ σκεπτέον πρῶτον τί ἐστι καὶ πῶς ἔχει
πρὸς τὸ ἑκούσιον καὶ ἀκούσιον. δοκεῖ δὴ τὸ 4
βίαιον καὶ τὸ ἀναγκαῖον ἀντικεῖσθαι, καὶ ἡ βία
καὶ ἡ ἀνάγκη, τῷ ἑκουσίῳ καὶ τῇ πειθοῖ ἐπὶ
τῶν πραττομένων. καθόλου δὲ τὸ βίαιον καὶ τὴν
ἀνάγκην καὶ ἐπὶ τῶν ἀψύχων λέγομεν· καὶ γὰρ
τὸν λίθον ἄνω καὶ τὸ πῦρ κάτω βίᾳ καὶ ἀναγκαζό-
μενα φέρεσθαι φαμέν, ταῦτα[1] δ' ὅταν κατὰ τὴν
φύσει[2] καὶ τὴν καθ' αὑτὰ ὁρμὴν φέρηται, οὐ βίᾳ
—οὐ μὴν οὐδ' ἑκούσια λέγεται, ἀλλ' ἀνώνυμος
ἡ ἀντίθεσις, ὅταν δὲ παρὰ ταύτην, βίᾳ φαμέν.
ὁμοίως δὲ καὶ ἐπὶ ἐμψύχων καὶ ἐπὶ τῶν ζῴων 5
ὁρῶμεν βίᾳ πολλὰ καὶ πάσχοντα καὶ ποιοῦντα,
ὅταν παρὰ τὴν ἐν αὐτῷ ὁρμὴν ἔξωθέν τι κινῇ. ἐν
μὲν τοῖς ἀψύχοις ἁπλῆ ἡ ἀρχή, ἐν δὲ τοῖς ἐμψύχοις
πλεονάζει· οὐ γὰρ ἀεὶ ἡ ὄρεξις καὶ ὁ λόγος συμ-
φωνεῖ. ὥστ' ἐπὶ μὲν τῶν ἄλλων ζῴων ἁπλοῦν 6
τὸ βίαιον, ὥσπερ ἐπὶ τῶν ἀψύχων (οὐ γὰρ ἔχει

[1] Fr.: τοῦτο.
[2] v.l. φύσιν.

and if it is not the two former, it remains that voluntariness consists in acting with some kind of thought. *cf.* 1323 a 21) the Voluntary depends on thought.

3 Moreover, let us put a conclusion to our delimitation of the voluntary and involuntary by carrying the argument a little further. Acting under compulsion and not under compulsion seem to be terms akin to the ones mentioned; for we say that everything forced is involuntary and everything involuntary is forced. So we must first consider the exact meaning of 'forced,' and how what is forced is related to the
4 voluntary and involuntary. It seems, then, that in the sphere of conduct 'forced' or 'necessary,' and force or necessity, are the opposite of 'voluntary,' and of persuasion. And we employ the terms force and necessity in a general sense even in the case of inanimate objects: we say that a stone travels upwards and fire downwards by force and under necessity, whereas when they travel according to their natural and intrinsic impulse we say that they do not move under force—although nevertheless they are not spoken of as moving voluntarily: the state opposite to forced motion has no name, but when they travel contrary to their natural impulse we say
5 that they move by force. Similarly also in the case of living things and of animals, we see many being acted on by force, and also acting under force when something moves them from outside, contrary to the impulse within the thing itself. In inanimate things the moving principle is simple, but in living things it is multiple, for appetition and rational principle are
6 not always in harmony. Hence whereas in the case of the other animals the factor of force is simple, as it is in the case of inanimate objects, for animals do not possess rational principle and appetition in

Compulsion is from without; whereas the control of impulse by reason is internal, and therefore voluntary.

1224 a
λόγον καὶ ὄρεξιν ἐναντίαν, ἀλλὰ τῇ ὀρέξει ζῇ)· ἐν
δ' ἀνθρώπῳ ἔνεστιν ἄμφω, καὶ ἔν τινι ἡλικίᾳ, ᾗ
καὶ τὸ πράττειν ἀποδίδομεν (οὐ γάρ φαμεν τὸ
παιδίον πράττειν, οὐδὲ τὸ θηρίον, ἀλλὰ τὸν[1] ἤδη
διὰ λογισμὸν πράττοντα). δοκεῖ δὴ τὸ βίαιον 7
ἅπαν λυπηρὸν εἶναι, καὶ οὐθεὶς βίᾳ μὲν ποιεῖ
χαίρων δέ. διὸ περὶ τὸν ἐγκρατῆ καὶ τὸν ἀκρατῆ
πλείστη ἀμφισβήτησίς ἐστιν. ἐναντίας γὰρ ὁρμὰς
ἔχων αὐτὸς ἑκάτερος[2] αὑτῷ πράττει, ὥσθ' ὅ τ'
ἐγκρατὴς βίᾳ, φασίν, ἀφέλκων[3] αὑτὸν ἀπὸ τῶν
ἡδέων ἐπιθυμῶν[4] (ἀλγεῖ γὰρ ἀφέλκων πρὸς ἀντι-
τείνουσαν τὴν ὄρεξιν), ὅ τ' ἀκρατὴς βίᾳ παρὰ τὸν
λογισμόν. ἧττον δὲ δοκεῖ λυπεῖσθαι, ἡ γὰρ ἐπι- 8
θυμία τοῦ ἡδέος, ᾗ ἀκολουθεῖ χαίρων· ὥσθ' ὁ
ἀκρατὴς μᾶλλον ἑκὼν καὶ οὐ βίᾳ, ὅτι οὐ λυπηρῶς.
ἡ δὲ πειθὼ τῇ βίᾳ καὶ ἀνάγκῃ ἀντιτίθεται, ὁ δ'
1224 b ἐγκρατὴς ἐφ' ἃ πέπεισται ἄγεται,[5] καὶ πορεύεται
οὐ βίᾳ ἀλλ' ἑκών· ἡ δ' ἐπιθυμία οὐ πείσασα ἄγει,
οὐ γὰρ μετέχει λόγου. ὅτι μὲν οὖν δοκοῦσιν οὗτοι 9
μόνον[6] βίᾳ καὶ ἄκοντες ποιεῖν, καὶ διὰ τίν' αἰτίαν,
ὅτι καθ' ὁμοιότητά τινα τοῦ βίᾳ, καθ' ἣν καὶ ἐπὶ
τῶν ἀψύχων λέγομεν, εἴρηται. οὐ μὴν ἀλλ' εἴ 10
τις προσθείη[7] τὸ ἐν τῷ διορισμῷ προσκείμενον

[1] Iac.: ἀλλ' ὅταν. [2] Sp.: ἕκαστος.
[3] Sp.: ἀφέλκει.
[4] Bek.: ἐπιθυμιῶν (τῶν <τῶν> ἡδέων ἐπιθυμιῶν Fr.).
[5] ἄγεται ? Sol. (ὁρμᾷ ? Ric.): ἄγει.
[6] Rac.: μόνοι. [7] Sp.: προσθῇ.

[a] Or 'conduct.'

opposition to it, but live by their appetition, in man both forms of force are present—that is, at a certain age, the age to which we attribute action [a] in the proper sense; for we do not speak of a child as acting, any more than a wild animal, but only a person who has attained to acting by rational calculation.
7 So what is forced always seems to be painful, and no one acting under force acts gladly. Consequently there is a great deal of dispute about the self-controlled man and the uncontrolled. For each of them acts under a conflict of impulses within him, so that the self-controlled man, they say, acts under force in dragging himself away from the pleasures that he covets (for he feels pain in dragging himself away against the resistance of appetition), while the uncontrolled man acts under force in going contrary
8 to his rational faculty. But he seems to feel less pain, because desire is for what is pleasant, and he follows his desire; so that the uncontrolled man rather acts voluntarily and not under force, because not painfully. On the other hand persuasion is thought to be the opposite of force and necessity; and the self-controlled man is led towards things that he has been persuaded to pursue, and proceeds not under force but voluntarily; whereas desire leads a man on without employing persuasion, since
9 it possesses no element of rational principle. It has, then, been stated that these men only seem to act under force and involuntarily; and we have shown the reason—it is because their action has a certain resemblance to forced action, just as we speak of forced action even in the case of inanimate objects
10 too. Yet nevertheless if one added there also the addition made in our definition, the statement is

1224 b κἀκεῖ, λύεται τὸ λεχθέν. ὅταν μὲν γάρ τι τῶν
ἔξωθεν παρὰ τὴν ἐν αὐτῷ ὁρμὴν κινῇ ἢ ἠρεμίζῃ,
βίᾳ φαμέν, ὅταν δὲ μή, οὐ βίᾳ· ἐν δὲ τῷ ἐγκρατεῖ
καὶ ἀκρατεῖ ἡ καθ' αὑτὸν ὁρμὴ ἐνοῦσα ἄγει (ἄμφω
γὰρ ἔχει), ὥστ' οὐ βίᾳ οὐδέτερος ἀλλ' ἑκὼν διά
γε ταῦτα πράττοι ἄν· οὐδ' ἀναγκαζόμενος, τὴν 11
γὰρ ἔξωθεν ἀρχὴν τὴν παρὰ τὴν ὁρμὴν ἢ ἐμποδί-
ζουσαν ἢ κινοῦσαν ἀνάγκην λέγομεν, ὥσπερ εἴ τις
λαβὼν τὴν χεῖρα τύπτοι τινὰ ἀντιτείνοντος καὶ
τῷ βούλεσθαι καὶ τῷ ἐπιθυμεῖν· ὅταν δ' ἔσωθεν
ἡ ἀρχή, οὐ βίᾳ. ἔτι[1] καὶ ἡδονὴ καὶ λύπη ἐν
ἀμφοτέροις ἔνεστιν· καὶ γὰρ ὁ ἐγκρατευόμενος 12
λυπεῖται παρὰ τὴν ἐπιθυμίαν πράττων ἤδη καὶ
χαίρει τὴν ἀπ' ἐλπίδος ἡδονὴν ὅτι ὕστερον ὠφελη-
θήσεται ἢ καὶ ἤδη ὠφελεῖται ὑγιαίνων, καὶ ὁ
ἀκρατὴς χαίρει μὲν τυγχάνων ἀκρατευόμενος οὗ
ἐπιθυμεῖ λυπεῖται δὲ τὴν ἀπ' ἐλπίδος λύπην, οἴεται
γὰρ κακὸν πράττειν. ὥστε τὸ μὲν βίᾳ ἑκάτερον 13
φάναι ποιεῖν ἔχει λόγον, καὶ διὰ τὴν ὄρεξιν καὶ
διὰ τὸν λογισμὸν ἑκάτερον ἄκοντα ποτὲ πράττειν·
κεχωρισμένα γὰρ ὄντα ἑκάτερα ἐκκρούεται ὑπ'
ἀλλήλων. ὅθεν καὶ ἐπὶ τὴν ὅλην μεταφέρουσι
ψυχήν, ὅτι ἐπὶ[2] τῶν ἐν ψυχῇ τι τοιοῦτον ὁρῶσιν.
ἐπὶ μὲν οὖν τῶν μορίων ἐνδέχεται τοῦτο λέγειν, ἡ 14
δ' ὅλη ἑκοῦσα ψυχὴ καὶ τοῦ ἀκρατοῦς καὶ τοῦ

[1] Sus.: ὅτι.

[2] ὅτι ἐπὶ Sol.: ὅτι.

refuted. For we speak of a thing as being forced to act when something external moves it or brings it to rest, acting against the impulse within the thing itself—when there is no external motive, we do not say that it acts under force ; and in the uncontrolled man and the self-controlled it is the impulse present in the man himself that drives him (for he has both impulses), so that as far as these considerations go neither of them would be acting under force, but
11 voluntarily ; nor yet are they acting of necessity, for by necessity we mean an external principle that either checks or moves a man in opposition to his impulse—as if A were to take hold of B's hand and with it strike C, B's will and desire both resisting ; whereas when the source of action is from within, we
12 do not speak of the act as done under force. Again, both pleasure and pain are present in both cases ; for a man exercising self-control both feels pain when he finally acts in opposition to his desire and enjoys the pleasure of hoping that he will be benefited later on, or is even being benefited already, by being in good health ; and the uncontrolled man enjoys getting what he desires owing to his lack of self-control, but feels prospective pain because he thinks he is
13 doing a bad thing. Hence it is reasonable to say that each does what he does under compulsion, and that each is at one point acting involuntarily, from motives both of appetition and of rational calculation —for calculation and appetition are things quite separate, and each is pushed aside by the other. Hence men transfer this to the spirit as a whole, because they see something of this sort in the ex-
14 periences of the spirit. Now it is admissible to say this in the case of the parts, but the spirit as a whole

1224 b ἐγκρατοῦς πράττει, βίᾳ δ' οὐδέτερος,[1] ἀλλὰ τῶν
ἐν ἐκείνοις τι, ἐπεὶ καὶ φύσει ἀμφότερα ἔχομεν·
καὶ γὰρ ὁ λόγος φύσει ὑπάρχει[2] ὅτι ἐωμένης τῆς
γενέσεως καὶ μὴ πηρωθείσης ἐνέσται, καὶ ἡ ἐπιθυμία ὅτι εὐθὺς ἐκ γενετῆς ἀκολουθεῖ καὶ ἔνεστιν·
σχεδὸν δὲ τούτοις δυσὶ τὸ φύσει διορίζομεν, τῷ τε 15
ὅσα εὐθὺς γινομένοις ἀκολουθεῖ πᾶσι, καὶ ὅσα
ἐωμένης τῆς γενέσεως εὐθυπορεῖν γίνεται ἡμῖν,
οἷον πολιὰ καὶ γῆρας καὶ τἆλλα τὰ τοιαῦτα. ὥστε
μὴ κατὰ φύσιν ἑκάτερος πράττει πώς,[3] ἁπλῶς δὲ
κατὰ φύσιν ἑκάτερος, οὐ τὴν αὐτήν. αἱ μὲν οὖν 16
περὶ τὸν ἐγκρατῆ καὶ ἀκρατῆ ἀπορίαι αὗται,[4] περὶ
τοῦ βίᾳ πράττειν ἢ ἀμφοτέρους ἢ τὸν ἕτερον,
ὥστε ἢ μὴ ἑκόντας ἢ ἅμα βίᾳ καὶ ἑκόντας,[5] εἰ
δὲ τὸ βίᾳ ἀκούσιον,[6] ἅμα ἑκόντας καὶ ἄκοντας
1225 a πράττειν· σχεδὸν δὲ ἐκ τῶν εἰρημένων δῆλον ἡμῖν
ὡς ἀπαντητέον.

Λέγονται δὲ κατ' ἄλλον τρόπον βίᾳ καὶ ἀναγκα- 17
σθέντες πρᾶξαι οὐ διαφωνοῦντος τοῦ λόγου καὶ
τῆς ὀρέξεως, ὅταν πράττωσιν ὃ καὶ λυπηρὸν καὶ
φαῦλον ὑπολαμβάνουσιν ἀλλὰ[7] μὴ τοῦτο πράττουσιν[8] πληγαὶ ἢ δεσμοὶ ἢ θάνατοι ὦσιν· ταῦτα
γάρ φασιν ἀναγκασθέντες πρᾶξαι. ἢ οὔ, ἀλλὰ 18
πάντες ἑκόντες ποιοῦσιν αὐτὰ ταῦτα,[9] ἔξεστι γὰρ

[1] οὐδετέρου ? Rac.
[2] ὑπάρχει Ras.: ἄρχων.
[3] πώς add. ante μὴ Sus., hic Sol. (cf. 1225 a 12 ed.).
[4] αὗται add. Bus.
[5] Sp.: ἄκοντας.
[6] Bz.: ἑκούσιον.
[7] Rac.: ἀλλ' ἄν.
[8] Sp.: πράττωσι.
[9] Sp.: αὐτὸ τοῦτο.

both in the uncontrolled and in the self-controlled
man acts voluntarily, and in neither case does the
man act under compulsion, but one of the parts in
them so acts—for we possess by nature both parts;
since rational principle is a natural property, because
it will be present in us if our growth is allowed and
not stunted, and also desire is natural, because it
15 accompanies and is present in us from birth; and
these are pretty nearly the two things by which we
define the natural—it is what accompanies everybody as soon as he is born, or else what comes to
us if development is allowed to go on regularly, for
example grey hair, old age, etc. Therefore each of
the two persons in a way acts not in accordance with
nature, but absolutely each does act according to
nature, though not according to the same nature.
16 The difficulties, then, raised about the uncontrolled
and the self-controlled man are these: do both, or
does one of them, act under compulsion, so that
they either act not voluntarily or else voluntarily
and under compulsion at the same time—and if what
is done under compulsion is involuntary, act voluntarily and involuntarily at the same time? And it
is fairly clear from what has been said how these
difficulties are to be met.

Mixed acts are voluntary (excepting some caused by overpowering motives).

17 But there is another way in which people are said
to act under compulsion and of necessity without
disagreement between rational principle and appetition, when they do something that they consider
actually painful and bad but they are faced by
flogging or imprisonment or execution if they do not
do it; for in these cases they say that they are acting
18 under necessity. Possibly, however, this is not the
case, but they all do the actual deeds willingly, since

1225 a μὴ ποιεῖν ἀλλ' ἐκεῖνο ὑπομεῖναι τὸ πάθος. ἔτι 19
ἴσως τούτων τὰ μὲν φαίη τις ἂν τὰ δ' οὔ. ὅσα
μὲν γὰρ ἐφ' αὑτῷ τῶν τοιούτων μὴ ὑπάρξαι ἢ
ὑπάρξαι,[1] καὶ[2] ὅσα πράττει ἃ μὴ βούλεται ἑκὼν
πράττει καὶ οὐ βίᾳ· ὅσα δὲ μὴ ἐφ' αὑτῷ τῶν
τοιούτων, βίᾳ πώς, οὐ μέντοι γ' ἁπλῶς ὅτι οὐκ
αὐτὸ τοῦτο προαιρεῖται ὃ πράττει ἀλλ' οὗ ἕνε-
κα· ἐπεὶ καὶ ἐν τούτοις ἐστί τις διαφορά. εἰ γὰρ 20
ἵνα μὴ λάβῃ ψηλαφῶν ἀποκτείνῃ, γελοῖος ἂν εἴη
εἰ λέγοι ὅτι βίᾳ καὶ ἀναγκαζόμενος, ἀλλὰ δεῖ
μεῖζον κακὸν καὶ λυπηρότερον εἶναι ὃ πείσεται
μὴ ποιήσας. οὕτω γὰρ ἀναγκαζόμενος καὶ ἢ[3] βίᾳ
πράξει ἢ οὐ φύσει ὅταν κακὸν ἀγαθοῦ ἕνεκα ἢ
μείζονος κακοῦ ἀπολύσεως πράττῃ, καὶ ἄκων γε·
οὐ γὰρ ἐφ' αὑτῷ ταῦτα. διὸ καὶ τὸν ἔρωτα 21
πολλοὶ ἀκούσιον τιθέασιν καὶ θυμοὺς ἐνίους καὶ
τὰ φυσικά, ὅτι ἰσχυρὰ καὶ ὑπὲρ τὴν φύσιν· καὶ
συγγνώμην ἔχομεν ὡς πεφυκότα βιάζεσθαι τὴν
φύσιν. καὶ μᾶλλον ἂν δόξειε βίᾳ καὶ ἄκων
πράττειν ἵνα μὴ ἀλγῇ ἰσχυρῶς ἢ ἵνα μὴ ἠρέμα,
καὶ ὅλως ἵνα μὴ ἀλγῇ ἢ ἵνα χαίρῃ. τὸ γὰρ ἐφ'

[1] μὴ πρᾶξαι ἢ πρᾶξαι Sp. [2] καὶ (vel ἀεὶ) Bz.: δεῖ.
[3] Bz.: μή.

---

[a] Or 'for in those of such acts which it rests with himself to do or not.'

[b] *i.e.* in blind-man's-buff, μυΐνδα or χαλκῆ μυῖα.

it is open to them not to do them but to endure
19 the penalty threatened. Moreover, perhaps someone
might say that in some cases these actions are done
of necessity and in others not. For in cases where
the presence or absence of such circumstances depends on the agent himself,[a] even the actions that he does without wishing to do them he does willingly and not under compulsion ; but where in such cases the circumstances do not rest with himself, he acts under compulsion in a sense, though not indeed under compulsion absolutely, because he does not definitely choose the actual thing that he does but
the object for which he does it ; since even in the
20 objects of action there is a certain difference. For
if someone were to kill a man to prevent his catching him by groping for him,[b] it would be ridiculous for him to say that he had done it under compulsion and of necessity—there must be some greater and more painful evil that he will suffer if he does not do it. It is when a man does something evil for the sake of something good, or for deliverance from another evil, that he will be acting under necessity and by compulsion, or at all events not by nature ; and then he will really be acting unwillingly, for
21 these actions do not rest with himself. On this
account many reckon even love as involuntary, and some forms of anger, and natural impulses, because their power is even beyond nature ; and we pardon them as naturally capable of constraining nature. And it would be thought that a man is acting more under compulsion and involuntarily when his object is to avoid violent pain than when it is to avoid mild pain, and in general more when his object is the avoidance of pain than when it is to gain enjoyment.

1225 a αὑτῷ, εἰς ὃ ἀνάγεται ὅλον, τοῦτ' ἐστὶν ὃ ἡ αὐτοῦ
φύσις οἵα τε φέρειν· ὃ δὲ μὴ οἵα τε μηδ' ἐστὶ
τῆς ἐκείνου φύσει ὀρέξεως ἢ λογισμοῦ, οὐκ ἐφ'
αὑτῷ. διὸ καὶ τοὺς ἐνθουσιῶντας καὶ προλέγοντας, 22
καίπερ διανοίας ἔργον ποιοῦντας, ὅμως οὔ φαμεν
ἐφ' αὑτοῖς εἶναι οὔτ' εἰπεῖν ἃ εἶπον οὔτε πρᾶξαι
ἃ ἔπραξαν. ἀλλὰ μὴν οὐδὲ δι' ἐπιθυμίαν· ὥστε 23
ἢ[1] διάνοιαί τινες καὶ πάθη οὐκ ἐφ' ἡμῖν εἰσὶν
ἢ πράξεις αἱ κατὰ τὰς τοιαύτας διανοίας καὶ
λογισμούς, ἀλλ' ὥσπερ Φιλόλαος ἔφη εἶναί τινας
λόγους κρείττους ἡμῶν.

Ὥστ' εἰ τὸ ἑκούσιον καὶ ἀκούσιον καὶ πρὸς τὸ βίᾳ ἔδει σκέψασθαι, τοῦτο μὲν οὕτω διῃρήσθω (οἱ γὰρ μάλιστ' ἐμποδίζοντες τὸ ἑκούσιον . . .[2] ὡς βίᾳ πράττοντες, ἀλλ' ἑκόντες).

IX. Ἐπεὶ δὲ τοῦτ' ἔχει τέλος, καὶ οὔτε τῇ 1
ὀρέξει οὔτε τῇ προαιρέσει τὸ ἑκούσιον ὥρισται,
1225 b λοιπὸν δὴ ὁρίσασθαι τὸ[3] κατὰ τὴν διάνοιαν. δοκεῖ 2
δὴ ἐναντίον εἶναι τὸ ἑκούσιον τῷ ἀκουσίῳ, καὶ τὸ
εἰδότα ἢ ὃν ἢ ᾧ ἢ οὗ ἕνεκα (ἐνίοτε γὰρ οἶδε μὲν
ὅτι πατὴρ ἀλλ' οὐχ ἵνα ἀποκτείνῃ ἀλλ' ἵνα σώσῃ,
ὥσπερ αἱ Πελιάδες, ἤτοι ὡς τοδὶ[4] μὲν πόμα ἀλλ'
ὡς φίλτρον καὶ οἶνον, τὸ δ' ἦν κώνειον) τῷ
ἀγνοοῦντα[5] καὶ ὃν καὶ ᾧ καὶ ὃ δι' ἄγνοιαν, μὴ

[1] ἢ ? Ric.: καὶ. [2] lacunam edd.
[3] τὸ e *M.M.* 1188 b 26 Sp.: τὰ.
[4] τοδὶ Fr.: ὅτι. [5] Rieckher: ἀγνοοῦντι.

---

[a] Pythagorean philosopher contemporary with Socrates.
[b] Some words seem to have been lost here (ἀλλά suggests that they contained a negative).
[c] The daughters of Pelias, King of Iolchus, cut him up and boiled him, having been told by Medea (who wanted Jason to leave his throne) that this would restore his youth.

For what rests with himself—and it wholly turns on this—means what his nature is able to bear; what his nature is not able to bear and what is not a matter of his own natural appetition or calculation
22 does not rest with himself. On this account also in the case of persons who are inspired and utter prophecies, although they perform an act of thought, nevertheless we do not say that saying what they said and doing what they did rested with themselves.
23 Nor yet do we say that what men do because of desire rests with themselves; so that some thoughts and emotions, or the actions that are guided by such thoughts and calculations, do not rest with ourselves, but it is as Philolaus [a] said—'some arguments are too strong for us.'

Hence if it was necessary to consider the voluntary and involuntary with reference also to acting under compulsion, let this be our decision of the matter (for those who cause most hindrance . . . the voluntary . . .[b] as acting under compulsion, but voluntarily).

Definition of Voluntary and Involuntary. An act done in ignorance due to oneself is involuntary.

1 IX. Now that this is concluded, and as the voluntary has been found not to be defined by appetition, nor yet by purposive choice, it therefore remains to define it as that which is in accordance with thought.
2 Now the voluntary seems to be the opposite of the involuntary; and acting with knowledge of either the person acted on or the instrument or the result (for sometimes the agent knows that it is his father but does not intend to kill him but to save him—as the Peliads [c] did—or knows that what he is offering is a drink but offers it as a love-charm or wine, when really it is hemlock) seems to be the opposite of acting without knowing the person acted on, the instrument and the nature of the act, through

1225 b κατὰ συμβεβηκός. τὸ δὲ δι' ἄγνοιαν καὶ ὃ καὶ ᾧ
καὶ ὃν ἀκούσιον. τὸ ἐναντίον ἄρ' ἑκούσιον. ὅσα 3
μὲν οὖν ἐφ' ἑαυτῷ ὂν μὴ πράττειν πράττει μὴ
ἀγνοῶν καὶ δι' αὑτόν, ἑκούσια ταῦτ' ἀνάγκη εἶναι,
καὶ τὸ ἑκούσιον τοῦτ' ἐστίν· ὅσα δ' ἀγνοῶν καὶ
διὰ τὸ ἀγνοεῖν, ἄκων. ἐπεὶ δὲ τὸ ἐπίστασθαι καὶ 4
τὸ εἰδέναι διττόν, ἓν μὲν τὸ ἔχειν, ἓν δὲ τὸ χρῆσθαι
τῇ ἐπιστήμῃ, ὁ ἔχων μὴ χρώμενος δὲ ἔστι μὲν
ὡς δικαίως ἂν[1] ἀγνοῶν λέγοιτο, ἔστι δ' ὡς οὐ
δικαίως, οἷον εἰ δι' ἀμέλειαν μὴ ἐχρῆτο. ὁμοίως
δὲ καὶ μὴ ἔχων τις ψέγοιτο ἄν, εἰ ὃ ῥᾴδιον ἢ
ἀναγκαῖον ἦν μὴ ἔχει[2] δι' ἀμέλειαν ἢ ἡδονὴν ἢ
λύπην. ταῦτ' οὖν προσδιοριστέον.

Περὶ μὲν οὖν τοῦ ἑκουσίου καὶ ἀκουσίου διωρίσθω[3] τοῦτον τὸν τρόπον.

X. Περὶ δὲ προαιρέσεως μετὰ τοῦτο λέγωμεν, 1
διαπορήσαντες πρῶτον τῷ λόγῳ περὶ αὐτῆς.
διστάσειε γὰρ ἄν τις ἐν τῷ γένει πέφυκε καὶ ἐν
ποίῳ θεῖναι αὐτὴν χρή, καὶ πότερον οὐ ταὐτὸν
τὸ ἑκούσιον καὶ τὸ προαιρετὸν ἢ ταὐτόν ἐστιν.
μάλιστα δὲ λέγεται παρά τινων καὶ ζητοῦντι 2
δόξειεν[4] ἂν δυοῖν εἶναι θάτερον ἡ προαίρεσις, ἤτοι
δόξα ἢ ὄρεξις· ἀμφότερα γὰρ φαίνεται παρακολουθοῦντα. ὅτι μὲν οὖν οὐκ ἔστιν ὄρεξις, φανερόν. 3

[1] ἂν add. Ras. [2] εἴη μὴ ἔχοι ? Ric.
[3] διηρήσθω ? Rac. [4] Fr.: δόξειε δ'.

[a] Perhaps the Greek should be altered to give 'Let this be our decision.'

[b] The term denotes not the deliberate choice of an object but the selection of means to attain an object: see § 7.

ignorance and not by accident. But to act through ignorance of the act, the means and the person acted
3 on is involuntary action. Therefore the opposite is voluntary. It follows then that all the things that a man does not in ignorance, and through his own agency, when it is in his power not to do them, are voluntary acts, and it is in this that the voluntary consists; and all the things that he does in ignorance, and through being in ignorance, he does involun-
4 tarily. But since to understand or know has two meanings, one being to have the knowledge and the other to use it, a man who has knowledge but is not using it would in one case be justly described as acting in ignorance but in another case unjustly—namely, if his non-employment of the knowledge were due to carelessness. And similarly one would be blamed for not having the knowledge, if it were something that was easy or necessary and his not having it is due to carelessness or pleasure or pain. These points therefore must be added to our definition.

Let this, then, be our mode of definition [a] about the voluntary and involuntary.

1 X. Next let us speak about purposive choice,[b] first raising various difficulties about it. For one might doubt to which class it naturally belongs and in what class it ought to be put, and whether the voluntary and the purposely chosen are different
2 things or the same thing. And a view specially put forward from some quarters, which on inquiry may seem correct, is that purposive choice is one of two things, either opinion or appetition; for
3 both are seen to accompany it. Now it is evident that it is not appetition; for in that case it

PURPOSE.

It is not appetition, since it is

1225 b ἢ γὰρ βούλησις ἂν εἴη ἢ ἐπιθυμία ἢ θυμός· οὐθεὶς γὰρ ὀρέγεται μηθὲν πεπονθὼς τούτων. θυμὸς
μὲν οὖν καὶ ἐπιθυμία καὶ τοῖς θηρίοις ὑπάρχει,
προαίρεσις δ' οὔ. ἔτι δὲ καὶ οἷς ὑπάρχει ἄμφω
ταῦτα, πολλὰ καὶ ἄνευ θυμοῦ καὶ ἐπιθυμίας προ-
αιροῦνται· καὶ ἐν τοῖς πάθεσιν ὄντες οὐ προαιροῦνται ἀλλὰ καρτεροῦσιν. ἔτι ἐπιθυμία μὲν καὶ
θυμὸς ἀεὶ μετὰ λύπης, προαιρούμεθα δὲ πολλὰ
καὶ ἄνευ λύπης. ἀλλὰ μὴν οὐδὲ βούλησις καὶ 4
προαίρεσις ταὐτόν· βούλονται μὲν γὰρ ἔνια καὶ
τῶν ἀδυνάτων εἰδότες, οἷον βασιλεύειν τε πάντων
ἀνθρώπων καὶ ἀθάνατοι εἶναι, προαιρεῖται δ' οὐθεὶς μὴ ἀγνοῶν ὅτι ἀδύνατον, οὐδ' ὅλως ὃ δυνατὸν μέν, μὴ ἐφ' αὑτῷ δ' οἴεται πρᾶξαι ἢ μὴ
πρᾶξαι. ὥστε τοῦτο μὲν φανερόν, ὅτι ἀνάγκη[1]
τὸ προαιρετὸν τῶν ἐφ' αὑτῷ τι εἶναι. ὁμοίως δὲ
1226 a δῆλον ὅτι οὐδὲ δόξα, οὐδ' ἁπλῶς εἴ τις οἴεταί τι·
τῶν γὰρ ἐφ' αὑτῷ τι ἦν[2] τὸ προαιρετόν, δοξάζομεν
δὲ πολλὰ καὶ τῶν οὐκ ὄντων ἐφ' ἡμῖν, οἷον τὴν
διάμετρον ἀσύμμετρον[3]· ἔτι οὐκ ἔστι προαίρεσις
ἀληθὴς ἢ ψευδής. οὐδὲ δὴ ἡ τῶν ἐφ' αὑτῷ ὄν- 6
των πρακτῶν δόξα ᾗ τυγχάνομεν οἰόμενοι δεῖν τι
πράττειν ἢ οὐ πράττειν· κοινὸν δὲ περὶ δόξης
τοῦτο καὶ βουλήσεως. οὐθεὶς γὰρ τέλος οὐθὲν 7
προαιρεῖται, ἀλλὰ τὰ πρὸς τὸ τέλος. λέγω δ' οἷον

[1] Pᵇ: ἀνάγκη μὲν Mᵇ: ἀνάγκη ἦν Fr.
[2] Bz.: εἶναι. [3] Rac.: σύμμετρον.

---

[a] 1223 a 16-19.
[b] The MSS. give 'commensurable,' but there is no point in specifying an untrue opinion. *Cf. N.E.* 1112 a 22 περὶ δὴ

would be either wish or desire or passion, since nobody wants to get a thing without having experienced one of those feelings. Now even animals possess passion and desire, but they do not have purposive choice. And again, beings that possess both of these often make choices even without passion and desire; and while they are experiencing these feelings do not make a choice but hold out. Again, desire and passion are always accompanied by pain,

not passion nor desire;

4 but we often make a choice even without pain. But moreover purposive choice is not the same as wish either; for men wish for some things that they know to be impossible, for instance to be king of all mankind and to be immortal, but nobody purposively chooses a thing knowing it to be impossible, nor in general a thing that, though possible, he does not think in his own power to do or not to do. So that this much is clear—a thing purposively chosen must necessarily be something that rests with oneself.

nor is it wish, nor opinion,

5 And similarly it is manifest that purposive choice is not opinion either, nor something that one simply thinks; for we saw [a] that a thing chosen is something in one's own power, but we have opinions as to many things that do not depend on us, for instance that the diagonal of a square is incommensurable [b] with

6 the side; and again, choice is not true or false. Nor yet is purposive choice an opinion about practicable things within one's own power that makes us think that we ought to do or not to do something; but this characteristic is common to opinion and to wish.

since it applies to means only, not to Ends;

7 For no one purposively chooses any End, but the means to his End—I mean for instance no one

τῶν ἀϊδίων οὐδεὶς βουλεύεται, οἷον περὶ τοῦ κόσμου, ἢ τῆς διαμέτρου καὶ τῆς πλευρᾶς ὅτι ἀσύμμετροι (where K[b] has σύμμετροι).

1226 a
οὐθεὶς ὑγιαίνειν προαιρεῖται, ἀλλὰ περιπατεῖν ἢ
καθῆσθαι τοῦ ὑγιαίνειν ἕνεκεν, οὐδ' εὐδαιμονεῖν,
ἀλλὰ χρηματίζεσθαι ἢ κινδυνεύειν τοῦ εὐδαιμονεῖν
ἕνεκα, καὶ ὅλως δηλοῖ ἀεὶ ὁ[1] προαιρούμενος τί τε
καὶ τίνος ἕνεκα προαιρεῖται, ἔστι δὲ τὸ μὲν τίνος[2]
οὗ ἕνεκα προαιρεῖται ἄλλο, τὸ δὲ τί, ὃ προαιρεῖται
ἕνεκα ἄλλου. βούλεται δέ γε μάλιστα τὸ τέλος, 8
καὶ δοξάζει[3] δεῖν καὶ ὑγιαίνειν καὶ εὖ πράττειν.
ὥστε φανερὸν διὰ τούτων ὅτι ἄλλο καὶ δόξης καὶ
βουλήσεως. βούλεσθαι μὲν γὰρ[4] καὶ δοξάζειν[5]
μάλιστα τοῦ τέλους, προαίρεσις δ' οὐκ ἔστιν.
Ὅτι μὲν οὖν οὐκ ἔστιν οὔτε βούλησις οὔτε δόξα 9
οὔθ' ὑπόληψις ἁπλῶς ἡ προαίρεσις, δῆλον· τί δὲ
διαφέρει τούτων; καὶ πῶς ἔχει πρὸς τὸ ἑκούσιον;
ἅμα δὲ δῆλον ἔσται καὶ τί ἐστι προαίρεσις. ἔστι 10
δὴ τῶν δυνατῶν καὶ εἶναι καὶ μὴ τὰ μὲν τοιαῦτα
ὥστε ἐνδέχεσθαι βουλεύσασθαι περὶ αὐτῶν, περὶ
ἐνίων δ' οὐκ ἐνδέχεται. τὰ μὲν γὰρ δυνατὰ μέν
ἐστι καὶ εἶναι καὶ μὴ εἶναι, ἀλλ' οὐκ ἐφ' ἡμῖν
αὐτῶν ἡ γένεσίς ἐστιν ἀλλὰ τὰ μὲν διὰ φύσιν τὰ
δὲ δι' ἄλλας αἰτίας γίνεται· περὶ ὧν οὐδεὶς ἂν
οὐδ' ἐγχειρήσειε βουλεύεσθαι μὴ ἀγνοῶν. περὶ 11
ἐνίων[6] δ' ἐνδέχεται μὴ μόνον τὸ εἶναι καὶ μή, ἀλλὰ
καὶ τὸ[7] βουλεύσασθαι τοῖς ἀνθρώποις· ταῦτα δ'
ἐστὶν ὅσα ἐφ' ἡμῖν ἐστὶ πρᾶξαι ἢ μὴ πρᾶξαι. διὸ
οὐ βουλευόμεθα περὶ τῶν ἐν Ἰνδοῖς, οὐδὲ πῶς ἂν
ὁ κύκλος τετραγωνισθείη· τὰ μὲν γὰρ οὐκ ἐφ'

[1] ὁ add. Fr. [2] τίνος <ἕνεκα>? Rac. [3] Vic.: δοξάζειν.
[4] γὰρ add. Sp. [5] Sp.: δόξα.
[6] sic Sol.: ὧν. [7] lacunam hic edd.

[a] See p. 199, note c.

chooses to be healthy, but to take a walk or sit down for the sake of being healthy, no one chooses to be well off,[a] but to go into business or to speculate for the sake of being well off; and generally, one who makes a choice always makes it clear both what his choice is and what its object is, 'object' meaning that for the sake of which he chooses something else and 'choice' meaning that which he chooses for the
8 sake of something else. Whereas clearly it is specially an End that a man wishes, and the feeling that he ought to be healthy and prosperous is an opinion. So these considerations make it clear that purposive choice is different from both opinion and wish. Forming wishes and forming opinions apply specially to one's End; purposive choice is not of Ends.

9 It is clear, then, that purposive choice is not either wish or opinion or judgement simply; but in what does it differ from them? and how is it related to the voluntary? To answer these questions will make
10 it clear what purposive choice is. Now of things that can both be and not be, some are such that it is possible to deliberate about them, but about others it is not possible. Some things can either be or not be but their coming into being does not rest with us, but in some cases is due to the operation of nature and in others to other causes; and about these things nobody would deliberate unless in ignorance
11 of the facts. But with some things not only their existence or non-existence is possible, but also for human beings to deliberate about them; and these are all the things that it rests with us to do or not to do. Hence we do not deliberate about affairs in India, or about how to square the circle; for affairs in India do not rest with us, whereas the objects of

but it arises from deliberate opinion prompted by wish.

1226 a ἡμῖν,[1] τὰ δὲ προαιρετὰ καὶ πρακτὰ τῶν ἐφ' ἡμῖν
ὄντων ἐστί, τὸ δ' ὅλως οὐ πρακτόν (ᾗ καὶ δῆλον
ὅτι οὐδὲ δόξα ἁπλῶς ἡ προαίρεσίς ἐστιν). ἀλλ' 12
οὐδὲ τῶν[2] ἡμῖν πρακτῶν περὶ ἁπάντων. διὸ καὶ 13
ἀπορήσειεν ἄν τις, τί δή ποθ' οἱ μὲν ἰατροὶ βουλεύονται περὶ ὧν ἔχουσι τὴν ἐπιστήμην οἱ δὲ
γραμματικοὶ οὔ; αἴτιον δ' ὅτι διχῇ γινομένης
τῆς ἁμαρτίας (ἢ γὰρ λογιζόμενοι ἁμαρτάνομεν, ἢ
κατὰ τὴν αἴσθησιν αὐτὸ δρῶντες) ἐν μὲν τῇ ἰατρικῇ ἀμφοτέρως ἐνδέχεται ἁμαρτεῖν, ἐν δὲ τῇ
1226 b γραμματικῇ κατὰ τὴν αἴσθησιν καὶ πρᾶξιν, περὶ
ἧς ἂν σκοπῶσιν, εἰς ἄπειρον[3] ἥξουσιν. ἐπειδὴ 14
οὖν οὔτε δόξα οὔτε βούλησις ἡ[4] προαίρεσίς ἐστιν
ὡς ἑκάτερον, οὐδ' ἄμφω (ἐξαίφνης γὰρ προαιρεῖται
μὲν οὐθείς, δοκεῖ δὲ δεῖν[5] πράττειν καὶ βούλονται),
ὡς[6] ἐξ ἀμφοῖν ἄρα· ἄμφω γὰρ ὑπάρχει τῷ προ-
αιρουμένῳ ταῦτα. ἀλλὰ πῶς ἐκ τούτων σκε-
πτέον· δηλοῖ δέ πως καὶ τὸ ὄνομα αὐτό. ἡ γὰρ 15
προαίρεσις αἵρεσις μέν ἐστιν, οὐχ ἁπλῶς δέ, ἀλλ'
ἑτέρου πρὸ ἑτέρου· τοῦτο δὲ οὐχ οἷόν τε ἄνευ
σκέψεως καὶ βουλῆς. διὸ ἐκ δόξης βουλευτικῆς
ἐστὶν ἡ προαίρεσις.

Περὶ μὲν δὴ τοῦ τέλους οὐδεὶς βουλεύεται, ἀλλὰ 16
τοῦτο κεῖται πᾶσι, περὶ δὲ τῶν εἰς τοῦτο τεινόν-
των, πότερον τόδε ἢ τόδε συντείνει, ἢ δεδογμένον
τοῦτο πῶς ἔσται. βουλευόμεθα δὲ πάντες[7] τοῦτο

[1] ll. 30-33 traiecit Bz.: ἡμῖν, τὸ δ' ὅλως οὐ πρακτόν· ἀλλ' οὐδὲ περὶ τῶν ἐν ἡμῖν πρακτῶν περὶ ἁπάντων· ᾗ καὶ δῆλον ὅτι οὐδὲ δόξα ἁπλῶς ἡ προαίρεσίς ἐστι· τὰ δὲ προαιρετὰ καὶ πρακτὰ τῶν ἐν ἡμῖν ὄντων ἐστίν, διὸ κτλ.

[2] τῶν Rac.: περὶ τῶν ἐν.

[3] εἰς ἀκριβῆ πεῖραν Bus.

[4] ἡ Bz.: ἐστι.

[5] δεῖν add. ? Sus.

[6] [ὡς] aut <δῆλον> ὡς Sp.

choice and things practicable are among things resting with us, and squaring the circle is entirely impracticable (and thus it is clear that purposive choice
12 is not simply opinion either). But purposive choice does not deal with all the practicable things resting
13 with us either. Hence one might also raise the question, why is it exactly that, whereas doctors deliberate about things in their field of science, scholars do not? The reason is that since error occurs in two ways (for we err either in reasoning, or in perception when actually doing the thing), in medicine it is possible to err in both ways, but in grammar error only occurs in our perception and action, to investigate which would be an endless undertaking.

14 Since then purposive choice is not either opinion nor wish separately, nor yet both (for no one makes a deliberate choice suddenly, but men do suddenly think they ought to act and wish to act), therefore it arises as from both, for both of them are present
15 with a person choosing. But how purposive choice arises out of opinion and wish must be considered. And indeed in a manner the actual term 'choice' makes this clear. 'Choice' is 'taking,' but not taking simply—it is taking one thing in preference to another; but this cannot be done without consideration and deliberation; hence purposive choice arises out of deliberative opinion.

16 Now nobody deliberates about his End—this everybody has fixed; but men deliberate about the means leading to their End—does *this* contribute to it, or does *this*? or when a means has been decided on, how will that be procured? and this deliberation

---

[7] M[b]: πάντως P[b] (sed cf. *N.E.* 1113 a 5 ἕκαστος).

1226 b
ἕως ἂν εἰς ἡμᾶς ἀναγάγωμεν τῆς γενέσεως τὴν
ἀρχήν. εἰ δὴ προαιρεῖται μὲν μηθεὶς μὴ παρα- 17
σκευασάμενος μηδὲ βουλευσάμενος εἰ[1] χεῖρον ἢ
βέλτιον, βουλεύεται[2] δ᾽ ὅσα ἐφ᾽ ἡμῖν ἐστὶ τῶν
δυνατῶν καὶ εἶναι καὶ μὴ τῶν πρὸς τὸ τέλος,
δῆλον ὅτι ἡ προαίρεσις μέν ἐστιν ὄρεξις τῶν ἐφ᾽
αὑτῷ βουλευτική. ἅπαντα[3] γὰρ βουλευόμεθα ἃ
καὶ προαιρούμεθα, οὐ μέντοι γε ἃ βουλευόμεθα
πάντα προαιρούμεθα. λέγω δὲ βουλευτικὴν ἧς
ἀρχὴ καὶ αἰτία βούλευσίς ἐστι, καὶ ὀρέγεται διὰ
τὸ βουλεύσασθαι. διὸ οὔτε ἐν τοῖς ἄλλοις ζῴοις 18
ἐστὶν ἡ προαίρεσις οὔτε ἐν πάσῃ ἡλικίᾳ οὔτε
πάντως[4] ἔχοντος ἀνθρώπου· οὐδὲ γὰρ τὸ βουλεύσασθαι, οὐδ᾽ ὑπόληψις τοῦ διὰ τί, ἀλλὰ δοξάσαι
μὲν εἰ ποιητέον ἢ μὴ ποιητέον οὐθὲν κωλύει πολλοῖς ὑπάρχειν τὸ δὲ διὰ λογισμοῦ οὐκέτι. ἔστι γὰρ 19
τὸ[5] βουλευτικὸν τῆς ψυχῆς τὸ θεωρητικὸν αἰτίας
τινός· ἡ γὰρ οὗ ἕνεκα μία τῶν αἰτιῶν ἐστίν·
τὸ μὲν γὰρ διὰ τί αἰτία, οὗ δ᾽ ἕνεκα ἐστὶν ἢ
γίγνεταί τι, τοῦτ᾽ αἴτιόν φαμεν εἶναι, οἷον τοῦ
βαδίζειν ἡ κομιδὴ τῶν χρημάτων, εἰ τούτου ἕνεκα
βαδίζει. διὸ οἷς μηθεὶς κεῖται σκοπός, οὐ
βουλευτικοί. ὥστ᾽ ἐπεὶ τὸ μὲν ἐφ᾽ αὑτῷ ὂν ἢ 20
πράττειν ἢ μὴ πράττειν ἐάν τις πράττῃ ἢ ἀπρακτῇ
δι᾽ αὑτὸν καὶ μὴ δι᾽ ἄγνοιαν, ἑκὼν πράττει ἢ

[1] Fr.: ᾗ.
[2] v.l. βούλεται.
[3] Bz.: ἅπαντες.
[4] Bz.: παντὸς (παντὸς <λόγου> Sp.).
[5] τὸ add. Sus.

as to means we all pursue until we have carried the starting-point in the process of producing the End
17 back to ourselves. If, then, nobody chooses without first preparing, and deliberating as to the comparative merits of the alternatives, and a man deliberates as to those among the means to the End capable of existing or not existing that are within our power, it is clear that purposive choice is deliberative appetition of things within one's power. For we deliberate about everything that we choose, although of course we do not choose everything that we deliberate about. I call appetition deliberative when its origin or cause is deliberation, and when a man
18 desires because of having deliberated. Therefore the faculty of purposive choice is not present in the other animals, nor in man at every age nor in every condition, for no more is the act of deliberation, nor yet the concept of cause: it is quite possible that many men may possess the faculty of forming an opinion whether to do or not to do a thing without also having the power of forming this opinion by
19 process of reasoning. For the deliberative faculty is the spirit's power of contemplating a kind of cause—for one sort of cause is the final cause, as although cause means anything because of which a thing comes about, it is the object of a thing's existence or production that we specially designate as its cause: for instance, if a man walks in order to fetch things, fetching things is the cause of his walking. Consequently people who have no fixed aim are not
20 given to deliberation. Hence inasmuch as if a man of his own accord and not through ignorance does or refrains from doing something resting with himself either to do or not to do, he acts or refrains from

Definition of Purposive Choice.

Deliberation.

1226 b ἀπρακτεῖ, πολλὰ δὲ τῶν τοιούτων πράττομεν οὐ
βουλευσάμενοι οὐδὲ προνοήσαντες, ἀνάγκη τὸ μὲν
προαιρετὸν ἅπαν ἑκούσιον εἶναι, τὸ δ' ἑκούσιον
μὴ[1] προαιρετόν, καὶ τὰ μὲν κατὰ προαίρεσιν πάντα
ἑκούσια εἶναι, τὰ δ' ἑκούσια μὴ πάντα κατὰ
προαίρεσιν. ἅμα δ' ἐκ τούτων φανερὸν καὶ ὅτι 21
καλῶς διορίζονται οἱ τῶν ἀδικημάτων[2] τὰ μὲν
ἀκούσια τὰ δ' ἑκούσια[3] τὰ δ' ἐκ προνοίας
1227 a νομοθετοῦσιν· εἰ γὰρ καὶ μὴ διακριβοῦσιν, ἀλλ'
ἅπτονταί γέ πῃ τῆς ἀληθείας. ἀλλὰ περὶ μὲν 22
τούτων ἐροῦμεν ἐν τῇ περὶ τῶν δικαίων ἐπισκέψει·
ἡ δὲ προαίρεσις ὅτι οὔτε ἁπλῶς βούλησις οὔτε
δόξα ἐστί, δῆλον, ἀλλὰ δόξα τε καὶ ὄρεξις ὅταν
ἐκ τοῦ βουλεύσασθαι συμπερανθῶσιν.

Ἐπεὶ δὲ βουλεύεται ἀεὶ ὁ βουλευόμενος ἕνεκά
τινος, καὶ ἐστὶ σκοπός τις ἀεὶ τῷ βουλευομένῳ
πρὸς ὃν σκοπεῖ τὸ συμφέρον, περὶ μὲν τοῦ τέλους
οὐθεὶς βουλεύεται, ἀλλὰ τοῦτ' ἐστὶν ἀρχὴ καὶ
ὑπόθεσις, ὥσπερ ἐν ταῖς θεωρητικαῖς ἐπιστήμαις 23
ὑποθέσεις (εἴρηται δὲ περὶ αὐτῶν ἐν μὲν τοῖς ἐν
ἀρχῇ βραχέως, ἐν δὲ τοῖς ἀναλυτικοῖς δι' ἀκριβείας)· περὶ δὲ τῶν πρὸς τὸ τέλος φερόντων ἡ
σκέψις καὶ μετὰ τέχνης καὶ ἄνευ τέχνης πᾶσίν
ἐστιν, οἷον εἰ πολεμῶσιν ἢ μὴ πολεμῶσι τούτῳ[4]
βουλευομένοις. ἐκ προτέρου δὲ μᾶλλον ἔσται τὸ 24
δι' ὅ, τοῦτ' ἐστὶ τὸ οὗ ἕνεκα, οἷον πλοῦτος ἢ
ἡδονὴ ἤ τι ἄλλο τοιοῦτον ὃ τυγχάνει οὗ ἕνεκα.

[1] μὴ <ἅπαν> ? Sus.
[2] Bz.: παθημάτων.
[3] Rac.: τὰ μὲν ἑκούσια τὰ δ' ἀκούσια.
[4] τούτῳ Fr. (τουτῳί ? Rac.): τοῦτο.

[a] Not in *E.E.*, but *cf.* *N.E.* 1135 a 16 ff.

acting voluntarily, but yet we do many such things without deliberation or previous thought, it necessarily follows that, although all that has been purposively chosen is voluntary, 'voluntary' is not the same as 'chosen,' and, although all things done by purposive choice are voluntary, not all things
21 voluntary are done by purposive choice. And at the same time it is clear from these considerations that the classification of offences made by legislators as involuntary, voluntary and premeditated is a good one; for even if it is not precisely accurate, yet at all events
22 it approximates to the truth in a way. But we will speak about this in our examination of justice.[a] As to purposive choice, it is clear that it is not absolutely identical with wish nor with opinion, but is opinion plus appetition when these follow as a conclusion from deliberation.

But since one who deliberates always deliberates for the sake of some object, and a man deliberating always has some aim in view with reference to which he considers what is expedient, nobody deliberates about his End, but this is a starting-point or assump-
23 tion, like the postulates in the theoretic sciences (we have spoken about this briefly at the beginning of this discourse, and in detail in *Analytics*[b]); whereas with all men deliberation whether technical or untechnical is about the means that lead to their End, *e.g.* when they deliberate about whether to go
24 to war or not to go to war with a given person. And the question of means will depend rather on a prior question, that is, the question of object, for instance wealth or pleasure or something else of that kind which happens to be our object. For one who deliberates

Deliberation considers Means to Ends.

[b] See 1214 b 6 ff., and *Anal. Post.* i., 72 a 20 and context.

1227 a
βουλεύεται γὰρ ὁ βουλευόμενος εἰ[1] ἀπὸ τοῦ τέλους
ἔσκεπται ᾗ[2] ὅτι ἐκεῖσε[3] συντείνει ὅπως εἰς αὐτὸν
ἀναγάγῃ[4] ἢ ᾗ[5] αὐτὸς δύναται ἰέναι[6] πρὸς τὸ τέλος.
τὸ δὲ τέλος ἐστὶ φύσει μὲν ἀεὶ ἀγαθὸν καὶ περὶ 25
οὗ κατὰ μέρος βουλεύονται (οἷον ἰατρὸς βουλεύσαιτο
ἂν εἰ δῷ[7] φάρμακον, καὶ στρατηγὸς ποῦ στρατο-
πεδεύσηται) οἷς ἀγαθὸν τὸ τέλος τὸ ἁπλῶς ἄριστόν
ἐστιν· παρὰ φύσιν δὲ καὶ κατὰ[8] διαστροφὴν οὐ τὸ 26
ἀγαθὸν ἀλλὰ τὸ φαινόμενον ἀγαθόν. αἴτιον δ' ὅτι
τῶν ὄντων τοῖς[9] μὲν οὐκ ἔστιν ἐπ' ἄλλῳ χρήσασθαι
ἢ πρὸς ἃ πέφυκεν, οἷον ὄψει· οὐ γὰρ οἷόν τ' ἰδεῖν
οὗ μή ἐστιν ὄψις, οὐδ' ἀκοῦσαι οὗ μή ἐστιν ἀκοή·
ἀλλ' ἀπὸ ἐπιστήμης ποιῆσαι καὶ οὗ μή ἐστιν ἡ
ἐπιστήμη. οὐ γὰρ ὁμοίως τῆς ὑγιείας ἡ αὐτὴ
ἐπιστήμη καὶ νόσου, ἀλλὰ τῆς μὲν κατὰ φύσιν
τῆς δὲ παρὰ φύσιν. ὁμοίως δὲ καὶ ἡ βούλησις 27
φύσει μὲν τοῦ ἀγαθοῦ ἐστί, παρὰ φύσιν δὲ καὶ
τοῦ κακοῦ, καὶ βούλεται φύσει μὲν τὸ ἀγαθόν,
παρὰ φύσιν δὲ καὶ κατὰ[10] διαστροφὴν καὶ τὸ
κακόν.

Ἀλλὰ μὴν ἑκάστου γε φθορὰ καὶ διαστροφὴ οὐκ εἰς τὸ τυχὸν ἀλλ' εἰς τὰ ἐναντία καὶ τὰ μεταξύ. οὐ γὰρ ἔστιν ἐκβῆναι ἐκ τούτων, ἐπεὶ καὶ ἡ ἀπάτη οὐκ εἰς τὰ τυχόντα γίνεται, ἀλλ' εἰς τὰ ἐναντία ὅσοις ἐστὶν ἐναντία, καὶ εἰς ταῦτα τῶν ἐναντίων ἃ κατὰ τὴν ἐπιστήμην ἐναντία ἐστίν.

[1] Mᵇ ἤ.
[2] ᾗ add. Fr.
[3] Rac.: ἐκεῖ.
[4] Ric.: ἀγάγῃ.
[5] ῃ add. Rac.
[6] ἰέναι add. Rac.
[7] Sp.: δώη.
[8] κατὰ add. Syl.: διὰ στροφὴν Iac., διαστροφῇ Fr.
[9] Ric.: τὰ.
[10] κατὰ add. Syl.

deliberates if he has considered, from the standpoint
of the End, either what tends to enable him to bring
the End to himself or how he can himself go to the
25 End.[a] And by nature the End is always a good and Wish for
a thing about which men deliberate step by step (for Ends
example a doctor may deliberate whether he shall
give a drug, and a general where he shall pitch his
camp) when their End is the good that is the absolute
26 best ; but in contravention of nature and by perversion not the good but the apparent good is the End.
The reason is that there are some things that cannot
be employed for something other than their natural
objects, for instance sight—it is not possible to see a
thing that is not visible, or to hear a thing that is not
audible ; but a science does enable us to do a thing
that is not the object of the science. For health
and disease are not the objects of the same science
in the same way : health is its object in accordance
with nature, and disease in contravention of nature.
27 And similarly, by nature good is the object of wish,
but evil is also its object in contravention of nature ;
by nature one wishes good, against nature and by
perversion one even wishes evil.

But moreover with everything its corruption and perversion are not in any chance direction, but leads to the contrary and intermediate states. For it is not possible to go outside these, since even error does not lead to any chance thing, but, in the case of things that have contraries, to the contraries, and to those contraries that are contrary according to

[a] *i.e.* he works back in thought from his intended End to some means to its attainment that is already within his power.

1227 a
ἀνάγκη ἄρα καὶ τὴν ἀπάτην καὶ τὴν προαίρεσιν 28
ἀπὸ τοῦ μέσου ἐπὶ τὰ ἐναντία γίνεσθαι (ἐναντία
δὲ τῷ μέσῳ τὸ πλέον καὶ τὸ ἔλαττον).—αἴτιον δὲ
τὸ ἡδὺ καὶ τὸ λυπηρόν· οὕτω γὰρ ἔχει ὥστε τῇ
ψυχῇ φαίνεσθαι τὸ μὲν ἡδὺ ἀγαθὸν καὶ τὸ ἥδιον
ἄμεινον, καὶ τὸ λυπηρὸν κακὸν καὶ τὸ λυπηρότερον
1227 b χεῖρον. ὥστε καὶ ἐκ τούτων δῆλον ὅτι περὶ ἡδονὰς 29
καὶ λύπας ἡ ἀρετὴ καὶ ἡ κακία· περὶ μὲν γὰρ
τὰ προαιρετὰ τυγχάνουσιν οὖσαι, ἡ δὲ προαίρεσις
περὶ τὸ ἀγαθὸν καὶ κακὸν καὶ τὰ φαινόμενα,
τοιαῦτα δὲ φύσει ἡδονὴ καὶ λύπη.

Ἀνάγκη τοίνυν, ἐπειδὴ ἡ ἀρετὴ μὲν ἡ ἠθικὴ 30
αὐτή τε μεσότης τίς ἐστι καὶ περὶ ἡδονὰς καὶ
λύπας πᾶσα, ἡ δὲ κακία ἐν ὑπερβολῇ καὶ ἐλλείψει
καὶ περὶ ταὐτὰ τῇ ἀρετῇ, τὴν ἀρετὴν εἶναι τὴν
ἠθικὴν ἕξιν προαιρετικὴν μεσότητος τῆς πρὸς ἡμᾶς
ἐν ἡδέσι καὶ λυπηροῖς καθ' ὅσα ποιός τις λέγεται
τὸ ἦθος ἢ χαίρων ἢ λυπούμενος (ὁ γὰρ φιλόγλυκυς
ἢ φιλόπικρος οὐ λέγεται ποιός τις τὸ ἦθος).

XI. Τούτων δὲ διωρισμένων λέγωμεν πότερον 1
ἡ ἀρετὴ ἀναμάρτητον ποιεῖ τὴν προαίρεσιν καὶ τὸ
τέλος ὀρθὸν οὕτως ὥστε οὗ ἕνεκα δεῖ προαιρεῖσθαι,
ἤ, ὥσπερ δοκεῖ τισί, τὸν λόγον. ἔστι δὲ τοῦτο
ἐγκράτεια, αὕτη γὰρ οὐ διαφθείρει τὸν λόγον· ἔστι
δ' ἀρετὴ καὶ ἐγκράτεια ἕτερον. λεκτέον δ' ὕστερον 2

[a] This division of contraries is unusual: elsewhere (*e.g. Met.* K, 1061 a 18) Aristotle merely states that contraries are the objects of the same science.

[b] The connexion of pleasure and pain with virtue is here clearer than in *N.E.*, and forms part of the definition (Stocks).

perverted by pleasure and pain.

28 their science.[a] It therefore necessarily follows that both error and purposive choice take place from the middle point to the contraries (the contraries of the middle being the more and the less).—And the cause is pleasure and pain; for things are so constituted that the pleasant appears to the spirit good and the more pleasant better, the painful bad
29 and the more painful worse. So from these things also it is clear that goodness and badness have to do with pleasures and pains; for they occur in connexion with the objects of purposive choice, and this has to do with good and bad and what appears to be good and bad, and pleasure and pain are by nature things of that kind.

Definition of Moral Goodness or Virtue.

30 It therefore follows that since moral goodness is itself a middle state and is entirely concerned with pleasures and pains, and badness consists in excess and defect and is concerned with the same things as goodness, moral goodness or virtue is a state of purposively choosing the mean in relation to ourselves in all those pleasant and painful things in regard to which according as a person feels pleasure or pain he is described as having some particular moral quality[b] (for a person is not said to have a particular moral character merely for being fond of sweets or savouries).

Virtue and vice being voluntary, moral judgement applies to purposive choice, which depends on character,

1 XI. These things having been settled, let us say whether goodness makes the purposive choice correct and the End right in the sense of making the agent choose for the sake of the proper End, or whether (as some hold) it makes the rational principle right. But what does this is self-control—for that saves the rational principle from being corrupted; and good-
2 ness and self-control are different. But we must

1227 b
περὶ αὐτῶν, ἐπεὶ ὅσοις γε δοκεῖ τὸν λόγον ὀρθὸν
παρέχειν ἡ ἀρετή, τοῦτο αἴτιον· ἡ μὲν ἐγκράτεια
τοιοῦτον, τῶν ἐπαινετῶν δ' ἡ ἐγκράτεια. λέγωμεν 3
δὲ προαπορήσαντες. ἔστι γὰρ τὸν μὲν σκοπὸν
ὀρθὸν εἶναι, ἐν δὲ τοῖς πρὸς τὸν σκοπὸν διαμαρτάνειν· ἔστι δὲ τὸν μὲν σκοπὸν ἡμαρτῆσθαι,
τὰ δὲ πρὸς ἐκεῖνον περαίνοντα ὀρθῶς ἔχειν· καὶ
μηδέτερον. πότερον δ' ἡ ἀρετὴ ποιεῖ τὸν σκοπὸν[1] 4
ἢ τὰ πρὸς τὸν σκοπόν; τιθέμεθα δὴ ὅτι τὸν
σκοπόν, διότι τούτου οὐκ ἔστι συλλογισμὸς οὐδὲ
λόγος, ἀλλὰ δὴ ὥσπερ ἀρχὴ τοῦτο ὑποκείσθω.
οὔτε γὰρ ἰατρὸς σκοπεῖ εἰ δεῖ ὑγιαίνειν ἢ μή,
ἀλλ' εἰ περιπατεῖν ἢ μή, οὔτε ὁ γυμναστικὸς εἰ
δεῖ εὖ ἔχειν ἢ μή, ἀλλ' εἰ παλαῖσαι ἢ μή. ὁμοίως 5
δ' οὐδ' ἄλλη[2] οὐδεμία περὶ τοῦ τέλους. ὥσπερ
γὰρ ταῖς θεωρητικαῖς αἱ ὑποθέσεις ἀρχαί, οὕτω
καὶ ταῖς ποιητικαῖς τὸ τέλος ἀρχὴ καὶ ὑπόθεσις·
ἐπειδὴ δεῖ τονδὶ[3] ὑγιαίνειν, ἀνάγκη τοδὶ ὑπάρξαι
εἰ ἔσται ἐκεῖνο, ὥσπερ ἐκεῖ, εἰ ἔστι τὸ τρίγωνον
δύο ὀρθαί, ἀνάγκη τοδὶ εἶναι. τῆς μὲν οὖν νοήσεως 6
ἀρχὴ τὸ τέλος, τῆς δὲ πράξεως ἡ τῆς νοήσεως
τελευτή. εἰ οὖν πάσης ὀρθότητος ἢ ὁ λόγος ἢ ἡ
ἀρετὴ αἰτία, εἰ μὴ ὁ λόγος, διὰ τὴν ἀρετὴν ἂν

[1] σκοπὸν ⟨ὀρθὸν⟩? Rac.
[2] ἄλλη ⟨τέχνη⟩? Rac.
[3] Sp.: τόδε.

[a] Or, altering the text, 'makes the aim right.'

speak about this later, since all who do hold that goodness makes the rational principle right think so on the ground that that is the nature of self-control
3 and self-control is a praiseworthy thing. Having raised this preliminary question let us continue. It is possible to have one's aim right but to be entirely wrong in one's means to the end aimed at ; and it is possible for the aim to have been wrongly chosen but the means conducing to it to be right ; and for
4 neither to be right. But does goodness decide the aim [a] or the means to it ? Well, our position is that it decides the aim, because this is not a matter of logical inference or rational principle, but in fact this must be assumed as a starting-point. For a doctor does not consider whether his patient ought to be healthy or not, but whether he ought to take walking exercise or not, and the gymnastic trainer does not consider whether his pupil ought to be in good condition or not, but whether he ought to go in for
5 wrestling or not ; and similarly no other science either deliberates about its End. For as in the theoretic sciences the assumptions are first principles, so in the productive sciences the End is a starting-point and assumption : since it is required that so-and-so is to be in good health, if that is to be secured it is necessary for such-and-such a thing to be provided—just as in mathematics, if the angles of a triangle are together equal to two right angles, such-and-such a consequence necessarily follows.
6 Therefore the End is the starting-point of the process of thought, but the conclusion of the process of thought is the starting-point of action. If, then, of all rightness either rational principle or goodness is the cause, if rational principle is not the cause of

and not to actions, which may be done under compulsion.

1227 b ὀρθὸν εἴη τὸ τέλος, ἀλλ' οὐ τὰ πρὸς τὸ τέλος.
τέλος δ' ἐστὶ τὸ οὗ ἕνεκα· ἔστι γὰρ πᾶσα προαίρεσις 7
τινὸς καὶ ἕνεκά τινος. οὗ μὲν οὖν ἕνεκα τὸ μέσον
ἐστίν, οὗ αἰτία ἡ ἀρετὴ τῷ[1] προαιρεῖσθαι[2]· ἔστι
μέντοι ἡ προαίρεσις οὐ τούτου, ἀλλὰ τῶν τούτου
ἕνεκα. τὸ μὲν οὖν τυγχάνειν τούτων ἄλλης δυ- 8
1228 a νάμεως ὅσα ἕνεκα τοῦ τέλους δεῖ πράττειν, τοῦ
δὲ τὸ τέλος ὀρθὸν εἶναι τῆς προαιρέσεως ἡ[3] ἀρετὴ
αἰτία. καὶ διὰ τοῦτο ἐκ τῆς προαιρέσεως κρίνομεν 9
ποῖός τις, τοῦτο δ' ἐστὶ τὸ τίνος ἕνεκα πράττει
ἀλλ' οὐ τί πράττει. ὁμοίως δὲ καὶ ἡ κακία τῶν ἐν- 10
αντίων ἕνεκα ποιεῖ τὴν προαίρεσιν. εἰ[4] δή τις, ἐφ'
αὑτῷ ὂν πράττειν μὲν τὰ καλὰ ἀπρακτεῖν δὲ τὰ
αἰσχρά, τοὐναντίον ποιεῖ, δῆλον ὅτι οὐ σπουδαῖός
ἐστιν οὗτος ὁ ἄνθρωπος. ὥστ' ἀνάγκη τήν τε
κακίαν ἑκούσιον εἶναι καὶ τὴν ἀρετήν· οὐδεμία
γὰρ ἀνάγκη τὰ μοχθηρὰ πράττειν. διὰ ταῦτα 11
καὶ ψεκτὸν ἡ κακία καὶ ἡ ἀρετὴ ἐπαινετόν· τὰ
γὰρ ἀκούσια αἰσχρὰ καὶ κακὰ οὐ ψέγεται[5] οὐδὲ
τὰ ἀγαθὰ ἐπαινεῖται,[6] ἀλλὰ τὰ ἑκούσια. ἔτι
πάντας ἐπαινοῦμεν καὶ ψέγομεν εἰς τὴν προαίρεσιν
βλέποντες μᾶλλον ἢ εἰς τὰ ἔργα (καίτοι αἱρετώτερον
ἡ ἐνέργεια τῆς ἀρετῆς), ὅτι[7] πράττουσι μὲν φαῦλα
καὶ ἀναγκαζόμενοι, προαιρεῖται δ' οὐδείς. ἔτι διὰ 12
τὸ μὴ ῥᾴδιον εἶναι ἰδεῖν τὴν προαίρεσιν ὁποία τις,

[1] Fr.: τό.
[2] Ric.: προαιρεῖσθαι οὗ ἕνεκα.
[3] ἡ Fr.: οὗ ἡ.
[4] προαίρεσιν ⟨εἶναι⟩. εἰ? Rac.
[5] Pb: ψεκτὰ Mb.
[6] Pb: ἐπαινετά Mb.
[7] ἔτι Ald.

the rightness of the End, then the End (though not the means to the End) will be right owing to goodness.
7 But the End is the object for which one acts ; for every purposive choice is a choice of something and for some object. The End is therefore the object for which the thing chosen is the mean, of which End goodness is the cause [a] by its act of choice—though the choice is not of the End but of the means
8 adopted for the sake of the End. Therefore though it belongs to another faculty to hit on the things that must be done for the sake of the End, goodness is the cause of the End aimed at by choice being right.
9 And owing to this it is by a man's purposive choice that we judge his character—that is, not by what he
10 does but what he does it for. Similarly also badness causes purposive choice to be made from the opposite motives. If therefore, when a man has it in his power to do what is honourable and refrain from doing what is base, he does the opposite, it is clear that this man is not virtuous. Hence it necessarily follows that both badness and goodness are voluntary ; for there is no necessity to do wicked things.
11 For this reason badness is a blameworthy thing and goodness praiseworthy ; for involuntary baseness and evil are not blamed nor involuntary good things praised, but voluntary ones are. Moreover we praise and blame all men with regard to their purpose rather than with regard to their actions (although activity is a more desirable thing than goodness), because men may do bad acts under compulsion,
12 but no one is compelled to choose to do them. Moreover because it is not easy to see the quality of

[a] Virtue by choosing the right means to achieve the End causes the End to be realized.

1228 a διὰ ταῦτα ἐκ τῶν ἔργων ἀναγκαζόμεθα κρίνειν
ὁποῖός τις· αἱρετώτερον μὲν οὖν ἡ ἐνέργεια, 13
ἐπαινετώτερον δ' ἡ προαίρεσις. ἔκ τε τῶν κειμένων
οὖν συμβαίνει ταῦτα καὶ ἔτι ὁμολογεῖται τοῖς
φαινομένοις.

a man's purpose we are forced to judge his char-
13 acter from his actions; therefore activity is more desirable, but purpose more praiseworthy. And this not only follows from our assumptions but also agrees with observation.

Γ

1228 a
I. Ὅτι μὲν οὖν μεσότητές τ' εἰσὶ[1] ἐν ταῖς 1
ἀρεταῖς καὶ αὗται προαιρετικαί, καὶ αἱ ἐναντίαι
κακίαι καὶ τίνες εἰσὶν αὗται, καθόλου εἴρηται·
καθ' ἑκάστην δὲ λαμβάνοντες λέγωμεν ἐφεξῆς,
καὶ πρῶτον εἴπωμεν περὶ ἀνδρείας.
Σχεδὸν δὴ δοκεῖ πᾶσιν ὅ τ' ἀνδρεῖος εἶναι περὶ 2
φόβους καὶ ἡ ἀνδρεία μία τῶν ἀρετῶν. διείλομεν
δ' ἐν τῇ διαγραφῇ πρότερον[2] θράσος καὶ φόβον[3]
ἐναντία· καὶ γάρ ἐστί πως ἀντικείμενα ἀλλήλοις.
δῆλον οὖν ὅτι καὶ οἱ κατὰ τὰς ἕξεις ταύτας 3
λεγόμενοι ὁμοίως ἀντικείσονται σφίσιν αὐτοῖς,
οἷον ὁ δειλός (οὗτος γὰρ λέγεται κατὰ τὸ φοβεῖσθαι
μᾶλλον ἢ δεῖ καὶ θαρρεῖν ἧττον ἢ δεῖ) καὶ ὁ θρασύς
(καὶ γὰρ οὗτος κατὰ τὸ τοιοῦτος εἶναι οἷος
φοβεῖσθαι μὲν ἧττον ἢ δεῖ θαρρεῖν δὲ μᾶλλον ἢ
δεῖ· διὸ καὶ παρωνυμιάζεται, ὁ γὰρ θρασὺς παρὰ
τὸ θράσος λέγεται παρωνύμως). ὥστ' ἐπεὶ ἡ 4
ἀνδρεία ἐστὶν ἡ βελτίστη ἕξις περὶ φόβους καὶ
θάρρη, δεῖ δὲ μήθ' οὕτως ὡς οἱ θρασεῖς (τὰ μὲν
γὰρ ἐλλείπουσι τὰ δ' ὑπερβάλλουσι) μήθ' οὕτως
1228 b
ὡς οἱ δειλοί (καὶ γὰρ οὗτοι ταὐτὸ ποιοῦσι, πλὴν

[1] τ' εἰσὶ Rac.: εἰσί τε.
[2] Bz.: πότερον.
[3] Bz.: φόβος.

[a] 1220 b 39, 1221 a 17-19.

BOOK III

1 I. It has then been stated in general terms that there are middle states in the virtues and that these are purposive, and also that the opposite dispositions are vices and what these are. But let us take them separately and discuss them seriatim. And first let us speak about Courage.

The Moral Virtues.

2 Now almost everybody holds that the brave man is concerned with fears, and that courage is one of the virtues. And in our schedule [a] previously we distinguished daring and fear as contraries, for they are indeed in a manner opposed to one another.

Courage, the mean between rashness and cowardice.

3 It is clear, therefore, that the persons named after these states of character will also be similarly opposed to each other—that is, the coward (for that is the term that denotes being more afraid than is proper and less daring than is proper) and the daring man (for that denotes the characteristic of being less afraid than is proper and more daring than is proper—and from this the name is derived, as the word ' daring ' is cognate with the
4 word ' dare '). So that since courage is the best state of character in relation to feelings of fear and daring, and the proper character is neither that of the daring (for they fall short in one respect and exceed in another) nor that of the cowardly (for they also do the same, only not as regards the same things

1228 b οὐ περὶ ταὐτὰ ἀλλ' ἐξ ἐναντίας, τῷ μὲν γὰρ θαρρεῖν
ἐλλείπουσι τῷ δὲ φοβεῖσθαι ὑπερβάλλουσι), δῆλον
ὡς ἡ μέση διάθεσις θρασύτητος καὶ δειλίας ἐστὶν
ἀνδρεία· αὕτη γὰρ βελτίστη.

Δοκεῖ δ' ὁ ἀνδρεῖος ἄφοβος εἶναι ὡς ἐπὶ τὸ 5
πολύ, ὁ δὲ δειλὸς φοβητικός, καὶ ὁ μὲν καὶ πολλὰ
καὶ ὀλίγα καὶ μεγάλα καὶ μικρὰ φοβεῖσθαι καὶ
σφόδρα καὶ ταχύ, ὁ δὲ τὸ ἐναντίον ἢ οὐ φοβεῖσθαι
ἢ ἠρέμα καὶ μόλις καὶ ὀλιγάκις καὶ μεγάλα· καὶ
ὁ μὲν ὑπομένει τὰ φοβερὰ σφόδρα, ὁ δὲ οὐδὲ τὰ
ἠρέμα. ποῖα οὖν ὑπομένει ὁ ἀνδρεῖος; πρῶτον, 6
πότερον τὰ αὑτῷ φοβερὰ ἢ τὰ ἑτέρῳ; εἰ μὲν δὴ
τὰ ἑτέρῳ φοβερά, οὐθὲν σεμνὸν φαίη ἄν τις εἶναι·
εἰ δὲ τὰ αὑτῷ, εἴη ἂν αὐτῷ μεγάλα καὶ πολλὰ[1]
φοβερά· τὰ δὲ φοβερὰ[2] φόβου ποιητικὰ ἑκάστῳ ᾧ
φοβερά, οἷον εἰ μὲν σφόδρα φοβερά, εἴη ἂν ἰσχυρὸς
ὁ φόβος, εἰ δ' ἠρέμα, ἀσθενής· ὥστε συμβαίνει
τὸν ἀνδρεῖον μεγάλους φόβους καὶ πολλοὺς φοβεῖσθαι.[3] ἐδόκει δὲ τοὐναντίον ἡ ἀνδρεία ἄφοβον
παρασκευάζειν, τοῦτο δ' εἶναι ἐν τῷ ἢ μηθὲν ἢ
ὀλίγα φοβεῖσθαι καὶ ἠρέμα καὶ μόλις. ἀλλ' ἴσως 7
τὸ φοβερὸν λέγεται, ὥσπερ καὶ τὸ ἡδὺ καὶ τἀγαθόν,
διχῶς. τὰ μὲν γὰρ ἁπλῶς, τὰ δὲ τινὶ μὲν καὶ ἡδέα

[1] πολλὰ om. M^b.
[2] τὰ δὲ φοβερὰ add. Bz. (τὰ δὲ φοβερὰ τοιούτου add. ? Rac.).
[3] v.l. ποιεῖσθαι vulg.

[a] Or, emending the text, 'of corresponding fear.'

but inversely—they fall short in daring and exceed in being afraid), it is clear that the middle state of character between daring and cowardice is courage, for this is the best state.

5 And it seems that the brave man is in general fearless, and the coward liable to fear; and that the latter fears things when they are few in number and small in size as well as when numerous and great, and fears violently, and gets frightened quickly, whereas the former on the contrary either never feels fear at all or only slightly and reluctantly and seldom, and in regard to things of magnitude; and he endures things that are extremely formidable, whereas the other does not endure even those that

What terrors does the brave man endure?

6 are slightly formidable. What sort of things, then, does the brave man endure? First, is it the things that are formidable to himself or formidable to somebody else? If the things formidable to somebody else, one would not indeed call it anything remarkable; but if it is those that are formidable to himself, what is formidable to him must be things of great magnitude and number. But formidable things are productive of fear [a] in the particular person to whom they are formidable—that is, if they are very formidable, the fear they produce will be violent, if slightly formidable, it will be weak; so it follows that the brave man's fears are great and many. Yet on the contrary it appeared that courage makes a man fearless, and that fearlessness

7 consists in fearing nothing, or else few things, and those slightly and reluctantly. But perhaps 'formidable' is an ambiguous term, like 'pleasant' and 'good.' Some things are pleasant and good absolutely, whereas others are so to a particular

1228 b
καὶ ἀγαθά ἐστιν, ἁπλῶς δ' οὔ, ἀλλὰ τοὐναντίον
φαῦλα καὶ οὐχ ἡδέα, ὅσα τοῖς πονηροῖς ὠφέλιμα,
καὶ ὅσα ἡδέα τοῖς παιδίοις ᾗ παιδία. ὁμοίως δὲ 8
καὶ τὰ φοβερὰ τὰ μὲν ἁπλῶς ἐστί, τὰ δὲ τινί· ἃ
μὲν δὴ ὁ[1] δειλὸς φοβεῖται ᾗ δειλός, τὰ μὲν οὐδενί
ἐστι φοβερά, τὰ δ' ἠρέμα· τὰ δὲ τοῖς πλείστοις
φοβερά, καὶ ὅσα τῇ ἀνθρωπίνῃ φύσει, ταῦθ'
ἁπλῶς φοβερὰ λέγομεν. ὁ δ' ἀνδρεῖος πρὸς ταῦτ' 9
ἔχει ἀφόβως, καὶ ὑπομένει τὰ τοιαῦτα φοβερά,
ἃ ἔστι μὲν ὡς φοβερὰ αὐτῷ ἔστι δ' ὡς οὔ, ᾗ μὲν
ἄνθρωπος φοβερά, ᾗ δ' ἀνδρεῖος οὐ φοβερὰ ἀλλ'
ἢ ἠρέμα, ἢ οὐδαμῶς. ἔστι μέντοι φοβερὰ ταῦτα·
τοῖς γὰρ πλείστοις φοβερά. διὸ καὶ ἐπαινεῖται ἡ 10
ἕξις· ὥσπερ γὰρ ὁ ἰσχυρὸς καὶ ὑγιεινὸς ἔχει. καὶ
γὰρ οὗτοι οὐ τῷ ὑπὸ μηθενὸς ὁ μὲν πόνου τρίβεσθαι
ὁ δ' ὑπὸ μηδεμιᾶς ὑπερβολῆς τοιοῦτοί εἰσιν, ἀλλὰ
τῷ ὑπὸ τούτων ἀπαθεῖς εἶναι ἢ ἁπλῶς ἢ ἠρέμα
ὑφ' ὧν οἱ πολλοὶ καὶ[2] οἱ πλεῖστοι. οἱ μὲν οὖν 11
νοσώδεις καὶ ἀσθενεῖς καὶ δειλοὶ καὶ ὑπὸ τῶν
κοινῶν παθημάτων πάσχουσί τι, πλὴν θᾶττόν τε
καὶ μᾶλλον ἢ οἱ πολλοί, . . . [3] καὶ ἔτι ὑφ' ὧν οἱ
πολλοὶ πάσχουσιν, ὑπὸ τούτων ἀπαθεῖς ἢ ὅλως ἢ
ἠρέμα.
Ἀπορεῖται δ' εἰ τῷ ἀνδρείῳ οὐθέν ἐστι φοβερόν, 12

[1] ὁ add. Fr. [2] οἱ πολλοὶ <ἢ> καὶ vel οἱ ἄλλοι καὶ ? Ric.
[3] <οἱ δ' ὑγιεινοὶ καὶ ἰσχυροὶ καὶ ἀνδρεῖοι ὑπὸ τῶν μεγίστων πάσχουσιν, ἀλλὰ βραδύτερόν τε καὶ ἧττον ἢ οἱ πολλοί> Bz. (aut secl. καὶ ἔτι . . . ἠρέμα ut prave e ll. 34 seq. repetita).

---

[a] The words 'the healthy, strong and brave . . . mass of men' are a conjectural addition to the ms. text.

person but absolutely are not so, but on the contrary are bad and unpleasant—all the things that are beneficial for the base, and all those that are pleasant
8 to children *qua* children. And similarly some things are formidable absolutely and others to a particular person : thus the things that the coward *qua* coward fears are some of them not formidable to anybody and others only slightly formidable, but things that are formidable to most men, and all that are formidable to human nature, we pronounce to be for-
9 midable absolutely. But the brave man is fearless in regard to them, and endures formidable things of this sort, which are formidable to him in one way but in another way are not—they are formidable to him *qua* human being, but *qua* brave not formidable except slightly, or not at all. Yet such things really are formidable, for they are formidable to
10 most men. Owing to this the brave man's state of character is praised, because it resembles that of the strong and the healthy. These have those characters not because no labour in the one case or extreme of temperature in the other can crush them, but because they are not affected at all, or only affected slightly, by the things that affect the many
11 or the majority. Therefore whereas the sickly and weak and cowardly are affected also by the afflictions commonly felt, only more quickly and to a greater extent than the mass of men, the healthy, strong and brave, although affected by the very great afflictions, are affected by them more slowly and less than the mass of men,[a] and moreover they are entirely unaffected or only slightly affected by things that affect the mass.

Analogy of health and strength.

12 But the question is raised whether to the brave

1228 b οὐδ᾽ ἂν φοβηθείη. ἢ οὐθὲν κωλύει τὸν εἰρημένον
1229 a τρόπον; ἡ γὰρ ἀνδρεία ἀκολούθησις[1] τῷ λόγῳ
ἐστίν, ὁ δὲ λόγος τὸ καλὸν αἱρεῖσθαι κελεύει. διὸ
καὶ ὁ μὴ διὰ τοῦτον[2] ὑπομένων αὐτά, οὗτος ἤτοι
ἐξέστηκεν ἢ θρασύς· ὁ δὲ διὰ τὸ καλὸν ἄφοβος 13
καὶ ἀνδρεῖος μόνος. ὁ μὲν οὖν δειλὸς καὶ ἃ μὴ
δεῖ φοβεῖται, ὁ δὲ θρασὺς καὶ ἃ μὴ δεῖ θαρρεῖ· ὁ
δ᾽ ἀνδρεῖος ἄμφω ἃ δεῖ, καὶ ταύτῃ μέσος ἐστίν,
ἃ γὰρ ἂν ὁ λόγος κελεύῃ, ταῦτα καὶ θαρρεῖ καὶ
φοβεῖται· ὁ δὲ λόγος τὰ μεγάλα λυπηρὰ καὶ
φθαρτικὰ οὐ κελεύει ὑπομένειν, ἂν μὴ καλὰ ᾖ. ὁ 14
μὲν οὖν θρασύς, καὶ εἰ μὴ κελεύει, ταῦτα θαρρεῖ,
ὁ δὲ δειλὸς οὐδ᾽ ἂν κελεύῃ· ὁ δ᾽ ἀνδρεῖος μόνος[3]
ἐὰν κελεύῃ.

Ἔστι δ᾽ εἴδη ἀνδρείας πέντε λεγόμενα καθ᾽ 15
ὁμοιότητα· τὰ αὐτὰ γὰρ ὑπομένουσιν, ἀλλ᾽ οὐ διὰ
τὰ αὐτά. μία μὲν πολιτική· αὕτη δ᾽ ἐστὶν ἡ δι᾽
αἰδῶ οὖσα. δευτέρα ἡ στρατιωτική· αὕτη δὲ δι᾽
ἐμπειρίαν καὶ τὸ εἰδέναι, οὐχ ὥσπερ Σωκράτης
ἔφη, τὰ δεινά, ἀλλὰ[4] τὰς βοηθείας τῶν δεινῶν.
τρίτη δ᾽ ἡ δι᾽ ἀπειρίαν καὶ ἄγνοιαν, δι᾽ ἣν τὰ 16
παιδία καὶ οἱ μαινόμενοι οἱ μὲν ὑπομένουσι τὰ
φερόμενα[5] οἱ δὲ λαμβάνουσι τοὺς ὄφεις. ἄλλη δ᾽
ἡ κατ᾽ ἐλπίδα, καθ᾽ ἣν οἵ τε κατευτυχηκότες
πολλάκις ὑπομένουσι τοὺς κινδύνους καὶ οἱ
μεθύοντες· εὐέλπιδας γὰρ ποιεῖ ὁ οἶνος. ἄλλη δὲ 17

[1] ἀκολουθητικὴ Bus. [2] v.l. τοῦτο: τούτων Cas.
[3] Rac.: μόνον. [4] Syl. (ἀλλὰ τὸ lac.): ἀλλ᾽ ὅτι.
[5] ἐπιφερόμενα ? (cf. b 27) Rac.

[a] Plato, *Protagoras* 360 D.

The brave man fears when reasonable.

man nothing is formidable, and whether he would
be insensible to fear. Or is it not possible that he
may feel fear in the way described ? For courage is
following reason, and reason bids us choose what is
fine. Hence he who endures formidable things not on
account of reason is either out of his mind or daring,
13 but only he who does so from motives of honour
is fearless and brave. The coward, therefore, fears
even things that he ought not to fear, and the daring
man is bold even about things about which he ought
not to be bold, but the brave man alone does both
as he ought, and is intermediate in this respect,
for he feels both confidence and fear about whatever things reason bids ; but reason does not bid
him endure things that are extremely painful and
14 destructive, unless they are fine. The daring man,
therefore, faces such things with confidence even if
reason does not bid him face them, and the coward
does not face them even if it does, but only the brave
man faces them if reason bids.

Five unreal forms of Courage.

15 There are five kinds of courage so called by analogy,
because brave men of these kinds endure the same
things as the really courageous but not for the same
reasons. One is civic courage ; this is courage due
to a sense of shame. Second is military courage ;
this is due to experience and to knowledge, not of
what is formidable, as Socrates said,[a] but of ways
16 of encountering what is formidable. Third is the
courage due to inexperience and ignorance, that
makes children and madmen face things rushing on
them, or grasp snakes. Another is the courage
caused by hope, which often makes those who have
had a stroke of luck endure dangers, and those who
are intoxicated—for wine makes men sanguine.

1229 a διὰ πάθος ἀλόγιστον, οἷον δι' ἔρωτα καὶ θυμόν.
ἄν τε γὰρ ἐρᾷ, θρασὺς μᾶλλον ἢ δειλός, καὶ
ὑπομένει πολλοὺς κινδύνους, ὥσπερ ὁ ἐν Μετα-
ποντίῳ τὸν τύραννον ἀποκτείνας καὶ ὁ ἐν Κρήτῃ
μυθολογούμενος· καὶ δι' ὀργὴν καὶ θυμὸν ὡσ-
αύτως· ἐκστατικὸν γὰρ ὁ θυμός. διὸ καὶ οἱ ἄγριοι
σύες[1] ἀνδρεῖοι δοκοῦσιν εἶναι, οὐκ ὄντες· ὅταν γὰρ
ἐκστῶσι, τοιοῦτοι εἰσίν, εἰ δὲ μή, ἀνώμαλοι,
ὥσπερ οἱ θρασεῖς. ὅμως δὲ μάλιστα φυσικὴ ἡ 18
τοῦ θυμοῦ· ἀήττητον γὰρ ὁ θυμός, διὸ καὶ οἱ
παῖδες ἄριστα μάχονται. διὰ νόμον δὲ ἡ πολιτικὴ 19
ἀνδρεία. κατ' ἀλήθειαν δὲ οὐδεμία τούτων, ἀλλὰ
πρὸς τὰς παρακελεύσεις τὰς ἐν τοῖς κινδύνοις χρήσιμα ταῦτα πάντα.

Περὶ δὲ τῶν φοβερῶν νῦν μὲν ἁπλῶς εἰρήκαμεν, 20
βέλτιον δὲ διορίσασθαι μᾶλλον. ὅλως μὲν οὖν
φοβερὰ λέγεται τὰ ποιητικὰ φόβου, τοιαῦτα δ'
ἐστὶν ὅσα φαίνεται ποιητικὰ λύπης φθαρτικῆς·
τοῖς γὰρ ἄλλην τινὰ προσδεχομένοις λύπην ἑτέρα
μὲν ἄν τις ἴσως λύπη γένοιτο καὶ πάθος ἕτερον,
φόβος δ' οὐκ ἔσται, οἷον εἴ τις προορῷτο ὅτι
λυπήσεται λύπην ἣν οἱ φθονοῦντες λυποῦνται, ἢ
τοιαύτην οἵαν οἱ ζηλοῦντες ἢ οἱ αἰσχυνόμενοι.
ἀλλ' ἐπὶ μόναις ταῖς τοιαύταις φαινομέναις ἔσεσθαι 21
λύπαις φόβος γίνεται ὅσων ἡ φύσις ἀναιρετικὴ τοῦ
1229 b ζῆν. διὸ καὶ σφόδρα τινὲς ὄντες μαλακοὶ περὶ
ἔνια ἀνδρεῖοί εἰσι, καὶ ἔνιοι σκληροὶ καὶ[2] καρτερικοὶ
καὶ δειλοί. καὶ δὴ καὶ δοκεῖ σχεδὸν ἴδιον τῆς 22

[1] P^b: M^b θῆρες. [2] καὶ secl. Vic.

[a] Unknown.

17 Another is due to some irrational emotion, for example love or passion. For if a man is in love he is more daring than cowardly, and endures many dangers, like the man [a] who murdered the tyrant at Metapontium and the person in Crete in the story [a]; and similarly if a man is under the influence of anger and passion, for passion is a thing that makes him beside himself. Hence wild boars are thought to be brave, though they are not really, for they are so when they are beside themselves, but otherwise
18 they are variable, like daring men. But nevertheless the courage of passion is in the highest degree natural; passion is a thing that does not know defeat, owing to which the young are the best fighters.
19 Civic courage is due to law. But none of these is truly courage, though they are all useful for encouragement in dangers.

Only extreme terrors are the sphere of Courage.

20 Up to this point we have spoken about things formidable in general terms, but it will be better to define them more precisely. As a general term 'formidable' denotes what causes fear, and that is a property of things that appear capable of causing pain of a destructive kind: for persons expecting some other pain might perhaps experience a different sort of pain and a different feeling, but will not have fear—for example if a man foresaw that he was going to feel the pain felt by the jealous, or the sort of pain felt by the envious or by those who are ashamed.
21 But fear only occurs in the case of pains that seem likely to be of the kind whose nature it is to destroy life. Hence some people who are even very soft about certain things are brave, and some who are
22 hard and enduring are also cowardly. Moreover it is thought to be almost a special property of courage

1229 b ἀνδρείας εἶναι τὸ περὶ τὸν θάνατον καὶ τὴν τούτου
λύπην ἔχειν πώς· εἰ γάρ τις εἴη τοιοῦτος οἷος πρὸς
ἀλέας καὶ ψύχη καὶ τὰς τοιαύτας λύπας ὑπομενε-
τικός[1] ὡς ὁ λόγος, ἀκινδύνους οὔσας, πρὸς δὲ τὸν
θάνατον καὶ μαλακὸς καὶ περίφοβος, μὴ δι' ἄλλο
τι πάθος ἀλλὰ δι' αὐτὴν τὴν φθοράν, ἄλλος δὲ
πρὸς μὲν ἐκείνας μαλακός, πρὸς δὲ τὸν θάνατον
ἀπαθής, ἐκεῖνος μὲν ἂν εἶναι δόξειε δειλός, οὗτος
δ' ἀνδρεῖος. καὶ γὰρ κίνδυνος ἐπὶ τοῖς τοιούτοις 23
λέγεται μόνοις τῶν φοβερῶν ὅταν πλησίον ᾖ τὸ
τῆς τοιαύτης φθορᾶς ποιητικόν, φαίνεται δὲ
κίνδυνος ὅταν πλησίον φαίνηται.[2]

Τὰ μὲν οὖν φοβερὰ περὶ ὅσα φαμὲν εἶναι τὸν
ἀνδρεῖον εἴρηται δὴ ὅτι τὰ φαινόμενα ποιητικὰ
λύπης τῆς φθαρτικῆς, ταῦτα μέντοι πλησίον τε
φαινόμενα καὶ μὴ πόρρω, καὶ τοσαῦτα τῷ μεγέθει
ὄντα ἢ φαινόμενα ὥστ' εἶναι σύμμετρα πρὸς
ἄνθρωπον· ἔνια γὰρ ἀνάγκη παντὶ φαίνεσθαι 24
ἀνθρώπῳ φοβερὰ καὶ διαταράττειν, οὐθὲν γὰρ
κωλύει, ὥσπερ θερμὰ καὶ ψυχρὰ καὶ τῶν ἄλλων
δυνάμεων ἐνίας ὑπὲρ ἡμᾶς εἶναι καὶ τὰς τοῦ
ἀνθρωπίνου σώματος ἕξεις, οὕτω καὶ τῶν περὶ
τὴν ψυχὴν παθημάτων.

Οἱ μὲν οὖν[3] δειλοὶ καὶ θρασεῖς διαψεύδονται διὰ
τὰς ἕξεις, τῷ μὲν γὰρ δειλῷ τά τε μὴ φοβερὰ δοκεῖ
φοβερὰ εἶναι καὶ τὰ ἠρέμα σφόδρα, τῷ δὲ θρασεῖ
τοὐναντίον τά τε φοβερὰ θαρραλέα καὶ τὰ σφόδρα
ἠρέμα· τῷ δ' ἀνδρείῳ τἀληθῆ μάλιστα. διόπερ οὔτ' 25
εἴ τις ὑπομένει[4] τὰ φοβερὰ δι' ἄγνοιαν, ἀνδρεῖος,

[1] ὑπομενετικὸς <εἶναι> ? Ric.
[2] Syl.: φαίνεται.
[3] οὖν add. Bz.
[4] ὑπομένει Pᵇ: -νοι Mᵇ, Syl.

to be of a certain disposition in regard to death and the pain of death; for if a man were such as to be capable of rational endurance in respect of heat and cold and pains of that sort that are not dangerous, but at the same time soft and excessively timid about death, not because of any other feeling but just because it brings destruction, while another man was soft in regard to those pains but impassive as regards death, the former would be thought a coward and
23 the latter brave. For we speak of danger only in the case of such formidable things as bring near to us what causes destruction of that sort, and when this appears near it appears to be danger.

The formidable things, therefore, in relation to which we speak of a man as brave are, we have said, those that appear likely to cause pain of the destructive kind—provided that these appear close at hand and not far off, and are or appear to be of
24 a magnitude proportionate to a human being; for some things must necessarily appear fearful to every human being and throw everybody into alarm, since it is quite possible that, just as heat and cold and some of the other forces are above us and above the conditions of the human body, so also are some mental sufferings.

The opposed extremes.

Therefore whereas the cowardly and the daring are mistaken owing to their characters, since the coward thinks things not formidable formidable and things slightly formidable extremely formidable, and the daring man on the contrary thinks formidable things perfectly safe and extremely formidable things only slightly formidable, to the brave man on the other hand things seem exactly what they are.
25 Hence a man is not brave if he endures formidable

1229 b
οἷον εἴ τις τοὺς κεραυνοὺς ὑπομένοι[1] φερομένους[2]
διὰ μανίαν, οὔτ' εἰ γινώσκων ὅσος ὁ κίνδυνος,
διὰ θυμόν, οἷον οἱ Κελτοὶ πρὸς τὰ κύματα ὅπλα
ἀπαντῶσι λαβόντες· καὶ ὅλως ἡ βαρβαρικὴ ἀνδρεία
μετὰ θυμοῦ ἐστίν. ἔνιοι δὲ καὶ δι' ἄλλας ἡδονὰς 26
ὑπομένουσιν· καὶ γὰρ ὁ θυμὸς ἡδονὴν ἔχει τινά,
μετ' ἐλπίδος γάρ ἐστι τιμωρίας. ἀλλ' ὅμως οὔτ'
εἰ διὰ ταύτην οὔτ' εἰ δι' ἄλλην ἡδονὴν ὑπομένει
τις τὸν θάνατον, ἢ φυγὴν[3] μειζόνων λυπῶν, οὐδεὶς
δικαίως ἂν[4] ἀνδρεῖος λέγοιτο τούτων. εἰ γὰρ ἦν 27
ἡδὺ τὸ ἀποθνήσκειν, πολλάκις ἂν δι' ἀκρασίαν
ἀπέθνησκον οἱ ἀκόλαστοι, ὥσπερ καὶ νῦν αὐτοῦ
μὲν τοῦ ἀποθνήσκειν οὐκ ὄντος ἡδέος, τῶν
ποιητικῶν δ' αὐτοῦ, πολλοὶ δι' ἀκρασίαν περι-
πίπτουσιν εἰδότες, ὧν οὐδεὶς ἂν[4] ἀνδρεῖος εἶναι
δόξειεν, εἰ καὶ πάνυ ἑτοίμως[5] ἀποθνήσκειν.[6] οὔτ'
εἰ φεύγοντες τὸ πονεῖν, ὅπερ πολλοὶ ποιοῦσιν, οὐδὲ
τῶν τοιούτων οὐθεὶς ἀνδρεῖος, καθάπερ καὶ
1230 a Ἀγάθων φησὶ

> φαῦλοι βροτῶν γὰρ τοῦ πονεῖν ἡσσώμενοι
> θανεῖν ἐρῶσιν.

ὥσπερ καὶ τὸν Χείρωνα μυθολογοῦσιν οἱ ποιηταὶ
διὰ τὴν ἀπὸ τοῦ ἕλκους ὀδύνην εὔξασθαι ἀποθανεῖν
ἀθάνατον ὄντα. παραπλησίως δὲ τούτοις καὶ ὅσοι 28
δι' ἐμπειρίαν ὑπομένουσι τοὺς κινδύνους, ὅνπερ τρό-

[1] ὑπομένοι Syl.: ὑπομένει.
[2] ἐπιφερομένους ? (cf. a 17) Rac.
[3] ‹διὰ› φυγὴν ? Rac.
[4] ἂν bis add. Sp. [5] v.l. ἑτοῖμος.
[6] ἀποθνήσκει Vic.: -κοι ? Rac.

[a] This appears to be loosely quoted from a verse passage:

things through ignorance (for instance, if owing to madness he were to endure a flight of thunderbolts), nor if he does so owing to passion when knowing the greatness of the danger, as the Celts 'take arms and march against the waves '[a]; and in general, the courage of barbarians has an element of passion. The motives of true Courage.

26 And some men endure terrors for the sake of other pleasures also—for even passion contains pleasure of a sort, since it is combined with hope of revenge. But nevertheless neither if a man endures death for the sake of this pleasure nor for another, nor for the sake of avoiding greater pains, would any of these

27 persons justly be termed brave. For if dying were pleasant, profligates would be dying constantly, owing to lack of self-control, just as even as it is, when, although death itself is not pleasant, things that cause it are, many men through lack of self-control knowingly encounter it; none of whom would be thought brave, even though he were thought to die quite readily. Nor yet are any of those brave who, as many men do, commit suicide to escape from trouble, as Agathon[b] says:

> The base among mankind, by toil o'ercome,
> Conceive a love of death.

As also Cheiron,[c] in the legendary story of the poets, because of the pain from his wound prayed that

28 though immortal he might die. And in like manner to these, all who face dangers because of experience

cf. N.E. iii. 7. 7. An echo of the story survives in Shakespeare's metaphor, 'to take arms against a sea of troubles.'

[b] Athenian tragic poet, friend of Plato.

[c] The Centaur sage and physician, accidentally wounded by a poisoned arrow of Heracles, transferred his immortality to Prometheus.

1230 a
πον σχεδὸν οἱ πλεῖστοι τῶν στρατιωτικῶν ἀνθρώπων ὑπομένουσιν. αὐτὸ γὰρ τοὐναντίον ἔχει ἢ ὡς
ᾤετο Σωκράτης, ἐπιστήμην οἰόμενος εἶναι τὴν ἀνδρείαν. οὔτε γὰρ διὰ τὸ εἰδέναι τὰ φοβερὰ θαρ-
ροῦσιν οἱ ἐπὶ τοὺς ἱστοὺς ἀναβαίνειν ἐπιστάμενοι,
ἀλλ' ὅτι ἴσασι τὰς βοηθείας τῶν δεινῶν· οὔτε δι' ὃ
θαρραλεώτερον ἀγωνίζονται, τοῦτο ἀνδρεία, καὶ γὰρ 29
ἂν ἡ ἰσχὺς καὶ ὁ πλοῦτος κατὰ Θέογνιν ἀνδρεία
εἶεν·

πᾶς γὰρ ἀνὴρ πενίῃ δεδμημένος.

φανερῶς δ'[1] ἔνιοι δειλοὶ ὄντες ὅμως ὑπομένουσι
δι' ἐμπειρίαν, τοῦτο δὲ ὅτι οὐκ οἴονται κίνδυνον
εἶναι, ἴσασι γὰρ τὰς βοηθείας. σημεῖον δέ· ὅταν
γὰρ μὴ ἔχειν οἴωνται βοήθειαν ἀλλ' ἤδη πλησίον
ᾖ τὸ δεινόν, οὐχ ὑπομένουσιν. ἀλλὰ πάντων τῶν 30
τοιούτων αἰτίων[2] οἱ διὰ τὴν αἰδῶ ὑπομένοντες
μάλιστα φανεῖεν ἂν[3] ἀνδρεῖοι, καθάπερ καὶ Ὅμηρος
τὸν Ἕκτορά φησιν ὑπομεῖναι τὸν κίνδυνον τὸν
πρὸς τὸν Ἀχιλλέα·

Ἕκτορα δ' αἰδὼς εἷλε·

καὶ[4]

Πουλυδάμας μοι πρῶτος ἐλεγχείην ἀναθήσει.

καὶ ἐστὶν ἡ πολιτικὴ ἀνδρεία αὕτη. ἡ δ' ἀληθὴς 31
οὔτε αὕτη οὔτ' ἐκείνων οὐδεμία, ἀλλ' ὁμοία μέν,
ὥσπερ καὶ ἡ τῶν θηρίων, ἃ διὰ τὸν θυμὸν ὁμόσε
τῇ πληγῇ φέρεται. οὔτε γὰρ ὅτι ἀδοξήσει δεῖ

[1] δ' add. Rieckher.
[2] [αἰτίων] ? Ric.: ἀνδρείων Sp.
[3] ἂν add. Sus.
[4] καὶ add. Fr.

are not brave ; this is how perhaps most of the military class face dangers. For the fact is the exact opposite of the view of Socrates, who thought that bravery was knowledge : sailors who know how to go aloft are not daring through knowing what things are formidable, but because they know how to protect themselves against the dangers ; also courage is not merely what makes men more daring fighters,
29 for in that case strength and wealth would be courage —as Theognis puts it :

For every man by poverty subdued.[a]

But manifestly some men do face emergencies in spite of being cowards, owing to experience, and they do so because they do not think that there is any danger, as they know how to protect themselves. A proof of this is that when they think that they have no protection and that the cause of alarm is now
30 close at hand, they turn tail. But among all such causes, it is when shame makes men face what is alarming that they would appear to be bravest, as Homer says Hector faced the danger of encountering Achilles :

And shame on Hector seized——[b]

and

Polydamas will be the first to taunt me.[c]

31 Civic courage is this kind. But true courage is neither this nor any of the others, though it resembles them, as does the courage of wild animals, which are led by passion to rush to meet the blow. For it is not from fear that he will incur disgrace that a

[a] Theognis 177.
[b] Not in our Homer.
[c] *Iliad* xxii. 100.

1230 a μένειν φοβούμενον,[1] οὔτε δι' ὀργήν, οὔτε διὰ τὸ
μὴ νομίζειν ἀποθανεῖσθαι ἢ διὰ τὸ δυνάμεις ἔχειν
φυλακτικάς· οὐδὲ γὰρ οἰήσεται οὕτω γε φοβερὸν
εἶναι οὐθέν. ἀλλ' ἐπειδὴ πᾶσά γ'[2] ἀρετὴ προαιρε- 32
τική (τοῦτο δὲ πῶς λέγομεν, εἴρηται πρότερον,
ὅτι ἕνεκά τινος πάντα αἱρεῖσθαι ποιεῖ, καὶ τοῦτό
ἐστι τὸ οὗ ἕνεκα τὸ καλόν), δῆλον ὅτι καὶ ἡ
ἀνδρεία ἀρετή τις οὖσα ἕνεκά τινος ποιήσει τὰ
φοβερὰ ὑπομένειν, ὥστ' οὔτε δι' ἄγνοιαν (ὀρθῶς
γὰρ μᾶλλον ποιεῖ κρίνειν) οὔτε δι' ἡδονήν, ἀλλ'
ὅτι καλόν, ἐπεί, ἄν γε μὴ καλὸν ᾖ ἀλλὰ μανικόν,
οὐχ ὑπομενεῖ[3]· αἰσχρὸν γάρ.

Περὶ ποῖα μὲν οὖν ἐστὶν ἡ ἀνδρεία μεσότης καὶ 33
τίνων καὶ διὰ τί, καὶ τὰ φοβερὰ τίνα δύναμιν
ἔχει, σχεδὸν εἴρηται κατὰ τὴν παροῦσαν ἔφοδον
ἱκανῶς.

II. Περὶ δὲ σωφροσύνης καὶ ἀκολασίας μετὰ 1
ταῦτα διελέσθαι πειρατέον. λέγεται δ' ὁ ἀκόλαστος
πολλαχῶς. ὅ τε γὰρ μὴ κεκολασμένος πως[4] μηδ'
1230 b ἰατρευμένος,[5] ὥσπερ ἄτμητος ὁ μὴ τετμημένος·
καὶ τούτων ὁ μὲν δυνατὸς ὁ δ' ἀδύνατος· ἄτμητον
γὰρ τό τε μὴ δυνάμενον τμηθῆναι καὶ τὸ δυνατὸν
μὲν μὴ τετμημένον δέ, τὸν αὐτὸν δὲ τρόπον καὶ
τὸ ἀκόλαστον· καὶ γὰρ τὸ μὴ πεφυκὸς δέχεσθαι 2
κόλασιν, καὶ τὸ πεφυκὸς μὲν μὴ κεκολασμένον δὲ

[1] Cas.: φοβουμένους.
[2] γ' add. Mb.
[3] Ric.: ὑπομένει.
[4] πω Vict.
[5] Sp.: ἰατρευόμενος.

man ought to stand his ground, nor from motives of anger, nor because he does not think that he will be killed or because he has forces to protect him, for in that case he will not think that there is really any-
32 thing to be afraid of. But, since indeed all goodness involves purposive choice (it has been said before what we mean by this—goodness makes a man choose everything for the sake of some object, and that object is what is fine), it is clear that courage being a form of goodness will make a man face formidable things for some object, so that he does not do it through ignorance (for it rather makes him judge correctly), nor yet for pleasure, but because it is fine, since in a case where it is not fine but insane he will not face them, for then it would be base to do so.

33 We have now given an account that is fairly adequate for our present procedure of the kind of things in relation to which Courage is a middle state, and between what vices and for what reason it is this, and what is the power that formidable things exercise.

1 II. We must next attempt to decide about Temperance and Profligacy. The term 'profligate' (unchaste) has a variety of meanings. It means the man who has not been (as it were) 'chastized' or cured, just as 'undivided' means one that has not been divided; and these terms include both one capable of the process and one not capable of it: 'undivided' means both that which cannot be divided and that which though it can be has not been;
2 and similarly with 'unchaste'—it denotes both that which is by nature incapable of chastening and that which, though capable, has not actually been chast-

TEMPERANCE. Profligacy, its meaning.

1230 b
περὶ ἁμαρτίας περὶ ἃς ὀρθοπραγεῖ ὁ σώφρων,
ὥσπερ οἱ παῖδες· κατὰ ταύτην γὰρ ἀκόλαστοι
λέγονται τὴν ἀκολασίαν, ἔτι δ' ἄλλον τρόπον οἱ 3
δυσίατοι καὶ οἱ ἀνίατοι πάμπαν διὰ κολάσεως.
πλεοναχῶς δὲ λεγομένης τῆς ἀκολασίας, ὅτι μὲν
περὶ ἡδονάς τινας καὶ λύπας εἰσί, φανερόν, καὶ
ὅτι ἐν τῷ περὶ ταύτας διακεῖσθαί πως καὶ ἀλλήλων
διαφέρουσι καὶ τῶν ἄλλων· διεγράψαμεν δὲ πρότερον πῶς τὴν ἀκολασίαν ὀνομάζοντες μεταφέρομεν.
τοὺς δὲ[1] ἀκινήτως ἔχοντας δι' ἀναισθησίαν πρὸς 4
ταύτας τὰς[2] ἡδονὰς οἱ μὲν καλοῦσιν ἀναισθήτους,
οἱ δ' ἄλλοις ὀνόμασι τοιούτοις προσαγορεύουσιν[3]·
ἔστι δ' οὐ πάνυ γνώριμον τὸ πάθος οὐδ' ἐπιπόλαιον 5
διὰ τὸ πάντας ἐπὶ θάτερον ἁμαρτάνειν μᾶλλον καὶ
πᾶσιν εἶναι σύμφυτον τὴν τῶν τοιούτων ἡδέων ἧτ-
ταν καὶ αἴσθησιν. μάλιστα δ' εἰσὶ τοιοῦτοι οἵους
οἱ κωμῳδοδιδάσκαλοι παράγουσιν ἀγροίκους, οἳ
οὐδὲ[4] τὰ μέτρια καὶ τὰ ἀναγκαῖα πλησιάζουσι τοῖς
ἡδέσιν.

Ἐπεὶ δ' ὁ σώφρων ἐστὶ περὶ ἡδονάς, ἀνάγκη 6
καὶ περὶ ἐπιθυμίας τινὰς αὐτὸν εἶναι. δεῖ δὴ λαβεῖν περὶ τίνας. οὐ γὰρ περὶ πάσας οὐδὲ περὶ
ἅπαντα τὰ ἡδέα ὁ σώφρων σώφρων ἐστίν, ἀλλὰ
τῇ μὲν δόξῃ περὶ δύο τῶν αἰσθητῶν, περί τε τὸ
γευστὸν καὶ τὸ ἁπτόν, τῇ δ' ἀληθείᾳ περὶ τὸ

[1] Sus.: γὰρ.
[2] ταύτας τὰς Sp.: τὰς αὐτάς.
[3] προσαγορεύουσιν <οἷον . . . > Sus. (cf. 1231 b 1).
[4] οὐδ' ε<ἰ> vel οὐδ' ἐ<ς>? Rac.

[a] ἀκόλαστος (lit. ' incorrigible ') often means no more than ' naughty ' (Solomon).

ened in respect of the errors as regards which the temperate man acts rightly, as is the case with children; for of them it is in this sense that the
3 term 'unchaste'[a] is used, whereas another use of it again refers to persons hard to cure or entirely incurable by chastisement. But though 'profligacy' has more than one sense, it is clear that the profligate are concerned with certain pleasures and pains and that they differ from one another and from the other vicious characters in being disposed in a certain manner towards these; and we described previously the way in which we apply the term 'profligacy'
4 by analogy.[b] Persons on the other hand who owing to insensitiveness are uninfluenced by these pleasures are called by some people 'insensitive' and by others are designated by other names of the same
5 sort; but the state is not a very familiar one nor of common occurrence, because all men err more in the other direction, and susceptibility and sensitiveness to pleasures of this sort are natural to everybody. It specially attaches to persons like the boors who are a stock character in comedy—people who steer clear of pleasures even in moderate and necessary indulgences.

Its opposite, Insensitiveness, rare.

6 And since the temperate character is shown in connexion with pleasures, it follows that it is also related to certain desires. We must, therefore, ascertain what these are. For the temperate man is not temperate about all pleasures nor about everything pleasant, but apparently about the objects of two of the senses, taste and touch, and in reality about

Only some pleasures the sphere of Temperance.

[b] This seems to refer to words which must have been lost at 1221 a 20 (Solomon).

1230 b ἁπτόν· περὶ γὰρ τὴν διὰ τῆς ὄψεως ἡδονὴν τῶν 7
καλῶν (ἄνευ ἐπιθυμίας ἀφροδισίων) ἢ λύπην τῶν
αἰσχρῶν, καὶ περὶ τὴν διὰ τῆς ἀκοῆς τῶν εὐ-
αρμόστων ἢ ἀναρμόστων, ἔτι δὲ πρὸς τὰς δι'
ὀσφρήσεως, τάς τε ἀπὸ εὐωδίας καὶ τὰς ἀπὸ δυσ-
ωδίας, οὐκ ἔστιν ὁ σώφρων· οὐδὲ γὰρ ἀκόλαστος
οὐδεὶς λέγεται τῷ πάσχειν ⟨ὑπὸ τούτων⟩[1] ἢ μὴ
πάσχειν· εἰ γοῦν τις ἢ καλὸν ἀνδριάντα θεώμενος 8
ἢ ἵππον ἢ ἄνθρωπον, ἢ ἀκροώμενος ᾄδοντος, μὴ
βούλοιτο μήτε ἐσθίειν μήτε πίνειν μήτε ἀφροδισιά-
ζειν, ἀλλὰ τὰ μὲν καλὰ θεωρεῖν τῶν δ' ᾀδόντων
ἀκούειν, οὐκ ἂν δόξειεν ἀκόλαστος εἶναι, ὥσπερ
οὐδ' οἱ κηλούμενοι παρὰ ταῖς Σειρῆσιν. ἀλλὰ 9
περὶ τὰ δύο τῶν αἰσθητῶν ταῦτα περὶ ἅπερ καὶ
τἆλλα θηρία μόνα τυγχάνει αἰσθητικῶς ἔχοντα καὶ
χαίροντα καὶ λυπούμενα, περὶ τὰ γευστὰ καὶ
ἁπτά, περὶ δὲ τὰ τῶν ἄλλων αἰσθήσεων[2] ἡδέα 10
1231 a σχεδὸν ὁμοίως ἅπαντα φαίνεται ἀναισθήτως δια-
κείμενα, οἷον περὶ εὐαρμοστίαν ἢ κάλλος· οὐθὲν
γὰρ ὅ τι καὶ ἄξιον λόγου φαίνεται πάσχοντα αὐτῇ
τῇ θεωρίᾳ τῶν καλῶν ἢ τῇ ἀκροάσει τῶν εὐαρ-
μόστων, εἰ μή τί που συμβέβηκε τερατῶδες. ἀλλ'
οὐδὲ πρὸς τὰ εὐώδη ἢ δυσώδη· καίτοι τάς γε
αἰσθήσεις ὀξυτέρας ἔχουσι πάσας, ἀλλὰ καὶ τῶν 11
ὀσμῶν ταύταις χαίρουσιν ὅσαι κατὰ συμβεβηκὸς
εὐφραίνουσιν, ἀλλὰ μὴ καθ' αὑτάς· λέγω δὲ μὴ[3]
καθ' αὑτὰς αἷς ἢ[4] ἐλπίζοντες χαίρομεν ἢ μεμνημέ-

[1] Fr.
[2] Pb: αἰσθητῶν Mb.
[3] μὴ add. Fr.
[4] Fr.: μή.

7 the objects of touch. For the temperate man is not concerned with the pleasure of beautiful things (apart from sexual desire) or pain caused by ugly things, the medium of which is sight, nor with the pleasure of harmonious sounds or pain of discords conveyed through the medium of hearing, nor yet with the pleasures and pains of smell, derived from good and bad scents; for neither is anyone termed profligate because of being sensitive or not sensitive
8 to sensations of that sort—for example, a man would not be considered profligate if when looking at a beautiful statue or horse or person, or listening to someone singing, he did not wish for food or drink or sexual indulgence but only wished to look at the beautiful objects or listen to the music,—any more than the persons held spell-bound in the abode of the
9 Sirens. Temperance and profligacy have to do with those two sorts of sensory objects in relation to which alone the lower animals also happen to be sensitive and to feel pleasure and pain—the objects of taste
10 and of touch, whereas about virtually all the pleasures of the other senses alike animals are clearly so constituted as to be insensitive—*e.g.* harmonious sound, or beauty; for clearly they are not affected in any degree worth speaking of by the mere sight of beautiful objects or by listening to musical sounds, except possibly in the case of some miraculous occurrences. Nor yet are they sensitive to good or bad smells, although it is true that all their senses are
11 keener than man's; but even the smells they enjoy are those that have agreeable associations, and are not intrinsically agreeable. By smells not intrinsically agreeable I mean those that we enjoy because of either anticipation or recollection, for example the

1231 a
νοι, οἷον ὄψων καὶ ποτῶν, δι' ἑτέραν γὰρ ἡδονὴν
ταύταις χαίρομεν, τὴν τοῦ φαγεῖν ἢ πιεῖν· καθ'
αὑτὰς δὲ οἷαι αἱ τῶν ἀνθῶν εἰσίν (διὸ ἐμμελῶς
ἔφη Στρατόνικος τὰ[1] μὲν καλὸν ὄζειν, τὰ[1] δὲ ἡδύ).
ἐπεὶ καὶ τῶν περὶ τὸ γευστὸν οὐ περὶ πᾶσαν 12
ἡδονὴν ἐπτόηται τὰ θηρία, οὐδ' ὅσων τῷ ἄκρῳ
τῆς γλώττης ἡ αἴσθησις, ἀλλ' ὅσων τῷ φάρυγγι,
καὶ ἔοικεν ἁφῇ μᾶλλον ἢ γεύσει τὸ πάθος· διὸ οἱ
ὀψοφάγοι οὐκ εὔχονται τὴν γλῶτταν ἔχειν μακρὰν
ἀλλὰ τὸν φάρυγγα γεράνου, ὥσπερ Φιλόξενος ὁ
Ἐρύξιδος.[2] ὥστε περὶ τὰ ἁπτόμενα ὡς ἁπλῶς 13
εἰπεῖν θετέον τὴν ἀκολασίαν, ὁμοίως δὲ καὶ ὁ
ἀκόλαστος περὶ τὰς τοιαύτας ἐστίν· οἰνοφλυγία
γὰρ καὶ γαστριμαργία καὶ λαγνεία καὶ ὀψοφαγία[3]
καὶ πάντα τὰ τοιαῦτα περὶ τὰς εἰρημένας ἐστὶν
αἰσθήσεις, εἰς ἅπερ μόρια ἡ ἀκολασία διαιρεῖται.
περὶ δὲ τὰς δι' ὄψεως ἢ ἀκοῆς ἢ ὀσφρήσεως 14
ἡδονὰς οὐθεὶς λέγεται ἀκόλαστος ἐὰν ὑπερβάλλῃ,
ἀλλ' ἄνευ ὀνείδους τὰς ἁμαρτίας ψέγομεν ταύτας,
καὶ ὅλως περὶ ὅσα μὴ λέγονται ἐγκρατεῖς· οἱ δ'
ἀκρατεῖς οὐκ εἰσὶν ἀκόλαστοι οὐδὲ σώφρονες.
Ἀναίσθητος μὲν οὖν, ἢ ὅπως δεῖ ὀνομάζειν, ὁ 15
οὕτως ἔχων ὥστε καὶ ἐλλείπειν ὅσων ἀνάγκη
κοινωνεῖν ὡς ἐπὶ τὸ πολὺ πάντας καὶ χαίρειν· ὁ
δ' ὑπερβάλλων ἀκόλαστος. πάντες γὰρ τούτοις 16
φύσει τε χαίρουσι καὶ ἐπιθυμίας λαμβάνουσι, καὶ

[1] τὰ . . . τὰ Cas.: τὰς . . . τὰς.
[2] Syl.: ἐρύξιος, ἐξ ὕριδος. [3] ὀψοφαγία καὶ λαγνεία Ric.

[a] A contemporary musician, a number of whose smart sayings are recorded by Athenaeus viii. 347 f–352 d.

smell of things to eat or drink, for we enjoy these scents on account of a different pleasure, that of eating or drinking; by intrinsically agreeable I mean scents such as those of flowers (this is the reason of Stratonicus's[a] neat remark that the scent of flowers is beautiful but that of things to eat and drink sweet).

12 For even the pleasures of taste are not all attractive to animals, nor are those perceived with the tip of the tongue, but those perceived by the throat, the sensation of which seems more like touch than taste; so that gourmands do not pray that they may have a long tongue but a crane's gullet, like Philo-

13 xenus son of Eryxis.[b] It follows that broadly speaking profligacy must be considered to be related to the objects of touch, and likewise it is with pleasures of that sort that the profligate is concerned; for tippling and gluttony and lechery and gormandizing and the like all have to do with the sensations specified, and these are the departments into which pro-

Profligacy distinguished from Incontinence.

14 fligacy is divided. But nobody is called profligate if he exceeds in regard to the pleasures of sight or hearing or smell; those errors we criticize without severe rebuke, and generally all the things included under the term 'lack of self-control': the uncontrolled are not profligate, yet they are not temperate.

15 Therefore the person of such a character as to be deficient in all the enjoyments which practically everybody must share and must enjoy, is insensitive (or whatever the proper term is), and he that ex-

16 ceeds in them is profligate. For all people by nature enjoy these things, and conceive desires for them,

[b] Mr. Hospitable, son of Mistress Belch—presumably a character in comedy.

1231 a
οὐκ εἰσὶν οὐδὲ λέγονται ἀκόλαστοι, οὐ γὰρ ὑπερβάλλουσι τῷ χαίρειν μᾶλλον ἢ δεῖ τυγχάνοντες
καὶ λυπεῖσθαι μᾶλλον ἢ δεῖ μὴ τυγχάνοντες· οὐδ'
ἀνάλγητοι, οὐ γὰρ ἐλλείπουσι τῷ χαίρειν ἢ λυπεῖσθαι, ἀλλὰ μᾶλλον ὑπερβάλλουσιν.
'Επεὶ δ' ἔστιν ὑπερβολὴ καὶ ἔλλειψις περὶ αὐτά, 17
δῆλον ὅτι καὶ μεσότης, καὶ βελτίστη αὕτη ἡ ἕξις,
καὶ ἀμφοῖν ἐναντία. ὥστ' εἰ[1] σωφροσύνη ἡ
βελτίστη ἕξις περὶ ἃ ὁ ἀκόλαστος, ἡ περὶ τὰ
ἡδέα τὰ εἰρημένα τῶν αἰσθητῶν μεσότης σωφροσύνη
ἂν εἴη, μεσότης οὖσα ἀκολασίας καὶ ἀναισθησίας·
1231 b ἡ δ' ὑπερβολὴ ἀκολασία, ἡ δ' ἔλλειψις ἤτοι
ἀνώνυμος ἢ τοῖς εἰρημένοις ὀνόμασι προσαγορευο-
μένη. ἀκριβέστερον δὲ περὶ τοῦ γένους τῶν 18
ἡδονῶν ἔσται διαιρετέον ἐν τοῖς λεγομένοις ὕστερον
περὶ ἐγκρατείας καὶ ἀκρασίας.
III. Τὸν αὐτὸν δὲ τρόπον ληπτέον καὶ περὶ 1
πραότητος καὶ χαλεπότητος. καὶ γὰρ τὸν πρᾶον
περὶ λύπην τὴν ἀπὸ θυμοῦ γιγνομένην ὁρῶμεν
ὄντα, τῷ πρὸς ταύτην ἔχειν πώς. διεγράψαμεν
δὲ καὶ ἀντεθήκαμεν τῷ ὀργίλῳ καὶ χαλεπῷ καὶ
ἀγρίῳ (πάντα γὰρ τὰ τοιαῦτα τῆς αὐτῆς ἐστὶ
διαθέσεως) τὸν ἀνδραποδώδη καὶ τὸν ἀνόργητον[2]·
σχεδὸν γὰρ ταῦτα μάλιστα καλοῦσι τοὺς μηδ' ἐφ' 2
ὅσοις δεῖ κινουμένους τὸν θυμόν, ἀλλὰ προπηλακι-
ζομένους εὐχερῶς καὶ ταπεινοὺς πρὸς τὰς ὀλι-
γωρίας· ἔστι γὰρ ἀντικείμενον τῷ μὲν ταχὺ τὸ

[1] Sp.: ὥστε. [2] Rac. (cf. 1220 b 38, 1221 a 17): ἀνόητον.

[a] ἀνάλγητοι is thrown in as a possible synonym for ἀναίσθητοι, see § 15.

[b] Perhaps in a sentence lost at 1230 b 15.

[c] See 1220 b 38, 1221 b 12-15.

without being or being called profligate, for they do not exceed by feeling more joy than they ought when they get them nor more pain than they ought when they do not get them; nor yet are they unfeeling,[a] for they do not fall short in feeling joy or pain, but rather exceed.

17 And since there are excess and deficiency in regard to these things, it is clear that there is also a middle state, and that this state of character is the best one, and is the opposite of both the others. Hence if temperance is the best state of character in relation to the things with which the profligate is concerned, the middle state in regard to the pleasant objects of sense mentioned will be Temperance, being a middle state between profligacy and insensitiveness: the excess will be Profligacy, and the deficiency will either be nameless or will be denoted
18 by the terms mentioned.[b] We shall have to define the class of pleasures concerned more exactly in our discussion of Self-control and Lack of Control later on.

1 III. And also the nature of Gentleness and Harshness must be ascertained in the same way. For we see that the term 'gentle' is concerned with the pain that arises from passion—a man is gentle by being disposed in a certain way towards that pain. And in our diagram[c] we opposed to the irascible and harsh and fierce man (for all such traits belong to the same disposition) the slavish and spiritless[d]
2 man; for these are perhaps the most usual words to denote those whose passion is not aroused even at all the things at which it ought to be, but who undergo insulting treatment readily and meet slights with humility; since as opposed to feeling the pain that

GENTLENESS: proper resentment of insult.

[d] The MSS. give 'slavish and senseless.'

1231 b μόλις, τῷ δ' ἠρέμα τὸ σφόδρα, τῷ δὲ πολὺν
χρόνον τὸ ὀλίγον λυπεῖσθαι ταύτην τὴν λύπην ἣν
καλοῦμεν θυμόν. ἐπεὶ δ' ὥσπερ καὶ ἐπὶ τῶν 3
ἄλλων εἴπομεν, καὶ ἐνταῦθ' ἐστὶν ὑπερβολὴ καὶ
ἔλλειψις (ὁ μὲν γὰρ χαλεπὸς τοιοῦτός ἐστιν, ὁ καὶ
θᾶττον καὶ μᾶλλον πάσχων[1] καὶ πλείω χρόνον καὶ
ὅτ' οὐ δεῖ καὶ ὁποίοις οὐ δεῖ καὶ ἐπὶ πολλοῖς,
ὁ δ' ἀνδραποδώδης τοὐναντίον), δῆλον ὅτι ἔστι
τις καὶ ὁ[2] μέσος τῆς ἀνισότητος. ἐπεὶ οὖν ἡμαρτη- 4
μέναι ἀμφότεραι αἱ ἕξεις ἐκεῖναι, φανερὸν ὅτι ἐπι-
εικὴς ἡ μέση τούτων ἕξις· οὔτε γὰρ προτερεῖ
οὔθ' ὑστερίζει, οὔτε οἷς οὐ δεῖ ὀργίζεται οὔτε
οἷς δεῖ οὐκ ὀργίζεται. ὥστ' ἐπεὶ καὶ πραότης ἡ
βελτίστη ἕξις περὶ ταῦτα τὰ πάθη ἐστίν, εἴη ἂν
καὶ ἡ πραότης μεσότης τις, καὶ ὁ πρᾶος μέσος τοῦ
χαλεποῦ καὶ τοῦ ἀνδραποδώδους.

IV. Ἔστι δὲ καὶ ἡ μεγαλοψυχία καὶ ἡ μεγα- 1
λοπρέπεια καὶ ἡ ἐλευθεριότης μεσότητες, ἡ μὲν
ἐλευθεριότης περὶ χρημάτων κτῆσιν καὶ ἀποβολήν.
ὁ μὲν γὰρ κτήσει μὲν πάσῃ μᾶλλον χαίρων ἢ δεῖ
ἀποβολῇ δὲ πάσῃ λυπούμενος μᾶλλον ἢ δεῖ
ἀνελεύθερος, ὁ δ' ἀμφότερα ἧττον ἢ δεῖ ἄσωτος,
ὁ δ' ἄμφω ὡς δεῖ ἐλευθέριος (τοῦτο δὲ λέγω τὸ
ὡς δεῖ, καὶ ἐπὶ τούτων καὶ ἐπὶ τῶν ἄλλων, τὸ
ὡς ὁ λόγος ὁ ὀρθός). ἐπεὶ δ' ἐκεῖνοι μέν εἰσιν ἐν 2
ὑπερβολῇ καὶ ἐλλείψει, ὅπου δὲ ἔσχατά εἰσι, καὶ
μέσον, καὶ τοῦτο βέλτιστον, ἓν δὲ περὶ ἕκαστον
τῷ εἴδει τὸ βέλτιστον, ἀνάγκη καὶ τὴν ἐλευθεριότητα

[1] ὁ καὶ . . . πάσχων: οἷος καὶ . . . πάσχειν Sp.
[2] [ὁ] ? Rac.

[a] *i.e.* half-way between excess and defect.

we call passion quickly, extremely or for a long time there is feeling it slowly, slightly, or for a short time.
3 And since, as we said in the other cases, so here also there is excess and deficiency (for the harsh man is the sort of man that feels this emotion too quickly, too long, at the wrong time, with the wrong kind of people, and with many people, while the slavish man is the opposite), it is clear that there is also somebody who is at the middle point in the inequality.[a]
4 Since, therefore, both those states of character are wrong, it is clear that the state midway between them is right, for it is neither too hasty nor too slow-tempered, nor does it get angry with the people with whom it ought not nor fail to get angry with those with whom it ought. So that since the best state of character in regard to those feelings is gentleness, Gentleness also would be a middle state, and the gentle man would be midway between the harsh man and the slavish man.

Liberality, the mean between Meanness and Prodigality in getting and spending.

1 IV. Greatness of Spirit and Magnificence and Liberality are also middle states. Liberality is the mean in regard to the acquisition and expenditure of wealth. The man who is more pleased than he ought to be by all acquisition and more pained than he ought to be by all expenditure is mean, he that feels both feelings less than he ought is prodigal, and he that feels both as he ought is liberal (what I mean by 'as he ought,' both in this and in the other
2 cases, is 'as right principle directs'). And since the two former characters consist in excess and deficiency, and where there are extremes there is also a mean, and that mean is best, there being a single best for each kind of action, a single thing, it necessarily follows that liberality is a middle state between

1231 b μεσότητα εἶναι ἀσωτίας καὶ ἀνελευθερίας περὶ
χρημάτων κτῆσιν καὶ ἀποβολήν. διχῶς δὲ τὰ 3
χρήματα λέγομεν καὶ τὴν χρηματιστικήν· ἡ μὲν
1232 a γὰρ καθ' αὑτὸ χρῆσις τοῦ κτήματός ἐστιν, οἷον
ὑποδήματος ἢ ἱματίου, ἡ δὲ κατὰ συμβεβηκὸς
μέν, οὐ μέντοι οὕτως ὡς ἂν εἴ τις σταθμῷ
χρήσαιτο τῷ ὑποδήματι, ἀλλ' οἷον ἡ πώλησις καὶ
ἡ μίσθωσις· χρῆται γὰρ ᾗ ὑπόδημα.[1] ὁ δὲ φιλ- 4
άργυρος ὁ περὶ τὸ νόμισμά ἐστιν ἐσπουδακώς, τὸ
δὲ νόμισμα τῆς κτήσεως ἀντὶ τῆς κατὰ συμβεβηκὸς
χρήσεώς ἐστιν. ὁ δ' ἀνελεύθερος εἴη ἂν[2] καὶ 5
ἄσωτος περὶ τὸν κατὰ συμβεβηκὸς τρόπον τοῦ
χρηματισμοῦ· καὶ γὰρ ἐπὶ τοῦ κατὰ φύσιν χρη-
ματισμοῦ τὴν αὔξησιν διώκει. ὁ δ' ἄσωτος
ἐλλείπει τῶν ἀναγκαίων, ὁ δ' ἐλευθέριος τὴν
περιουσίαν δίδωσιν. αὐτῶν δὲ τούτων εἴδη 6
λέγονται διαφέροντα τῷ μᾶλλον καὶ ἧττον περὶ
μόρια· οἷον ἀνελεύθερος φειδωλὸς καὶ κίμβιξ καὶ
αἰσχροκερδής, φειδωλὸς μὲν ἐν τῷ μὴ προΐεσθαι,
αἰσχροκερδὴς δ' ἐν τῷ ὁτιοῦν προσίεσθαι, κίμβιξ
δὲ ὁ σφόδρα περὶ μικρὰ διατεινόμενος, παραλογισ-
τὴς δὲ καὶ ἀποστερητὴς ὁ ἄδικος κατ' ἀνελευθερίαν·
καὶ τοῦ ἀσώτου ὡσαύτως λαφύκτης μὲν ὁ ἐν τῷ 7
ἀτάκτως ἀναλίσκειν, ἀλόγιστος δὲ ὁ ἐν τῷ μὴ
ὑπομένειν τὴν ἀπὸ λογισμοῦ λύπην.

V. Περὶ δὲ μεγαλοψυχίας ἐκ τῶν τοῖς μεγαλο- 1
ψύχοις ἀποδιδομένων δεῖ διορίσαι τὸ ἴδιον. ὥσπερ[3]

[1] <ᾗ> ὑπόδημα Rac. (ὑποδήματι Vic., ὑποδήματι <ᾗ ὑπόδημα> Sus.): ὑποδήματος aut -τα. [2] v.l. ἂν εἴη. [3] Bz.: αἴτιον.

---

[a] *Cf. Pol.* i., 1257 a 14, where the use of a shoe for sale is included with its use for wear under χρῆσις καθ' αὑτό, but dis-

prodigality and meanness as regards getting and
3 parting with wealth. But the terms 'wealth' and 'art of wealth' we use in two senses, since one way of using an article of property, for example a shoe or a cloak, is proper to the article itself,[a] another is accidental, though not as using a shoe for a weight would be an accidental use of it, but for example selling it or letting it on hire, for these uses
4 do employ it as a shoe. The covetous man is the party whose interest centres on money, and money is a thing of ownership instead of accidental use.
5 But the mean man might be even prodigal in regard to the accidental mode of getting wealth, inasmuch as it is in the natural acquisition of wealth that he pursues increase. The prodigal man lacks necessities, but the liberal man gives his super-
6 fluity. And of these classes themselves there are species designated as exceeding or deficient in respect of parts of the matter concerned: for example, the stingy man, the skinflint and the profiteer are mean—the stingy in not parting with money, the profiteer in accepting anything, the skinflint is he who is very excited about small sums; also the man who offends by way of meanness is a
7 false reckoner and a cheat. Similarly 'prodigal' includes the spendthrift who is prodigal in unregulated spending and the reckless man who is prodigal in not being able to endure the pain of calculation.

1 V. On the subject of Greatness of Spirit we must define its characteristic from the attributes of the

MAGNANIMITY. It implies all the virtues.

[a] tinguished from it as οὐχ ὁμοίως καθ' αὑτό, because not its οἰκεία χρῆσις, οὐ γὰρ ἀλλαγῆς ἕνεκα γέγονεν. The term χρήματα itself denotes to the Greek ear 'useful things.'

1232 a γὰρ καὶ τὰ ἄλλα ⟨ἃ⟩[1] κατὰ τὴν γειτνίασιν καὶ
ὁμοιότητα μέχρι του λανθάνει[2] ⟨διαφέροντα⟩[3]
πόρρω προϊόντα, καὶ περὶ τὴν μεγαλοψυχίαν ταὐτὸ
συμβέβηκεν. διὸ ἐνίοτε οἱ ἐναντίοι τοῦ αὐτοῦ 2
ἀντιποιοῦνται, οἷον ὁ ἄσωτος τῷ ἐλευθερίῳ καὶ ὁ
αὐθάδης τῷ σεμνῷ καὶ ὁ θρασὺς τῷ ἀνδρείῳ· εἰσὶ
γὰρ καὶ περὶ ταὐτὰ καὶ ὅμοροι μέχρι τινός, ὥσπερ
ὁ ἀνδρεῖος ὑπομενετικὸς κινδύνων καὶ ὁ θρασύς,
ἀλλ' ὁ μὲν ὧδε ὁ δ' ὧδε· ταῦτα δὲ διαφέρει
πλεῖστον. λέγομεν δὲ τὸν μεγαλόψυχον κατὰ τὴν 3
τοῦ ὀνόματος προσηγορίαν, ὥσπερ ἐν μεγέθει τινὶ
ψυχῆς καὶ δυνάμει.[4] ὥστε καὶ τῷ σεμνῷ καὶ τῷ
μεγαλοπρεπεῖ ὅμοιος εἶναι δοκεῖ, ὅτι[5] καὶ πάσαις
ταῖς ἀρεταῖς ἀκολουθεῖν φαίνεται. καὶ γὰρ τὸ 4
ὀρθῶς κρῖναι τὰ μεγάλα καὶ μικρὰ τῶν ἀγαθῶν
ἐπαινετόν· δοκεῖ δὲ ταῦτ' εἶναι μεγάλα ἃ διώκει
ὁ τὴν κρατίστην ἔχων ἕξιν περὶ τὰ τοιαῦτα[6] ἡδέα,
ἡ δὲ μεγαλοψυχία κρατίστη. κρίνει δ' ἡ περὶ 5
ἕκαστον ἀρετὴ τὸ μεῖζον καὶ τὸ ἔλαττον ὀρθῶς,
ἅπερ[7] ὁ φρόνιμος ἂν κελεύσειε καὶ ἡ ἀρετή,[8] ὥστε
ἕπεσθαι αὐτῇ πάσας τὰς ἀρετάς, ἢ αὐτὴν ἕπεσθαι
πάσαις.

Ἔτι δοκεῖ μεγαλοψύχου εἶναι τὸ καταφρονητικὸν 6
εἶναι. ἑκάστη δ' ἀρετὴ καταφρονητικοὺς ποιεῖ τῶν
1232 b παρὰ τὸν λόγον μεγάλων, οἷον ἀνδρεία[9] κινδύνων
(μέγα γὰρ ἡγεῖσθαι[10] οἴεται εἶναι τῶν αἰσχρῶν
καὶ πλῆθος οὐ πᾶν φοβερόν), καὶ σώφρων ἡδονῶν

[1] Fr. [2] Cas.: τοῦ λανθάνειν. [3] Rac.
[4] Γ: δυνάμεως. [5] Sus.: ὅτε.
[6] τοιαῦτα Ric.: τοιαῦτ' εἶναι (e priore linea).
[7] κάθαπερ ? Sp.
[8] ἡ ⟨τοιαύτη⟩ ἀρετὴ vel ἡ φρόνησις ? Rac.
[9] ἀνδρεῖος Sp. [10] ἡγεῖσθαι (cf. 1233 a 31) add. Sol.

great-spirited man. For just as in the other cases of things that, owing to their affinity and similarity up to a point, are not noticed to differ when they advance further, the same has happened about great-
2 ness of spirit. Hence sometimes the opposite characters claim the same quality, for instance the extravagant man claims to be the same as the liberal, the self-willed as the proud, the daring as the brave; for they are concerned with the same things, and also are neighbours up to a point, as the brave man can endure dangers and so can the daring man, but the former in one way and the latter in another, and
3 that makes a very great difference. And we use the term 'great-spirited' according to the designation of the word, as consisting in a certain greatness or power of spirit. So that the great-spirited man seems to resemble both the proud man and the magnificent, because greatness of spirit seems to go
4 with all the virtues also. For it is praiseworthy to judge great and small goods rightly; and those goods seem great which a man pursues who possesses the best state of character in relation to such pleas-
5 ures, and greatness of spirit is the best. And the virtue concerned with each thing judges rightly the greater and the smaller good, just as the wise man and virtue would bid, so that all the virtues go with it, or it goes with all the virtues.

6 Again, it is thought characteristic of the great-spirited man to be disdainful. Each virtue makes men disdainful of things irrationally deemed great: for example, courage makes a man disdainful of dangers, for he thinks that to consider danger a great matter is a disgraceful thing, and that numbers are not always formidable; and the sober-minded man dis- Indifferent to popularity,

1232 b
μεγάλων καὶ πολλῶν, καὶ ἐλευθέριος χρημάτων.
μεγαλοψύχου δὲ τοῦτο δοκεῖ εἶναι[1] διὰ τὸ περὶ 7
ὀλίγα σπουδάζειν καὶ ταῦτα μεγάλα, καὶ οὐχ
ὅ τι[2] δοκεῖ ἑτέρῳ τινί. καὶ μᾶλλον ἂν φροντίσειεν
ἀνὴρ μεγαλόψυχος τί δοκεῖ ἑνὶ σπουδαίῳ ἢ πολλοῖς τοῖς τυγχάνουσιν,[3] ὥσπερ Ἀντιφῶν ἔφη
πρὸς Ἀγάθωνα κατεψηφισμένος[4] τὴν ἀπολογίαν
ἐπαινέσαντα. καὶ τὸ ὀλίγωρον τοῦ μεγαλοψύχου
μάλιστ᾽ εἶναι πάθος ἴδιον. πάλιν περὶ τιμῆς καὶ 8
τοῦ ζῆν καὶ πλούτου, περὶ ὧν σπουδάζειν δοκοῦσιν
οἱ ἄνθρωποι, οὐθὲν φροντίζειν[5] περὶ τῶν ἄλλων πλὴν
περὶ τιμῆς· καὶ λυποῖτ᾽ ἂν[6] ἀτιμαζόμενος καὶ ἀρχόμενος ὑπὸ ἀναξίου, καὶ χαίρει μάλιστα τυγχάνων.
Οὕτω μὲν οὖν δόξειεν ἂν ἐναντίως ἔχειν, τὸ 9
γὰρ εἶναί τε μάλιστα περὶ τιμὴν καὶ καταφρονητικὸν εἶναι τῶν πολλῶν καὶ δόξης[7] οὐχ ὁμολογεῖσθαι.
δεῖ δὲ τοῦτο διορίσαντας εἰπεῖν. ἔστι γὰρ τιμὴ 10
καὶ μικρὰ καὶ μεγάλη διχῶς· ἢ γὰρ τῷ ὑπὸ πολλῶν
τῶν τυχόντων ἢ καὶ[8] ὑπὸ[9] τῶν ἀξίων λόγου, καὶ
πάλιν τῷ ἐπὶ τίνι ἡ τιμὴ διαφέρει· μεγάλη γὰρ
οὐ τῷ πλήθει τῶν τιμώντων οὐδὲ τῷ ποιῷ μόνον,
ἀλλὰ καὶ τῷ τιμία[10] εἶναι· τῇ ἀληθείᾳ δὲ καὶ αἱ
ἀρχαὶ καὶ τἆλλα ἀγαθὰ τίμια καὶ ἄξια σπουδῆς
ταῦτα ὅσα μεγάλα ἀληθῶς ἐστίν, ὥστε καὶ ἀρετὴ

[1] εἶναι add. Rac.: τοῦτο δοκεῖ aut δοκεῖ τοῦτο.
[2] Rac.: ὅτι edd. [3] τυχοῦσιν Cas.
[4] v.l. κατεψευσμένως. [5] φροντίζει Cas.
[6] Ric. (vel λυπηθήσεται): λυπηθήσοιτ᾽ ἄν.
[7] εἶναι τῆς τῶν πολλῶν δόξης ? (καὶ om. Γ) Rac.
[8] Ric.: ἤ. [9] ὑπὸ ? Ric.: τῷ ὑπὸ.
[10] Sol. (τίμια ? Ric.): τιμίαν.

[a] A variant reading gives ‘ as A. said to A. when he in-

dains great and numerous pleasures, and the liberal
7 man wealth. But the reason why this is thought characteristic of the great-spirited man is because of his caring about few things and those great ones, and not about whatever somebody else thinks. And a great-spirited man would consider more what one virtuous man thinks than what many ordinary people think, as Antiphon after his condemnation said to Agathon when he praised his speech for his defence.[a] And a feeling thought to be specially characteristic of the great-spirited man is disdain.
8 On the other hand, as to the accepted objects of human interest, honour, life, wealth, he is thought to care nothing about any of them except honour; it would grieve him to be dishonoured and ruled by someone unworthy, and his greatest joy is to obtain honour.

but loves honour

9 Thus he might therefore be thought inconsistent, on the ground that to be specially concerned about honour and to be disdainful of the multitude and of
10 reputation do not go together. But in saying this we must distinguish. Honour is small or great in two ways: it differs in being conferred either by many ordinary people or by persons of consideration, and again it differs in what it is conferred for, since its greatness does not depend only on the number or the quality of those who confer it, but also on its being honourable; and in reality those offices and other good things are honourable and worthy of serious pursuit that are truly great, so that there is

of the noble kind.

sincerely praised his defence.' For Antiphon's indictment as a leader in the revolution of the Four Hundred at Athens see Thuc. viii. 68. Agathon is presumably the tragic poet, see Plato's *Symposium*. The anecdote is not recorded elsewhere.

1232 b οὐδεμία ἄνευ μεγέθους· διὸ δοκοῦσι μεγαλοψύχους ποιεῖν ἑκάστη περὶ ὅ ἐστιν ἑκάστη αὐτῶν, ὥσπερ εἴπομεν. ἀλλ' ὅμως ἐστί τις παρὰ τὰς ἄλλας 11
ἀρετὰς μία μεγαλοψυχία, ὥστε[1] καὶ ἰδίᾳ μεγαλόψυχον τοῦτον λεκτέον τὸν ἔχοντα ταύτην. ἐπεὶ δ' ἐστὶν ἔνια τῶν ἀγαθῶν τὰ μὲν τίμια τὰ δ' οὔ,[2] ὡς διωρίσθη πρότερον, τῶν τοιούτων δ' ἀγαθῶν ἐστὶ τὰ μὲν μεγάλα κατ' ἀλήθειαν τὰ δὲ μικρά, καὶ τούτων ἔνιοι ἄξιοι καὶ ἀξιοῦσιν αὑτούς, ἐν τούτοις ζητητέος ὁ μεγαλόψυχος. τετραχῶς δ' 12
ἀνάγκη διαφέρειν· ἔστι μὲν γὰρ ἄξιον εἶναι μεγάλων καὶ ἀξιοῦν ἑαυτὸν τούτων, ἔστι δὲ μικρὰ καὶ ἄξιον εἶναι[3] τηλικούτων καὶ ἀξιοῦν ἑαυτὸν τούτων, ἔστι δ' ἀνάπαλιν πρὸς ἑκάτερα αὐτῶν· ὁ μὲν γὰρ ἂν εἴη τοιοῦτος οἷος ἄξιος ὢν μικρῶν μεγάλων[4] ἀξιοῦν ἑαυτὸν τῶν ἐντίμων ἀγαθῶν, ὁ δὲ ἄξιος ὢν μεγάλων ἀξιοίη ἂν μικρῶν ἑαυτόν. ὁ μὲν οὖν ἄξιος μικρῶν, μεγάλων δ' ἀξιῶν ἑαυτόν, 13
ψεκτός· ἀνόητον γὰρ καὶ οὐ καλὸν τὸ παρὰ τὴν ἀξίαν[5] τυγχάνειν. ψεκτὸς δὲ καὶ ὅστις ἄξιος ὢν
1233 a ὑπαρχόντων αὐτῷ τῶν τοιούτων μετέχειν μὴ ἀξιοῖ ἑαυτόν. λείπεται δὲ ἐνταῦθα ἐναντίος τούτοις 14
ἀμφοτέροις ὅστις ὢν ἄξιος μεγάλων ἀξιοῖ αὐτὸς ἑαυτὸν τούτων, καὶ τοιοῦτός ἐστιν οἷος ἀξιοῦν[6]

[1] Γ: ὥσπερ. [2] οὔ add. Sol.
[3] εἶναι (vel εἶναί τινα) Ric.: τινα.
[4] [μεγάλων] ? Rac.
[5] ἀξίαν <ἀξιοῦντα vel οἰόμενον vel χαυνούμενον> Ric.
[6] οἷον ἀξιοῖ Ric. (οἷος ἀξιοῖ Sp.).

[a] See a 39. [b] *i.e.* ll. 17 ff.
[c] Perhaps the lecturer points to a diagram (Solomon).

no goodness without greatness ; owing to which each of the virtues seems to make men great-spirited in regard to the things with which that virtue is con-
11 cerned, as we said.[a] But nevertheless there is a single virtue of greatness of spirit side by side with the other virtues, so that the possessor of this virtue must be termed great-spirited in a special sense. And since there are certain goods which are in some cases honourable and in others not, according to the distinction made before,[b] and of goods of this sort some are truly great and others small, and some men deserve and claim the former, it is among these men that the great-spirited man must be
12 looked for. And there are necessarily four varieties of claim : it is possible to deserve great things and to claim them as one's desert ; and there are small things and a man may deserve and claim things of that size ; and as regards each of these two classes of things the reverse is possible—one man may be of such a character that although deserving small things he claims great ones—the goods held in high honour, and another man though deserving great
13 things may claim small ones. Now the man worthy of small things but claiming great ones is blameworthy, for it is foolish and not fine to obtain what does not correspond to one's deserts. And he also is blameworthy who though worthy of such things does not deem himself worthy to partake of them
14 although they are available for him. But there is left here [c] the man who is the opposite of both of these, who being worthy of great things claims them as his desert,[d] and is of such a character as to deem

Four attitudes towards honour.

Definition of Magnanimity.

[d] The Greek phrase combines the senses of rating one's deserts high and asserting one's claims.

1233 a ἑαυτόν· οὗτος ἐπαινετὸς καὶ μέσος τούτων. ἐπεὶ 15
οὖν περὶ τιμῆς αἵρεσιν καὶ χρῆσιν καὶ τῶν ἄλλων ἀγαθῶν τῶν ἐντίμων ἀρίστη ἐστὶ διάθεσις ἡ
μεγαλοψυχία καὶ οὐ περὶ τὰ χρήσιμα,[1] καὶ τοῦτ᾿
ἀποδίδομεν τῷ μεγαλοψύχῳ,[2] ἅμα δὲ καὶ ἡ μεσότης
[αὕτη][3] ἐπαινετωτάτη, δῆλον ὅτι καὶ ἡ μεγαλοψυχία
μεσότης ἂν εἴη. τῶν δ᾿ ἐναντίων, ὥσπερ διεγρά- 16
ψαμεν, ἡ μὲν ἐπὶ τὸ ἀξιοῦν ἑαυτὸν ἀγαθῶν μεγάλων
ἀνάξιον ὄντα χαυνότης (τοὺς τοιούτους γὰρ χαύ-
νους λέγομεν ὅσοι μεγάλων οἴονται ἄξιοι εἶναι οὐκ
ὄντες), ἡ δὲ περὶ τὸ ἄξιον ὄντα μὴ ἀξιοῦν ἑαυτὸν
μεγάλων μικροψυχία (μικρόψυχος[4] γὰρ εἶναι δοκεῖ
ὅστις ὑπαρχόντων δι᾿ ἃ δικαίως ἂν ἀξιοῖτο μὴ
ἀξιοῖ μηθενὸς μεγάλου ἑαυτόν), ὥστ᾿ ἀνάγκη καὶ
τὴν μεγαλοψυχίαν εἶναι μεσότητα χαυνότητος καὶ
μικροψυχίας. ὁ δὲ τέταρτος τῶν διορισθέντων 17
οὔτε πάμπαν ψεκτὸς οὔτε μεγαλόψυχος, περὶ
οὐδὲν ὢν ἔχον[5] μέγεθος· οὔτε γὰρ ἄξιος οὔτε ἀξιοῖ
μεγάλων, διὸ οὐκ ἐναντίος· καίτοι δόξειεν ἂν
ἐναντίον εἶναι τῷ μεγάλων ἄξιον ὄντα μεγάλων τὸ
μικρῶν ὄντα ἄξιον μικρῶν[6] ἀξιοῦν ἑαυτόν. οὐκ 18
ἔστι δ᾿ ἐναντίος οὐδὲ[7] τῷ μεμπτὸς εἶναι, ὡς γὰρ ὁ

[1] οὐ περὶ τὰ χρήσιμα hic Ric.: post ἀποδίδομεν.
[2] Fr.: τὸν μεγαλόψυχον. [3] Rac.
[4] Fr.: μικροψύχου.
[5] ὢν ἔχον Rac. (ἔχον ὢν Sus.): ἔχων.
[6] μικρῶν add. Sus. [7] Sp.: οὔτε.

[a] Or, emending the text, 'and is as worthy as he claims to be.'

himself worthy[a]: he is praiseworthy, and he is in
15 the middle between the two. Since, therefore, greatness of spirit is the best disposition in relation to the
choice and the employment of honour and of the other
good things that are esteemed, and not in relation
to useful things, and since we assign this to the
great-spirited man, and since also at the same time
the middle state is most praiseworthy, it is clear that
even greatness of spirit must be a middle state.
16 And of the opposites as shown in our diagram, the Vanity.
one in the direction of deeming oneself worthy of
great goods when one is not worthy is vanity (for
the sort of men that fancy themselves worthy of
great things though they are not we call vain), and
the one that is concerned with not deeming oneself
worthy of great things when one is worthy of them
is smallness of spirit (for if a man does not think
himself worthy of anything great although he possesses qualities which would justly make him considered worthy of it, he is thought small-spirited);
so that it follows that greatness of spirit is a middle
17 state between vanity and smallness of spirit. But Modest Self-esteem.
the fourth of the persons in our classification is
neither entirely reprehensible nor is he great-
spirited, as he is concerned with nothing possessing
greatness, for he neither is nor thinks himself worthy
of great things; owing to which he is not the opposite of the man of great spirit. Yet thinking
oneself worthy of small things when one is worthy
of small things might be thought the opposite of
thinking oneself worthy of great ones when one is
18 worthy of great ones; but he is not opposite to the
great-spirited man because he is not blameworthy

1233 a λόγος κελεύει ἔχει· καὶ ὁ αὐτός ἐστι τῇ φύσει τῷ
μεγαλοψύχῳ· ὧν γὰρ ἄξιοι, τούτων ἀξιοῦσιν αὑτοὺς
ἄμφω. καὶ ὁ μὲν γένοιτ' ἂν μεγαλόψυχος, ἀξιώσει 19
γὰρ ὧν ἐστὶν ἄξιος· ὁ δὲ μικρόψυχος, ὃς ὑπαρχόντων αὐτῷ μεγάλων κατὰ τιμὴν ἀγαθῶν οὐκ
ἀξιοῖ, τί ἂν ἐποίει[1] εἰ μικρῶν ἄξιος ἦν; ἢ[2] γὰρ
ἂν[3] μεγάλων ἀξιῶν χαῦνος ἦν,[4] ἢ ἔτι ἐλαττόνων.
διὸ καὶ οὐθεὶς ἂν εἴποι μικρόψυχον εἴ τις μέτοικος 20
ὢν ἄρχειν μὴ ἀξιοῖ ἑαυτὸν ἀλλ' ὑπείκει, ἀλλ' εἴ
τις εὐγενὴς ὢν καὶ ἡγούμενος μέγα εἶναι τὸ ἄρχειν.
VI. Ἔστι δὲ καὶ ὁ μεγαλοπρεπὴς οὐ περὶ τὴν 1
τυχοῦσαν πρᾶξιν καὶ προαίρεσιν, ἀλλὰ τὴν δαπάνην,[5] εἰ μή που κατὰ μεταφορὰν λέγομεν· ἄνευ
δὲ δαπάνης μεγαλοπρέπεια οὐκ ἔστιν, τὸ μὲν γὰρ
πρέπον ἐν κόσμῳ ἐστίν, ὁ δὲ κόσμος οὐκ ἐκ τῶν
τυχόντων ἀναλωμάτων, ἀλλ' ἐν ὑπερβολῇ τῶν
ἀναγκαίων ἐστίν. ὁ δὴ ἐν μεγάλῃ δαπάνῃ τοῦ 2
πρέποντος μεγέθους προαιρετικός, καὶ τῆς τοιαύτης
μεσότητος καὶ ἐπὶ τῇ τοιαύτῃ ἡδονῇ[6] ὀρεκτικός,
μεγαλοπρεπής. ὁ δ' ἐπὶ τὸ μεῖζον καὶ παρὰ μέλος 3
1233 b ἀνώνυμος· οὐ μὴν ἀλλ' ἔχουσι[7] τινὰ γειτνίασιν
οὓς καλοῦσί τινες ἀπειροκάλους καὶ σαλάκωνας.

[1] Γ: εἴποι. [2] Mᵇ: εἰ Pᵇ.
[3] ἂν om. Mᵇ: εἰ γὰρ μεγάλων ἀξιῶν <αὐτὸν ἀνάξιον> ὢν Sp.
[4] post ἦν lacunam Sus.
[5] ἀλλὰ τὴν δαπάνην infra post λέγομεν Ric.
[6] δαπάνῃ? Ric. [7] Cas.: ἔχει.

[a] The MS. reading hardly gives a sense. An emendation gives 'for if he conceitedly thought himself worthy of great things when unworthy,' and supposes a gap in the text before the following words.

[b] A probable emendation substitutes 'expenditure' for 'pleasure.'

[c] The MS. text gives 'he has a certain set of neighbours

either, for his character is as reason bids, and in nature he is the same as the great-spirited man, for both claim as their desert the things that they are
19 worthy of. And he might become great-spirited, for he will claim the things that he is worthy of; whereas the small-spirited man, who when great goods corresponding to his worth are available does not think himself worthy of them,—what would he have done if his deserts were small? For either he would have conceitedly thought himself worthy of
20 great things, or of still less.[a] Hence nobody would call a man small-spirited for not claiming to hold office and submitting to authority if he is a resident alien, but one would do so if he were of noble birth and attached great importance to office.

Mean-spiritedness.

1 VI. The Magnificent Man also (except in a case when we are using the term metaphorically) is not concerned with any and every action and purposive choice, but with expenditure. Without expenditure there is no magnificence, for it is what is appropriate in ornament, and ornament does not result from any chance expenditure, but consists in going
2 beyond the merely necessary. Therefore the magnificent man is the man who purposively chooses the appropriate greatness in great expenditure, and who even on the occasion of a pleasure[b] of this
3 nature aims at this sort of moderation. There is no name denoting the man who likes spending to excess and inappropriately; however the persons whom some people call tasteless and swaggering have a certain affinity to him.[c] For instance if a

Magnificence.

Its excess and defect.

whom some people call . . .': but γειτνίασις is abstract at 1232 a 21 and *Pol.* i., 1257 a 2. Its concrete use in later Greek, 'neighbourhood' = 'set of neighbours' (Plutarch, etc.) has led to corruption here.

1233 b
οἷον εἰ εἰς γάμον δαπανῶν τις τοῦ ἀγαπητοῦ,
πλούσιος ὤν, δοκεῖ πρέπειν ἑαυτῷ τοιαύτην κατασκευὴν οἵαν[1] ἀγαθοδαιμονιστὰς ἑστιῶντι, οὗτος
μὲν μικροπρεπής, ὁ δὲ τοιούτους δεχόμενος ἐκείνως
μὴ δόξης χάριν μηδὲ δι' ἐξουσίαν ὅμοιος τῷ
σαλάκωνι, ὁ δὲ κατ' ἀξίαν καὶ ὡς ὁ λόγος μεγαλο-
πρεπής· τὸ γὰρ πρέπον κατ' ἀξίαν ἐστίν· οὐθὲν
γὰρ πρέπει τῶν παρὰ τὴν ἀξίαν. δεῖ δὲ πρέπον 4
⟨καθ' ἕκαστον⟩[2] εἶναι· καὶ γὰρ τοῦ πράττοντος[3]
κατ' ἀξίαν, καὶ περὶ ὅν[4] καὶ περὶ ὅ, οἷον περὶ οἰκέτου
γάμον ἕτερον τὸ πρέπον καὶ περὶ ἐρωμένου· καὶ
αὐτῷ, εἴπερ ἐστὶ[5] τοσοῦτον ἢ τοιοῦτον, οἷον τὴν
θεωρίαν οὐκ ᾤοντο[6] Θεμιστοκλεῖ πρέπειν ἣν ἐποιήσατο Ὀλυμπίαζε, διὰ τὴν προϋπάρξασαν ταπεινό-
τητα, ἀλλὰ Κίμωνι. ὁ δ' ὅπως ἔτυχεν ἔχων πρὸς 5
τὴν ἀξίαν οὐθεὶς[7] τούτων.

Καὶ ἐπ' ἐλευθεριότητος ὡσαύτως· ἔστι γάρ τις
οὔτ' ἐλευθέριος οὔτ' ἀνελεύθερος.[8]

VII. Σχεδὸν δὲ καὶ τῶν ἄλλων ἕκαστα τῶν περὶ 1
τὸ ἦθος ἐπαινετῶν καὶ ψεκτῶν τὰ μὲν ὑπερβολαὶ
τὰ δ' ἐλλείψεις τὰ δὲ μεσότητές εἰσι παθητικαί,
οἷον ὁ φθονερὸς καὶ ὁ[9] ἐπιχαιρέκακος. καθ' ἃς
γὰρ ἕξεις λέγονται, ὁ μὲν φθόνος τὸ λυπεῖσθαι ἐπὶ

[1] Rac.: οἷον.
[2] Iac.
[3] Bus.: πρέποντος.
[4] Iac.: καὶ πρέπον.
[5] ἐστὶ ? Iac.: ἐπὶ. (ἐστὶ τοσοῦτος καὶ τοιοῦτος, aut εἴπερ ἐστὶ τοσοῦτον καὶ τοιοῦτον tr. supra post 9 περὶ ὅ Ric.)
[6] Sp. (vel ᾤετο . . . comici nomine omisso): ᾤετο.
[7] οὐδεὶς Γ: ὁ οὐδεὶς.
[8] Cas.: τις ὡς ἐλευθέριος ὅταν ἐλεύθερος.
[9] ὁ add. Rac.

[a] *i.e.* persons who only drink the formal toast (' Here's to Good Luck '), with which dinner ended.

rich man spending money on the wedding of a favourite thinks it fitting for him to have the sort of arrangements that would be fitting when entertaining abstainers,[a] he is shabby, while one who entertains guests of that sort after the manner of a wedding feast, if he does not do it for the sake of reputation or to gain an office, resembles the swaggerer; but he that entertains suitably and as reason directs is magnificent, for the fitting is the suitable, as nothing is fitting that is unsuitable.
4 But it must be fitting in each particular, that is, in suitability to the agent and to the recipient and to the occasion—for example, what is fitting at the wedding of a servant is not what is fitting at that of a favourite; and it is fitting for the agent himself, if it is of an amount or quality suitable to him—for example people thought that the mission that Themistocles conducted to Olympia was not fitting for him, because of his former low station, but would
5 have been for Cimon.[b] But he who is casual in regard to the question of suitability is not in any of these classes.

Similarly in regard to liberality: a man may be neither liberal nor illiberal.

Moderate and praiseworthy States of Feeling.

1 VII. Generally speaking the other praiseworthy and blameworthy states of character also are excesses or deficiencies or middle states, but in respect of an emotion: for instance, the envious man and the malicious. For—to take the states of character after which they are named—Envy means being

[b] The story of Themistocles at the Olympic festival incurring disapproval by vying with Cimon in the splendour of his equipment and entertainments is told by Plutarch, *Vit. Them.* 5.

1233 b τοῖς κατ' ἀξίαν εὖ πράττουσίν ἐστιν, τὸ δὲ τοῦ ἐπιχαιρεκάκου πάθος ἐστὶν[1] αὐτὸ ἀνώνυμον, ἀλλ' ὁ ἔχων δῆλός ἐστι[2] τῷ χαίρειν[3] ταῖς παρὰ τὴν
ἀξίαν κακοπραγίαις· μέσος δὲ τούτων ὁ νεμεση- 2
τικός, καὶ ὃ ἐκάλουν οἱ ἀρχαῖοι τὴν νέμεσιν, τὸ λυπεῖσθαι μὲν ἐπὶ ταῖς παρὰ τὴν ἀξίαν κακοπραγίαις καὶ εὐπραγίαις, χαίρειν δ' ἐπὶ ταῖς ἀξίαις· διὸ καὶ θεὸν οἴονται εἶναι τὴν νέμεσιν.

Αἰδὼς δὲ μεσότης ἀναισχυντίας καὶ καταπλήξεως· 3
ὁ μὲν γὰρ μηδεμιᾶς φροντίζων δόξης ἀναίσχυντος, ὁ δὲ πάσης ὁμοίως καταπλήξ, ὁ δὲ τῆς τῶν φαινομένων ἐπιεικῶν αἰδήμων.

Φιλία δὲ μεσότης ἔχθρας καὶ κολακείας· ὁ μὲν 4
γὰρ εὐχερῶς ἅπαντα πρὸς τὰς ἐπιθυμίας ὁμιλῶν κόλαξ, ὁ δὲ πρὸς ἁπάσας ἀντικρούων ἀπεχθητικός, ὁ δὲ μὴ[4] πρὸς ἅπασαν ἡδονὴν μήτ' ἀκολουθῶν μήτ' ἀντιτείνων, ἀλλὰ πρὸς τὸ φαινόμενον βέλτιστον, φίλος.

Σεμνότης δὲ μεσότης αὐθαδείας καὶ ἀρεσκείας· 5
ὁ μὲν γὰρ μηδὲν πρὸς ἕτερον ζῶν ἀλλὰ[5] καταφρονητικὸς αὐθάδης, ὁ δὲ πάντα πρὸς ἄλλον καὶ[6] πάντων ἐλάττων ἄρεσκος, ὁ δὲ τὰ μὲν τὰ δὲ μή, καὶ πρὸς τοὺς ἀξίους οὕτως ἔχων, σεμνός.

Ὁ δ' ἀληθὴς καὶ ἁπλοῦς, ὃν καλοῦσιν αὐθέκαστον, 6
μέσος τοῦ εἴρωνος καὶ ἀλαζόνος· ὁ μὲν γὰρ ἐπὶ τὰ
1234 a χείρω καθ' αὑτοῦ ψευδόμενος μὴ ἀγνοῶν εἴρων, ὁ δ' ἐπὶ τὰ βελτίω ἀλαζών, ὁ δ' ὡς ἔχει, ἀληθὴς

[1] ἐστὶν Sp.: ἐπὶ τὸ. [2] ἐστι Cas.: ἐπὶ.
[3] ὁ χαίρων Ric. [4] μὴ Sp.: μήτε.
[5] ἀλλὰ Γ: om. codd. (nonnulli ἀκαταφρονητικὸς).
[6] καὶ Sp.: ἢ καί.

[a] The man who calls each thing itself, *i.e.* what it really is, calls a spade a spade.

pained at people who are deservedly prosperous, while the emotion of the malicious man is itself nameless, but the possessor of it is shown by his
2 feeling joy at undeserved adversities ; and midway between them is the righteously indignant man, and what the ancients called Righteous Indignation —feeling pain at undeserved adversities and prosperities and pleasure at those that are deserved ; hence the idea that Nemesis is a deity.

3 Modesty is a middle state between Shamelessness and Bashfulness : the man who pays regard to nobody's opinion is shameless, he who regards everybody's is bashful, he who regards the opinion of those who appear good is modest.

4 Friendliness is a middle state between Animosity and Flattery ; the man who accommodates himself readily to his associates' desires in everything is a flatterer, he who runs counter to them all shows animosity, he who neither falls in with nor resists every pleasure, but falls in with what seems to be the best, is friendly.

5 Dignity is a middle state between Self-will and Obsequiousness. A man who in his conduct pays no regard at all to another but is contemptuous is self-willed ; he who regards another in everything and is inferior to everybody is obsequious ; he who regards another in some things but not in others, and is regardful of persons worthy of regard, is dignified.

6 The truthful and sincere man, called 'downright,'[a] is midway between the dissembler and the charlatan. He that wittingly makes a false statement against himself that is depreciatory is a dissembler, he that exaggerates his merits is a charlatan, he that speaks

1234 a
καὶ καθ' Ὅμηρον πεπνυμένος· καὶ ὅλως ὁ μὲν φιλ-
αλήθης, οἱ δὲ φιλοψευδεῖς.[1]
Ἔστι δὲ καὶ ἡ εὐτραπελία μεσότης, καὶ ὁ εὐ- 7
τράπελος μέσος τοῦ ἀγροίκου καὶ δυστραπέλου
καὶ τοῦ βωμολόχου. ὥσπερ γὰρ περὶ τροφὴν ὁ
σικχὸς τοῦ παμφάγου διαφέρει τῷ ὁ μὲν μηθὲν ἢ
ὀλίγα καὶ χαλεπῶς προσίεσθαι, ὁ δὲ πάντα εὐχερῶς,
οὕτω καὶ ὁ ἄγροικος ἔχει πρὸς τὸν φορτικὸν καὶ
βωμολόχον· ὁ μὲν γὰρ οὐθὲν γελοῖον ἀλλ' ἢ[2] χαλεπῶς προσίεται, ὁ δὲ πάντα εὐχερῶς καὶ ἡδέως.
δεῖ δ' οὐδέτερον, ἀλλὰ τὰ μὲν τὰ δὲ μή, καὶ κατὰ
λόγον· οὗτος δ' ὁ[3] εὐτράπελος. ἡ δ' ἀπόδειξις ἡ 8
αὐτή· ἥ τε γὰρ εὐτραπελία ἡ τοιαύτη, καὶ μὴ ἣν
μεταφέροντες λέγομεν, ἐπιεικεστάτη ἕξις, καὶ ἡ
μεσότης ἐπαινετή, τὰ δ' ἄκρα ψεκτά. οὔσης δὲ
διττῆς τῆς εὐτραπελίας (ἡ μὲν γὰρ ἐν τῷ χαίρειν
ἐστὶ τῷ γελοίῳ, καὶ[4] τῷ εἰς αὐτὸν ἐὰν ᾖ τοιονδί,
ὧν ἓν καὶ τὸ σκῶμμά ἐστιν, ἡ δ' ἐν τῷ δύνασθαι
τοιαῦτα πορίζεσθαι), ἕτεραι μέν εἰσιν ἀλλήλων, ἀμφότεραι μέντοι μεσότητες· καὶ γὰρ ὁ δυνάμενος[5] 9
τοιαῦτα πορίζεσθαι ἐφ' οἵοις[6] ἡσθήσεται ὁ[7] εὖ
κρίνων κἂν εἰς αὐτὸν ᾖ τὸ γελοῖον, μέσος ἔσται
τοῦ φορτικοῦ καὶ τοῦ ψυχροῦ. ὁ δ' ὅρος οὗτος
βελτίων ἢ τὸ μὴ[8] λυπηρὸν εἶναι τὸ λεχθὲν τῷ σκω-
πτομένῳ ὄντι ὁποιῳοῦν· μᾶλλον γὰρ δεῖ τῷ ἐν
μεσότητι ὄντι ἀρέσκειν· οὗτος γὰρ κρίνει εὖ.

[1] Rac.: ὁ δὲ φιλοψευδής.
[2] ἀλλ' ἢ Rac. (ἢ Sp).: ἀλλά.
[3] ὁ add. Fr.
[4] καὶ <δὴ καὶ> ? Rac.
[5] Syl.: τὸν δυνάμενον.
[6] Rac.: ὅσοις.
[7] ὁ add. Fr.
[8] μὴ add. Cas.

[a] The term εὐτράπελος means literally 'able to turn easily,' versatile; it denotes both 'witty' and 'easy-going.'

of himself as he is is truthful and in Homer's phrase 'sagacious'; and in general the one is a lover of truth and the others lovers of falsehood.

7 Wittiness[a] also is a middle state, and the witty man is midway between the boorish or stiff man and the buffoon. For just as in the matter of food the squeamish man differs from the omnivorous in that the former takes nothing or little, and that reluctantly, and the latter accepts everything readily, so the boor stands in relation to the vulgar man or buffoon—the former takes no joke except with difficulty, the latter accepts everything easily and with pleasure. Neither course is right: one should allow some things and not others, and on principle,
8 —that constitutes the witty man. The proof of the formula is the same as in the other cases: wittiness of this kind (not the quality[b] to which we apply the term in a transferred sense) is a very becoming sort of character, and also a middle state is praiseworthy, whereas extremes are blameworthy. But as there are two kinds of wit (one consisting in liking a joke, even one that tells against oneself if it is funny, for instance a jeer, the other in the ability to produce things of this sort), these kinds of wit differ from one
9 another, but both are middle states; for a man who can produce jokes of a sort that will give pleasure to a person of good judgement even though the laugh is against himself will be midway between the vulgar man and the frigid. This is a better definition than that the thing said must not be painful to the victim whatever sort of man he may be—rather, it must give pleasure to the man in the middle position, since his judgement is good.

[b] Viz. βωμολοχία, 'buffoonery,' *N.E.* 1128 a 15.

1234 a
Πᾶσαι δ' αὗται αἱ μεσότητες ἐπαινεταὶ μέν, 10
οὐκ εἰσὶ δ' ἀρεταί, οὐδ' αἱ ἐναντίαι κακίαι, ἄνευ
προαιρέσεως γάρ· ταῦτα δὲ πάντ' ἐστὶν ἐν ταῖς
τῶν παθημάτων διαιρέσεσιν, ἕκαστον γὰρ αὐτῶν
πάθος τί ἐστιν. διὰ δὲ τὸ φυσικὰ εἶναι ἰς τὰς 11
φυσικὰς συμβάλλεται ἀρετάς· ἔστι γάρ, ὥσπερ
λεχθήσεται ἐν τοῖς ὕστερον, ἑκάστη πως ἀρετὴ
καὶ φύσει καὶ ἄλλως, μετὰ φρονήσεως. ὁ μὲν οὖν 12
φθόνος εἰς ἀδικίαν συμβάλλεται (πρὸς γὰρ ἄλλον
αἱ πράξεις αἱ ἀπ' αὐτοῦ) καὶ ἡ νέμεσις εἰς δικαιοσύνην καὶ[1] ἡ αἰδὼς εἰς σωφροσύνην (διὸ καὶ ὁρί-
ζονται ἐν τῷ γένει τούτῳ τὴν σωφροσύνην), ὁ δ'
ἀληθὴς καὶ ψευδὴς ὁ μὲν ἔμφρων ὁ δ' ἄφρων.
1234 b
Ἔστι δ' ἐναντιώτερον τοῖς ἄκροις τὸ μέσον ἢ 13
ἐκεῖνα ἀλλήλοις, διότι τὸ μὲν μετ' οὐδετέρου γίνεται αὐτῶν, τὰ δὲ πολλάκις μετ' ἀλλήλων, καὶ εἰσὶν
ἐνίοτε οἱ αὐτοὶ θρασύδειλοι, καὶ τὰ μὲν ἄσωτοι τὰ
δὲ ἀνελεύθεροι, καὶ ὅλως ἀνώμαλοι κακῶς· ὅταν μὲν 14
γὰρ καλῶς ἀνώμαλοι ὦσιν, μέσοι γίνονται, ἐν τῷ
μέσῳ γάρ ἐστί πως τὰ ἄκρα.
Αἱ δ' ἐναντιώσεις οὐ δοκοῦσιν ὑπάρχειν τοῖς
ἄκροις πρὸς τὸ μέσον ὁμοίως ἀμφότεραι, ἀλλ' ὁτὲ
μὲν καθ' ὑπερβολὴν ὁτὲ δὲ κατ' ἔλλειψιν. αἴτια 15
δὲ τά τε πρῶτα ῥηθέντα δύο, ὀλιγότης τε, οἷον
τῶν πρὸς τὰ ἡδέα ἀναισθήτων, καὶ ὅτι ἐφ' ὃ ἁμαρτάνομεν μᾶλλον, τοῦτο ἐναντιώτερον εἶναι δοκεῖ· τὸ 16

[1] καὶ add. Rac.

---

[a] Not in *E.E.*, but *cf.* *N.E.* vi., 1144 b 1-17.

[b] Truthfulness and mendacity contribute to wisdom and folly as νέμεσις and φθόνος do to δικαιοσύνη and ἀδικία, and αἰδώς (and ἀναιδεία) to σωφροσύνη (and ἀκολασία).

[c] *Cf.* 1222 a 22–b 4.

These praiseworthy States of Feeling promote the virtues.

10 None of these middle states, though praiseworthy,
are virtues, nor are the opposite states vices, for they
do not involve purposive choice ; they are all in the
classification of the emotions, for each of them is an
11 emotion. But because they are natural they contribute to the natural virtues ; for, as will be said
in what follows,[a] each virtue exists both naturally
and otherwise, that is, in conjunction with thought.
12 Therefore envy contributes to injustice (for the
actions that spring from it affect another person),
and righteous indignation to justice, and modesty to
temperance (owing to which people even define temperance as a species of emotion), and the sincere and
false are respectively wise and foolish.[b]

Extremes that meet.

13 And the mean is more opposed to the extremes
than the extremes are to one another, because the
mean does not occur in combination with either extreme, whereas the extremes often do occur in
combination with one another, and sometimes the
same men are venturesome cowards, or extravagant
in some things and illiberal in others, and in general
14 not uniform in a bad way—for when men lack uni-
formity in a good way, this results in men of the
middle characters, since the mean contains both
extremes.

Appendix to II. v. 4 ff.

The opposition existing between the mean and
the extremes does not seem to be the same in the
case of both the extremes, but sometimes the greater
opposition is by way of excess, sometimes by way
15 of deficiency. The causes of this are partly the two
first mentioned,[c] rarity (for example, the rarity of
people insensitive to pleasant things) and the fact
that the error to which we are more prone seems
16 more opposite to the mean, and thirdly the fact that

1234 b δὲ τρίτον, ὅτι τὸ ὁμοιότερον ἧττον ἐναντίον φαίνεται, οἷον πέπονθε τὸ θράσος πρὸς τὸ θάρσος[1] καὶ ἀσωτία πρὸς ἐλευθεριότητα.

Περὶ μὲν οὖν τῶν ἄλλων ἀρετῶν τῶν ἐπαινετῶν εἴρηται σχεδόν, περὶ δὲ δικαιοσύνης ἤδη λεκτέον.

[1] τὸ θάρσος πρὸς τὸ θράσος Mb (sed cf. 1220 b 39): τὸ θάρσος (potius θράσος Rac.) πρὸς τὴν ἀνδρείαν Bz.

[a] Or, 'confidence'; but perhaps the Greek should be altered to give 'courage.'

the extreme that more resembles the mean seems less opposite to it, as is the case with daring in relation to boldness [a] and extravagance in relation to liberality.

We have therefore sufficiently discussed the other praiseworthy virtues, and must now speak about Justice.

(Books IV, V, VI are omitted, as they are identical with Books V, VI, VII of the *Nicomachean Ethics*.)

H

1234 b

I. Περὶ φιλίας, τί ἐστι καὶ ποῖόν τι, καὶ τίς ὁ 1
φίλος, καὶ πότερον ἡ φιλία μοναχῶς λέγεται ἢ
πλεοναχῶς, καὶ εἰ πλεοναχῶς, πόσα ἐστίν,[1] ἔτι δὲ
πῶς χρηστέον τῷ φίλῳ καὶ τί τὸ δίκαιον τὸ φιλικόν,
ἐπισκεπτέον οὐθενὸς ἧττον τῶν περὶ τὰ ἤθη καλῶν
καὶ αἱρετῶν. τῆς τε γὰρ πολιτικῆς ἔργον εἶναι 2
δοκεῖ μάλιστα ποιῆσαι φιλίαν, καὶ τὴν ἀρετὴν διὰ
τοῦτό φασιν εἶναι χρήσιμον· οὐ γὰρ ἐνδέχεσθαι
φίλους ἑαυτοῖς εἶναι τοὺς ἀδικουμένους ὑπ' ἀλλήλων. ἔτι τὸ δίκαιον καὶ τὸ ἄδικον περὶ τοὺς φίλους 3
εἶναι μάλιστα πάντες φαμέν, καὶ ὁ αὐτὸς δοκεῖ
ἀνὴρ εἶναι καὶ ἀγαθὸς καὶ φίλος, καὶ φιλία ἠθική
τις εἶναι ἕξις· καὶ ἐάν τις βούληται ποιῆσαι[2] ὥστε
μὴ ἀδικεῖν, ἄλις[3] φίλους ποιῆσαι, οἱ γὰρ ἀληθινοὶ
φίλοι οὐκ ἀδικοῦσιν. ἀλλὰ μὴν καὶ ἐὰν δίκαιοι 4
ὦσιν, οὐκ ἀδικήσουσιν· ἢ ταὐτὸν ἄρα ἢ ἐγγύς τι ἡ
δικαιοσύνη καὶ ἡ φιλία. πρὸς δὲ τούτοις τῶν 5
μεγίστων ἀγαθῶν τὸν φίλον εἶναι ὑπολαμβάνομεν,
τὴν δὲ ἀφιλίαν καὶ τὴν ἐρημίαν δεινότατον, ὅτι ὁ
1235 a βίος ἅπας καὶ ἡ ἑκούσιος ὁμιλία μετὰ τούτων· μετ'
οἰκείων γὰρ ἢ μετὰ συγγενῶν ἢ μεθ' ἑταίρων

[1] πόσαι εἰσίν Sp.: ποσαχῶς ? Rac. (ποσαχῶς ἐστίν vel πόσα ἐστὶν <εἴδη> Bz.).

[2] πεῖσαι ? Ric.

[3] ἄλις Iac.: ἀλλ' εἰς. (ἄλλους, φίλους ποιήσει Sp., ἄλλους φίλους ποιῆσαι δεῖν Fr.)

BOOK VII

1 I. Friendship—its nature and qualities, what constitutes a friend, and whether the term friendship has one or several meanings, and if several, how many, and also what is our duty towards a friend and what are the just claims of friendship—is a matter that calls for investigation no less than any of the things that are fine and desirable in men's
2 characters. For to promote friendship is thought to be the special task of the art of government; and people say that it is on this account that goodness is a valuable thing, for persons wrongfully treated by one another cannot be each other's friends.
3 Furthermore we all say that justice and injustice are chiefly displayed towards friends; it is thought that a good man is a friendly man, and that friendship is a state of the moral character; and if one wishes to make men not act unjustly, it is enough to make them friends, for true friends do not wrong one
4 another. But neither will men act unjustly if they are just; therefore justice and friendship are either
5 the same or nearly the same thing. In addition to this, we consider a friend to be one of the greatest goods, and friendlessness and solitude a very terrible thing, because the whole of life and voluntary association is with friends; for we pass our days with our

FRIENDSHIP. Its nature and value.

(a) (b) (c)

1235 a

συνδιημερεύομεν, ἢ τέκνων ἢ γονέων ἢ γυναικός. καὶ τὰ ἴδια δίκαια τὰ πρὸς τοὺς φίλους ἐστὶν ἐφ' ἡμῖν μόνον, τὰ δὲ πρὸς τοὺς ἄλλους νενομοθέτηται καὶ οὐκ ἐφ' ἡμῖν.

Ἀπορεῖται δὲ πολλὰ περὶ τῆς φιλίας, πρῶτον μὲν 7
ὡς οἱ ἔξωθεν περιλαμβάνοντες καὶ ἐπὶ πλέον λέγοντες. δοκεῖ γὰρ τοῖς μὲν τὸ ὅμοιον τῷ ὁμοίῳ εἶναι φίλον, ὅθεν εἴρηται

ὡς αἰεὶ τὸν ὅμοιον ἄγει θεὸς ὡς τὸν ὅμοιον·
καὶ γὰρ κολοιὸς παρὰ κολοιόν . . .
ἔγνω δὲ φώρ τε φῶρα καὶ λύκος λύκον.

οἱ δὲ φυσιολόγοι καὶ τὴν ὅλην φύσιν διακοσμοῦσιν 8
ἀρχὴν λαβόντες τὸ τὸ ὅμοιον ἰέναι πρὸς τὸ ὅμοιον, διὸ Ἐμπεδοκλῆς καὶ τὴν κύν' ἔφη καθῆσθαι ἐπὶ τῆς κεραμίδος διὰ τὸ ἔχειν πλεῖστον ὅμοιον.

Οἱ μὲν οὖν οὕτω τὸν[1] φίλον λέγουσιν· οἱ δὲ τὸ 9
ἐναντίον τῷ ἐναντίῳ φασὶν εἶναι φίλον, τὸ μὲν γὰρ ἐρώμενον καὶ ἐπιθυμητὸν πᾶσιν εἶναι φίλον, ἐπιθυμεῖν[2] δὲ οὐ τὸ ξηρὸν τοῦ ξηροῦ ἀλλὰ τοῦ[3] ὑγροῦ (ὅθεν εἴρηται

ἐρᾷ μὲν ὄμβρου γαῖα,

καὶ τὸ

μεταβολὴ πάντων γλυκύ·

[1] v.l. τό. [2] Fr.: ἐπιθυμεῖ. [3] τοῦ add. M^b.

[a] *Od.* xvii. 218.

[b] 'Birds of a feather flock together.' *Sc.* ἱζάνει, 'perches': an iambic verse quoted in full *M.M.* 1208 b 9, and in the form κολοιὸν ποτὶ κολοιόν *N.E.* viii., 1155 a 35, where the dialect suggests that it is from a Doric poet (unknown).

family or relations or comrades, children, parents or
6 wife. And our private right conduct towards our friends depends only on ourselves, whereas right actions in relation to the rest of men are established by law and do not depend on us. (*d*)

7 Many questions are raised about friendship—first, on the line of those who take in wider considerations and extend the term. For some hold that like is friend to like, whence the sayings :

Is friendship based on likeness?

> Mark how God ever brings like men together[a];
> For jackdaw by the side of jackdaw . . .[b];
> And thief knows thief and wolf his fellow wolf.[c]

8 And the natural philosophers even arrange the whole of nature in a system by assuming as a first principle that like goes to like, owing to which Empedocles[d] said that the dog sits on the tiling because it is most like him.[e]

9 Some people then give this account of a friend ; but others say that opposite is dear to opposite, since it is what is loved and desired that is dear to everybody, and the dry does not desire the dry but the wet (whence the sayings—

or on contrast?

> Earth loveth rain,[f]

and

> In all things change is sweet—[g]

[c] 'Set a thief to catch a thief.' The origin of the verse is unknown.

[d] Mystic philosopher, man of science and statesman of Agrigentum (Girgenti), *fl.* 490 B.C.

[e] Presumably, like in colour ; true of Greek dogs to-day. Empedocles does not appear to have gone on to infer protective mimicry.

[f] Quoted as from Euripides, *N.E.* viii., 1155 a 34 ; the play is not known.

[g] Euripides, *Orestes* 234.

1235 a
ἡ δὲ μεταβολὴ εἰς τοὐναντίον)· τὸ δ' ὅμοιον ἐχθρὸν
τῷ ὁμοίῳ, καὶ γὰρ

κεραμεὺς κεραμεῖ κοτέει,

καὶ τὰ ἀπὸ τῶν αὐτῶν τρεφόμενα πολέμια ἀλλήλοις
ζῷα. αὗται μὲν οὖν αἱ ὑπολήψεις τοσοῦτον δι- 10
εστᾶσιν· οἱ[1] μὲν γὰρ τὸ ὅμοιον φίλον,[2] τὸ δ' ἐναντίον
πολέμιον—

τῷ πλέονι δ' αἰεὶ πολέμιον καθίσταται
τοὔλασσον, ἔχθρας θ' ἡμέρας κατάρχεται,

ἔτι δὲ καὶ οἱ τόποι κεχωρισμένοι τῶν ἐναντίων, ἡ 11
δὲ φιλία δοκεῖ συνάγειν· οἱ δὲ τὰ ἐναντία φίλα, καὶ
Ἡράκλειτος ἐπιτιμᾷ τῷ ποιήσαντι

ὡς ἔρις ἔκ τε θεῶν κἀξ[3] ἀνθρώπων ἀπόλοιτο,

οὐ γὰρ ἂν εἶναι ἁρμονίαν μὴ ὄντος ὀξέος καὶ βαρέος,
οὐδὲ τὰ ζῷα ἄνευ θήλεος καὶ ἄρρενος ἐναντίων
ὄντων.

Δύο μὲν οὖν[4] αὗται δόξαι περὶ φιλίας εἰσί, λίαν 12
τε καθόλου κεχωρισμέναι[5] τοσοῦτον, ἄλλαι δὲ ἤδη
ἐγγυτέρω[6] καὶ οἰκειότεραι[7] τῶν φαινομένων. τοῖς
μὲν γὰρ οὐκ ἐνδέχεσθαι δοκεῖ τοὺς φαύλους εἶναι
φίλους, ἀλλὰ μόνον τοὺς ἀγαθούς· τοῖς δ' ἄτοπον
εἰ μὴ φιλοῦσιν αἱ μητέρες τὰ τέκνα (φαίνεται 13
δ' ἥδε[8] καὶ ἐν τοῖς θηρίοις ἐνοῦσα φιλία· προαπο-
θνήσκειν γοῦν[9] αἱροῦνται τῶν τέκνων). τοῖς δὲ τὸ 14
χρήσιμον δοκεῖ φίλον εἶναι μόνον· σημεῖον δ' ὅτι

[1] Fr.: αἱ.
[2] φίλον <φασὶ> vel <οἴονται> Ric.
[3] Rac.: καὶ (ἔκ τ' *Il.* xviii. 107).
[4] οὖν add. Sus.
[5] καὶ κεχωρισμέναι Cas.
[6] ἐγγύτεραι M^b.
[7] οἰκειότεραι Rac.: οἰκεῖαι.
[8] δ' ἥδε Rac.: δὲ (γὰρ Γ).
[9] Fr.: οὖν.

change being transition to the opposite), whereas like hates like, for

Potter 'gainst potter hath a grudge,[a]

and animals that live on the same food are hostile
10 to one another. These opinions, therefore, are thus widely variant. One party thinks that the like is friend and the opposite foe—

The less is rooted enemy to the more
For ever, and begins the day of hate,[b]

11 and moreover adversaries are separated in locality, whereas friendship seems to bring men together. The other party say that opposites are friends, and Heracleitus[c] rebukes the poet who wrote—

Would strife might perish out of heaven and earth,[d]

for, he says, there would be no harmony without high and low notes, and no animals without male and female, which are opposites.

12 These, then, are two opinions about friendship, and being so widely separated they are too general[e]; but there are others that are closer together and more akin to the facts of observation. Some persons think that it is not possible for bad men to be friends, but only for the good. Others think it strange that *or on virtue?*
13 mothers should not love their own children (and maternal affection we see existing even among animals—at least, animals deliberately die for their
14 young). Others hold that only what is useful is a friend, the proof being that all men actually do *or on utility?*

[a] Hesiod, *Works and Days* 25 ('Two of a trade never agree').

[b] Euripides, *Phoenissae* 539 f. (ἐχθρᾶς ἡμέρας = ἔχθρας, *cf.* δούλιον ἦμαρ = δουλεία, Paley).

[c] The natural philosopher of Ephesus, *fl.* end of 6th cent. B.C.

[d] *Iliad* xviii. 107.

[e] *i.e.* being so absolutely opposite to one another, they are too sweeping, and do not really correspond with the facts.

1235 a καὶ διώκουσι ταῦτα πάντες, τὰ δὲ ἄχρηστα καὶ
αὐτοὶ αὑτῶν[1] ἀποβάλλουσιν (ὥσπερ Σωκράτης ὁ
γέρων ἔλεγε τὸν πτύελον καὶ τὰς τρίχας καὶ τοὺς
ὄνυχας παραβάλλων), καὶ[2] τὰ μόρια ὅτι ῥιπτοῦμεν
1235 b τὰ ἄχρηστα, καὶ τέλος τὸ σῶμα, ὅταν ἀποθάνῃ,
ἄχρηστος γὰρ ὁ νεκρός· οἷς δὲ χρήσιμον, φυλάτ-
τουσιν, ὥσπερ ἐν Αἰγύπτῳ. ταῦτα δὴ πάντα δοκεῖ 15
μὲν ὑπεναντία ἀλλήλοις εἶναι. τό τε γὰρ ὅμοιον[3]
ἄχρηστον τῷ ὁμοίῳ καὶ ἐναντιότης ὁμοιότητος
ἀπέχει πλεῖστον, καὶ τὸ ἐναντίον ἀχρηστότατον τῷ
ἐναντίῳ, φθαρτικὸν γὰρ τοῦ ἐναντίου τὸ ἐναντίον.
ἔτι δοκεῖ τοῖς μὲν ῥᾴδιον τὸ κτήσασθαι φίλον, τοῖς 16
δὲ σπανιώτατον γνῶναι, καὶ οὐκ ἐνδέχεσθαι ἄνευ
ἀτυχίας[4], τοῖς γὰρ εὖ πράττουσι βούλονται πάντες
δοκεῖν φίλοι εἶναι· οἱ δ' οὐδὲ τοῖς συνδιαμένουσιν 17
ἐν ταῖς ἀτυχίαις ἀξιοῦσι πιστεύειν, ὡς ἐξαπα-
τῶντας καὶ προσποιουμένους, ἵνα κτήσωνται διὰ
τῆς τῶν ἀτυχούντων ὁμιλίας πάλιν εὐτυχούντων
φιλίαν.

II. Ληπτέος δὴ λόγος[5] ὅστις ἡμῖν ἅμα τά τε 1
δοκοῦντα περὶ τούτων μάλιστα ἀποδώσει καὶ τὰς
ἀπορίας λύσει καὶ τὰς ἐναντιώσεις. τοῦτο δ' ἔσται
ἐὰν εὐλόγως φαίνηται τὰ ἐναντία δοκοῦντα. μάλιστα
γὰρ ὁμολογούμενος ὁ τοιοῦτος ἔσται λόγος τοῖς
φαινομένοις· συμβαίνει δὲ μένειν τὰς ἐναντιώσεις
ἐὰν ἔστι μὲν ὡς ἀληθὲς ᾖ τὸ λεγόμενον ἔστι δ'
ὡς οὔ.

Ἔχει δ' ἀπορίαν καὶ πότερον τὸ ἡδὺ ἢ τὸ ἀγαθόν 2

[1] ἀφ' ἑαυτῶν Iac. [2] [καὶ] ? Rac.
[3] ὅμοιον add. Fr. [4] Vict.: εὐτυχίας.
[5] Cas.: λοιπὸς. (λοιπὸς <λόγος> Sp., τρόπος Syl.)

pursue the useful, and discard what is useless even
in their own persons (as the old Socrates [a] used to
say, instancing spittle, hair and nails), and that we
throw away even parts of the body that are of no
use, and finally the body itself, when it dies, as a
corpse is useless—but people that have a use for it
15 keep it, as in Egypt. Now all these factors [b] seem
to be somewhat opposed to one another. For like
is of no use to like and opposition is farthest
removed from likeness, and at the same time opposite is most useless to opposite, since opposite is
16 destructive of opposite. Moreover some think that Is it
to gain a friend is easy, but others that it is the frequent?
rarest thing to recognize a friend, and not possible
without misfortune, as everybody wants to be thought
17 a friend of the prosperous; and others maintain
that we must not trust even those who stay with us
in our misfortunes, because they are deceiving us
and pretending, in order that by associating with
us when unfortunate they may gain our friendship
when we are again prosperous.

1 II. Accordingly a line of argument must be taken
that will best explain to us the views held on these
matters and at the same time solve the difficulties
and contradictions. And this will be secured if the
contradictory views are shown to be held with some
reason. For such a line of argument will be most
in agreement with the observed facts: and in the
upshot, if what is said is true in one sense but not
true in another, both the contradictory views stand
good.

2 There is also a question as to whether what is Friendship
is based on

[a] *Cf.* 1216 b 3.

[b] *i.e.* likeness, contrariety, utility (Solomon).

1235 b

ἔστι τὸ φιλούμενον. εἰ μὲν γὰρ φιλοῦμεν οὗ ἐπιθυμοῦμεν (καὶ μάλιστα ὁ ἔρως τοιοῦτον, οὐδεὶς γὰρ

ἐραστὴς ὅστις οὐκ ἀεὶ φιλεῖ),

ἡ δ' ἐπιθυμία τοῦ ἡδέος, ταύτῃ μὲν τὸ φιλούμενον
τὸ ἡδύ, εἰ δὲ ὃ βουλόμεθα, τὸ ἀγαθόν· ἔστι δ'
ἕτερον τὸ ἡδὺ καὶ τὸ ἀγαθόν.

Περὶ δὴ[1] τούτων καὶ τῶν ἄλλων τῶν συγγενῶν 3
τούτοις πειρατέον διορίσαι, λαβοῦσιν ἀρχὴν τήνδε.
τὸ γὰρ ὀρεκτὸν καὶ βουλητὸν ἢ τὸ ἀγαθὸν ἢ τὸ
φαινόμενον ἀγαθόν. διὸ καὶ τὸ ἡδὺ ὀρεκτόν, φαινόμενον
γάρ τι ἀγαθόν· τοῖς μὲν γὰρ δοκεῖ, τοῖς
δὲ φαίνεται κἂν μὴ δοκῇ (οὐ γὰρ ἐν ταὐτῷ τῆς
ψυχῆς ἡ φαντασία καὶ ἡ δόξα). ὅτι μέντοι φίλον
καὶ τὸ ἀγαθὸν καὶ τὸ ἡδὺ δῆλον.

Τούτου δὲ διωρισμένου ληπτέον ὑπόθεσιν ἑτέραν. 4
τῶν γὰρ ἀγαθῶν τὰ μὲν ἁπλῶς ἐστὶν ἀγαθά, τὰ δὲ
τινί, ἁπλῶς δ' οὔ· καὶ τὰ αὐτὰ ἁπλῶς ἀγαθὰ καὶ
ἁπλῶς ἡδέα. τὰ μὲν γὰρ τῷ ὑγιαίνοντί φαμεν
σώματι συμφέροντα ἁπλῶς εἶναι σώματι ἀγαθά, τὰ
δὲ τῷ κάμνοντι οὔ, οἷον φαρμακείας καὶ τομάς·
ὁμοίως δὲ καὶ ἡδέα ἁπλῶς σώματι τὰ τῷ ὑγιαίνοντι 5
καὶ ὁλοκλήρῳ, οἷον τὸ ἐν τῷ φωτὶ ζῆν[2] καὶ οὐ τὸ
ἐν τῷ σκότει· καίτοι τῷ ὀφθαλμιῶντι ἐναντίως.
καὶ οἶνος ἡδίων οὐχ ὁ τῷ διεφθαρμένῳ τὴν γλῶτταν
ὑπὸ οἰνοφλυγίας, ἐπεὶ ἐνίοτε[3] ὄξος παρεγχέουσιν,

[1] Sus.: δὲ Pᵇ, om. Mᵇ.
[2] Iac. (cf. *Hist. An.* 488 a 26 τὰ μὲν νυκτερόβια . . . τὰ δ' ἐν τῷ φωτὶ ζῇ): ὁρᾶν.
[3] Ric.: οὔτε.

[a] Euripides, *Troades* 1051.
[b] *i.e.* are different psychological experiences.

dear to us is the pleasant or the good. If we hold dear what we *desire* (and that is specially characteristic of love, for

both goodness and pleasantness (absolute or relative).

None lover is that loveth not for aye [a]),

and desire is for what is pleasant, on this showing it is the pleasant that is dear ; whereas if we hold dear what we *wish*, it is the good ; but the pleasant and the good are different things.

3 We must therefore attempt to decide about these matters and others akin to them, taking as a starting-point the following. The thing desired and wished is either the good or the apparent good. Therefore also the pleasant is desired, for it is an apparent good, since some people think it good, and to others it appears good even though they do not think it so (as appearance and opinion are not in the same part of the spirit).[b] Yet it is clear that both the good and the pleasant are dear.

4 This being decided, we must make another assumption. Things good are some of them absolutely good, others good for someone but not good absolutely ; and the same things are absolutely good and absolutely pleasant. For things advantageous for a healthy body we pronounce good for the body absolutely, but things good for a sick body not—for example doses of medicine and surgical operations ;
5 and likewise also the things pleasant for a healthy and perfect body are pleasant for the body absolutely, for example to live in the light and not in the dark, although the reverse is the case for a man with ophthalmia. And the pleasanter wine is not the wine pleasant to a man whose palate has been corrupted by tippling, since sometimes they pour

1236 a ἀλλὰ τῇ ἀδιαφθόρῳ αἰσθήσει. ὁμοίως δὲ καὶ ἐπὶ 6
ψυχῆς, καὶ οὐχ ἃ τοῖς παιδίοις καὶ τοῖς θηρίοις,
ἀλλ' ἃ τοῖς καθεστῶσιν· ἀμφοτέρων γοῦν μεμνη-
μένοι ταῦθ' αἱρούμεθα. ὡς δ' ἔχει παιδίον καὶ 7
θηρίον πρὸς ἄνθρωπον καθεστῶτα, οὕτως ἔχει ὁ
φαῦλος καὶ ἄφρων πρὸς τὸν ἐπιεικῆ καὶ φρόνιμον·
τούτοις δὲ ἡδέα τὰ κατὰ τὰς ἕξεις, ταῦτα δ' ἐστὶ
τὰ ἀγαθὰ καὶ τὰ καλά.

'Επεὶ οὖν τὸ ἀγαθὸν[1] πλεοναχῶς (τὸ μὲν γὰρ τῷ 8
τοιόνδ' εἶναι λέγομεν ἀγαθόν, τὸ δὲ τῷ ὠφέλιμον
καὶ χρήσιμον), ἔτι δὲ[2] τὸ ἡδὺ τὸ μὲν ἁπλῶς καὶ
ἀγαθὸν ἁπλῶς, τὸ δὲ τινὶ καὶ[3] φαινόμενον ἀγαθόν,
ὥσπερ καὶ ἐπὶ τῶν ἀψύχων δι' ἕκαστον τούτων
ἐνδέχεται ἡμᾶς αἱρεῖσθαί τι καὶ φιλεῖν, οὕτω[4] καὶ
ἄνθρωπον· τὸν μὲν γὰρ ὅτι τοιόσδε[5] καὶ δι' ἀρετήν,
τὸν δ' ὅτι ὠφέλιμος καὶ χρήσιμος, τὸν δ' ὅτι ἡδὺς
καὶ δι' ἡδονήν. φίλος δὲ[6] γίνεται ὅταν φιλούμενος
ἀντιφιλῇ καὶ τοῦτο μὴ λανθάνῃ πως αὐτούς.

'Ανάγκη ἄρα τρία φιλίας εἴδη εἶναι, καὶ μήτε 9
καθ' ἓν ἁπάσας μηδ'[7] ὡς εἴδη ἑνὸς γένους μήτε
πάμπαν λέγεσθαι ὁμωνύμως. πρὸς μίαν γάρ τινα
λέγονται καὶ πρώτην, ὥσπερ τὸ ἰατρικόν, καὶ ψυχὴν
ἰατρικὴν καὶ σῶμα λέγομεν καὶ ὄργανον καὶ ἔργον,

[1] Sp.: τὰ ἀγαθά.
[2] ἔτι δὲ Bz.: ἐπεὶ δὲ P^b, ἐπεὶ M^b.
[3] καὶ Beier: ᾗ (om. Γ).
[4] οὕτω Bz.: ὥσπερ.
[5] Ric.: τὸν μὲν γὰρ τοιόνδε.
[6] Iac.: δή.
[7] Sus.: μήθ'.

in a dash of vinegar, but to the uncorrupted taste.
6 And similarly also in the case of the spirit, the really pleasant things are not those pleasant to children and animals, but those pleasant to the adult; at least it is these that we prefer when we remember
7 both. And as a child or animal stands to an adult human being, so the bad and foolish man stands to the good and wise man; and these take pleasure in things that correspond to their characters, and these are things good and fine.

8 Since therefore good is a term of more than one meaning (for we call one thing good because that is its essential nature, but another because it is serviceable and useful), and furthermore pleasant includes both what is absolutely pleasant and absolutely good and what is pleasant for somebody and apparently good—, as in the case of inanimate objects we may choose a thing and love it for each of these reasons, so also in the case of a human being, one man we love because of his character, and for goodness, another because he is serviceable and useful, another because he is pleasant, and for pleasure. And a man becomes a friend when while receiving affection he returns it, and when he and the other are in some way aware of this.

Definition of friend.

9 It follows, therefore, that there are three sorts of friendship, and that they are not all so termed in respect of one thing or as species of one genus, nor yet have they the same name entirely by accident. For all these uses of the term are related to one particular sort of friendship which is primary—as with the term 'surgical,'—we speak of a surgical mind and a surgical hand and a surgical instrument and a surgical operation, but we apply the term

Three kinds of Friendship,

1236 a ἀλλὰ κυρίως τὸ πρῶτον. πρῶτον δ' οὗ ὁ[1] λόγος 10
ἐν πᾶσιν[2] ὑπάρχει, οἷον ὄργανον ἰατρικὸν ᾧ ἂν ὁ
ἰατρὸς χρήσαιτο, ἐν δὲ τῷ τοῦ ἰατροῦ λόγῳ οὐκ
ἔστιν ὁ τοῦ ὀργάνου. ζητεῖται μὲν οὖν πανταχοῦ 11
τὸ πρῶτον, διὰ δὲ τὸ τὸ καθόλου εἶναι[3] πρῶτον
λαμβάνουσι καὶ τὸ[4] πρῶτον καθόλου· τοῦτο δ'
ἐστὶ ψεῦδος. ὥστε καὶ περὶ τῆς φιλίας οὐ δύνανται
πάντ' ἀποδιδόναι τὰ φαινόμενα· οὐ γὰρ[5] ἐφ-
αρμόττοντος ἑνὸς λόγου οὐκ οἴονται τὰς[6] ἄλλας
φιλίας εἶναι· αἱ δ' εἰσὶ μέν, ἀλλ' οὐχ ὁμοίως εἰσίν.
οἱ δ' ὅταν ἡ πρώτη μὴ ἐφαρμόττῃ, ὡς οὖσαν 12
καθόλου ἂν εἴπερ ἦν πρώτη, οὐδ' εἶναι φιλίας τὰς
ἄλλας φασίν. ἔστι δὲ πολλὰ εἴδη φιλίας· τῶν γὰρ 13
ῥηθέντων ἦν ἤδη, ἐπειδὴ διώρισται τριχῶς λέγεσθαι
τὴν φιλίαν, ἡ μὲν γὰρ διώρισται δι' ἀρετὴν ἡ δὲ διὰ
τὸ χρήσιμον ἡ δὲ διὰ τὸ ἡδύ.

Τούτων ἡ μὲν διὰ τὸ χρήσιμόν ἐστι νὴ Δία[7] τῶν 14
πλείστων φιλία· διὰ γὰρ τὸ χρήσιμοι εἶναι φιλοῦσιν
ἀλλήλους, καὶ μέχρι τούτου, ὥσπερ ἡ παροιμία

> Γλαῦκ', ἐπίκουρος ἀνὴρ τόσσον φίλος[8] ἔς κε[9]
> μάχηται,

καὶ

> οὐκέτι γιγνώσκουσιν Ἀθηναῖοι Μεγαρῆας.

ἡ δὲ δι' ἡδονὴν τῶν νέων, τούτου γὰρ αἴσθησιν
ἔχουσιν· διὸ εὐμετάβολος φιλία ἡ τῶν νέων, 15
μεταβαλλόντων γὰρ τὰ ἤθη κατὰ τὰς ἡλικίας

[1] ὁ add. Ric. [2] πᾶσιν Sus.: ἡμῖν.
[3] τὸ τὸ καθόλου εἶναι Sus.: τὸ καθόλου εἶναι τὸ.
[4] τὸ add. Sp. [5] οὐκ οὖν ? Rac.
[6] τὰς add. Bz. [7] ἐστι νὴ Δία Iac.: ἐστιν ἡ.
[8] τόσσον φίλος Fr.: τὸν σόφον φίλον. [9] ἔστε Sol.

[a] ll. 7-17. [b] A friend in need is a friend indeed.

10 properly to that which is primarily so called. The primary is that of which the definition is implicit in the definition of all, for example a surgical instrument is an instrument that a surgeon would use, whereas the definition of the instrument is not
11 implicit in that of surgeon. Therefore in every case people seek the primary, and because the universal is primary they assume that also the primary is universal; but this is untrue. Hence in the case of friendship, they cannot take account of all the observed facts. For as one definition does not fit, they think that the other kinds of friendship are not friendships at all; but really they are, although
12 not in the same way, but when they find that the primary friendship does not fit, assuming that it would be universal if it really were primary, they
13 say that the others are not friendships at all. But in reality there are many kinds of friendships: this was one of the things said already,[a] as we have distinguished three senses of the term friendship—one sort has been defined as based on goodness, another on utility, another on pleasure.

based on utility, pleasure, and goodness.

14 Of these the one based on utility is assuredly the friendship of most people; for they love one another because they are useful, and in so far as they are so, as says the proverb—

> Glaucus, an ally is a friend
> As long as he our battle fights,[b]

and

> Athens no longer knoweth Megara.

15 On the other hand friendship based on pleasure is the friendship of the young, for they are sensitive to what is pleasant; hence young people's friendship easily changes, for since their characters change as

1236 b μεταβάλλει καὶ τὸ ἡδύ. ἡ δὲ κατ' ἀρετὴν τῶν
βελτίστων.

Φανερὸν δ' ἐκ τούτων ὅτι ἡ πρώτη φιλία, ἡ τῶν 16
ἀγαθῶν, ἐστὶν ἀντιφιλία καὶ ἀντιπροαίρεσις πρὸς
ἀλλήλους. φίλον μὲν γὰρ τὸ φιλούμενον τῷ φι-
λοῦντι, φίλος δὲ τῷ φιλουμένῳ καὶ αὐτὸς ὁ φιλῶν.[1]
αὕτη μὲν οὖν ἐν ἀνθρώπῳ[2] μόνον ὑπάρχει ἡ[3] φιλία, 17
μόνος[4] γὰρ αἰσθάνεται προαιρέσεως· αἱ δ' ἄλλαι
καὶ ἐν τοῖς θηρίοις. καὶ γὰρ[5] τὸ χρήσιμον ἐπὶ
μικρόν τι φαίνεται ἐνυπάρχον καὶ πρὸς ἄνθρωπον
τοῖς ἡμέροις καὶ πρὸς ἄλληλα, οἷον τὸν[6] τροχίλον
φησὶν Ἡρόδοτος τῷ κροκοδείλῳ, καὶ ὡς οἱ μάντεις
τὰς συνεδρίας καὶ διεδρίας λέγουσιν. καὶ οἱ φαῦλοι 18
ἂν εἶεν φίλοι ἀλλήλοις καὶ διὰ τὸ χρήσιμον καὶ διὰ
τὸ ἡδύ· οἱ δ', ὅτι ἡ πρώτη οὐχ ὑπάρχει αὐτοῖς, οὔ 19
φασι φίλους εἶναι· ἀδικήσει γὰρ ὅ γε φαῦλος τὸν
φαῦλον, οἱ δ' ἀδικούμενοι οὐ φιλοῦσι σφᾶς αὐτούς.
οἱ δὲ φιλοῦσι μέν, ἀλλ' οὐ τὴν πρώτην φιλίαν, ἐπεὶ 20
τάς γε ἑτέρας οὐθὲν κωλύει· δι' ἡδονὴν γὰρ
ὑπομένουσιν[7] ἀλλήλους βλαπτόμενοι, ἕως[8] ἂν ὦσιν
ἀκρατεῖς. οὐ δοκοῦσι δ' οὐδ' οἱ δι' ἡδονὴν φιλοῦν- 21
τες ἀλλήλους φίλοι εἶναι, ὅταν κατ' ἀκρίβειαν
ζητῶσιν, ὅτι οὐχ ἡ πρώτη· ἐκείνη μὲν γὰρ βέβαιος,

[1] αὐτὸς ὁ φιλῶν Ross: ἀντιφιλῶν.
[2] ἀνθρώπῳ ? Sp.: ἀνθρώποις.
[3] ἡ add. Ric.
[4] Sp.: μόνον.
[5] γὰρ add. Ric.
[6] <πρὸς> τὸν ? Rac.
[7] Bz.: ὑπονοοῦσιν.
[8] Iac.: ὡς (ἧς Ric.).

[a] Herodotus, ii. 68, says that the *trochilus* picks leeches out of the crocodile's throat, Aristotle, *Hist. An.* ix. 6. 6, that it picks the crocodile's teeth. In reality it picks gnats from the crocodile's open mouth.

they grow up, their taste in pleasure also changes. But the friendship in conformity with goodness is the friendship of the best men.

16 It is clear from this that the primary friendship, that of the good, is mutual reciprocity of affection and purpose. For the object of affection is dear to the giver of it, but also the giver of affection is him-
17 self dear to the object. This friendship, therefore, only occurs in man, for he alone has conscious purpose; but the other forms occur also in the lower animals. Indeed mutual utility manifestly exists to some small extent between the domestic animals and man, and between animals themselves, for instance Herodotus's account of the friendship between the crocodile and the sandpiper,[a] and the perching together and separating of birds of which soothsayers speak.
18 The bad may be each other's friends from motives
19 both of utility and of pleasure; though some say that they are not really friends, because the primary kind of friendship does not belong to them, since obviously a bad man will do harm to a bad man, and those who suffer harm from one another
20 do not feel affection for one another. But as a matter of fact bad men do feel affection for one another, though not according to the primary form of friendship—because clearly nothing hinders their being friends under the other forms, since for the sake of pleasure they put up with one another although they are being harmed, so long as they are
21 lacking in self-restraint. The view is also held, when people look into the matter closely, that those who feel affection for each other on account of pleasure are not friends, because it is not the primary friendship, since that is reliable but this is unreliable.

The last peculiar to virtuous men; the two former occur among animals, and bad men.

1236 b
αὕτη δὲ ἀβέβαιος. ἡ δ' ἐστὶ μέν, ὥσπερ εἴρηται,
φιλία, οὐκ ἐκείνη δὲ ἀλλ' ἀπ' ἐκείνης. τὸ μὲν οὖν 22
ἐκείνως μόνον λέγειν τὸν φίλον βιάζεσθαι τὰ φαι-
νόμενά ἐστι, καὶ παράδοξα λέγειν ἀναγκαῖον· καθ'
ἕνα δὲ λόγον πάσας ἀδυνατόν.[1] λείπεται τοίνυν 23
οὕτως, ὅτι ἔστι μὲν ὡς μόνη ἡ πρώτη φιλία, ἔστι
δ' ὡς πᾶσαι, οὔτε ὡς ὁμώνυμοι καὶ ὡς ἔτυχεν
ἔχουσαι πρὸς αὑτάς, οὔτε καθ' ἓν εἶδος, ἀλλὰ
μᾶλλον πρὸς ἕν.

Ἐπεὶ δ' ἁπλῶς ἀγαθὸν καὶ ἁπλῶς ἡδὺ τὸ αὐτὸ 24
καὶ ἅμα ἂν μή τι[2] ἐμποδίζῃ, ὁ δ' ἀληθινὸς φίλος
καὶ ἁπλῶς ὁ πρῶτός ἐστιν, ἔστι δὲ τοιοῦτος ὁ
αὐτὸς δι' αὑτὸν αἱρετός (ἀνάγκη δ' εἶναι τοιοῦτον, ᾧ[3]
γὰρ βούλεταί τις δι' αὐτὸν εἶναι τἀγαθά, ἀνάγκη
καὶ δι'[4] αὑτὸν αἱρετὸν[5] εἶναι), ὅ[6] ἀληθινὸς φίλος 25
καὶ ἡδύς ἐστιν ἁπλῶς· διὸ δοκεῖ καὶ ὁ ὁπωσοῦν
φίλος ἡδύς. ἔτι δὲ διοριστέον περὶ τούτου μᾶλλον· 26
ἔχει γὰρ ἐπίστασιν, πότερον[7] τὸ γ' αὑτῷ ἀγαθὸν
ἢ τὸ ἁπλῶς ἀγαθὸν φίλον, καὶ πότερον τὸ κατ'
ἐνέργειαν φιλεῖν μεθ' ἡδονῆς, ὥστε καὶ τὸ φιλητὸν
ἡδύ,[8] ἢ οὔ. ἄμφω γὰρ εἰς ταὐτὸ συνακτέον· τά τε
γὰρ μὴ ἁπλῶς ἀγαθὰ ἀλλὰ κακὰ ἄν πως[9] τύχῃ
φευκτά, καὶ τὸ μὴ αὑτῷ ἀγαθὸν οὐθὲν πρὸς αὐτόν,
ἀλλὰ τοῦτ' ἐστὶν ὃ ζητεῖται, τὰ ἁπλῶς ἀγαθὰ
1237 a οὕτως εἶναι ἀγαθά. ἔστι γὰρ αἱρετὸν μὲν[10] τὸ 27
ἁπλῶς ἀγαθόν, αὑτῷ δὲ τὸ αὑτῷ ἀγαθόν· ἃ δεῖ

[1] Bz.: δυνατόν.
[2] Γ: τις.
[3] Sp.: ὡς.
[4] δι' add. Sp.
[5] Sp.: αἱρεῖσθαι.
[6] Sp.: ὁ δ'.
[7] Erasmus: ἔχει ἐπίστασιν. πότερον γάρ.
[8] ὥστε τὸ φιλητὸν καὶ ἡδύ ? Rac.
[9] ἄν πως Iac.: ἁπλῶς (ἁπλῶς <κἂν ἡδέα ὄντα> Ric.).
[10] μὲν <ἁπλῶς> ? Rac.

But as a matter of fact it is friendship, as has been said, though not the primary sort of friendship but
22 one derived from it. Therefore to confine the use of the term friend to primary friendship is to do violence to observed facts, and compels one to talk paradoxes ; though it is not possible to bring
23 all friendship under one definition. The only remaining alternative, therefore, is, that in a sense the primary sort of friendship alone is friendship, but in a sense all sorts are, not as having a common name by accident and standing in a merely chance relationship to one another, nor yet as falling under one species, but rather as related to one thing.

24 And since the same thing is absolutely good and absolutely pleasant at the same time if nothing interferes, and the true friend and friend absolutely is the primary friend, and such is a friend chosen in and for himself (and he must necessarily be such, for he for whom one wishes good for his own sake must
25 necessarily be desirable for his own sake), a true friend is also absolutely pleasant ; owing to which it
26 is thought that a friend of any sort is pleasant. But we must define this still further, for it is debatable whether what is good merely for oneself is dear or what is absolutely good, and whether the actual exercise of affection is accompanied by pleasure, so that an object of affection is also pleasant, or not. Both questions must be brought to the same issue ; for things not absolutely good but possibly evil are to be avoided, and also a thing not good for oneself is no concern of oneself, but what is sought for is that things absolutely good shall be good for oneself.
27 For the absolutely good is absolutely desirable, but what is good for oneself is desirable for oneself ;

Pleasantness and goodness.

1237 a

συμφωνῆσαι. καὶ τοῦτο ἡ ἀρετὴ ποιεῖ· καὶ ἡ
πολιτικὴ ἐπὶ τούτῳ, ὅπως οἷς μήπω ἐστὶ γένηται.
εὔθετος[1] δὲ καὶ πρὸ ὁδοῦ ὁ[2] ἄνθρωπος ὢν (φύσει
γὰρ αὐτῷ ἀγαθὰ τὰ ἁπλῶς ἀγαθά), ὁμοίως δὲ καὶ 28
ἀνὴρ ἀντὶ γυναικὸς καὶ εὐφυὴς ἀφυοῦς[3]· διὰ τοῦ
ἡδέος δὲ ἡ ὁδός· ἀνάγκη εἶναι τὰ καλὰ ἡδέα. ὅταν
δὲ ταῦτα[4] διαφωνῇ, οὔπω σπουδαῖος[5] τελέως· ἐνδέχεται γὰρ ἐγγενέσθαι ἀκρασίαν· τῷ[6] γὰρ δια-
φωνεῖν τἀγαθὸν τῷ ἡδεῖ ἐν τοῖς πάθεσιν ἀκρασία
ἐστίν.

Ὥστ' ἐπειδὴ ἡ πρώτη φιλία κατ' ἀρετήν, ἔσον- 29
ται καὶ αὐτοὶ ἁπλῶς ἀγαθοί, τοῦτο δ' οὐχ ὅτι
χρήσιμοι, ἀλλ' ἄλλον τρόπον. διχῶς γὰρ ἔχει τὸ 30
τῳδὶ ἀγαθὸν καὶ τὸ[7] ἁπλῶς ἀγαθόν· καὶ ὁμοίως,
ὥσπερ ἐπὶ τοῦ ὠφελίμου, καὶ ἐπὶ τῶν ἕξεων·
ἄλλο γὰρ τὸ ἁπλῶς ὠφέλιμον καὶ τὸ τοισδί (ὃν
τρόπον[8] τὸ γυμνάζεσθαι πρὸς τὸ φαρμακεύεσθαι)·
ὥστε καὶ ἡ ἕξις, ἡ ἀνθρώπου ἀρετή (ἔστω γὰρ ὁ 31
ἄνθρωπος τῶν φύσει σπουδαίων)· ἡ ἄρα τοῦ φύσει
σπουδαίου ἀρετὴ ἁπλῶς ἀγαθόν, ἡ δὲ τοῦ μὴ
ἐκείνῳ.

Ὁμοίως δὴ ἔχει καὶ τὸ ἡδύ. ἐνταῦθα γὰρ 32
ἐπιστατέον καὶ σκεπτέον πότερόν ἐστιν ἄνευ ἡδονῆς
φιλία, καὶ τί διαφέρει, καὶ ἐν ποτέρῳ ποτ' ἐστὶ

[1] Rac.: εὐθέτως (ante quod lacunam Sp., initium protaseos cuius apodosis l. 6 ἀνάγκη).
[2] ὁ add. Iac.
[3] Bus.: ἀφυὴς εὐφυοῦς.
[4] Bus.: τοῦτο.
[5] sic versio Solomonis: σπουδαῖον.
[6] M^{b} τό.
[7] τὸ add. Rac.
[8] τὸ . . . τρόπον Iac. (τὸ add. Rac.): τὸ καλὸν τοιοῦτον.

and the two ought to come into agreement. This is effected by goodness; and the purpose of political science is to bring it about in cases where it does not yet exist. And one who is a human being is well adapted to this and on the way to it (for by nature things that are absolutely good are good to him),
28 and similarly a man rather than a woman and a gifted man rather than a dull one; but the road is through pleasure—it is necessary that fine things shall be pleasant. When there is discord between them, a man is not yet perfectly good; for it is possible for unrestraint to be engendered in him, as unrestraint is caused by discord between the good and the pleasant in the emotions.

Friendship based on virtue the primary kind.

29 Therefore since the primary sort of friendship is in accordance with goodness, friends of this sort will be absolutely good in themselves also, and this not because of being useful, but in another manner.
30 For good for a given person and good absolutely are separate; and the same is the case with states of character as with profitableness—what is profitable absolutely and what is profitable for given persons are different things (just as taking exercise is a different thing from taking drugs). So the state of character called human goodness is of two kinds—
31 for let us assume that man is one of the things that are excellent by nature: consequently the goodness of a thing excellent by nature is good absolutely, but that of a thing not excellent by nature is only good for that thing.

Problems as to the factor of pleasantness.

32 The case of the pleasant also, therefore, is similar. For here we must pause and consider whether there is any friendship without pleasure, and how such a friendship differs from other friendship, and on which

1237 a
τὸ φιλεῖν, πότερον[1] ὅτι ἀγαθὸς κἂν εἰ μὴ ἡδύς,
ἀλλ' οὐ[2] διὰ τοῦτο; διχῶς δὴ λεγομένου τοῦ
φιλεῖν, πότερον ὅτι ἀγαθὸν τὸ κατ' ἐνέργειαν οὐκ
ἄνευ ἡδονῆς φαίνεται; δῆλον δ' ὅτι ὥσπερ ἐπὶ 33
τῆς ἐπιστήμης αἱ πρόσφατοι θεωρίαι καὶ μαθήσεις
αἰσθηταὶ μάλιστα τῷ ἡδεῖ, οὕτω καὶ αἱ τῶν
συνήθων ἀναγνωρίσεις, καὶ ὁ λόγος ὁ αὐτὸς ἐπ'
ἀμφοῖν. φύσει γοῦν τὸ ἁπλῶς ἀγαθὸν ἡδὺ ἁπλῶς,
καὶ οἷς ἀγαθόν, τούτοις ἡδύ. διὸ εὐθὺς τὰ ὅμοια 34
ἀλλήλοις χαίρει, καὶ ἀνθρώπῳ ἥδιστον ἄνθρωπος·
ὥστ' ἐπεὶ καὶ ἀτελῆ, δῆλον ὅτι καὶ τελειωθέντα·
ὁ δὲ σπουδαῖος τέλειος. εἰ δὲ τὸ κατ' ἐνέργειαν
φιλεῖν μεθ' ἡδονῆς ἀντιπροαίρεσις τῆς ἀλλήλων
γνωρίσεως, δῆλον ὅτι καὶ ὅλως ἡ φιλία ἡ πρώτη
ἀντιπροαίρεσις τῶν ἁπλῶς ἀγαθῶν καὶ ἡδέων ὅτι
ἀγαθὰ καὶ ἡδέα· ἔστι δ' αὐτὴ ἡ φιλία ἕξις ἀφ' 35
ἧς ἡ τοιαύτη προαίρεσις. τὸ γὰρ ἔργον αὐτῆς
ἐνέργεια, αὕτη δ' οὐκ ἔξω ἀλλ' ἐν αὐτῷ τῷ
φιλοῦντι· δυνάμεως δὲ πάσης[3] ἔξω, ἢ γὰρ ἐν
ἑτέρῳ ἢ ᾗ[4] ἕτερον. διὸ τὸ φιλεῖν χαίρειν ἀλλ'
οὐ τὸ φιλεῖσθαί ἐστιν· τὸ μὲν γὰρ φιλεῖσθαι οὐ 36
τοῦ[5] φιλητοῦ ἐνέργεια, τὸ δὲ καὶ φιλίας, καὶ τὸ
μὲν ἐν ἐμψύχῳ, τὸ δὲ καὶ ἐν ἀψύχῳ· φιλεῖται γὰρ
καὶ τὰ ἄψυχα. ἐπεὶ δὲ τὸ φιλεῖν τὸ κατ' ἐνέργειαν 37

[1] καὶ πότερον M^b.
[2] ἀλλ' οὐ] ἢ οὔ, ἀλλὰ Sp.
[3] ⟨σωματικῆς⟩ πάσης ? Ric.
[4] ᾗ add. Bz.
[5] οὐ τοῦ add. Rac.

---

[a] Goodness and pleasantness.

[b] Perhaps the Greek should be altered to give 'or not, but because he is pleasant.'

[c] Potential and actual (Solomon).

[d] Ross marks this clause as corrupted.

exactly of the two things [a] the affection depends—do we love a man because he is good even if he is not pleasant, but not because he is pleasant? [b] Then, affection having two meanings,[c] does actual affection seem to involve pleasure because activity
33 is good? It is clear that as in science recent studies and acquirements are most fully apprehended, because of their pleasantness,[d] so with the recognition of familiar things, and the principle is the same in both cases. By nature at all events the absolutely good is absolutely pleasant, and the relatively good
34 is pleasant to those for whom it is good.[e] Hence *ipso facto* like takes pleasure in like, and man is the thing most pleasant to man; so that as this is so even with imperfect things, it is clearly so with things when perfected, and a good man is a perfect man. And if active affection is the reciprocal choice, accompanied by pleasure, of one another's acquaintance, it is clear that friendship of the primary kind is in general the reciprocal choice of things absolutely good and pleasant because they are good and
35 pleasant; and friendship itself is a state from which such choice arises. For its function is an activity, but this not external but within the lover himself; whereas the function of every faculty is external, for it is either in another or in oneself *qua* other.
36 Hence to love is to feel pleasure but to be loved is not; for being loved is not an activity of the thing loved, whereas loving is an activity—the activity of friendship; and loving occurs only in an animate thing, whereas being loved occurs with an inanimate thing also, for even inanimate things are loved.
37 And since to love actively is to treat the loved

[e] Sc. (τὸ τοισδὶ ἀγαθὸν) οἷς ἀγαθόν, τούτοις ἡδύ.

1237 b τῷ φιλουμένῳ[1] ἐστὶ χρῆσθαι ᾗ φιλούμενον, ὁ δὲ φίλος φιλούμενον τῷ[2] φίλῳ ᾗ φίλος ἀλλὰ μὴ ᾗ μουσικὸς ἢ ἰατρός, ἡδονὴ τοίνυν ἡ ἀπ' αὐτοῦ ᾗ αὐτός, αὕτη φιλική· αὐτὸν γὰρ φιλεῖ, οὐχ ὅτι ἄλλο.[3] ὥστ' ἂν μὴ χαίρῃ ᾗ ἀγαθός, οὐχ ἡ πρώτη φιλία. οὐδὲ δεῖ ἐμποδίζειν οὐθὲν τῶν συμβεβηκότων 38
μᾶλλον ἢ τὸ ἀγαθὸν εὐφραίνει[4]· τί γάρ; σφόδρα δυσώδης λείπεται[5]· ἀγαπητὸν[6] γὰρ τὸ εὐνοεῖν συζῆν[7] δὲ μή.

Αὕτη μὲν οὖν ἡ πρώτη φιλία, ἣν[8] πάντες ὁμολογοῦσιν. αἱ δ' ἄλλαι δι' αὐτὴν καὶ δοκοῦσι καὶ 39
ἀμφισβητοῦνται, βέβαιον γάρ τι δοκεῖ ἡ φιλία, μόνη δ' αὕτη βέβαιος· τὸ γὰρ κεκριμένον βέβαιον, τὰ δὲ μὴ ταχὺ γινόμενα μηδὲ ῥᾳδίως ποιεῖ[9] τὴν κρίσιν ὀρθήν. οὐκ ἔστι δ' ἄνευ πίστεως φιλία 40
βέβαιος, ἡ δὲ πίστις οὐκ ἄνευ χρόνου· δεῖ γὰρ πεῖραν λαβεῖν, ὥσπερ λέγει καὶ Θέογνις·

οὐ γὰρ ἂν εἰδείης ἀνδρὸς νόον οὐδὲ γυναικός,
πρὶν πειραθείης ὥσπερ ὑποζυγίου.

οἱ δ' ἄνευ χρόνου οὐ φίλοι[10] ἀλλὰ βούλονται εἶναι[11] φίλοι. καὶ μάλιστα λανθάνει ἡ τοιαύτη ἕξις ὡς φιλία· ὅταν γὰρ προθύμως ἔχωσι φίλοι εἶναι, διὰ 41
τὸ πάνθ' ὑπηρετεῖν τὰ φιλικὰ ἀλλήλοις οἴονται οὐ βούλεσθαι εἶναι[12] φίλοι ἀλλ' εἶναι φίλοι. τὸ δ' ὥσπερ ἐπὶ τῶν ἄλλων συμβαίνει καὶ ἐπὶ τῆς

[1] Fr.: τὸ φιλούμενον ὅ.
[2] Bz.: καί.
[3] Iac.: ἄλλῳ.
[4] Rac.: εὐφραίνειν.
[5] οἷον εἰ σφόδρα δυσώδης γίνεται Ric.
[6] Ross: ἀγαπᾶται.
[7] Sol.: συζῇ.
[8] Fr.: ᾗ.
[9] Bz.: οὐ ποιεῖ.
[10] οἱ δ' . . . φίλοι Fr.: οὐδ' ἄνευ χρόνου φίλος.
[11] εἶναι add. Fr.
[12] εἶναι add. Rac.

object *qua* loved, and the friend is an object of love to the friend *qua* dear to him but not *qua* musician or medical man, the pleasure of friendship is the pleasure derived from the person himself *qua* himself; for the friend loves him as himself, not because he is something else. Consequently if he does not take pleasure in him *qua* good, it is not the primary
38 friendship. Nor ought any accidental quality to cause more hindrance than the friend's goodness causes delight; for surely, if a person is very evil-smelling, people cut him—he must be content with our goodwill, he must not expect our society!

Permanence of true friendship.

This then is the primary friendship, which all people
39 recognize. It is on account of it that the other sorts are considered to be friendship, and also that their claim is disputed—for friendship seems to be something stable, and only this friendship is stable; for a formed judgement is stable, and not doing things
40 quickly or easily makes the judgement right. And there is no stable friendship without confidence, and confidence only comes with time; for it is necessary to make trial, as Theognis says:

> Thou canst not know the mind of man nor woman
> E'er thou hast tried them as thou triest cattle.

Those who become friends without the test of time are not real friends but only wish to be friends; and such a character very readily passes for friend-
41 ship, because when eager to be friends they think that by rendering each other all friendly services they do not merely wish to be friends but actually are friends. But as a matter of fact it happens in friendship as in everything else; people are not

1237 b
φιλίας· οὐ γὰρ εἰ βούλονται ὑγιαίνειν ὑγιαίνουσιν,
ὥστ' οὐδ' εἰ εἶναι[1] φίλοι βούλονται ἤδη καὶ φίλοι
εἰσίν. σημεῖον δέ· εὐδιάβλητοι γὰρ οἱ διακείμενοι 42
ἄνευ πείρας τοῦτον τὸν τρόπον· περὶ ὧν μὲν γὰρ
πεῖραν δεδώκασιν ἀλλήλοις, οὐκ εὐδιάβλητοι, περὶ
ὧν δὲ μή, πεισθεῖεν ἂν ὅταν σύμβολα λέγωσιν οἱ
διαβάλλοντες. ἅμα δὲ φανερὸν ὅτι οὐδ' ἐν τοῖς 43
φαύλοις αὕτη ἡ φιλία· ἄπιστος γὰρ ὁ φαῦλος καὶ
κακοήθης πρὸς πάντας· αὑτῷ γὰρ μετρεῖ τοὺς
ἄλλους. διὸ εὐεξαπατητότεροί εἰσιν οἱ ἀγαθοί,
ἂν μὴ διὰ πεῖραν ἀπιστῶσιν. οἱ δὲ φαῦλοι 44
αἱροῦνται τὰ φύσει ἀγαθὰ ἀντὶ τοῦ φίλου, καὶ οὐθεὶς φιλεῖ μᾶλλον ἄνθρωπον ἢ πράγματα, ὥστ'
οὐ φίλοι· οὐ γὰρ γίνεται οὕτω κοινὰ τὰ φίλων,
προσνέμεται γὰρ ὁ φίλος τοῖς πράγμασιν, οὐ τὰ
πράγματα τοῖς φίλοις.

Οὐ γίνεται ἄρ' ἡ φιλία ἡ πρώτη ἐν πολλοῖς, 45
ὅτι χαλεπὸν πολλῶν πεῖραν λαβεῖν· ἑκάστῳ γὰρ
ἂν ἔδει[2] συζῆσαι. οὐδὲ δὴ αἱρετέον ὁμοίως περὶ
ἱματίου καὶ φίλου· καίτοι ἐν πᾶσι δοκεῖ τοῦ νοῦν 46
ἔχοντος δυοῖν τὸ βέλτιον αἱρεῖσθαι, καὶ εἰ μὲν τῷ
χείρονι πάλαι ἐχρῆτο, τῷ βελτίονι δὲ μηδέπω,
τοῦθ' αἱρετέον, ἀλλ' οὐκ ἀντὶ τοῦ πάλαι φίλου
1238 a τὸν ἀγνῶτα εἰ βελτίων. οὐ γάρ ἐστιν ἄνευ πείρας

[1] εἶναι add. Rac.

[2] Bus.: ἂν δεῖ (δεῖ? Rac.).

healthy merely if they wish to be healthy, so that even if people wish to be friends they are not actually
42 friends already. A proof of this is that people who have come into this position without first testing one another are easily set at variance; for though men are not set at variance easily about things in which they have allowed each other to test them, in cases where they have not, whenever those who are attempting to set them at variance produce evidence
43 they may be convinced. At the same time it is manifest that this friendship does not occur between base people either; for the base and evil-natured man is distrustful towards everybody, because he measures other people by himself. Hence good men are more easily cheated, unless as a result of
44 trial they are distrustful. But the base prefer the goods of nature to a friend, and none of them love people more than things; and so they are not friends, for the proverbial 'common property as between friends' is not realized in this way—the friend is made an appendage of the things, not the things of the friends.

45 Therefore the first kind of friendship does not Its rarity.
occur between many men, because it is difficult to test many—one would have to go and live with each of them. Nor indeed should one exercise choice in the case of a friend in the same way as about a
46 coat; although in all matters it seems the mark of a sensible man to choose the better of two things, and if he had been wearing his worse coat for a long time and had not yet worn his better one, the better one ought to be chosen—but you ought not in place of an old friend to choose one whom you do not know to be a better man. For a friend is

1238 a
οὐδὲ μιᾶς ἡμέρας ὁ φίλος, ἀλλὰ χρόνου δεῖ· διὸ
εἰς παροιμίαν ἐλήλυθεν ὁ μέδιμνος τῶν ἁλῶν.
ἅμα δὲ δεῖ[1] μὴ μόνον ἁπλῶς ἀγαθὸν εἶναι ἀλλὰ 47
καὶ σοί, εἰ ὁ[2] φίλος ἔσται σοι φίλος· ἀγαθὸς μὲν
γὰρ ἁπλῶς ἐστὶ τῷ ἀγαθὸς εἶναι, φίλος δὲ τῷ
ἄλλῳ ἀγαθός· ἁπλῶς τε δ'[3] ἀγαθὸς καὶ φίλος ὅταν
συμφωνήσῃ ταῦτα ἄμφω, ὥστε ὅ ἐστιν ἁπλῶς
ἀγαθόν, τὸ αὐτὸ[4] ἄλλῳ· ἢ καὶ μὴ ἁπλῶς μὲν
σπουδαῖος,[5] ἄλλῳ δ' ἀγαθὸς ὅτι χρήσιμος. τὸ 48
δὲ πολλοῖς ἅμα εἶναι φίλον[6] καὶ τὸ φιλεῖν κωλύει·
οὐ γὰρ οἷόν τε ἅμα πρὸς πολλοὺς ἐνεργεῖν.

Ἐκ δὴ τούτων φανερὸν ὅτι ὀρθῶς λέγεται ὅτι 49
ἡ φιλία τῶν βεβαίων, ὥσπερ ἡ εὐδαιμονία τῶν
αὐτάρκων. καὶ ὀρθῶς εἴρηται

ἡ γὰρ φύσις βέβαιον, οὐ τὰ χρήματα—

πολὺ δὲ κάλλιον εἰπεῖν ὅτι ἡ[7] ἀρετὴ τῆς φύσεως. 50
καὶ ὅ τε χρόνος λέγεται δεικνύναι τὸν φίλον καὶ
αἱ ἀτυχίαι μᾶλλον τῶν εὐτυχιῶν. τότε γὰρ δῆλον
ὅτι κοινὰ τὰ τῶν φίλων, οὗτοι γὰρ μόνοι ἀντὶ
τῶν φύσει ἀγαθῶν καὶ φύσει κακῶν, περὶ ἃ αἱ
εὐτυχίαι καὶ αἱ δυστυχίαι, αἱροῦνται μᾶλλον
ἄνθρωπον ἢ τούτων τὰ μὲν εἶναι τὰ δὲ μὴ εἶναι·
ἡ δ' ἀτυχία δηλοῖ τοὺς μὴ ὄντως ὄντας φίλους 51
ἀλλὰ διὰ τὸ χρήσιμον τυχόν.[8] ὁ δὲ χρόνος δηλοῖ
ἀμφοτέρους· οὐδὲ γὰρ ὁ χρήσιμος ταχὺ δῆλος,

[1] Bz.: εἰ. [2] εἰ ὁ Bus.: εἶναι (εἰ δὴ et ἔσται <καὶ> Ric.).
[3] τε δ' add. Rac. (δ' add. Γ). [4] Ric.: τούτου.
[5] Fr.: σπουδαίῳ. [6] Syl.: φίλον.
[7] [ἡ] Ric. [8] τυχόντας Γ.

[a] Euripides, *Electra* 941.
[b] Or, emending the MS. text, 'that friendship is goodness of nature.'

not to be had without trial and is not a matter of a single day, but time is needed; hence the 'peck
47 of salt' has come to be proverbial. At the same time if a friend is really to be your friend he must be not only good absolutely but also good to you; for a man is good absolutely by being good, but he is a friend by being good to another, and he is both good absolutely and a friend when both these attributes harmonize together, so that what is good absolutely is also good for another person; or also he may be not good absolutely yet good to another
48 because useful. But being a friend of many people at once is prevented even by the factor of affection, for it is not possible for affection to be active in relation to many at once.

49 These things, therefore, show the correctness of the saying that friendship is a thing to be relied on, just as happiness is a thing that is self-sufficing. And it has been rightly said [a]:

Its trustworthiness.

> Nature is permanent, but wealth is not—

although it would be much finer to say 'Friend-
50 ship' than 'Nature.' [b] And it is proverbial that time shows a friend, and also misfortunes more than good fortune. For then the truth of the saying 'friends' possessions are common property' is clear, for only friends, instead of the natural goods and natural evils on which good and bad fortune turn, choose a human being rather than the presence of
51 the former and the absence of the latter; and misfortune shows those who are not friends really but only because of some casual utility. And both are shown by time; for even the useful friend is not shown quickly, but rather the pleasant one—

1238 a
ἀλλ᾽ ὁ ἡδὺς μᾶλλον, πλὴν οὐδ᾽ ὁ ἁπλῶς ἡδὺς
ταχύς.[1] ὅμοιοι γὰρ οἱ ἄνθρωποι τοῖς οἴνοις καὶ
ἐδέσμασιν· ἐκείνων τε γὰρ τὸ μὲν γλυκὺ[2] ταχὺ
δηλοῖ, πλείω δὲ χρόνον γινόμενον ἀηδὲς καὶ οὐ
γλυκύ, καὶ ἐπὶ τῶν ἀνθρώπων ὁμοίως. ἔστι γὰρ
τὸ ἁπλῶς ἡδὺ τῷ τέλει ὁριστέον καὶ τῷ χρόνῳ.
ὁμολογήσαιεν δ᾽ ἂν καὶ οἱ πολλοί, οὐκ ἐκ τῶν 52
ἀποβαινόντων μόνον, ἀλλ᾽ ὥσπερ ἐπὶ τοῦ πόματος
καλοῦσι γλύκιον· τοῦτο γὰρ οὐ[3] διὰ τὸ ἀποβαῖνον
οὐχ ἡδὺ ἀλλὰ διὰ τὸ μὴ συνεχὲς ἀλλὰ τὸ πρῶτον
ἐξαπατᾶν.

Ἡ μὲν οὖν πρώτη φιλία καὶ δι᾽ ἣν αἱ ἄλλαι 53
λέγονται ἡ κατ᾽ ἀρετήν ἐστι καὶ δι᾽ ἡδονὴν τὴν
ἀρετῆς, ὥσπερ εἴρηται πρότερον. αἱ δ᾽ ἄλλαι
ἐγγίνονται φιλίαι καὶ ἐν παισὶ καὶ θηρίοις καὶ τοῖς
φαύλοις· ὅθεν λέγεται "ἧλιξ ἥλικα τέρπει" καὶ
"κακὸς κακῷ συντέτηκεν ἡδονῇ." ἐνδέχεται δὲ 54
καὶ ἡδεῖς ἀλλήλοις εἶναι τοὺς φαύλους, οὐχ[4] ᾗ
φαῦλοι ἢ μηδέτεροι, ἀλλ᾽ οἷον εἰ[5] ᾠδικοὶ ἄμφω,
ἢ ὁ μὲν φιλῳδὸς[6] ὁ δ᾽ ᾠδικός ἐστιν, καὶ ᾗ πάντες
ἔχουσί τι[7] ἀγαθὸν καὶ ταύτῃ συναρμόττουσιν ἀλλήλοις. ἔτι χρήσιμοι ἂν εἶεν ἀλλήλοις καὶ ὠφέλιμοι 55
1238 b (οὐχ ἁπλῶς ἀλλὰ πρὸς τὴν προαίρεσιν) οὐχ ᾗ
φαῦλοι[8] ἢ οὐδέτεροι. ἐνδέχεται δὲ καὶ τῷ ἐπι- 56
εικεῖ[9] φαῦλον εἶναι φίλον· καὶ γὰρ χρήσιμος ἂν
εἴη πρὸς τὴν προαίρεσιν ὁ μὲν φαῦλος πρὸς τὴν

[1] ταχύ Guil.
[2] Ric.: ἡδύ.
[3] οὐ add. Rac.
[4] οὐχ Γ: καί.
[5] εἰ (vel ᾗ) add. Ric.
[6] Vict.: φειδωλός.
[7] ἔχουσί τι Fr.: ἔχουσιν.
[8] οὐχ ᾗ φαῦλοι add. Rac. (<φαῦλοι> Ric.).
[9] Γ: τὸν ἐπιεικῆ.

except that one who is absolutely pleasant is also not quick to show himself. For men are like wines and foods ; the sweetness of those is quickly evident, but when lasting longer it is unpleasant and not sweet, and similarly in the case of men. For absolute pleasantness is a thing to be defined by the
52 End it effects and the time it lasts. And even the multitude would agree, not in consequence of results only, but in the same way as in the case of a drink they call it sweeter—for a drink fails to be pleasant not because of its result, but because its pleasantness is not continuous, although at first it quite takes one in.

53 The primary form of friendship therefore, and the one that causes the name to be given to the others, is friendship based on goodness and due to the pleasure of goodness, as has been said before. The other friendships occur even among children and animals and wicked people : whence the sayings—

The two lower forms of Friendship.

> Two of an age each other gladden

and

> Pleasure welds the bad man to the bad.[a]

54 And also the bad may be pleasant to each other not as being bad or neutral,[b] but if for instance both are musicians or one fond of music and the other a musician, and in the way in which all men have some
55 good in them and so fit in with one another. Further they might be mutually useful and beneficial (not absolutely but for their purpose) not as being bad
56 or neutral. It is also possible for a bad man to be friends with a good man, for the bad man may be useful to the good man for his purpose at the time

[a] Euripides, *Bellerophontes*, fr. 298 (Nauck).
[b] *i.e.* neither good nor bad.

1238 b
ὑπάρχουσαν τῷ σπουδαίῳ, ὁ δὲ τῷ μὲν ἀκρατεῖ
πρὸς τὴν ὑπάρχουσαν τῷ δὲ φαύλῳ πρὸς τὴν
κατὰ φύσιν· καὶ βουλήσεται τὰ ἀγαθά, ἁπλῶς μὲν
τὰ ἁπλᾶ,[1] τὰ δ' ἐκείνῳ ἐξ ὑποθέσεως, ᾗ πενία
συμφέρει ἢ νόσος—ταῦτα τῶν ἁπλῶν[1] ἀγαθῶν
ἕνεκα, ὥσπερ καὶ τὸ φάρμακον πιεῖν· οὐ γὰρ αὐτὸ[2]
βούλεται, ἀλλὰ τοῦδ' ἕνεκα βούλεται. ἔτι καθ' 57
οὓς τρόπους καὶ ἀλλήλοις οἱ μὴ σπουδαῖοι εἶεν ἂν
φίλοι· εἴη γὰρ ἂν ἡδὺς οὐχ ᾗ φαῦλος, ἀλλ' ᾗ τῶν
κοινῶν τινὸς μετέχει, οἷον εἰ μουσικός. ἔτι ᾗ
ἔνι τι πᾶσιν ἐπιεικές (διὸ ἔνιοι ὁμιλητικοί εἰσιν[3]
ἂν καὶ σπουδαῖοι[4]), ἢ ᾗ προσαρμόττουσιν ἑκάστῳ·
ἔχουσι γάρ τι πάντες τοῦ ἀγαθοῦ.

III. Τρία μὲν οὖν εἴδη ταῦτα φιλίας· ἐν πᾶσι δὲ 1
τούτοις κατ' ἰσότητά πως λέγεται ἡ φιλία· καὶ
γὰρ οἱ κατ' ἀρετὴν φίλοι ἐν ἰσότητί πως ἀρετῆς
εἰσὶ φίλοι ἀλλήλοις.

Ἄλλη δὲ διαφορὰ τούτων ἡ καθ' ὑπερβολήν, 2
ὥσπερ θεοῦ [ἀρετὴ][5] πρὸς ἄνθρωπον, τοῦτο γὰρ
ἕτερον εἶδος φιλίας, καὶ ὅλως ἄρχοντος καὶ ἀρχομένου· καθάπερ καὶ τὸ δίκαιον ἕτερον, κατ'
ἀναλογίαν γὰρ ἴσον, κατ' ἀριθμὸν δ' οὐκ ἴσον. ἐν
τούτῳ τῷ γένει πατὴρ πρὸς υἱὸν καὶ ὁ εὐεργέτης

[1] ἁπλῶς Rieckher.
[2] αὐτὸ hic Rac.: ante τὸ φάρμακον.
εἶεν Ald. [4] Pᵇ: σπουδαίῳ Mᵇ, <μὴ> σπουδαῖοι Bz.
[5] [ἀρετὴ] Rac. (vel ἀρετῇ vel κατ' ἀρετὴν subaudito φιλία).

[a] *i.e.* ready to associate with all and sundry, regardless of moral inferiority. But perhaps the Greek should be altered to give 'some (bad men) might be worthy to associate with, even in the judgement of a good man,' or 'some might be worthy to associate with even though not good.'

[b] Between two unequal persons justice divides benefits in proportion to their deserts, so that the two shares are not

and the good man to the uncontrolled man for his purpose at the time and to the bad man for the purpose natural to him ; and he will wish his friend what is good—wish absolutely things absolutely good, and under a given condition things good for him, as poverty or disease may be beneficial : things good for him he will wish for the sake of the absolute goods, in the way in which he wishes his friend to drink medicine—he does not wish the action in
57 itself but wishes it for the given purpose. Moreover a bad man may also be friends with a good one in the ways in which men not good may be friends with one another : he may be pleasant to him not as being bad but as sharing some common characteristic, for instance if he is musical. Again they may be friends in the way in which there is some good in everybody (owing to which some men are sociable [a] even though good), or in the way in which they suit each particular person, for all men have something of good.

1 III. These then are three kinds of friendship ; and in all of these the term friendship in a manner indicates equality, for even with those who are friends on the ground of goodness the friendship is in a manner based on equality of goodness. **Friendship between unequals.**

2 But another variety of these kinds is friendship on a basis of superiority, as in that of a god for a man, for that is a different kind of friendship, and generally of a ruler and subject ; just as the principle of justice between them is also different, being one of equality proportionally but not of equality numerically.[b] The friendship of father for son is in this

equal to each other but each equal to its recipient's merit. The word ἴσον itself connotes 'fair,' just, reasonable.

1238 b
πρὸς τὸν εὐεργετηθέντα. αὐτῶν δὲ τούτων 3
διαφοραί εἰσιν· ἄλλη[1] πατρὸς πρὸς υἱὸν καὶ ἀνδρὸς
πρὸς γυναῖκα, αὕτη μὲν ὡς ἄρχοντος καὶ ἀρχομένου, ἡ δὲ[2] εὐεργέτου πρὸς εὐεργετηθέντα. ἐν
ταύταις δὲ ἢ οὐκ ἔνεστιν ἢ οὐχ ὁμοίως τὸ ἀντιφιλεῖσθαι. γελοῖον γὰρ εἴ τις ἐγκαλοίη τῷ θεῷ 4
ὅτι οὐχ ὁμοίως ἀντιφιλεῖ[3] ὡς φιλεῖται, ἢ τῷ
ἄρχοντι ὁ ἀρχόμενος[4]· φιλεῖσθαι γάρ, οὐ φιλεῖν,
τοῦ ἄρχοντος, ἢ φιλεῖν ἄλλον τρόπον. καὶ ἡ[5] 5
ἡδονὴ διαφέρει, οὐδ' ἓν[6] ἥ τε τοῦ αὐτάρκους ἐπὶ
τῷ αὑτοῦ κτήματι ἢ παιδὶ καὶ ἡ[5] τοῦ ἐνδεοῦς
ἐπὶ τῷ γινομένῳ. ὡς δ' αὕτως καὶ ἐπὶ τῶν διὰ 6
τὴν χρῆσιν φίλων καὶ ἐπὶ τῶν δι' ἡδονήν, οἱ μὲν
κατ' ἰσότητα εἰσίν, οἱ δὲ καθ' ὑπεροχήν. διὸ καὶ
οἱ ἐκείνως οἰόμενοι ἐγκαλοῦσιν ἐὰν μὴ ὁμοίως
ὦσι[7] χρήσιμοι καὶ εὖ ποιῶσιν· καὶ[8] ἐπὶ τῆς ἡδονῆς. δῆλον δ' ἐν τοῖς ἐρωτικοῖς· τοῦτο γὰρ αἴτιον 7
τοῦ μάχεσθαι ἀλλήλοις πολλάκις, ἀγνοεῖ γὰρ ὁ
ἐρῶν ὅτι οὐχ ὁ αὐτὸς λόγος ἐστὶ τῆς προθυμίας.[9]
διὸ εἴρηκεν Αἴνικος[10]·

ἐρώμενος τοιαῦτ' ἄν, οὐκ ἐρῶν λέγοι.

οἱ δὲ νομίζουσι τὸν αὐτὸν εἶναι λόγον.

1239 a
IV. Ὥσπερ οὖν εἴρηται τριῶν ὄντων εἰδῶν 1

[1] Mb: ἄλλην Pb, ἄλλαι <καὶ> Sp.
[2] δὲ <ὡς> Sp.
[3] Γ: τῷ ἀντιφιλεῖσθαι.
[4] ὁ ἀρχόμενος Bz.: καὶ ἀρχομένῳ.
[5] ἡ add. Iac.
[6] οὐδ' ἓν Iac.: οὐδέν.
[7] ὦσι add. Cas.
[8] καὶ <ὁμοίως> vel <ὡσαυτὼς> ? Rac.
[9] Fr.: λόγος τῆς ἐπὶ τὴν προθυμίαν.
[10] Iac.: διὸ εὑρηκέναι νεῖκος ὁ.

[a] *i.e.* they complain if the pleasure or benefit they get from their friend is not equal (absolutely, not merely in pro-

3 class, and that of benefactor for beneficiary. And of these sorts of friendship themselves there are varieties: the friendship of father for son is different from that of husband for wife—the former is friendship as between ruler and subject, the latter that of benefactor for beneficiary. And in these varieties either there is no return of affection or it is not
4 returned in a similar way. For it would be ludicrous if one were to accuse God because he does not return love in the same way as he is loved, or for a subject to make this accusation against a ruler; for it is the part of a ruler to be loved, not to love, or else to
5 love in another way. And the pleasure differs; the pleasure that a man of independent position has in his own property or son and that which one who lacks them feels in an estate or a child coming to him
6 are not one and the same. And in the same way also in the case of those who are friends for utility or for pleasure—some are on a footing of equality, others one of superiority. Owing to this those who think they are on the former footing complain if they are not useful and beneficial in a similar
7 manner; and also in the case of pleasure.[a] This is clear in cases of passionate affection, for this is often a cause of conflict between the lover and his beloved: the lover does not see that they have not the same reason for their affection. Hence Aenicus [b] has said:

A loved one so would speak, but not a lover.

But they think that the reason is the same.

1 IV. There being then, as has been said,[c] three

portion to a supposed difference of merit) to that which they give to him. [b] A dramatist of the Old Comedy.

[c] See 1236 a 7—1237 b 15.

1239 a
φιλίας, κατ' ἀρετὴν καὶ[1] κατὰ τὸ χρήσιμον καὶ
κατὰ τὸ ἡδύ, αὗται πάλιν διῄρηνται εἰς δύο· αἱ
μὲν γὰρ κατὰ τὸ ἴσον αἱ δὲ καθ' ὑπεροχήν εἰσιν.
φιλίαι μὲν οὖν ἀμφότεραι, φίλοι δ' οἱ κατὰ τὴν 2
ἰσότητα· ἄτοπον γὰρ ἂν εἴη εἰ ἀνὴρ παιδίῳ φίλος,
φιλεῖ δέ γε καὶ φιλεῖται. ἐνιαχοῦ δὲ φιλεῖσθαι
μὲν δεῖ τὸν ὑπερέχοντα, ἐὰν δὲ φιλῇ, ὀνειδίζεται
ὡς ἀνάξιον φιλῶν· τῇ γὰρ ἀξίᾳ τῶν φίλων[2]
μετρεῖται καί τινι ἴσῳ. τὰ μὲν οὖν δι' ἡλικίας 3
ἔλλειψιν ἀνάξια ὁμοίως φιλεῖσθαι, τὰ δὲ κατ' ἀρετὴν ἢ γένος ἢ κατὰ ἄλλην τοιαύτην ὑπεροχήν· δεῖ[3]
δὲ τὸν ὑπερέχοντα ἢ ἧττον ἢ μὴ φιλεῖν ἀξιοῦν,
καὶ ἐν τῷ χρησίμῳ καὶ ἐν τῷ ἡδεῖ καὶ κατ' ἀρετήν.
ἐν μὲν οὖν ταῖς μικραῖς ὑπεροχαῖς εἰκότως γίνονται 4
ἀμφισβητήσεις (τὸ γὰρ μικρὸν ἐνιαχοῦ οὐδὲν
ἰσχύει, ὥσπερ ἐν ξύλου σταθμῷ, ἀλλ' ἐν χρυσίῳ[4]·
ἀλλὰ τὸ μικρὸν κακῶς κρίνουσιν, φαίνεται γὰρ
τὸ μὲν οἰκεῖον ἀγαθὸν διὰ τὸ ἐγγὺς μέγα τὸ δ'
ἀλλότριον διὰ τὸ πόρρω μικρόν)· ὅταν δὲ ὑπερβολὴ 5
ᾖ, οὐδ' αὐτοὶ ἐπιζητοῦσιν ὡς δεῖ ἢ ἀντιφιλεῖσθαι
ἢ ὁμοίως ἀντιφιλεῖσθαι, οἷον εἴ τις ἀξιοῖ τὸν θεόν.
φανερὸν δὴ ὅτι φίλοι μὲν ὅταν ἐν τῷ ἴσῳ, τὸ 6
ἀντιφιλεῖν δ' ἐστὶν ἄνευ τοῦ φίλους εἶναι. δῆλον 7
δὲ καὶ διὰ τί ζητοῦσι μᾶλλον οἱ ἄνθρωποι τὴν καθ'
ὑπεροχὴν φιλίαν τῆς κατ' ἰσότητα· ἅμα γὰρ

[1] καὶ add. Rac.
[2] τῷ φιλεῖν: τὸ φιλεῖν Bz.
[3] Wilson: ἀεί.
[4] χρυσίου Sp.

[a] *i.e.* proportional equality: see note on 1238 b 21.
[b] Or 'one ought to expect the superior to feel . . .'

kinds of friendship, based on goodness, utility and pleasantness, these are again divided in two, one set being on a footing of equality and the other on
2 one of superiority. Though both sets, therefore, are friendships, only when they are on an equality are the parties friends; for it would be absurd for a man to be a friend of a child, though he does feel affection for him and receive it from him. In some cases, while the superior partner ought to receive affection, if he gives it he is reproached as loving an unworthy object; for affection is measured by the worth of the friends and by one sort of equality.[a]
3 So in some cases there is properly a dissimilarity of affection because of inferiority of age, in others on the ground of goodness or birth or some other such superiority; it is right for the superior to claim to feel[b] either less affection or none, alike in a friendship of utility and in one of pleasure and
4 one based on goodness. So in cases of small degrees of superiority disputes naturally occur (for a small amount is not of importance in some matters, as in weighing timber, though in gold plate it is; but people judge smallness of amount badly, since one's own good because of its nearness appears big and that of others because of its remoteness small);
5 but when there is an excessive amount of difference, then even the parties themselves do not demand that they ought to be loved in return, or not loved alike—for example, if one were claiming a return
6 of love from God. It is manifest, therefore, that men are friends when they are on an equality, but that a return of affection is possible without their
7 being friends. And it is clear why men seek friendship on a basis of superiority more than that on one

Friendship between unequals possible in all three forms;

but these are not true friends.

1239 a
ὑπάρχει οὕτως αὐτοῖς τό τε φιλεῖσθαι καὶ ἡ
ὑπεροχή. διὸ ὁ κόλαξ παρ' ἐνίοις ἐντιμότερος τοῦ
φίλου· ἄμφω γὰρ φαίνεσθαι ποιεῖ ὑπάρχειν τῷ
κολακευομένῳ. μάλιστα δ' οἱ φιλότιμοι τοιοῦτοι·
τὸ γὰρ θαυμάζεσθαι ἐν ὑπεροχῇ. φύσει δὲ 8
γίνονται οἱ μὲν φιλητικοὶ οἱ δὲ φιλότιμοι· φιλητικὸς
δὲ ὁ τῷ φιλεῖν χαίρων μᾶλλον ἢ τῷ φιλεῖσθαι,
ἐκεῖνος δὲ φιλούμενος[1] μᾶλλον. ὁ μὲν οὖν χαίρων
τῷ θαυμάζεσθαι καὶ φιλεῖσθαι τῆς ὑπεροχῆς φίλος,
ὁ δὲ τῆς ἐν τῷ φιλεῖν ἡδονῆς[2] ὁ φιλητικός. ἔνεστι
γὰρ ἀνάγκῃ ἐνεργοῦντι[3]· τὸ μὲν γὰρ φιλεῖσθαι
συμβεβηκός, ἔστι γὰρ λανθάνειν φιλούμενον,
φιλοῦντα δ' οὔ. ἔστι δὲ καὶ κατὰ τὴν φιλίαν τὸ 9
φιλεῖν μᾶλλον ἢ τὸ φιλεῖσθαι,[4] τὸ δὲ φιλεῖσθαι
κατὰ τὸ φιλητόν. σημεῖον δέ· ἕλοιτ' ἂν ὁ φίλος
μᾶλλον, εἰ μὴ ἐνδέχοιτ' ἄμφω, γινώσκειν ἢ
γινώσκεσθαι, οἷον ἐν ταῖς ὑποβολαῖς[5] αἱ γυναῖκες
ποιοῦσι, καὶ ἡ Ἀνδρομάχη ἡ Ἀντιφῶντος. καὶ
γὰρ ἔοικε τὸ μὲν ἐθέλειν γινώσκεσθαι αὑτοῦ ἕνεκα,
καὶ τοῦ πάσχειν τι ἀγαθὸν ἀλλὰ μὴ ποιεῖν, τὸ δὲ
γινώσκειν τοῦ ποιεῖν καὶ τοῦ φιλεῖν ἕνεκα. διὸ 10
1239 b καὶ τοὺς ἐμμένοντας τῷ φιλεῖν πρὸς τοὺς τεθνεῶτας
ἐπαινοῦμεν· γινώσκουσι γάρ, ἀλλ' οὐ γινώσκονται.
Ὅτι μὲν οὖν πλείονες τρόποι φιλίας, καὶ πόσοι

[1] Rac.: φιλότιμος.
[2] τῇ . . . ἡδονῇ Sp. (et Ric. om. ὁ).
[3] Ric. et Sol.: ἀνάγκη ἐνεργοῦντα.
[4] [ἢ τὸ φιλεῖσθαι] ? Rac.
[5] Vict.: ὑπερβολαῖς.

[a] This poet lived at Syracuse at the court of Dionysius the elder (who came into power 406 B.C.). He is said to have written tragedies in collaboration with the tyrant; and he was sentenced by him to death by flogging (*Rhet.* 1384 a 9).

of equality ; for in the former case they score both affection and a sense of superiority at the same time. Hence with some men the flatterer is more esteemed than the friend, for he makes the person flattered appear to score both advantages. And this most of all characterizes men ambitious of honours, since
8 to be admired implies superiority. Some persons grow up by nature affectionate and others ambitious ; one who enjoys loving more than being loved is affectionate, whereas the other enjoys being loved more. So the man who enjoys being admired and loved is a lover of superiority, whereas the other, the affectionate man, loves the pleasure of loving. For this he necessarily possesses by the mere activity of loving ; for being loved is an accident, as one can be loved without knowing it, but one cannot love
9 without knowing it. Loving depends, more than being loved, on the actual feeling, whereas being loved corresponds with the nature of the object. A sign of this is that a friend, if both things were not possible, would choose to know the other person rather than to be known by him, as for example women do when they allow others to adopt their children, and Andromache in the tragedy of Antiphon.[a] Indeed the wish to be known seems to be selfish, and its motive a desire to receive and not to confer some benefit, whereas to wish to know a person is for the sake of conferring benefit and
10 bestowing affection. For this reason we praise those who remain constant in affection towards the dead ; for they know, but are not known.

It has, then, been stated that there are several modes of friendship, and how many modes there

1239 b
τρόποι, ὅτι τρεῖς, καὶ ὅτι τὸ φιλεῖσθαι καὶ ἀντιφιλεῖσθαι καὶ οἱ φίλοι διαφέρουσιν οἵ τε κατ'
ἰσότητα καὶ οἱ καθ' ὑπεροχήν, εἴρηται.
V. Ἐπεὶ δὲ τὸ φίλον λέγεται καὶ καθόλου 1
μᾶλλον, ὥσπερ καὶ κατ' ἀρχὰς ἐλέχθη, ὑπὸ τῶν
ἔξωθεν συμπαραλαμβανόντων[1] (οἱ μὲν γὰρ τὸ
ὅμοιόν φασιν εἶναι φίλον, οἱ δὲ τὸ ἐναντίον),
λεκτέον καὶ περὶ τούτων πῶς εἰσὶ πρὸς τὰς
εἰρημένας φιλίας. ἀνάγεται δὲ τὸ μὲν ὅμοιον καὶ 2
εἰς τὸ ἡδὺ καὶ εἰς τὸ ἀγαθόν. τό τε γὰρ ἀγαθὸν
ἁπλοῦν τὸ δὲ κακὸν πολύμορφον· καὶ ὁ ἀγαθὸς
μὲν ὅμοιος ἀεὶ καὶ οὐ μεταβάλλεται τὸ ἦθος, ὁ
δὲ φαῦλος καὶ ὁ ἄφρων οὐθὲν ἔοικεν ἕωθεν καὶ
ἑσπέρας. διὸ ἐὰν μὴ συμβάλλωσιν οἱ φαῦλοι, οὐ 3
φίλοι ἑαυτοῖς ἀλλὰ διίστανται· ἡ δ' οὐ βέβαιος
φιλία οὐ φιλία. ὥστε οὕτω μὲν τὸ ὅμοιον φίλον,
ὅτι τὸ[2] ἀγαθὸν ὅμοιον. ἔστι δὲ ὡς καὶ κατὰ τὸ
ἡδύ· τοῖς γὰρ ὁμοίοις ταὔθ' ἡδέα, καὶ ἕκαστον δὲ
φύσει αὐτὸ αὑτῷ ἡδύ. διὸ καὶ φωναὶ καὶ ἕξεις[3] 4
καὶ συνημερεύσεις τοῖς ὁμογενέσιν ἥδισται ἀλλήλοις,
καὶ τοῖς ἄλλοις ζῴοις· καὶ ταύτῃ ἐνδέχεται καὶ
τοὺς φαύλους ἀλλήλους φιλεῖν·

κακὸς κακῷ δὲ συντέτηκεν ἡδονῇ.

Τὸ δ' ἐναντίον τῷ ἐναντίῳ φίλον κατὰ[4] τὸ 5
χρήσιμον. αὐτὸ γὰρ αὑτῷ τὸ ὅμοιον ἄχρηστον,
διὸ δεσπότης δούλου δεῖται καὶ δοῦλος δεσπότου
καὶ γυνὴ καὶ ἀνὴρ ἀλλήλων· καὶ ἡδὺ καὶ ἐπι-

[1] Sp.: συμπεριλαμβανόντων. [2] τὸ add. Bz.
[3] v.l. αἱ ἕξεις: πράξεις? Rac. (διαλέξεις vel διάλεξις Ric., sed cf. l. 20). [4] Rac.: ὡς.

[a] 1235 a 4 ff. [b] *Cf.* 1238 a 34 note.

are, namely three, and that receiving affection and having one's affection returned, and friends on an equality and those on a footing of superiority, are different.

Friendship of the like and of opposites (see c. i. §§ 7, 8).

1 V. But as the term 'friend' is used in a more universal sense as well, as was also said at the beginning,[a] by those who take in wider considerations (some saying that what is like is dear, others what is opposite), we must also speak about these forms of friendship and their relation to the kinds that have
2 been discussed. As for likeness, it connects with pleasantness and also with goodness. For the good is simple, whereas the bad is multiform; and also the good man is always alike and does not change in character, whereas the wicked and the foolish are quite different in the evening from what they were
3 in the morning. Hence if wicked men do not hit it off together, they are not friends with one another but they separate; yet an insecure friendship is not friendship at all. So the like is dear to us in this way, because the good is like. But in a way it is also dear on the score of pleasantness; for to those who are alike the same things are pleasant, and also everything is by nature pleasant to itself.
4 Owing to this relations find one another's voices and characters and society pleasantest, and so with the lower animals; and in this way it is possible even for bad men to feel affection for each other:

> But pleasure welds the bad man to the bad.[b]

5 But opposite is dear to opposite on the score of utility. For the like is useless to itself, and therefore master needs slave and slave master, man and wife need one another; and the opposite is pleasant

1239 b θυμητὸν τὸ ἐναντίον ὡς χρήσιμον, καὶ οὐχ ὡς ἐν
τῷ[1] τέλει ἀλλ' ὡς πρὸς τὸ τέλος· ὅταν γὰρ τύχῃ
οὗ ἐπιθυμεῖ, ἐν τῷ τέλει μέν ἐστιν οὐκ ὀρέγεται
δὲ τοῦ ἐναντίου, οἷον τὸ θερμὸν τοῦ ψυχροῦ καὶ
τὸ ξηρὸν τοῦ ὑγροῦ.

Ἔστι δέ πως καὶ ἡ τοῦ ἐναντίου φιλία τοῦ 6
ἀγαθοῦ. ὀρέγεται γὰρ ἀλλήλων διὰ τὸ μέσον· ὡς
σύμβολα γὰρ ὀρέγεται ἀλλήλων, διὰ τὸ οὕτω[2]
γίνεσθαι ἐξ ἀμφοῖν ἓν μέσον. ὥστε[3] κατὰ συμ- 7
βεβηκός ἐστι τοῦ ἐναντίου, καθ' αὑτὸ δὲ τῆς μεσότητος, ὀρέγονται γὰρ οὐκ ἀλλήλων τἀναντία ἀλλὰ
τοῦ μέσου. ὑπερψυχθέντες γὰρ ἐὰν θερμανθῶσιν εἰς
τὸ μέσον καθίστανται, καὶ ὑπερθερμανθέντες ἐὰν
ψυχθῶσιν, ὁμοίως δὲ καὶ ἐπὶ τῶν ἄλλων· εἰ δὲ μή,
ἀεὶ ἐν ἐπιθυμίᾳ, ὅτι[4] οὐκ ἐν τοῖς μέσοις. ἀλλὰ 8
χαίρει ὁ ἐν τῷ μέσῳ ἄνευ ἐπιθυμίας τοῖς φύσει
ἡδέσιν, οἱ δὲ πᾶσι τοῖς ἐξιστᾶσι τῆς φύσει ἕξεως.
τοῦτο μὲν οὖν τὸ εἶδος καὶ ἐπὶ τῶν ἀψύχων ἐστίν· 9
1240 a τὸ φιλεῖν δὲ γίνεται ὅταν ᾖ ἐπὶ τῶν ἐμψύχων.
διὸ ἐνίοτε[5] ἀνομοίοις χαίρουσιν, οἷον αὐστηροὶ εὐ-
τραπέλοις καὶ ὀξεῖς ῥαθύμοις· εἰς τὸ μέσον γὰρ
καθίστανται ὑπ' ἀλλήλων. κατὰ συμβεβηκὸς οὖν, 10
ὥσπερ ἐλέχθη, τὰ ἐναντία φίλα καὶ διὰ τὸ ἀγαθόν.

Πόσα μὲν οὖν εἴδη φιλίας, καὶ τίνες διαφοραὶ
καθ' ἃς λέγονται οἵ τε φίλοι καὶ οἱ φιλοῦντες καὶ

[1] τῷ add. Rac. (cf. 1333 a 10).
[2] Sp.: διὸ οὐ τῷ.
[3] Sus.: ἔτι.
[4] ὅτι add. Sp.
[5] ἔνιοι τοῖς Fr.

[a] The two halves of a bone or coin broken in half by two contracting parties and one kept by each, to serve as a token of identification when found to fit together.

and desirable as useful, not as contained in the End but as a means to the End—for when a thing has got what it desires it has arrived at its End, and does not strive to get its opposite, for example the hot the cold and the wet the dry.

6 But in a way love of the opposite is also love of the
good. For opposites strive to reach one another
through the middle point, for they strive after each
other as tallies,[a] because in that way one middle
7 thing results from the two. Hence accidentally love
of the good is love of the opposite, but essentially
it is love of the middle, for opposites do not strive
to reach one another but the middle. If when
people have got too cold they are subjected to heat,
and when they have got too hot to cold, they reach
a mean temperature, and similarly in other matters;
but without such treatment they are always in a
state of desire, because they are not at the middle
8 points. But a man in the middle enjoys without
passionate desire things by nature pleasant, whereas
the others enjoy everything that takes them outside
9 their natural state. This kind of relationship, then,
exists even between inanimate things; but when it
occurs in the case of living things it becomes affection. Hence sometimes people take delight in
persons unlike themselves, the stiff for instance in
the witty and the active in the lazy, for they are
brought by one another into the middle state.
10 Hence accidentally, as was said,[b] opposites are dear
to opposites also on account of the good.

It has, then, been said how many kinds of friendship there are, and what are the different senses in which people are termed friends, and also givers

[b] 1239 b 32.

1240 a οἱ φιλούμενοι, καὶ οὕτως ὥστε φίλοι εἶναι καὶ
ἄνευ τούτου, εἴρηται.

VI. Περὶ δὲ τοῦ αὐτὸν αὑτῷ φίλον εἶναι ἢ μὴ 1
πολλὴν ἔχει ἐπίσκεψιν. δοκεῖ γὰρ ἐνίοις μάλιστα
ἕκαστος αὐτὸς αὑτῷ φίλος εἶναι, καὶ τούτῳ
χρώμενοι κανόνι κρίνουσι τὴν πρὸς τοὺς ἄλλους
φίλους φιλίαν. κατὰ δὲ τοὺς λόγους καὶ τὰ
δοκοῦνθ' ὑπάρχειν τοῖς φίλοις τὰ μὲν ὑπεναντιοῦται,
τὰ δ' ὅμοια φαίνεται ὄντα. ἔστι γάρ πως κατ' 2
ἀναλογίαν αὕτη[1] φιλία ἁπλῶς δ' οὔ. ἐν δυσὶ γὰρ
διῃρημένοις τὸ φιλεῖσθαι καὶ φιλεῖν· δι' ἃ μᾶλλον
οὕτως[2] αὐτὸς αὑτῷ φίλος ὡς[3] ἐπὶ τοῦ ἀκρατοῦς
καὶ ἐγκρατοῦς εἴρηται πῶς ἑκὼν ἢ ἄκων, τῷ τὰ
μέρη ἔχειν πως πρὸς ἄλληλα τὰ τῆς ψυχῆς. καὶ
ὅμοιον[4] τὰ τοιαῦτα πάντα, εἰ φίλος αὐτὸς αὑτῷ
καὶ ἐχθρός, καὶ εἰ ἀδικεῖ τις αὐτὸς αὑτόν· πάντα
γὰρ ἐν δυσὶ ταῦτα καὶ διῃρημένοις[5]· ᾗ[6] δὴ[7] δύο 3
πως καὶ ἡ ψυχή, ὑπάρχει πως ταῦτα, ᾗ[8] δ' οὐ
διῃρημένα, οὐχ ὑπάρχει.

Ἀπὸ δὲ τῆς πρὸς αὑτὸν ἕξεώς εἰσιν[9] οἱ λοιποὶ
τρόποι τοῦ φίλον εἶναι ὡρισμένοι[10] καθ' οὓς ἐν
τοῖς λόγοις ἐπισκοπεῖν εἰώθαμεν. δοκεῖ γὰρ φίλος
εἶναι ὁ βουλόμενός τινι τἀγαθά, ἢ οἷα οἴεται
ἀγαθά, μὴ δι' αὑτὸν ἀλλ' ἐκείνου ἕνεκα· ἄλλον δὲ 4

[1] Ric.: *αὕτη ἡ*. [2] *οὗτος* Mᵇ. [3] *ὡς* add. Γ.
[4] *ὁμοῖα* Sp. [5] Bz.: *διῃρημένως*. [6] Fr.: *εἰ* Pᵇ, *ἡ* Mᵇ.
[7] Sp. (*enim* Guil.): *δὲ*. [8] *ἡ* codd, *εἰ* Bk.
[9] Sp.: *ὡς* (*καὶ* Ric.). [10] Iac.: *φιλεῖσθαι διωρισμένοι*.

[a] *Cf.* 1223 a 36–b 17. Self-restraint (or the lack of it) indicates that a man's personality has in a sense two parts, one of which may control the other; and similarly self-love implies that one part of the personality can have a certain feeling in regard to another part.

and objects of affection, both in a manner that makes them actually friends and without being friends.

Self-love

1 VI. The question whether one is one's own friend or not involves much consideration. Some think that every man is his own best friend, and they use this friendship as a standard by which to judge his friendship for his other friends. On theoretical grounds, and in view of the accepted attributes of friends, self-love and love of others are in some respects opposed but in others manifestly similar.

only metaphorical friendship;

2 For in a way self-love is friendship by analogy, but not absolutely. For being loved and loving involve two separate factors; owing to which a man is his own friend rather in the way in which, in the case of the unrestrained and the self-restrained man, we have said [a] how one has those qualities voluntarily or involuntarily—namely by the parts of one's spirit being related to each other in a certain way; and all such matters are a similar thing,—whether a man can be his own friend or foe, and whether a man can treat himself unjustly. For all these relations
3 involve two separate factors; in so far then as the spirit is in a manner two, these relations do in a manner belong to it, but in so far as the two are not separate, they do not.

but the four notes of true friendship

From the state of friendship for oneself are determined the remaining modes of friendship under which we usually study it in our discourses.[b] For a man is thought to be a friend who wishes for somebody things that are good, or that he believes to be good, not on his own account but for the other's sake;

[b] *Cf.* 1244 a 20. Perhaps a reference to Aristotle's lectures (Stock).

1240 a
τρόπον ᾧ τὸ εἶναι βούλεται δι' ἐκεῖνον καὶ μὴ δι'
αὑτόν, κἂν εἰ μὴ διανέμων τἀγαθά, μήτοι[1] τὸ
εἶναι, τούτῳ ἂν δόξειε μάλιστα φίλος εἶναι[2]·
ἄλλον δὲ τρόπον ᾧ συζῆν αἱρεῖται δι' αὐτὴν τὴν 5
ὁμιλίαν καὶ μὴ δι' ἕτερόν τι, οἷον οἱ πατέρες τὸ
μὲν εἶναι τοῖς τέκνοις, συζῶσι δ' ἑτέροις. μάχεται 6
δὲ[3] ταῦτα πάντα πρὸς ἄλληλα· οἱ μὲν γὰρ ἂν μὴ
τοδὶ αὑτοῖς,[4] οἱ δὲ ἂν μὴ τὸ εἶναι, οἱ δὲ τὸ συζῆν,
οὐκ οἴονται φιλεῖσθαι. ἔτι τὸ τῷ[5] ἀλγοῦντι συν- 7
αλγεῖν μὴ δι' ἕτερόν τι ἀγαπᾶν θήσομεν—οἷον οἱ
δοῦλοι πρὸς τοὺς δεσπότας ὅτι χαλεποὶ ἀλγοῦντες,
ἀλλ' οὐ δι' αὐτούς, ὥσπερ αἱ μητέρες τοῖς τέκνοις
καὶ οἱ συνωδίνοντες ὄρνιθες. βούλεται γὰρ μάλιστά 8
τε οὐ μόνον συλλυπεῖσθαι ὁ φίλος τῷ φίλῳ ἀλλὰ
καὶ τὴν αὐτὴν λύπην (οἷον διψῶντι συνδιψῆν) εἰ
ἐνεδέχετο, εἴτε μή, ὅτι[6] ἐγγύτατα. ὁ δ' αὐτὸς 9
λόγος καὶ ἐπὶ τοῦ χαίρειν· τὸ γὰρ χαίρειν[7] μὴ δι'
1240 b ἕτερόν τι ἀλλὰ δι' ἐκεῖνον ὅτι χαίρει φιλικόν. ἔτι
τὰ τοιάδε λέγεται περὶ φιλίας, ὡς ἰσότης φιλότης,
καὶ μίαν ψυχὴν[8] εἶναι τοῖς ἀληθῶς φίλοις.[9] ἅπαντα 10
ταῦτα ἐπαναφέρεται πρὸς τὸν ἕνα· καὶ γὰρ βούλεται
τἀγαθὰ αὑτῷ[10] τοῦτον τὸν τρόπον, οὐθεὶς γὰρ
αὐτὸς αὑτὸν εὖ ποιεῖ διά τι ἕτερον, οὐδὲ χάριν
τοσουδὶ εὖ[11] λέγει, ὅτι ἐποίησεν ᾗ εἷς· δοκεῖν[12] γὰρ

[1] Iac.: μὴ τῷ.
[2] Iac.: μάλιστα φιλεῖν.
[3] Sp. δή.
[4] Iac.: μὴ τὸ ἑαυτοῖς.
[5] τὸ τῷ Fr.: τῷ.
[6] εἴτε μή, ὅτι Rac.: ὅτι μὴ (εἴτε μὴ Iac.).
[7] τὸ γὰρ χαίρειν add. Γ.
[8] Cas.: καὶ μὴ μίαν φιλίαν.
[9] Rac.: τοὺς . . . φίλους.
[10] Bek.: αὐτῷ.
[11] χάριν τοσουδὶ εὖ Rac.: χάριτος οὐδὲ (χάριν τοσοῦδε Iac.).
[12] Iac.: δοκεῖ.

4 and in another way when a man wishes another's
existence — even though not bestowing goods on
him, let alone existence—for that other's sake and
not for his own, he would be thought to be in a high
5 degree the friend of that other ; and in another
way a man is a friend of one whose society he desires
merely for the sake of his company and not for something else, as fathers, though they desire their
children's existence, associate with other people. All
6 these cases conflict with one another ; some men
do not think they are loved unless the friend wishes
them this or that particular good, others unless their
existence is desired, others unless their society.
7 Again we shall reckon it affection to grieve with
one who grieves not for some ulterior motive—as
for instance slaves in relation to their masters share
their grief because when in grief they are harsh, and
not for their masters' own sake, as mothers grieve
with their children, and birds that share each other's
8 pain. For a friend wishes most of all that he might
not only feel pain when his friend is in pain but feel
actually the same pain—for example when he is
thirsty, share his thirst—if this were possible, and
9 if not, as nearly the same as may be. The same
principle applies also in the case of joy ; it is characteristic of a friend to rejoice for no other reason
than because the other is rejoicing. Again there
are sayings about friendship such as 'Amity is
10 equality' and 'True friends have one spirit.' All
these sayings refer back to the single individual ;
for that is the way in which the individual wishes
good to himself, as nobody benefits himself for some
ulterior motive, nor speaks well of himself for such
and such a consideration, because he acted as an

1240 b
φιλεῖν βούλεται ὁ δῆλον ποιῶν ὅτι φιλεῖ, ἀλλ'
οὐ φιλεῖν.[1] καὶ τὸ εἶναι βούλεσθαι[2] καὶ τὸ συζῆν 11
καὶ τὸ συγχαίρειν καὶ τὸ συναλγεῖν, καὶ μία δὴ
ψυχή, καὶ τὸ μὴ δύνασθαι ἄνευ ἀλλήλων μηδὲ
ζῆν, ἀλλὰ συναποθνήσκειν—οὕτω γὰρ ἔχει ὁ εἷς,
καὶ οὕτως[3] ὁμιλεῖ αὐτὸς αὑτῷ—πάντα δὴ[4] ταῦτα
τῷ ἀγαθῷ ὑπάρχει πρὸς αὑτόν. ἐν δὲ τῷ πονηρῷ 12
διαφωνεῖ, οἷον ἐν τῷ ἀκρατεῖ, καὶ διὰ τοῦτο δοκεῖ
καὶ ἐχθρὸν ἐνδέχεσθαι αὐτὸν αὑτῷ εἶναι· ᾗ δ' εἷς
καὶ ἀδιαίρετος, ὀρεκτὸς αὐτὸς αὑτῷ. τοιοῦτος ὁ 13
ἀγαθὸς καὶ ὁ κατ' ἀρετὴν φίλος· ἐπεὶ ὅ γε μοχθηρὸς
οὐχ εἷς ἀλλὰ πολλοί, καὶ τῆς αὐτῆς ἡμέρας ἕτερος
καὶ ἔμπληκτος. ὥστε καὶ ἡ αὑτοῦ πρὸς αὑτὸν
φιλία ἀνάγεται πρὸς τὴν τοῦ ἀγαθοῦ· ὅτι γάρ πῃ
ὅμοιος[5] καὶ εἷς καὶ αὐτὸς αὑτῷ ἀγαθός, ταύτῃ
αὐτὸς αὑτῷ φίλος καὶ ὀρεκτός. φύσει δὲ τοιοῦτος,
ἀλλ' ὁ πονηρὸς παρὰ φύσιν. ὁ δ'[6] ἀγαθὸς οὔθ' 14
ἅμα λοιδορεῖται ἑαυτῷ, ὥσπερ ὁ ἀκρατής, οὔθ' ὁ
ὕστερος τῷ πρότερον, ὥσπερ ὁ μεταμελητικός,[7]
οὔτε ὁ ἔμπροσθεν τῷ ὕστερον, ὥσπερ ὁ ψεύστης
(ὅλως τε εἰ δεῖ ὥσπερ οἱ σοφισταὶ διορίζουσιν, 15
ὥσπερ τὸ Κορίσκος καὶ Κορίσκος σπουδαῖος,
δῆλον γὰρ ὡς τὸ αὐτὸ πόσον σπουδαῖον αὐτῶν[8])·
ἐπεὶ ὅταν ἐγκαλέσωσιν αὑτοῖς,[9] ἀποκτιννύασιν
αὑτούς,[10] ἀλλὰ δοκεῖ πᾶς αὐτὸς αὑτῷ ἀγαθός.

[1] φιλεῖ? Rac.
[2] Rac.: μάλιστα.
[3] Rac.: ἴσως.
[4] Iac.: γὰρ (δὲ Γ).
[5] Bk.: ὅμοιοι.
[6] Syl.: οὐδέ.
[7] Cas.: μεταληπτικός.
[8] Fr.: αὐτόν.
[9] Fr.: αὐτοῖς.
[10] Fr.: αὐτούς.

[a] *Cf.* l. 3: δή marks a quotation.

[b] See *Sophistici Elenchi*, 175 b 15 ff. 'Coriscus' is used for any imaginary person, *cf.* 1220 a 19 f.

individual; for one who displays his affection wishes
11 not to be but to be thought affectionate. And wishing for the other to exist, and associating together, and sharing joy and grief, and 'being one spirit'[a] and being unable even to live without one another but dying together—for this is the case with the single individual, and he associates with himself in this way,—all these characteristics then belong to the good man in relation to himself. all apply to the good man's love of self.
12 In a wicked man on the other hand, for instance in one who lacks self-control, there is discord, and because of this it is thought to be possible for a man actually to be his own enemy; but as being one and
13 indivisible he is desirable to himself. This is the case with a good man and one whose friendship is based on goodness, because assuredly an evil man is not a single individual but many, and a different person in the same day, and unstable. Hence even a man's affection for himself carries back to the good man's self-love; for because he is in a way like himself, a single person, good to himself, he is in this way dear and desirable to himself. And a man is like that by nature, but a wicked man is contrary to
14 nature. But a good man does not rebuke himself either at the time, like the uncontrolled, nor yet his former self his later, like the penitent, nor his later
15 self his former, like the liar—(and generally, if it is necessary to distinguish as the sophists do, he is related to himself as 'John Styles' is related to 'good John Styles'[b]; for it is clear that the same amount of 'John Styles' is good as of 'good John Styles')—because when men blame themselves they are murdering their own personalities, whereas everybody seems to himself good. And he who is

1240 b
ζητεῖ δὲ ὁ ἁπλῶς ὢν ἀγαθὸς εἶναι καὶ αὐτὸς αὑτῷ
φίλος, ὥσπερ εἴρηται, ὅτι δύ' ἔχει ἐν αὑτῷ ἃ
φύσει βούλεται εἶναι φίλα καὶ διασπάσαι ἀδύνατον.
διὸ ἐπ' ἀνθρώπου μὲν δοκεῖ ἕκαστος αὐτὸς αὑτῷ 16
φίλος, ἐπὶ δὲ τῶν ἄλλων ζῴων οὔ,[1] οἷον ἵππος
αὐτὸς αὑτῷ . . .[2] οὐκ ἄρα φίλος. ἀλλ' οὐδὲ τὰ
παιδία, ἀλλ' ὅταν ἤδη ἔχῃ προαίρεσιν· ἤδη γὰρ
τότε διαφωνεῖ ὁ νοῦς[3] πρὸς τὴν ἐπιθυμίαν. ἔοικε 17
δ' ἡ φιλία ἡ πρὸς αὑτὸν[4] τῇ κατὰ συγγένειαν·
οὐθέτερον γὰρ ἐφ' αὑτοῖς λῦσαι, ἀλλὰ κἂν δια-
φέρωνται ὅμως οὗτοι μὲν συγγενεῖς ἔτι,[5] ὁ δὲ
ἔτι εἷς ἕως ἂν ζῇ.

Ποσαχῶς μὲν οὖν τὸ φιλεῖν λέγεται, καὶ ὅτι
πᾶσαι αἱ φιλίαι ἀνάγονται πρὸς τὴν πρώτην, δῆλον
ἐκ τῶν εἰρημένων.

1241 a VII. Οἰκεῖον δὲ τῇ σκέψει θεωρῆσαι καὶ περὶ 1
ὁμονοίας καὶ εὐνοίας· δοκεῖ γὰρ τοῖς μὲν εἶναι
ταὐτό,[6] τοῖς δ' οὐκ ἄνευ ἀλλήλων. ἔστι δ' ἡ εὔνοια τῆς φιλίας οὔτε πάμπαν ἕτερον οὔτε ταὐτόν.
διῃρημένης γὰρ τῆς φιλίας κατὰ τρεῖς τρόπους, 2
οὔτ' ἐν τῇ χρησίμῃ οὔτ' ἐν τῇ καθ' ἡδονήν ἐστιν.
εἴτε γὰρ ὅτι χρήσιμος[7] βούλεται αὐτῷ τἀγαθά, οὐ
δι' ἐκεῖνον ἀλλὰ δι' αὑτὸν βούλοιτ' ἄν, δοκεῖ δ'
ὥσπερ . . .[8] καὶ ἡ εὔνοια οὐκ αὐτοῦ ἕνεκα[9] τοῦ

[1] οὐ add. Sp. [2] lacunam Sus. [3] Fr.: παῖς.
[4] Syl.: αὐτὸν. [5] εἰσί Sp.
[6] Rac.: ταὐτά. [7] Sp.: χρήσιμον.
[8] lacunam edd.: ⟨καὶ ἡ κατ' ἀρετὴν φιλία⟩ Sus.
[9] Iac.: εὔνοια.

[a] ll. 13-21.
[b] Some words seem to have been lost here.

absolutely good seeks to be dear even to himself, as has been said,[a] because he has two factors within him which by nature desire to be friendly and which
16 it is impossible to draw asunder. Therefore in the case of man each individual seems dear to himself, although in the case of other animals it is not so, for example a horse to itself . . .[b] so it is not dear to itself. But neither are children, but only when they have come to possess purposive choice; for when that point is reached the mind is at variance with
17 the appetite. And affection for oneself resembles the affection of relationship: neither connexion is in people's own power to dissolve, but even if the parties quarrel, nevertheless relatives are still relatives and the individual is still one as long as he lives.

From what has been said, then, it is clear how many meanings there are of the term 'affection,' and that all the forms of friendship carry back to the first one.

Goodwill the basis of friendship founded on Goodness.

1 VII. It is relative to our inquiry to consider also the subject of agreement of feeling and kindly feeling[c]; for some people think that they are the same thing, and others that they cannot exist apart. Kindly feeling is neither entirely distinct from friend-
2 ship nor yet identical with it. If friendship is divided into three modes, kindly feeling is not found in the friendship of utility nor in friendship for pleasure. If A wishes B prosperity because he is useful, the motive of his wish would be not B's interest but his own, whereas it is thought that kindly feeling like . . .[d] is not for the sake of the person

[c] These are Solomon's versions of the terms usually rendered 'concord and goodwill.'

[d] Perhaps 'virtuous friendship' should be supplied.

1241 a εὐνοϊζομένου εἶναι ἀλλὰ τοῦ ᾧ εὐνοεῖ· εἴτ'[1] ἐν τῇ
τοῦ ἡδέος φιλίᾳ, κἂν τοῖς ἀψύχοις ηὐνόουν· ὥστε
δῆλον ὅτι περὶ τὴν ἠθικὴν φιλίαν ἡ εὔνοιά ἐστιν.
ἀλλὰ τοῦ μὲν εὐνοοῦντος βούλεσθαι μόνον ἐστί, τοῦ 3
δὲ φίλου καὶ πράττειν ἃ βούλεται· ἔστι γὰρ ἡ
εὔνοια ἀρχὴ φιλίας. ὁ μὲν γὰρ φίλος πᾶς εὔνους, ὁ
δ' εὔνους οὐ πᾶς φίλος, ἀρχομένῳ γὰρ ἔοικεν ὁ
εὐνοῶν μόνον. διὸ ἀρχὴ φιλίας, ἀλλ' οὐ φιλία.

Δοκοῦσι γὰρ οἵ τε φίλοι ὁμονοεῖν καὶ οἱ ὁμονοοῦντες φίλοι εἶναι. ἔστι δ' οὐ περὶ πάντα ἡ ὁμόνοια 4
ἡ φιλική, ἀλλὰ περὶ τὰ πρακτὰ τοῖς ὁμονοοῦσι καὶ
ὅσα εἰς τὸ συζῆν συντείνει. οὐδὲ[2] μόνον κατὰ διάνοιαν ἢ κατὰ ὄρεξιν· ἔστι γὰρ τἀναντία νοεῖν καὶ[3]
ἐπιθυμεῖν, ὥσπερ ἐν τῷ ἀκρατεῖ διαφωνεῖ τοῦτο·
οὐδ' εἰ[4] κατὰ τὴν προαίρεσιν ὁμονοεῖ,[5] καὶ κατὰ
τὴν ἐπιθυμίαν. ἐπὶ δὲ τῶν ἀγαθῶν ἡ ὁμόνοια· οἵ 5
γε φαῦλοι ταὐτὰ προαιρούμενοι καὶ ἐπιθυμοῦντες
βλάπτουσιν ἀλλήλους. ἔοικε δὲ καὶ ἡ ὁμόνοια οὐχ 6
ἁπλῶς λέγεσθαι, ὥσπερ οὐδ' ἡ φιλία, ἀλλ' ἡ μὲν
πρώτη καὶ φύσει σπουδαία, διὸ οὐκ ἔστι τοὺς
φαύλους οὕτως[6] ὁμονοεῖν, ἑτέρα δὲ καθ' ἣν καὶ οἱ
φαῦλοι ὁμονοοῦσιν, ὅταν τῶν αὐτῶν τὴν προαίρεσιν
καὶ τὴν ἐπιθυμίαν ἔχωσιν. οὕτω δὲ δεῖ τῶν αὐτῶν 7
ὀρέγεσθαι ὥστ' ἐνδέχεσθαι ἀμφοτέροις ὑπάρχειν

[1] Sp.: εἰ δ' aut εἰ δή.
[2] Sus.: οὔτε
[3] νοεῖν καὶ Sol.: τὸ κινοῦν.
[4] οὐ δεῖ M^b
[5] ὁμονοεῖν P^b.
[6] <οὕτως> add. Rac.

who feels it himself but for the sake of him for whom he feels kindly ; and if kindly feeling were found in friendship for the pleasant, men would feel kindly even towards inanimate objects. So that it is clear that kindly feeling has to do with the
3 friendship that is based on character. But it is the mark of one who feels kindly only to wish good, whereas it is the mark of the friend also to do the good that he wishes ; for kindly feeling is the beginning of friendship, as every friend feels kindly, but not everyone who feels kindly is a friend, since the kindly man is only as it were making a beginning. Therefore kindly feeling is the beginning of friendship, but it is not friendship.

Concord in social conduct is confined to the good.

For it is thought that friends agree in feeling,
4 and that those who agree in feeling are friends. But the agreement of friendship is not in regard to everything, but to things practicable for the parties, and to all that contributes to their association. Nor is it only agreement in thought or in appetition, for it is possible to think and to desire opposite things, as in the man lacking self-control this discord occurs ; if a man agrees with another in purposive choice he does not necessarily agree with him in desire also.
5 Agreement occurs in the case of good men—at all events when bad men purpose and desire the same
6 things they harm one another. And it appears that agreement, like friendship, is not a term of single meaning, but whereas the primary and natural form of it is good, so that it is not possible for bad men to agree in this way, there is another sort of agreement shown even by bad men when their purpose and
7 desire are for the same objects. But it is only proper for them to aim at the same objects in cases when

1241 a
οὗ ὀρέγονται· ἂν γὰρ τοιούτου ὀρέγωνται ὃ μὴ
ἐνδέχεται ἀμφοῖν, μαχοῦνται. οἱ ὁμονοοῦντες δ'
οὐ μάχονται.[1]
Ἔστι δὴ[2] ὁμόνοια ὅταν περὶ τοῦ ἄρχειν καὶ 8
ἄρχεσθαι[3] ἡ αὐτὴ προαίρεσις ᾖ, μὴ τοῦ ἑκάτερον,
ἀλλὰ τοῦ τὸν αὐτόν. καὶ ἔστιν ἡ ὁμόνοια φιλία
πολιτική.

Περὶ μὲν οὖν ὁμονοίας καὶ εὐνοίας εἰρήσθω
τοσαῦτα.

VIII. Ἀπορεῖται δὲ διὰ τί μᾶλλον φιλοῦσιν οἱ 1
ποιήσαντες εὖ τοὺς παθόντας ἢ οἱ παθόντες εὖ τοὺς
ποιήσαντας· δοκεῖ δὲ δίκαιον εἶναι τοὐναντίον.
τοῦτο δ' ὑπολάβοι μὲν ἄν τις διὰ τὸ χρήσιμον 2
καὶ τὸ αὑτῷ ὠφέλιμον συμβαίνειν· τῷ[4] μὲν
γὰρ ὀφείλεται[5] τὸν δ' ἀποδοῦναι δεῖ. οὐκ ἔστι δὲ
τοῦτο μόνον, ἀλλὰ καὶ φυσικόν· ἡ γὰρ ἐνέργεια 3
1241 b
αἱρετώτερον, τὸν αὐτὸν δὲ[6] λόγον ἔχει τὸ ἔργον καὶ
ἡ ἐνέργεια, ὁ δ' εὖ παθὼν ὥσπερ ἔργον τοῦ εὖ
ποιήσαντος. διὸ καὶ ἐν τοῖς ζῴοις ἡ περὶ τὰ τέκνα
σπουδή ἐστι καὶ τοῦ γεννῆσαι καὶ τοῦ[7] τὰ[8] γεννώ-
μενα σῴζειν. καὶ φιλοῦσι δὴ μᾶλλον οἱ πατέρες 4
τὰ τέκνα (καὶ αἱ μητέρες τῶν πατέρων)[9] ἢ φι-
λοῦνται, καὶ οὗτοι πάλιν τὰ αὑτῶν ἢ τοὺς γεννή-
σαντας, διὰ τὸ τὴν ἐνέργειαν εἶναι τὸ ἄριστον. καὶ
αἱ μητέρες τῶν πατέρων, ὅτι μᾶλλον οἴονται αὑτῶν
εἶναι ἔργον τὰ τέκνα· τὸ γὰρ ἔργον τῷ χαλεπῷ 5

[1] Rac.: μαχοῦνται.
[2] Sp.: δ' ᾖ.
[3] [καὶ ἄρχεσθαι] ? Rac.
[4] Fr.: τὸ (τὸν edd.).
[5] Fr.: ὠφελεῖται.
[6] Sp.: δὴ.
[7] τοῦ add. Rac.
[8] τὰ add. Sp.
[9] [καὶ . . . πατέρων] Sp.

it is possible for both to have the things aimed at, since if they aim at a thing of a kind that it is not possible for both to have, they will quarrel; but those who agree in mind do not quarrel.

8 Therefore agreement exists when there is the same purposive choice as to ruling and being ruled—not each choosing himself to rule but both the same one. Agreement is civic friendship.

So much for the subject of agreement in feeling and kindly feeling.

Love of benefactor for beneficiary.

1 VIII. The question is raised, why those who have conferred a benefit feel more affection for those who have received it than those who have received it feel for those who have conferred it; whereas justice
2 seems to require the opposite. One might conceive that it occurs for reasons of utility and personal benefit; for benefit is owing to one party and it is the other party's duty to repay it. But really it is not
3 this alone; it is also a law of nature—activity is a more desirable thing, and there is the same relation between effect and activity as between the parties here: the person benefited is as it were the product of the benefactor. This is why even animals have the philoprogenitive instinct, which urges them to produce offspring and also to protect the offspring
4 produced. And in fact fathers love their children more than they are loved by them (mothers more so than fathers)[a] and these in their turn love *their* children more than their parents, because activity is the greatest good. And mothers love their children more than fathers, because they think that the
5 children are more their work; for people estimate

[a] This clause is probably an interpolation in the Greek.

1241 b διορίζουσιν, πλείω δὲ λυπεῖται περὶ τὴν γένεσιν
ἡ[1] μήτηρ.

Καὶ περὶ μὲν φιλίας τῆς πρὸς αὑτὸν καὶ τῆς ἐν
πλείοσι διωρίσθω τὸν τρόπον τοῦτον.

IX. Δοκεῖ δὲ τό τε δίκαιον εἶναι ἴσον τι καὶ ἡ 1
φιλία ἐν ἰσότητι, εἰ μὴ μάτην λέγεται ἰσότης ἡ
φιλότης. αἱ δὲ πολιτεῖαι πᾶσαι δικαίου τι εἶδος·
κοινωνίαι[2] γάρ, τὸ δὲ κοινὸν πᾶν διὰ τοῦ δικαίου
συνέστηκεν, ὥστε ὅσα εἴδη[3] φιλίας, τοσαῦτα[4] καὶ
δικαίου καὶ κοινωνίας, καὶ πάντα ταῦτα σύνορα
ἀλλήλοις καὶ ἐγγὺς ἔχει τὰς διαφοράς. ἐπεὶ δ'[5] 2
ὁμοίως ἔχει ψυχὴ πρὸς σῶμα καὶ τεχνίτης πρὸς
ὄργανον καὶ δεσπότης πρὸς δοῦλον, τούτων μὲν
οὐκ ἔστι κοινωνία· οὐ γὰρ δύ' ἐστίν, ἀλλὰ τὸ μὲν
ἕν, τὸ δὲ τοῦ ἑνὸς οὐδ' ἕν[6]· οὐδὲ διαιρετὸν τὸ
ἀγαθὸν ἑκατέρῳ, ἀλλὰ τὸ ἀμφοτέρων τοῦ ἑνὸς οὗ
ἕνεκά ἐστιν. τό τε γὰρ σῶμά ἐστιν ὄργανον σύμφυτον, καὶ τοῦ δεσπότου ὁ δοῦλος ὥσπερ μόριον
καὶ ὄργανον[7] ἀφαιρετόν, τὸ δ' ὄργανον ὥσπερ
δοῦλος ἄψυχος.

Αἱ δ' ἄλλαι κοινωνίαι εἰσὶν[8] μόριον τῶν τῆς 3
πόλεως κοινωνιῶν, οἷον ἡ τῶν φρατέρων ἢ τῶν
ὀργέων[9] ἢ αἱ χρηματιστικαὶ [ἔτι πολιτεῖαι].[10] αἱ
δὲ πολιτεῖαι πᾶσαι ἐν ταῖς οἰκίαις[11] συνυπάρχουσι,
καὶ αἱ ὀρθαὶ καὶ αἱ παρεκβάσεις (ἔστι γὰρ τὸ

[1] ἡ add. Rac. (et olim Fr.).
[2] Bz.: κοινωνία.
[3] ὥστε ὅσα εἴδη Bz.: ὅστις ἀεὶ δὴ (διὰ Mb).
[4] τοσαῦτα add. Rac. (cf. *M.M.* 1211 a).
[5] δ' <οὐχ> ? Rac.
[6] Iac.: οὐδέν.
[7] [καὶ ὄργανον] ? Rac.
[8] Bz.: εἰσὶν ἤ.
[9] Sol. (et v. L. & S.): ὀργίων (ὀργεώνων Dietsche).
[10] Fr.
[11] <ταῖς> οἰκίαις (cf. *N.E.* 1160 b 24) Fr.: οἰκείοις.

work by its difficulty, and in the production of a child the mother suffers more pain.

Such may be our decision on the subject of friendship for oneself and of friendship among more than one.

1 IX. It is thought that what is just is something that is equal, and also that friendship is based on equality, if there is truth in the saying 'Amity is equality.' And all constitutions are some species of justice; for they are partnerships, and every partnership is founded on justice, so that there are as many species of justice and of partnership as there are of friendship, and all these species border on each
2 other and have their differentia closely related. But since the relations of soul and body, craftsman and tool, and master and slave are similar,[a] between the two terms of each of these pairs there is no partnership; for they are not two, but the former is one and the latter a part of that one, not one itself; nor is the good divisible between them, but that of both belongs to the one for whose sake they exist. For the body is the soul's tool born with it, a slave is as it were a member or tool of his master, a tool is a sort of inanimate slave.

Forms of partnerships.

3 The other partnerships are a constituent part of the partnerships of the state—for example that of the members of a brotherhood or a priesthood, or business partnerships. All forms of constitution exist together in the household, both the correct forms and the deviations (for the same thing is found in

Analogy of private relationships with constitutions.

[a] *i.e.* to one another. Perhaps the Greek should be emended to give 'not similar' (to those just mentioned).

1241 b αὐτό, ὥσπερ ἐπὶ τῶν ἁρμονιῶν, καὶ ἐν[1] ταῖς πολιτείαις), βασιλικὴ μὲν ἡ τοῦ γεννήσαντος, ἀριστο- 4
κρατικὴ δ' ἡ ἀνδρὸς καὶ γυναικός, πολιτεία δ' ἡ τῶν
ἀδελφῶν, παρέκβασις δὲ τούτων τυραννίς, ὀλιγαρχία,
δῆμος· καὶ τὰ δίκαια δὴ τοσαῦτα.

Ἐπεὶ δὲ τὸ ἴσον τὸ μὲν κατ' ἀριθμὸν τὸ δὲ κατ' 5
ἀναλογίαν, καὶ τοῦ δικαίου εἴδη ἔσται καὶ τῆς
φιλίας καὶ τῆς κοινωνίας. κατ' ἀριθμὸν μὲν γὰρ
ἡ ⟨δημοκρατικὴ⟩[2] κοινωνία, καὶ ἡ ἑταιρικὴ φιλία
(τῷ γὰρ αὐτῷ ὅρῳ μετρεῖται), κατ' ἀναλογίαν δὲ
ἡ ἀριστοκρατικὴ ἡ[3] ἀρίστη καὶ ἡ[4] βασιλική (οὐ
γὰρ ταὐτὸν δίκαιον τῷ ὑπερέχοντι καὶ ὑπερεχο-
μένῳ ἀλλὰ τὸ ἀνάλογον)· καὶ ἡ φιλία δὲ ὁμοίως 6
πατρὸς καὶ παιδός, καὶ ἐν ταῖς κοινωνίαις ὁ αὐτὸς
τρόπος.

1242 a X. Λέγονται δὴ[5] φιλίαι συγγενική, ἑταιρική, κοι- 1
νωνική, ἡ λεγομένη πολιτική. ἔστι μὲν συγγενι-
κὴ πολλὰ ἔχουσα εἴδη, ἡ μὲν ὡς ἀδελφῶν, ἡ
δ' ὡς πατρὸς καὶ υἱῶν[6]· καὶ γὰρ κατ' ἀναλογίαν,
οἷον ἡ πατρική, καὶ κατ' ἀριθμόν, οἷον ἡ τῶν
ἀδελφῶν. ἐγγὺς γὰρ αὕτη τῆς ἑταιρικῆς· ἐπι-
λαμβάνουσι γὰρ καὶ ἐνταῦθα πρεσβείων. ἡ δὲ 2
πολιτικὴ συνέστηκε μὲν κατὰ τὸ χρήσιμον καὶ
μάλιστα· διὰ γὰρ τὸ μὴ αὔταρκες[7] δοκοῦσι συμ-

[1] Sp.: τῶν ἐν.
[2] Sus.
[3] ἡ add. Ross.
[4] ἡ add. Rac.
[5] Sp.: δέ.
[6] [ἡ μὲν ὡς . . . υἱῶν] ? Rac.
[7] Rac.: αὐτάρκη.

[a] *Cf. Politics* viii., 1342 a 24 τῶν ἁρμονιῶν παρεκβάσεις εἰσὶ

constitutions as in the case of musical modes [a])—
4 paternal authority being royal, the relationship of man and wife aristocratic, that of brothers a republic, while the deviation-forms of these are tyranny, oligarchy and democracy ; and there are therefore as many varieties of justice.

5 And since there are two sorts of equality, numerical and proportional, there will also be various species of justice and of partnership and friendship. The partnership of democracy is based on numerical equality, and so is the friendship of comrades, as it is measured by the same standard ; whereas the aristocratic partnership (which is the best) and the royal are proportional, for it is just for superior and inferior to have not the same share but proportional
6 shares ; and similarly also the friendship of father and son, and the same way in partnerships.

Friendships and Justice. The claims of various friendships differ.

1 X. Specified sorts of friendship are therefore the friendship of relatives, that of comrades, that of partners and what is termed civic friendship. Really friendship of relatives has more than one species, one as between brothers, another as of father and son [b] : it may be proportional, for example paternal friendship, or based on number, for example the friendship of brothers—for this is near the friendship of comrades, as in this also they claim privileges of
2 seniority. Civic friendship on the other hand is constituted in the fullest degree on the principle of utility, for it seems to be the individual's lack of self-sufficiency that makes these unions permanent—

καὶ τῶν μελῶν τὰ σύντονα καὶ παρακεχρωσμένα, 'those harmonies and melodies that are highly strung and irregular in coloration (*i.e.* divergent from the regular scale in having smaller intervals) are deviations.'

[b] These two clauses look like an interpolation.

1242 a
μένειν,[1] ἐπεὶ συνῆλθόν γ' ἂν καὶ τοῦ συζῆν χάριν.
μόνη δ' ἡ πολιτικὴ καὶ ἡ παρ' αὐτὴν παρέκβασις
οὐ μόνον φιλίαι, ἀλλὰ καὶ ὡς φίλοι κοινωνοῦσιν,
αἱ δ' ἄλλαι καθ' ὑπεροχήν. μάλιστα δὲ δίκαιον τὸ 3
ἐν τῇ τῶν χρησίμων φιλίᾳ, διὰ τὸ τοῦτ' εἶναι τὸ
πολιτικὸν δίκαιον. ἄλλον γὰρ τρόπον συνῆλθον
πρίων καὶ τέχνη, οὐχ ἕνεκα κοινοῦ τινός (οἷον[2] γὰρ
ὄργανον καὶ ψυχή) ἀλλὰ τοῦ χρωμένου ἕνεκεν.
συμβαίνει δὲ καὶ αὐτὸ τὸ[3] ὄργανον ἐπιμελείας 4
τυγχάνειν ἧς δίκαιον πρὸς τὸ ἔργον· ἐκείνου γὰρ
ἕνεκέν ἐστι, καὶ τὸ τρυπάνῳ εἶναι διττόν, ὧν τὸ
κυριώτερον ἐνέργεια, ἡ τρύπησις. καὶ ἐν τούτῳ τῷ
εἴδει σῶμα καὶ δοῦλος, ὥσπερ εἴρηται πρότερον.

Τὸ δὴ ζητεῖν πῶς δεῖ τῷ φίλῳ ὁμιλεῖν, τὸ ζητεῖν 5
δίκαιόν τι ἐστίν. καὶ γὰρ ὅλως τὸ δίκαιον ἅπαν
πρὸς φίλον· τό τε γὰρ δίκαιόν τισι καὶ κοινωνοῖς,
καὶ ὁ φίλος κοινωνός, ὁ μὲν γένους, ὁ δὲ βίου. ὁ
γὰρ ἄνθρωπος οὐ μόνον πολιτικὸν[4] ἀλλὰ καὶ
οἰκονομικὸν ζῷον, καὶ οὐχ ὥσπερ τἆλλά ποτε
συνδυάζεται καὶ τῷ τυχόντι καὶ θήλει καὶ ἄρρενι,
ἀλλ' ἰδίᾳ οὐ μοναυλικὸν[5] ἀλλὰ κοινωνικὸν ἄνθρωπος 6
ζῷον πρὸς οὓς φύσει συγγένειά ἐστιν· καὶ κοινωνία
τοίνυν καὶ δίκαιόν τι καὶ εἰ μὴ πόλις εἴη. οἰκία 7
δ' ἐστί τις φιλία· δεσπότου μὲν οὖν καὶ δούλου

[1] Sus.: συνελθεῖν. [2] Γ: ὅλον. [3] αὐτὸ τὸ Bz.: τοῦτο.
[4] Cas.: ἀνθρώπου μόνον οὐ πολιτικὸς (ἄνθρωπος οὐ μόνον πολιτικὸς Γ).
[5] Sp.: ἀλλ' αἱ διάδυμον αὐλικόν.

[a] Not its ἕξις, its shape, hardness, etc.
[b] 1241 b 17-24.
[c] *i.e.* 'friend' in the sense of 'relation.'

since they would have been formed in any case merely for the sake of society. Only civic friendship and the deviation from it are not merely friendships but also partnerships on a friendly footing; the
3 others are on a basis of superiority. The justice that underlies a friendship of utility is in the highest degree just, because this is the civic principle of justice. The coming together of a saw with the craft that uses it is on different lines—it is not for the sake of some common object, for saw and craft are like instrument and spirit, but for the sake of
4 the man who employs them. It does indeed come about that even the tool itself receives attention which it deserves with a view to its work, since it exists for the sake of its work, and the essential nature of a gimlet is twofold, the more important half being its activity, boring.[a] And the body and the slave are in the class of tool, as has been said before.[b]

5 Therefore to seek the proper way of associating with a friend is to seek for a particular kind of justice. In fact the whole of justice in general is in relation to a friend, for what is just is just for certain persons, and persons who are partners, and a friend is a partner, either in one's family [c] or in one's life. For man is not only a political but also a house-holding animal, and does not, like the other animals, couple occasionally and with any chance female or male,
6 but man is in a special way not a solitary but a gregarious animal, associating with the persons with whom he has a natural kinship; accordingly there would be partnership, and justice of a sort, even if
7 there were no state. And a household is a sort of friendship—or rather the relationship of master and

Domestic relations.

1242 a ἥπερ καὶ τέχνης καὶ ὀργάνων καὶ ψυχῆς καὶ
σώματος, αἱ δὲ τοιαῦται οὔτε φιλίαι οὔτε δικαιο-
σύναι ἀλλ' ἀνάλογον, ὥσπερ καὶ τὸ ὑγιεινὸν[1] οὐ
δίκαιον ἀλλ' ἀνάλογον. γυναικὸς δὲ καὶ ἀνδρὸς 8
φιλία ὡς χρήσιμον καὶ κοινωνία· πατρὸς δὲ καὶ
υἱοῦ ἡ αὐτὴ ἥπερ θεοῦ πρὸς ἄνθρωπον καὶ τοῦ εὖ
ποιήσαντος πρὸς τὸν παθόντα καὶ ὅλως τοῦ φύσει
ἄρχοντος πρὸς τὸν φύσει ἀρχόμενον. ἡ δὲ τῶν 9
ἀδελφῶν πρὸς ἀλλήλους ἑταιρικὴ μάλιστα, ᾗ[2] κατ'
ἰσότητα—

> οὐ γάρ τι νόθος τῷδ' ἀπεδείχθην,[3]
> ἀμφοῖν δὲ πατὴρ[4] αὐτὸς[5] ἐκλήθη
> Ζεὺς ἐμὸς ἄρχων—

ταῦτα γὰρ ὡς τὸ ἴσον ζητούντων λέγεται. διὸ ἐν
1242 b οἰκίᾳ πρῶτον ἀρχαὶ καὶ πηγαὶ φιλίας καὶ πολιτείας
καὶ δικαίου.

Ἐπεὶ δὲ φιλίαι τρεῖς, κατ' ἀρετήν, κατὰ τὸ 10
χρήσιμον, κατὰ τὸ ἡδύ, τούτων δὲ ἑκάστης δύο
διαφοραί (ἡ μὲν γὰρ καθ' ὑπεροχὴν ἡ δὲ κατ'
ἰσότητά ἐστιν ἑκάστη αὐτῶν), τὸ δὲ δίκαιον τὸ περὶ
αὐτὰς ἐκ τῶν ἀμφισβητήσεων[6] δῆλον, ἐν μὲν τῇ[7]
καθ' ὑπεροχὴν ἀξιοῦται τὸ ἀνάλογον οὐχ ὡσαύτως,
ἀλλ' ὁ μὲν ὑπερέχων ἀνεστραμμένως τὸ ἀνάλογον,
ὡς αὐτὸς πρὸς τὸν ἐλάττω, οὕτω τὸ παρὰ τοῦ ἐλάττονος γινόμενον πρὸς τὸ παρ' αὐτοῦ,[8] διακείμενος[9] ὥσπερ ἄρχων πρὸς ἀρχόμενον· εἰ δὲ μὴ τοῦτο, ἀλλὰ 11
τὸ ἴσον κατ' ἀριθμὸν ἀξιοῖ (καὶ γὰρ δὴ καὶ ἐπὶ

[1] ὑγιεινὸν corruptum edd.: ἐπιεικὲς ? Sus.
[2] Iac.: ἡ.
[3] Cas.: ἀπεδείχθη.
[4] Γ: πατρὸς.
[5] Nauck: αὐτός.
[6] Fr.: ἀμφισβητησάντων (ἀμφισβητηθέντων Bz.).
[7] Fr.: τῷ.
[8] Rac.: αὐτοῦ.
[9] Bz.: διακείμενον.

slave is that of craft and tools, and of spirit and body, and such relationships are not friendships or forms of justice but something analogous, just as
8 health[a] is not justice but analogous to it. But the friendship of man and wife is one of utility, a partnership; that of father and son is the same as that between god and man and between benefactor and beneficiary, and generally between natural
9 ruler and natural subject. That between brothers is principally the friendship of comrades, as being on a footing of equality—

> For never did he make me out a bastard,
> But the same Zeus, my lord, was called the sire
> Of both—,[b]

for these are the words of men seeking equality. Hence in the household are first found the origins and springs of friendship, of political organization and of justice.

10 And since there are three sorts of friendship, based on goodness, on utility and on pleasure, and two varieties of each sort (for each of them is either on a basis of superiority or of equality), and what is just in relation to them is clear from our discussions, in the variety based on superiority the proportionate claims are not on the same lines, but the superior party claims by inverse proportion—the contribution of the inferior to stand in the same ratio to his own as he himself stands in to the inferior, his attitude
11 being that of ruler to subject; or if not that, at all events he claims a numerically equal share (for in

Unequal friendships of all three forms.

[a] Perhaps the text is corrupt.

[b] Sophocles fr. 755 Jebb and Pearson (684 Nauck). The third line is completed in a quotation by Philo, *θνητῶν δ' οὐδείς*. (For *τῷδε* dative of agent see Kühner-Gerth, i. 422).

1242 b τῶν ἄλλων κοινωνιῶν οὕτω συμβαίνει, ὁτὲ μὲν γὰρ ἀριθμῷ τὸ ἴσον[1] μετέχουσιν, ὁτὲ δὲ λόγῳ· εἰ μὲν γὰρ ἴσον ἀριθμῷ εἰσήνεγκον ἀργύριον, ἴσον καὶ τῷ ἴσῳ ἀριθμῷ διαλαμβάνουσιν, εἰ δὲ μὴ ἴσον, ἀνάλογον), ὁ δ' ὑπερεχόμενος τοὐναντίον στρέφει τὸ ἀνάλογον καὶ κατὰ διάμετρον συζεύγνυσιν· δόξειε 12
δ' ἂν οὕτως ἐλαττοῦσθαι ὁ ὑπερέχων, καὶ λειτουργία ἡ φιλία καὶ ἡ[2] κοινωνία. δεῖ ἄρα τινὶ ἑτέρῳ ἀνισάσαι καὶ ποιῆσαι ἀνάλογον· τοῦτο δ' ἐστὶν ἡ 13
τιμή, ὅπερ καὶ τῷ ἄρχοντι φύσει καὶ θεῷ πρὸς τὸ ἀρχόμενον. δεῖ δὲ ἰσασθῆναι τὸ κέρδος πρὸς τὴν τιμήν.

Ἡ δὲ κατ' ἴσα φιλία ἐστὶν ἡ πολιτική. ἡ δὲ 14
πολιτικὴ ἐστὶ μὲν κατὰ τὸ χρήσιμον, καὶ ὥσπερ αἱ πόλεις ἀλλήλαις φίλαι, οὕτω καὶ οἱ πολῖται, καὶ ὁμοίως

οὐκέτι γιγνώσκουσιν Ἀθηναῖοι Μεγαρῆας

καὶ οἱ πολῖται, ὅταν μὴ χρήσιμοι ἀλλήλοις, ἀλλ' ἐκ

[1] Rac.: τοῦ ἴσου. [2] ἡ] οὐ Fr. (cf. *N.E.* 1163 a 29).

[a] The inferior party p claims to draw a larger share of benefit B and to leave the smaller share b to the superior party P, the result of which would be p + B and P + b. The superior party P also invokes the principle of inverse proportion (line 7), but applies it to their contributions to the common cause, not to the benefits drawn from it: he claims to make a smaller contribution c, while the inferior party makes a larger one C, the result of which would be P − c and p − C. The proposed conjunctions are in fact both of

fact it happens in this way in other associations too—sometimes the shares are numerically equal, sometimes proportionally : if the parties contributed a numerically equal sum of money, they also take a share equal by numerical equality, if an unequal sum, a share proportionally equal). The inferior party on the contrary inverts the proportion, and
12 makes a diagonal conjunction[a]; but it would seem that in this way the superior comes off worse, and the friendship or partnership is a charitable service.[b] Therefore equality must be restored and proportion
13 secured by some other means ; and this means is honour, which belongs by nature to a ruler and god in relation to a subject. But the profit[c] must be made equal to the honour.

14 Friendship on a footing of equality is civic friendship. Civic friendship is, it is true, based on utility, and fellow-citizens are one another's friends in the same way as different cities are, and

Political friendship

Athens no longer knoweth Megara,[d]

nor similarly do citizens know one another, when they are not useful to one another ; their friend-

them diagonal, connecting the larger person with the smaller thing and *vice versa* :

[b] Perhaps the Greek should be altered to give 'friendship is a charity and not a partnership.'

[c] *i.e.* the advantage in the shape of protection, guidance, etc., that the inferior party derives from the friendship.

[d] Lit. 'the Athenians no longer recognize the Megarians.' Author unknown (Bergk, *Fr. Eleg.*, Adespota 6).

1242 b
χειρὸς εἰς χεῖρα ἡ φιλία. ἔστι δὲ ἐνταῦθα καὶ 15
ἄρχον καὶ ἀρχόμενον, οὔτε τὸ φυσικὸν οὔτε τὸ
βασιλικόν, ἀλλὰ τὸ ἐν τῷ μέρει, οὐδὲ τούτου
ἕνεκα ὅπως εὖ ποιῇ ὡς ὁ θεός, ἀλλὰ ἵνα ἴσον ᾖ[1]
τοῦ ἀγαθοῦ καὶ[2] τῆς λειτουργίας. κατ' ἰσότητα δὴ
βούλεται εἶναι ἡ πολιτικὴ φιλία. ἔστι δὲ τῆς 16
χρησίμου φιλίας εἴδη δύο, ἡ μὲν νομικὴ ἡ δ' ἠθική.
βλέπει δ' ἡ μὲν πολιτικὴ εἰς τὸ ἴσον καὶ εἰς τὸ
πρᾶγμα, ὥσπερ οἱ πωλοῦντες καὶ οἱ ὠνούμενοι·
διὸ εἴρηται

μισθὸς ἀνδρὶ φίλῳ.

ὅταν μὲν οὖν καθ' ὁμολογίαν ᾖ,[3] πολιτικὴ αὕτη 17
φιλία καὶ νομική· ὅταν δ' ἐπιτρέπωσιν αὑτοῖς,[4]
ἠθικὴ βούλεται εἶναι φιλία καὶ ἑταιρική. διὸ
μάλιστα τὰ ἐγκλήματα[5] ἐν ταύτῃ τῇ φιλίᾳ· αἴτιον
δ' ὅτι παρὰ φύσιν· ἕτεραι γὰρ φιλίαι ἡ κατὰ τὸ
χρήσιμον καὶ ἡ κατὰ τὴν ἀρετήν, οἱ δ' ἀμφότερα[6]
βούλονται ἅμα ἔχειν, καὶ ὁμιλοῦσι μὲν τοῦ χρησίμου
1243 a
ἕνεκα, ἠθικὴν δὲ ποιοῦσιν ὡς ἐπιεικεῖς, διὸ ὡς
πιστεύοντες οὐ νομικὴν ποιοῦσιν.

Ὅλως μὲν γὰρ ἐν τῇ χρησίμῃ τῶν τριῶν πλεῖστα[7] 18
ἐγκλήματα (ἡ μὲν γὰρ ἀρετὴ ἀνέγκλητος[8] οἱ δ'
ἡδεῖς ἔχοντες καὶ δόντες ἀπαλλάττονται, οἱ δὲ
χρήσιμοι οὐκ εὐθὺς διαλύονται, ἂν μὴ νομικῶς
καὶ[9] ἑταιρικῶς προσφέρωνται)· ὅμως δὲ τῆς 19

[1] ἔχῃ ? Rac.
[2] καὶ Γ: ᾗ (ἴσον ᾖ τὸ ἀγαθὸν τῇ λειτουργίᾳ ? Rac.).
[3] Fr. (et Γ): ἡ.
[4] Rac.: αὐτοῖς.
[5] τὰ ἐγκλήματα Sp.: ἔγκλημα.
[6] ἀμφοτέρας ? Rac.
[7] πλεῖστα τὰ Sp.
[8] Sp.: ἀνέγκλητον.
[9] καὶ: ἀλλ' ? Rac.

[a] *Cf. N.E.* 1262 b 26.
[b] *N.E.* 1164 a 28. Hesiod, *W.D.* 371 μισθὸς δ' ἀνδρὶ φίλῳ

15 ship is a ready-money transaction.[a] Nevertheless there is present here a ruling factor and a ruled—not a natural ruler or a royal one, but one that rules in his turn, and not for the purpose of conferring benefit, as God rules, but in order that he may have an equal share of the benefit and of the burden. Therefore civic friendship aims at being on a footing of equality.

16 But useful friendship is of two kinds, the merely legal and the moral. Civic friendship looks to equality and to the object, as buyers and sellers do —hence the saying

Unto a friend his wage—.[b]

17 When, therefore, it is based on a definite agreement, this is civic and legal friendship ; but when they trust each other for repayment, it tends to be moral friendship, that of comrades. Hence this is the kind of friendship in which recriminations most occur, the reason being that it is contrary to nature ; for friendship based on utility and friendship based on goodness are different, but these people wish to have it both ways at once—they associate together for the sake of utility but make it out to be a moral friendship as between good men, and so represent it as not merely legal, pretending that it is a matter of trust.

Complaints frequent in friendships of utility on a moral basis.

18 For in general, of the three kinds of friendship, it is in useful friendship that most recriminations occur (for goodness is not given to recrimination, and pleasant friends having got and given their share break it off, but useful friends do not dissolve the association at once, if their intercourse is on comradely and not

19 merely legal lines) ; nevertheless the legal sort of

εἰρημένος ἄρκιος ἔστω 'et the wage stated for a friend stand good.'

1243 a

χρησίμου ἡ νομικὴ ἀνέγκλητος. ἔστι δ' ἡ μὲν νομικὴ διάλυσις πρὸς νόμισμα (μετρεῖται γὰρ τούτῳ τὸ ἴσον), ἡ δ' ἠθικὴ ἑκούσιος. διὸ ἐνιαχοῦ νόμος ἐστὶ τοῖς οὕτως ὁμιλοῦσι φιλικῶς μὴ εἶναι δίκας τῶν ἑκουσίων συναλλαγμάτων, ὀρθῶς· τοῖς γὰρ ἀγαθοῖς οὐ πέφυκε δίκη[1] εἶναι, οἱ δ' ὡς
ἀγαθοὶ καὶ πιστοῖς[2] συναλλάττουσιν. ἔστι δ' ἐν 20
ταύτῃ τῇ φιλίᾳ τὰ ἐγκλήματα ἀμφιβάλλοντα αὐτοῖς ἀμφότερα, πῶς ἑκάτερος ἐγκαλεῖ,[3] ὅταν ἠθικῶς ἀλλὰ μὴ νομικῶς πιστεύσωσιν.

Καὶ ἔχει δὴ ἀπορίαν ποτέρως δεῖ κρίνειν τὸ[4] 21
δίκαιον, πότερα πρὸς τὸ πρᾶγμα βλέποντα τὸ ὑπηρετηθὲν πόσον ἢ ποῖον, ἢ[5] τῷ πεπονθότι· ἐνδέχεται γὰρ[6] εἶναι ὅπερ λέγει Θέογνις—

σοὶ μὲν τοῦτο, θεά, σμικρόν, ἐμοὶ δὲ μέγα,

ἐνδέχεται δὲ[7] καὶ τοὐναντίον γενέσθαι, ὥσπερ ἐν τῷ λόγῳ, σοὶ μὲν παιδιὰν τοῦτ' εἶναι, ἐμοὶ δὲ
θάνατον. ἐντεῦθεν δ' ὥσπερ[8] εἴρηται[9] ἐγκλήματα· 22
ὁ μὲν γὰρ ἀξιοῖ ἀντιπαθεῖν ὡς μέγα ὑπηρετήσας ὅτι δεομένῳ ἐποίησεν, ἤ τι ἄλλο τοιοῦτο λέγων πρὸς τὴν ἐκείνου ὠφέλειαν πόσον ἐδύνατο ἀλλ' οὐ τί ἦν αὐτῷ,[10] ὁ δὲ τοὐναντίον ὅσον ἐκείνῳ ἀλλ'

[1] Sol.: δίκαιον (ἀγαθοῖς αὐτοῖς πέφυκε δικαίοις Sp.).
[2] Iac.: τοῖς.
[3] [πῶς . . . ἐγκαλεῖ] ? gloss. (an lege ἐγκαλέσει?) Rac.
[4] Sp.: τὸν. [5] ἦν Fr. [6] Γ: δὲ.
[7] Fr.: γὰρ. [8] ὥσπερ add. Fr.
[9] Rac.: εἴρηται τὰ. [10] Rac.: αὐτῷ.

[a] Or, adopting another conjectural emendation, 'since it is natural for good men to be just of their own accord.'

[b] Solomon renders 'It is uncertain how either will recriminate on the other, seeing that they trust each other, not

useful friendship is not given to recrimination. The legal method of discharging the obligation is a matter of money, for that serves as a measure of equality; but the moral method is voluntary. Hence in some places there is a law prohibiting friendly associates of this sort from actions as to their voluntary contracts—rightly, since it is not natural for good men to go to law,[a] and these men make their contracts as good
20 men and as dealing with trustworthy people. And in fact in this sort of friendship the recriminations are doubtful on both sides—what line of accusation each party will take, inasmuch as their confidence was of a moral kind and not merely legal.[b]

Estimate of claims.

21 Indeed it is a question in which of two ways one ought to judge what is a just return, whether by looking at the actual amount or quality of the service rendered, or by its amount or quality for the recipient; for it may be as Theognis says—

> Goddess, 'tis small to thee, but great to me,[c]

and also the result may be opposite, as in the saying
22 'This is sport to you but death to me.' Hence recriminations, as has been said [d]; for one party claims recompense as having rendered a great service, because he did it for his friend in need, or saying something else of the sort as to how much it was worth in relation to the benefit given to the recipient and not what it was to himself, while the other party on the contrary speaks of how much it was to the

in a limited legal way but on the basis of their characters.' But the Greek text may be questioned.

[c] Theognis 14. This quotation illustrates that the amount of a service is 'subjective,' the next quotation shows that its quality is.

[d] 1242 b 37.

οὐχ ὅσον αὐτῷ.[1] ὁτὲ δὲ καὶ μεταβάλλει[2]· ὁ μὲν 23
γὰρ ὅσον αὐτῷ[1] μικρὸν ἀπέβη, ὁ δ' ὅσον αὐτῷ[3]
μέγα[3] ἐδύνατο, οἷον, εἰ κινδυνεύσας δραχμῆς ἄξιον
ὠφέλησεν, ὁ μὲν τὸ τοῦ κινδύνου μέγεθος ὁ δὲ τὸ
τοῦ ἀργυρίου, ὥσπερ ἐν τῇ τῶν νομισμάτων ἀποδόσει
—καὶ γὰρ ἐνταῦθα περὶ τούτων ἡ ἀμφισβήτησις·
ὁ μὲν γὰρ ἀξιοῖ πῶς τότ' ἦν, ὁ δὲ πῶς νῦν, ἂν
μὴ διείπωνται.

Ἡ μὲν οὖν πολιτικὴ βλέπει εἰς τὴν ὁμολογίαν 24
καὶ εἰς τὸ πρᾶγμα, ἡ δ' ἠθικὴ εἰς τὴν προαίρεσιν·
ὥστε καὶ δίκαιον τοῦτο μᾶλλόν ἐστι, καὶ δικαιοσύνη φιλική. αἴτιον δὲ τοῦ μάχεσθαι διότι καλλίων 25
μὲν ἡ ἠθικὴ φιλία ἀναγκαιοτέρα δὲ ἡ χρησίμη· οἱ
δ' ἄρχονται[4] μὲν ὡς ἠθικοὶ φίλοι καὶ δι' ἀρετὴν
ὄντες, ὅταν δ' ἀντικρούσῃ[5] τι τῶν ἰδίων, δῆλοι γίνονται ὅτι ἕτεροι ἦσαν. ἐκ περιουσίας γὰρ διώ-
κουσιν οἱ πολλοὶ τὸ καλόν, διὸ καὶ τὴν καλλίω
φιλίαν. ὥστε φανερὸν πῶς διαιρετέον περὶ τούτων. 26
εἰ μὲν γὰρ ἠθικοὶ φίλοι, εἰς τὴν προαίρεσιν.
βλεπτέον εἰ ἴση, καὶ οὐθὲν ἄλλο ἀξιωτέον θατέρῳ
παρὰ θατέρου· εἰ δ' ὡς χρήσιμοι καὶ πολιτικοί,
ὡς ἂν ἐλυσιτέλει[6] ὁμολογοῦσιν. ἂν δ' ὁ μὲν
φῇ ὧδε ὁ δ' ἐκείνως, οὐ καλόν,[7] ἀντιποιῆσαι
δέον, τοὺς καλοὺς λέγειν λόγους, ὁμοίως δὲ καὶ

[1] (bis) Rac.: αὑτῷ.

[2] μεταβάλλει (vel μεταλαμβάνει) Rac.: μεταλαμβάνων καὶ ἀμφιβάλλει.

[3] [μέγα] Sol.

[4] Bus.: ἔρχονται.

[5] Iac.: ἄντικρυς ᾖ.

[6] ἕως ἂν λυσιτελῇ ? Rac. (ὡς ἂν λυσιτελῇ Sp.).

[7] Rac.: καλὸν μέν.

---

[a] Or, altering the Greek, 'they agree for as long as it profits them.'

23 donor and not how much it was to himself. And at other times the position is reversed: the one says how little he got out of it, the other how much the service was worth to him—for instance, if by taking a risk he did the other a shilling's worth of benefit, the one talks about the amount of the risk and the other about the amount of the cash; just as in the repayment of a money loan, for there too the dispute turns on this—one claims to be repaid the value that the money had when lent, the other claims to repay it at the present value, unless they have put a proviso in the contract.

24 Civic friendship, then, looks at the agreement and to the thing, but moral friendship at the intention; hence the latter is more just—it is friendly justice.

25 The cause of conflict is that moral friendship is nobler but friendship of utility more necessary; and men begin as being moral friends and friends on grounds of goodness, but when some private interest comes into collision it becomes clear that really they were different. For most men pursue what is fine only when they have a good margin in hand, and so with the finer sort of friendship too.

26 Hence it is clear how these cases must be decided. If they are moral friends, we must consider if their intentions are equal, and nothing else must be claimed by either from the other; and if they are friends on the ground of utility or civic friends, we must consider what form of agreement would have been profitable for them.[a] But if one says they are friends on one footing and the other on another, it is not honourable, when an active return is due, merely to make fine speeches, and similarly also in

1243 b ἐπὶ θατέρου· ἀλλ' ἐπειδὴ οὐ διείποντο ὡς ἠθικῶς, 27
δεῖ κρίνειν τινά, μηδ' ὑποκρινόμενον μηδέτερον[1]
αὐτῶν ἐξαπατᾶν· ὥστε δεῖ στέργειν ἑκάτερον τὴν
τύχην. ὅτι δ' ἐστὶν ἡ ἠθικὴ κατὰ προαίρεσιν 28
δῆλον, ἐπεὶ κἂν εἰ μεγάλα παθὼν μὴ ἀποδῴη δι'
ἀδυναμίαν ἀλλ' ὅσ'[2] ἐδύνατο, καλῶς· καὶ γὰρ[3] ὁ
θεὸς ἀνέχεται κατὰ δύναμιν λαμβάνων τὰς θυσίας.
ἀλλὰ τῷ πωλοῦντι οὐχ ἱκανῶς ἕξει ἂν μὴ φήσῃ 29
δύνασθαι πλέον δοῦναι, οὐδὲ τῷ δανείσαντι.
Πολλὰ ἐγκλήματα γίνεται ἐν ταῖς φιλίαις ταῖς[4] 30
μὴ κατ' εὐθυωρίαν, καὶ τὸ δίκαιον ἰδεῖν οὐ ῥᾴδιον·
χαλεπὸν γὰρ[5] μετρῆσαι ἑνὶ τῷδε τὰ[6] μὴ κατ' εὐθυ-
ωρίαν· οἷον συμβαίνει ἐπὶ τῶν ἐρωτικῶν, ὁ μὲν 31
γὰρ διώκει ὡς τὸν[7] ἡδὺν ἐπὶ τὸ συζῆν, ὁ δ'
ἐκεῖνον ἐνίοτε ὡς χρήσιμον, ὅταν δὲ παύσηται τοῦ
ἐρᾶν, ἄλλου γενομένου[8] ἄλλος γίνεται, καὶ τότε
λογίζονται τί ἀντὶ[9] τίνος, καὶ ὡς Πύθων καὶ
Παμμένης διεφέροντο, καὶ ὅλως διδάσκαλος καὶ
μαθητής (ἐπιστήμη γὰρ καὶ χρήματα οὐχ ἑνὶ
μετρεῖται), καὶ ὡς Ἡρόδικος[10] ὁ ἰατρὸς πρὸς τὸν
ἀποδιδόντα μικρὸν τὸν μισθόν, καὶ ὡς ὁ κιθαρῳδὸς
καὶ ὁ βασιλεύς. ὁ μὲν γὰρ ὡς ἡδεῖ ὁ δ' ὡς 32

[1] Syl.: ὑποκρινόμενος μηδέτερος. [2] Rac.: ὡς.
[3] καὶ γὰρ Fr.: καί. [4] Bz.: τοῖς.
[5] Γ: γὰρ χαλεπὸν. [6] Γ: τῷ.
[7] [τὸν] Sp. [8] Rac.: γινομένου.
[9] τί ἀντὶ Iac.: παντὶ. [10] Sp.: Πρόδικος.

[a] *i.e.* in a moral friendship it is not honourable to insist on a return on a business footing.

[b] 'Dissimilar friendships, where action and reaction are not in the same straight line' (Solomon).

[c] The distinguished Theban general, friend of Epaminondas. Pytho may be a dramatist of Catana, or a Byzantine rhetorician of the period.

27 the other case[a];—but since they did not provide for this in the contract, on the ground that it was a moral friendship, somebody must judge, and neither party must cheat by pretending; so that each must
28 be content with his luck. But it is clear that moral friendship is a matter of intention, since even if a man after having received great benefits owing to inability did not repay them, but only repaid as much as he was able, he acts honourably; for even God is content with getting sacrifices in accordance
29 with our ability. But a seller will not be satisfied if a man says he cannot pay more, nor will one who has made a loan.

30 In friendships not based on direct reciprocity[b] many causes of recrimination occur, and it is not easy to see what is just; for it is difficult to measure by one given thing relations that are not directly
31 reciprocal. This is how it happens in love affairs, since in them one party pursues the other as a pleasant person to live with, but sometimes the other the one as useful, and when the lover ceases to love, he having changed the other changes, and then they calculate the *quid pro quo*, and quarrel as Pytho and Pammenes[c] used, and as teacher and pupil do in general (for knowledge and money have no common measure), and as Herodicus[d] the doctor did with the patient who offered to pay his fee with a discount, and as the harpist and the king fell out.
32 The king associated with the harpist as pleasant and the harpist with the king as useful; but the

Causes and settlement of disputes

[d] Born in Thrace, practised in Athens fifth cent. B.C.; tutor of Hippocrates. The MSS. give 'Prodicus' (the sophist, who figures frequently in Plato), and possibly the text has suffered haplography, and both names should be read.

1243 b
χρησίμῳ ὡμίλει· ὁ δ', ἐπειδὴ[1] ἔδει ἀποδιδόναι,
αὐτὸν αὐτὸν ὡς ἡδὺν ἐποίησεν, καὶ ἔφη, ὥσπερ
ἐκεῖνον ᾄσαντα εὐφρᾶναι, οὕτω καὶ αὐτὸς ὑποσχόμενος ἐκείνῳ. ὅμως δὲ φανερὸν καὶ ἐνταῦθα 33
πῶς γνωριστέον· ἑνὶ γὰρ μετρητέον καὶ ἐνταῦθ',
ἀλλ' οὐκ ἀρίθμῳ[2] ἀλλὰ λόγῳ. τῷ[3] ἀνάλογον
γὰρ μετρητέον, ὥσπερ καὶ ἡ πολιτικὴ μετρεῖται
κοινωνία· πῶς γὰρ κοινωνήσει γεωργῷ σκυτο-
τόμος, εἰ μὴ τῷ ἀνάλογον ἰσασθήσεται τὰ ἔργα;
ταῖς δὴ[4] μὴ κατ' εὐθυωρίαν τὸ ἀνάλογον μέτρον, 34
οἷον εἰ ὁ μὲν σοφίαν δοῦναι ἐγκαλεῖ, ὁ δ' ἐκείνῳ
ἀργύριον, τί[5] σοφία[6] πρὸς τὸ πλούσιον εἶναι[7];
εἶτα τί δοθὲν πρὸς ἑκάτερον[8]; εἰ γὰρ ὁ μὲν τοῦ
ἐλάττονος ἥμισυ ἔδωκεν, ὁ δὲ τοῦ μείζονος μὴ
πολλοστὸν μέρος, δῆλον ὅτι οὗτος ἀδικεῖ. ἔστι 35
δὲ κἀνταῦθα ἐν ἀρχῇ ἀμφισβήτησις, ἂν φῇ ὁ μὲν[9]
ὡς χρησίμους συνελθεῖν αὐτούς, ὁ δὲ μή, ἀλλ' ὡς
κατ' ἄλλην τινὰ φιλίαν.

1244 a XI. Περὶ δὲ τοῦ ἀγαθοῦ καὶ κατ' ἀρετὴν φίλου, 1
σκεπτέον πότερον δεῖ ἐκείνῳ τὰ χρήσιμα ὑπηρετεῖν
καὶ βοηθεῖν ἢ τῷ ἀντιποιεῖν τὰ ἴσα[10] δυναμένῳ. τοῦτο δὲ τὸ αὐτὸ πρόβλημά ἐστι, πότερον τὸν φίλον
ἢ τὸν σπουδαῖον εὖ ποιητέον μᾶλλον. ἂν μὲν 2
γὰρ φίλος[11] καὶ σπουδαῖος, ἴσως οὐ λίαν χαλεπόν,

[1] Rac.: ἐπεί.
[2] Iac.: οὐχ ὅρῳ. [3] Fr.: τό.
[4] Rac.: τοῖς δὲ (δὴ ? Sus.). [5] Bz.: τῇ.
[6] Sol.: σοφίᾳ. [7] εἶναι add. Rac.
[8] πρὸς ἑκατέρου Fr.: <ἑκατέρου> πρὸς ἑκάτερον ? Rac.
Bk.: φήσωμεν. [10] Iac.: ἀντιποιοῦντι καί.
[11] <καὶ> φίλος ? Rac.: <ὁ> φίλος Rieckher.

[a] The story (also told *N.E.* ix., 1164 a 16) is related by

king, when the time came for him to pay, made out that he was himself of the pleasant sort, and said that just as the harpist had given him pleasure by his singing, so he had given the harpist pleasure by
33 his promises to him.[a] Nevertheless here too it is clear how we must decide : here too we must measure by one standard, but by a ratio, not a number. For we must measure by proportion, as also the civic partnership is measured. For how is a shoemaker to be partner with a farmer unless their
34 products are equalized by proportion ? Therefore the measure for partnerships not directly reciprocal is proportion—for example if one party complains that he has given wisdom and the other says he has given the former money, what is the ratio of wisdom to being rich ? and then, what is the amount given for each ? for if one party has given half of the smaller amount but the other not even a small fraction of the larger, it is clear that the latter is
35 cheating. But here too there is a dispute at the outset, if one says that they came together on grounds of utility and the other denies it and says it was on the basis of some other kind of friendship.

Casuistry of Friendship.

1 XI. About the good friend and the friend on the basis of goodness, we must consider whether one ought to render useful services and assistance to him or to the friend who is able to make an equal return. This is the same problem as whether it is more one's duty to benefit a friend or a virtuous
2 man. If a man is a friend and virtuous, perhaps[b]

Plutarch, *De Alexandri fortuna* ii. 1, of the tyrant Dionysius of Syracuse.

[b] Or, altering the punctuation with Fritsche, 'is a friend and virtuous equally.'

1244 a ἂν μή τις τὸ μὲν αὐξήσῃ τὸ δὲ ταπεινώσῃ, φίλον μὲν σφόδρα εὖ[1] ποιῶν, ἐπιεικῆ δὲ ἠρέμα. εἰ δὲ μή, πολλὰ προβλήματα γίνεται, οἷον εἰ ὁ μὲν ἦν οὐκ ἔσται δέ, ὁ δὲ ἔσται οὔπω δέ, ἢ ὁ μὲν ἐγένετο ἔστι δ' οὔ, ὁ δ'[2] ἔστιν οὐκ ἦν δὲ οὐδὲ ἔσται. ἀλλ'
ἐκεῖνο ἐργωδέστερον. μὴ γάρ τι λέγει Εὐριπίδης 3
ποιήσας

λόγων[3] δίκαιον μισθὸν ἂν λόγους φέροις,[4]
ἔργον δ' ἐκεῖνος[5] ἔργον ὃς[6] παρέσχετο·

καὶ οὐ πάντα δεῖ τῷ πατρί, ἀλλ' ἔστιν ἄλλ' ἃ δεῖ[7] τῇ μητρί, καίτοι βελτίων ὁ πατήρ· οὐδὲ γὰρ τῷ Διὶ πάντα θύεται, οὐδ' ἔχει πάσας τὰς τιμὰς ἀλλὰ
τινάς. ἴσως οὖν ἔστιν ἃ δεῖ τῷ χρησίμῳ, ἄλλα 4
δὲ τῷ ἀγαθῷ· οἷον οὐκ εἰ σῖτον δίδωσι καὶ τἀναγκαῖα, καὶ συζῆν τούτῳ δεῖ· οὐδ' ᾧ τοίνυν τὸ συζῆν,[8] τούτῳ ἃ μὴ οὗτος δίδωσιν ἀλλ' ὁ[9] χρήσιμος· ἀλλ' οἱ τοῦτο ποιοῦντες [τούτῳ][10] πάντα τῷ ἐρωμένῳ διδόασιν οὐ δέον, οὐδενός[11] εἰσιν ἄξιοι.

Καὶ οἱ ἐν τοῖς λόγοις ὅροι τῆς φιλίας πάντες
μέν πώς εἰσι φιλίας, ἀλλ' οὐ τῆς αὐτῆς. τῷ μὲν 5
γὰρ χρησίμῳ τὸ βούλεσθαι τἀκείνῳ ἀγαθά, καὶ τῷ εὖ ποιήσαντι, καὶ τῷ ὁποίῳ δή[12] (οὐ γὰρ ἐπισημαίνει οὗτος ὁ ὁρισμὸς τῆς φιλίας), ἄλλῳ δὲ

[1] εὖ add. Rac. [2] ὁ δ' Syl.: διό.
[3] Bus.: λόγον.
[4] Bus.: λόγου εἰσφέροις (λόγου φέροις Bk.).
[5] Musgrave: ἐκείνοις. [6] ἔργον δὲ Meineke: ἔργα.
[7] ἄλλ' ἃ δεῖ Sus.: ἄλλα δέ. [8] Bz.: τὸ εὖ ζῆν.
[9] Sus.: ἀλλά. [10] Rac. [11] Fr.: οὐδ'.
[12] Iac.: ὁποῖος δεῖ.

[a] See the first sentence of the chapter.
[b] Fr. 882 Nauck.

it is not over-difficult, provided one does not exaggerate the one factor and underrate the other, benefiting him greatly as friend but only slightly as good. But in other cases many problems arise, for instance, if A was a friend but is going not to be and B is going to be but is not now, or if A became one but is not one now and B is one now but was not and is going not to be. But the former problem[a]
3 is more difficult. For possibly there is something in the lines of Euripides[b]:

> Prithee take words as thy just pay for words,
> But he, that gave a deed, a deed shall have;

and it is not one's duty to give everything to one's father, but there are other things that one ought to give to one's mother, although the father is the superior; for even to Zeus not all the sacrifices are offered, nor does he have all the honours but some
4 particular ones. Perhaps, therefore, there are some services that ought to be rendered to the useful friend and others to the good friend: for instance, if a friend gives you food and necessaries you are not therefore bound to give him your society, and accordingly also you are not bound to render to the friend to whom you give your society the things that you do not get from him but from the useful friend; but those who by so doing wrongly give everything to one whom they love are good-for-nothing people.

Different kinds of friendship have different claims.

And the defining marks of friendship stated in the discourses all belong to friendship in some sense,
5 but not to the same kind of friendship. It is a mark of the useful friend that one wishes the things good for him, and so of the benefactor, and in fact a friend of any sort (for this definition of friendship is not distinctive); of another friend, that one

1244 a
τὸ εἶναι καὶ ἄλλῳ τὸ συζῆν, τῷ δὲ καθ' ἡδονὴν
τὸ συναλγεῖν καὶ συγχαίρειν. πάντες δ' οὗτοι οἱ 6
ὅροι κατὰ φιλίαν μὲν λέγονταί τινα, οὐ πρὸς μίαν
δ' οὐδείς. διὸ πολλοί εἰσι, καὶ ἕκαστος μιᾶς
εἶναι δοκεῖ φιλίας, οὐκ ὤν, οἷον ἡ τοῦ εἶναι προ-
αίρεσις· καὶ γὰρ ὁ καθ' ὑπεροχὴν καὶ ποιήσας εὖ
βούλεται τῷ ἔργῳ τῷ αὐτοῦ ὑπάρχειν (καὶ τῷ
δόντι τὸ εἶναι δεῖ καὶ ἀνταποδιδόναι), ἀλλὰ συζῆν
οὐ τούτῳ ἀλλὰ τῷ ἡδεῖ.

Ἀδικοῦσιν οἱ φίλοι ἔνιοι ἀλλήλους, τὰ γὰρ 7
πράγματα μᾶλλον, ἀλλ' οὐ φιλοῦσι τὸν[1] ἔχοντα·
διὸ φίλοι[2] κἀκείνῳ[3] (οἷον διότι ἡδὺς τὸν οἶνον
εἵλετο καὶ ὅτι χρήσιμος τὸν πλοῦτον εἵλετο), χρησι-
μώτερος γάρ. διὸ δὴ ἀγανακτεῖ,[4] ὥσπερ ἂν εἰ
μᾶλλον εἵλοντο[5] ἀντὶ ἥττονος· οἱ δ'[6] ἐγκαλοῦσιν,
ἐκεῖνον γὰρ νῦν ζητοῦσι τὸν ἀγαθόν, πρότερον ζητή-
σαντες τὸν ἡδὺν ἢ τὸν χρήσιμον.

1244 b
XII. Σκεπτέον δὲ καὶ περὶ αὐταρκείας καὶ 1
φιλίας, πῶς ἔχουσι πρὸς τὰς ἀλλήλων δυνάμεις.
ἀπορήσειε γὰρ ἄν τις πότερον, εἴ τις εἴη κατὰ
πάντα αὐτάρκης, ἔσται τούτῳ φίλος, ἢ[7] κατ'
ἔνδειαν ζητεῖται φίλος καὶ[8] ἔσται ἁγαθὸς[9] αὐτ-
αρκέστατος. εἰ ὁ μετ' ἀρετῆς βίος[10] εὐδαίμων,
τί ἂν δέοι φίλου; οὔτε γὰρ τῶν χρησίμων δεῖσθαι αὐτάρκους, οὔτε τῶν εὐφρανούντων[11] οὔτε τοῦ

[1] Bz.: τά. [2] edd.: φιλεῖ. [3] Rac.: κἀκείνοις.
[4] rec. Pb: δεῖ. [5] Rac.: εἵλετο. [6] Vict.: ὁ δ'.
[7] Ald.: εἰ. [8] Fr.: ᾗ. [9] Ross: ἀγαθός.
[10] βίος add. Syl. [11] Sp.: εὖ φρονούντων.

[a] *i.e.* the beneficiary.

[b] This also means the beneficiary, who is the cause of the benefactor's *being* a benefactor; so the benefactor ought to repay him in kind by wishing *his* existence (as he does also for the reason that he is his own product).

wishes his existence, of another that one wishes his society ; of the friend on the ground of pleasure, that
6 one shares his grief and his joy. All these defining marks are predicated in the case of some friendship, but none of them with reference to friendship as a single thing. Hence there are many of them, and each is thought to belong to friendship as one, though it does not: for instance, the desire for the friend's existence—for the superior friend and benefactor wishes existence to belong to his own work[a]—and to him who gave one existence[b] it is one's duty to give existence in return; but he wishes the society not of this friend but of the pleasant one.

7 Friends in some cases wrong each other, because they love things more, not the possessor of them, and are friends of the possessor too on this account (just as a man chose his wine because it was sweet and chose his wealth because it was useful), for he is more useful.[c] Hence naturally he is annoyed, just as if they had preferred his possessions to himself as being inferior ; and they complain, for now they look to find in him the good man, having previously looked for the pleasant or the useful man.

Self-sufficiency and the need for friends.

1 XII. We must also consider self-sufficiency and friendship, and the interrelationship of their potentialities. For one may raise the question whether if a person be self-sufficing in every respect he will have a friend, or whether on the contrary a friend is sought for in need, and the good man will be most self-sufficing. If the life that is combined with goodness is happy, what need would there be of a friend? For it does not belong to the self-sufficing man to need either useful friends or friends to amuse

[c] *Sc.* on account of his possessions.

1244 b
συζῆν, αὐτὸς[1] γὰρ αὑτῷ ἱκανὸς συνεῖναι. μάλιστα 2
δὲ τοῦτο φανερὸν ἐπὶ θεοῦ· δῆλον γὰρ ὡς οὐδενὸς προσδεόμενος οὐδὲ φίλου δεήσεται, οὐδ' ἔσται
αὐτῷ εἴ γε μηθὲν δέοιτό του.[2] ὥστε καὶ ἄνθρωπος
ὁ εὐδαιμονέστατος ἥκιστα δεήσεται φίλου, ἀλλ' ᾗ
καθ' ὅσον ἀδύνατον εἶναι αὐτάρκη. ἀνάγκη ἄρα 3
ἐλαχίστους εἶναι φίλους τῷ ἄριστα ζῶντι, καὶ
ἀεὶ[3] ἐλάττους γίνεσθαι, καὶ μὴ σπουδάζειν ὅπως
ὦσι φίλοι, ἀλλ' ὀλιγωρεῖν μὴ μόνον τῶν χρησίμων
ἀλλὰ καὶ τῶν[4] εἰς τὸ συζῆν αἱρετῶν. ἀλλὰ μὴν
καὶ τότε[5] φανερὸν ἂν εἶναι δόξειεν ὡς οὐ χρήσεως
ἕνεκα ὁ φίλος οὐδ' ὠφελείας, ἀλλ' ὁ[6] δι' ἀρετὴν
φίλος μόνος. ὅταν γὰρ μηθενὸς ἐνδεεῖς ὦμεν, 4
τότε τοὺς συναπολαυσομένους ζητοῦμεν[7] πάντες,
καὶ τοὺς εὖ πεισομένους μᾶλλον ἢ τοὺς ποιήσοντας[8]·
ἀμείνω δ' ἔχομεν κρίσιν αὐτάρκεις ὄντες ἢ μετ'
ἐνδείας, μάλιστά τε[9] τῶν συζῆν ἀξίων δεόμεθα
φίλων.

Περὶ δὲ τῆς ἀπορίας ταύτης σκεπτέον μή ποτε 5
τὸ μέν τι λέγεται καλῶς τὸ δὲ λανθάνει διὰ τὴν
παραβολήν. δῆλον δὲ λαβοῦσι τί τὸ ζῆν τὸ κατ'
ἐνέργειαν καὶ ὡς τέλος. φανερὸν οὖν ὅτι τὸ 6
αἰσθάνεσθαι καὶ τὸ γνωρίζειν, ὥστε καὶ τὸ συζῆν
τὸ συναισθάνεσθαι καὶ τὸ συγγνωρίζειν ἐστίν.
ἔστι δὲ αὐτὸ τὸ[10] αἰσθάνεσθαι καὶ αὐτὸ τὸ[10] γνωρίζειν αἱρετώτατον ἑκάστῳ (καὶ διὰ τοῦτο τοῦ ζῆν
πᾶσιν ἔμφυτος ἡ ὄρεξις, τὸ γὰρ ζῆν δεῖ τιθέναι[11]

[1] Sp.: οὗτος.
[2] Iac.: αὐτῷ οὔτε μηθὲν δεσπότου.
[3] Sp.: δεῖ.
[4] τῶν add. Sp.
[5] τῷδε Rieckher, τούτῳ Sus.
[6] ὁ add. Ald.
[7] Rac.: ζητοῦσι.
[8] Syl.: ποιήσαντας.
[9] Syl.: τε μάλιστα.
[10] (bis) Sol.: τὸ αὐτὸ (τὸ αὑτοῦ Bz.).
[11] Bz.: διατιθέναι.

him and society, for he is sufficient society for him-
2 self. This is most manifest in the case of God; for it is clear that as he needs nothing more he will not need a friend, and that inasmuch as he has no need of one he will not have one. Consequently the happiest human being also will very little need a friend, except in so far as to be self-sufficing is
3 impossible. Of necessity, therefore, he who lives the best life will have fewest friends, and they will constantly become fewer, and he will not be eager to have friends but will think lightly not only of useful friends but also of those desirable for society. But assuredly even his case would seem to show that a friend is not for the sake of utility or benefit but that the only real friend is one loved on account of
4 goodness. For when we are not in need of something, then we all seek people to share our enjoyments, and beneficiaries rather than benefactors; and we can judge them better when we are self-sufficing than when in need, and we most need friends who are worthy of our society.

5 But about this question we must consider whether perhaps, although the view stated is partly sound, in part the truth escapes us because of the comparison.[a] The matter is clear if we ascertain what life
6 in the active sense and as an End is. It is manifest Psychology of social life.
that life is perception and knowledge, and that consequently social life is perception and knowledge in common. But perception and knowledge themselves are the thing most desirable for each individually (and it is owing to this that the appetition for life is implanted by nature in all, for living must

[a] *i.e.* of man with God, l. 8 above; *cf.* 1245 b 13.

1244 b
γνῶσίν τινα). εἰ οὖν τις ἀποτέμοι καὶ ποιήσειε 7
τὸ γινώσκειν αὐτὸ καθ' αὑτὸ καὶ τὸ[1] μή (ἀλλὰ
τοῦτο μὲν λανθάνει ὥσπερ ἐν τῷ λόγῳ γέγραπται,
τῷ μέντοι πράγματι ἔστι μὴ λανθάνειν), οὐθὲν
ἂν διαφέροι ἢ τὸ γινώσκειν ἄλλον ἀνθ' αὑτοῦ· τὸ
δ' ὅμοιον τῷ[2] ζῆν ἀνθ' αὑτοῦ ἄλλον, εὐλόγως δὲ
τὸ ἑαυτοῦ αἰσθάνεσθαι καὶ[3] γνωρίζειν αἱρετώτερον.
δεῖ γὰρ ἅμα συνθεῖναι δύο ἐν τῷ λόγῳ, ὅτι τε τὸ
ζῆν αἱρετὸν[4] καὶ ὅτι τὸ ἀγαθόν, καὶ ἐκ τούτων
1245 a ὅτι τὸ αὐτοῖς[5] ὑπάρχειν τὴν τοιαύτην φύσιν. εἰ 8
οὖν ἐστὶν ἀεὶ τῆς τοιαύτης συστοιχίας ἡ ἑτέρα
ἐν τῇ τοῦ αἱρετοῦ τάξει, καὶ τὸ γνωστὸν καὶ τὸ
αἰσθητόν[6] ἐστιν ὡς ὅλως εἰπεῖν τῷ[7] κοινωνεῖν τῆς
ὡρισμένης φύσεως,[8] ὥστε τὸ αὑτοῦ βούλεσθαι
αἰσθάνεσθαι τὸ αὑτὸν εἶναι τοιονδὶ βούλεσθαι
ἐστίν, ἐπεὶ οὖν οὐ κατ' αὐτούς ἐσμεν ἕκαστον
τούτων ἀλλὰ κατὰ μετάληψιν τῶν δυνάμεων ἐν
τῷ αἰσθάνεσθαι ἢ γνωρίζειν (αἰσθανόμενος γὰρ
αἰσθητὸς γίνεται τούτῳ καὶ[9] ταύτῃ καὶ κατὰ
τοῦτο καθ' ὃ[10] πρότερον αἰσθάνεται καὶ ᾗ καὶ οὗ,
γνωστὸς δὲ γινώσκων)—ὥστε διὰ τοῦτο καὶ ζῆν
ἀεὶ βούλεται ὅτι βούλεται ἀεὶ γνωρίζειν, τοῦτο δὲ
ὅτι αὐτὸς εἶναι τὸ γνωστόν. τὸ δὴ συζῆν αἱρεῖσθαι 9
δόξειε μὲν ἂν εἶναι σκοπουμένοις πως εὔηθες—

[1] τὸ add. Wilson.
[2] Sol.: τοῦ.
[3] καὶ <ἑαυτὸν> Sp.
[4] Fr.: καὶ αἱρετὸν.
[5] Brandis: τὸ αὐτὸ τοῖς.
[6] corr. Pᵇ: αἱρετόν.
[7] Fr.: τὸ.
[8] hic lacunam Sus.
[9] τούτῳ καὶ add. Rac.
[10] Fr.: καθὰ.

[a] τοιαύτην = ἀγαθήν.
[b] *e.g.* the Pythagorean pair of series, One, Good, etc. opposed to Many, Bad, etc. (Solomon). 'The Determined'

7 be deemed a mode of knowing). If therefore one were to abstract and posit absolute knowledge and its negation (though this, it is true, is obscure in the argument as we have written it, but it may be observed in experience), there would be no difference between absolute knowledge and another person's knowing instead of oneself; but that is like another person's living instead of oneself, whereas perceiving and knowing oneself is reasonably more desirable. For two things must be taken into consideration together, that life is desirable and that good is desirable, and as a consequence that it is desirable for
8 ourselves to possess a nature of that quality.[a] If, therefore, of the pair of corresponding series [b] of this kind one is always in the class of the desirable, and the known and the perceived are generally speaking constituted by their participation in the 'determined' nature, so that to wish to perceive oneself is to wish oneself to be of a certain character,—since, then, we are not each of these things in ourselves but only by participating in these faculties in the process of perceiving or knowing (for when perceiving one becomes perceived by means of what one previously perceives,[c] in the manner and in the respect in which one perceives it, and when knowing one becomes known) —hence owing to this one wishes always to live because one wishes always to know; and this is because one wishes to be oneself the object known.
9 To choose to live in the society of others might, therefore, from a certain point of view seem foolish

Reasons for the pleasure of society.

(opposed to 'the Indeterminate') belonged to the 'desirable' series.

[c] *i.e.* perception of something outside oneself causes consciousness of self.

1245 a (ἐπὶ τῶν κοινῶν[1] πρῶτον καὶ τοῖς ἄλλοις ζῴοις, οἷον τοῦ συνεσθίειν ἢ τοῦ[2] συμπίνειν· τί γὰρ διαφέρει τὸ πλησίον οὖσι ταῦτα συμβαίνειν ἢ χωρὶς ἂν ἀφέλῃς τὸν λόγον; ἀλλὰ μὴν[3] καὶ τοῦ λόγου κοινωνεῖν τοῦ τυχόντος ἕτερον τοιοῦτον, ἅμα τ' οὔτε διδάσκειν οὔτε μανθάνειν τοῖς αὐταρκέσι φίλοις οἷόν τε, μανθάνων μὲν γὰρ αὐτὸς οὐκ ἔχει ὡς δεῖ, διδάσκοντος δ' ὁ[4] φίλος, ἡ δ' ὁμοιότης
φιλία)—ἀλλὰ μὴν φαίνεταί γε ὅτι[5] καὶ πάντες 10
ἥδιον τῶν ἀγαθῶν μετὰ τῶν φίλων κοινωνοῦμεν, καθ' ὅσον ἐπιβάλλει ἑκάστῳ[6] καὶ οὗ δύναται ἀρίστου, ἀλλὰ τούτων τῷ μὲν ἡδονῆς σωματικῆς 11
τῷ δὲ θεωρίας μουσικῆς τῷ δὲ φιλοσοφίας· καὶ τὸ ἅμα δὴ[7] εἶναι τῷ φίλῳ (διό φησι 'μόχθος οἱ τηλοῦ φίλοι'), ὥστ'[8] οὐ δεῖ γενέσθαι ἀπ' ἀλλήλων τούτου γινομένου. ὅθεν καὶ ὁ ἔρως δοκεῖ φιλίᾳ ὅμοιον εἶναι· τοῦ γὰρ συζῆν ὀρέγεται ὁ ἐρῶν, ἀλλ' οὐχ ᾗ μάλιστα δεῖ, ἀλλὰ κατ' αἴσθησιν.

Ὁ μὲν τοίνυν λόγος ἐκεῖνά φησι διαπορῶν, τὸ 12
δ' ἔργον οὕτω φαίνεται γινόμενον, ὥστε δῆλον ὅτι παρακρούεταί πως ἡμᾶς ὁ διαπορῶν. σκεπτέον 13
οὖν[9] ἐντεῦθεν[10] τἀληθές· ὁ γὰρ φίλος βούλεται εἶναι, ὥσπερ ἡ παροιμία φησίν, 'ἄλλος Ἡρακλῆς,' ἄλλος

[1] Bz.: κοινωνῶν.
[2] Bz.: οἷον τὸ . . . ἢ τό.
[3] Bk.: μή.
[4] Bz.: οὐ.
[5] ὅτι add. (et καὶ om.) Fr.
[6] Ross: ἕκαστον.
[7] Rac. (καὶ τὸ ἅμα δεῖ Camerarius): καὶ τολμᾷ δὴ (δεῖ Γ).
[8] Fr.: ὡς.
[9] οὖν add. Fr.
[10] Sp.: ἔνθεν.

[a] This proverb looks like a quotation, being half a line of verse.

[b] See 1244 b 2 ff., 1245 a 27.

[c] *Ib.* 22 ff.

(first in the case of the things common to the other animals also, for instance eating together or drinking together, for what difference does it make whether these things take place when we are near together or apart, if you take away speech? but even to share in speech that is merely casual is a thing indifferent, and also neither to impart nor to receive information is possible for friends who are self-sufficing, since receiving information implies a deficiency in oneself and imparting it a deficiency in
10 one's friend, and likeness is friendship)—but nevertheless it surely seems that we all find it pleasanter to share good things with our friends, as far as these fall to each, and the best that each can—
11 but among these, it falls to one to share bodily pleasure, to another artistic study, to another philosophy—; and so it is pleasanter to be with one's friend (whence the saying 'Distant friends a burden are '[a]), so that they must not be separated when this is taking place. Hence also love seems to resemble friendship, for the lover is eager to share the life of the loved one, although not in the most proper way but in a sensuous manner.

12 Therefore the argument in raising the question asserts the former position,[b] but the facts of experience are obviously on the latter lines,[c] so that it is clear that the raiser of the question in a way mis-
13 leads us. We must therefore examine the truth from the following consideration: 'friend' really denotes, in the language of the proverb,[d] 'another Hercules'—another self; but the characteristics are

The *Alter Ego.*

[d] Quoted elsewhere in the same connexion, but one may conjecture that the phrase originally meant 'as strong as Hercules.'

1245 a αὐτός· διέσπασται δέ, καὶ χαλεπὸν πάντα[1] ἐφ᾽
ἑνὸς γενέσθαι, ἀλλὰ κατὰ μὲν τὴν φύσιν ὃ συγ-
γενέστατον, κατὰ δὲ τὸ σῶμα ὅμοιος ἕτερος, ἄλλος
δὲ κατὰ τὴν ψυχήν, καὶ τούτων κατὰ μόριον ἕτερος
ἕτερον. ἀλλ᾽ οὐθέν γε[2] ἧττον βούλεται ὥσπερ
αὐτὸς διαιρετὸς εἶναι ὁ φίλος. τὸ οὖν τοῦ φίλου 14
αἰσθάνεσθαι ⟨καὶ τὸ τὸν φίλον γνωρίζειν⟩[3] τὸ
αὑτοῦ πως ἀνάγκη αἰσθάνεσθαι εἶναι καὶ τὸ αὑτόν
πως γνωρίζειν. ὥστε καὶ τὰ φορτικὰ μὲν συνήδεσ-
θαι καὶ συζῆν τῷ φίλῳ ἡδὺ εὐλόγως (συμβαίνει γὰρ
ἐκείνου ἅμα αἴσθησις ἀεί), μᾶλλον δὲ τὰς θειοτέρας
1245 b ἡδονάς· αἴτιον δ᾽ ὅτι ἀεὶ ἥδιον ἑαυτὸν θεωρεῖν ἐν
τῷ βελτίονι ἀγαθῷ, τοῦτο δ᾽ ἐστὶν ὁτὲ μὲν πάθος,
ὁτὲ δὲ πρᾶξις, ὁτὲ δὲ ἕτερόν τι. εἰ δ᾽ αὐτὸν[4] εὖ ζῆν
καὶ οὕτω καὶ τὸν φίλον, ἐν δὲ τῷ[5] συζῆν συνεργεῖν,
ἡ κοινωνία τῶν ἐν τέλει μάλιστά γε. διὸ δεῖ[6]
συνθεωρεῖν καὶ συνευωχεῖσθαι, οὐ τὰ διὰ τροφὴν
καὶ τὰ ἀναγκαῖα (αἱ τοιαῦται γὰρ κοινωνίαι οὐχ[7]
ὁμιλίαι δοκοῦσιν εἶναι ἀλλ᾽ ἀπολαύσεις), ἀλλ᾽
ἕκαστος οὗ δύναται τυγχάνειν τέλους, ἐν τούτῳ 15
βούλεται συζῆν, εἰ δὲ μή, καὶ ποιεῖν εὖ καὶ πάσχειν
ὑπὸ τῶν φίλων αἱροῦνται μάλιστα. ὅτι μὲν τοίνυν
καὶ δεῖ συζῆν, καὶ ὅτι μάλιστα βούλονται πάντες,
καὶ ὅτι ὁ εὐδαιμονέστατος καὶ ἄριστος μάλιστα
τοιοῦτος, φανερόν. ὅτι δὲ κατὰ τὸν λόγον οὐκ
ἐφαίνετο, καὶ τοῦτ᾽ εὐλόγως συνέβαινε, λέγοντος

[1] Rac.: τά. [2] Syl.: τε. [3] Rac.
[4] v.l. εἰ δυνατὸν (εἰ δ᾽ αὐτὸν δυνατὸν εὖ ζῆν οὕτω καὶ τὸν φίλον Sus.).
[5] εἰ δὲ τὸ Fr. [6] δεῖ add. Fr.
[7] γὰρ κοινωνίαι οὐχ add. Rac. (ὁμιλίαι γὰρ οὐχ Sus.).

[a] *Cf.* 1244 b 2 ff., 1245 a 27.

scattered, and it is difficult for all to be realized in the case of one person; though by nature a friend is what is most akin, yet one resembles his friend in body and another in spirit, and one in one part of the body or spirit, another in another. But still none the less a friend really means as it were a
14 separate self. To perceive and to know a friend, therefore, is necessarily in a manner to perceive and in a manner to know oneself. Consequently to share even vulgar pleasures and ordinary life with a friend is naturally pleasant (for it always involves our simultaneously perceiving the friend), but more so to share the more divine pleasures; the reason of which is that it is always more pleasant to behold oneself enjoying the superior good, and this is sometimes a passive, sometimes an active experience, sometimes something else. But if it is pleasant to live well oneself and for one's friend also to live well, and if living together involves working together, surely their partnership will be preeminently in things included in the End. Hence we should study together, and feast together—not on the pleasures of food and the necessary pleasures (for such partnerships do not seem to be real social
15 intercourse but mere enjoyment), but each really wishes to share with his friends the End that he is capable of attaining, or failing this, men choose most of all to benefit their friends and to be benefited by them. It is therefore manifest that to live together is actually a duty, and that all people wish it very much, and that this is most the case with the man that is the happiest and best. But that the contrary appeared to be the conclusion of the argument [a] was also reasonable, the statement being

1245 b
ἀληθῆ. κατὰ τὴν σύνθεσιν γὰρ τῆς παραβολῆς
ἀληθοῦς οὔσης ἡ λύσις ἐστίν· ὅτι γὰρ ὁ θεὸς οὐ
τοιοῦτος οἷος δεῖσθαι φίλου, καὶ τὸν ὅμοιον ἀξιοῖ.[1]
καίτοι κατὰ τοῦτον τὸν λόγον οὐδὲν[2] νοήσει ὁ 16
σπουδαῖος· οὐ γὰρ οὕτως ὁ θεὸς εὖ ἔχει, ἀλλὰ
βέλτιον ἢ ὥστε ἄλλο τι νοεῖν παρ' αὐτὸς αὑτόν.
αἴτιον δ' ὅτι ἡμῖν μὲν τὸ εὖ καθ' ἕτερον, ἐκείνῳ[3]
δὲ αὐτὸς αὑτοῦ τὸ εὖ ἐστίν.

Καὶ τὸ ζητεῖν ἡμῖν καὶ εὔχεσθαι πολλοὺς φίλους, 17
ἅμα δὲ λέγειν ὡς οὐθεὶς φίλος ᾧ πολλοὶ φίλοι,
ἄμφω λέγεται ὀρθῶς. ἐνδεχόμενον[4] γὰρ πολλοῖς
συζῆν ἅμα καὶ συναισθάνεσθαι, ὡς πλείστοις[5]
αἱρετώτατον· ἐπεὶ δὲ χαλεπώτατον, ἐν ἐλάττοσιν
ἀνάγκη τὴν ἐνέργειαν τῆς συναισθήσεως εἶναι, ὥστ' 18
οὐ μόνον χαλεπὸν τὸ πολλοὺς κτήσασθαι (πείρας
γὰρ δεῖ[6]), ἀλλὰ καὶ οὖσι χρήσασθαι.

Καὶ ὁτὲ μὲν ἀπεῖναι εὖ πράττοντα τὸν φιλούμενον
βουλόμεθα, ὁτὲ δὲ μετέχειν τῶν αὐτῶν. καὶ τὸ
ἅμα βούλεσθαι εἶναι φιλικόν· ἐνδεχόμενον[4] μὲν γὰρ
ἅμα καὶ εὖ, τοῦτο πάντες αἱροῦνται· μὴ ἐνδεχόμενον[4] δὲ ἅμα,[7] ὥσπερ τὸν Ἡρακλῆ[8] ἴσως ἂν ἡ
μήτηρ εἵλετο θεὸν εἶναι μᾶλλον ἢ μετ' αὐτῆς ὄντα
τῷ Εὐρυσθεῖ θητεύειν. ὁμοίως γὰρ ἂν εἴποιεν καὶ 19
ὅ[9] ὁ Λάκων ἔσκωψεν, ἐπεί τις ἐκέλευσεν αὐτὸν
χειμαζόμενον ἐπικαλέσασθαι τοὺς Διοσκούρους.

[1] Bz.: ἀξίου. [2] Rac.: οὐδὲ. [3] ἐκεῖνος ? Rac.
[4] Rac.: ἐνδεχομένου. [5] Sp.: πλείστους.
[6] Syl.: ἀεί. [7] Iac.: ἀλλὰ.
[8] Γ: τῷ Ἡρακλεῖ. [9] Iac.: ὃν.

[a] *i.e.* of man with God, 1244 b 7.
[b] He doubtless said that being in trouble himself he did not wish to involve the Dioscuri in it (Solomon).

true. For the solution is on the line of the comparison,[a] the correspondence being true; for the fact that God is not of such a nature as to need a friend postulates that man, who is like God, also
16 does not need one. Yet according to this argument the virtuous man will not think of anything; for God's perfection does not permit of this, but he is too perfect to think of anything else beside himself. And the reason is that for us well-being has reference to something other than ourselves, but in his case he is himself his own well-being.

17 As to seeking for ourselves and praying for many friends, and at the same time saying that one who has many friends has no friend, both statements are correct. For if it is possible to live with and share the perceptions of many at once, it is most desirable for them to be the largest possible number; but as that is very difficult, active community of perception must
18 of necessity be in a smaller circle, so that it is not only difficult to acquire many friends (for probation is needed), but also to use them when one has got them.

Practical limitations.

One for whom we feel affection we sometimes wish to prosper in absence from us, but sometimes to share the same experiences. And to wish to be together is a mark of friendship, for if it is possible to be together and to prosper all choose this; but if it is not possible to prosper together, then we choose as the mother of Heracles perhaps would have chosen for her son, to be a god rather than to
19 be with her but in service to Eurystheus. For men would say things like the jest which the Spartan made when somebody told him to invoke the Dioscuri in a storm.[b]

Presence and absence of friends in prosperity and in adversity.

1245 b Δοκεῖ δὲ τοῦ μὲν φιλοῦντος τὸ ἀπείργειν εἶναι τῆς
συμμεθέξεως τῶν χαλεπῶν, τοῦ δὲ φιλουμένου τὸ
βούλεσθαι συμμετέχειν. καὶ ταῦτα ἀμφότερα συμβαίνει εὐλόγως· δεῖ γὰρ τῷ φίλῳ μηθὲν εἶναι οὕτω
λυπηρὸν ὡς ἡδὺ τὸν φίλον, δοκεῖ δὲ δεῖν αἱρεῖσθαι
μὴ τὸ αὑτοῦ. διὸ κωλύουσι συμμετέχειν· ἱκανοὶ 20
γὰρ αὐτοὶ κακοπαθοῦντες, ἵνα μὴ φαίνωνται τὸ
1246 a αὑτῶν σκοποῦντες καὶ αἱρεῖσθαι τὸ χαίρειν λυπου-
μένου τοῦ φίλου, ἔτι δὲ[1] κουφότεροι εἶναι μὴ μόνοι
φέροντες τὰ κακά. ἐπεὶ δ᾿ αἱρετὸν τό τ᾿ εὖ καὶ τὸ 21
ἅμα, δῆλον ὅτι καὶ τὸ ἅμα εἶναι μετ᾿ ἐλάττονος
ἀγαθοῦ αἱρετώτερόν[2] πως ἢ χωρὶς μετὰ μείζονος.
ἐπεὶ δὲ[3] ἄδηλον τὸ πόσον δύναται τὸ ἅμα, ἤδη
διαφέρονται, καὶ οἱ μὲν[4] οἴονται[5] τὸ μετέχειν ἅμα
πάντων φιλικόν, καὶ[6] ὥσπερ συνδειπνεῖν ἅμα φασὶν
ἥδιον[7] ταὐτὰ ἔχοντας· οἱ δ᾿ ἅμα[8] μὲν τοῦ εὖ[9] βούλονται, ἐπειδὴ εἴ[10] τις ὑπερβολὰς ποιήσει, ὁμολόγους
εἶναι[11] ἅμα κακῶς πράττοντας σφόδρα ἢ[12] εὖ
σφόδρα χωρίς. παραπλήσιον δὲ τούτῳ καὶ περὶ τὰς 22
ἀτυχίας· ὁτὲ μὲν γὰρ βουλόμεθα τοὺς φίλους ἀπεῖναι,[13] οὐδὲ λυπεῖν ὅταν μηθὲν μέλλωσι ποιήσειν
πλέον, ὁτὲ δὲ αὐτοὺς[14] ἥδιστον παρεῖναι. τὸ δὲ[15]
τῆς ὑπεναντιώσεως ταύτης καὶ μάλ᾿ εὔλογον. διὰ
γὰρ τὰ προειρημένα τοῦτο συμβαίνει, καὶ ὅτι μὲν
τὸ λυπούμενον ἢ ἐν φαύλῃ ὄντα ἕξει τὸν φίλον

1 δὲ (et lacunam ante ἔτι) Bk.: δὲ τὸ.
2 Sp.: αἱρετὸν.
3 Sp.: ἐπειδὴ.
4 οἱ μὲν add. Sus.
5 Cas.: οἷον καί.
6 καὶ om. Γ.
7 ἥδιον <ἢ ἰδίᾳ> Fr.
8 Sp.: ἂν.
9 Iac.: μέντοι οὐ.
10 Iac.: ἐπεὶ δέ γέ.
11 Iac.: ὁμολογοῦσιν.
12 ἢ] καὶ ? Rac.
13 Cas.: εἶναι.
14 Syl.: τούς.
15 τὸ δ᾿ <αἴτιον> Fr.

It seems to be characteristic of one who feels affection for another to debar him from sharing his troubles, and of the person for whom affection is felt to wish to share them. Both these things happen reasonably; for to a friend nothing ought to give so much pain as his friend gives pleasure, yet it is felt that he ought not to choose his own interest.
20 Hence people hinder their friends from sharing their sorrows; they are content to be in trouble by themselves, in order that they may not appear from selfish considerations actually to choose the joy of their friend's grief and furthermore to find it a
21 relief not to bear their misfortunes alone. And as both well-being and companionship are desirable, it is clear that companionship combined with even a lesser good is in a way more desirable than separation with a greater good. But as it is not clear how much value companionship has, at this point men differ, and some think it is friendly to share everything in company, and say, for instance, that it is pleasanter to dine with company though having the same food; others wish to share only in well-being, because, they say, if one supposes extreme cases, people experiencing great adversity in company or great pro-
22 sperity separately are on a par. And it is much the same as this in regard to misfortunes also; sometimes we wish our friends to be absent, and do not want to give them pain when their presence is not going to do any good, but at other times for them to be present is most pleasant. And the reason of this contrariety is very easily explained; it comes about because of the things stated before,[a] and because to behold a friend in pain or in a bad state is a thing

[a] *Cf.* 1245 b 26—1246 a 2.

1246 a θεωρεῖν φεύγομεν ἁπλῶς, ὥσπερ καὶ ἡμᾶς αὐτούς, τὸ δ' ὁρᾶν τὸν φίλον ἡδὺ ὥσπερ ἄλλο τι τῶν ἡδίστων, διὰ τὴν εἰρημένην αἰτίαν, καὶ μὴν[1] κάμνοντα εἰ αὐτός· ὥστε ὁπότερον ἂν τούτων ᾖ μᾶλλον ἡδύ, 23
ποιεῖ τὴν ῥοπὴν τοῦ βούλεσθαι παρεῖναι ἢ μή. καὶ τοῦτο[2] ἐπὶ τῶν χειρόνων συμβαίνει[3] καὶ διὰ τὴν αὐτὴν αἰτίαν γίνεσθαι· μάλιστα γὰρ φιλοτιμοῦνται τοὺς φίλους μὴ πράττειν εὖ μηδ' ἀπεῖναι[4] ἂν[5] ἀνάγκη ᾖ[6] αὐτοῖς κακῶς. διὸ ἐνίοτε τοὺς ἐρωμένους συναποκτιννύασιν· μᾶλλον γὰρ τοῦ οἰκείου αἰσθάνεσθαι κακοῦ, ὥσπερ ἄν, εἰ καὶ μεμνημένος ὅτι ποτὲ εὖ ἔπραττε, μᾶλλον ἢ εἰ ᾤετο ἀεὶ κακῶς πράττειν.

[1] Sol.: μή.
[2] Fr.: τότε.
[3] Camot: συμβαίνειν.
[4] Rac.: εἶναι.
[5] ἂν add. Fr.
[6] ᾖ add. Fr.

we absolutely shun, as we shun it in our own case, but to see a friend is as pleasant as anything can be, for the reason stated,[a] and indeed to see him ill
23 if one is ill oneself; so that whichever of these is more pleasant, it sways the balance of wishing him to be present or not. And it fits in that the former occurs in the case of inferior people, and for the same reason; they are most eager for their friends not to prosper and not to be absent if they themselves have to suffer adversity. Hence sometimes suicides kill those whom they love with themselves, as they think that they feel their own misfortune more if their loved ones are to survive[b]; just as, if a man in trouble had the memory that he had once been prosperous, he would be more conscious of his trouble than if he thought that he had always done badly.

[a] *Cf.* 1245 a 26–b 9.

[b] In the Greek this clause is left to be understood.

Θ

1246 a
I. Ἀπορήσειε δ' ἄν τις εἰ ἔστιν ἑκάστῳ[1] χρήσα- 1
σθαι καὶ ἐφ' ὃ[2] πέφυκε καὶ ἄλλως, καὶ τοῦτο ᾗ
αὐτὸ ἢ αὖ[3] κατὰ συμβεβηκός· οἷον ᾗ[4] ὀφθαλμός,
ἰδεῖν ἢ καὶ ἄλλως παριδεῖν διαστρέψαντα ὥστε δύο
τὸ ἓν φανῆναι, αὗται μὲν δὴ χρεῖαι[5] ἄμφω ὅτι μὲν
ὀφθαλμός ἐστιν,[6] ἦν δ' ὀφθαλμῷ ἄλλῃ[7] δέ, κατὰ
συμβεβηκός, οἷον εἰ ἦν ἀποδόσθαι ἢ φαγεῖν. ὁμοίως 2
δὲ[8] καὶ ἐπιστήμῃ[9]· καὶ γὰρ ἀληθῶς καὶ ἁμαρτεῖν,
οἷον ὅταν ἑκὼν μὴ ὀρθῶς γράψῃ, ὡς ἀγνοίᾳ δὴ νῦν
χρῆσθαι, ὥσπερ μεταστρέψασαι[10] τὴν χεῖρα καὶ
τὸν ποδα[11] τῷ ποδί ποτε ὡς χειρὶ καὶ ταύτῃ ὡς
ποδὶ χρῶνται αἱ[12] ὀρχηστρίδες. εἰ δὴ πᾶσαι αἱ 3
ἀρεταὶ[13] ἐπιστῆμαι, εἴη ἂν[14] καὶ τῇ δικαιοσύνῃ ὡς
ἀδικίᾳ χρῆσθαι· ἀδικήσει[15] ἄρα ἀπὸ δικαιοσύνης
τὰ ἄδικα πράττων, ὥσπερ καὶ τὰ ἀγνοητικὰ ἀπὸ
1246 b ἐπιστήμης· εἰ δὲ τοῦτ' ἀδύνατον, φανερὸν ὅτι οὐκ

[1] Pb: ἑκάστῳ φίλῳ Mb.
[2] Sp.: ᾧ aut ἃ.
[3] Iac.: τοῦτο ἢ αὐτὸ ἡδύ.
[4] Iac.: ἤ.
[5] χρεῖαι add. Sp.
[6] ἐστιν Iac.: ὅτι.
[7] Iac.: ἄλλη.
[8] Sp.: δή.
[9] Sp.: ἐπιστήμη.
[10] Iac.: μεταστρέψας.
[11] τὸν πόδα add. Iac.
[12] αἱ add. Sp.
[13] Sp.: ἄρισται.
[14] εἴη ἂν Sp.: εἶπαν.
[15] Sp.: εἰ δίκης εἰ.

[a] In Mb the remainder of the work forms part of the pre-

BOOK VIII [a]

1 I. But one may raise the question whether it is possible to use any given thing both for its natural purpose and otherwise, and in the latter case to use it *qua* itself or on the contrary incidentally: for instance, with an eye *qua* eye, to see, or also just to see wrong, by squinting so that one object appears two—both these uses of the eye, then, use it because it is an eye, but it would be possible to make use of an eye but to use it in another way, incidentally, for example, if it were possible to sell it or to eat it.

c. i. GOODNESS AND KNOWLEDGE. The virtues are not branches of knowledge, which is capable of misuse.

2 And similarly with the use of knowledge: one can use it truly, and one can use it wrongly—for instance, when one spells a word incorrectly on purpose, then at the time one is using knowledge as ignorance, just as dancing-girls sometimes interchange the hand and

3 the foot and use foot as hand and hand as foot.[b] If then all the virtues are forms of knowledge, it would be possible to use even justice as injustice—in that case a man will be behaving unjustly by doing unjust acts as a result of justice, as when one makes ignorant mistakes from knowledge; but if this is impossible, it is clear that the virtues cannot

ceding Book, and some editors print it as cc. xiii.-xv. of Book VII. The text has been fully treated by Jackson, *J. Phil.* xxii. 170.

[b] *i.e.* stand on their hands and wave their feet in the air, see *Dict Ant.*, "Saltatio.'

1246 b ἂν εἶεν ἐπιστῆμαι αἱ ἀρεταί. οὐδ' εἰ μὴ ἔστιν
ἀγνοεῖν ἀπὸ ἐπιστήμης ἀλλ' ἁμαρτάνειν μόνον καὶ
τὰ αὐτὰ καὶ ἀπὸ ἀγνοίας ποιεῖν, οὔτι ἀπὸ
δικαιοσύνης γε ὡς ἀπὸ ἀδικίας πράξει. ἀλλ' ἐπεὶ[1]
φρόνησις ἐπιστήμη καὶ ἀληθές τι, τὸ αὐτὸ ποιήσει
κἀκείνη· ἐνδέχοιτο γὰρ ἂν ἀφρόνως ἀπὸ φρονήσεως
καὶ ἁμαρτάνειν ταὐτὰ ἅπερ ὁ ἄφρων· εἰ δὲ ἁπλῆ
ἦν[2] ἡ ἑκάστου χρεία ᾗ ἕκαστον, κἂν φρονίμως
ἔπραττον οὕτω πράττοντες. ἐπὶ μὲν οὖν ταῖς 4
ἄλλαις ἐπιστήμαις ἄλλη κυρία ποιεῖ τὴν στροφήν·
αὐτῆς δὲ τῆς πασῶν κυρίας τίς; οὐ γὰρ ἔτι ἐπιστήμη γε ἢ νοῦς. ἀλλὰ μὴν οὐδ' ἀρετή· χρῆται
γὰρ αὐτῇ,[3] ἡ γὰρ τοῦ ἄρχοντος ἀρετὴ τῇ τοῦ
ἀρχομένου χρῆται. τίς οὖν ἐστίν; ἢ ὥσπερ λέγεται 5
ἀκρασία ἡ[4] κακία τοῦ ἀλόγου τῆς ψυχῆς, καί πως[5]
ἀκόλαστος ὁ ἀκρατής, ἔχων νοῦν, ἀλλ' ἤδη ἂν
ἰσχυρὰ ᾖ ἡ ἐπιθυμία, στρέψει καὶ λογιεῖται τἀναντία; ἢ ἔστι[6] δῆλον ὅτι, κἂν ἐν μὲν τούτῳ ἀρετὴ ἐν
δὲ τῷ λόγῳ ἄνοια ᾖ, ἑτέρᾳ[7] μεταποιοῦνται; ὥστε
ἔσται δικαιοσύνῃ τ' οὐ[8] δικαίως χρῆσθαι καὶ κακῶς
καὶ φρονήσει ἀφρόνως· ὥστε καὶ τἀναντία. ἄτοπον
γὰρ εἰ τὴν μὲν ἐν τῷ λογιστικῷ ἀρετὴν[9] μοχθηρία
ποτὲ ἐγγενομένη ἐν[10] τῷ ἀλόγῳ[11] στρέψει καὶ

[1] ἐπεὶ ἡ ? Rac.
[2] ἦν add. Rac. (ἦν pro ἡ Bus.)
[3] αὐτὴ αὐτῇ ? Rac.
[4] ἡ add. Rac.
[5] Iac.: πῶς.
[6] Iac.: ἡ σφι.
[7] Iac.: ἕτεραι.
[8] τ' οὐ Iac.: τό.
[9] Γ: τῆς . . . ἀρετῆς.
[10] Sp.: μέν.
[11] Sus.: λόγῳ.

be branches of knowledge. And also if it is not possible from knowledge to be ignorant, but only to make mistakes and do the same things as one does from ignorance, a man will assuredly never act from justice in the same way as he will act from injustice. But since wisdom is knowledge and a form of truth, wisdom also will produce the same effect as knowledge, that is, it would be possible from wisdom to act unwisely and to make the same mistakes as the unwise man does; but if the use of anything *qua* itself were single,[a] when so acting men would
4 be acting wisely. In the case of the other forms of knowledge, therefore, another higher form causes their diversion; but what knowledge causes the diversion of the actually highest of all? Obviously there is no longer any knowledge or any mind to do it. But moreover goodness does not cause it either; for wisdom makes use of goodness, since the goodness
5 of the ruling part uses that of the ruled. Who then is there in whom this occurs? or is it in the same way as the vice of the irrational part of the spirit is termed lack of control, and the uncontrolled man is in a manner profligate—possessing reason, but ultimately if his appetite is powerful it will turn him round, and he will draw the opposite inference? Or is it manifest that also if there is goodness in the irrational part but folly in the reason, goodness and folly are transformed in another way? so that it will be possible to use justice unjustly and badly, and wisdom unwisely; and therefore the opposite uses also will be possible. For it is strange if whereas when wickedness at any time arises in the irrational part it will pervert the goodness in

[a] As in § 1 above it was shown not to be.

1246 b
ποιήσει ἀγνοεῖν, ἡ δ' ἀρετὴ ἡ[1] ἐν τῷ ἀλόγῳ
ἐν τῷ λογιστικῷ[2] ἀνοίας ἐνούσης οὐ στρέψει ταύτην
καὶ ποιήσει φρονίμως κρίνειν καὶ τὰ δέοντα,[3] καὶ
πάλιν ἡ φρόνησις ἡ ἐν τῷ λογιστικῷ τὴν ἐν τῷ
ἀλόγῳ ἀκολασίαν[4] σωφρόνως πράττειν, ὅπερ δοκεῖ
εἶναι[5] ἡ ἐγκράτεια. ὥστ' ἔσται καὶ[6] ἀπὸ ἀνοίας[7]
φρονίμως. ἔστι δὲ[8] ταῦτα ἄτοπα, ἄλλως τε καὶ 6
ἀπὸ ἀνοίας[7] χρῆσθαι φρονήσει[9] φρονίμως· τοῦτο
γὰρ ἐπὶ τῶν ἄλλων οὐδαμῶς ὁρῶμεν· ὥσπερ τὴν
ἰατρικὴν ἢ γραμματικὴν στρέφει ἀκολασία, ἀλλ'
οὐ[10] τὴν ἄγνοιαν, ἐὰν ᾖ ἐναντία διὰ τὸ μὴ ἐνεῖναι
τὴν ὑπεροχήν, ἀλλὰ τὴν ἀρετὴν ὅλως μᾶλλον εἶναι
πρὸς τὴν κακίαν οὕτως ἔχουσαν· καὶ γὰρ ἃ[11] ὁ
ἄδικος πάντα ὁ δίκαιος δύναται, καὶ ὅλως ἔνεστιν
ἐν τῇ δυνάμει ἡ ἀδυναμία. ὥστε δῆλον ὅτι ἅμα φρό- 7
νιμοι καὶ ἀγαθοί, ἐκεῖναι[12] δ' ἄλλου ἕξεις, καὶ ὀρθὸν[13]
τὸ Σωκρατικὸν[14] ὅτι οὐδὲν ἰσχυρότερον φρονήσεως.
ἀλλ' ὅτι ἐπιστήμην ἔφη, οὐκ ὀρθῶς[15]· ἀρετὴ γάρ
ἐστι, καὶ οὐκ ἐπιστήμη ἀλλὰ γένος ἄλλο γνώσεως.[16]
II. Ἐπεὶ δ' οὐ μόνον ἡ φρόνησις ποιεῖ τὴν 1
εὐπραγίαν κατ' ἀρετήν,[17] ἀλλὰ φαμὲν καὶ τοὺς εὐ-
1247 a τυχεῖς εὖ πράττειν ὡς καὶ τῆς εὐτυχίας ἐμποιούσης[18]
εὐπραγίαν κατὰ[19] τὰ αὐτὰ τῇ ἐπιστήμῃ,[20] σκεπτέον

[1] ἡ add. Rac. [2] ἐν τῷ λογιστικῷ add. Sus.
[3] δέονται <πράττειν> vel <ποιεῖν> ? Rac.
[4] Γ: κόλασιν ἄν. [5] εἶναι add. Rac.
[6] καὶ Γ: καὶ ἡ. [7] (bis) Iac.: ἀγνοίας.
[8] ἔστι δὲ Sp.: ἐπί τε. [9] φρονήσει add. Sp.
[10] οὐ Rac.: οὖν ὁ (οὖν οὐ Iac.).
[11] ἃ add. Iac. (post πάντα Γ).
[12] Iac.: καὶ ἀγαθαὶ ἐκεῖναι αἱ.
[13] Rac.: ὀρθῶς. [14] Bek.: τὸ σῶμα κρατητικόν.
[15] Rac.: ὀρθόν. [16] Sp.: γνωσ . . .
[17] Iac.: καὶ ἀρετήν (καὶ ἀρετή Sp.).

the rational and cause it to be ignorant, yet goodness in the irrational part when there is folly in
the rational should not convert the folly and make
it form wise and proper judgements, and again
wisdom in the rational part should not make profligacy in the irrational act temperately—which seems
to be what self-control essentially is. So that there
6 will actually be wise action arising from folly. But
these consequences are absurd, especially that of
using wisdom wisely as a result of folly ; for that
is a thing which we certainly do not see in other
cases—for instance profligacy perverts one's medical
knowledge or scholarship, but it does not pervert
one's ignorance if it be opposed to it, because it
does not contain superiority, but rather it is goodness in general that stands in this relation to badness ; for example, the just man is capable of all
that the unjust man is, and in general inability
7 is contained in ability. So that it is clear that
men are wise and good simultaneously, and that
the states of character above described belong to
a different person, and the Socratic dictum 'Nothing
is mightier than wisdom,' is right. But in that by
'wisdom' he meant 'knowledge,' he was wrong ;
for wisdom is a form of goodness, and is not scientific knowledge but another kind of cognition.

c. ii. Good Fortune. Luck seems to come by nature, not by wisdom or providence.

1 II. But wisdom is not the only thing which
acting in accordance with goodness causes welfare,
but we also speak of the fortunate as faring well,
which implies that good fortune also engenders
welfare in the same way as knowledge does ; we
must therefore consider whether one man is fortu-

[18] ἐμποιούσης Fr.: εὖ ποιούσης.

[19] Sp.: καί.

[20] Sp.: τῆς ἐπιστήμης.

1247 a ἆρ' ἐστὶ φύσει ὁ μὲν εὐτυχὴς ὁ δ' ἀτυχὴς ἢ οὔ,
καὶ πῶς ἔχει περὶ τούτων. ὅτι μὲν γάρ εἰσί τινες 2
εὐτυχεῖς ὁρῶμεν· ἄφρονες γὰρ ὄντες κατορθοῦσι
πολλοὶ[1] ἐν οἷς ἡ τύχη κυρία, οἱ δὲ καὶ ἐν οἷς τέχνη
ἐστί, πολλὴ[2] μέντοι καὶ τύχη[3] ἐνυπάρχει, οἷον ἐν
στρατηγίᾳ καὶ κυβερνητικῇ. πότερον οὖν ἀπό τινος 3
ἕξεως οὗτοί εἰσιν, ἢ οὐ τῷ[4] αὐτοὶ ποιοί τινες εἶναι
πρακτικοί εἰσι τῶν εὐτυχημάτων; νῦν μὲν γὰρ
οὕτως οἴονται ὡς φύσει τινῶν ὄντων· ἡ δὲ φύσις
ποιούς τινας ποιεῖ, καὶ εὐθὺς ἐκ γενετῆς διαφέρουσιν, ὥσπερ οἱ μὲν γλαυκοὶ οἱ δὲ μελανόμματοι
τῷ τοδὶ[5] τοιονδὶ ἔχειν, οὕτω καὶ οἱ εὐτυχεῖς καὶ
ἀτυχεῖς. ὅτι μὲν γὰρ οὐ φρονήσει κατορθοῦσι 4
δῆλον, οὐ γὰρ ἄλογος ἡ φρόνησις ἀλλ' ἔχει λόγον
διὰ τί οὕτω πράττει, οἱ δ' οὐκ ἂν ἔχοιεν εἰπεῖν διὰ
τί κατορθοῦσι, τέχνη γὰρ ἂν ἦν· ἔτι δὲ φανερὸν ὅτι[6] 5
ὄντες ἄφρονες, οὐχ ὅτι περὶ ἄλλα (τοῦτο μὲν γὰρ
οὐθὲν ἄτοπον, οἷον Ἱπποκράτης γεωμετρικὸς ὤν,
ἀλλὰ περὶ τὰ ἄλλα ἐδόκει[7] βλὰξ καὶ ἄφρων εἶναι,
καὶ πολὺ χρυσίον πλέων[8] ἀπώλεσεν ὑπὸ τῶν ἐν
Βυζαντίῳ πεντηκοστολόγων δι' εὐήθειαν, ὡς λέγουσιν) ἀλλ' ὅτι καὶ ἐν οἷς[9] εὐτυχοῦσιν ἄφρονες.
περὶ γὰρ ναυκληρίαν οὐχ οἱ δεινότατοι εὐτυχεῖς, 6
ἀλλ' (ὥσπερ ἐν κύβων πτώσει ὁ μὲν οὐδέν, ἄλλος

[1] Iac.: πολλά. [2] Rac.: πολλοὶ (πολὺ Cas.).
[3] Rac.: τύχης. [4] Γ: οὕτω.
[5] Sp.: τὸ δεῖν. [6] ὅτι add. Sp.
[7] B^f: δοκεῖ. [8] Sp.: πλέον. [9] B^f: ἐνίοις.

nate and another unfortunate by nature or not, and
2 how it stands with these matters. For that some men are fortunate we see, since many though foolish succeed in things in which luck is paramount, and some even in things which involve skill although also containing a large element of luck—for ex-
3 ample strategy and navigation. Are, then, these men fortunate as a result of a certain state of character, or are they enabled to achieve fortunate results not by reason of a certain quality in themselves? As it is, people think the latter, holding that some men are successful by natural causes; but nature makes men of a certain quality, and the fortunate and unfortunate are different even from birth, in the same way as some men are blue-eyed and others black-eyed because a particular part of them is of a par-
4 ticular quality. For it is clear that they do not succeed by means of wisdom, because wisdom is not irrational but can give reason why it acts as it does, whereas they could not say why they succeed
5 —for that would be science; and moreover it is manifest that they succeed in spite of being unwise—not unwise about other matters (for that would not be anything strange, for example Hippocrates[a] was skilled in geometry but was thought to be stupid and unwise in other matters, and it is said that on a voyage owing to foolishness he lost a great deal of money, taken from him by the collectors of the two-per-cent duty at Byzantium), but even though they are unwise about
6 the matters in which they are fortunate. For in navigation it is not the cleverest who are fortunate, but (just as in throwing dice one man throws a

[a] A Pythagorean philosopher of Chios, *fl.* 460 B.C.

1247 a δ' ἒξ[1] βάλλει) καθὰ ἦν[2] φύσει ἐστὶν εὐτυχής. ἢ τῷ
φιλεῖσθαι, ὥσπερ φασίν, ὑπὸ θεοῦ, καὶ ἔξωθέν τι
εἶναι τὸ κατορθοῦν, οἷον πλοῖον κακῶς νεναυπη-
γημένον ἄμεινον πολλάκις διαπλεῖ,[3] ἀλλ' οὐ δι'
αὐτὸ ἀλλ' ὅτι ἔχει κυβερνήτην ἀγαθόν; ἀλλ' οὕτως
ὁ εὐτυχῶν[4] τὸν δαίμον' ἔχει κυβερνήτην.[5] ἀλλ' 7
ἄτοπον θεὸν ἢ δαίμονα φιλεῖν τὸν τοιοῦτον, ἀλλὰ
μὴ τὸν βέλτιστον καὶ τὸν φρονιμώτατον. εἰ δὴ
ἀνάγκη ἢ φύσει ἢ νόῳ ἢ ἐπιτροπίᾳ τινὶ κατορθοῦν,
τὰ δὲ δύο μή ἐστι, φύσει ἂν εἶεν οἱ εὐτυχεῖς. ἀλλὰ 8
μὴν ἥ γε φύσις αἰτία ἢ τοῦ ἀεὶ ὡσαύτως ἢ τοῦ ὡς
ἐπὶ τὸ πολύ, ἡ δὲ τύχη τοὐναντίον. εἰ μὲν οὖν τὸ[6]
παραλόγως ἐπιτυγχάνειν τύχης δοκεῖ εἶναι,[7] ἀλλ',
εἴπερ διὰ τύχην εὐτυχής, οὐκ ἂν δόξειε[8] τοιοῦτον
εἶναι τὸ αἴτιον οἷον ἀεὶ τοῦ αὐτοῦ ἢ ὡς ἐπὶ τὸ πολύ—
ἔτι εἰ ὅτι[9] τοιοσδὶ ἐπιτυγχάνει ἢ ἀποτυγχάνει,[10] 9
ὥσπερ ὅτι[11] γλαυκὸς οὐκ ὀξὺ ὁρᾷ, οὐ τύχη αἰτία
ἀλλὰ φύσις· οὐκ ἄρα ἐστὶν εὐτυχὴς ἀλλ' οἷον εὐ-
φυής. ὥστε τοῦτ' ἂν εἴη λεκτέον, ὅτι οὓς λέγομεν
1247 b εὐτυχεῖς, οὐ διὰ τύχην εἰσίν· οὐκ ἄρα εἰσὶν εὐτυχεῖς,
εὐτυχεῖς[12] γὰρ ὅσοις[13] αἰτία τύχη ἀγαθὴ ἀγαθῶν.

[1] ἒξ add. hic Rac. (post βάλλει Bf, Iac.).
[2] Iac. (et post φύσει, ⟨τ ῷ τὴν φύσιν ἔχειν εὐτυχῆ⟩): καθ' ἥν.
[3] Syl.: δὲ πλεῖ.
[4] Syl.: οὗτος εὐτυχὴς (εὐτυχῶν edd.).
[5] post κυβερνήτην add. ἀγαθὸν codd. plur.
[6] οὖν ⟨οὕτω⟩ τὸ Bus.
[7] εἶναι ⟨ὁ δὲ διὰ τύχην εὐτυχὴς⟩ Iac., ⟨ὁ δὲ διὰ τύχην ἐπιτυγχάνων εὐτυχὴς⟩ ? Rac.
[8] δόξειε add. Iac.
[9] ὅτι add. Fr.
[10] ἢ ἀποτυγχάνει add. Sus.
[11] ὅτι ὁ codd. plur.
[12] Bf: εὐτύχὴς.
[13] Iac.: ὅσων.

blank and another a six) a man is fortunate according as things were arranged by nature.[a] Or is it because he is loved by God, as the phrase goes, and because success is something from outside? as for instance a badly built ship often gets through a voyage better, though not owing to itself, but be-
7 cause it has a good man at the helm. But on this showing the fortunate man has the deity as steersman. But it is strange that a god or deity should love a man of this sort, and not the best and most prudent. If, then, the success of the lucky must necessarily be due to either nature or intellect or some guardianship, and of these three causes two are ruled out, those who are fortunate will be so by

Yet nature is uniform, luck is not.

8 nature. But again, nature of course is the cause of a thing that happens either always or generally in the same way, whereas fortune is the opposite. If, then, unexpected achievement seems a matter of fortune, but, if a man is fortunate owing to fortune, it would seem that the cause is not of such a sort as to produce the same result always or generally
9 —further, if a man's succeeding or not succeeding is due to his being of a certain sort, as a man does not see clearly because he has blue eyes, not fortune but nature is the cause; therefore he is not a man who has good fortune but one who has as it were a good nature. Hence we should have to say that the people we call fortunate are so not by reason of fortune; therefore they are not fortunate, for the fortunate are those for whom good fortune is a cause of good things.

[a] Or, with Jackson's emendations, 'another a six according as nature determines, so here a man is lucky because his nature is such.'

1247 b Εἰ δ' οὕτω, πότερον οὐκ[1] ἔσται τύχη ὅλως, ἢ
ἔσται μέν, ἀλλ' οὐκ αἰτία[2]; ἀλλ' ἀνάγκη καὶ εἶναι
καὶ αἰτίαν εἶναι. ἔσται ἄρα καὶ ἀγαθῶν τισὶν 10
αἰτία ἢ κακῶν· εἰ δ' ὅλως ἐξαιρετέον, καὶ[3]
οὐδὲν[4] ἀπὸ τύχης φατέον γίνεσθαι, ἀλλ' ἡμεῖς
ἄλλης οὔσης αἰτίας διὰ τὸ μὴ ὁρᾶν τύχην εἶναί
φαμεν αἰτίαν· διὸ καὶ ὁριζόμενοι τὴν τύχην τιθέασιν
αἰτίαν ἄλογον[5] ἀνθρωπίνῳ λογισμῷ, ὡς οὔσης τινὸς
φύσεως. τοῦτο μὲν οὖν ἄλλο πρόβλημ' ἂν εἴη·
ἐπεὶ δὲ[6] ὁρῶμέν τινας ἅπαξ εὐτυχήσαντες, διὰ τί
οὐ καὶ πάλιν ἂν διὰ τὸ αὐτὸ κατορθώσαιεν,[7] καὶ
πάλιν, καὶ πάλιν[8]; τοῦ γὰρ αὐτοῦ τὸ αὐτὸ[9] αἴτιον.
οὐκ ἄρα ἔσται τύχης τοῦτο[10]· ἀλλ' ὅταν τὸ αὐτὸ 11
ἀποβαίνῃ ἀπ'[11] ἀπείρων καὶ ἀορίστων, ἔσται μέν
τῳ[12] ἀγαθὸν ἢ κακόν, ἐπιστήμη δ' οὐκ ἔσται αὐτοῦ
ἡ δι' ἐμπειρίαν,[13] ἐπεὶ ἐμάνθανον ἄν τινες εὐτυχεῖς,[14]
ἢ καὶ πᾶσαι ἂν αἱ ἐπιστῆμαι, ὥσπερ ἔφη Σωκράτης,
εὐτυχίαι ἦσαν. τί οὖν κωλύει συμβῆναί τινι ἐφ- 12
εξῆς τὰ τοιαῦτα πολλάκις οὐχ ὅτι τοιοσδί,[15] ἀλλ'
οἷον ἂν εἴη[16] τὸ κύβους ἀεὶ μακαρίαν[17] βάλλειν;
τί δὲ δή; ἆρ' οὐκ ἔνεισιν ὁρμαὶ ἐν τῇ ψυχῇ αἱ μὲν
ἀπὸ λογισμοῦ αἱ δ' ἀπὸ ὀρέξεως ἀλόγου; καὶ
πρότεραι αὗται; εἰ γάρ ἐστι φύσει ἡ δι' ἐπιθυμίαν

[1] οὐκ Sp.: ἤ.
[2] Sp.: ἀλλ' οὐκέτι.
[3] [καὶ] Sp.
[4] μηδὲν Sus.
[5] Iac.: ἀνάλογον.
[6] Bf: ἐπειδή.
[7] Iac.: διὰ τὸ ἀποκατορθῶσαι (*propter idem dirigere unum* Bf).
[8] καὶ πάλιν καὶ πάλιν Mb: καὶ πάλιν Pb.
[9] Bf: τὸ γὰρ αὐτὸ τοῦτ'.
[10] Bf: οὐ τό.
[11] Bf: ἀπ' om. codd.
[12] Iac.: τὸ.
[13] Bf: ἀπειρίαν.
[14] εὐτυχεῖν Sp.
[15] Iac.: τοῖς δεῖ.
[16] Syl.: εἶεν.
[17] Fr.: μακρὰν.

But if so, shall we say that there is no such thing
as fortune at all, or that it does exist but is not a
10 cause? No, it must both exist and be a cause. Consequently it will furthermore be a cause of goods or
evils to certain persons; whereas if fortune is to be
eliminated altogether, then nothing must be said
to come about from fortune, in spite of the fact that,
although there is another cause, because we do not
see it we say that fortune is a cause—owing to which
people give it as a definition of fortune that it is a
cause incalculable to human reasoning, implying that
it is a real natural principle. This, then, would be a
matter for another inquiry. But since we see that
some people have good fortune on one occasion, why
should they not succeed a second time too owing
to the same cause? and a third time? and a fourth?
11 for the same cause produces the same effect. Therefore this will not be a matter of fortune; but when
the same result follows from indeterminate and in-
definite antecedents, it will be good or bad for somebody, but there will not be the knowledge of it that
comes by experience, since, if there were, some fortunate persons would learn it, or indeed all branches
of knowledge would, as Socrates said,[a] be forms of
12 good fortune. What, then, prevents such things from
happening to somebody a number of times running
not because he has a certain character, but in the
way in which for instance it would be possible to
make the highest throw at dice every time? And
what then? are there not some impulses in the
spirit that arise from reasoning and others from irrational appetition? and are not the latter prior?
because if the impulse caused by desire for what is

[a] Plato, *Euthydemus* 279 D.

1247 b
ἡδέος, καὶ ἡ ὄρεξις φύσει γε ἐπὶ τὸ ἀγαθὸν βαδίζοι
ἂν πάντοτε.[1] εἰ δή τινές εἰσιν εὐφυεῖς (ὥσπερ οἱ 13
ᾠδικοὶ[2] οὐκ ἐπιστάμενοι ᾄδειν οὕτως εὖ πεφύκασι)
καὶ ἄνευ λόγου ὁρμῶσιν ᾗ[3] ἡ φύσις πέφυκε καὶ
ἐπιθυμοῦσι καὶ τούτου καὶ τότε[4] καὶ οὕτως ὡς δεῖ
καὶ οὗ δεῖ καὶ ὅτε, οὗτοι κατορθώσουσι[5] κἂν
τύχωσιν ἄφρονες ὄντες καὶ ἄλογοι, ὥσπερ καὶ εὖ
ᾄσονται[6] οὐ[7] διδασκαλικοὶ ὄντες. οἱ δέ γε τοιοῦτοι
εὐτυχεῖς, ὅσοι ἄνευ λόγου κατορθοῦσιν ὡς ἐπὶ τὸ
πολύ. φύσει ἄρα οἱ εὐτυχεῖς εἶεν ἄν.
Ἢ πλεοναχῶς λέγεται ἡ εὐτυχία; τὰ μὲν γὰρ 14
πράττεται ἀπὸ τῆς ὁρμῆς καὶ προελομένων πρᾶξαι,
τὰ δ' οὔ, ἀλλὰ τοὐναντίον· καὶ εἰ[8] ἐν ἐκείνοις
κακῶς λογίσασθαι δοκοῦσι κατορθοῦντες, καὶ[9] εὐ-
τυχῆσαί φαμεν· καὶ πάλιν ἐν τούτοις, εἰ ἐβούλοντο
ἄλλο[10] ἢ ἔλαττον ἢ[11] ἔλαβον τἀγαθόν. ἐκείνους 15
μὲν τοίνυν εὐτυχεῖν διὰ φύσιν ἐνδέχεται· ἡ γὰρ
ὁρμὴ καὶ ἡ ὄρεξις οὖσα οὗ ἔδει[12] κατώρθωσεν, ὁ
δὲ λογισμὸς ἦν ἠλίθιος· καὶ τοὺς μὲν ἐνταῦθα,
ὅταν ὁ[13] μὲν λογισμὸς μὴ δοκῶν ὀρθὸς[14] εἶναι τύχῃ,[15]
ὁρμὴ[16] δ' αὐτοῦ αἰτία οὖσα, αὕτη[17] ὀρθὴ οὖσα
ἔσωσεν[18]· ἀλλ' ἐνίοτε δι' ἐπιθυμίαν ἐλογίσαντο[19]
πάλιν οὕτω καὶ ἠτύχησαν.[20] ἐν δὲ δὴ τοῖς ἑτέροις 16

[1] Iac. (*semper* B[f]): πᾶν.
[2] Syl.: ἄδικοι (ἀδίδακτοι ᾠδικοὶ Iac., *indocti* B[f]).
[3] ᾗ add. Iac. (*secundum quod* B[f]).
[4] Sp. (*tunc* B[f]): ποτέ.
[5] Fr. (*dirigent* B[f]): κατορθοῦσι.
[6] Syl.: ἔσονται.
[7] Fr. (*non* B[f]): οἱ P[b], εἰ M[b].
[8] εἰ add. Rac. (post ἐκείνοις Sp.).
[9] [καὶ] (vel κατευτυχῆσαι) Bus.
[10] Iac.: ἂν.
[11] ἢ add. Iac.
[12] Fr.: δεῖ.
[13] ὁ add. Rac.
[14] v.l.: ὀρθῶς P[b], M[b].
[15] Sp.: τύχη.
[16] ὁρμὴ add. Rac. (ἡ add. Sp.).
[17] Sp.: αὕτη δ'.
[18] Sp. (*saluauit* B[f]): ἔξωσεν.

pleasant exists by nature, appetition also would merely by nature proceed towards what is good in every
13 case. If, therefore, some men have good natures—just as musical people though they have not learnt to sing [a] have a natural aptitude for it—and without the aid of reason have an impulse in the direction of the natural order of things and desire the right thing in the right way at the right time, these men will succeed even although they are in fact foolish and irrational, just as the others will sing well although unable to teach singing. And men of this sort obviously are fortunate—men who without the aid of reason are usually successful. Hence it will follow that the fortunate are so by nature.

14 Or has the term 'good fortune' more than one meaning? For some things are done from impulse and as a result of the agents' purposive choice, other things not so but on the contrary; and if in the former cases when the agents succeed they seem to have reasoned badly, we say that in fact they have had good fortune; and again in the latter cases, if they wished for a different good or less good than they
15 have got. The former persons then may possibly owe their good fortune to nature, for their impulse and appetition, being for the right object, succeeded, but their reasoning was foolish; and in their case, when it happens that their reasoning seems to be incorrect but that impulse is the cause of it, this impulse being right has saved them; although sometimes on the contrary owing to appetite they have reasoned in this way and come to misfortune.

Luck an ambiguous term: it includes success really caused by nature.

[a] Or, with Jackson's additions, 'just as untaught musical geniuses, without professional knowledge of singing.'

[19] Sp.: ἐλογίσατο. [20] Sp.: ἠτύχησεν.

1247 b πῶς ἔσται ἡ εὐτυχία κατ' εὐφυΐαν ὀρέξεως καὶ
1248 a ἐπιθυμίας; ἀλλὰ μὴν ἡ ἐνταῦθα εὐτυχία κἀκείνη
ἡ αὐτή. ἢ πλείους αἱ εὐτυχίαι καὶ τύχη διττή[1];
ἐπεὶ δ' ὁρῶμεν παρὰ πάσας τὰς ἐπιστήμας καὶ τοὺς 17
λογισμοὺς τοὺς ὀρθοὺς εὐτυχοῦντάς τινας, δῆλον
ὅτι ἕτερον ἄν τι εἴη τὸ αἴτιον τῆς εὐτυχίας. ἐκείνη
δὲ πότερον ἔστιν[2] εὐτυχία ἢ οὐκ ἔστιν, ᾗ[3] ἐπεθύμη-
σεν ὧν ἔδει καὶ ὅτε ἔδει ᾧ[4] λογισμὸς ἀνθρώπινος
οὐκ ἂν τούτου εἴη; οὐ γὰρ δὴ πάμπαν ἀλόγιστον
τοῦτο οὗ γε[5] φυσική ἐστιν ἡ ἐπιθυμία, ἀλλὰ δια-
φθείρεται ὑπό τινος. εὐτυχεῖν μὲν οὖν δοκεῖ ὅτι ἡ 18
τύχη τῶν παρὰ λόγον αἰτία, τοῦτο[6] δὲ παρὰ λόγον,
παρὰ γὰρ τὴν ἐπιστήμην καὶ τὸ καθόλου. ἀλλ' ὡς 19
ἔοικεν, οὐκ ἀπὸ τύχης, ἀλλὰ δοκεῖ διὰ τοῦτο.
ὥσθ' οὗτος μὲν ὁ λόγος οὐ δείκνυσιν ὅτι φύσει εὐ-
τυχεῖται,[7] ἀλλ' ὅτι οὐ πάντες οἱ δοκοῦντες εὐτυχεῖν
διὰ τύχην κατορθοῦσιν, ἀλλὰ[8] διὰ φύσιν· οὐδ' ὅτι
οὐδέν ἐστι τύχη ⟨οὐδ' ὅτι οὐκ ἔστι τύχη⟩[9] αἰτία
οὐθενὸς δείκνυσιν, ἀλλ' ὅτι[10] οὐ τῶν πάντων ὧν
δοκεῖ.

Τοῦτο μέντ' ἂν ἀπορήσειέ τις, ἆρ' αὐτοῦ τούτου 20
τύχη αἰτία, τοῦ ἐπιθυμῆσαι οὗ δεῖ καὶ ὅτε δεῖ; ἢ
οὕτω γε πάντων ἔσται; καὶ γὰρ τοῦ νοῆσαι καὶ
βουλεύσασθαι· οὐ γὰρ δὴ ἐβουλεύσατο βουλευσάμενος καὶ πρὶν[11] τοῦτ' ἐβουλεύσατο οὐδ' ἐνόησε

1 καὶ τύχη διττή hic Sp.: ante κἀκείνη codd.
2 ἔστιν Sp.: ἡ Mᵇ, om. Pᵇ. 3 Fr.: ἡ. 4 Iac.: τό.
5 οὗ γε Iac.: οὔτε. 6 Vict. (*hoc* Bᶠ): τούτου.
7 Iac. (*bene fortunate agatur* Bᶠ): εὐτυχεῖν.
8 ἀλλ' <ἐνίοτε> ? Rac.: ἀλλὰ <πολλοὶ> ? Sus.
9 Iac. 10 ὅτι add. Cas.
11 πρὶν add. Rac. (*antequam consiliaretur* Bᶠ).

---

a *Cf.* 1247 b 30 τὰ δ' οὔ (Solomon).

16 But in the case of the others,[a] then, how will good fortune be due to natural goodness of appetition and desire? The fact is that the good fortune here and that in the other case are the same. Or is good fortune of more than one kind, and is fortune two-
17 fold? But since we see some people being fortunate contrary to all the teachings of science and correct calculation, it is clear that the cause of good fortune must be something different. But is it or is it not good fortune whereby a man formed a desire for the right thing and at the right time when in his case human reasoning could not make this calculation? For a thing the desire for which is natural is not altogether uncalculated, but the reasoning
18 is perverted by something. So no doubt he seems fortunate, because fortune is the cause of things contrary to reason, and this is contrary to reason, for it is contrary to knowledge and to general prin-
19 ciple. But probably it does not really come from fortune, but seems to do so from the above cause. So that this argument does not prove that good fortune comes by nature, but that not all those who seem fortunate succeed because of fortune, but because of nature; nor does it prove that there is no such thing as fortune, nor that fortune is not the cause of anything, but that it is not the cause of all the things of which it seems to be the cause.

Right desire not due to chance but a gift of heaven.

20 Yet someone may raise the question whether fortune is the cause of precisely this—our forming a desire for the right thing at the right time. Or, on that showing, will not fortune be the cause of everything—even of thought and deliberation? since it is not the case that one only deliberates when one has deliberated even previously to that

1248 a
νοήσας πρότερον ἢ[1] νοῆσαι, καὶ τοῦτ' εἰς ἄπειρον,
ἀλλ' ἔστιν ἀρχή τις.[2] οὐκ ἄρα τοῦ νοῆσαι ὁ νοῦς[3]
ἀρχή, οὐδὲ τοῦ βουλεύσασθαι βουλή. τί οὖν ἄλλο
πλὴν τύχη; ὥστ' ἀπὸ τύχης ἅπαντα ἔσται. ἢ[4] ἔστι
τις ἀρχὴ ἧς οὐκ ἔστιν ἄλλη ἔξω, αὕτη δὲ διὰ τὸ
τοιαύτη γε εἶναι τοιοῦτο[5] δύναται[6] ποιεῖν; τὸ 21
δὲ ζητούμενον τοῦτ' ἐστί, τίς ἡ τῆς κινήσεως ἀρχὴ
ἐν τῇ ψυχῇ. δῆλον δή· ὥσπερ ἐν τῷ ὅλῳ, θεὸς καὶ
πᾶν ἐκεῖ κινεῖ[7]· κινεῖ γάρ πως πάντα[8] τὸ ἐν ἡμῖν
θεῖον. λόγου δ' ἀρχὴ οὐ λόγος ἀλλά τι κρεῖττον. 22
τί οὖν ἂν κρεῖττον καὶ ἐπιστήμης εἴη[9] καὶ νοῦ[10]
πλὴν θεός; ἡ γὰρ ἀρετὴ τοῦ νοῦ ὄργανον· καὶ διὰ
τοῦτο, ὃ[11] πάλαι ἔλεγον, εὐτυχεῖς καλοῦνται οἳ
οἳ[12] ἂν ὁρμήσωσι κατορθοῦσιν[13] ἄλογοι ὄντες. καὶ
βουλεύεσθαι οὐ συμφέρει αὐτοῖς· ἔχουσι γὰρ ἀρχὴν
τοιαύτην ἣ κρείττων[14] τοῦ νοῦ καὶ βουλεύσεως
(οἱ δὲ τὸν λόγον, τοῦτο δ' οὐκ ἔχουσι), καὶ ἐν- 23
θουσιασμόν,[15] τοῦτο δ' οὐ δύνανται, ἄλογοι γὰρ
ὄντες ἐπιτυγχάνουσι[16] καὶ τοῦ τῶν[17] φρονίμων καὶ
σοφῶν ταχεῖαν εἶναι τὴν μαντικήν· καὶ μόνον οὐ
τὴν ἀπὸ τοῦ λόγου δεῖ ἀπολαβεῖν, ἀλλ' οἱ μὲν δι'
ἐμπειρίαν, οἱ δὲ διὰ συνήθειαν τοῦ[18] τῷ σκοπεῖν

[1] ἢ add. Sp.
[2] ἀλλ' . . . τις hic Rac.: ante οὐδ' ἐνόησε codd.
[3] ὁ νοῦς Cas.: συνοῦσα.
[4] ἢ Sus. (*aut* Bf): εἰ (εἰ <μὴ> Sp.).
[5] Iac.: διὰ τί τοιαύτη τὸ εἶναι τὸ τοῦτο.
[6] Syl. (*potest* Bf): δύνασθαι.
[7] ἐκεῖ κινεῖ Iac.: ἐκείνῳ.
[8] πάντα <τὰ ἐν ἡμῖν> Iac.
[9] Sp.: εἴποι.
[10] καὶ νοῦ add. Sp. (*et intellectu* Bf).
[11] Iac.: οἱ.
[12] οἳ add. Ross.
[13] Fr. (*dirigunt* Bf): κατορθοῦν.
[14] Ald.: κρεῖττον.
[15] Sp.: ἐνθουσιασμοί.
[16] Syl.: ἀποτυγχάνουσι.
[17] τοῦ τῶν Syl.: τούτων (*horum* Bf).
[18] τοῦ Sol.: τε ἐν.

deliberation, nor does one only think when one has previously thought before thinking, and so on to infinity, but there is some starting-point; therefore thought is not the starting-point of thinking, nor deliberation of deliberating. Then what else is, save fortune? It will follow that everything originates from fortune. Or shall we say that there is a certain starting-point outside which there is no other, and that this, merely owing to its being of such and such a nature, can produce a result of such
21 and such a nature? But this is what we are investigating—what is the starting-point of motion in the spirit? The answer then is clear: as in the universe, so there, everything is moved by God; for in a manner the divine element in us is the cause
22 of all our motions. And the starting-point of reason is not reason but something superior to reason. What, then, could be superior even to knowledge and to intellect, except God? Not goodness, for goodness is an instrument of the mind; and owing to this, as I was saying some time ago,[a] those are called fortunate who although irrational succeed in whatever they start on. And it does not pay them to deliberate, for they have within them a principle of a kind that is better than mind and deliberation
23 (whereas the others have reason but have not this): they have inspiration, but they cannot deliberate. For although irrational they attain even what belongs to the prudent and wise—swiftness of divination: only the divination that is based on reason we must not specify, but some of them attain it by experience and others by practice in the use of observation;

[a] See 1247 b 26.

1248 a
χρῆσθαι· τῷ θείῳ[1] δὲ οὗτοι.[2] τοῦτο γάρ[3] εὖ
ὁρᾷ καὶ τὸ μέλλον καὶ τὸ ὄν, καὶ ὧν ἀπολύεται ὁ
λόγος οὗτοι.[4] διὸ οἱ μελαγχολικοὶ καὶ εὐθυόνειροι·
1248 b ἔοικε γὰρ ἡ ἀρχὴ ἀπολυομένου τοῦ λόγου[5] ἰσχύειν
μᾶλλον, ὥσπερ[6] οἱ τυφλοὶ μνημονεύουσι μᾶλλον,
ἀπολυθέντες τοῦ πρὸς τοῖς ὁρωμένοις[7] εἶναι τὸ
μνημονεῦον.[8]

Φανερὸν δή[9] ὅτι δύο εἴδη εὐτυχίας, ἡ μὲν θεία· 24
διὸ καὶ δοκεῖ ὁ εὐτυχὴς διὰ θεὸν κατορθοῦν, οὗτος
δ' ἐστὶν ὁ κατὰ τὴν ὁρμὴν κατορθωτικός,[10] ὁ δ'
ἕτερος ὁ παρὰ τὴν ὁρμήν. ἄλογοι δ' ἀμφότεροι.
καὶ ἡ μὲν συνεχὴς εὐτυχία μᾶλλον, αὕτη δὲ οὐ συν-
εχής.

III. Κατὰ μέρος μὲν οὖν περὶ ἑκάστης ἀρετῆς 1
εἴρηται πρότερον· ἐπεὶ δὲ χωρὶς διείλομεν τὴν
δύναμιν αὐτῶν, καὶ περὶ τῆς ἀρετῆς διαρθρωτέον[11]
τῆς ἐκ τούτων ἣν καλοῦμεν[12] ἤδη καλοκἀγαθίαν.

[1] Sp.: *θεῷ.* [2] Von Arnim: *αὗται.* [3] Von Arnim: *καί.*

[4] Sol.: *οὗτος* (ll. 37 ff. *συνήθειαν τὸ ἐν τῷ σκοπεῖν χρῆσθαι τῷ θεῷ δύνανται τοῦτο καὶ εὖ ὁρᾶν καὶ τὸ μέλλον καὶ τὸ ὄν, καὶ ὧν ἀπολύεται ὁ λόγος οὕτως* Iac.).

[5] Sp. (cum B^f): *ἀπολυομένους τοὺς λόγους.*

[6] Von Arnim: *καὶ ὥσπερ.*

[7] Rac.: *εἰρημένοις* (*τοῦ πρὸς τοῖς <ὁρατοῖς εἶναι τῷ πρὸς τοῖς> εἰρημένοις <σπουδαιότερον> εἶναι τὸ μνημονεῦον* Iac., *ad mirabilia uirtuosius esse quod memoratur* B^f).

[8] [*τὸ μνημονεῦον*] ? Rac. [9] Fr. (*itaque* B^f): *δέ.*

[10] Von Arnim: *διορθωτικός.* [11] v.l. *διορθωτέον.*

[12] Γ, Iac. (*uocamus* B^f): *ἐκαλοῦμεν.*

---

[a] The ms. reading gives 'and experience and habit use God.'

[b] Or, with Jackson's text, 'But some of them by experi-

and these men use the divine.[a] For this quality discerns aright the future as well as the present, and these are the men whose reason is disengaged.[b] This is why the melancholic even have dreams that are true; for it seems that when the reason is disengaged principle has more strength—just as the blind remember better, being released from having their faculty of memory engaged with objects of sight.[c]

24 It is clear, then, that there are two kinds of good fortune—one divine, owing to which the fortunate man's success is thought to be due to the aid of God, and this is the man who is successful in accordance with his impulse, while the other is he who succeeds against his impulse. Both persons are irrational. The former kind is more continuous good fortune, the latter is not continuous.

1 III. We have, then, previously spoken about each virtue in particular; and as we have distinguished their meaning separately, we must also describe in detail the virtue constituted from them, to which we
2 now give the name [d] of nobility.[e] Now it is mani-

c. iii. NOBILITY. The combination of all virtues.

ence and others by habituation have this capacity of consulting God in examining things, and of discerning aright both the future and the present; and those also have it whose reason is disengaged in the manner described.'

[c] Jackson (with some hints from the Latin version) emends to give 'just as blind men, who are released from attention to visibles, remember better than others, because the faculty of memory is thus more earnestly addressed to what has been said.'

[d] The MS. reading gives, 'we were already giving the name,' but if that is correct, the passage referred to has been lost.

[e] Καλοκἀγαθία, like 'nobility', connotes both social status and moral excellence; so καλοκἀγαθός may be rendered 'gentleman.'

1248 b
ὅτι μὲν οὖν ἀνάγκη τὸν ταύτης ἀληθῶς τευξόμενον 2
τῆς προσηγορίας ἔχειν τὰς κατὰ μέρος ἀρετάς,
φανερόν· οὐδὲ γὰρ ἐπὶ τῶν ἄλλων οὐθενὸς οἷόν τ'
ἄλλως ἔχειν, οὐθεὶς γὰρ ὅλον μὲν τὸ σῶμα ὑγιαίνει
μέρος δ' οὐθέν, ἀλλ' ἀναγκαῖον πάντα ἢ τὰ πλεῖστα
καὶ κυριώτατα τὸν αὐτὸν ἔχειν τρόπον τῷ ὅλῳ.
ἔστι δὴ τὸ ἀγαθὸν εἶναι καὶ τὸ καλὸν κἀγαθὸν οὐ 3
μόνον κατὰ τὰ ὀνόματα ἀλλὰ καὶ[1] καθ' αὑτὰ
ἔχοντα διαφοράν. τῶν γὰρ ἀγαθῶν πάντων τέλη
ἐστὶν ἃ αὐτὰ αὑτῶν ἕνεκά ἐστιν αἱρετά. τούτων δὲ 4
καλὰ ὅσα δι' αὑτὰ ὄντα πάντα[2] ἐπαινετά ἐστιν·
ταῦτα γάρ ἐστιν ἀφ'[3] ὧν αἵ τε πράξεις εἰσὶν
ἐπαινεταὶ καὶ αὐτὰ ἐπαινετά, δικαιοσύνη[4] καὶ
αὐτὴ καὶ αἱ πράξεις, καὶ αἱ[5] σώφρονες, ἐπαινετὴ
γὰρ καὶ ἡ σωφροσύνη· ἀλλ' οὐχ ὑγίεια ἐπαινετόν,
οὐδὲ γὰρ τὸ ἔργον, οὐδὲ τὸ ἰσχυρῶς, οὐδὲ γὰρ ἡ
ἰσχύς, ἀλλ' ἀγαθὰ μέν, ἐπαινετὰ δ' οὔ. ὁμοίως 5
δὲ τοῦτο δῆλον καὶ ἐπὶ τῶν ἄλλων διὰ τῆς
ἐπαγωγῆς. ἀγαθὸς μὲν οὖν ἐστὶν ᾧ τὰ φύσει
ἀγαθά ἐστιν ἀγαθά. τὰ γὰρ περιμάχητα καὶ
μέγιστα εἶναι δοκοῦντα ἀγαθά, τιμὴ καὶ πλοῦτος
καὶ σώματος ἀρεταὶ καὶ εὐτυχίαι καὶ δυνάμεις,
ἀγαθὰ μὲν φύσει ἐστίν, ἐνδέχεται δ' εἶναι βλαβερά
τισι διὰ τὰς ἕξεις. οὔτε γὰρ ἄφρων οὔτ' ἄδικος ἢ
ἀκόλαστος ὢν οὐδὲν ἂν ὀνήσειε[6] χρώμενος αὐτοῖς,
ὥσπερ οὐδ' ὁ κάμνων τῇ τοῦ ὑγιαίνοντος τροφῇ
χρώμενος, οὐδ' ὁ ἀσθενὴς καὶ ἀνάπηρος τοῖς τοῦ
ὑγιοῦς καὶ τοῖς τοῦ ὁλοκλήρου κόσμοις. καλὸς 6
δὲ κἀγαθὸς τῷ τῶν ἀγαθῶν τὰ καλὰ ὑπάρχειν
αὐτῷ δι' αὑτά, καὶ τῷ πρακτικὸς εἶναι τῶν καλῶν

[1] καὶ add. Bus.
[2] αἱρετὰ pro πάντα? Sp.
[3] Syl.: ἐφ'.
[4] <οἷον> δικαιοσύνη Syl.

fest that one who is to obtain this appellation truly must possess the particular virtues; for it is impossible for it to be otherwise in the case of any other matter either—for instance, no one is healthy in his whole body but not in any part of it, but all the parts, or most of them and the most important, must necessarily be in the same condition as the
3 whole. Now being good and being noble are really different not only in their names but also in themselves. For all goods have Ends that are desirable
4 in and for themselves. Of these, all those are fine which are laudable as existing for their own sakes, for these are the Ends which are both the motives of laudable actions and laudable themselves—justice itself and its actions, and temperate actions, for temperance also is laudable; but health is not laudable, for its effect is not, nor is vigorous action laudable, for strength is not—these things are good
5 but they are not laudable. And similarly induction makes this clear in the other cases also. Therefore a man is good for whom the things good by nature are good. For the things men fight about and think the greatest, honour and wealth and bodily excellences and pieces of good fortune and powers, are good by nature but may possibly be harmful to some men owing to their characters. If a man is foolish or unjust or profligate he would gain no profit by employing them, any more than an invalid would benefit from using the diet of a man in good health, or a weakling and cripple from the equipment of a
6 healthy man and of a sound one. A man is noble because he possesses those good things that are fine for their own sake and because he is a doer of

More than mere goodness.

Its psychology.

[5] Sol.: οἱ. [6] Γ, Sp.: οὐδ' ὀνήσειε.

1248 b
καὶ αὑτῶν ἕνεκα· καλὰ δ' ἐστὶν αἵ τε ἀρεταὶ καὶ
τὰ ἔργα τὰ ἀπὸ τῆς ἀρετῆς.
Ἔστι δέ τις ἕξις πολιτική, οἵαν οἱ Λάκωνες 7
ἔχουσιν ἢ ἄλλοι τοιοῦτοι ἔχοιεν ἄν, αὕτη δ' ἐστὶν
ἕξις τοιαύτη. εἰσὶ γὰρ οἳ οἴονται τὴν ἀρετὴν δεῖν
1249 a μὲν ἔχειν, ἀλλὰ τῶν φύσει ἀγαθῶν ἕνεκεν· διὸ
ἀγαθοὶ μὲν ἄνδρες εἰσίν (τὰ γὰρ φύσει μὲν[1] ἀγαθὰ
ἀγαθὰ[2] αὐτοῖς ἐστίν), καλοκἀγαθίαν δὲ[3] οὐκ
ἔχουσιν· οὐ γὰρ ὑπάρχει αὐτοῖς τὰ καλὰ δι' αὑτὰ
καὶ προαιροῦνται καλὰ κἀγαθά[4]· καὶ οὐ μόνον
ταῦτα, ἀλλὰ καὶ τὰ μὴ καλὰ μὲν φύσει ὄντα,
ἀγαθὰ δὲ φύσει ὄντα, τούτοις καλά. καλὰ γάρ 8
ἐστιν ὅταν οὗ ἕνεκα πράττουσι καὶ αἱροῦνται
καλὸν ᾖ. διὸ τῷ καλῷ κἀγαθῷ καλά ἐστι τὰ
φύσει ἀγαθά· καλὸν γὰρ τὸ δίκαιον, τοῦτο δὲ τὸ
κατ' ἀξίαν, ἄξιος δ' οὗτος τούτων· καὶ τὸ πρέπον 9
καλόν, πρέπει δὲ ταῦτα τούτῳ,[5] πλοῦτος εὐγένεια
δύναμις. ὥστε τῷ καλῷ κἀγαθῷ τὰ αὐτὰ καὶ[6]
συμφέροντα καὶ καλά ἐστιν· τοῖς δὲ πολλοῖς διαφωνεῖ ταῦτα,[7] οὐ γὰρ τὰ ἁπλῶς ἀγαθὰ κἀκείνοις
ἀγαθά ἐστι, τῷ δ' ἀγαθῷ ἀγαθά· τῷ δὲ καλῷ
κἀγαθῷ[8] καὶ καλά, πολλὰς γὰρ καὶ καλὰς πράξεις
δι' αὐτὰ ἔπραξεν. ὁ δ' οἰόμενος τὰς ἀρετὰς ἔχειν 10
δεῖν ἕνεκα τῶν ἐκτὸς ἀγαθῶν κατὰ τὸ συμβεβηκὸς καλὰ πράττει.
Ἔστιν οὖν καλοκἀγαθία ἀρετὴ τέλειος.
Καὶ περὶ ἡδονῆς δ' εἴρηται ποῖόν τι καὶ πῶς 11

1 [μὲν] ? Rac.
2 ἀγαθὰ alterum add. Sol. (cf. 1248 b 26).
3 Γ: γάρ.
4 Ross: καλοὶ κἀγαθοί.
5 Γ: πλούτῳ.
6 Brandis: καὶ αὐτὰ τὰ aut καὶ αὐτά.
7 Rac.: τοῦτο.
8 Sp.: τῷ δ' ἀγαθῷ.

fine deeds even for their own sake; and the fine things are the virtues and the actions that arise from virtue.

7 But there is also a state of character that is the 'civic' character, such as the Spartans have or others like them may have; and this character is of the following sort. There are those who think that one ought, it is true, to possess goodness, but for the sake of the things that are naturally good; hence though they are good men (for the things naturally good are good for them), yet they have not nobility, for it is not the case with them that they possess fine things for their own sake and that they purpose fine actions, and not only this, but also that things not fine by nature but good by nature are
8 fine for them. For things are fine when that for which men do them and choose them is fine. Therefore to the noble man the things good by nature are fine; for what is just is fine, and what is according to worth is just, and he is worthy of these things;
9 and what is befitting is fine, and these things befit him—wealth, birth, power. Hence for the noble man the same things are both advantageous and fine; but for the multitude these things do not coincide, for things absolutely good are not also good for them, whereas they are good for the good man; and to the noble man they are also fine, for he performs many fine actions because of them.
10 But he who thinks that one ought to possess the virtues for the sake of external goods does fine things only by accident.

It is non-utilitarian.

Nobility then is perfect goodness.

11 We have also spoken about the nature of pleasure

Its pleasantness.

1249 a ἀγαθόν, καὶ ὅτι τά τε ἁπλῶς ἡδέα καὶ καλὰ τά τε
ἁπλῶς ἀγαθὰ καὶ[1] ἡδέα. οὐ γίνεται δὲ ἡδονὴ μὴ
ἐν πράξει· διὰ τοῦτο ὁ ἀληθῶς εὐδαίμων καὶ ἥδιστα
ζήσει, καὶ τοῦτο οὐ μάτην οἱ ἄνθρωποι ἀξιοῦσιν.
Ἐπεὶ δ' ἐστί τις ὅρος καὶ τῷ ἰατρῷ πρὸς ὃν 12
ἀναφέρων κρίνει τὸ ὑγιαῖνον[2] σῶμα καὶ τὸ[3] μή,
καὶ πρὸς ὃν μέχρι ποσοῦ ποιητέον ἕκαστον καὶ
ὑγιεινόν,[4] εἰ δὲ ἔλαττον ἢ πλέον οὐκέτι, οὕτω καὶ
τῷ σπουδαίῳ περὶ τὰς πράξεις καὶ αἱρέσεις τῶν
1249 b φύσει μὲν ἀγαθῶν οὐκ ἐπαινετῶν δὲ δεῖ τινὰ εἶναι
ὅρον καὶ ἕξεως καὶ τῆς αἱρέσεως καὶ φυγῆς, καὶ
περὶ χρημάτων πλῆθος καὶ ὀλιγότητα[5] καὶ τῶν εὐτυχημάτων. ἐν μὲν οὖν τοῖς πρότερον ἐλέχθη τὸ 13
ὡς ὁ λόγος· τοῦτο δ' ἐστὶν ὥσπερ ἂν εἴ τις
ἐν τοῖς περὶ τὴν τροφὴν εἴπειεν ὡς ἡ ἰατρικὴ καὶ
ὁ λόγος ταύτης, τοῦτο δ' ἀληθὲς μὲν οὐ σαφὲς
δέ. δεῖ δὴ ὥσπερ καὶ ἐν τοῖς ἄλλοις πρὸς τὸ 14
ἄρχον ζῆν, καὶ πρὸς τὴν ἕξιν καὶ[6] τὴν ἐνέργειαν
τὴν τοῦ ἄρχοντες, οἷον δοῦλον πρὸς δεσπότου καὶ
ἕκαστον πρὸς τὴν ἑκάστῳ[7] καθήκουσαν ἀρχήν. ἐπεὶ 15
δὲ καὶ ἄνθρωπος φύσει συνέστηκεν ἐξ ἄρχοντος
καὶ ἀρχομένου, καὶ ἕκαστον ἂν[8] δέοι πρὸς τὴν
αὑτοῦ[9] ἀρχὴν ζῆν (αὕτη δὲ διττή, ἄλλως γὰρ ἡ
ἰατρικὴ ἀρχὴ καὶ ἄλλως ἡ ὑγίεια, ταύτης δὲ ἕνεκα
ἐκείνη), οὕτω δὴ[10] ἔχει καὶ[11] κατὰ τὸ θεωρητικόν.
οὐ γὰρ ἐπιτακτικῶς ἄρχων ὁ θεός, ἀλλ' οὗ ἕνεκα

[1] καὶ hic Rac.: ante τά τε ἁπλῶς. [2] Vat.: ὑγιεινόν.
[3] τὸ add. Rac. [4] Ross: καὶ εὖ ὑγιαῖνον.
[5] Zeller: καὶ περὶ φυγῆς χρημάτων πλήθους καὶ ὀλιγότητος.
[6] καὶ Ross: κατὰ. [7] Rac.: ἑκάστου.
[8] ἂν Sp.: δή. [9] Sp.: ἑαυτῶν (ἐν αὐτῷ ? Rac.).
[10] Rieckher: δεῖ. [11] καὶ add. Sus.

[a] 1222 a 6-10, b 7, 1232 a 32 f.

and the manner in which it is a good, and have said that things pleasant absolutely are also fine and that things good absolutely are also pleasant. Pleasure does not occur except in action ; on this account the truly happy man will also live most pleasantly, and it is not without reason that people demand this.

12 But since a doctor has a certain standard by referring to which he judges the healthy body and the unhealthy, and in relation to which each thing up to a certain point ought to be done and is wholesome, but if less is done, or more, it ceases to be wholesome, so in regard to actions and choices of things good by nature but not laudable a virtuous man ought to have a certain standard both of character and of choice and avoidance ; and also in regard to large and small amount of property and of good

Limit of external goods

13 fortune. Now in what preceded[a] we stated the standard 'as reason directs' ; but this is as if in matters of diet one were to say 'as medical science and its principles direct,' and this though true is

14 not clear. It is proper, therefore, here as in other matters to live with reference to the ruling factor, and to the state and the activity of the ruling factor, as for example slave must live with reference to the rule of master, and each person with reference to the rule

15 appropriate to each. And since man consists by nature of a ruling part and a subject part, and each would properly live with reference to the ruling principle within him (and this is twofold, for medical science is a ruling principle in one way and health is in another, and the former is a means to the latter), this is therefore the case in regard to the faculty of contemplation. For God is not a ruler in the sense of issuing commands, but is the End as a means

1249 b

ἡ φρόνησις ἐπιτάττει (διττὸν δὲ τὸ οὗ ἕνεκα, διώρισται δ' ἐν ἄλλοις), ἐπεὶ ἐκεῖνός γε[1] οὐθενὸς
δεῖται. ἥτις οὖν αἵρεσις καὶ κτῆσις τῶν φύσει 16
ἀγαθῶν ποιήσει μάλιστα τὴν τοῦ θεοῦ θεωρίαν, ἢ σώματος ἢ χρημάτων ἢ φίλων ἢ τῶν ἄλλων ἀγαθῶν, αὕτη ἀρίστη καὶ οὗτος ὁ ὅρος κάλλιστος· εἴ τις δ' ἢ δι' ἔνδειαν ἢ δι' ὑπερβολὴν κωλύει τὸν
θεὸν θεραπεύειν καὶ θεωρεῖν, αὕτη δὲ φαύλη. ἔχει 17
δὲ τοῦτο οὕτω[2] τῇ ψυχῇ, καὶ οὗτος τῆς ψυχῆς ὅρος ἄριστος, τὸ[3] ἥκιστα αἰσθάνεσθαι τοῦ ἀλόγου[4] μέρους τῆς ψυχῆς, ᾗ τοιοῦτον.

Τίς μὲν οὖν ὅρος τῆς καλοκἀγαθίας καὶ τίς ὁ σκοπὸς τῶν ἁπλῶς ἀγαθῶν ἔστω εἰρημένον.

[1] Syl.: τε.
[2] οὕτω add. Rac.
[3] Zeller: τὰ.
[4] Fr.: ἄλλου.

[a] End or 'final cause' (οὗ ἕνεκα) denotes (1) the person or thing for whose good something is done, (2) the purpose for which it is done. God is the Final Cause in the latter sense:

to which wisdom gives commands (and the term 'End' has two meanings, but these have been distinguished elsewhere[a]); since clearly God is in
16 need of nothing. Therefore whatever mode of choosing and of acquiring things good by nature—whether goods of body or wealth or friends or the other goods—will best promote the contemplation of God, that is the best mode, and that standard is the finest; and any mode of choice and acquisition that either through deficiency or excess hinders us from serving and from contemplating God—that is a
17 bad one. This is how it is for the spirit, and this is the best spiritual standard—to be as far as possible unconscious of the irrational part of the spirit, as such.

as means to the contemplation of God.

Let this, then, be our statement of what is the standard of nobility and what is the aim of things absolutely good.

[a] *cf. Phys.* 194 a 32-36, *De An.* 415 b 2, *Met.* 1072 b 2 (Solomon).

INDEX I.—PROPER NAMES

References are to the pages, columns (a and b) and lines of the Berlin edition of Aristotle, 1831, *marked in the left-hand margin of the text. The two first figures of the page-numbers are omitted,* 14 *a to* 51 *b standing for* 1214 *a to* 1251 *b. The first line only of each passage referred to is given in most cases.*

Short foot-notes on some of the names will be found below the translation.

INDEX II.—SUBJECTS

References as in Index I.

INDEX II. TO THE EUDEMIAN ETHICS

ON VIRTUES AND VICES

INTRODUCTION

Contents

This essay is of interest as an example of the way in which Aristotle's reduction to scientific form of the ethical system adumbrated by Plato was later systematized and stereotyped by smaller minds. It classifies the various kinds of good and bad conduct under the virtues and vices of which they are manifestations. It starts from the ethical psychology of Plato, dividing the Soul or personality of man into three parts, the reason, the passions and the appetites. Then turning to conduct, it ranges the various actions and emotions under the virtues and vices which they exemplify.

Affinities

The list of Virtues or forms of Goodness [a] is Aristotelian, as in addition to the four cardinal virtues of Plato, Wisdom or prudence, Courage or manliness, Temperance or sobriety of mind, and Justice or righteousness, it includes Gentleness, Self-control, Liber-

[a] The word 'virtue' to the modern English ear denotes only one department of ἀρετή, viz. ἠθικὴ ἀρετή or 'moral goodness.' The Greek mind saw the unity of human excellence behind its various forms.

ality or generosity, and Magnanimity or greatness of spirit. But the analysis of these virtues adopted is not Aristotle's. He exhibited them as forms of moderation, lying midway between vicious extremes of excess and deficiency ; but here each virtue is merely contrasted with a single vice as its opposite. And near the end of the essay (c. viii.) there is an allusion to the comparison drawn by Plato in the *Republic* between the well-ordered Soul and the well-constituted State.

It is true that the rigorously systematic arrangement of the matter and the concise fullness of detail (in cc. vii., viii. three of the Vices are neatly subdivided into three species each) are more characteristic of the Peripatetic School than of the Academy ; the formal exposition of a subject already fully explored has replaced the tentative heuristic method which Plato in his dialogues inherited from Socrates. The descriptive treatment of the virtues and vices (a method that had been first foreshadowed in the *Nicomachean Ethics*, in for instance the portrait of the Magnanimous Man) links the work with the *Characters* of Theophrastus, and seems to have been customary in the Peripatetic School from his time onward. Zeller [a] points out that the recognition of an order of beings between gods and men, the *daimones*, in the passages dealing with piety and godliness (cc. v., vii.), also indicates a late period. A faint trace of Stoic influence may be seen in the formal antithesis of praiseworthy and blameworthy actions at the beginning and the end of the treatise.

[a] *Eclectics*, p. 145.

Date

Susemihl [a] agrees with Zeller that the book probably belongs to the eclectic period ; he dates it not earlier than the first century B.C. and perhaps in the first century A.D., and sees in it an author of no great ability, apparently a Peripatetic, attempting to reconcile the moral philosophy of Aristotle with that of Plato.

The earlier date suggested brings it within range of Andronicus of Rhodes, who was head of the Peripatetic School at Athens in Cicero's student days. Andronicus edited and commentated on the Master's works, making some modifications of his own in logic and psychology. Under his name, though scholars usually assign it to a later date, there has come down to us a treatise Περὶ παθῶν, and appended to this treatise is an essay *On Virtues and Vices* which is a copy of the one before us, though the order of the contents has been rearranged. This book serves as additional evidence for our text.

Some further evidence is supplied by the MSS. of the *Florilegium* of Joannes Stobaeus (John of Stobi in Macedonia, fifth century A.D. or later), of which miscellany the present essay forms c. xviii of Book I.

Manuscripts and Texts

The text of this edition is based on that of Bekker in the Berlin Aristotle, 1833, where Περὶ ἀρετῶν καὶ κακιῶν occupies pp. 1249-1251 in the second volume ; Bekker gives no critical notes. The Berlin

[a] Teubner ed., p. xxxi.

page-numbers, columns (*a* and *b*) and lines are printed in the margin here. The only considerable later work on the text is that of Susemihl, who included this essay in the volume containing the *Eudemian Ethics* (Teubner, Leipzig, 1884); his text has full critical notes, a few selections from which are given here. Susemihl uses chiefly four MSS.: L^b, the twelfth-century Paris MS. of the *Nicomachean Ethics* which, has *Of Virtues and Vices* appended, in a hand dating probably at the beginning of the thirteenth century; F^c, the fourteenth-century Laurentian MS.; and two at Madrid, one grouping with F^c and the other with L^b, as do six others of the fifteenth and sixteenth centuries (one in the Bodleian) which he has collated, and the oldest extant edition, published at Basel in 1539: an older edition has now disappeared.

In the brief critical notes beneath the present text the variants of L^b and F^c are sometimes quoted, and the readings of one or more other MSS. are denoted by v.l. The sources of conjectural emendations are indicated by the following abbreviations:

And. = Andronicus
Rac. = Rackham
St. = Stobaeus
Sus. = Susemihl

A few conjectures of Bussemaker and of Sylburg are quoted from Susemihl.

H. R.

December 1934.

ΠΕΡΙ ΑΡΕΤΩΝ ΚΑΙ ΚΑΚΙΩΝ

1249 a
26 I. Ἐπαινετὰ μέν ἐστιν τὰ καλά, ψεκτὰ δὲ τὰ 1
αἰσχρά· καὶ τῶν μὲν καλῶν ἡγοῦνται αἱ ἀρεταί,
τῶν δὲ αἰσχρῶν αἱ κακίαι· ὥστε ἐπαινεταὶ μὲν αἱ 2
ἀρεταί,[1] ἐπαινετὰ δέ ἐστι καὶ τὰ αἴτια τῶν ἀρετῶν
καὶ τὰ παρεπόμενα ταῖς ἀρεταῖς καὶ τὰ γινόμενα ἀπ᾿
αὐτῶν καὶ τὰ ἔργα αὐτῶν,[2] ψεκτὰ δὲ τὰ ἐναντία.
Τριμεροῦς δὲ τῆς ψυχῆς λαμβανομένης κατὰ 3
1249 b Πλάτωνα, τοῦ μὲν λογιστικοῦ ἀρετή ἐστιν ἡ
27 φρόνησις, τοῦ δὲ θυμοειδοῦς ἥ τε πραότης καὶ ἡ
ἀνδρεία, τοῦ δὲ ἐπιθυμητικοῦ ἥ τε σωφροσύνη καὶ
ἡ ἐγκράτεια, ὅλης δὲ τῆς ψυχῆς ἥ τε δικαιοσύνη
καὶ ἡ ἐλευθεριότης καὶ ἡ μεγαλοψυχία· κακία δέ 4
ἐστιν τοῦ μὲν λογιστικοῦ ἡ ἀφροσύνη, τοῦ δὲ
θυμοειδοῦς ἥ τε ὀργιλότης καὶ ἡ δειλία, τοῦ δὲ
1250 a ἐπιθυμητικοῦ ἥ τε ἀκολασία καὶ ἡ ἀκρασία, ὅλης
δὲ τῆς ψυχῆς ἥ τε ἀδικία καὶ ἡ ἀνελευθερία καὶ
ἡ μικροψυχία.

II. Ἔστιν δὲ φρόνησις μὲν ἀρετὴ τοῦ λογιστικοῦ 1
παρασκευαστικὴ τῶν πρὸς εὐδαιμονίαν συντεινόν-
των. πραότης δέ ἐστιν ἀρετὴ τοῦ θυμοειδοῦς καθ᾿ 2
ἣν πρὸς ὀργὰς γίνονται δυσκίνητοι. ἀνδρεία δέ 3

ON VIRTUES AND VICES

Moral values

1 I. Fine things are the objects of praise, base things
of blame; and at the head of the fine stand the
2 virtues, at the head of the base the vices; consequently the virtues are objects of praise, and also the causes of the virtues are objects of praise, and the things that accompany the virtues and that result from them, and their works, while the opposite are the objects of blame.

Psychology of ethics

3 If in accordance with Plato the spirit is taken as having three parts, wisdom is goodness of the rational part, gentleness and courage of the passionate, of the appetitive sobriety of mind and self-control, and of the spirit as a whole righteousness, liberality and
4 great-spiritedness; while badness of the rational part is folly, of the passionate ill-temper and cowardice, of the appetitive profligacy and uncontrol, and of the spirit as a whole unrighteousness, meanness and smallmindedness.

applied to the Virtues

1 II. Wisdom is goodness of the rational part that is
productive of the things contributing to happiness.
2 Gentleness is goodness of the passionate part that
3 makes people difficult to move to anger. Courage is

---

[1] ὥστε . . . ἀρεταί And.: om. codd.
[2] καὶ τὰ ἔργα αὐτῶν om. F^{c}.

1250 a

ἐστιν ἀρετὴ τοῦ θυμοειδοῦς καθ' ἣν δυσέκπληκτοί
εἰσιν ὑπὸ φόβων τῶν περὶ θάνατον. σωφροσύνη 4
δέ ἐστιν ἀρετὴ τοῦ ἐπιθυμητικοῦ καθ' ἣν ἀνόρεκτοι
γίνονται τῶν περὶ τὰς ἀπολαύσεις φαύλων ἡδονῶν.
ἐγκράτεια δέ ἐστιν ἀρετὴ τοῦ ἐπιθυμητικοῦ καθ' 5
ἣν κατέχουσι τῷ λογισμῷ τὴν ἐπιθυμίαν ὁρμῶσαν
ἐπὶ φαύλας ἡδονάς. δικαιοσύνη δέ ἐστιν ἀρετὴ 6
ψυχῆς διανεμητικὴ τοῦ κατ' ἀξίαν. ἐλευθεριότης 7
δέ ἐστιν ἀρετὴ ψυχῆς εὐδάπανος εἰς τὰ καλά.
μεγαλοψυχία δέ ἐστιν ἀρετὴ ψυχῆς καθ' ἣν δύνανται φέρειν εὐτυχίαν καὶ ἀτυχίαν, τιμὴν καὶ ἀτιμίαν.
III. Ἀφροσύνη δέ ἐστιν κακία τοῦ λογιστικοῦ 1
αἰτία τοῦ ζῆν κακῶς. ὀργιλότης δέ ἐστι κακία 2
τοῦ θυμοειδοῦς καθ' ἣν εὐκίνητοι γίνονται πρὸς
ὀργήν. δειλία δέ ἐστι κακία τοῦ θυμοειδοῦς καθ' 3
ἣν ἐκπλήττονται ὑπὸ φόβων, καὶ μάλιστα τῶν
περὶ θάνατον. ἀκολασία δέ ἐστι κακία τοῦ ἐπι- 4
θυμητικοῦ καθ' ἣν ὀρεκτικοὶ γίνονται τῶν περὶ
τὰς ἀπολαυσεις φαύλων ἡδονῶν.[1] ἀκρασία δέ ἐστι 5
κακία τοῦ ἐπιθυμητικοῦ καθ' ἣν αἱροῦνται τὰς
φαύλας ἡδονὰς κωλύοντος[2] τοῦ λογισμοῦ.[3] ἀδικία 6
δέ ἐστι κακία ψυχῆς καθ' ἣν πλεονεκτικοὶ γίνονται
τοῦ[4] παρὰ τὴν ἀξίαν. ἀνελευθερία δέ ἐστιν κακία 7
ψυχῆς καθ' ἣν ὀρέγονται τοῦ πανταχόθεν κέρδους.
μικροψυχία δέ ἐστι κακία ψυχῆς καθ' ἣν ἀδύνατοί 8
εἰσι φέρειν εὐτυχίαν καὶ ἀτυχίαν καὶ τιμὴν καὶ
ἀτιμίαν.
IV. Τῆς δὲ φρονήσεώς ἐστι τὸ βουλεύσασθαι, 1
τὸ κρῖναι τὰ ἀγαθὰ καὶ τὰ κακὰ καὶ πάντα τὰ[5] ἐν

[1] ὀρεκτικοὶ . . . ἡδονῶν: v.l. αἱροῦνται τὰς φαύλας ἡδονάς.
[2] ⟨μὴ⟩ κωλύοντος St.

goodness of the passionate part that makes them un-
4 dismayed by fear of death. Sobriety of mind is goodness of the appetitive part that makes them not
desirous of the base pleasures of sensual enjoyment.
5 Self-control is goodness of the appetitive part that
enables men by means of reason to restrain their
6 appetite when it is set on base pleasures. Righteousness is goodness of the spirit shown in distributing
7 what is according to desert. Liberality is goodness of
spirit shown in spending rightly on fine objects. Great-
spiritedness is goodness of spirit that enables men to
bear good fortune and bad, honour and dishonour.

and to the Vices.

1 III. On the other hand folly is badness of the
2 rational part that causes bad living. Ill-temper is
badness of the passionate part that makes men easy
3 to provoke to anger. Cowardice is badness of the
passionate part that causes men to be dismayed by
4 fear, and especially by fear of death. Profligacy is
badness of the appetitive part that makes men desirous of the base pleasures of sensual enjoyment.
5 Uncontrol is badness of the appetitive part that
makes men choose base pleasures when reason tries
6 to hinder. Unrighteousness is badness of spirit that
makes men covetous of what is contrary to their
7 desert. Meanness is badness of spirit that makes
8 men try to get profit from all sources. Smallmindedness is badness of spirit that makes men unable to
bear good fortune and bad, honour and dishonour.

Virtuous actions and feelings classified.

1 IV. It belongs to wisdom to take counsel, to judge
the goods and evils and all the things in life that are

[3] αἱροῦνται . . . λογισμοῦ: v.l. παρασύρουσι τῇ ἀλογίᾳ τὴν ἐπιθυμίαν ὠθοῦσαν ἐπὶ τὰς τῶν φαύλων ἡδονῶν ἀπολαύσεις.

[4] τοῦ add. Rac. (cf. l. 13).

[5] τὰ add. Rac.

1250 a
τῷ βίῳ αἱρετὰ καὶ φευκτά, τὸ χρήσασθαι καλῶς
πᾶσιν τοῖς ὑπάρχουσιν ἀγαθοῖς, τὸ ὁμιλῆσαι ὀρθῶς,
τὸ συνιδεῖν τοὺς καιρούς, τὸ ἀγχίνως χρήσασθαι
καὶ λόγῳ καὶ ἔργῳ, τὸ τὴν ἐμπειρίαν ἔχειν τῶν
χρησίμων πάντων. μνήμη δὲ καὶ ἐμπειρία καὶ 2
ἀγχίνοια ἤτοι ἀπὸ τῆς φρονήσεως ἑκάστη αὐτῶν
ἐστιν ἢ παρέπεται τῇ φρονήσει· ἢ τὰ μὲν αὐτῶν
οἷον συναίτια τῆς φρονήσεώς ἐστι, καθάπερ ἡ ἐμπειρία καὶ ἡ μνήμη, τὰ δὲ οἷον μέρη,[1] οἷον εὐβουλία
καὶ ἀγχίνοια.

Πραότητος δέ ἐστι τὸ δύνασθαι φέρειν μετρίως 3
ἐγκλήματα καὶ ὀλιγωρίας, καὶ τὸ μὴ ταχέως
ὁρμᾶν ἐπὶ τὰς τιμωρίας, καὶ τὸ μὴ εὐκίνητον εἶναι
πρὸς τὰς ὀργάς, ἄπικρον δὲ τῷ ἤθει καὶ ἀφιλόνεικον, ἔχοντα τὸ ἠρεμαῖον ἐν τῇ ψυχῇ καὶ
στάσιμον.

Ἀνδρείας δέ ἐστι τὸ δυσέκπληκτον εἶναι ὑπὸ 4
φόβων τῶν περὶ θάνατον καὶ εὐθαρσῆ[2] ἐν τοῖς
1250 b δεινοῖς καὶ εὔτολμον πρὸς τοὺς κινδύνους, καὶ τὸ
μᾶλλον αἱρεῖσθαι τεθνάναι καλῶς ἢ αἰσχρῶς
σωθῆναι, καὶ τὸ νίκης αἴτιον εἶναι. ἔτι δὲ ἀνδρείας
ἐστὶ καὶ τὸ πονεῖν καὶ καρτερεῖν καὶ ἀνδραγαθίζεσθαι.[3] παρέπεται δὲ τῇ ἀνδρείᾳ ἥ τε εὐτολμία
καὶ ἡ εὐψυχία καὶ τὸ θάρσος,[4] ἔτι δὲ ἥ τε φιλο-
πονία καὶ ἡ καρτερία.

Σωφροσύνης δέ ἐστι τὸ μὴ θαυμάζειν τὰς ἀπο- 5
λαύσεις τῶν σωματικῶν ἡδονῶν,[5] καὶ τὸ εἶναι
πάσης ἀπολαυστικῆς [αἰσχρᾶς][6] ἡδονῆς ἀνόρεκτον,
καὶ τὸ φοβεῖσθαι τὴν ἀταξίαν,[7] καὶ τὸ τετάχθαι
περὶ τὸν βίον ὁμοίως ἔν τε μικροῖς καὶ μεγάλοις.
παρέπεται δὲ τῇ σωφροσύνῃ εὐταξία, κοσμιότης,
αἰδώς, εὐλάβεια.

desirable and to be avoided, to use all the available goods finely, to behave rightly in society, to observe due occasions, to employ both speech and action with sagacity, to have expert knowledge of all things that
2 are useful. Memory and experience and acuteness are each of them either a consequence or a concomitant of wisdom; or some of them are as it were subsidiary causes of wisdom, as for instance experience and memory, others as it were parts of it, for example good counsel and acuteness.

3 To gentleness belongs ability to bear reproaches and slights with moderation, and not to embark on revenge quickly, and not to be easily provoked to anger, but free from bitterness and contentiousness, having tranquillity and stability in the spirit.

4 To courage it belongs to be undismayed by fears of death and confident in alarms and brave in face of dangers, and to prefer a fine death to base security, and to be a cause of victory. It also belongs to courage to labour and endure and play a manly part. Courage is accompanied by confidence and bravery and daring, and also by perseverance and endurance.

5 To sobriety of mind it belongs not to value highly bodily pleasures and enjoyments, not to be covetous of every enjoyable pleasure, to fear disorder, and to live an orderly life in small things and great alike. Sobriety of mind is accompanied by orderliness, regularity, modesty, caution.

---

1 *μέρη* Sus.: *μέρη τῆς φρονήσεως* aut *φρονήσεως* aut *αὐτῆς*.
2 *εὐθαρσῆ* v.l.: *τὸ εὐθαρσῆ εἶναι*.
3 *ἀνδραγαθίζεσθαι* St.: *αἱρεῖσθαι καὶ δύνασθαι* (viz. lipography + gloss).
4 *τὸ θάρσος καὶ τὸ θράσος* codd. plur.
5 *ἡδονῶν*: *ἐπιθυμιῶν* St.
6 [*αἰσχρᾶς*] Rac.: v.l. *καὶ αἰσχρᾶς*.
7 St.: *τὴν* (*καὶ τὴν* F[c]) *δικαίαν ἀδοξίαν* (aut *ἄδειαν*).

1250 b

V. Ἐγκρατείας δέ ἐστι τὸ δύνασθαι κατασχεῖν 1
τῷ λογισμῷ τὴν ἐπιθυμίαν ὁρμῶσαν ἐπὶ φαύλας
ἀπολαύσεις καὶ ἡδονάς,[1] καὶ[2] καρτερεῖν, καὶ τὸ
ὑπομενετικὸν εἶναι τῆς κατὰ φύσιν ἐνδείας τε[3]
καὶ λύπης.

Δικαιοσύνης δέ ἐστι τὸ διανεμητικὸν εἶναι τοῦ 2
κατ᾽ ἀξίαν, καὶ τὸ σῴζειν τὰ πάτρια ἔθη καὶ τὰ
νόμιμα καὶ[4] τοὺς γεγραμμένους νόμους, καὶ τὸ
ἀληθεύειν ἐν τῷ διαφέροντι, καὶ τὸ διαφυλάττειν
τὰς ὁμολογίας. ἔστι δὲ πρῶτα τῶν δικαίων[5] τὰ
πρὸς τοὺς θεούς, εἶτα τὰ πρὸς δαίμονας, εἶτα τὰ
πρὸς πατρίδα καὶ γονεῖς, εἶτα τὰ πρὸς τοὺς κατ-
οιχομένους· ἐν οἷς ἐστι καὶ ἡ εὐσέβεια, ἤτοι
μέρος οὖσα τῆς δικαιοσύνης ἢ παρακολουθοῦσα.
ἀκολουθεῖ δὲ τῇ δικαιοσύνῃ καὶ ἡ ὁσιότης καὶ 3
ἡ ἀλήθεια καὶ ἡ πίστις καὶ ἡ μισοπονηρία.

Ἐλευθεριότητος δέ ἐστι τὸ προετικὸν εἶναι 4
χρημάτων εἰς τὰ ἐπαινετὰ καὶ δαψιλῆ[6] ἐπὶ τῷ εἰς
τὰ δέοντα[7] ἀναλωθῆναι, καὶ τὸ βοηθητικὸν εἶναι
ἐν τῷ διαφόρῳ, καὶ τὸ μὴ λαβεῖν ὅθεν μὴ δεῖ.
ἔστι δὲ ὁ ἐλευθέριος καὶ περὶ ἐσθῆτα καθάριος
καὶ περὶ οἴκησιν,[8] καὶ κατασκευαστικὸς τῶν περιτ-
τῶν καὶ καλῶν καὶ διαγωγὴν ἐχόντων ἡδεῖαν ἄνευ
τοῦ λυσιτελοῦντος, καὶ θρεπτικὸς τῶν ζῴων τῶν
ἴδιον ἐχόντων τι ἢ θαυμαστόν. ἀκολουθεῖ δὲ τῇ 5
ἐλευθεριότητι ἡ τοῦ ἤθους ὑγρότης καὶ εὐαγωγία
καὶ φιλανθρωπία καὶ τὸ εἶναι ἐλεητικὸν καὶ φιλό-
φιλον καὶ φιλόξενον καὶ φιλόκαλον.

[1] Lb: ἀπολαύσεις ἡδονῶν.

[2] Lb: καὶ τό.

[3] τε add. St., And.

[4] καὶ Rac.: τὸ (aut καὶ τὸ) σῴζειν.

[5] v.l. ἔστι δὲ πρώτη τῶν δικαιοσυνῶν.

1 V. To self-control belongs ability to restrain desire by reason when it is set on base enjoyments and pleasures, and to be resolute, and readiness to endure natural want and pain.

2 To righteousness it belongs to be ready to distribute according to desert, and to preserve ancestral customs and institutions and the established laws, and to tell the truth when interest is at stake, and to keep agreements. First among the claims of righteousness are our duties to the gods, then our duties to the spirits,[a] then those to country and parents, then those to the departed; and among these claims is piety, which is either a part of righteousness or a
3 concomitant of it. Righteousness is also accompanied by holiness and truth and loyalty and hatred of wickedness.

4 To liberality it belongs to be profuse of money on praiseworthy objects and lavish in spending on what is necessary, and to be helpful in a matter of dispute, and not to take from wrong sources. The liberal man is cleanly in his dress and dwelling, and fond of providing himself with things that are above the ordinary and fine and that afford entertainment without being profitable; and he is fond of keeping animals that have something special or remarkable
5 about them. Liberality is accompanied by elasticity and ductility of character, and kindness, and a compassionate and affectionate and hospitable and honourable nature.

[a] Deities of a minor order, in some cases the souls of dead men of the heroic age; often the object of only local worship.

---

[6] δαψιλῆ Sylburg: ἐπιδαψιλεία Fc, δαψιλεῖ Lb, ἐπιδαψιλεύειν Gaisford.

[7] τὰ δέοντα v.l.: δέοντι Lb, δέον Fc, δέον τι edd.

[8] καὶ περὶ οἴκησιν om. v.l.

1250 b
Μεγαλοψυχίας δέ ἐστι τὸ καλῶς ἐνεγκεῖν καὶ 6
εὐτυχίαν καὶ ἀτυχίαν, καὶ τιμὴν καὶ ἀτιμίαν, καὶ
τὸ μὴ θαυμάζειν μήτε τρυφὴν μήτε θεραπείαν μήτε
ἐξουσίαν μήτε τὰς νίκας τὰς ἐναγωνίους, ἔχειν
δέ τι βάθος τῆς ψυχῆς καὶ μέγεθος. ἔστι δὲ[1]
μεγαλόψυχος οὔθ' ὁ[2] τὸ ζῆν περὶ πολλοῦ ποιούμενος οὔθ' ὁ[2] φιλόζωος. ἁπλοῦς δὲ τῷ ἤθει
καὶ γενναῖος ἀδικεῖσθαι δυνάμενος καὶ οὐ τιμωρη-
τικός. ἀκολουθεῖ δὲ τῇ μεγαλοψυχίᾳ ἁπλότης καὶ 7
ἀλήθεια.

VI. Ἀφροσύνης δέ ἐστι τὸ κρῖναι κακῶς τὰ 1
πράγματα, τὸ βουλεύσασθαι κακῶς, τὸ ὁμιλῆσαι
κακῶς, τὸ χρήσασθαι κακῶς τοῖς παροῦσιν ἀγαθοῖς,
1251 a τὸ ψευδῶς δοξάζειν περὶ τῶν εἰς τὸν βίον καλῶν
καὶ ἀγαθῶν. παρακολουθεῖ δὲ τῇ ἀφροσύνῃ 2
ἀπειρία, ἀμαθία, ἀκρασία, ἐπαριστερότης, ἀμνη-
μοσύνη.

Ὀργιλότητος δέ ἐστιν εἴδη τρία, ἀκροχολία 3
πικρία βαρυθυμία. ἔστι δὲ τοῦ ὀργίλου τὸ μὴ
δύνασθαι φέρειν μήτε[3] τὰς μικρὰς ὀλιγωρίας μήτε
τὰς ἐλαττώσεις,[4] εἶναι δὲ κολαστικὸν καὶ τιμωρη-
τικὸν καὶ εὐκίνητον πρὸς ὀργὴν καὶ ὑπὸ ἔργου καὶ
ὑπὸ λόγου τοῦ τυχόντος. ἀκολουθεῖ δὲ τῇ ὀρ- 4
γιλότητι τὸ παροξυντικὸν τοῦ ἤθους καὶ τὸ[5]
εὐμετάβολον καὶ ἡ πικρολογία[6] καὶ τὸ ἐπὶ μικροῖς
λυπεῖσθαι καὶ ταῦτα πάσχειν ταχέως καὶ παρὰ
βραχὺν καιρόν.

Δειλίας δέ ἐστι τὸ ὑπὸ τῶν τυχόντων φόβων 5
εὐκίνητον εἶναι, καὶ μάλιστα τῶν περὶ θάνατον
καὶ τὰς σωματικὰς πηρώσεις, καὶ τὸ ὑπολαμβάνειν
κρεῖττον εἶναι ὁπωσοῦν σωθῆναι ἢ τελευτῆσαι
καλῶς. ἀκολουθεῖ δὲ τῇ δειλίᾳ μαλακία, ἀνανδρία, 6

6 To greatness of spirit it belongs to bear finely both
good fortune and bad, honour and disgrace, and not
to think highly of luxury or attention or power or
victories in contests, and to possess a certain depth
and magnitude of spirit. He who values life highly
and who is fond of life is not great-spirited. The
great-spirited man is simple and noble in character,
7 able to bear injustice and not revengeful. Greatness
of spirit is accompanied by simplicity and sincerity.

Vicious actions and feelings classified.

1 VI. To folly belongs bad judgement of affairs, bad
counsel, bad fellowship, bad use of one's resources,
false opinions about what is fine and good in life.
2 Folly is accompanied by unskilfulness, ignorance, uncontrol, awkwardness, forgetfulness.

3 Of ill-temper there are three kinds, irascibility,
bitterness, sullenness. It belongs to the ill-tempered
man to be unable to bear either small slights or
defeats but to be given to retaliation and revenge,
and easily moved to anger by any chance deed or
4 word. Ill-temper is accompanied by excitability
of character, instability, bitter speech, and liability to
take offence at trifles and to feel these feelings quickly
and on slight occasions.

5 To cowardice it belongs to be easily excited by
chance alarms, and especially by fear of death or of
bodily injuries, and to think it better to save oneself
6 by any means than to meet a fine end. Cowardice is
accompanied by softness, unmanliness, faint-hearted-

---

[1] *δὲ ὁ* L^{b}.

[2] *οὔθ' ὁ* (bis) Bekker: *οὐδ' ὁ* L^{b}, *οὐδὲ* F^{c}.

[3] *μηδὲ* Bussemaker.

[4] [*μήτε τὰς ἐλαττώσεις*] idem: *τὰς <μεγάλας> ἐλαττώσεις* Sus.

[5] *καὶ τὸ* And.: *καὶ*.

[6] St.: *μικρολογία καὶ ἡ μεταμέλεια* codd.

1251 a
ἀπόνοια, φιλοψυχία· ὕπεστι δέ τις καὶ εὐλάβεια
καὶ τὸ ἀφιλόνεικον τοῦ ἤθους.[1]
Ἀκολασίας δέ ἐστι τὸ αἱρεῖσθαι τὰς ἀπολαύσεις 7
τῶν ἡδονῶν τῶν βλαβερῶν καὶ αἰσχρῶν καὶ[2]
ὑπολαμβάνειν εὐδαιμονεῖν μάλιστα τοὺς ἐν ταῖς
τοιαύταις ἡδοναῖς ζῶντας, καὶ τὸ φιλογέλοιον εἶναι
καὶ φιλοσκώπτην καὶ φιλευτράπελον καὶ τὸ ῥᾳδιουρ-
γὸν εἶναι ἐν τοῖς λόγοις καὶ ἐν τοῖς ἔργοις. ἀκο- 8
λουθεῖ δὲ τῇ ἀκολασίᾳ ἀταξία, ἀναίδεια, ἀκοσμία,
τρυφή, ῥᾳθυμία, ἀμέλεια, ὀλιγωρία, ἔκλυσις.
Ἀκρασίας δέ ἐστι τὸ κωλύοντος τοῦ λογισμοῦ 9
τὰς ἀπολαύσεις τῶν ἡδονῶν αἱρεῖσθαι, καὶ τὸ ὑπολαμβάνοντα κρεῖττον εἶναι μὴ μετασχεῖν αὐτῶν
μετέχειν[3] μηδὲν ἧττον, καὶ τὸ οἴεσθαι μὲν δεῖν
πράττειν καὶ τὰ καλὰ καὶ τὰ συμφέροντα ἀφ-
ίστασθαι δὲ αὐτῶν διὰ τὰς ἡδονάς. ἀκολουθεῖ δὲ 10
τῇ ἀκρασίᾳ μαλακία καὶ[4] ἀμέλεια καὶ τὰ πλεῖστα
ταὐτὰ ἃ καὶ τῇ ἀκολασίᾳ.
VII. Ἀδικίας δέ ἐστιν εἴδη τρία, ἀσέβεια πλεον- 1
εξία ὕβρις. ἀσέβεια μὲν ἡ περὶ θεοὺς πλημ- 2
μέλεια καὶ περὶ δαίμονας, ἢ[5] περὶ τοὺς κατοιχο-
μένους καὶ περὶ γονεῖς καὶ πατρίδα· πλεονεξία δὲ 3
ἡ περὶ τὰ συμβόλαια, παρὰ τὴν ἀξίαν αἱρουμένη
τὸ διάφορον· ὕβρις δὲ καθ' ἣν τὰς ἡδονὰς αὑτοῖς 4
παρασκευάζουσιν εἰς ὄνειδος ἄγοντες ἑτέρους, ὅθεν
Εὔηνος περὶ αὐτῆς λέγει

ἥτις κερδαίνουσ' οὐδὲν ὅμως ἀδικεῖ.

ἔστι δὲ τῆς ἀδικίας τὸ παραβαίνειν τὰ πάτρια 5
ἔθη[6] καὶ τὰ νόμιμα, τὸ ἀπειθεῖν τοῖς νόμοις καὶ
1251 b τοῖς ἄρχουσι, τὸ ψεύδεσθαι, τὸ ἐπιορκεῖν, τὸ παρα-

[1] καὶ . . . ἤθους om. v.l. [2] καὶ cet.: καὶ τὸ L^bF^c.

ness, fondness of life; and it also has an element of
cautiousness and submissiveness of character.
7 To profligacy belongs choosing harmful and base
pleasures and enjoyments, and thinking that the
happiest people are those who pass their lives in
pleasures of that kind, and being fond of laughter and
mockery and jokes and levity in words and deeds.
8 Profligacy is accompanied by disorder, shamelessness,
irregularity, luxury, slackness, carelessness, negligence, remissness.
9 To uncontrol it belongs to choose the enjoyment of
pleasures when reason would restrain, and although
one believes that it would be better not to participate
in them, to participate in them all the same, and
while thinking one ought to do fine and expedient
things yet to abstain from them for the sake of one's
10 pleasures. The concomitants of uncontrol are softness and negligence and in general the same as those
of profligacy.
1 VII. Of unrighteousness there are three kinds,
2 impiety, greed, outrage. Transgression in regard to
gods and spirits, or even in regard to the departed
3 and to parents and country, is impiety. Transgression in regard to contracts, taking what is in dispute
4 contrary to one's desert, is greed. Outrage is the
unrighteousness that makes men procure pleasures
for themselves while leading others into disgrace; in
consequence of which Evenus says about outrage:

She that wrongs others e'en when she gaineth nought.

5 And it belongs to unrighteousness to transgress
ancestral customs and regulations, to disobey the
laws and the rulers, to lie, to perjure, to transgress

[3] And.: μετέχειν δὲ.

[4] καὶ v.l.: om. L^bF^c.

[5] v.ll. καὶ ἡ, καί.

[6] ἔθη om. $L^b F^c$.

1251 b
βαίνειν τὰς ὁμολογίας καὶ τὰς πίστεις. ἀκολουθεῖ 6
δὲ τῇ ἀδικίᾳ συκοφαντία, ἀλαζονεία, φιλανθρωπία
προσποίητος, κακοήθεια, πανουργία.
Ἀνελευθερίας δέ ἐστιν εἴδη τρία, αἰσχροκέρδεια 7
φειδωλία κιμβικία. αἰσχροκέρδεια μὲν καθ' ἣν 8
κερδαίνειν ζητοῦσι πανταχόθεν καὶ τὸ κέρδος τῆς
αἰσχύνης περὶ πλείονος ποιοῦνται· φειδωλία δὲ 9
καθ' ἣν ἀδάπανοι γίνονται τῶν χρημάτων εἰς τὸ
δέον· κιμβικία δὲ καθ' ἣν δαπανῶσι μέν, κατὰ 10
μικρὸν δὲ καὶ κακῶς, καὶ πλείω βλάπτονται τῷ
μὴ κατὰ καιρὸν προέσθαι τὸ διάφορον. ἔστι δὲ 11
τῆς ἀνελευθερίας τὸ περὶ πλείστου ποιεῖσθαι χρήματα καὶ τὸ μηδὲν ὄνειδος ἡγεῖσθαι τῶν ποιούντων
κέρδος, βίος θητικὸς καὶ δουλοπρεπὴς καὶ ῥυπαρός,
φιλοτιμίας καὶ ἐλευθερίας ἀλλότριος. ἀκολουθεῖ 12
δὲ τῇ ἀνελευθερίᾳ μικρολογία, βαρυθυμία [μικρο-
ψυχία],[1] ταπεινότης, ἀμετρία, ἀγένεια, μισαν-
θρωπία.
Μικροψυχίας δέ ἐστι τὸ μήτε τιμὴν μήτε ἀτιμίαν, 13
μήτε εὐτυχίαν μήτε ἀτυχίαν δύνασθαι φέρειν, ἀλλὰ
τιμώμενον μὲν χαυνοῦσθαι[2] μικρὰ δὲ εὐτυχήσαντα
ἐξαίρεσθαι, ἀτιμίαν δὲ μηδὲ τὴν ἐλαχίστην ἐνεγκεῖν
δύνασθαι ἀπότευγμα δὲ ὁτιοῦν ἀτυχίαν κρίνειν
μεγάλην, ὀδύρεσθαι δὲ ἐπὶ πᾶσιν καὶ δυσφορεῖν.
ἔτι δὲ τοιοῦτός ἐστιν ὁ μικρόψυχος οἷος πάντα τὰ
ὀλιγωρήματα καλεῖν ὕβριν καὶ ἀτιμίαν, καὶ τὰ δι'
ἄγνοιαν ἢ λήθην γινόμενα. ἀκολουθεῖ δὲ τῇ μικρο- 14
ψυχίᾳ μικρολογία, μεμψιμοιρία, δυσελπιστία, ταπεινότης.
VIII. Καθόλου δὲ τῆς μὲν ἀρετῆς ἐστι τὸ ποιεῖν 1
σπουδαίαν τὴν διάθεσιν περὶ τὴν ψυχήν, ἠρεμαίαις
καὶ τεταγμέναις κινήσεσι χρωμένην καὶ συμφωνοῦ-

6 covenants and pledges. Unrighteousness is accompanied by slander, imposture, pretence of kindness,
malignity, unscrupulousness.
7 Of meanness there are three kinds, love of base
8 gain, parsimony, niggardliness. Love of base gain
makes men seek profit from all sources and pay more
9 regard to the profit than to the disgrace ; parsimony
makes them unwilling to spend money on a necessary
10 object ; niggardliness causes them only to spend in
driblets and in a bad way, and to lose more than
they gain by not at the proper moment letting go
11 the difference. It belongs to meanness to set a
very high value on money and to think nothing
that brings profit a disgrace—a menial and servile
and squalid mode of life, alien to ambition and to
12 liberality. Meanness is accompanied by pettiness,
sulkiness, self-abasement, lack of proportion, ignoble-
ness, misanthropy.

13 It belongs to small-mindedness to be unable to bear either honour or dishonour, either good fortune or bad, but to be filled with conceit when honoured and puffed up by trifling good fortune, and to be unable to bear even the smallest dishonour and to deem any chance failure a great misfortune, and to be distressed and annoyed at everything. Moreover the small-minded man is the sort of person to call all slights an insult and dishonour, even those that are
14 due to ignorance or forgetfulness. Small-mindedness
is accompanied by pettiness, querulousness, pessim-
ism, self-abasement.

1 VIII. In general it belongs to goodness to make the spirit's disposition virtuous, experiencing tranquil and ordered emotions and in harmony throughout all its

Psychology of ethics.

[1] Sylburg.

[2] v.l. ἀναχαυνοῦσθαι LᵇF: cet.

1251 b

σαν κατὰ πάντα τὰ μέρη· διὸ καὶ δοκεῖ παράδειγμα πολιτείας ἀγαθῆς εἶναι ψυχῆς σπουδαίας
διάθεσις. ἔστι δὲ τῆς ἀρετῆς καὶ τὸ εὐεργετεῖν 2
τοὺς ἀξίους καὶ τὸ φιλεῖν τοὺς ἀγαθοὺς καὶ τὸ
μισεῖν τοὺς φαύλους,[1] καὶ τὸ μήτε κολαστικὸν
εἶναι μήτε τιμωρητικόν, ἀλλὰ ἵλεων καὶ εὐμενικὸν
καὶ συγγνωμονικόν. ἀκολουθεῖ δὲ τῇ ἀρετῇ χρη- 3
στότης, ἐπιείκεια, εὐγνωμοσύνη, ἐλπὶς ἀγαθή,[2] ἔτι
δὲ καὶ τὰ τοιαῦτα οἷον φίλοικειον εἶναι καὶ φιλό-
φιλον καὶ φιλέταιρον καὶ φιλόξενον καὶ φιλάνθρωπον καὶ φιλόκαλον· ἃ δὴ πάντα τῶν ἐπαινουμένων
ἐστί.

Τῆς δὲ κακίας ἐστὶ τὰ ἐναντία, καὶ παρακολουθεῖ 4
τὰ ἐναντία αὐτῇ· ἅπαντα δὲ τὰ τῆς κακίας καὶ τὰ
παρακολουθοῦντα αὐτῇ τῶν ψεγομένων ἐστίν.

[1] καὶ τὸ μισεῖν τοὺς φαύλους om. v.l.
[2] post ἀγαθὴ add. μνήμη ἀγαθὴ F^{c}.

parts ; this is the cause of the opinion that the disposition of a good spirit is a pattern of a good constitu-
2 tion of the state. It also belongs to goodness to do good to the deserving and love the good and hate the wicked, and not to be eager to inflict punishment or take vengeance, but gracious and kindly and for-
3 giving. Goodness is accompanied by honesty, reasonableness, kindness, hopefulness, and also by such traits as love of home and of friends and comrades and guests, and of one's fellow-men, and love of what is noble—all of which qualities are among those that are praised.

4 To badness belong the opposite qualities, and it has the opposite concomitants : all the qualities and concomitants of badness are among the things that are blamed.

INDEX